BATMAN

A VISUAL HISTORY

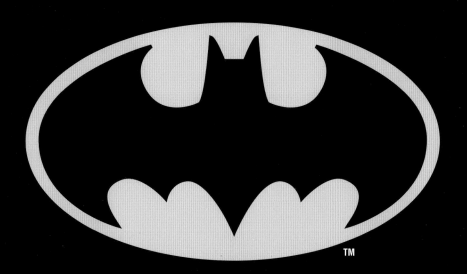

Senior Editor **Alastair Dougall**
Senior Art Editor **Robert Perry**
Editors **Kathryn Hill, Laura Nickoll, Julia March**
Designers **Nick Avery, Simon Murrell**
Editorial Assistant **Beth Davies**
Senior Pre-Production Producer **Jennifer Murray**
Senior Producer **Alex Bell**
Managing Editor **Sadie Smith**
Managing Art Editor **Ron Stobbart**
Creative Manager **Sarah Harland**
Art Director **Lisa Lanzarini**
Publisher **Julie Ferris**
Publishing Director **Simon Beecroft**

This edition published in 2016
First published in Great Britain in 2014
by Dorling Kindersley Limited
80 Strand, London WC2R 0RL

Page design copyright © 2016 Dorling Kindersley Limited
A Penguin Random House Company

002-193692-09/15

A CIP catalogue record for this book is available from the British Library.

ISBN: 978-0-2412-4200-1

Printed in China.

www.dk.com

A WORLD OF IDEAS:
SEE ALL THERE IS TO KNOW

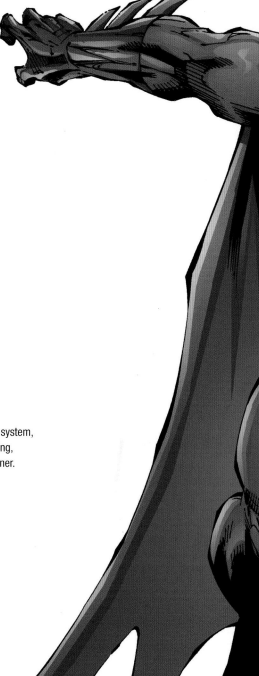

BATMAN
A VISUAL HISTORY

WRITTEN BY
MATTHEW K. MANNING

ADDITIONAL TEXT BY MATT FORBECK

CONTENTS

NB: Dating of comic books: This has followed cover date where possible.
If issues on a page are all from the same month, the month is not repeated each time.

FOREWORD

He scared me as a child, amused me as an adolescent, and thrilled me as an adult. He still thrills me, scary as he remains.

Batman is just plain scary. But only when interpreted as such.

Me, I tried to kill him twice. I failed both times.

The first time I tried to kill Batman was in my graphic novel THE DARK KNIGHT RETURNS. That was my intended climax to the series: that Batman would die in a hail of police bullets. But I couldn't pull it off. Batman, as my character Commisioner Yindel said, was "too big." To kill, that is.

The next time—and the final time—I tried to kill Batman was in my sequel to THE DARK KNIGHT RETURNS, called THE DARK KNIGHT STRIKES AGAIN. The good Commissioner was again proven true to her word. There's no killing this guy.

Just like Wonder Woman and Superman, Batman is immortal.

Immortal, and as undestroyable as a many-faceted diamond.

Keep with the diamond reference. You can toss Batman across the room. You can crash him against the ceiling, against the floor, against the wall.

You can interpret him in a hundred ways, and they all work.

Before you stand many versions of Batman. From creator Bob Kane, to talents Jerry Robinson and Bill Finger and Dick Sprang and many more, most notably Dennis O'Neil, Neal Adams, and Dick Giordano.

FRANK MILLER

INTRODUCTION

As I write this from my home office, the room is lit by a Batman leg lamp. That's right, it's Batman's leg with a light bulb and shade attached to it, à la *A Christmas Story*. To my right is a framed Michael Keaton autograph, and behind me are more Batman action figures than any rational man has a right to own.

Batman has been a major part of my life since the release of the 1989 Tim Burton film. Twenty-five years and over 10,000 comic books later, and I keep going to the comic book store every Wednesday for the latest news from Gotham City. I've even been lucky enough to write my fair share of Batman comics and books. And I hope to write plenty more in the future. There's just something about the famed Caped Crusader that I can never get bored with. Something fascinating about the giant moons and purple skies of Gotham City. Something about this Super Hero, who really isn't super at all.

When DK asked me if I was interested in writing this book, the only question in my mind was what eras I wanted to tackle. I have a soft spot for the 1980s, for the innovations in storytelling and breakout artwork of some of the industry's finest creators. But then I'm also quite attached to the 1970s. Some of my first Batman comics were from that bold age of a globetrotting Batman. The 1930s and 1940s were a given, as I'd become interested in Batman's first tales since I was a kid wondering how it all came into being. And the 1950s was a time of sci-fi and fun that was only topped in bright dynamics by the comics of the 1960s. And of course, the 1990s, 2000s, and 2010s I just had to write, as they represented hours of enjoyment during high school, college, and my modern life. So I thought it over, and there really wasn't much of a choice. I had to write the whole thing.

Unfortunately, there wasn't enough time. I had to sacrifice the 1960s for the sake of the deadline, but thankfully, Matthew Forbeck stepped up to the plate and got to enjoy writing about one of the Caped Crusader's most iconic decades. I'd like to thank him for his hard work as well as my editors, Alastair

1930s

It was the dawn of the comic book, the introduction of the Super Hero. The 1930s gave the world a new medium and that medium's biggest stars. And right there, among the first, was Batman.

In 1935, a man named Major Malcolm Wheeler-Nicholson founded National Allied Publishing after noticing how well newspaper comic strips were selling when repackaged in comic book form with a front and back cover. Instead of purchasing the rights to established characters, Nicholson took a less expensive route and released *New Fun Comics*, a collection of all-new strips and characters. Soon Nicholson debuted another corporation, Detective Comics, Inc., with a bit of help from his distributor Harry Donenfeld. Under that new sister company, *Detective Comics* #1 (March 1937) would soon see publication, and later, both of Nicholson's business endeavors became known as DC Comics.

Inspired by pulp characters and crime fiction comic strips like "Dick Tracy," *Detective Comics* introduced readers to Slam Bradley, an "ace free lance sleuth" who would be adopted into Batman's supporting cast decades later in the 2000s. But perhaps more importantly, the new title paved the way for *Action Comics* #1 (June 1938), an issue that would change the direction of comic books to this day. Its cover depicted a man lifting up a car with his bare hands while wearing something akin to a wrestler's costume and a red cape. The man in the red cape was none other than Superman.

Superman was a runaway success, one that was soon repeated in the pages of *Detective Comics* #27 (May 1939) when editor Vin Sullivan commissioned a young artist named Bob Kane to deliver a Superman-like strip. Kane returned to DC Comics with a new adventure hero called Batman. The rest would soon be history.

The hyphen that had originally appeared in the character's name was dropped and, with a few tweaks, his costume became very similar to the uniform fans see in comic stores today. While only existing in the 1930s for the better part of a year, Batman managed to acquire an ally at police headquarters in Commissioner Gordon, as well as a fiancée in the glamorous form of socialite Julie Madison. He gained quite an arsenal, fought his first few super-villains, and even received an origin story. Batman had arrived, and even Bob Kane could have had little idea of the phenomenon that he had unleashed.

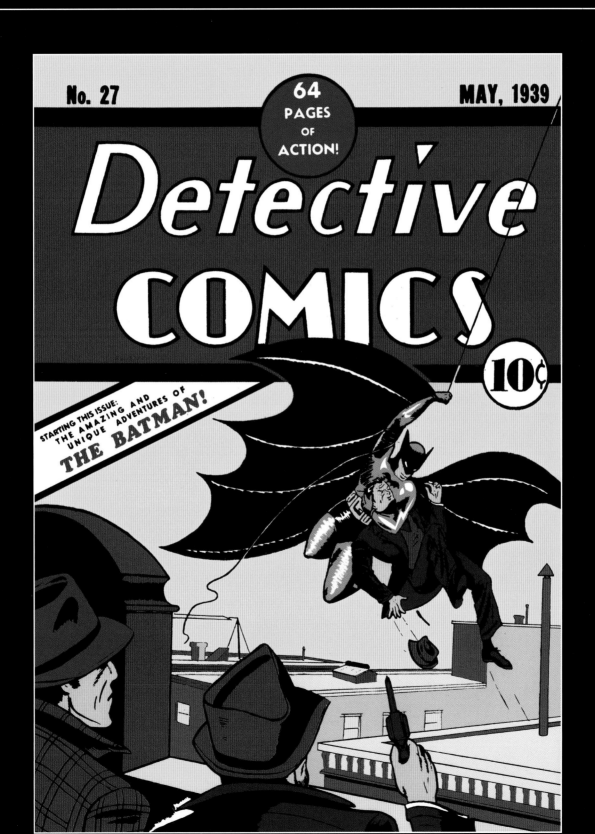

THE BATMAN
DETECTIVE COMICS #27

As soon as DC Comics' new character, Batman, made his debut, artist Bob Kane knew he had a hit on his hands.

Bob Kane was a young freelance artist who had worked on several comic book features including "Rusty and His Pals" in *Adventure Comics* and "Clip Carson" in *Action Comics*. When editor Vin Sullivan, who worked for the company that would one day be known as DC Comics, wanted a new character in the vein of his company's hit Superman character, he approached Kane. Over a weekend, Kane began work on developing artwork for the new strip.

After the character was fully realized, and approved by Sullivan, Kane worked on a six-page story that not only debuted in this issue, but grabbed the cover spot as well. A tale called "The Case of the Chemical Syndicate" was drawn by Kane. The tale was the lead feature in this issue of *Detective Comics*, and was followed by a variety of other shorts, including spy and western stories, as well as another crime-fighting adventure.

Batman's premiere tale began with prominent playboy and pipe-smoker Bruce Wayne talking with his friend Commissioner Gordon about the city's new vigilante, Batman. Their conversation was interrupted by news of the murder of a chemical magnate named Lambert. Batman soon solved the case, tracking down the killer, who turned out to be Lambert's old business partner, Alfred Stryker. The story's final scene revealed that playboy Bruce Wayne had been the mysterious Batman all along.

1939

"A bat! That's it! It's an omen. I shall become a bat!"

Bruce Wayne, *Detective Comics* #33

Batman made his first comic book appearance in an ad in *Action Comics* #12 (May 1939), promising readers a "thrilling adventure strip." And after his first true appearance in that month's *Detective Comics* #27, readers agreed. Batman quickly became a regular strip in every issue of *Detective Comics*. The strip was soon expanded from six pages to ten, and a hyphen was removed from the character's name to become simply "Batman." Batman became the second hit for the company that would become known as DC Comics, and would not long be confined to simply one comic book title.

THE MURDER SCENE
When news came in that Lambert, CEO of Apex Chemical Corporation, had been murdered, Commissioner Gordon (in a herringbone suit and green hat) and his friend Bruce Wayne (in yellow check) were soon on the scene. Playing the role of bored playboy to perfection, Bruce remarked that solving the case might prove an amusing way of spending the evening.

THE FIRST BATMOBILE
The intrepid Batman cracked his first case with the help of a red sedan identical to one Bruce Wayne was seen driving earlier in the story.

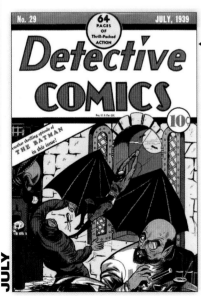

No. 29   64 PAGES OF Thrill-Packed ACTION   JULY, 1939

Detective COMICS

10¢

PAGING DOCTOR DEATH

Detective Comics #29 ■ A Super Hero is only as good as the villains in his Rogues Gallery, and Batman's first recurring foe, Doctor Death, said a lot about the state of the Dark Knight in 1939. In a story drawn by Bob Kane and written by Gardner Fox, Dr. Karl Hellfern was little more than a typical mad scientist running an extortion racket; Batman was clearly still finding his feet as a crime fighter. After testing out his Batrope in the previous issue, he added glass pellets of "choking gas" to his Utility Belt in this issue, and suction gloves and knee pads to his costume.

SPECIAL FEATURE

CHANGING GLOVES

In his first appearance in *Detective Comics* #27 (May 1939), Batman's gloves were purple. By the following issue they were beige, as if he wasn't wearing gloves at all. For this issue, Batman's sported blue gloves in the interior pages but was gloveless on the cover, his second for *Detective Comics*.

No. 30   64 PAGES OF Thrill-Packed ACTION   AUGUST, 1939

Detective COMICS

10¢

Another thrilling episode of THE BATMAN in this issue

MAN AND BAT BECOME ONE

Detective Comics #30 ■ After seemingly dying in a fiery blaze when he tangled with Batman in the last issue, Doctor Death returned, albeit hideously burned, in this issue illustrated by Bob Kane and Sheldon Moldoff and written by Gardner Fox. In a story that saw the hyphen removed from Batman, just as quietly as Batman's gloves had become a blue shade in the previous issue, Batman stopped Doctor Death from exacting his revenge. After a brief struggle, Batman overpowered Doctor Death, tied him up, and left him for the police to deal with.

SPECIAL FEATURE

THE FACE OF DEATH

Batman's declaration "Death... to Doctor Death!" at the end of the previous issue had been premature. The minor league threat would be Batman's first recurring enemy. The Doctor, now possessing a severely burnt, mask-like face, revealed his true appearance in this issue's final sequence.

A CHILLING ORIGIN
DETECTIVE COMICS #33

Undoubtedly the most famous story in Batman's history, the origin of the Dark Knight Detective was revealed to readers in this momentous issue.

Artists Bob Kane and Sheldon Moldoff and writer Bill Finger collaborated on an origin story that was near perfect in its simplicity. The tale began "some fifteen years ago" when Thomas and Martha Wayne were shot and killed by an anonymous mugger when walking home from a movie. (While he'd be nameless in this issue, the gunman would later be named Joe Chill.) Surviving the event, Thomas and Martha's young son Bruce pledged to avenge his parents' deaths by spending the remainder of his life battling criminals; all the money he'd ever need to wage his war had been left to him by his family. As the boy became a man, Bruce became a master scientist and trained his body to physical perfection. Noting that "criminals are a superstitious cowardly lot," he decided he needed a disguise to "strike terror into their hearts." While Bruce pondered this idea in his study, a bat flew through an open window. The omen was clear, and at the end of this 12-panel sequence, the Batman was born. Suddenly, readers could fully relate to this dark figure of the night; Batman had become more than just another mystery man. Also in this issue, Gardner Fox scripted the issue's main story, in which Batman battled the "Dirigible of Doom" and its villainous captain, Carl Kruger.

THE COMPLETE CRIME FIGHTER
Bruce Wayne's training was told through minimal snippets. This origin story would prove so important, it would later be included in *Batman* #1 (April 1940) to help introduce the Caped Crusader to new readers.

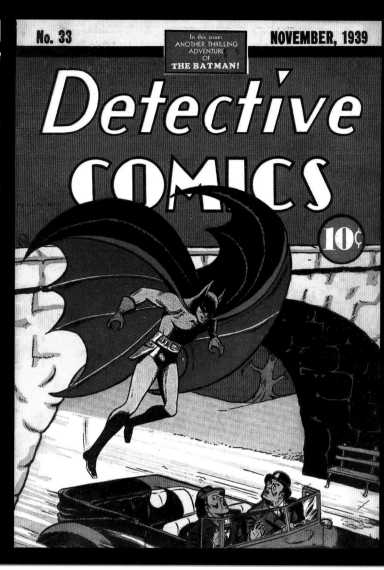

No. 33 — In this issue: ANOTHER THRILLING ADVENTURE OF THE BATMAN! — NOVEMBER, 1939

Detective COMICS 10¢

No. 31 — 64 PAGES OF Thrill-Packed ACTION — SEPTEMBER, 1939

Detective COMICS 10¢

THE PLANE AND THE DAME
Detective Comics #31 ■ Batman's second super-villain appeared on this famous cover and in a ten-page story by artists Bob Kane and Sheldon Moldoff and writer Gardner Fox. While the hypnotic Monk would be the main focus of the issue, the real addition to Batman's life was shown in the story's opening scene when readers were introduced to Bruce Wayne's fiancée, Julie Madison. This issue also debuted Batman's Batgyro (called the Batplane later in the story) and the earliest version of his famous Batarang.

SPECIAL FEATURE
TOOLS OF THE TRADE

Batman was developing quite an arsenal, but his equipment still needed work. His Batarang would change in size and shape over the years, and even alter its spelling—it was originally referred to as a "Baterang." Batman's Batgyro was also tweaked, becoming the Batplane, and later lost its top rotor.

No. 32 — THE BATMAN — OCTOBER, 1939

Detective COMICS 10¢

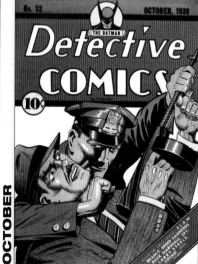

BATMAN WITH A GUN?
Detective Comics #32 ■ The Monk had hypnotized Batman's fiancée in the previous issue, so when Batman confronted him again in this tale illustrated by Bob Kane and Sheldon Moldoff and written by Gardner Fox, the gloves were off. (Despite the fact that Batman's gloves had been extended over his forearms in the last issue.) Following Julie to Hungary, Batman met the Monk's lackey, Dala, and discovered that both villains were vampires. In an unprecedented final scene, Batman used a handgun to shoot a silver bullet into the Monk and kill him.

SPECIAL FEATURE
VAMPIRE KILLER

Batman would soon grow to abhor firearms, a standpoint that would be retroactively credited to the callous shooting of his parents. However, in this issue, Batman shot dead the vampiric Monk. Despite Batman's later "no killing" rule, he would continue to view vampires as inhuman, and thus fair game, killing them in various stories in succeeding decades.

ROUGH JUSTICE

Detective Comics **#27 (May 1939)** ■ In his original incarnation, drawn by Bob Kane, Batman was a grimmer type of Super Hero. While he only killed on rare occasions in his first few appearances, he hadn't yet quite developed his respect for human life, either. In this issue, when Batman caught up to the villain Stryker, a left hook sent the criminal through a railing and into an acid tank. Rather than show regret for causing such a horrible death, Batman simply remarked: "A fitting ending for his kind."

1940s

From the start, artist Bob Kane had a knack for working with some of the best artists and writers in the fledging business of comic books. As the 1940s dawned, Kane and company would be ahead of the pack, creating a strong foundation for the Caped Crusader.

From the first appearance of the Dark Knight in *Detective Comics* #27 (May 1939), Kane had collaborated with writers to create new tales. He soon hired artist Sheldon Moldoff as his assistant to help him with some of the artistic tasks, including inking. When Moldoff went on to draw his own strips directly for DC Comics, Kane hired another assistant, artist Jerry Robinson. Robinson gave much to the polished look of the Batman mythos. In fact, Robinson would be working on the title when it debuted its next great character, Robin the Boy Wonder, in *Detective Comics* #38 (April 1940).

But Robin wasn't the only important character to debut in the 1940s. This impressive decade saw the creation of the Joker, Catwoman, Clayface, Scarecrow, the Penguin, Two-Face, the Riddler, and dozens of other memorable villains. This dawn of the Caped Crusader saw the introduction of the Batcave and the first appearance of Batman's faithful butler, Alfred. Batman gained two new titles in the form of *Batman* and *World's Finest Comics*, and Robin found himself starring in solo stories for a time in the pages of *Star Spangled Comics*.

It was this decade that first saw Batman venture to the silver screen for two different, 15-chapter serials that highly influenced aspects of the comics themselves. In what is now referred to fondly as the Golden Age of comic books, Batman was a shining star, rivaled at DC Comics only by the original Super Hero, Superman.

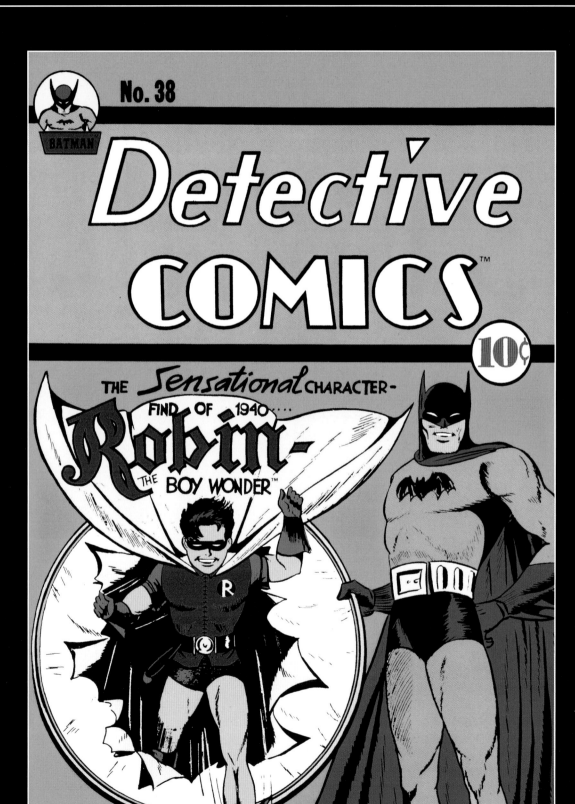

THE BOY WONDER
DETECTIVE COMICS #38

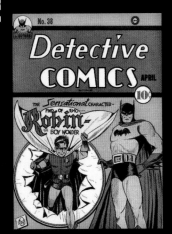

Touted as "The sensational character find of 1940" on the cover, Robin debuted in this issue. Batman's sidekick would go on to become an iconic Super Hero.

Before young Dick Grayson could become a world-famous, pop-culture superstar, he had to earn his spot by the Caped Crusader in this 12-page story by artists Bob Kane and Jerry Robinson and writer Bill Finger. Patterned, in part, on the famous Robin Hood of legend, the Boy Wonder's origin began on the first page. Introduced as the talented son of Haly's Circus' Flying Graysons trapeze act, young Dick Grayson overheard two criminals attempting to extort money from Mr. Haly, promising an "accident" if Haly didn't pay up. The next night, while John and Mary Grayson were performing their amazing "triple spin" act, their trapeze ropes unaccountably snapped, and Dick Grayson looked on in horror as both his parents fell to their deaths.

Before Dick could go to the police with what he knew, Batman met with the young boy, telling him that the town was run by his parents' killer, "Boss" Zucco. Sensing Dick's need to avenge his parents, Batman drove him to the Batcave (in his red sedan) and swore him into service by candlelight. A few boxing and jiu-jitsu lessons later and, by the end of the story's third page, Robin, the Boy Wonder was born.

Batman and Robin then took down Zucco and his organization. In the climax, Robin used his signature slingshot and aerial expertise to prevent Zucco's latest attempt at arson. Still occasionally resorting to lethal force, a trend the Dynamic Duo would quickly grow out of, Robin at one point flipped a henchman off a high girder.

1940

"No, I think Mother and Dad would like me to go on fighting crime—and as for me—well... I love adventure!"

Dick Grayson to Bruce Wayne, *Detective Comics* #38

1940 would be a breakout year for Batman. Sales of *Detective Comics* would increase dramatically when the Dark Knight's partner, Robin, debuted to lighten up his adventures, and many other comic book titles soon took on young sidekicks to accompany their heroes, hoping to net a bit of that Batman and Robin magic. Soon, the Dynamic Duo would go from a feature in an anthology comic to a comic book all their own, complete with two of the most famous super-villains in the long history of the Dark Knight Detective, the Joker and Catwoman.

KINDRED SPIRITS
The ringmaster comforted Dick Grayson on the night his parents were murdered. Dick had no idea that he would soon join forces with Batman to take down Zucco, the gangster responsible.

SWINGING INTO ACTION

Robin's amazing acrobatic skills soon helped him to earn a place at Batman's side. Robin also helped to brighten up Batman's moody world, giving younger readers a character they could easily identify with.

THE BAT, THE CAT, AND THE JOKER

BATMAN #1

Advertised in *Detective Comics* #39 (May 1940) was this premiere issue of *Batman*. After only a year in publication, Batman had earned his own comic book.

While the new title remained quarterly rather than monthly for the time being, *Batman* included four all-new Dynamic Duo adventures, beginning with this issue by artist Bob Kane and writer Bill Finger that introduced two of Batman's greatest foes. Opening with Batman's origin, first featured in *Detective Comics* #33, the issue then introduced readers to the Joker, Batman's arch enemy. The Joker returned in this issue's fourth story and was originally slated to die.

In the second story, readers met the Monster Men, Hugo Strange's new deadly creation. Called the Man-Monsters when they were advertised in *Detective Comics* #37 (March 1940), the behemoths were dealt with by Batman in an uncharacteristically lethal fashion. He even hanged one with a rope and his Batplane. Originally intended for *Detective Comics* #38 before the last-minute creation of Robin, the story prompted the establishment of a code against killing for Batman that would be adhered to from that point forward.

Catwoman made her first appearance in the third story. Simply called "the Cat," this soon-to-be-iconic female cat-burglar would quickly return.

> "You can't win anyway... You see, I hold the winning card."
>
> **The Joker, *Batman* #1**

THE SIGN OF THE JOKER
The Joker's first victim was Henry Claridge, a millionaire who owned a famous diamond. Despite police protection, at the strike of midnight, Henry collapsed to the floor, dying with a grotesque smile upon his face.

STRANGE DEVELOPMENTS

***Detective Comics* #36** ● Artist Bob Kane and his new assistant, Jerry Robinson, and writer Bill Finger introduced Batman to his first true arch foe, Professor Hugo Strange. Destined to become a recurring character who has endured even to this day, the impressively built Strange utilized a machine to create a fog that would better blanket his thefts, until Batman bested the criminal's gang with a gas pellet and toppled Strange with a left hook. This issue also saw Batman add the famous spikes to his gloves, continuing the triangle motif in his design.

SPECIAL FEATURE

DR. HUGO STRANGE

Pre-dating both the Joker and Catwoman, Professor Hugo Strange was Batman's first major super-villain, destined to recur time and time again. While his physical stature would change over the years, the professor never lost his trademark beard and glasses.

KILLER IN CLAY

***Detective Comics* #40** ● When his fiancée, Julie Madison, caught her big break as an actress in motion pictures, Bruce Wayne decided to visit her on set at Argus Pictures, only to meet the newest addition to his Rogues Gallery, the murderer known as Clayface. Illustrated by Bob Kane and written by Bill Finger, the Clayface who debuted in this tale was far removed from his modern day shape-shifting counterpart. This Clayface was Basil Karlo, a movie actor who was driven to commit murders in a clay-like mask.

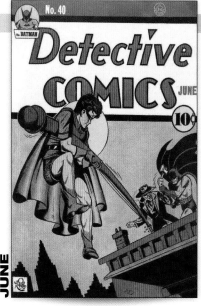

CAT-WOMAN AND COMPANY

***Batman* #2** ● This second installment of Batman's regular series featured four new stories, each drawn by Bob Kane and written by Bill Finger. The first tale starred both of Batman's main rogues, the Joker and the beautiful burglar formerly called "the Cat," here referred to as Cat-Woman for the first time, even though she still hadn't earned a proper costume. The second story introduced the nefarious mastermind called the Crime Master, while the third debuted yet another new criminal for Batman to face, the hook-handed villain known as Clubfoot.

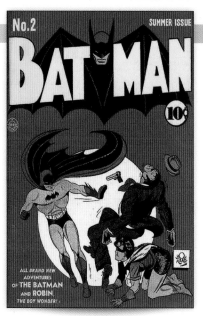

MASTER OF DISGUISE
Another of the Joker's victims, Judge Drake, was killed when the Clown Prince of Crime disguised himself as the chief of police. Holding up a Joker card, the villain then murdered his victim, leaving the Judge with a morbid grin.

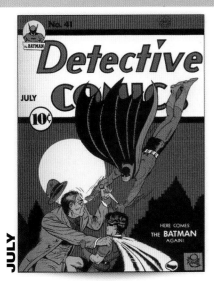

JULY

ROBIN BUCKLES UP
Detective Comics #41 ■ When a knife-wielding maniac made his escape from an asylum, and kidnapped a child from Blake's Boys School, Bruce Wayne enrolled Dick Grayson at the school to help capture the insane murderer in this tale by artists Bob Kane and Jerry Robinson and writer Bill Finger. In this Robin-centric tale that introduced the advancement of Robin's Utility Belt buckle's two-way radio, the Boy Wonder soon discovered that while the maniac had indeed killed the school's janitor, the kidnapper was someone else: the art teacher, Graves.

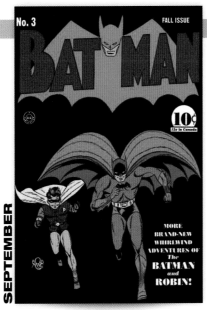

SEPTEMBER

CATWOMAN GETS INTO CHARACTER
Batman #3 ■ Batman's top feline villain would finally gain a costume in this issue that contained four stories by artist Bob Kane and writer Bill Finger. Cat-Woman's new look consisted of a cat-head mask, a red cape, and an orange dress, teamed with a pair of sensible heels. The femme fatale's wardrobe must have impressed, as she managed to steal her first kiss from the Dark Knight by the story's end. This issue also introduced a new Batman supporting character in the person of bumbling cop Detective McGonigle.

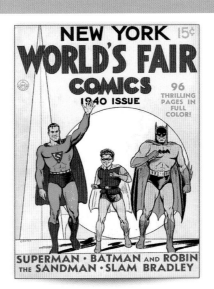

FAIR FARE
New York World's Fair Comics 1940 Issue
In the company's second attempt at selling a comic book at the New York World's Fair, this 96-page special served as a precursor to the Superman/Batman team-up title *World's Finest Comics* that would debut in the following year. While Superman, Batman, and Robin appeared together on this issue's cover, Superman and Batman appeared in two separate stories. Drawn by Bob Kane and written by Bill Finger, Batman's tale saw trouble strike as Bruce Wayne and Dick Grayson headed to the famous fair.

ALSO THIS YEAR

January—*Detective Comics* #35:
In this issue, Batman's sedan was upgraded to a blue convertible.

March—*Detective Comics* #37:
Night-vision goggles were added to the contents of Batman's Utility Belt.

December—*All Star Comics* #3:
While Batman was not yet a member, the first Super Hero team, the Justice Society of America, debuted in this issue.

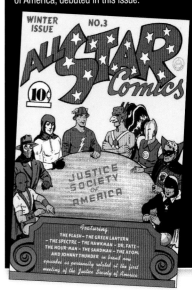

PRESENTING... THE PENGUIN
DETECTIVE COMICS #58

This issue of *Detective Comics* featured the debut of Batman's newest great rogue, whose very appearance made even the Caped Crusader laugh.

Artist Bob Kane had started his career with more playful, humorous cartoons, and maintained, even in his final years, that stylized characters worked better in comic books than realistic ones. The villain that this issue introduced was named the Penguin, a rather oddly proportioned character with a penchant for tuxedos and trick umbrellas. Memorable from the start in this Bill Finger-scripted tale, the Penguin would go on to be a frequent foe for the Dark Knight Detective, proving that appearances could be deceptive when it came to a flair for committing crimes.

In this first appearance, the Penguin stole two priceless paintings from right under the noses of Bruce Wayne and Dick Grayson. After hiding the artworks in the hollow handle of his umbrella, the Penguin used them as leverage to secure himself a position with a local gang. The highly intelligent villain then began a crime spree in which he fired gas from a trick umbrella to escape Batman's clutches. Though the Caped Crusader caught up with the Penguin, he failed to apprehend the wily, bird-loving fiend, who fled via a speeding train. Despite his eccentric appearance, the Penguin had proven himself a major threat to the Dark Knight, and would return the following month for a rematch.

THE BIRD IS THE WORD
Although he didn't appear on this issue's cover, the Penguin's arrival was dramatically announced on this splash page image. It would be years before the criminal was depicted in a threatening manner. At this time, the Penguin could not really be said to inspire terror in his enemies.

> "Why not call me the Penguin? It does fit... hee... hee!"
>
> The Penguin, *Detective Comics #58*

1941

> "Ha! Ha! He does look like a penguin at that!"
>
> Bruce Wayne to Dick Grayson upon seeing the Penguin for the first time, *Detective Comics #58*

With a self-titled quarterly comic book, as well as continued appearances in *Detective Comics*' lead feature, Batman was proving quite a hot commodity, just as Superman had in both his own title and in the pages of *Action Comics*. To further capitalize on these popular characters, *World's Best Comics* (soon to be *World's Finest Comics*) was devised, containing adventures of the two icons, even as both were elected as honorary members of the Justice Society of America in the pages of *All Star Comics*. Batman was a big seller for DC Comics, yet in 1941 he still fell short of the Man of Steel, who had nabbed his own radio show the year before.

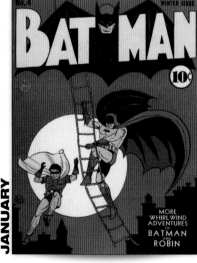

GAINING GOTHAM CITY
Batman #4 ▪ The Joker donned a proper clown costume for his latest scheme in this issue by artist Bob Kane and writer Bill Finger. There was also a tale starring new pirate villain Blackbeard. However the real star of the show was a newspaper masthead plastered on page five, because that particular newspaper was titled the *Gotham City Gazette*. Referred to as "New York" a few times in the past, as of this issue and *Detective Comics* #48 (published a few weeks earlier), Batman's hometown was finally awarded its proper, now-famous name.

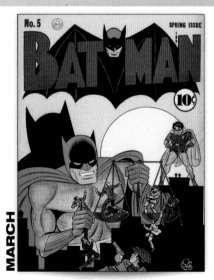

A REAL PAGE-TURNER
Batman #5 ▪ Artist Bob Kane and writer Bill Finger packed plenty of developments into the four stories in this spring issue of *Batman*. In the Joker tale, "The Riddle of the Missing Card," the Batmobile gained its iconic oversized hood ornament and fin. In the second tale, Batman and Robin were transported into a fairy-tale world. In the third tale, Robin was nearly killed, sending Batman on a quest for vengeance. And in the final story, Bruce Wayne literally bumped into his new love interest—beautiful society girl turned nurse, Linda Page.

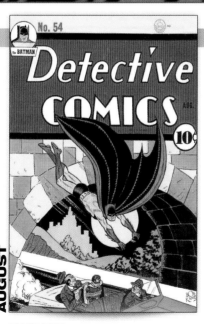

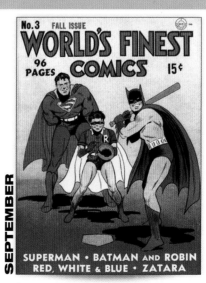

SPRING

AUGUST

SEPTEMBER

DC COMICS' BEST

World's Best Comics #1 ■ After the release of the 1940 special, *New York World's Fair Comics*, DC continued pairing up its two most popular heroes, Superman and Batman, in a title that went on sale in February 1941. While the title would undergo a name change by its second issue, this 96-page first issue featured Superman, Batman, and Robin on the cover, but like *World's Fair* before it, Superman and Batman each kept to their own individual story. Batman's section was a 13-page tale drawn by Bob Kane and written by Bill Finger, involving new villain the Witch.

HIGH 'TEC

Detective Comics #54 ■ In a tale by artists Bob Kane, Jerry Robinson, and George Roussos, and writer Bill Finger, that pit the Dark Knight Detective against modern-day pirates, Batman saw his arsenal become just a little bit more advanced. When trapped in a refrigerator room, Batman employed a new acid capsule from his Utility Belt, followed quickly by a wireless two-way radio stored in the heel of his boot. But perhaps the best new innovation in Batman's war on crime was his first use of the Batplane's ability to transform into a speedboat.

AS THE SCARECROW FLIES

World's Finest Comics #3 ■ One of the biggest names in Batman's Rogues Gallery, Scarecrow, debuted in this issue, only to star in one more story before disappearing until 1967. A slow start to be sure, Scarecrow's origin was nevertheless quite dramatic thanks to pencillers Bob Kane and Jerry Robinson and writer Bill Finger. A disgruntled psychology professor obsessed with fear, Jonathan Crane became the murderous Scarecrow after shame drove him to sell his services as a fear monger in the hopes of gaining more money.

TWO-FACES OF HARVEY DENT

DETECTIVE COMICS #66

Two-Face, one of Batman's most tragic and tortured villains, debuted in this issue by penciller Bob Kane and writer Bill Finger.

Kane and Finger immediately drew parallels between Two-Face and the protagonist in the R. L. Stevenson novella *The Strange Case of Dr. Jekyll and Mr. Hyde*, even having the villain hold that very book on the story's splash page.

Harvey "Apollo" Dent (he was called "Kent" in his first few appearances) was Gotham City's handsome district attorney, often seen about town with his beautiful fiancée Gilda. When trying the case of "Boss" Moroni (changed to "Maroni" in later versions), Harvey presented evidence of the crime boss's guilt by showing the courtroom a two-headed silver dollar with the criminal's fingerprints on it. As an act of revenge, Moroni threw acid in Dent's face, ruining the D.A.'s "pretty boy" appearance.

After Gilda reacted in horror to seeing his face, Harvey's fragile mind snapped, and he scarred one side of Moroni's two-sided coin to match his own visage. Wearing a suit of two different colors split down the middle, he began calling himself Two-Face and embarked on a life of crime. However, before attempting each illegal activity, Harvey would flip his trademark coin to determine if he would act on his basest violent desires, or opt for the path of a noble, upstanding citizen.

In an unusual move by the creators, the tale was left as a cliffhanger, and wouldn't be continued until issue #68 (October 1942). However, the story proved worth the wait, as readers would watch Batman eventually triumph, seeing Harvey placed securely behind bars.

EMOTIONALLY SCARRED
On hand for Moroni's trial, Batman did his best to stop the gangster's attack on Harvey Dent. However, despite the Caped Crusader's best efforts, the concentrated vitriol landed on Dent's face.

> "I've given up my fiancée, my career, everything. Now stay out of my way…"
>
> **Two-Face to Batman,** *Detective Comics* #66

1942

"War savings bonds and stamps keep 'em rolling!"

Batman, *Batman* #12

The United States had officially entered World War II after the bombing of Pearl Harbor in December of 1941. As a result, Batman became more patriotic, especially on his comic books' covers. He was shown saluting soldiers, shaking hands with U.S. troops, and selling war bonds on the front of many issues. And there would be plenty of those covers as *Batman* began a bi-monthly schedule during the second half of 1941, bringing many more comics to its readership than the previous quarterly schedule had allowed. The world was changing fast, and Batman was going to change with it.

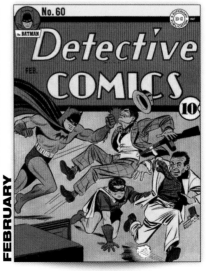

HE GAVE US A SIGNAL
Detective Comics #60 ■ The Joker once again reared his gruesome head in Gotham City in this issue by artist Bob Kane and writer Jack Schiff. Luckily, the Dynamic Duo was ready for him, and so was the police department, because in this tale the police introduced the Bat-Signal, a giant spotlight that displayed the bat-symbol on the night sky in order to summon the hero. While not quite as significant, this issue also introduced a stylish red stripe down the side of the Batmobile, one that was given to the Batplane in the following issue as well.

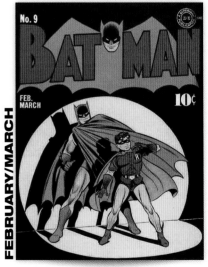

COVER SPOTLIGHT
Batman #9 ■ Artists Fred Ray and Jerry Robinson supplied one of the most iconic covers of the era with this issue of Batman. Featuring the Dynamic Duo caught in a spotlight, this image would be paid homage to many times, including on the almost identical cover of *Batman* #16 (May 1943) by artist Jerry Robinson. Inside this issue were four stories illustrated by Bob Kane and written by Bill Finger that included such outlandish elements as Batman killing a whale with a harpoon and the Joker escaping prison via a breathing apparatus that looked like a duck decoy.

OF TWO MINDS
The acid scarred Harvey Dent symmetrically, giving him reason to indulge his split personality. This obsession with duality would continue into the present day.

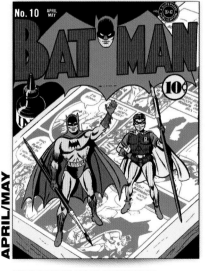

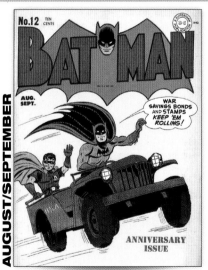

ALSO THIS YEAR

January—*Sensation Comics* #1: Readers met the crime fighter Wildcat, a future ally of the Dark Knight.

June—*World's Finest Comics* #6: An actor accepted the role of the Dark Knight in order to fool a reporter close to unmasking Bruce Wayne's secret identity.

September—*World's Finest Comics* #7: Batman and Robin donned all-white costumes (including white hair for Robin) in order to blend in with the snowy terrain.

BIRTHDAY BOY WONDER
***Batman* #10** ▪ While most kids his age would have been happy with a bicycle, Robin received his very own Batplane for his birthday in the first story in this issue by artist Bob Kane and writer Joe Greene. This issue also featured a tale memorably titled "The Princess of Plunder," written by Jack Schiff and drawn by Fred Ray and Jerry Robinson, in which the Catwoman adopted a black version of her realistic cat mask and costume complete with a purple cape. The issue featured two more Kane-illustrated stories, one by Greene and the other by writer Bill Finger.

BEFORE THE BATCAVE
***Batman* #12** ▪ In the first of this issue's four stories, writer Don Cameron and artist Jerry Robinson introduced Batman's Hall of Trophies, a room in Wayne Manor crowded with mementos from the Dark Knight's many cases. Surprisingly, this wasn't the only precursor to the Batcave shown in this issue. In the second story by artist Bob Kane and writer Bill Finger, a secret garage of sorts was shown under Wayne Manor that contained Batman's Batmobiles and Batplanes. This issue also featured the work of penciller Jack Burnley.

A BIRD IN HAND
***Detective Comics* #67** ▪ If his ultimate goal was to be taken seriously, the Penguin certainly wasn't helping his case in this memorable lead story by artist Bob Kane and writer Bill Finger. While his new liquid-flame-spewing umbrella stopped Batman in his tracks, riding an ostrich to escape the scene didn't exactly strike fear into the heart of the Caped Crusader. If nothing else, the Penguin was certainly committed to his bird theme. As part of his scheme, he even trained a parrot to memorize the safe combination of its rich owner.

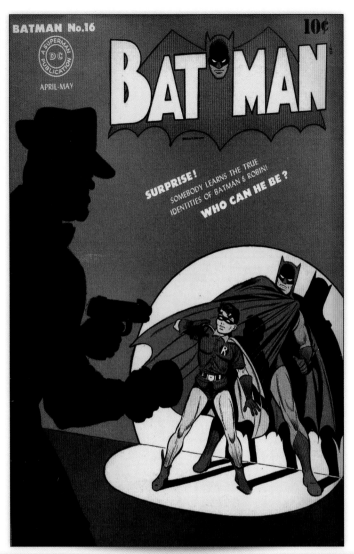

BATMAN No.16

SURPRISE! SOMEBODY LEARNS THE TRUE IDENTITIES OF BATMAN & ROBIN!

WHO CAN HE BE?

HERE COMES ALFRED
BATMAN #16

He was the man behind the man behind the Batman. Practically as well-known as the Dynamic Duo he aids on a daily basis, Bruce Wayne's faithful butler Alfred first appeared in the final tale of the four stories presented in this volume, an effort by artist Bob Kane and writer Don Cameron.

Made famous by his inclusion in the *Batman* television show of the 1960s, as well as in every Batman movie since, the Alfred that first appeared in this issue was a far cry from the svelte gentleman's gentleman we all know. This Alfred was a wannabe detective, but his bumbling nature and rotund appearance were obstacles for that particular ambition. Traveling to Gotham City from his native England, Alfred barged into Wayne Manor, declaring himself Bruce Wayne's new butler. When he accidentally discovered a sliding panel in the wall with a secret stairway that led to Batman's "underground hangar," Alfred quickly put two and two together, and realized that his new life included helping out the famed Caped Crusaders in their adventures.

The remainder of this issue featured a Joker story illustrated by Bob Kane, two other tales by writer Don Cameron, and an adventure at a sawmill illustrated by Jack Burnley. It also featured the work of writer Ruth Lyon Kaufman, whose tale of a criminal milk truck operation was also illustrated by Burnley.

> "Oh-h—a bally stickup, such as I've seen in the cinema!"
>
> Alfred, *Batman #16*

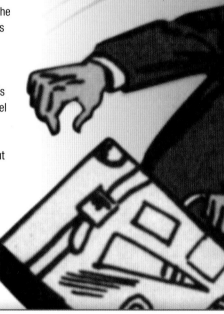

1943

"Mr. Bruce Wayne is the Batman, and the young mawster is Robin! How clever of me to have discovered it...!" Alfred, *Batman #16*

The Caped Crusader began to move into the mainstream in 1943. While Superman ruled the airways with his radio show, Batman beat the hero in the race to live action, securing his first 15-chapter movie serial years before the Man of Steel. And while Superman was the first to make a splash in the world of comic strips, Batman would follow suit this year. In the 1940s, comic books were considered a kids' medium and comic strips were viewed as the "major leagues." Batman's arrival in his own strip was a source of pride for artist Bob Kane, and he began to focus his energy on the daily cartoon for the majority of its four-year run.

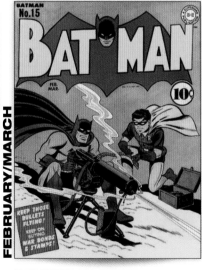

A MATTER OF STYLE
Batman #15 ▪ Catwoman was having trouble deciding exactly what to wear. In the first story of this issue, which featured a very uncharacteristic image of Batman firing a machine gun on its cover, Catwoman (now no longer spelled Cat-Woman) fought Batman once again wearing her black cat mask, but now clad in a green dress with an orange cape. Featuring tales by artists Bob Kane and Jack Burnley and writers Don Cameron and Jack Schiff, this issue also saw Batman convert his Batplane into a Christmas-themed flying sleigh.

MEET THE TWEEDS
Detective Comics #74 ▪ While not destined to rise to the level of Batman's other main foes from this era like the Joker or Catwoman, Tweedledee and Tweedledum, who premiered in this issue, would continue to be a part of the Batman mythos into the present day. Pencilled by Bob Kane and Jerry Robinson and written by Don Cameron, this tale featured cousins Deever and Dumfree Tweed, two thieves who dressed themselves as characters out of Lewis Carroll's *Through the Looking-Glass*, complete with henchmen dressed as disturbing white rabbits.

A GENTLEMAN'S GENTLEMAN
The son of Thomas Wayne's butler Jarvis, Alfred had promised his dying father that he would follow in his footsteps as the Wayne family butler—whether Bruce Wayne wanted him there or not!

PRESCRIPTIONS FOR PLUNDER
Detective Comics #77 ▪ Batman's Rogues Gallery grew by one more member with the introduction of surgeon Matthew Thorne alias the Crime Doctor in this tale by artist Bob Kane and writer Bill Finger. Running his so-called Crime Clinic, the Crime Doctor prescribed ways to "cure" any criminal operation in order to help it run smoothly. Despite his hand-to-hand combat skills and use of blinding light from his head reflector, the Crime Doctor proved no match for Batman and Robin during a fight atop a massive atom smasher vacuum tube.

THE END OF TWO-FACE?
Detective Comics #80 ▪ When Two-Face broke out of jail, Batman and Robin feared the worst in this story drawn by Bob Kane and penned by Bill Finger. In order to learn Two-Face's location, Batman disguised himself as a criminal and interrupted the villain's robbery at Tarnegie Hall. The Caped Crusader then talked some sense into Harvey Dent (named "Kent" at this time, until 1949). By the story's end, Harvey's face was reconstructed by famed plastic surgeon Dr. Ekhart. Afterwards, Two-Face's retired trademark coin was placed in its new home: Batman's trophy room.

A CAVALIER BEGINNING
Detective Comics #81 ▪ Artist Bob Kane and writer Don Cameron gave Batman a new recurring foe in the form of Mortimer Drake, alias the swashbuckling Cavalier, in this issue's memorable lead feature. Hoping to be an "even greater inconvenience" to Batman and Robin than the Joker or the Penguin, the Cavalier started out small, stealing a baseball from a small boy. He soon upped the ante, however, and his robberies grew in scale and ambition. The Cavalier even fought off Batman with an electrical sword.

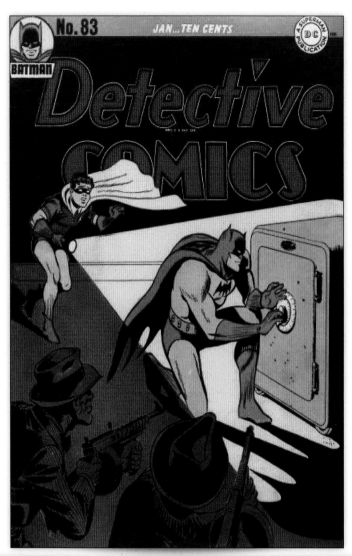

BREAKING IN THE BATCAVE

DETECTIVE COMICS #83

This landmark issue by writer Don Cameron and artist Jack Burnley introduced Batman's secret hideout, the famous Batcave.

Before this issue, a hangar of sorts had been situated underneath Wayne Manor. Connected to the mansion by a hidden elevator and staircase, this garage included a repair shop and storage for Batman's various cars and planes. The vehicles could exit via an underground tunnel that connected to a neighboring barn. Batman also had a Hall of Trophies, but that was located in a locked chamber in Wayne Manor itself.

However, in the previous year's Batman movie serials, one memorable chapter was called "The Bat's Cave." It introduced the concept of Batman setting up a base in a cave under his mansion. The Batcave was accessible through a secret entrance in Wayne Manor inside a grandfather clock. This issue expanded on that Batcave idea, giving a bit more character to some of the elements already established in previous comics, although it left out the clock for the time being.

This issue also saw Alfred go from being overweight to the lanky butler that has served Batman ever since, thanks to a quick trip to a health resort. Although he still managed to retain his trademark clumsiness, Alfred now more closely resembled his counterpart from the Batman serials.

> "The alarm from the Batcave! Someone must be down there!"
>
> Dick Grayson to Bruce Wayne, Detective Comics #83

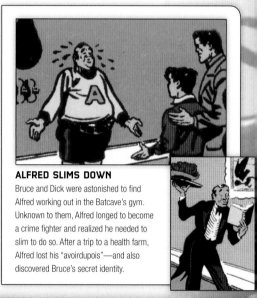

ALFRED SLIMS DOWN
Bruce and Dick were astonished to find Alfred working out in the Batcave's gym. Unknown to them, Alfred longed to become a crime fighter and realized he needed to slim to do so. After a trip to a health farm, Alfred lost his "avoirdupois"—and also discovered Bruce's secret identity.

1944

> "You ought to hide your silly, grinning face in shame. I'm the king of crime in these parts."
>
> The Penguin to the Joker, Batman #25

Today it's commonplace for a Batman film or TV show to influence events in the comics themselves. For instance, Harley Quinn debuted in *Batman: The Animated Series* before becoming a star in the comics. The first of time this happened was in 1944, when Batman's hideout and his butler Alfred both received makeovers thanks to a popular Batman movie serial from the previous year. This year also saw time travel become a regular part of Batman's life, even as his old villains continued to haunt him in the present.

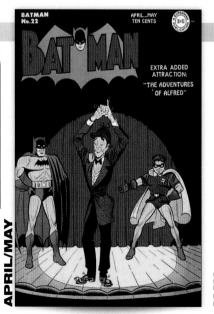

THE ADVENTURES OF ALFRED
Batman #22 ● Alfred nabbed his own back-up tale thanks to writer Mort Weisinger and artist Jerry Robinson. Not quite the crime fighter that his employers are, Alfred spent his tale accusing an innocent pair of writers of criminal activity before being taken hostage by an actual criminal whom Alfred had mistaken for a college professor. Nevertheless, the butler's clumsiness helped catch the crooks in the end of this four-page tale that accompanied other stories by artists Bob Kane and Jack Burnley and writers Alvin Schwartz and Bill Finger.

UMBRELLA UPGRADE
Detective Comics #87 ● Umbrellas had long been the Penguin's weapons of choice. He'd often used trick bumbershoots to fire gas and "liquid flame" at the Dynamic Duo in the past. In this tale by writer Joseph Greene and penciller Dick Sprang, the Penguin toyed with a few new umbrella-based gadgets to add firepower to his arsenal: The super-villain debuted an umbrella with a welding torch handle, a radio umbrella, a glider umbrella, a sword umbrella, and even one that could serve as a mini-helicopter for a quick getaway.

AUGUST

"NICH" OF TIME

Batman #24 ▪ Professor Carter Nichols, a recurring member of Batman's supporting cast, first appeared in this time-spanning epic by writer Joe Samachson and artist Dick Sprang. Having devised a way to send Batman back in time via hypnosis, Nichols sent the Caped Crusader to ancient Rome. He then dispatched Robin to help Batman escape from a Roman jail cell. After meeting a Joker-like jester and being dubbed "Batmanus," the Dark Knight returned to the present in this issue that also featured stories by writer Don Cameron and artist Jerry Robinson.

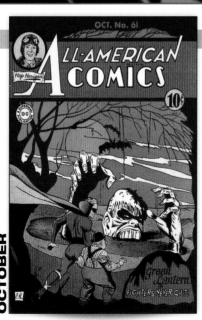

OCTOBER

STEALING SOLOMON

All-American Comics #61 ▪ While many of the members of Batman's Rogues Gallery debuted in the pages of the Dark Knight's regular titles, a few of his villains were appropriated from other heroes' casts. One example was Solomon Grundy, a pale monster who rose from the muck of Slaughter Swamp to plague the original Golden Age Green Lantern, Alan Scott, in this issue by writer Alfred Bester and penciller Paul Reinman. Years later, Grundy would find his way into Batman's world, forcing the original Green Lantern to share his most famous foe.

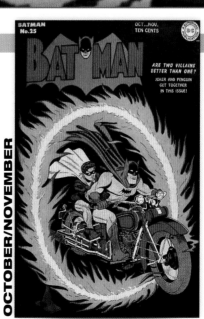

OCTOBER/NOVEMBER

THE JOKER VS. THE PENGUIN

Batman #25 ▪ The Caped Crusader's two best known enemies would form an uneasy alliance for the first time in "Knights of Knavery," the lead story of this issue by writer Don Cameron and artist Jack Burnley. While this comic also featured the work of writers Alvin Schwartz and Bill Finger and artist Jerry Robinson, the main focus was the story that paired the Joker and the Penguin. Meeting in prison, the two super-villains decided to work together in order to prove which of them was the smartest crook in Gotham City's underworld.

ALSO THIS YEAR

March—*Detective Comics* #85: The Joker was forced to clear his own name when an imposter Clown Prince of Crime plagued Gotham.

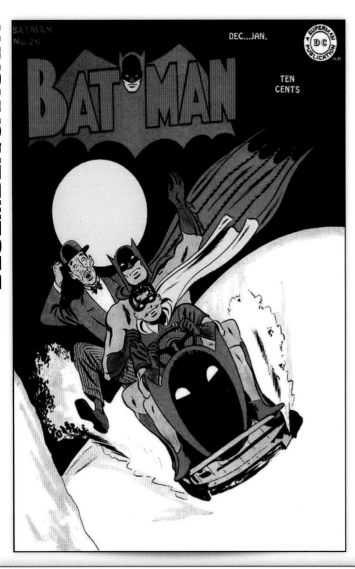

IN THE YEAR 3000
BATMAN #26

Wrapped in a Jerry Robinson-drawn cover that showed off a new sled for Batman, this issue contained four new stories, one of which introduced a new version of Batman himself.

In this issue, readers were introduced to the Batman of the year 3000 by writer Joe Greene and artist Dick Sprang. A descendant of Bruce Wayne named Brane (a contraction of "Bruce" and "Wayne") was forced to act when he saw his world conquered by aliens from Saturn. Brane would become inspired to combat these tyrants when he and his young companion, Ricky, discovered a time capsule from the 1939 World's Fair that contained newsreels of Batman and Robin in action.

Donning their own Batman and Robin costumes, Brane and Ricky trained the populace to combat the invaders. The heroes soon discovered that the alien soldiers were robots controlled by a single, mad Saturnian named Fura. It was probably no accident that this character's name sounded suspiciously like "führer," a common synonym for Adolf Hitler. The events of World War II were still uppermost in the minds of the era's comic book creators. Before Brane and Ricky brought an end to Fura's reign of terror, the alien had even begun herding humans into concentration camps.

A spirited tale of triumph over oppression, Brane was an intriguing new sci-fi addition to Batman mythology.

FREEDOM FIGHTERS
Ricky and Brane witnessed the aliens rounding up political prisoners, scientists, and "honest writers." A time capsule from 1939 containing the story of the 1776 War of Independence and newsreels of Batman and Robin inspired their fight for freedom.

1945

"Hold on to your scalp... here we go again!"

Batman, *Batman* #29

This year consolidated Batman and Robin's look in the comics. The Dynamic Duo looked more polished and finished than ever before. Artist Dick Sprang's memorable style became clearly evident, as did the artwork of Jerry Robinson. *Detective Comics* reached its landmark 100th issue, and Batman and Robin also managed to make a major impact in other mediums, guest-starring in the first of 13 episodes that would pair the heroes with the Man of Steel on the popular radio show *The Adventures of Superman*.

BECOMING A BEAGLE
Detective Comics #96 ● Batman's faithful manservant Alfred was finally rewarded with a last name in this story by writer Don Cameron and artist Dick Sprang. After completing a mail-order course in criminology, Alfred was determined to assist Batman and Robin on their missions. However, the Dynamic Duo declined his help, inspiring Alfred to start his own private investigation business. It was when the naïve butler placed an ad for his services in the local newspaper that readers finally learned that his last name was Beagle (Pennyworth from the late 1960s).

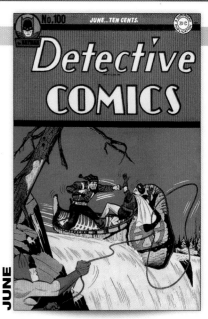

DETECTING 100 ISSUES
Detective Comics #100 ● In the early days of comic books, not much attention was given to seemingly monumental numbers on a title's cover. In later years, a 100th issue might herald an extra-sized comic, an embossed or foil cover, or the start or end of a major storyline. But *Detective Comics* 100th issue came and went with no extra fanfare. The story was a fairly routine tale of gem smugglers by writer Don Cameron and penciller Jack Burnley. Not even one of Batman's many rogues bothered to stop by on this, *Detective Comics*' centennial issue.

LIBERATORS OF EARTH
The Batman and Robin of the year 3000 took on "grotesque space invaders" from the planet Saturn who were determined to conquer first Earth and then the entire solar system.

JUNE/JULY

THE NOT-SO-DYNAMIC DUO

Batman #29 ■ Batman and Robin found themselves up against doppelganger imposters in "Heroes by Proxy," a tale by writer Don Cameron and artist Dick Sprang. Two washed-up detectives named Hawke and Wrenn decided to gain publicity for their agency by posing as a rather odd-looking Batman and Robin, and the real Dynamic Duo had to intervene and save the pair's lives when crime-fighting proved a bit too dangerous for the rather clumsy sleuths. This issue also featured stories by Bill Finger and artist Jerry Robinson.

AUGUST/SEPTEMBER

BABBLE ON

Batman #30 ■ Bill Finger introduced the humorous new character Ally Babble to Gotham City in his script for this issue drawn by artist Dick Sprang. In an attempt to earn $5,000 from an elderly man with a list of 14 "Peeves," the talkative Ally set out giving annoying folks a taste of their own medicine. Writer Don Cameron and artist Jerry Robinson also contributed to this issue, which featured a cover showing Batman passing a firearm to a soldier. Batman had no problem with soldiers or police using guns in the line of duty.

LOUD MOUTH

A play on the classic "Arabian Nights" story of "Ali Baba and the 40 Thieves," the tale that introduced criminal chatterbox Ally Babble was titled "Ally Babble and the Fourteen Peeves." The comical Babble would later return in a future Batman yarn titled "Ally Babble and the Four Tea Leaves" in *Batman* #34 (April 1946).

ALSO THIS YEAR

January—*Detective Comics* #95: The new crime kingpin known as the Blaze heated up Gotham City.

March—*World's Finest Comics* #17: The villain Dr. Dreemo debuted, using the dreams of others as a source of information to inspire his criminal schemes.

★ **September 10th:** Batman and Robin made their radio debuts as guest stars on *The Adventures of Superman*, marking the first time Batman and Superman ever truly worked together.

Batman #11 (June 1942) ● The Joker has been a major presence in Batman's life from his debut in *Batman* #1 (April 1940) to the present day. Batman is a dark figure of the night. The Joker is his opposite: a brightly clad clown. The Joker comes on like a children's entertainer but is a disturbed, murderous villain, contrasting with Batman in every possible way. This cover image of the Golden Age Joker getting his just deserts was drawn by Jerry Robinson.

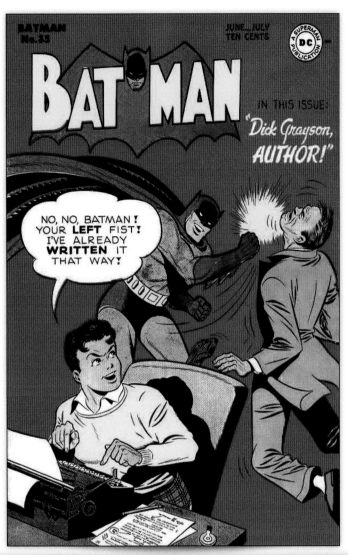

"I LOVE PURPLE"
BATMAN #35

Catwoman was quickly becoming known for changing her outfit every time she encountered the Caped Crusader.

First appearing in ordinary clothes, Catwoman soon took to wearing a furry cat mask and a cape and dress that were constantly switching hues. The villainess needed a wardrobe as iconic as her name, and in a story in this issue by writer Bill Finger and artists Dick Sprang and Ray Burnley, Catwoman got closer to that goal.

Unusually rendered with blonde hair in this tale, Catwoman donned a purple, Batman-like cowl, purple gloves, boots and dress, and a green cape as she attempted to prove to the underworld that, like a cat, she had nine lives. While her hair color and gloves would soon receive some design tweaking, Catwoman retained her purple dress for some time, and years later, it would become her definitive Bronze Age look.

This issue also featured a Dick Sprang-illustrated tale that saw Dick Grayson try his hand at writing, and the classic "Dinosaur Island" story by writer Bill Finger and artists Dick Sprang and Ray Burnley in which Batman and Robin journeyed to a theme park that featured robotic dinosaurs. The island's dinosaurs eventually went haywire, forcing the Dynamic Duo to step up and save the day. It would later be explained that this story was how Batman obtained the giant T. Rex that stands in the Batcave's trophy room to this day.

1946

"The underworld is superstitious—so I will prove to them that I can't be killed!" *Catwoman, Batman #35*

Batman and Robin were a finely tuned institution by 1946, brought to life by a highly regarded group of writers and artists. But like all successful institutions, the Dynamic Duo were constantly evolving. This year saw the debuts of Batman's Batboat and the Joker's first two vehicles of his own. Catwoman's look grew closer to what would be her most iconic costume until the Modern Age of comics, and new villains continued to spring up, even in unexpected titles. While merchandising wasn't yet a big part of the Caped Crusader's life, the innovations introduced this year would later influence the creation of many toys—in some cases decades after the fact.

H.M.S. *BATBOAT*
***Detective Comics* #110** ▪ Batman and Robin christened the H.M.S. *Batboat*, during a trip to England in this story by writer Don Cameron and penciller Win Mortimer. The ship was special transportation arranged by Scotland Yard for the Dynamic Duo and it even included a Batarang gun. The crime fighters must have liked the ship, because it seems that they brought it home across the pond with them. They were on board again in that month's *Batman* #34, in a story by writer Bill Finger and artist Dick Sprang.

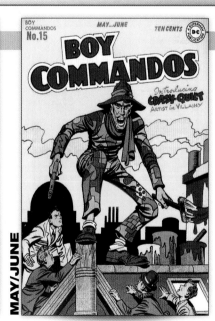

CRIME IN TECHNICOLOR
***Boy Commandos* #15** ▪ One of Robin's greatest future villains first formed his grudge against teenagers when he came up against the Boy Commandos in this issue by legendary writer/artist Jack Kirby. Fans of the Caped Crusader were probably already aware of the Boy Commandos, as the team had debuted in their own feature in *Detective Comics* #64 (June 1942). In *Boy Commandos* #15, they met Crazy-Quilt, an artistic villain who was only able to see colors after a gun battle and subsequent operation injured his vision.

BLONDES HAVE MORE FUN
Catwoman was given blonde hair in this issue, a first for the villain. In later years, Catwoman would again become a blonde in both *Batman: The Animated Series*, and the film *Batman Returns*.

ALSO THIS YEAR

December/January—*Batman* #32: Robin's origin was retold in this issue that also featured the Joker and a tale of the Dynamic Duo meeting the Three Musketeers.

★ **February—**The *Batman and Robin* Sunday strip revealed that Penguin's real name was Oswald Chesterfield Cobblepot.

JUNE

COPY CAT
Detective Comics #112 ● Writer Alvin Schwartz and artist Win Mortimer presented Batman and Robin with "A Case Without a Crime" when the duo caught Catwoman stealing a fake necklace at a costume party. But when Batman unmasked the "criminal," he discovered that the feline fatale in question was actually an innocent young woman named Corinne, an overzealous entrant in the evening's costume contest. Corinne's outfit included a mask similar to Batman's that influenced the next incarnation of Catwoman's ever-changing costume.

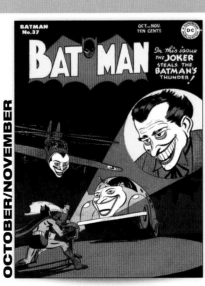

OCTOBER/NOVEMBER

TWO CAN PLAY THAT GAME
Batman #37 ● In an issue drawn completely by Jerry Robinson, readers were treated to "The Joker Follows Suit," a story that saw the Clown Prince of Crime attempt to match Batman's crime-fighting equipment. The Joker not only debuted his famous Jokermobile, but he also introduced a Jokergyro and a Joker Signal as well. This departure was all part of the Joker's bizarre new scheme to try to even out the playing field against his longtime foe. However, Batman turned the tables on the Joker by using the villain's own equipment against him.

NOVEMBER/DECEMBER

STRANGER THAN FICTION
Real Fact Comics #5 ● In a five-page feature, artist Bob Kane was placed in the spotlight usually reserved for Batman and Robin. This short tale focused on Kane's creative contributions to the character of Batman. Fictionalizing actual events, the tale suggested that Kane had first sketched Batman after having a friend try on a costume that his mother had made. This short story was actually written by a team of behind-the-scenes contributors: writers Jack Schiff, Mort Weisinger and Bernie Breslauer, and artist Win Mortimer.

ROBIN FLIES SOLO

STAR SPANGLED COMICS #65

While Superman was DC's number one Super Hero, Batman came a close second. And for a long time, the playing field was more or less even, with each Super Hero starring in two comics as well as their shared title, *World's Finest Comics*.

In January 1945, Superman earned a new title when Superboy's feature debuted in *More Fun Comics* and then quickly switched over to *Adventure Comics*. Exploring Superman's life as a boy, these adventures proved popular, so DC Comics decided to give Batman a similar treatment. That meant it was time for Robin to spread his wings and head into the pages of *Star Spangled Comics* #65.

Drawn by Win Mortimer, this ten-page story saw Robin try his hand at a solo adventure when he investigated corruption at the Boyville Reform School. While Batman's shadow appeared on the cover, Batman and Alfred only made cameo appearances, proving that the Boy Wonder was truly adventuring on his own. Robin's new starring role would become a successful monthly effort: The young hero soon faced his first super-villain in the form of No-Face in the following issue, also drawn by Mortimer.

While proving popular, Robin's adventures would not achieve the popularity of the Boy of Steel, who'd receive his own ongoing title *Superboy* in March of 1949. Robin's feature would still go on to run over half a decade, which was much longer than any sidekick's strip at that time, proving that the popularity of the Dynamic Duo didn't all rest on Batman's shoulders.

MAKING A SPLASH
Robin was thrust into action on the splash page of his first solo story, his adventures titled with a bat-shaped Robin logo, that let readers know in no uncertain terms the character's connection to the popular Batman.

1947

"Betrayed by pennies!"

Joe Coyne, the Penny Plunderer, *World's Finest Comics* #30

The popularity of Batman and Robin was such that they were becoming bigger than their three main titles. As *Batman*, *Detective Comics*, and *World's Finest Comics* attempted to contain the larger-than-life adventures of the Dynamic Duo, it seemed clear that readers wanted to see more of them. Robin soon received his own solo feature in the pages of *Star Spangled Comics*, and Batman popped into *All Star Comics* to make a rare guest appearance. Not only that, but a future Batman foe and an ally—Gentleman Ghost and Black Canary—appeared over in *Flash Comics*. Both characters were destined to be linked to the Caped Crusader in the coming decades.

CATWOMAN: COVER GIRL
Detective Comics #122 ▪ At long last Catwoman settled on a costume when her look from *Batman* #35 (June 1946) was altered a little thanks to penciller Bob Kane. Now no longer a blonde, Catwoman proudly wore the newest variation of her purple dress/green cape attire in this issue, showing off claws on her gloves and earning her first cover appearance. Perhaps even more innovative than her clothing was Catwoman's newest accessory: her Kitty Car, a purple, cat-shaped equivalent to the Batmobile that was capable of leaping.

LIKE CLOCKWORK
Star Spangled Comics #70 ▪ Robin faced the sinister Clock in this issue written by Bill Finger and pencilled by Win Mortimer. Obsessed with time down to the second, the Clock ran his criminal organization from the clock tower of a clock shop. While he looked merely like a man with a mustache in this debut story, when the Clock returned to plague Robin in issue #74 (November 1947), his face would take on a perfectly round shape, and his mustache would appear more like the hands of a clock, giving him a proper super-villain visage.

A PENNY FOR YOUR THOUGHTS
WORLDS FINEST COMICS #30

Batman gained one of the most iconic trophies in his Batcave when he encountered the new villain dubbed the Penny Plunderer in this issue.

The two most iconic items in depictions of the Batcave were the giant penny and the robotic Tyrannosaurus Rex—the largest trophies in Batman's collection of mementos from his past capers. The Caped Crusader had encountered the faux dinosaur in the pages of *Batman* #35 (July 1946); in *World's Finest* #30, artist Bob Kane and writer Bill Finger revealed how Batman added the giant penny to his intriguing collection.

A criminal named Joe Coyne became obsessed with pennies at a young age when he made a meager income as a paperboy. After robbing a cash register and only getting pennies for his efforts, he adopted the name of the Penny Plunderer. Later, Coyne encountered Batman and Robin when the villain and his gang attempted to rob a rare coin and stamp exhibit. Batman skittled the Penny Plunderer and his thugs with a giant penny prop. After Coyne was defeated, Batman moved the penny to the Batcave. And that is why the mammoth coin displayed a date of 1947. (The coin's history later changed; it became an item that Two-Face had used to try to crush Batman.)

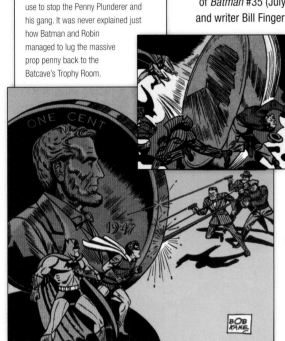

COIN TOSS
Batman put the giant penny to good use to stop the Penny Plunderer and his gang. It was never explained just how Batman and Robin managed to lug the massive prop penny back to the Batcave's Trophy Room.

No.30 SEPT...OCT. 15¢
WORLD'S FINEST COMICS

THE ORIGINAL BIRD OF PREY
Flash Comics #86 ▪ One of DC Comics' first female Super Heroes, Black Canary debuted in the Johnny Thunder feature by writer Robert Kanigher and artist Carmine Infantino. Originally appearing as a villain, it was later explained that the female vigilante was merely attempting to infiltrate the criminal underworld. A future member of the Justice Society, Justice League and the Batman-related team Birds of Prey, it would later be established that there were two Black Canaries, with this early version accepting the role of the latter's mother.

ROBIN CRUSOE
Star Spangled Comics #72 ▪ When a tropical hurricane forced Robin to crash the Batplane, he found himself stranded on a desert island in this story, drawn by Curt Swan. To survive, Robin fashioned himself a few tools, including a boomerang, bamboo spear, and wooden fish hook. Robin dreamed of his days in Gotham City with Batman, his hair grew longer, and his costume grew frayed. Nevertheless, he was still heroic enough to defeat a group of Nazis and commandeer their submarine's radio when they landed on his temporary island home.

HAUNTING HAWKMAN
Flash Comics #88 ▪ Writer Robert Kanigher would create his second major Batman character (yet not realize it) in this issue's Hawkman tale drawn by comic book legend Joe Kubert. In it, the pair introduced the mysterious villain that would later be named the Gentleman Ghost, an invisible figure in white suit and top hat. Like Kanigher's other creation, Black Canary, the Ghost would later become a major player in Batman's world. But instead of being an ally, like Black Canary, the Gentleman Ghost would face Batman as one of his regular Rogues Gallery members.

ALSO THIS YEAR

January—*World's Finest Comics* #26: Prince Stefan of Valonia became Robin for a day when he switched places with the Boy Wonder.

May—*World's Finest Comics* #28: Wearing a misshapen mask of glass, the Glass Man debuted to challenge Batman and Robin.

August—*All Star Comics* #36: Batman and Superman made a rare guest appearance in the Justice Society of America's title.

October—*Batman* #43: The Penguin tried out a pirate costume and a flying penguin blimp, while Professor Nichols perfected his time ray.

BATMAN AND ROBIN!

No. 140 OCT. Ten Cents

Detective COMICS
A 52 PAGE MAGAZINE

Introducing A SENSATIONAL NEW ADVERSARY OF THE PARTNERS IN PERIL — The Prince of Puzzles "THE RIDDLER!"

THE FIRST RIDDLE
DETECTIVE COMICS #140

This issue by writer Bill Finger and artist Dick Sprang introduced the Riddler, the newest soon-to-be-iconic Batman villain.

Edward Nigma learned to cheat at an early age, when he snuck a look at a completed jigsaw puzzle in order to win a classroom contest. He soon created a reputation for himself as a master of puzzles, becoming a conman in the process. Needing more of a challenge, the now adult Nigma decided to pit himself against Batman, adopting a question mark-covered suit and adopting the name, the Riddler.

The Riddler soon struck, forcing Batman and Robin to solve crossword clues, assemble a giant jigsaw puzzle, and free a man from a giant wire puzzle. The heroes tracked Nigma to Gotham City's Amusement Pier, where they escaped a glass labyrinth only to discover the Riddler had disappeared during an explosion.

A true intellectual match for the Caped Crusader, the Riddler exited his first comic in mysterious fashion, but returned just two issues later to plague Gotham City and its guardians.

WORD PLAY

On his first outing, Riddler commandeered a giant crossword puzzle, sending three clues to Batman about the crime he was about to commit. Solving the clues led the Dynamic Duo to a banquet, not realizing that Riddler was flooding a nearby bank in order to rob it, hence the real solution to the puzzle: "bank wet."

1948

"Hmm-m! You make quite a nice picture yourself!"

Bruce Wayne to Vicki Vale, *Batman* #49

By 1948, the average *Batman* issue contained three stories rather than the former four tales per issue. However, now used to this format, the writers and artists seemed to pack more of a punch per tale, giving readers as much story as they could in every issue. It was a style that came in handy when introducing the major foes and supporting characters that debuted in this busy year. These included Batman's love interest, photographer Vicki Vale, and the major villain known as the Riddler, both of whom would go on to co-star with the Dark Knight Detective in future blockbuster films and cartoons.

BATMAN OR FROG MAN?

Detective Comics #132 ▪ In a story drawn by Jim Mooney, Batman met the Human Key, a former circus performer named Paul Bodin. With a knack for picking locks, Bodin had, in the past, taught the Caped Crusader a thing or two about safe-cracking. Yet in this story, Bodin was forced to commit crimes as the Human Key when criminals kidnapped his daughter. Batman managed to free Bodin and his child, fighting the blackmailers underwater at one point while wearing a new "Frog Man" variation of his famous Batman costume.

DEADLY CHILL

Batman #47 ▪ Artist Bob Kane and writer Bill Finger helped Batman finally put a name to the face of the man who killed his parents in this expansion on Batman's origin. Employing his new underwater helmet, Batman caught up with the man, whose name was Joe Chill, on a gambling ship. Batman then revealed his identity to the murderer, terrifying Chill and causing him to run to his friends, confessing that he had killed Batman's father. The criminals gunned down Chill, enraged that he had been responsible for creating their nemesis, Batman.

MAD LOVE
BATMAN #49

This issue introduced not only the new villain Mad Hatter to Batman's universe, but also the Dark Knight Detective's new love interest, Vicki Vale.

Batman hadn't seen his last girlfriend, Linda Page, in almost five years, but over in Superman's titles, the Clark Kent/Lois Lane relationship was proving a hit with readers. So it was decided that Bruce Wayne should once again try his hand at love. In this issue, which included work by artists Bob Kane and Lew Schwartz and writer Bill Finger, readers met Bruce's latest flame, photographer Vicki Vale, introduced to establish a character who was slated to appear in a 1949 movie serial. Vicki wasn't the only major character to debut in this 12-page tale. Making his entrance into Batman's Rogues Gallery was the Mad Hatter, a foe inspired by Lewis Carroll's children's story *Alice's Adventures in Wonderland*. In the comic book, this eccentric thief broke into Gotham City's exclusive yacht club and stole a trophy valued at more than $5,000. Armed with a suitably bizarre appearance and a penchant for trick hats, the Mad Hatter seemed a perfect addition to the ranks of Batman's recurring foes.

VICKI VALE, PHOTOGRAPHER
Like Lois Lane, Vicki Vale had a job that could potentially get her into a lot of trouble. She wasn't a news reporter, but she was the next best thing, a "girl photographer." She quickly became a recurring character in both Batman and Bruce Wayne's life and, thanks to her skill with a camera, soon came to suspect that they were one and the same person.

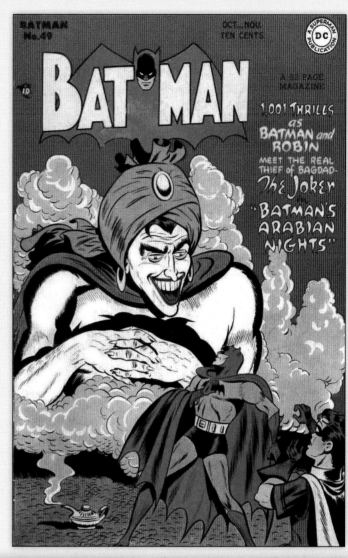

BOY OF MYSTERY
Star Spangled Comics #83 ▪ Robin adopted the identity of Mr. Mystery in this story illustrated by Jim Mooney. A radio show promoted U.S. savings bonds with a contest challenging readers to guess the identity of Mr. Mystery, and a new villain called Dictionary set out to solve the puzzle when he wasn't busy committing heists with his gang. While Dictionary was thwarted by Robin, this story gave readers a glimpse inside the Robin Fan Club Headquarters, a museum dedicated to the exploits of the Boy Wonder.

BREAKING IN THE BATCAVE
Batman #48 ▪ Writer Bill Finger brought readers inside the Batcave in the middle story of this issue drawn by Jim Mooney. Readers had gotten a quick glimpse of the Batcave in a diagram shown in July's *Detective Comics #137* by artist Dick Sprang. Now they were given an extensive tour when criminal Wolf Brando broke into Wayne Manor and chanced upon the grandfather clock entrance to the Batcave. Brando fought Batman through the cave's many rooms, including the relocated Hall of Trophies, before he fell into a whirlpool and drowned.

SPECIAL FEATURE

WHEN TROPHIES ATTACK
Wolf Brando tried to turn Batman's trophies against the Dynamic Duo, including the famous T. Rex robot from Dinosaur Island. Batman saved Robin's life by rolling his giant penny into the path of the toppling dinosaur.

ALSO THIS YEAR

January—*World's Finest Comics #32*: Batman and Robin fought new costumed foe Lucky Starr, the "Man Who Could Not Die."

February—*Batman #45*: After Batman, costumed as the biblical Samson, literally brought the house down in this issue's first tale, he met the long-necked, red-haired new villain Match.

March—*Star Spangled Comics #78*: The "Robin of India" debuted in the form of Robin's new ally, Rajah Rahbin.

BATMAN No. 50 — DEC...JAN. TEN CENTS — A SUPERMAN DC PUBLICATION — A 52 PAGE MAGAZINE

Special! ONCE AGAIN BATMAN and ROBIN BATTLE THE MOST BIZARRE VILLAIN OF ALL TIME in "The RETURN of TWO-FACE"

TWO-FACE'S RETURN
BATMAN #50

Two-Face was back in this thriller by artists Bob Kane and Lew Schwartz and writer Bill Finger, although how the villain had returned would remain a mystery for most of the story.

This issue marked the first time Two-Face's civilian identity was defined as Harvey Dent, rather than Harvey Kent. It was an intentional change by DC Comics, who gave Harvey a new last name so as not to confuse readers with DC's other famous Kent, Clark Kent, also known as Superman. (DC seemed to have a harder time cementing the name of the man who scarred Harvey's face, calling the gangster "Morony" here).

Sandwiched between two other Kane/Schwartz-drawn stories (one of which featured a new Robin of sorts, when Batman trained a blind boy named Jimmy and allowed him to wear Robin's costume), this tale saw Harvey Dent haunted by dreams of returning to his life of crime. Harvey's handsome features had been restored to him, and the scarred visage of Two-Face was seemingly a thing of the past, until Two-Face was spotted robbing Addison Stadium.

After a clash at the circus with Two-Face, Batman and Robin fought the villain atop a scarred statue of Harvey Dent that his wife Gilda Dent had been working on. They defeated their enemy only to discover that they hadn't been fighting the true Two-Face at all, but merely an impersonator in the form of Harvey's greedy butler, Wilkins. He had been using a silver dollar that was scarred on *both* sides, to ensure he always acted on the wrong side of the law.

THE COLOR OF EVIL
In his first appearance in *Detective Comics* #66 (August 1942), Two-Face's scarred half was green in color. But by this issue, it had shifted to a purple hue. The villain's face would continue to vary between those two colors throughout his career.

"The bad side wins! You're just unlucky, my friend!"

Two-Face, *Batman* #50

1949

"I may be a Merman, but I haven't forgotten to fight like Batman!"

Batman, *Batman* #53.

Gotham City was getting a larger budget. Thanks to the imagination of artists like Dick Sprang and Jim Mooney, Gotham City seemed to be full of giant props that Batman utilized whenever possible to fight his villains. Not just limited to the giant penny and the robotic Tyrannosaurus Rex in the Batcave's Hall of Trophies, Batman fought atop giant organs, roulette wheels, and even typewriters. Gotham City was becoming as unique as Batman himself, even if his second serial film, *Batman and Robin*, couldn't quite reflect the unlimited scope and unrestrained creativity of an artist's pencil.

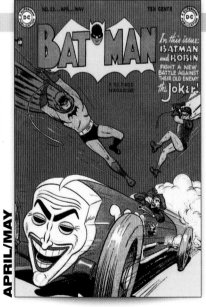

THE ART OF THE JOKE
Batman #52 ■ While this issue included the first appearance of a minor villain called the Thinker and featured the Caped Crusader journeying to the time of the Vikings with the help of Professor Carter Nichols, the real star of the issue (and any he appeared in) was the Joker. In the story "The Happy Victims," drawn by Bob Kane and written by Bill Finger, the Clown Prince of Crime attempted a career as a bizarre artist, donning a smock and beret. More importantly, he also debuted the latest spectacular version of his Jokermobile, a topless roadster.

SHARK ATTACK
Detective Comics #147 ■ The Dynamic Duo faced the menace of new villain Tiger Shark in this story drawn by Dick Sprang. A thief armed with a square helmet, a striped tiger-print scuba suit, and inflatable water "shoe skates," Tiger Shark nearly caused the end of Batman and Robin. However, after escaping a near-death experience when trapped in a bathysphere, Batman tried out his new submarine, and snagged the crafty villain in a steel mesh net. Batman discovered that Tiger Shark was actually famed oceanographer Dr. Gaige.

TWO SIDES OF THE SAME COIN
Batman deduced that Two-Face was an imposter when he noticed that the villain's trademark coin did not mesh with his obsession with the number two. Wilkins' coin was scarred on both sides to guarantee an "evil" outcome each time.

ALSO THIS YEAR

January—*Detective Comics* #143: While a different character entirely from the popular Silver Age Flash villain, the nefarious Pied Piper debuted to challenge the Dynamic Duo.

February—*Batman* #51: Batman and Robin met the daydreaming wannabe hero, Mr. Wimble.

★ **May 26th:** *Batman and Robin*, the Dynamic Duo's second and final movie serial debuted in 15 chapters, with Robert Lowery as Batman and Johnny Duncan as Robin.

June—*Detective Comics* #148: Batman and Robin were shrunk in size when they faced new menace Professor Zero.

MERMAN
Batman #53 ▪ In a comic that also included two other tales, drawn by Bob Kane and Lew Schwartz, writer Bill Finger and artist Jim Mooney saw Batman awaken under the ocean after a boat wreck. Surprisingly the Caped Crusader realized he could breathe underwater, and now had a Merman's tail instead of legs. Acting as a Merman, the Caped Crusader fought crime under the water until he entered a "converting chamber" and awoke back on land, never knowing if what he had experienced was a dream or reality.

CLOWN COLLEGE
Batman #55 ▪ When the Joker organized a syndicate of Jokers, one for every one of the then 48 states in the union, Batman was captured and forced to wear a floppy "clown" version of his own uniform. Soon, however, Batman managed to foil the Joker's plans and put an end to his clown college in this tale written by Bill Finger and drawn by Dick Sprang. This issue also contained two stories drawn by Bob Kane, one where Bruce Wayne became a temporary policeman, and another introducing a new villain, the Gong.

ON LEATHER WINGS
Detective Comics #153 ▪ The Caped Crusader briefly took to the sky in this story drawn by Dick Sprang. Batman attended a lecture by Professor Carl Wilde, a noted authority on bats, after which the professor fitted him with large blue wings controlled by Batman's shoulder muscles. Batman's flying adventures proved to be a dream he had experienced after a violent fall. This issue also featured the first appearance of TV detective Roy Raymond, thanks to artist Ruben Moreira. Raymond's son would become one of Batman's allies decades later.

1950s

The 1950s was a difficult time for comic books. The fashion for Super Heroes seemed to be dying, and the main reason for that was a popular misconception that comics were corrupting the nation's youth.

At the height of Cold War paranoia about the so-called Communist menace, as promulgated by Senator Joe McCarthy among others, Dr. Fredric Wertham published *Seduction of the Innocent*. This book seemed designed to instill fear and worry into the hearts of parents about what their children were reading. Crime and horror comics had become extremely popular, with the latter especially dealing in blood, gore, macabre humor, and revenge themes. These comics undoubtedly contained material that may not have been appropriate for children. Despite the fact that adults did read comics, the medium was still viewed as strictly for young audiences, and Wertham's book encouraged the public to tar Super Hero comics with the same brush as more questionable genres.

Wertham's book and its parallel media witch hunt coincided with the U.S. Senate's investigation of comics, resulting in the establishment of the self-regulating censors known as the Comics Code Authority. DC Comics adopted a C.C.A. logo on its comics, and suddenly, many of Batman's villains became less deadly, and more interested in pulling large-scale pranks. Batwoman and Batgirl were introduced in an attempt to create a more traditional family environment for the Dynamic Duo of Batman and Robin. Comics became tamer, and lost what edge they originally had. Batman even wandered into the world of sci-fi in an attempt to imitate Superman and solve intergalactic crimes that were so far-fetched they wouldn't "corrupt" the young minds of the era.

Luckily for the Caped Crusader, the next decade would see a major reinvention for Batman and a rise in mainstream popularity that was like nothing the character had ever seen before.

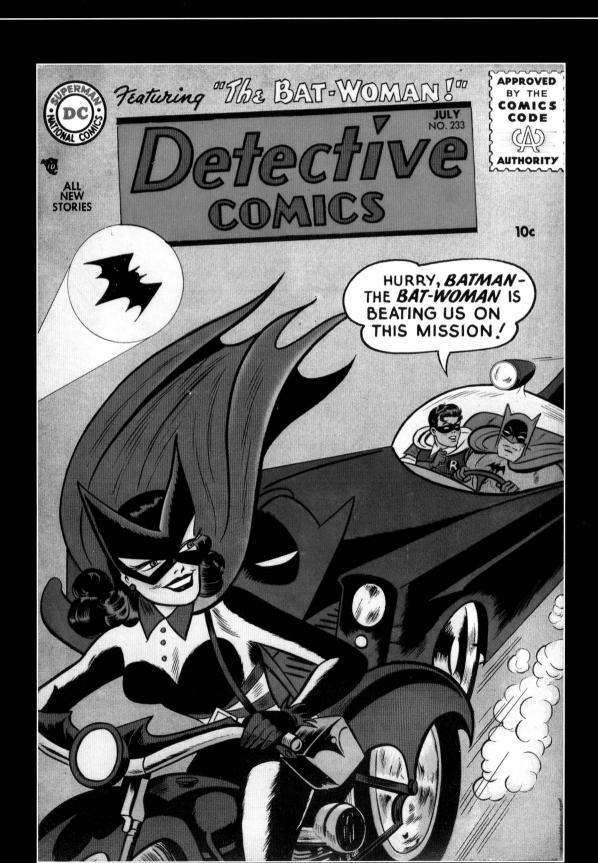

DOOM TO THE DOCTOR
DETECTIVE COMICS #158

Readers were treated to an insider's tour of the Hall of Trophies in this issue that featured a new minor villain named Dr. Doom.

Drawn by Bob Kane and written by Edmond Hamilton, this story was named "The Thousand and One Trophies of Batman." While this issue introduced smuggler Dr. Doom as a new villain, it was mostly concocted as a way of exploring Batman's trophy room now located in a locked chamber of the Batcave. Having accumulated 1000 trophies from their adventures, the Dynamic Duo took some time out from their busy schedule to look through their collection of mementos from the various crimes they had solved.

However Batman is rarely offered leisure time, and before long he was called into the city by Commissioner Gordon to confront a villain calling himself Dr. Doom who had smuggled a fortune of jewels by using faux Egyptian relics. Eluding Batman and Robin, Doom hid inside a mummy case that was scheduled for transportation to the Batcave's trophy room. There he rigged various trophies to attack the Dynamic Duo (including a robotic dinosaur that was clearly not a Tyrannosaurus Rex). Unfortunately for Dr. Doom he suffocated inside the same mummy case that he'd used as his makeshift Trojan horse.

DOOM'S DAY
While Batman and Robin were absent from their trophy room, Dr. Doom booby-trapped many of their larger than life props. Those death traps included a harpoon firing cannon, giant dice, and a robotic dinosaur.

1950

"And you call yourself Deadshot! Dudshot would be better!"

Batman to Deadshot, *Batman* #59

The major focus in 1950 was to clearly define the elements in Batman's environment. With so many interesting gadgets and equipment available to the hero, there seemed to be plenty of story potential in putting each unique innovation under the proverbial microscope. The Batmobile and Batplane were given facelifts, with each design thoroughly thought out. Readers were introduced to all the fun details and secrets that both vehicles possessed. The Hall of Trophies was explored, as were Batman's variant costumes. The spotlight was even cast on the Bat-Signal itself, as Batman's world was cataloged and explained like never before.

RIDE, BAT-HOMBRE, RIDE!
Batman #56 ▪ A frequent Batman writer during the 1950s and later the 1970s, David V. Reed penned this tale drawn by Dick Sprang. In it, Batman visited the tiny Latin American republic of Mantegua to help establish its new hero Bat-Hombre. After outfitting the hero with a masked horse, Batman discovered that Bat-Hombre was actually working for the country's criminals, and quickly put an end to his villainous ways. This issue also featured a pair of stories by Bill Finger; one illustrated by Sprang, and the other by Jim Mooney.

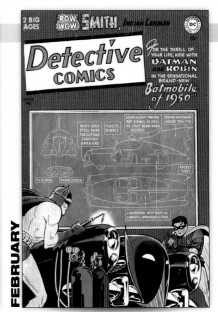

THE BATMOBILE OF 1950
Detective Comics #156 ▪ Introduced on a blueprint on this issue's cover, Batman's Batmobile received an upgrade in this story by writer Joe Samachson and penciller Dick Sprang. While earlier models had changed with little or no fanfare, this issue's entire lead story revolved around Batman crashing his former Batmobile and developing this new and improved model. One of Batman's most iconic cars, this particular Batmobile's most notable features were a searchlight on its roof and a crime lab in its back seat.

JUNE/JULY

DEADSHOT SETS HIS SIGHTS

Batman #59 ● This issue premiered Deadshot, a major Batman foe and future star of both the Suicide Squad and Secret Six. In this story by artists Bob Kane and Lew Sayre Schwartz and writer David V. Reed, Deadshot wore a top hat and tails rather than his later eye gunsight and wrist guns. Posing as a hero, Floyd Lawton's had his career cut short when Batman realized his corruption. This issue also featured work by artist Jim Mooney and writer Bill Finger, and introduced Chief Rokej, a policeman from the year 2050 who looked just like the Joker.

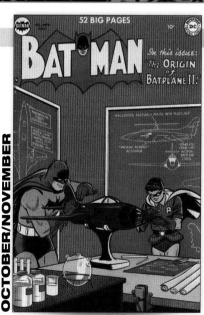

OCTOBER/NOVEMBER

THE NEW BATPLANE

Batman #61 ● In similar fashion to the Batmobile revealed in *Detective Comics* #156 (February 1950), Batman unveiled the Batplane II in this issue by writer David V. Reed and artist Dick Sprang. Also first showcased as a blueprint on the issue's cover, the Batplane II came into being when the Caped Crusaders lost their original model. The new Batplane could change into the Batmarine, and had a helicopter blade that folded into the fuselage. This issue also contained the work of artists Bob Kane and Lew Sayre Schwartz and writer Bill Finger.

NOVEMBER

EXPANDING THE WARDROBE

Detective Comics #165 ● Batman debuted several new Batsuits in this issue by writer Edmond Hamilton and artist Dick Sprang. In addition to Batman's white camouflage Batsuit, first glimpsed in *World's Finest Comics* #7 (September 1942), this issue saw a gold Batsuit Batman used to stop a Midas-inspired villain. It also debuted a super-thin cellophane Batsuit that he could keep in his boot heel, a glow-in-the-dark Batsuit, a space-suit, a suit with glider wings, a fireproof suit, an underwater suit, and a costume for Robin to appear as Batman!

ALSO THIS YEAR

October—*Detective Comics* #164: This issue featured the "Untold Tales of the Bat-Signal," including details on the newest bulletproof model.

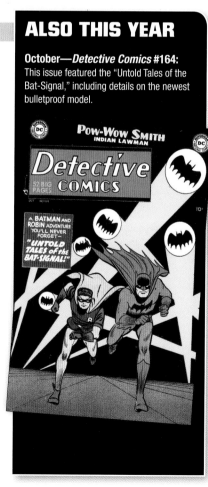

THE RED HOOD
DETECTIVE COMICS #168

Batman's greatest adversary, the Clown Prince of Crime, a.k.a. the Joker, received one of the most memorable origin stories in comic book history with this landmark tale.

Written by Bill Finger and drawn by Lew Sayre Schwartz, this 13-page tale introduced the idea of the Red Hood. Presented as a mystery for the reader, the question of the identity of the Red Hood was raised by Batman himself as he served as a guest professor of Criminology at State University. Having encountered the case of the Red Hood 10 years ago, Batman had still not succeeded in solving the mystery man's identity.

The Red Hood had escaped Batman's detection due to the fact that his face was covered completely by a red metal mask equipped with two-way mirrors. Active for over a month, the Red Hood continued his string of robberies until Batman caught up with him at the Monarch Playing Card Company. In order to elude Batman, the Red Hood dove into a vat of waste chemicals, and escaped into the river while the world presumed he had died.

Hearing that Batman had reopened the famous case, the Red Hood returned to plague the college campus, until Batman finally deduced his real identity as the Joker. Once captured, the Joker revealed that he had been a lab worker until he decided to steal one million dollars and then retire.

FROM RED HOOD TO THE JOKER
After he swam away from the scene of his final heist, the Red Hood's skin, lips, and hair had been permanently altered, and he now looked like a clown. So it made sense in his twisted mind to adopt the name of the clown from a deck of cards: the Joker.

1951

"Batman never carries a gun! But this is my little assistant right here, and it's worth six Robins! Ha, ha!"

Killer Moth, holding up a gun, *Batman* #63

It was a year of origins and debuts. Ever since *Batman* #1 (April 1940), fans had wondered about the backstories of the Joker and Catwoman. In 1951, these famous villains' origins were revealed in back-to-back months. However, the year wasn't just about familiar characters. Batman met a few heroes destined for future membership in the Batmen of All Nations, the mysterious Wingman, and England's own Knight and Squire. Meanwhile, new super-villain Killer Moth was inducted into the ranks of Batman's Rogues Gallery as Robin met one of his own arch foes, Crazy-Quilt.

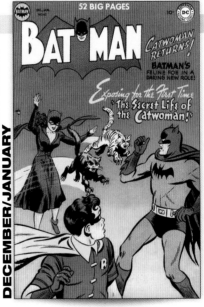

DECEMBER/JANUARY

THE END OF CATWOMAN?
Batman #62 • Artists Bob Kane and Lew Sayre Schwartz and writer Bill Finger collaborated on a Catwoman story that saw the feline fatale retire. Revealing her backstory for the first time, Catwoman admitted to being Selina Kyle, former airline stewardess who had been afflicted with amnesia. Now aware of her former life, Catwoman retired in this tale that also introduced the villain Mister X. In addition, this issue contained another major development when England's version of Batman and Robin, the Knight and the Squire, were introduced.

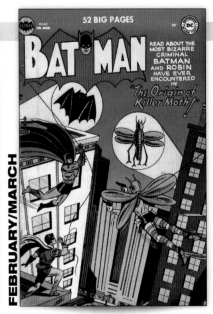

FEBRUARY/MARCH

LIKE A MOTH TO FLAME
Batman #63 • One of Batman's biggest foes of the 1950s debuted in this effort by artists Bob Kane and Lew Sayre Schwartz and writer Bill Finger. A criminal posing under the name Cameron van Cleer adopted the name of the Killer Moth and created his own Mothmobile, offering crooks his help for a fee when summoned by a Moth Signal. This issue also featured a collaboration between Finger and artist Dick Sprang, where the Joker tried out a variety of costumes after being inspired by Batman's own suits, including a futuristic Batman suit and a red fire suit.

EVERY HERO NEEDS A WINGMAN

Batman #65 ■ Robin came down with a severe case of jealousy when Batman adopted a new crime-fighting partner in this tale by artists Bob Kane and Lew Sayre Schwartz and writer Bill Finger. When the Boy Wonder fell and broke his leg, Batman teamed with a northern European Super Hero named Wingman. While Robin fretted that he had been replaced, Batman was merely training the hero, and soon the Dynamic Duo were reunited. This volume also contained the return of Catwoman as a secret ally of Batman in a story that debuted the Cat Signal.

BATMAN II AND ROBIN JUNIOR

Batman #66 ■ Artists Bob Kane and Lew Sayre Schwartz and writer Bill Finger teamed up again to introduce readers to Batman II and Robin II. This story gave us a glimpse of a future dreamt up by Robin where Batman retired, allowing Dick Grayson to take his place in a Batman costume complete with his Robin insignia on its chest. Stepping up to fill Robin's pixie boots was Dick's son, Dick Grayson Jr. The two were even aided by the masked Bruce Wayne, now working at International Police Headquarters. This issue also included art by Dick Sprang.

WHITEWASHED

Star Spangled Comics #123 ■ In a story written by France E. Herron and drawn by Jim Mooney, the villain Crazy-Quilt made his move from an enemy of the Boy Commandos to one of Robin's greatest foes. Armed with a color-projecting helmet that allowed him to see people clearly due to his unique affliction of only being able to see bright colors, Quilt set out to steal all colors in Gotham City. First bleaching the pennants at the yacht club and then cutting the color TV feed, Crazy-Quilt bleached Robin's costume white before he was defeated.

ALSO THIS YEAR

July—*Detective Comics* #173: Killer Moth returned in order to impersonate Bruce Wayne and Batman until finally losing memory of the event.

August—*Detective Comics* #174: Bruce Wayne tried his hand at boxing in a story that also introduced the new criminal called Dagger.

August—*World's Finest Comics* #53: Commissioner Gordon's private life was examined for the first time as his son Tony Gordon debuted.

October—*Batman* #67: Brane Taylor, Batman from the year 3051, traveled to the present to recruit Robin's help against the villain Yerxa.

WORLD'S FINEST
SUPERMAN #76

The World's Finest Super Heroes, Batman and Superman, finally came face-to-face in this landmark issue that teamed the Dark Knight Detective with the Man of Steel for the very first time in print.

Batman and Superman had both starred in *World's Finest Comics* for over a decade, but strangely enough, the two had never joined forces in the series' interior pages. While the covers often showed the two heroes playing sports or enjoying a bit of leisure time together, each issue contained solo tales of the heroes. They had appeared in the same story via cameo appearances in titles like *All Star Comics*, and had even joined forces on the popular *The Adventures of Superman* radio show, but that's as far as their friendship had gone.

This issue of *Superman* changed all that, thanks to writer Edmond Hamilton and iconic Superman artist Curt Swan. Featured on the issue's cover and in its lead 12-page story, Batman met Superman when the two took a cruise in their civilian identities. Forced to share a cabin together due to an overcrowded ship, the pair quickly learned each other's alter egos when they both changed into their Super Hero uniforms to save Lois from a blazing inferno. Despite Lois Lane nearly deducing both Superman and Batman's secret identities during the cruise, the two heroes became fast friends, even as they participated in a friendly competition for Lois' affections.

THE BIG REVEAL
Bruce Wayne and Clark Kent both changed to their alter egos after switching off the light in their room aboard the cruise ship. When flames outside unexpectedly illuminated the room, suddenly their secret identities were not so secret any longer.

1952

"Wait till they gaze upon the Firefly— genius of incredible lighting effects!"

Firefly, *Detective Comics* #184

It was par for the course in Gotham City. But par in Gotham City was anything from ordinary. In 1952, Batman faced two different Two-Faces, a handful of new villains, and finally partnered up with DC Comics' Superman. More of the Dark Knight Detective's gadgets were examined and invented, and the Joker did his best to keep up with his enemy in the invention department. And while Robin's solo adventures ended with *Star Spangled Comics* #130 (July 1952) when the title changed to *Star Spangled War Stories*, the Boy Wonder continued to fight by his mentor's side in their three regular titles.

A NEW TWO-FACE
Batman #68 ▪ In this story drawn by Bob Kane and Lew Sayre Schwartz and written by Bill Finger, a movie recreation of Harvey Dent's origin story created a new Two-Face when actor Paul Sloane had real acid thrown in his face while filming. History had repeated itself, and it was once again up to Batman to end the criminal's career with the help of a trick silver dollar. This issue also included a story featuring Batman's new Alfred-invented Sky Sled by the same writer and artist team, as well as another tale illustrated by Dick Sprang.

FLIGHT OF THE FIREFLY
Detective Comics #184 ▪ A far cry from the pyromaniac that plagues Batman in modern comics, Firefly made his debut in this issue, tricked out with a light-projecting belt. In a story written by France Herron and illustrated by Dick Sprang, the self-proclaimed world's foremost lighting-effects expert, Garfield Lynns, caused a fake stage fire at the musical "Aqua-Melodies of 1952" in order to rob the audience. Chasing Lynns through woodland, the light from a firefly distracted the Dynamic Duo, inspiring Lynns to adopt his costumed Firefly persona.

OCTOBER/NOVEMBER

BELTING THE JOKER
BATMAN #73

Not to be outdone by the Dynamic Duo's Utility Belts, the Joker received a Utility Belt of his very own in this tale that would later inspire an episode of the 1966-8 classic *Batman* TV show.

THE JOKER'S UTILITY BELT
Aware that Batman's Utility Belt relied on scientific devices, the Joker was determined to fill his belt with "jokes and trick novelties," including exploding cigarettes and a jack-in-the-box. He wore the belt outside his suit's vest to show it off.

When the Joker captured Batman and Robin after a scuffle at the Gotham Museum of Modern Art's Comedian Hall of Fame exhibit, the Dynamic Duo escaped the Clown Prince of Crime's clutches by the use of gas pellets from their Utility Belts. Angered that yet another caper was foiled by Batman's reliable belt, the Joker decided to turn the tables on the Caped Crusader and create a belt of tricks all his own in this story by writer David V. Reed and artist Dick Sprang. Instead of storing Batarangs and radios and the like, the Joker's belt boasted his own face as its buckle, and included gadgets that suited his own twisted sense of humor. It hosted trick cigarettes, fake snakes, a hand buzzer, sneezing powder, Mexican jumping beans, and plenty of other gags. This issue also featured a Vicki Vale story by artists Bob Kane and Lew Sayre Schwartz and writer David V. Reed that saw the suspicious photographer once again try to discover Batman's secret identity.

HIGH-FLYING HEROICS
Detective Comics #186 ■ Not content with a crime lab in his Batplane and Batmobile, Batman introduced the Flying Batcave in this issue by writer David V. Reed and artist Lew Sayre Schwartz. The mobile Batcave became a necessity to the Caped Crusader when he agreed not to set foot in Gotham City for a week in exchange for having the recently kidnapped Robin returned to him. Exploiting a loophole in the contract he signed, Batman debuted his Flying Batcave, a giant helicopter equipped with a powerful electromagnet to fight crime from the sky.

THE JUNGLE BATMAN
Batman #72 ■ Artists Bob Kane and Lew Sayre Schwartz collaborated with writer David V. Reed to deliver this fun romp through the jungle in a story that saw Batman and Robin strip off most of their costumes when they needed to make a long swim after surviving a shipwreck. As "Jungle Batman and Robin," the duo hunted down a group of criminals called the "Sinister 8" on a tropical island, before returning to civilization. This issue also featured the work of artists Dick Sprang and Jim Mooney in two other tales.

TWO-FACE OR FOUR-FACE?
Detective Comics #187 ■ The fourth villain to use the identity of Two-Face introduced himself thanks to writer Don Cameron and penciller Dick Sprang. When Two-Face began a new crime spree in Gotham City, the Dynamic Duo were left with quite a mystery on their hands. Batman finally deduced that this Two-Face was corrupt theater manager George Blake who'd used indelible paints to mimic Harvey Dent's formerly scarred visage, slipping up when he accidentally applied them to the wrong side of his face.

ALSO THIS YEAR

January—*Detective Comics* #179: Bruce Wayne became Mayor of Gotham City for a week and faced an imposter Batman.

February—*Batman* #69: Karl Kyle, the villainous King of the Cats, took up where his sister, the now reformed Catwoman, left off.

February—*Detective Comics* #180: Readers were treated to "The Joker's Millions," a famous Joker story that later inspired an episode of *The New Batman Adventures* cartoon.

March—*Detective Comics* #181: Batman and Robin faced the new costumed threat of the Human Magnet.

June—*Batman* #71: Two minor villains debuted this issue: the former magician known as the Masked Mystic and the man with the green, featureless mask, Mr. Cipher.

July—*Detective Comics* #185: Batman's Utility Belt and the gadgets it contained were spotlighted in this issue.

November—*Detective Comics* #189: Batman faced a new villain, the criminal smuggler Mr. Styx.

A BOLD NEW DIMENSION

BATMAN 3-D

Batman appropriately traveled to another dimension when two of his past stories were reprinted in 3-D for the first time.

Batman and Robin stood out like never before when DC Comics decided to give the Dynamic Duo the 3-D treatment. A popular novelty of the time, this type of printing made use of two overlapping colors of the same line image to create a three dimensional effect, causing various parts of the page to "pop out" at the reader.

Delivered to fans in an oversized magazine format, *Batman 3-D* was joined on the stands by *Superman 3-D*, and both issues came with 3-D glasses. However, Batman's particular glasses came bat-shaped, a fun bonus for fans of the Caped Crusader.

Batman 3-D included three stories. The first was a Penguin tale drawn by Jim Mooney that had originally been printed in full color in *Batman* #48 (August 1948). The third, from *Batman* #42 (September 1947), was "The Robot Raiders" by writer Bill Finger and artist Charles Paris. Oddly enough, sandwiched between the two tales was a science fiction story starring Tommy Tomorrow that had nothing to do with the Caped Crusader at all.

The 3-D fad soon died out. However, this issue would be reprinted in 1966 at the height of the so-called "Batmania" excitement surrounding the *Batman* live-action TV series. In addition "The Robot Raiders" would see 3-D print once more when it was included in the 1990 *Batman 3D* special.

ROBOT RAIDERS
In the 1950s, science fiction fascinated moviegoers, as did 3-D technology. Batman 3-D incorporated both elements when the Caped Crusader took a break from fighting common criminals to battle the likes of giant robots.

1953

"Batman, I told you to bring me flowers! Was that so hard to do?"

Vicki Vale, *Batman* #79

Current trends played a big part in Batman's year in 1953. 3-D movies had become a popular fad, and DC decided to capitalize on it. While audiences would soon complain of headaches and tire of wearing 3-D glasses at the theater, Batman had his own 3-D special released a good year before that particular trend faded away. Also all the rage in comics—and also popular in movies—were villains clad in robes and any story involving a monkey or ape. While they were known to follow a popular trend or two, overall when it came to Super Hero comics, DC would still remain the trendsetter.

FEBRUARY/MARCH

GOING APE
Batman #75 ▪ One of the most unique members of Batman's Rogues Gallery debuted in this issue that ushered in a new trend at DC Comics. DC soon realized that titles with gorillas on the cover tended to sell better than regular issues. In one of the first examples of this device, artists Bob Kane and Lew Sayre Schwartz and writer David V. Reed introduced Batman to the Gorilla Boss, the result of placing a criminal's mind inside the body of an ape. This issue also debuted another villain, Mr. Roulette, thanks to Reed and artist Dick Sprang.

MAY

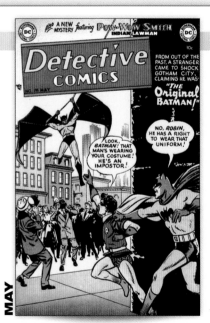

THE ORIGINAL BATMAN
Detective Comics #195 ▪ Penciller Dick Sprang showcased a different kind of Batman in this story that introduced a former circus performer who had laid claim to the Batman mantle long before Bruce Wayne. Arrested for impersonating Batman when he first showed up in Gotham City in costume, Hugo Marmon soon proved that he wore the uniform first, and therefore, by Gotham City law, had the exclusive right to wear a Batman uniform. He even briefly became a crime fighter before his renewed popularity caused him to return to his life in the circus.

APRIL

FOWL PLAY
BATMAN #76

One of Batman's most enduring foes, the Penguin starred in perhaps his most memorable adventure of the 1950s in this issue.

Following a story by artist Bob Kane and writer Edmond Hamilton about Batman and Robin encountering Gotham City's "Danger Club," came a tale of the Penguin by the same creative team. In this story, the Penguin was released from jail, and claimed to have renounced his criminal ways in order to study legendary winged creatures from the past. He said he planned to prove the continuing existence of mythical beasts such as the Phoenix and the Basilisk. But after supposedly discovering and capturing a winged lion, a basilisk, and a giant thunderbird, the Penguin resumed his criminal career, robbing stores as his giant creatures ran amuck in Gotham City. Batman and Robin had to don white asbestos suits to confront a fire-breathing phoenix. They also faced a threat called the "Man-Bat." The heroes soon discovered that the beasts were fakes, and brought the Penguin to justice. This issue concluded with a story featuring a gun-wielding Batman impersonator by writer Bill Finger and penciller Jim Mooney.

MYTHICAL MENACES
Often employing birds to commit his dastardly deeds, the Penguin flew into uncharted territory in this story, which involved mechanical versions of legendary flying creatures.

JULY

THE ROBES MAKE THE MAN
Detective Comics #197 ▪ Featuring a cover full of Batman toys that would make any kid green with envy, writer David V. Reed and penciller Dick Sprang introduced the new villain the Wrecker. The villain's look wasn't exactly unique—there had been a new, almost identical foe named the Exterminator in *Detective Comics* #191 (January 1953). However, the Wrecker at least boasted a large "W" on his purple robes, while the Exterminator's costume proudly displayed an "E." This trend of robed villains would be revived years later in the 1970s.

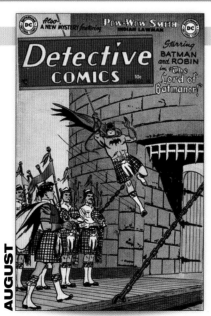
AUGUST

CAPE, COWL, AND KILT
Detective Comics #198 ▪ Thanks to husband-and-wife writers Edmond Hamilton and Leigh Brackett and penciller Dick Sprang, Batman changed up his wardrobe a bit when he became "The Lord of Batmanor." In a Scottish castle plagued with so many bats it was referred to as "Batmanor," a legend of hidden gold had existed for 400 years. The elderly lord of "Batmanor" decided that only Batman could discover the gold's location, and sent for him to crack the case. Batman not only proved successful, but even wore a traditional kilt during his adventure.

OCTOBER/NOVEMBER

BATMAN: ENGAGED?
Batman #79 ▪ When the Shah of Nairomi took a liking to Vicki Vale during his trip to Gotham City, Vicki pretended to be engaged to Batman in order to dodge his affections. In this story by writer David V. Reed and artist Dick Sprang, Batman played along with her game, but the lovestruck Vicki realized that she'd have to undergo extensive facial plastic surgery to disguise her identity if the pair ever truly married, or risk revealing Bruce Wayne as Batman. This issue also featured work by artists Bob Kane and Lew Sayre Schwartz and writer Bill Finger.

ALSO THIS YEAR

December/January—*Batman* #74: New villain Mr. Hydro plagued Batman with his "water crimes."

July—*World's Finest Comics* #65: When Batman was presumed dead, five different people told their versions of what the Caped Crusader was truly like.

October—*Detective Comics* #200: *Detective Comics* hit this milestone issue with little spectacle or fanfare.

November—*World's Finest Comics* #67: While his name seemed to imply he needed to work on his self-esteem, the new villain called the Zero proved a challenge for the Dynamic Duo.

53

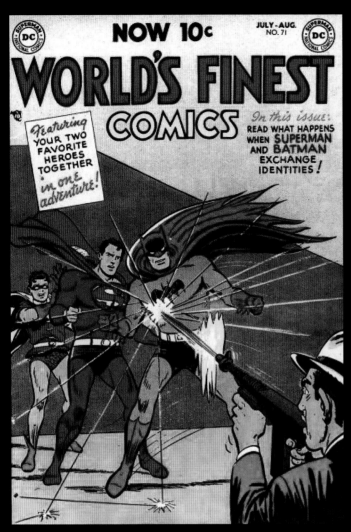

OLD TITLE, NEW FORMAT
WORLD'S FINEST COMICS #71

With this monumental issue, Batman and Superman ceased starring in solo adventures and finally paired up to become the World's Finest team. The two Super Heroes even swapped costumes in their first team-up tale, in an effort to confuse the inquisitive Lois Lane.

Despite first working together in *Superman* #76 (May 1952) and even learning each other's secret identities in that issue, Superman and Batman still kept to themselves in *World's Finest Comics*, the title they both starred in. They only paired up on the covers in order to attract readers. That situation changed with *World's Finest Comics* #71. This issue combined the two Super Heroes in a new format of 36 pages. The cover story was dedicated to Superman and Batman's adventure, a tale written by Alvin Schwartz and pencilled by Curt Swan, that saw them switch identities in order to fool Lois Lane, who had caught Clark Kent changing into his Man of Steel alter ego.

As Superman (now dressed as Batman) followed the trail of a criminal who had come into possession of a Kryptonite fragment, the only known material that could harm Superman, Batman made sure that Lois noticed him switching costumes in order to trick her into thinking that Superman was really Bruce Wayne.

THE LION SLEEPS TONIGHT
This entertaining story saw Bruce Wayne "punch" a trained lion in front of Lois Lane, helping to fool her into thinking he was Superman. By the story's end, she didn't know what to believe.

1954

"See him socking that crook? That's Batman—that's my pop!"

Tommy Wilson, *Batman* #88

In 1954, Batman continued to appear in three ongoing comic titles. As his adventures were combined with Superman's in the pages of *World's Finest Comics*, finally allowing the iconic Super Heroes to share adventures, his exploits in *Batman* went from three 12-page stories to three 8-pages stories. Meanwhile, Catwoman and Two-Face returned to their criminal ways, adding two of Batman's most important enemies to the fray. The popularity of Westerns in movies and on TV permeated the Caped Crusader's stories, and a few new minor villains and allies sprang up to keep Batman's world ever-expanding and exciting.

CATWOMAN RETURNS
Detective Comics #203 ▪ Catwoman returned to her roots in this issue when she could no longer resist the siren call of the criminal life. Illustrated by Bob Kane and written by Edmond Hamilton, this tale saw a newspaper reprint a past article about Batman's triumph over Catwoman. Angered by Batman's "gloating," Catwoman returned to crime and took up residence in her new Catacomb. In the end, the Dynamic Duo foiled her crime spree, only to have her escape when her boat crashed against a marshy shore.

THE REAL TWO-FACE
Batman #81 ▪ Batman thought Harvey Dent's life as Two-Face was a thing of the past. Dent's face had been reconstructed via plastic surgery, and the four different Two-Faces Batman had fought since then had been imposters. But in this issue by writer David V. Reed and artist Dick Sprang, an explosion undid Harvey's facial reconstruction, and he soon returned to a life of crime as Two-Face. This issue also included a story by Reed and artist Sheldon Moldoff that introduced the new villain Mr. Camera, as well as a tale by writer William Woolfolk and artist Sprang.

THE ORIGIN OF THE BATCAVE

Detective Comics #205 ■ Writer Bill Finger and artist Sheldon Moldoff told the backstory of Batman's famous headquarters in this memorable issue. When burying a wire in the cave floor for some new electronic devices, Robin chanced upon a piece of Native American pottery. Not only did this issue reveal that a pioneer named Jeremy Coe used to use the cave as his secret headquarters, it also showed how Bruce Wayne discovered the cave in the first place: by falling through the floor of the barn that neighbored his newly purchased mansion.

MAN-OF-THE-BATS

Batman #86 ■ Writer France Herron and penciller Sheldon Moldoff introduced readers to the Native American version of the Dynamic Duo in this issue that also featured work by writers Ed Hamilton and William Woolfolk and artist Dick Sprang. Chief Man-of-the-Bats and his sidekick Little Raven attracted the help of Batman and Robin when a bat-shaped smoke signal caught Batman's attention. Soon the Caped Crusader joined the Chief's cause by fighting in his place in order to throw off suspicions of Man-of-the-Bats' real identity.

THE MAN IN THE MIRROR

Detective Comics #213 ■ A wily criminal named Ventris broke free from his cell at the nearby state prison by using a shard of a broken mirror to shine the guards' spotlight back in their faces. While it wasn't the most dramatic origin story, this escape proved the inspiration for Batman's newest villain, the Mirror-Man, in this story written by Bill Finger and illustrated by Sheldon Moldoff. As he embarked on a series of mirror-themed heists, this foe's hopes were soon shattered by Batman, with a little help from a bizarre new cowl comprised of "crazy" distorting mirrors.

ALSO THIS YEAR

January—*World's Finest Comics* #68: Batman was challenged by the Crimesmith, a corrupt genius inventor.

April—*Detective Comics* #206: Batman faced the coonskin cap-wearing threat of the new villain Trapper, who just happened to be named Jason Bard.

August—*Batman* #85: Bat-Signal operator Sgt. Harvey Hainer debuted.

September—*Detective* #211: Catwoman debuted her own aircraft in the form of her cat-themed plane.

December—*Batman* #88: A young boy named Tommy mistakenly thought that Batman was his father, criminal Ed Wilson.

THE BATMEN OF ALL NATIONS

DETECTIVE COMICS #215

Batman's circle of allies grew larger in this story that saw him train "Batmen" from all over the world. Assuming different names, such as the Gaucho and the Musketeer, these heroes descended on Gotham City to learn crime-fighting skills from the Dark Knight Detective.

Writer Edmond Hamilton and artist Sheldon Moldoff created an international club of sorts for Super Heroes from other nations who had started a crime-fighting career patterned after that of Gotham City's own Dark Knight. Representing their homelands by their particular monikers and costume themes, these heroes traveled to Gotham City in order to study with the Caped Crusader.

While most of these "Batmen of All Nations" were new characters that debuted in this short 10-page story, two members, England's the Knight and Squire, were making their second comic book appearance, albeit in new costumes. The new heroes assembled for this tale included France's Musketeer, Italy's Legionary, South America's Gaucho, and Australia's Ranger.

The main story revolved around the Legionary being kidnapped and replaced by a local criminal, causing Batman to fail at stopping the capers of gangster "Knots" Caradine until the Caped Crusader's keen detective mind discovered the traitor in their midst. An interesting idea, this concept was revived, as were the characters, in writer Grant Morrison's *Batman* #667 (August 2007), a memorable collaboration with artist J.H. Williams III.

A CITY OF HEROES
Gotham City had never seen so many crime fighters. As Batman led his friends around the city, there were too many heroes to fit in the Batmobile.

1955

"They even have an ancient Batmobile, to comply with our law barring modern cars!"

An unnamed spectator, *Detective Comics* #219

On the cover of *Batman* #90 (March 1955) was a logo larger even than the DC bullet. The postage stamp-like image read: "Approved by the Comics Code Authority." In an era where groups of Americans were participating in mass comic book burnings in order to ensure the minds of their children were not "corrupted" by Batman and Superman's adventures, DC Comics was being as upfront about its self-censored comics as possible. Batman's stories would soon become more far-fetched than ever before.

SHE'S NO AGATHA CHRISTIE

Batman #89 • After his parents were killed, Bruce Wayne wasn't shown to have any other family. So it came as quite a surprise to readers that his Aunt Agatha made an appearance in the third story of this issue thanks to writer Bill Finger and artist Sheldon Moldoff. In a comic that also featured the art of Dick Sprang, Bruce Wayne's Aunt Agatha unwittingly unmasked him in front of a group of criminals, believing Bruce to be merely playing at being the Dark Knight Detective while on his way to attend a masquerade ball in Gotham City.

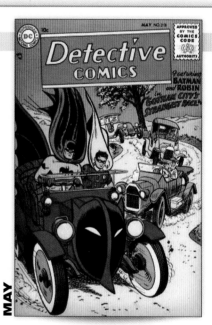

THE BATMOBILE OF 1905

Detective Comics #219 • The Batmobile had been upgraded on a few occasions in the past, but it received its most unusual revamp yet in the story "Gotham City's Strangest Race," drawn by penciller Sheldon Moldoff. In this unique tale, Batman debuted a 1905 Marmon model Batmobile in order to visit a car convention in the city of Millville. On the trail of a a gang of criminals spotted driving "ancient" cars, the Dynamic Duo marshaled a local race so that they could track down the thieves, who were after a fortune in stolen platinum.

JUNE

A BATMAN'S BEST FRIEND
BATMAN #92

Just a few months after Superboy gained a Superdog named Krypto, the Caped Crusader acquired his most loyal four-legged friend when the Batman Family grew to include a canine member, Ace the Bat-Hound.

This issue's new cover canine star found his way into the spotlight thanks to writer Bill Finger and artist Sheldon Moldoff. While patrolling the outskirts of Gotham City, Batman and Robin chanced upon a dog struggling to stay above water in a nearby river. Returning home with the dog, Batman, as Bruce Wayne, placed a lost dog notice in the local paper. But the mysterious canine seemed in no hurry to be claimed. In fact, he enjoyed his time with the Dynamic Duo so much, he began to follow them on patrol. Worried that the distinctive mark on the dog's forehead would give away Bruce Wayne's alter ego, Robin outfitted the animal with a black cowl, and Ace the Bat-Hound was born. After Ace proved his worth, he was promptly returned to his owner, John Wilker. But the Bat-Hound made several return appearances, and by issue #103 (October 1956), took up residence in the Batcave when Wilker traveled to Europe. Ace was finally able to join Batman on any case where the Dark Knight needed the dog's special brand of assistance.

ONE OF THE FAMILY
After Batman saved his life, Ace the Bat-Hound proved fiercely loyal to the Caped Crusaders, risking his life for them on many occasions.

SUPER BATMAN
***World's Finest Comics* #77** ● Now that Batman and Superman were teaming up on a regular basis in the pages of *World's Finest Comics*, it became challenging for writers and artists to tell a story without one hero overshadowing the other. A common gimmick was for Batman to swap powers with Superman, something he did for the first time in this issue. Written by Edmond Hamilton and drawn by Curt Swan, this wouldn't be the last time Batman gained superpowers. Batwoman also gained superpowers in issue #90 (October 1957).

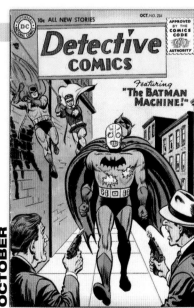

ROBO BATMAN
***Detective Comics* #224** ● Batman gained his own lifelike robot when he invented the so-called "Batman Machine" in this issue by writer Bill Finger and artist Dick Sprang. When a criminal exposed the body-reinforcing armor Batman was wearing under his costume to prevent injuries when testing a plane, the Gotham City underworld began to think Batman was merely a machine operated by Robin. Batman decided to make those fears a reality, creating a remote controlled Batman robot to help him in his war on crime.

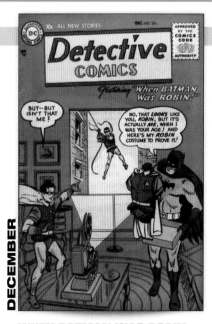

WHEN BATMAN WAS ROBIN
***Detective Comics* #226** ● Writer Edmond Hamilton and penciller Dick Sprang revealed that Dick Grayson wasn't the first Robin in this interesting issue that fleshed out Bruce Wayne's teenage years a bit more. In this tale, Batman revealed that he had once studied under Detective Harvey Harris, a legendary police investigator. In order to not compromise his identity while he was training, the young Bruce Wayne had adopted the costume that Dick Grayson would later wear, and was given the name Robin by Harris himself.

ALSO THIS YEAR

March—*Batman* #90: Robin teamed up with the baseball-themed Batboy, a new hero who retired by the issue's end.

April—*Detective Comics* #218: The Dynamic Duo became Batman Junior and Robin Senior when Robin was temporarily aged to an adult as Batman became a child.

June—*Detective Comics* #220: Marcus Tiller and his younger brother Guy, the medieval Batman and Robin, traveled to the future to meet their modern day counterparts.

August—*Batman* #93: Batman tried his hand at babysitting and met the Batman of a prehistoric era, Tiger Man.

September—*Batman* #94: While wearing Batman's costume, Alfred underwent an "amnesia shock," making him believe he was the true Caped Crusader.

October—*Batman* #95: Batman debuted his Bat Train, a traveling Batcave of sorts, when advertising anti-crime week.

December—*Batman* #96: Bruce Wayne's college years were examined in one story, while the Batmobile was converted into a fire truck in another.

FEATURING "The BAT-WOMAN!"

Detective COMICS

ALL NEW STORIES

SUPERMAN NATIONAL COMICS

JULY NO. 233

APPROVED BY THE COMICS CODE AUTHORITY

10¢

HURRY, BATMAN— THE BAT-WOMAN IS BEATING US ON THIS MISSION!

BRING ON THE BATWOMAN

DETECTIVE COMICS #233

Batman met the first female addition to his team of crime fighters when Batwoman raced onto the scene riding her motorcycle.

In an attempt to make Batman and Robin a more traditional family unit, DC Comics decided to introduce the Super Hero Batwoman as a love interest for the Caped Crusader. The first female equivalent to Batman, Batwoman wore a costume with a similar color scheme to Robin, rather than one based on the Dark Knight's blue and gray Batsuit.

Writer Edmond Hamilton and artist Sheldon Moldoff had the honor of introducing the original Batwoman to the readership. Mounted on a motorcycle and operating out of a tunnel underneath her home, Batwoman used a purse full of stereotypical women's items instead of a Utility Belt. This new crime fighter employed powder-puffs, a compact mirror, and handcuff charm bracelets to battle crooks.

Batwoman was quickly revealed to be heiress and former circus daredevil Kathy Kane, who used her fortune to fund her Batman-inspired war on crime. When Batman tracked her back to her hideout and discovered her secret identity, Ms. Kane decided to give up her life as a Super Hero; however, her claim of retirement would prove premature.

HEAR HER ROAR

While she may have accessorized differently from the Dynamic Duo, Batwoman was no damsel in distress. She was competition for Batman and Robin, rushing to solve crimes before them and proving her strength as a hero.

1956

"Hold it, Mad Hatter! You're not adding my cowl to your collection!"

Batman, *Detective Comics* #230

The second major period in comics, the Silver Age, had arrived, but Batman and Robin were not quite ready to leave the past behind. In *Detective Comics* #225 (November 1955), the Super Hero Martian Manhunter had debuted in his own back-up tale and was considered the first hero of the Silver Age by some. Others felt that honor went to the Flash (Barry Allen), who first appeared in *Showcase* #4 (October 1956). However, while the Silver Age had indeed begun by 1956, it could be argued that the Batman's Silver Age version really didn't appear until his redesign in *Detective Comics* #327 (May 1964). Until then, it was business as usual for Batman and Robin.

BATMAN VS. HATMAN
Detective Comics #230 ■ When the Mad Hatter first appeared, his diminutive stature made him seem like the character out of Lewis Carroll's fiction. However, the red-haired, mustachioed Mad Hatter that appeared in this issue by writer Bill Finger and penciller Sheldon Moldoff was so unlike his predecessor, it was declared in the mid-1980s that he was a different character altogether. Obsessed with hats in every form and Batman's cowl in particular, this Mad Hatter was later renamed Hatman in *Batman* #700 (August 2010).

BATMAN'S JUNIOR PARTNER
Detective Comics #231 ■ Writer Edmond Hamilton and artist Sheldon Moldoff revealed a bit more of Batman's history by introducing Batman Junior in this issue. When a criminal from Batman's past, Birrel Binter, escaped prison, Batman leaped into action, causing Robin to discover that his partner had years ago worked with a young boy named John Vance. To protect the boy's identity from the criminals he helped track down, Batman had outfitted Vance with a smaller version of his own costume and temporarily called him Batman Junior.

LIKE FATHER, LIKE SON
DETECTIVE COMICS #235

The Dark Knight Detective learned more about his parents' death in this issue, which revealed the true mastermind behind Thomas and Martha Wayne's mysterious assassination.

LOOKS FAMILIAR?

As Lew Moxon was killed before Batman could bring him to trial, there was nothing for the Dark Knight to do but hang up his father's costume in the Batcave's trophy room.

Writer Bill Finger and artist Sheldon Moldoff told one of the most memorable Batman stories of the 1950s with their landmark tale entitled "The First Batman." The story began as Dick Grayson discovered a hidden compartment in the desk of Bruce Wayne's father, Thomas Wayne. Inside was a costume Thomas wore years ago to a masquerade ball with a theme of "Flying Creatures." The costume was a blue and gray Batsuit, eerily similar to Batman's uniform. Studying the costume and reading Thomas Wayne's diary, Bruce realized that his father's old Batsuit had subconsciously inspired his own. Bruce also discovered that his father had been kidnapped from that costume party all those years ago by bank robber Lew Moxon. Moxon had been shot, and needed Thomas' surgical skills to remove the bullet. Instead of helping the gangster, Wayne attacked him and his men, delivering Moxon to the police and earning the robber's ire at the same time. Bruce discovered that, 10 years later, Moxon was a free man and had hired Joe Chill to do his dirty work and murder Thomas and Martha Wayne. Looking for a way to bring Moxon to justice, Bruce dressed in his father's Batman costume and startled the villain, causing Moxon to run out into the street and get hit by a moving truck.

WELCOME TO BATMANTOWN

Batman #100 ■ *Detective Comics* #100 and #200 had gone relatively unnoticed. Now one of Batman's anniversary issues was celebrated, running the words "100th Batman Issue!" over a cover created from some of the title's most iconic imagery. The stories inside weren't especially created for a 100th issue celebration. The most original, pencilled by Sheldon Moldoff, introduced Batmantown, when the mayor of the city of Plainville decided to change its name to attract tourists. He even organized the construction of an imitation Batmobile.

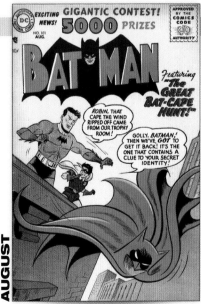

ROLLING OUT THE ROBINMOBILE

Batman #101 ■ It was Robin's time to shine in this story. Batman went undercover to bust a criminal gang, and the Boy Wonder was forced to step up to fill the Caped Crusader's boots in this tale by writer Edmond Hamilton and penciller Sheldon Moldoff. In this imaginative story, Robin drove a red version of Batman's Batmobile with an R on its hood (his Robinmobile), answered the Robin-Signal and even flew a Robin-Plane. This issue also featured two other stories drawn by Moldoff, one of which was written by Bill Finger.

THE NEW-MODEL BATMAN

Detective Comics #236 ■ Batman took his crime fighting to the next level with a tank, thanks to artist Sheldon Moldoff. After being stymied by a mirror that reflected the Bat-Signal to the wrong place, razor-sharp boomerangs that cut their Batlines, and oil slicks that caused the Batmobile to skid and swerve, Batman and Robin were forced to upgrade their equipment. Now with a tank, jumping springs attached to their boots, and a wingless aerodyne propelled by air jets, they were able to arrest the scientist responsible.

ALSO THIS YEAR

January—*World's Finest Comics* #80: Batman and Superman tracked down the mysterious new threat of the Mole when both heroes briefly worked for the *Gotham Gazette* in their civilian identities.

April—*Batman* #99: Batman introduced a Batman-themed stagecoach when Professor Carter Nichols sent the Dynamic Duo back in time to 1880.

October—*Batman* #103: The case of "The Broken Batman Trophies" consumed Batman's time in this issue that also guest-starred Ace the Bat-Hound.

November—*Detective Comics* #237: Batman was forced to temporarily adopt the secret identity of Barney Warren, and daydreamed of recruiting a new Robin.

December—*Detective Comics* #238: The checkered-suited new villain called Checkmate challenged Batman and Robin with elaborate death traps in this issue.

THE RAINBOW BATMAN

DETECTIVE COMICS #241

Perhaps partially responsible for all the multi-colored Batman action figures released over the years, this issue saw Batman try on a variety of bright Batsuits.

The team of writer Edmond Hamilton and artist Sheldon Moldoff took Batman's wardrobe into uncharted territories in this 12-page lead story. After Dick Grayson publicly saved the life of a young girl while in his civilian identity and injured his arm in the process, he noticed a few thieves fleeing the scene with a stolen TV camera. Batman suspected that the criminals had made off with the device in order to later pose as TV cameramen and steal something valuable.

Batman's solution to this potential problem was as over-the-top as most of his adventures of the time. He changed his Batsuit to an all-red version and attended a parade, a far cry from the publicity-avoiding Dark Knight of the present. Next, the hero switched to a light blue costume, followed by a gold one, an orange one, and then a green one, attending as many newsworthy public events as he could to flush out the TV camera crooks. He even wore a white outfit with a target on its chest to a shooting contest. Finally, wearing a rainbow striped costume to a museum display entitled "Moneys of the World," Batman discovered the crooks were planning to use their stolen camera to send tear gas into the room and raid the exhibit.

KNOCK-OUT COLORS
Batman's bright costumes also managed to draw attention to himself and away from his young partner, in order to prevent the public from noticing that Dick Grayson and Robin shared the same injury.

1957

"You deliberately tricked me—but you're a darling, Batman!"

Vicki Vale, *Detective Comics #245*

As Bob Kane was joined by returning talented artist Sheldon Moldoff to help Kane produce an impressive 365 pages of Batman stories per year, the Caped Crusader would not only adopt a variety of brightly colored Batsuits, he and Robin would also briefly change their identities. Robin became Owlman in one tale in April's *Batman* #107, while Batman adopted the role of Starman in another in September's *Detective Comics* #247. Commissioner Gordon also got in on the action, appearing as the costumed Mysteryman in a fondly remembered story in July's *Detective Comics #245*.

ROBIN GROWS UP
Batman #107 ● Following a story by penciller Sheldon Moldoff, where Batman and Robin gave a young boy a Batcycle, were two Moldoff-drawn tales written by Bill Finger. In the first of these, Robin fell in love with a young woman named Vera Lovely. In the final story, writer and artist paired up to tell a tale where Robin aged into adulthood when exposed to gas from an object Superman discovered in outer space. Adopting the name and costume of Owlman, Robin fought alongside his mentor until the effects of the "maturing gas" wore off and he was a boy again.

BATARANG X
Detective Comics #244 ● In a yarn written by Bill Finger and illustrated by Sheldon Moldoff, Batman prepared for a criminal who was using a Batarang against him by creating an inventory of his own Batarang collection. The Caped Crusader showed off the first Batarang given to him by Australian Lee Collins, a magnetic Batarang, a seeing-eye model, a flash bulb Batarang, a bomb version, a police whistle Batarang, a rope Batarang, and Batarang X, which was a giant version of Batman's famous weapon, able to be ridden by the Dark Knight Detective.

JUNE

WORLD'S WORST

WORLD'S FINEST COMICS #88

Batman's greatest foe, the Joker, joined forces with Superman's greatest enemy, Lex Luthor, in order to prove a fitting challenge for the World's Finest team.

THE JOKER AT THE WHEEL
While the Joker had tried out a new model of his Jokermobile in *World's Finest Comics* #61 (November 1952), he was back to his classic model by this issue, the perfect vehicle for chauffeuring Lex Luthor about town.

This story, written by Edmond Hamilton and illustrated by Dick Sprang, would be the first time these two notorious villains joined forces, a tradition that would continue into the modern era despite their having little in common besides a hatred for an iconic DC Super Hero. After serving time in jail, Lex Luthor decided to go into business with the Joker. As expected, Luthor and the Joker's application for a manufacturing license proved a part of a larger criminal scheme. Learning of their partnership, Superman paid a visit to Gotham City and recruited Batman, since the Caped Crusader was quite used to the Joker's antics by this point. Confronting the villains at their new factory, the World's Finest team discovered that their foes had created androids called Mechano-Men. The Joker and Luthor maintained that their invention was to be sold for the good of mankind, but later secretly attempted to break into the Sub-Treasury with their robots, only to be foiled by Batman and Superman.

Luthor and the Joker would pair up many times, and even team up in animated form years down the line. Just like Batman and Superman, their opposite character traits made for an interesting partnership, and their status as arch foes increased the popularity of titles they starred in together.

JULY

THE DYNAMIC TRIO

Detective Comics #245 ▪ The Dynamic Duo gained a third partner in the form of Mysteryman, a new Super Hero who perplexed reporter Vicki Vale all through this issue. Written by Edmond Hamilton and drawn by Sheldon Moldoff, this tale saw Gotham City's mayor berating Commissioner Gordon about wanted criminals being smuggled out of town. With strict orders to employ Batman and Robin on this case, the Commissioner had no other choice but to adopt the costumed identity of Mysteryman in order to help the heroes follow a plan he'd already devised.

SEPTEMBER

THE STARMAN OF 1957

Detective Comics #247 ▪ A source of inspiration for a memorable story arc in writer James Robinson's *Starman* series of the 1990s, this tale by writer Bill Finger and artist Sheldon Moldoff saw Batman temporarily become Starman when he was given an artificial phobia of bats. Equipped with a star-shaped Star-Plane and Star-Darts, Starman and Robin answered the Star-Signal when trouble arose. With Robin's help, Batman conquered his fear and vanquished Professor Milo, a villainous scientist who would prove a recurring thorn in Batman's side.

DECEMBER

A BAD SIGNAL

Batman #112 ▪ A new themed villain would enter Batman's life in the lead story of this issue by writer Bill Finger and artist Sheldon Moldoff that also showcased Batman's new Bat-Launch speedboat. Leaving symbol clues to his crimes, the Signalman would return many times to challenge the Dynamic Duo, even into the present day. This issue also featured a memorable tale of Batman facing the returning threat of Professor Milo by Finger and Moldoff, as well as a story about Batman being sent through time via time ray.

ALSO THIS YEAR

February—*Batman* #105: Batwoman returned to fighting crime only to retire again in this issue that also showed Batman trying out a missile sent to him from the future.

May—*Detective Comics* #243: An experimental invention called the "Maximizer" increased Batman's size to giant proportions for this issue.

June—*Batman* #108: Batman Jones debuted, a young boy who tried to emulate the hero on his own Batcycle after being named after Batman.

July—*World's Finest Comics* #89: John Mayhew gave the Batmen of All Nations a clubhouse in this issue that saw Superman elected Chairman of this so-called Club of Heroes.

August—*Batman* #109: Batman's many inventions were examined, including his Flying Eye, a human jet-power unit, a sleuth machine, and his Crime Calculator.

October—*Batman* #111: Batman and Robin donned knight's armor in order to hide the radiation suits they secretly wore to recover stolen atomic fuel.

THREE NEW FACES
BATMAN #113

The three stories in this memorable issue of *Batman* each introduced a new character into the Batman mythos: False Face, Fatman, and the Batman of Planet X.

Artist Sheldon Moldoff drew this first tale that debuted new villain False Face. False Face evaded capture from the Dynamic Duo for quite a while with his ability to impersonate other people by using masks and makeup. However, he would not become an established Batman villain until the character appeared on the 1966-68 *Batman* TV show, portrayed by actor Malachi Throne.

The second story introduced the parody character of Fatman thanks to Moldoff and writer Bill Finger. An obese version of Batman who had turned his clumsy display into a comedy act, Fatman used his clown skills to aid the Dynamic Duo when he unwittingly rescued them.

Perhaps the most important debut was the Batman of Planet X, a literally out-of-this-world hero who served as Batman's counterpart on the planet Zur-En-Arrh. Armed with a futuristic Batmobile, Batplane and Bat-Radia, a device that caused controlled disturbances in the atmosphere, Batman of Planet X wore a red, yellow, and purple costume. In this story by France Herron, with pencils by Dick Sprang, he recruited our Batman's help in order to take advantage of the Superman-like abilities Batman gained by traveling to his world. Despite being fairly inconsequential in its day, "Batman—The Superman of Planet X!" became a major part of writer Grant Morrison's epic saga on his run on *Batman* that began with issue #655 (September 2006).

THE BATMAN OF PLANET X
Arriving on the planet Zur-En-Arrh, Batman was astonished to encounter a colorful character with a remarkable likeness to himself. This Batman needed Earth's Batman to help battle an invasion of robots belonging to an alien race.

1958

"After all our cases together, how could Superman reject us like that?"

Robin to Batman, *World's Finest Comics* #94

One of the things the comic book censors, known as the Comics Code Authority, cracked down on in the 1950s was the use of realistic crimes in stories. It was believed by the public that showing these crimes in comics would cause children to want to imitate them. Batman and Robin normally battled this sort of "street level crime," so in order to make their adventures Code appropriate the Dynamic Duo ventured into the world of science fiction, an area more suited to Superman. No matter how odd it seemed for Batman to be battling aliens and facing oddly-powered villains, in the late 1950s it soon became the norm.

THE TERRIBLE TRIO
Detective Comics #253 • When they used a giant underground "burrow machine" to rob the Gotham Bank, the Terrible Trio made a name for themselves. Committing crimes on land, sea, and air, this group of masked criminals dubbed themselves the Fox, the Shark and the Vulture. Based in a lighthouse that contained the Vulture's sky nest, the Fox's den, and the Shark's cave, the Trio was defeated when Batman and Robin posed as mummies hidden in relics stolen by the villains in this tale by writer Dave Wood and artist Sheldon Moldoff.

WORLD'S FINEST ORIGIN
World's Finest Comics #94 • While readers had been led to believe that Superman and Batman first met in *Superman* #76 (May 1952), the origin of the World's Finest team was revealed in this issue by writer Edmond Hamilton and artist Curt Swan. When Superman rejected Batman's help in favor of a new Super Hero partner named Powerman (who turned out to be a robot Superman was using to protect the Caped Crusader), Batman reminisced about their partnership, revealing that he first met Superman when he saved him from Kryptonite smugglers.

OCTOBER

BOY WONDER OF STEEL
ADVENTURE COMICS #253

DC Comics' two top teenagers joined forces when Batman's popular sidekick, Robin the Boy Wonder, traveled back in time to meet Superman's younger version of himself, Superboy.

Since nearly the start of the Caped Crusader's career, the popular young counterpart to Batman had been Robin. The Boy Wonder had brought in many readers at the time, and was clearly the favorite sidekick in the entire world of comic books. However, when DC Comics added a youthful element to Superman's world, they did so, not with a sidekick, but in the form of flashback stories to Clark Kent's youth as Superboy. It was a popular concept, but Superboy's team-up potential was greatly diminished by the fact that his tales didn't exist in the present day. Luckily for readers everywhere, Robin had regular access to time travel, thanks to his friend and scientist Professor Carter Nichols. That made possible this tale by writer Dave Wood and artist Al Plastino, in which the Boy Wonder traveled back to Superboy's time. After Superman was caught in a Kryptonite explosion from a clock of his in the present, Robin decided to head back to the day Superboy received the item in order to destroy it and prevent Superman's death. Robin and the Boy of Steel did just that, and afterwards, parted ways as friends. A unique story in that Batman didn't participate in the adventure, this issue paved the way for the friendship between the third Robin, Tim Drake, and the modern Superboy, Kon-El.

TEEN TITANS
Witnessing Superman's tragic fate firsthand, Robin knew time travel was the only option to save the Man of Steel. Luckily, Superboy didn't find the Boy Wonder's story too far-fetched when Robin journeyed back to his time.

SEPTEMBER

CHECKING THE CALENDAR
Detective Comics #259 ▪ The Calendar Man made his debut thanks to the imaginations of writer Bill Finger and artist Sheldon Moldoff. The character's look has changed drastically through time from his costumed Bronze Age appearance to his tattooed modern visage. The Calendar Man's original method of operations required him to wear a different costume for each crime. In this issue, the Calendar Man designed his capers and outfits around the four seasons of the year and added a "fifth season," India's rainy season.

NOVEMBER

BOTH DOCTORS ARE IN
Detective Comics #261 ▪ Batman met one of his first Rogues Gallery additions whose origin was firmly based in science fiction when he encountered Dr. Double X in this issue written by Dave Wood and drawn by Sheldon Moldoff. Armed with a super-strong, super-fast glowing double, Dr. Double X proved quite a physical match for Batman until the Caped Crusader destroyed the machine that had produced the duplicate. Dr. Double X would return several times to haunt Batman, unlike the much less popular villain from the following issue, Jackal-Head.

DECEMBER

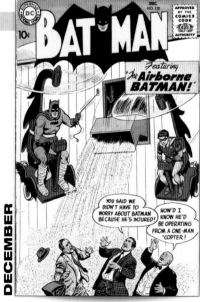

A WHIRLWIND HISTORY TOUR
Batman #120 ▪ Another of Bruce Wayne's relatives was revealed when Silas Wayne, Bruce's great uncle, paid him a visit in this story by writer Bill Finger and artist Sheldon Moldoff. Introducing the Wayne ancestral gallery, a hall of portraits that would return during writer Grant Morrison's Batman run in the 2000s, this story also saw Bruce reveal his double identity to his uncle when Silas was on his deathbed. This issue also debuted Batman and Robin's new mini-helicopters, the famous Whirly-Bats in another story drawn by Moldoff.

ALSO THIS YEAR

January—*Detective Comics #251:* The public began to distrust Batman when a pair of criminals framed the hero to appear like an alien from outer space.

March—*Batman #114:* Mogo the Bat-Ape joined Batman's extended family as the Mirage Maker joined his extended Rogues Gallery.

September—*Batman #118:* Batman gained the temporary ability to breathe underwater and had to wear a water-helmet while on dry land.

October—*Batman #119:* Batman fell asleep and seemingly hallucinated a future where he was an old man and a new Batman and Robin had taken his place.

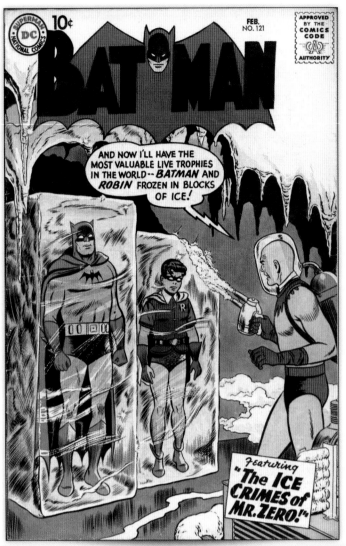

AND NOW I'LL HAVE THE MOST VALUABLE LIVE TROPHIES IN THE WORLD -- *BATMAN* AND *ROBIN* FROZEN IN BLOCKS OF ICE!

featuring "The ICE CRIMES of MR. ZERO!"

STARTING AT ZERO

BATMAN #121

The Dark Knight Detective met an important new foe in the form of Mr. Zero. This cold-projecting criminal would go on to be known as the super-villain Mr. Freeze, one of the best-known members of Batman's Rogues Gallery.

When Mr. Zero first appeared, he seemed little more than a new Batman foe with a pseudo-scientific gimmick. While his story did indeed capture the issue's cover, readers would have to first delve into two other Batman tales both written by Bill Finger and illustrated by Sheldon Moldoff before they arrived at the issue's main attraction. Mr. Zero's adventure was illustrated by Moldoff as well, yet written by Dave Wood.

When he wasn't operating out of the back of an ice cream truck and robbing places with his ice gas gun (that also shot heat), Mr. Zero was lounging about in a refrigerated mountain hideout. The victim of a scientific experiment on the ice gun he'd invented, Mr. Zero was forced to keep himself in freezing temperatures in order to breathe. However, in this issue's conclusion, Mr. Zero was exposed to steam that cured his condition, another factor in why the villain didn't make a return appearance for quite some time. Year later, when the character made repeat appearances in the 1966 Batman show under the name Mr. Freeze, he began to rise in the ranks of Batman's Rogues and would continue to do so in subsequent years.

KNOCKED COLD
A right hook from Batman sent Mr. Zero's ice gun spinning from his hand. Mr. Zero wore a purple robe that later inspired a scene from the 1997 movie, *Batman & Robin*.

1959

"That will stop you cold, officers!"

Mr. Zero, Batman #121

One of the most iconic Batman villains in the history of the character made his debut this year. That villain was Mr. Zero, whose popularity would soar in later years after the classic *Batman* TV show of the 1960s renamed him Mr. Freeze. Mr. Zero was essentially a reuse of the name of an unrelated criminal called Zero who debuted in *World's Finest Comics* #67 (November 1953). Several super-villains familiar to Batman devotees were given complete overhauls. The identities of the Clock and Firefly were adopted by new villains with no association to their original counterparts, creating exciting new foes for Batman and Robin to battle.

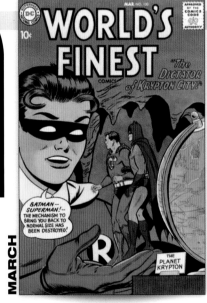

A TINY ANNIVERSARY
World's Finest Comics #100 ● Like so many other anniversary issues off the time, *World's Finest Comics* hit its 100th issue with little to differentiate it from other issues released up to that point. The comic simply featured an adventure where Batman and Superman teamed up to once again thwart the latest scheme of Lex Luthor. In the process, both the Man of Steel and the Dark Knight Detective were temporarily stuck in miniaturized form in this story by writer Bill Finger and artist Dick Sprang.

HERE COMES THE BRIDE
Batman #122 ● In an issue written entirely by Bill Finger and illustrated by Sheldon Moldoff, Batman fought pirates and met the new playing card-themed villain, Hijack. But the most memorable tale was advertised on this volume's cover: "The Marriage of Batman and Batwoman." When Bruce Wayne left for a date with Kathy Kane, Dick Grayson fell asleep and dreamed of a future where Batman and Batwoman married and the new Mrs. Wayne adopted a female version of Batman's Batsuit, down to its exact color scheme.

MAY

MITE MAKES RIGHT
DETECTIVE COMICS #267

Teetering on the brink for quite some time, Batman truly entered the realm of the fantastic when he met that other-dimensional imp, Bat-Mite.

MITE MAKES RIGHT

Bat-Mite was a prime example of how far Batman had strayed from his original dark roots. Bat-Mite has since developed into a popular character with several animated appearances and action figures to his credit.

Superman was DC Comics' strongest selling Super Hero from the moment he was concocted and often used as the template for other Super Heroes. Having already given the Caped Crusader a dog similar to Superboy's popular Krypto, it was only a matter of time before one of Superman's more interesting villains was cloned into Gotham City. That character was Superman's Mr. Mxyzptlk, a 5th dimensional imp who could warp reality as he saw fit. In this issue by writer Bill Finger and artist Sheldon Moldoff, Batman's own mischievous imp paid him a visit, in the form of Bat-Mite.

Bat-Mite immediately established himself as the Caped Crusader's number one fan. Described by Robin as "an elf dressed in a crazy-looking Batman costume," Bat-Mite came to Batman's dimension from his own in order to aid the Dynamic Duo with his "unearthly powers." The imp then tried to prove himself, turning a bridge into a rubber-like substance and levitating a giant record in order to help Batman and Robin catch a gang of crooks. Despite his interesting brand of assistance, Bat-Mite was rejected by the heroes. He returned to his dimension, only to later return much sooner than the Dynamic Duo would have preferred.

BATMAN BEATS THE CLOCK

Detective Comics #265 ■ Readers were given the chance to discover Batman's first case when they met a new villain calling himself the Clock in this story by writer Bill Finger and artist Sheldon Moldoff. Quite different from the Robin villain of the same name who first appeared in *Star Spangled Comics* #70 (July 1947), this Clock had adopted his costumed identity and begun using timepieces as a crime motif after Batman had made him "do time" in prison when the Dark Knight Detective nabbed the thief years ago on his first patrol.

LIGHTING FIRES

Batman #126 ■ Gotham City received its own version of the Statue of Liberty in a tale by writer Bill Finger and artist Sheldon Moldoff. Instead of Lady Liberty, the giant towering figure in Gotham Bay was in the image of the Dark Knight Detective, dubbed the Batman Lighthouse. This issue also featured a redesign of the Batboat, and a new short-lived version of Firefly. Wearing a different costume than the original who debuted in *Detective Comics* #184 (June 1952), this Firefly was Ted Carson, one of Bruce Wayne's rivals for the affections of Kathy Kane.

THORING WITH THE EAGLES

Batman #127 ■ Thor, the Thunder-God of Norse mythology, seemingly came to life in this tale by writer Bill Finger and artist Sheldon Moldoff. When unassuming museum curator Henry Meke came into contact with a replica of Thor's hammer that had been struck by a meteorite during a thunderstorm, he was transformed into the hulking villainous figure of Thor. This issue also included a story where Alfred adopted his own heroic identity as the Eagle and went on patrol with Batman and Robin, in a tale by Jerry Coleman and Dick Sprang.

ALSO THIS YEAR

August—*Batman* #125: Batman fought Mr. Midas, who specialized in gold robberies, and El Bolo, a caped international jewel thief.

September—*Detective Comics* #271: The Crimson Knight rivaled Batman for Gotham City's top crime fighter position before he was revealed to be a common crook.

1960s

The 1960s proved to be a turbulent decade for the entire world, and Batman was no exception. The comics that featured the Caped Crusader reflected the times. Batman stories started out by dabbling with science-fiction in the decade's early years. In the mid-1960s, they echoed the hugely successful *Batman* TV show's tongue-in-cheek nature. By the end of the decade, Batman had returned to his more serious, crime-fiction roots.

Bill Finger continued to write many of the Batman stories in the early years of the decade, but the advent of a new Batman editor, Julius Schwarz, in 1964 ushered in a new era. Schwartz brought in artist Carmine Infantino to redesign Batman and Robin. Infantino introduced what became known as the "New Look," streamlining Batman's physique and adding a yellow oval behind the bat-symbol on Batman's chest for the first time. Infantino's style was so recognizable that DC Comics fans who'd watched him work his magic on the Flash couldn't help but recognize it. Because of this he became the first artist besides Kane to have his name listed as the character's artist.

In 1966, the *Batman* show premiered on TV and introduced Gotham City and its greatest heroes and villains to the mass market, boosting Batman to new heights of popularity. To feed into this, the comics brought back many of Batman's classic villains who hadn't been seen for a long while—sometimes decades—including Scarecrow and Catwoman.

Artist Neal Adams began work on Batman in 1967, first on the cover of *The Brave and the Bold* #75 and then for the entire issue of *World's Finest Comics* #175. The "New Look" had updated Batman; Adams' work hauled the Dark Knight into the future, providing a new dynamism for the character in terms of fresh perspectives and daring panel design.

By the end of the decade, Robin had gone off to college, and Batman had left Wayne Manor. Both Robin and the new Batgirl had embarked on solo careers, and the Batman Family's ongoing battle against crime had become both broader and more sophisticated.

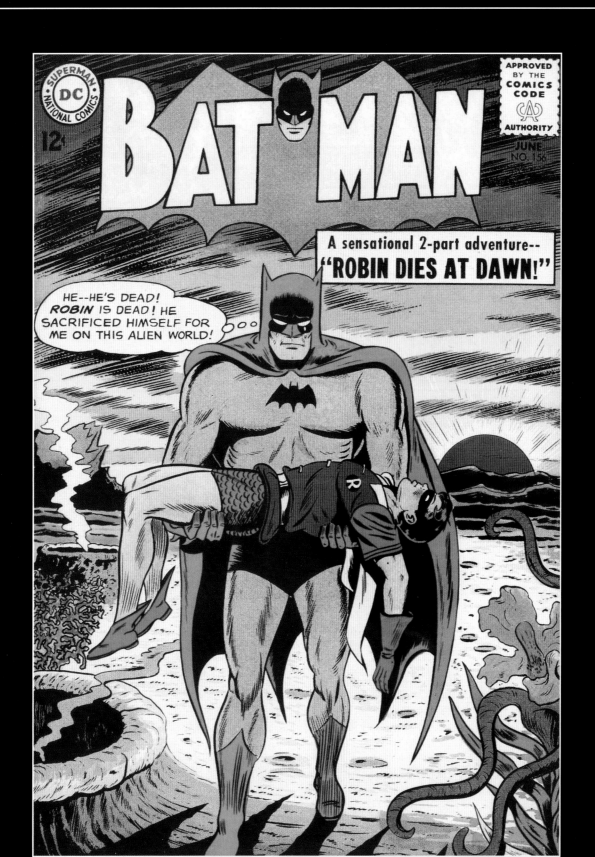

THE ZEBRA BATMAN
DETECTIVE COMICS #275

Bill Finger and Sheldon Moldoff brought us one of the first Batman and Robin tales of the 1960s, pitting the Dynamic Duo against the new villain Zebra-Man, whose magnetic powers covered him in black and white lines of force.

Zebra-Man controlled his incredible powers by means of a special belt. When the machine that gave Zebra-Man his powers was turned on Batman, the Caped Crusader, lacking this belt, found it impossible to control the powers the machine gave him, making him dangerous to everyone around him. Soon enough, however, Batman figured out how to reverse his powers' polarity and pull Zebra-Man straight to him—and then toss him in jail. This issue also featured back-up stories about Roy Raymond, TV Detective, and John Jones, Manhunter from Mars (a.k.a. the Martian Manhunter, J'onn J'onzz). On top of that, it contained a one-page comic about Casey the Cop, a half page called "Jail Jests," and even a couple of one-page public service comics.

ZEBRA MAN
Zebra-Man's control over lines of force extended beyond magnetism. He could affect any physical object with them.

ZEBRA-BATMAN
Batman and Robin tracked Zebra-Man to his hideout. As they tried to capture the criminal, Robin tripped and accidentally activated Zebra-Man's machine. It bathed Batman in a strange light and gave him Zebra-Man's uncontrolled magnetic powers.

1960

"Women are unpredictable, Robin... Men can never tell what they're going to do next."
Batman, *Detective Comics* #285

As well as tackling otherworldly creatures, Batman himself sometimes fell prey to bizarre occurrences, as in "The Zebra Batman" and "The Negative Batman" stories. Batman also moved from being the leader of the Batman family of heroes to a member of a much larger team: the Justice League of America. Although he only had the briefest of cameos in the Justice League's first appearance—appearing in only three panels because he was too busy chasing crooks in Gotham City—he was destined to become a marquee member of the greatest band of heroes in the world.

IRONIC STRIPES
The story ended with a visual gag. After Batman and Robin threw Zebra-Man in jail, the only stripes he had came from the shadows his cell's window cast upon him.

THE MIGHTIEST HERO TEAM

JUSTICE LEAGUE OF AMERICA #1

After three tryout issues in *The Brave and the Bold* #28–30 (March–July 1960), the Justice League of America, "The mightiest crime-fighting team that ever existed," finally got a first title of its own.

In common with previous Justice League stories, *Justice League of America* #1, written by Gardner Fox and illustrated by Mike Sekowsky and Bernard Sachs, featured a brand-new villain with a science-fiction bent. In this case it was Despero, a pink-skinned, fin-headed, dimension-traveling tyrant who dominated his homeworld with super-energy weapons and the power to control minds. After taking control of Aquaman, Batman, Green Lantern, the Martian Manhunter, Superman, and Wonder Woman, Despero challenged the Flash—who was temporarily immune to his powers—to a strange game played on a chessboard, with the lives of the others at stake.

Despero cheated at the game, sending each of the others to their doom in a distant dimension. The Flash, honorable as ever, lived up to his end of the bargain and allowed Despero to take him away in a dimension-spanning starship and dump him with the others. The heroes each managed to team up and escape from Despero's outlandish traps by employing clever scientific solutions.

Snapper Carr—a hip high school student who accidentally found protection from Despero's mind-control powers too—saved the day by stowing away on the starship when Despero left with the Flash. Using the anti-weaponry technology developed by the scientist who first alerted the Flash to the peril, Snapper paralyzed the tyrant. The rest of the heroes arrived soon after to send the captured Despero home, provoking his long vendetta against them.

THE SLY AND THE STRONG

Batman #129 ■ In the first of a pair of tales by writer Bill Finger and artist Sheldon Moldoff, Batman and Robin chased after the Spinner, a green-armored villain who used spinning or spun things—including a giant top, a buzzsaw gun, and a spider-web cannon—as weapons. With Batwoman's help, they tracked him to a windmill, only to discover he was a stooge whom the real villain had tricked into taking the fall for him. In the back-up, Batman and Robin helped Sardo, the strongman from Robin's circus days, clear up robbery charges against him and his son.

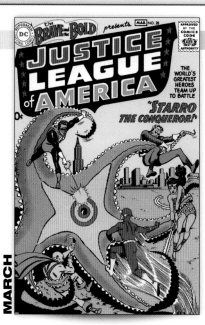

THE JUSTICE LEAGUE FORMS

The Brave and The Bold #28 ■ Writer Gardner Fox, alongside artists Mike Sekowsky and Murphy Anderson, introduced the greatest Super Hero team in the world, eight months before the JLA was awarded its own book. Aquaman alerted the entire JLA to the incursion of giant, mind-controlling alien starfish Starro the Conqueror. The most famous members—Batman and Superman—were too busy to join in. Lucas "Snapper" Carr, making his debut, became an honorary member of the Justice League. Starro returned to plague the JLA over the years.

GLIDERS, BOATS, AND FAME

Batman #133 ■ In the first of this trio of stories from writer Bill Finger and artists Dick Sprang and Sheldon Moldoff, the Dynamic Duo stopped the crimes of new villain Kite-Man, who traveled on what we'd recognize today as custom-made hang gliders. The second tale introduced the *S.S. Batman*, the crime-fighters' yacht, which quickly became the target of thieves. In the third, Bat-Mite declared himself Batwoman's partner and enlisted Ace the Bat-Hound to try to make her even more famous than Batman and Robin.

TEEN TEAM-UP

Adventure Comics #275 ■ In this issue, writer Jerry Coleman and artist George Papp revealed how Superboy and Bruce Wayne met in high school after the Wayne family moved to Smallville for a short while. With a time telescope, Superboy knew he would someday partner with Batman to fight crime. When Bruce spotted a crime in progress, he borrowed a witch doctor's costume from Lana Lang's father and became the Flying Fox. He later deduced Superboy's secret identity but he had his future Justice League partner hypnotize him to forget it.

SNAPPER

Although he had no powers or costume, young Snapper Carr played a key role in the Justice League's early adventures, sometimes providing the key to defeating the alien villains and saving his friends' lives.

SEPTEMBER

MONSTERS AND DUMMIES

Batman #134 ▪ Bill Finger and Sheldon Moldoff spun three exciting tales here. In the first, a Rainbow Beast emerged from a volcano and used powers keyed to its colors to rampage across a South American nation. In the next, a friend figured out who Batman and Robin were, and his taunting letters led them to stopping unrelated crimes. To wrap the issue up, a small person who performed a ventriloquism act with a large puppet became angry with those calling him the dummy in the act—so he turned to crime as the Dummy.

OCTOBER

GOING NEGATIVE

Detective Comics #284 ▪ In this classic Bill Finger and Sheldon Moldoff story, mad scientist Hal Durgin developed a camera that could shrink down and capture inside it any object that it took a picture of, including buildings. Robin stopped the camera from fully affecting Batman, but the half-finished process turned him into a negative version of himself. Light weakened him, and doctors gave him only days to live. In the end, Batman tricked Durgin into capturing him with the camera and then releasing him, reversing the effects.

NOVEMBER

A BEAST FROM THE PAST

Detective Comics #285 ▪ For this issue, Bill Finger and Sheldon Moldoff reached back into the far-distant past to thaw a caveman called Man-Beast from a block of ice. Freed from suspended animation, the Man-Beast went on a rampage until Batwoman brought him something to eat. Later, the scientists who were supposed to be studying him tried to frame him for a murder that they had committed while covering up the fact that they'd been stealing ancient artifacts. The Man-Beast himself later died bravely, saving Batwoman from a mountain lion.

ALSO THIS YEAR

January—*Superman's Girlfriend Lois Lane* #14: Lois tried on the Batwoman costume for an adventure.

April—*Batman* #131: In a tale told by Alfred, Batman and Batwoman married and retired, leaving their legacy to Robin (now Batman II) and their son (Robin II).

June—*Batman* #132: Batman and Robin captured SCUBA-diving enemy, Sea Fox.

June—*Strange Adventures* #117: The Atomic Knights debuted, including a future member of the Outsiders in their number.

June—*Detective Comics* #280: New foe Atomic-Man wore goggles that could change the atomic nature of any object, until Batman and Robin stopped him.

October—*Batman* #135: The Wheel sought revenge on Batman and Robin. Batman II and Robin II returned. A genie called the Sky Creature debuted.

November—*World's Finest* #113: Bat-Mite first encountered Mr. Mxyzptlk.

December—*Detective Comics* #286: The single appearance of Star-Man.

73

BATGIRL SURPRISE

BATMAN #139

Batgirl—whose name was hyphenated in this first incarnation—debuted in this issue, which saw Betty Kane try to follow in the footsteps of her aunt, Batwoman.

Like many DC Comics issues of the era, *Batman* contained not one story but three. Bill Finger wrote and Sheldon Moldoff drew each of them, with the cover story about the brand-new Batgirl coming third in the issue. In it Batwoman's niece Betty Kane came to visit. After figuring out her Aunt Kathy fought crime as Batwoman, Betty made her own costume and surprised Kathy as well as Batman and Robin by saving them from the Cobra Gang. Forbidden to fight crime again until she had completed rigorous training, Betty tried to prove herself by tracking down the Cobra Gang by herself—and was captured.

The first tale featured the return of the Signalman in the new identity of the Blue Bowman. In the second story, Batman and Robin took the Bat-Launch to a private island owned by the wealthy criminal George Milo. To get there, they had to bypass a mechanical shark, a steel-fisted tank, a gigantic octopus, and a radar-guided ballista.

NAUGHTY GIRL
Batwoman was shocked to learn that Batgirl was her niece Betty. Despite the fact that she grew to respect the girl and work with her regularly, her first instinct was to order her to give up being a hero instead.

1961

"If you can be Batwoman, I can certainly be Batgirl!"

Betty Kane, *Batman* #139

The Batman Family added another member with the introduction of Batgirl, who modeled herself on Batwoman (unlike the later Batgirl who followed in Batman's footsteps). The price of regular comics rose from a dime to 12¢, and DC Comics experimented with giant-sized (80-page) annuals, which mostly consisted of reprints. These annuals gave new fans a chance to catch up with ongoing stories, and for others to fill in holes in their collections. Sometimes, as with June's *Secret Origins* #1, these giant-size issues featured a variety of different heroes, enabling readers to sample characters they might not have discovered before.

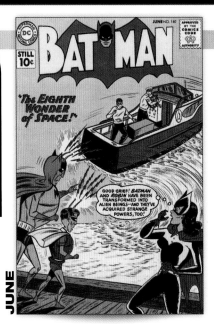

ALIENS AND ENEMIES

Batman #140 ▪ In the first of three tales served up by Bill Finger and Sheldon Moldoff, the Joker was thought to have been killed after escaping from jail. His ghost returned to haunt Batman and Robin, but it turned out to be a hoax he had pulled off with glowing paint and projected images. The second tale saw the Alchemist give Batman a secret potion for luck against a group of assassins. The Alchemist was Superman in disguise. In the cover story, green-skinned aliens accidentally kidnapped the heroes, who were briefly turned into aliens, too.

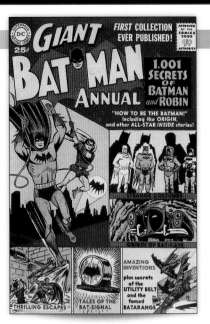

CATCHING UP

Batman Annual #1 ▪ The first *Batman* annual contained several reprinted stories and features written by Edmond Hamilton, David Vern Reed, and Bill Finger with art by Dick Sprang, Lew Sayre Schwartz, and Sheldon Moldoff. They covered Batman's origin and details about his costumes and crime-fighting tools. This proved popular enough that a second annual was released in November of the same year. Eventually the annuals would feature original stories, but they started out as a great way to read many stories in a giant, 80-page issue.

FACE OF CLAY
DETECTIVE COMICS #298

One of Batman's most iconic villains, Clayface—known here as Clay-Face—stormed into Batman's life. Able to morph into any shape he liked, the man of clay would return to haunt Batman for years to come.

After accidentally slipping into an underground pool of strange protoplasm, Matt Hagen discovered that his flesh had turned to clay in this story by writer/artist team Bill Finger and Sheldon Moldoff. At first, despair overwhelmed Hagen, but he soon realized he could control his shape with his mind. In the course of his first clash with Batman and Robin, Clayface turned himself into a giant python, a buzzsaw, and a giant eagle that flew away with a briefcase full of stolen cash. Later he showed that he could disguise himself as other people and could change into creatures that never existed, like a lion-dinosaur-unicorn. However, Clayface soon learned that his control over his powers faded with time and he had to return to the strange pool that gave him his power. Batman and Robin defeated him by running down the clock.

MASSIVE VILLAIN
Among Clayface's incredible powers was the ability to alter his overall mass. On top of being able to alter his appearance and shape, he could shrink or grow, making it even harder to tell him from the real thing.

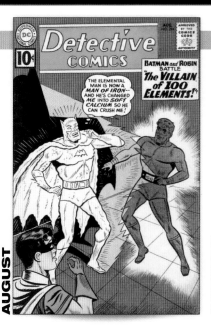

THE ELEMENTAL MAN
Detective Comics #294 ● Batman and Robin visited their friend Professor Higgins only to find that his new invention had been leaking power for weeks in this story written by Bill Finger with art by Sheldon Moldoff. This gave the professor's assistant, John Dolan, the power to change his body into different elements—and also drove him criminally insane. Calling himself the Elemental Man, he embarked on a crime spree that the heroes stopped with Higgins's help. The Elemental Man was a precursor to the similar hero Metamorpho, who debuted in 1964.

PLANET BUSTER
Detective Comics #296 ● Writer Dave Wood and penciller Jim Mooney introduced the Planet Master in this story. Using a series of powered costumes inspired by the nine planets, the mysterious criminal staged an inventive spree through Gotham City. The Dynamic Duo suspected the criminal to be Edward Burke, an assistant to scientist Irving Norbert. In fact, Norbett was the unwitting villain, under the influence of a strange gas from a meteorite. Burke discovered this and tried to take his place, but the recovering Norbett helped stop him.

LOVE AND CRIME
Batman #144 ● In the first of three stories, Bill Finger and Sheldon Moldoff spun a tale of two aliens dueling for the love of another, with Gotham City as their battleground. The heroes kept them from killing bystanders until the female arrived to break it off with both suitors. Arnold Drake took over the writing for a tale of the Joker dressed up as Batman as part of a test for new members of his gang—which Batman infiltrated in disguise. Finger stepped back in to tell how Batgirl and Robin patrolled Gotham City while Batman and Batwoman were away.

ALSO THIS YEAR

January—*Detective Comics* #287: Batman and Robin stopped a pair of aliens who each created a costumed villain to fight for them.

April—*Detective Comics* #290: When a scientist charged Batman and Robin with opposing energies so that they were unable to work near each other, Batman used a robot Robin to help him fight crime.

August—*Batman* #141: The Clockmaster taunted Batman and Robin by sending them a Crime Clock. The heroes entered an extreme race to prevent a murder. Batgirl helped capture the Moth—and revealed her crush on Robin.

June—*Secret Origins* #1: This comic featured a reprint of the origin of the Superman/Batman team.

November—*World's Finest Comics* #121: Batman fell into another universe through a mirror, and became a distorted version of himself until Superman and Robin rescued him.

IDENTITY CRISES

BATMAN #148

Many stories revolved around Batman and Robin's struggle to protect their secret identities and/or deal with copycats who wore their costumes or imitated their forms. This issue offered up three stories on this broad theme.

Writer Jerry Coleman and artist Jim Mooney led off the issue with Batman and Robin stumbling upon an alien settlement in a remote mountain range. The aliens' defense system consisted of swirling columns of energy that duplicated the heroes, forming powerful force twins who captured Batman and Robin. The aliens' vulnerability to water proved their downfall.

Artist Sheldon Moldoff and writer Bill Finger then introduced Bruce Wayne's cousin Vanderveer Wayne, a haughty member of the upper class who became Dick Grayson's rival during a weeklong visit. Wanting to prove himself a superior athlete, Vanderveer hired an actor to pretend to be Batman while he dressed up as Robin. After putting out a staged fire at a museum event, he revealed his supposed identity as Robin to Dick. When the actor decided to use the Batman costume to rob the payroll of an ice-cream plant, the real Batman and Robin worked with Vanderveer to stop him.

In the cover story by Finger and Moldoff, the Joker crashed his helicopter rather than let Batman capture him during a robbery. While Batman was stunned, the Joker unmasked him before Robin and the police chased him off. The Joker then threatened to reveal his identity to the world if Batman ever captured him again. Despite this, Batman pursued him harder than ever. In the end, he discovered the Joker had been blinded when his mask had been taken off, and his secret remained safe.

> "Now to unmask one clown and find another— the Joker!"
>
> Batman, *Batman* #148

1962

"Good thing we always carry crayon in our Utility Belts!"

Batman, *Batman* #149

Batman's partnerships became more important than ever this year, as the Justice League of America grew in popularity, dragging him into global troubles, often without Robin. Despite this, he and his young ward traveled widely and fought crime not just in Gotham City, but in Metropolis, Hawaii, and even other dimensions. The second team-up of Lex Luthor with the Joker to battle both Superman and Batman and Robin was an early instance of multiple heroes' foes joining forces, repeated by the likes of the Crime Champions in 1963 and the Injustice Gang and the Secret Society of Supervillains in the '70s.

LEAGUE ORIGINS

***Justice League of America* #9** ■ After eight issues of *JLA* and three appearances in *The Brave and the Bold*, the Justice League were given an origin story by writer Gardner Fox and artist Mike Sekowsky. When the planet Appellax lost its ruler, seven superpowered claimants to the throne came to Earth to wage a war for supremacy. Wonder Woman, the Martian Manhunter, Aquaman, Green Lantern, and the Flash each defeated one, then teamed up against another. They joined Superman and Batman, who defeated the seventh, to form the Justice League.

POLKA TIME

***Detective Comics* #300** ■ This milestone issue got zero fanfare, but writer Bill Finger and penciller Sheldon Moldoff served up a wacky tale introducing Mr. Polka-Dot, a villain whose spotted costume featured removable disks that could transform into amazing things, like a buzzsaw, a flying saucer, or a gigantic bubble. When captured by the villain and forced to write a note to Batman, to lead him into a trap, Robin used Braille letters to send Batman a secret warning as well. The duo then decoded Mr. Polka-Dot's plans and put an end to them, period.

FEB

MAY

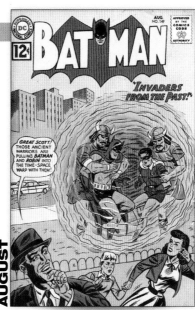

AUGUST

NEXT GENERATIONS

Batman #145 ■ Scribe Bill Finger and artist Sheldon Moldoff teamed up once more for this trio of tales. First, Batman and Robin traveled to Hawaii to hunt down a gangster known only as Mr. 50. In the next story, when a crook shrank himself to the size of a mouse to hide in a toy factory, Batman followed suit so he could go after him. In the cover story, Alfred recounted another imaginary tale of Batman II and Robin II, this time pitting them against a villainous protégé of the Joker, who was posing as the son of the Clown Prince of Crime.

FROM BATMAN TO BAT-BABY

Batman #147 ■ In the first of three tales in this issue, crooks took the plant seeds from an alien amnesiac disguised as a human and used them to commit wild crimes, until Batman and Robin stopped them. Next, a dying crime lord sent his men through a series of riddles to find his hidden loot, but the Dynamic Duo beat them to it. In the cover story, a scientist regressed Batman into a four-year-old body. Retaining his mind and strength, he kept fighting crime as "Bat-Baby." All three stories were written by Bill Finger with art by Sheldon Moldoff.

CRIMES AGAINST TIME

Batman #149 ■ Armed crooks posing as time travelers were swiftly dealt with by Batman and Robin when the pair, too, pretended to be pulled into the past in the cover story of this three-tale issue by writer Jerry Coleman and artist Sheldon Moldoff. In the other two stories, Batman and Robin teamed up with Professor Ambrose Weems—disguised as the Sparrow—to solve the musical clues that the Maestro of Crime had left; and a mysterious ray sent a garbled thought into Batman's head, helping him prevent the assassination of a foreign leader.

77

DEATH AND FAMILY
BATMAN #156

In the double-sized second story of this issue "Robin Dies at Dawn," Batman had to confront his own fears over the possibility of losing Robin permanently.

Like most of the Batman comics of the era, issue #156 featured stories by writer Bill Finger and artist Sheldon Moldoff. In the first of two stories, "The Secret of the Ant-Man," Robin found himself a new partner when Batman left town on a secret mission. The Ant-Man turned out to be a crook who'd shrunk down to doll size after being exposed to waste chemicals running out of Professor Hanson's lab. He fooled Robin into thinking he was a hero, right up until the moment he saw his chance to steal a satchel full of jewels.

The second story explained that Batman had disappeared during the first story to help U.S. Army doctors test out the effects of long-term isolation on astronauts. Toward the end of the test, Batman began to hallucinate that he was on a hostile alien planet, and he had a vision of his greatest fear: Robin dying to save him.

The vision proved so real that it induced post-traumatic stress disorder, causing Batman to have flashbacks while fighting criminals. Unable to trust himself any longer, he decided to hang up his cowl for good. Soon after, however, the Gorilla Gang captured Robin and sentenced him to death as a warning to Batman to leave them alone. Bruce donned his Batman costume again to track down the hoods. Seeing Robin in peril shocked Bruce out of his condition, and he returned to his crime-fighting career.

This powerful story influenced writer Grant Morrison during his run on the hero, starting in 2006. Morrison even used the doctor character as his main villain in the epic "Batman: R.I.P.," naming him Dr. Hurt.

1963

"Even a Batman can succumb to stress and shock! I just hope there won't be any after-effects." Dr. Hurt, *Batman #156*

Parallel worlds played a huge part in Batman's adventures this year. As part of the Justice League, he met the Justice Society and traveled from his Earth-One to their Earth-Two. Later in the year, he accidentally found himself in yet another reality, one in which he never existed. This proved to be a big part of laying the groundwork for the kind of multiversal continuity for all of DC Comics that would come to a head in 1985's *Crisis on Infinite Earths*. Romance became a stronger element in the stories, involving potential girlfriends not just for Batman but for Robin as well.

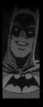

ROBIN'S "DEATH"
In Batman's hallucination, Robin came to rescue him from a giant, four-armed, stone statue. It killed Robin with a boulder as it fell to its death.

BATMAN'S DEEPEST FEAR
The U.S. Army doctor in charge of the isolation experiment explained the effects that long-term isolation had upon Batman's mind.

RETURN OF THE PENGUIN
BATMAN #155

The anchor in this pair of stories by writer Bill Finger and artist Sheldon Moldoff was the return of the Penguin, who hadn't been seen since *Batman* #99, back in April of 1956.

In the first tale, "Batman's Psychic Twin," Bruce Wayne was caught in an explosion with criminal Jo-Jo Gagan and formed a psychic bond with him. Whenever Jo-Jo was hurt, Bruce also felt the pain, even when dressed as Batman. When Jo-Jo's gangster friends realized this, they tried to kill Jo-Jo to cause Batman to die. Fortunately, Batman figured out an antidote to the psychic bonding. Jo-Jo then realized that he'd bonded with Bruce, which meant that Bruce had to be Batman. While trying to sell Batman's secret identity, Jo-Jo was killed.

In the second story, the Penguin returned after a seven-year hiatus, during which he'd served out his jail sentence. When other crooks called him a has-been, he came out of retirement to soothe his bruised ego. He lured Batman and Robin to a robbery in Chinatown by altering the Bat-Signal to show a Chinese-style bat, before escaping. He then sent them clues about an upcoming heist to make sure they'd try to stop him. When they did, he attacked them with his Penguin-Blimp, nearly killing Robin. Later, the Penguin attempted to rob a gala of the Friends of Birds Society, but the heroes cornered him by constructing scarecrows from Batman costumes.

FOR THE BIRDS
Because he was fascinated by birds, the Penguin often employed winged creatures of all kinds in his crimes, including (in this issue) gigantic animatronic birds.

CAT VS. BAT
Detective Comics #311 ■ In this issue, writer Bill Finger and artist Jim Mooney introduced a new Batman villain destined to return again and again: Cat-Man. Big-game hunter Tom Blake returned to Gotham City, bored by his long series of successes capturing large felines. To make money to cover his gambling debts, he turned to crime as the costumed Cat-Man. During his debut spree, he encountered Batwoman and invited her to join him, but she refused. After he fell into an underground waterfall, he was presumed dead.

CLAYFACE VS. CLAYFACE
Detective Comics #312 ■ In this Bill Finger and Sheldon Moldoff story, Clayface broke out of prison and returned to the mysterious pool that gave him his powers. He took to impersonating Batman in order to rob a bank run by people who trusted the hero. The Caped Crusader later followed Clayface to the power-giving pool, and both men fell in and began to battle by shifting into all sorts of dangerous shapes. After defeating Clayface, Batman destroyed the cavern containing the pool; however, this would not prevent Clayface's future return.

ENERGY CRISIS
Batman #153 ■ In this issue, Finger and Moldoff created a three-part tale in which Batman, Robin, Batwoman, and Batgirl confronted an alien in Gotham City. The alien teleported Robin and Batgirl to another dimension, but the teleportation machine separated Batman and Batwoman into weakened people on Earth and energy forms on another planet. As Batman's body began to die, he professed his love to Batwoman. At the same time, Robin and Batgirl kissed. After they beat the alien, Batman denied his feelings, but Robin and Batgirl did not.

MEETING OF WORLDS
Justice League of America #21 ■ In this instant classic by writer Gardner Fox and penciller Mike Sekowsky, the Justice League met the Justice Society for the first time, linking the Golden Age team of Earth-Two with the contemporary Silver Age heroes of Earth-One. Together, the heroes battled Earth-One villains Chronos, Doctor Alchemy, and Felix Faust and Earth-Two foes the Fiddler, the Icicle, and the Wizard. The two teams united on Earth-One at the end of this issue and defeated their combined foes in *Justice League of America* #22.

KILLER PENGUIN

While he may have seemed like a buffoon at times, the Penguin wasn't afraid to try to kill anyone who came after him. Fortunately Robin escaped from his busted "Whirly-Bat" just in time.

CAT-MAN RETURNS

Detective Comics #318 ● In this tale written by Jack Schiff and drawn by Jim Mooney, Cat-Man returned after his apparent death, declared his love for Batwoman, and embarked on a series of cat-related crimes. As a ruse to find his secret hideout, Batwoman pretended to fight with Batman, and Cat-Man took her in to become his Cat-Woman. When Cat-Man saw through the plan, he captured Batman and Robin, and kidnapped Batwoman, but the pair freed themselves in time to rescue her. Cat-Man's boat exploded, seeming to kill him once more.

FACELESS VILLAIN

Detective Comics #319 ● Writer Dave Wood joined artist Sheldon Moldoff to tell how Dr. Paul Dent accidentally erased his features when demonstrating his new skin rejuvenation ray. Driven mad, he called himself No-Face and went on a rampage, destroying faces on signs and artwork. Batman and Robin finally caught him as he attempted to deface the Batman-Face Monument carved into Mt. Gotham. He turned out to be not Dent at all, but a crook who'd used Dent's machine to remove his own face and then posed as the mad doctor while he committed crimes.

FEUDING FOES

Batman #159 ● Clayface broke out of jail in this story by Bill Finger and Sheldon Moldoff and used the last sample from the mysterious pool of protoplasm that originally gave him his power to synthesize a substitute. Soon after, he began a feud with the Joker over who was the greater crook, with each of them trying to top the other. Batman, Robin, Batwoman, and Batgirl exploited this disagreement to capture the Joker. They kept his capture a secret until they could lure Clayface into attacking the Joker—who was really Batman in disguise.

ALSO THIS YEAR

August—*Batman* #157**:** Batman and Robin pursued a villain called the Jackal, who turned out to be a reporter who'd developed a split personality. Then they faced off against the Mirror Man, who knew Batman was Bruce Wayne and meant to prove it to the world. When Vicki Vale tried to help, she made matters worse, and Alfred—dressed as Batman—ended up kissing her.

September—*World's Finest Comics* #136**:** After flying the Batplane through a lightning storm, Batman wound up in a parallel world in which he never existed and where Bruce Wayne was Superman's secret identity. After Batman convinced Superman and Robin that he was no criminal, they helped send him home.

October—*Detective Comics* #320**:** When Bruce Wayne and Dick Grayson were turned green by an alien ray, Batman and Robin had to wrap themselves up like mummies to keep their identities safe.

December—*Detective Comics* #322**:** Batman was transformed in the memorable tale "The Bizarre Batman-Genie."

MAY

THE NEW LOOK

DETECTIVE COMICS #327

Batman and *Detective Comics* both received makeovers when editor Julius Schwartz hired new creatives to update the books' style. Not only were Batman and Robin's outfits given redesigns, but Batman himself was given a subtle new look.

The New Look Batsuit featured a yellow oval around the bat symbol on Batman's chest. The edges of Robin's tunic hung lower, helping to show movement, even as the Boy Wonder grew taller and was now obviously a teenager. Batman also slimmed down from the burly brawler he'd been before to someone who looked more comfortable with judo than boxing.

In this first New Look issue, writer John Broome penned a tale, illustrated by Carmine Infantino, in which a jewel thief figured out a way to paralyze Batman and Robin any time they got within 10 feet of him. The Dynamic Duo hunted for him in Sub-Gotham Village, a labyrinth of caves beneath the city that people wanted destroyed because of all the criminals hiding out there. They found him, but he used his ability to paralyze the heroes to establish his criminal reputation. Fortunately, Batman figured out the thief's power, and disabled it.

The story stood out because Batman and Robin were the only people to wear a costume in the entire tale. This set the new tone for *Detective Comics*. It's no coincidence that the Elongated Man replaced the Martian Manhunter as the back-up feature that same issue, emphasizing a move from science fiction back to mystery.

LOOKING GOOD, HITTING HARD
Sporting their redesigned costumes, the Dynamic Duo made short work of a gang who thought they had Batman and Robin at their mercy.

1964

"I'd like to clear up that 'secret business' I've been on."
Batman, *Batman* #164

After successfully reinventing the Flash for the Silver Age, artist Carmine Infantino was brought in to work his magic on Batman and Robin, under the eye of editor Julius Schwartz. DC Comics dubbed this approach the "New Look" Batman and Robin. The sharp, modern style —which was accompanied by the return of the Batman titles to their mystery-story roots—brought about an upswing in popularity for the Dynamic Duo. This increase in public awareness for the characters would soon explode following the massive success of the *Batman* television series (1966–68).

JANUARY

A SUPERSTITIOUS LOT
Detective Comics #323 ● Writer Dave Wood and artist Sheldon Moldoff introduced the Zodiac Master, a character whose costume featured tear-off zodiacal symbols with strange powers. He predicted the crash of a ship, which came true, and then prevented a plane from taking off after he announced it would crash if it did. Superstitious criminals bought into his prophecies and paid him to predict the success of their heists. Batman and Robin stopped him by predicting where he would strike next with a theft of his own.

FEBRUARY

GHOST TRICKS
World's Finest Comics #139 ● Jim Mooney drew and Dave Wood wrote this story, "The Ghost of Batman," in which Batman and Superman tried to throw off the suspicions of Kathy Kane (Batwoman) that Batman was really Bruce Wayne. While Bruce was on a date with Kathy, Superman took his place as Batman. When a bomb blew him up, however, Superman realized that he would have to pretend that Batman had been killed. To cover their deception, the two heroes concocted a plan to have Superman act as Batman's ghost.

82

A SPOT OF BOTHER
Jewel thief Frank Fenton came up with a way to mark the foreheads of Batman and Robin with a symbol made from a rare isotope of phosphorus. They tracked Fenton to his home, where he paralyzed them with a signal sent to the glowing marks, which seemed to have vanished, but were in fact still there. Once the Dynamic Duo figured this out, they covered the now-invisible marks with lead and tricked Fenton into leading them to a gangster's den in Sub-Gotham Village. Fenton tried to paralyze them again, but thanks to the lead shielding, Batman and Robin rounded up the criminals.

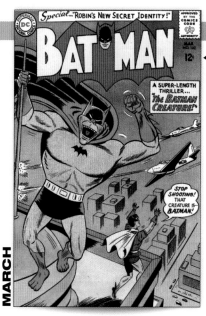

MARCH

THE BEAST AND THE BOY
Batman #162 ● In this issue's first extra-long story by writer Bill Finger and artist Sheldon Moldoff, a mad scientist used a strange machine to turn trained animals into powerful quasi-men who committed crimes for him. The villain later turned the device on Batman, transforming him into a massive, ape-like beast. In the issue's second tale, Robin wanted to see what life would be like as a regular boy and disguised himself to give it a try. Robin wound up with amnesia, but recovered before he accidentally revealed his secret identity to the world.

SPECIAL FEATURE

A GENTLE TOUCH
Batman went on a rampage when he was transformed into a beast. Nothing could stop him—not even Robin's pleas to calm down before the police were forced to shoot him—but Batwoman's tears made him as docile as a pet.

MAY

LOVE AND JUDGEMENT
Batman #163 ● In Bill Finger and Sheldon Moldoff's last issue of *Batman* before the New Look took hold, Alfred Pennyworth wrote an imaginary story in which Batgirl grew up to become Batwoman II and fell in love with her old crush, Robin, who was now Batman II. In the cover story, the Joker captured Batman and Robin and put them on trial with himself as the judge, along with a Joker district attorney and Joker jurors. Despite being found guilty (of course), the heroes escaped and managed to put the Joker back into a real cell.

DEAD FRIENDS
World's Finest Comics #141 ● Batman wore his old costume on the cover, but this issue marked the first appearance of the New Look Batman in this title. In the story by writer Edmond Hamilton and artist Curt Swan, Jimmy Olsen and Robin teamed up for the first time, faking their deaths to fool some crooks. To pay them back for the hoax, Superman and Batman put false bodies in the boys' coffins to shock them. Also, in a reprinted back-up story, from *Lois Lane* #29 (November 1961), Lois kissed Batman, Aquaman, and Green Arrow to help save Superman.

TEENS UNITE

THE BRAVE AND THE BOLD #54

Three popular Super Hero sidekicks—Aqualad, Kid Flash, and Robin—banded together for the first time. This issue became a test run for DC's next team book: *Teen Titans*.

In this story written by Bob Haney and drawn by Bruno Premiani, the three young heroes traveled to Hatton Corners to help the teenagers there work out their troubles with the town's adults. When they arrived, they discovered the teens had all disappeared, kidnapped by a villain known as Mr. Twister. He was actually a bitter descendant of the man who'd given the town the land on which it was built. In exchange, the town had to pay him a rent of one passenger pigeon per year or give him a youth to work in his service for that year.

No one had come to collect the rent for decades, and with the extinction of the passenger pigeon, it would have been impossible anyhow. When Mr. Twister came to claim the rent, the town laughed him to scorn—until he returned with a Native American staff that gave him magical powers.

The three teen heroes rescued the kids and saved the city, each proving themselves an important part of their nascent team. Better yet, the incident showed the adults and teens how much they valued each other, with the city promising to build the teens a new clubhouse to replace the one Mr. Twister had torn down.

THE FIRST NEMESIS
Bromwell Stikk, otherwise known as Mr. Twister, returned to plague the Teen Titans several times. A strange creature called the Antithesis transformed him into the Gargoyle for a while and sent him to battle their common foes.

GOODBYE, ALFRED
Detective Comics #328 ● Writer Bill Finger and artist Sheldon Moldoff returned to *Detective Comics* for their first "New Look" Batman tale. Gangsters hiding in the old, deserted Gotham Prison captured Alfred, and then grabbed Batman and Robin. The crooks told stories about their foiled crimes to determine which of them got to execute the heroes. Batman and Robin escaped, but Alfred sacrificed himself. Batman created the Alfred Foundation in memory of his fallen butler. In her first appearance, Dick Grayson's Aunt Harriet came to watch over them in Alfred's place.

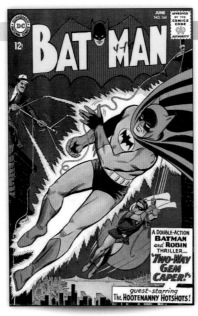

THE NEW WAY
Batman #164 ● Writer Ed Herron joined artist Sheldon Moldoff for this first issue of *Batman* featuring the "New Look", in which they introduced an elevator to the Batcave, a sleek new Batmobile, and a faster route from the Batcave via a tunnel with an automatic door. In the first story, Batman and Robin stopped a pearl thief, who seemed to anticipate their every move through excellent detective work. In the second, a private investigator tried to earn his spot in the Mystery Analysts of Gotham City by revealing a model of what he claimed was Batman's face.

ONE-MAN TEAM-UP
World's Finest Comics #142 ● In this tale from Edmond Hamilton and Curt Swan, an angry janitor received the powers of the entire Legion of Super-Heroes when a lightning bolt struck a nearby display of statuettes of them. Becoming the Composite Superman, he forced Superman and Batman to let him become their partner and then worked to outshine them. Just as he was about to expose their identities to the world, his powers finally faded—along with all his memories of being Composite Superman.

DEATHTRIP
Detective Comics #329 ● In this story by new *Detective Comics* regulars John Broome (script) and Carmine Infantino (art), Batman and Robin flew to England to track down an elusive thief they thought was in hiding there. They found his hospitable cousin instead, who put them up in the castle he'd refurbished while hunting for lost Nazi gold. The thief had secretly been holding his cousin's family hostage and was controlling his relative. The villain tried to kill the heroes with deathtraps, but Batman and Robin eventually foiled his efforts and captured him in the end.

AUGUST

TRIPLE TROUBLE
Justice League of America #29 • Writer Gardner Fox and artist Mike Sekowsky reunited the Justice League with the Justice Society of Earth-Two again, this time to face a dire new threat from Earth-Three: the Crime Syndicate of America. Tired of easily winning all their battles, the CSA villains attacked the JLA on Earth-One and were defeated. They then dragged the JLA back to Earth-Three with them and beat them there. In the next issue, the CSA fought the JSA, but they and the JLA managed to stop and capture them.

SPECIAL FEATURE

CRIME SYNDICATE
The Earth-Three equivalents of the regular Super Heroes were:
- Johnny Quick = The Flash
- Owlman = Batman
- Power Ring = Green Lantern
- Superwoman = Wonder Woman
- Ultraman = Superman

DECEMBER

THE OUTSIDER APPEARS
Detective Comics #334 • Gardner Fox wrote and Sheldon Moldoff illustrated this story in which a new costumed thief called the Grasshopper stole some of Batman's most valued possessions, including the Batmobile, a Batarang, the Batboat, and even Robin. The Grasshopper turned out to be not one man but twins faking superpowers by appearing to leap from place to place. After Batman stopped them, he learned that the brothers had been hired to commit their crimes by an important new villain called the Outsider, who promised to kill Batman.

ALSO THIS YEAR

August—*Batman* #165: Bruce Wayne's former college roommate, Governor Andrew Warner, discovered that he was a mutant, destined to become the next step of human evolution. He changed form, assumed incredible powers, and tried to conquer the world. In the second story, Batman met rookie cop Patricia Powell, who confessed that she had a crush on Bruce Wayne.

September—*World's Finest Comics* #144: Brainiac broke Clayface out of jail and attacked Superman with a Kryptonite ray, but Jimmy Olsen took the blast. With the material embedded in Jimmy's skin, Superman couldn't go near him, so Robin swapped places with Jimmy until the effects wore off. As part of the deal, Batman and Robin revealed their identities to Jimmy.

Featuring
"REMARKABLE RUSE of the RIDDLER!"

RIDDLED GOOD
BATMAN #171

Last seen in *Detective Comics* #142 back in 1948, the Riddler returned, presenting Batman and Robin with their most puzzling problems to date in this story written by Gardner Fox and illustrated by Sheldon Moldoff.

Not wanting to launch another crime spree until he had Batman's full attention, the Riddler claimed to be reformed and offered to help Batman catch his current quarry—the members of the Molehill Mob—and put them behind bars. He even wore his costume while he helped. He then left Batman and Robin a series of riddles that lured them into making fools of themselves by accusing him of crimes he wasn't committing. Once he'd played with them long enough, he struck for real, but the heroes anticipated this move, and they caught him red-handed robbing a safe.

The Riddler was ready for the heroes, however, and activated a new feature of his costume. This electrified it so that anyone who touched him got a nasty shock; it also rooted the Riddler's feet to the floor. Batman and Robin took to punching him in the jaw instead, but he'd numbed his face so that he couldn't feel the blows, and he bounced around like a punching bag. In due course, Batman figured out how to shut the suit off, and knocked the Riddler flat.

The return of the Riddler proved so popular that he became a staple of Batman's Rogues Gallery, making countless entertaining appearances down the decades.

SHOCKING COSTUME
The Riddler came up with a costume that shocked anyone who touched it, but Batman figured out where the Riddler had hidden its off switch.

1965

"My ruse worked! Batman solved the riddle I left him—but not the riddle *within* the riddle"
The Riddler, *Batman #171*

DC Comics continued to revamp its Batman titles, and *Batman* #170 featured a new, updated Batman logo to alert readers to that fact. Having moved solidly toward detective stories (and away from sci-fi) the previous year, the Batman creators continued to explore tales of that type; however, they also allowed themselves a bit more leeway with fantastic elements. A number of new tales involved parallel worlds with strange twists that made them different from those featured in the regular stories. Others embraced science fiction once again, but with stories that offered more than simply new aliens to beat.

ENTER METAMORPHO
The Brave and the Bold #57 ● Batman didn't appear in this issue, written by Bob Haney with art by Ramona Fradon. This story introduced Metamorpho, the Element Man and recounted his origin. An adventurer named Rex Mason became affected by the radiation from a meteor buried inside a pyramid, and transformed into a reluctant Super Hero with the ability to change his body into different chemical forms. Metamorpho would subsequently go on to be a founding member of the Outsiders, a strike force originally led by the Dark Knight.

BAT PLANNING
Batman #169 ● The Penguin returned from prison in the first of these stories written by Ed Herron and drawn by Sheldon Moldoff. Unable to think of a new heist worthy of Batman's attention, the Penguin unleashed dozens of his trick umbrellas on the city. When Batman spotted an unintended pattern and came up with a theory about the Penguin's plan the Penguin listened in and then proceeded to implement it. The issue's second story showed how even Batman could have a bad day trying to catch crooks—but that he always pushed through anyhow.

TEEN HEROES

World's Finest Comics #147 ■ In this story written by Edmond Hamilton and drawn by Curt Swan, Robin and Jimmy Olsen became Super Heroes in their own right rather than simply sidekicks. The pair set up their own headquarters and created new costumes for themselves. They then set out to build and fuel a rocket ship to take them to the stars, even going so far as to collect reward money to fund their efforts. Before things could go too far, Superman realized that a pair of jewels he'd given Jimmy had taken over the boys' minds, and removed them.

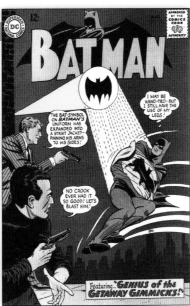

JUST GET AWAY

Batman #170 ■ In the first story, written by Gardner Fox and drawn by Sheldon Moldoff, a trio of thieves led by Roy Reynolds, the Getaway Genius, eluded capture by employing various tricks. Reynolds then caused Batman and Robin's symbols to expand, making the Dynamic Duo easy targets. However, two of the gang were captured and turned in Reynolds. In the second story by writer Bill Finger and artist Joe Giella, Aunt Harriet asked Bruce to check out how her friend had managed to win a contest that she hadn't entered, and they accidentally stopped a crime ring.

TRAPPED IN TIME

The Brave and the Bold #59 ■ In this tale from writer Bob Haney and artist Ramona Fradon, a fugitive styling himself the Time Commander asked Batman to help clear his name. The Time Commander then tricked Green Lantern into giving him part of his ring's power. Combining that with his own time-controlling hourglass, he sent Batman a day into the future and Green Lantern a day into the past. Green Lantern used his ring to tell Batman to set an air-raid siren at the right frequency to shatter the hourglass and return them to the proper time.

DUST TO DUST

Detective Comics #340 ■ Writer John Broome joined artist Sheldon Moldoff for this story, in which Batman and Robin's own crime-fighting equipment worked against them. This was caused by the Outsider, who had figured out a way to animate the things the Super Heroes owned and turn them into deadly weapons—until they turned to dust. Batman realized that the dust from the destroyed objects could be used to protect him, and managed to put an end to the Outsider's attacks. The Batcopter was first named in this issue.

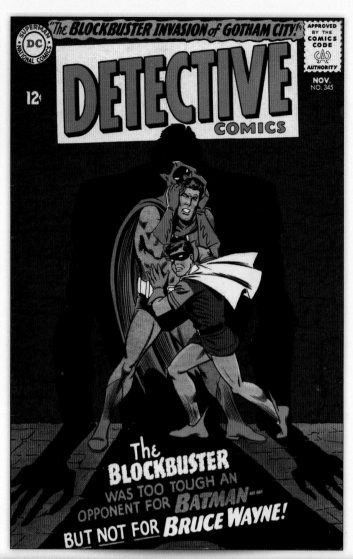

THE BLOCKBUSTER INVASION of GOTHAM CITY!

DC

SUPERMAN NATIONAL COMICS

DETECTIVE COMICS

12¢

NOV. NO. 345

The BLOCKBUSTER WAS TOO TOUGH AN OPPONENT FOR BATMAN --- BUT NOT FOR BRUCE WAYNE!

BIG BROTHER

DETECTIVE COMICS #345

Writer Gardner Fox and penciller Carmine Infantino introduced the villain Blockbuster in this issue which included a rare instance of Bruce Wayne proving more effective than Batman.

While deep-sea fishing alone, Bruce encountered a freak storm and was shipwrecked on a remote island. As he looked for shelter, he found young Mark Desmond, who'd fallen into quicksand, and rescued him. Mark's grateful older brother Roland took Bruce in for the night and returned him home in the morning.

Months later, a super-strong, bulletproof villain called Blockbuster robbed a bank. Although he was mute, he took everything Batman and Robin could throw at him, beat them down, and fled. The heroes followed Blockbuster to the same island on which Bruce had been shipwrecked. Bruce recognized young Mark's face in Blockbuster and unmasked himself to appeal to the boy inside.

Meanwhile, Robin captured Roland, who revealed that the young genius Mark had accidentally turned himself into the low-intelligence Blockbuster with a growth serum the boy had developed. Roland had taken advantage of this to order his brother to steal things for him. When Batman returned to the island to capture Blockbuster, he had already disappeared.

FULLY GROWN
Although he was a little boy at heart, Blockbuster proved to be too strong for Batman and Robin to handle with their fists. Only Bruce Wayne could calm him down.

OLD JOKES

Detective Comics #341 ▪ In "The Joker's Comedy Capers" by writer John Broome and artist Carmine Infantino, the Joker was hired by wealthy film director Van-Van Laugh to make old-time silent comedies. Disguised as Mr. DeNil, the Joker launched a series of robberies starring himself, impersonating various famous silent comedians. The Joker then had his hirelings film the results. This was part of the Joker's plot to gain an invite to the millionaire movie fan's mansion for the films' premiere so that he could rob him, a plan that Batman and Robin stopped cold.

PAST AND FUTURE

World's Finest Comics #151 ▪ Hamilton and Swan spun this wild tale, in which a Kryptonian evolution acceleration machine devolved Superman into a caveman and evolved Batman into a big-brained genius. The process removed Batman's ability to empathize with others, and he tried to rule the world. He sent Superman to live with other cavemen in the distant past and then sent himself into the far future, where he would fit in. Superman chased after him, and Krypto the Superdog turned the beam on Batman, restoring him to normal.

THUNDERBOLT CRISIS

Justice League of America #37 ▪ Writer Gardner Fox and artist Mike Sekowsky created another multiversal tale in which Johnny Thunder of Earth-Two decided to visit his counterpart in Earth-One—who turned out to be a crook. This issue marked the debut of Earth-A's Bill Gore Batman and included a moment where Johnny Thunder almost convinced Golden Age Batman not to be Batman. Luckily the JSA came to the rescue, beating the evil Thunder so often he wished everything back to normal by the next issue.

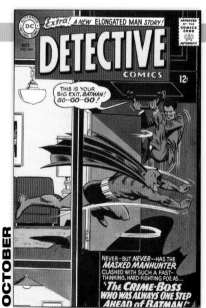

A DUEL OF WITTS

Detective Comics #344 ▪ In this story by Gardner Fox and Sheldon Moldoff, Batman and Robin faced off against the clever Johnny Witts, a criminal mastermind who anticipated the heroes' actions at every turn. Every time they made a move against him, he was ready for them. Once they figured this out, however, the heroes doubled up on their moves, putting them a step ahead of Witts. Undeterred by this setback, however, Johnny Witts would later return, to plague the Dynamic Duo again by trying to prove himself smarter than them.

SONS OF HEROES

WORLD'S FINEST COMICS #154

This imaginary story of an alternate world depicted a future in which Batman and Superman had gotten married to Kathy Kane (Batwoman) and Lois Lane, respectively, and each had sons.

In this story, written by Edmond Hamilton and illustrated by Curt Swan, Batman and Superman's sons grew up to be friends, but over the years resentment grew between their mothers, Kathy and Lois. When this reached breaking point, the women forbade their sons from seeing each other. Fearful that this disagreement would spell the end of their fathers' famed friendship, the young pals decided to run away together until matters could be sorted out.

While the boys were missing, the Napoleon of Crime—an old foe of their fathers—captured them and tricked them into giving away their fathers' secret identities. Fortunately, the boys broke free from the super-villain's trap before he could target their families. United in their relief, their mothers were able to put an end to the hard feelings between them. This entertaining tale proved to be the first of several adventures that used the idea of second-generation Super Heroes Batman Jr. and Superman Jr.

PROUD SONS
Batman and Superman's sons were proud of their fathers' heroic achievements and studied their adventures with glee. That is why they knew how important their fathers' friendship was to each other—and to the world.

THE BAD BATMAN

***World's Finest Comics* #153** ▪ In this imaginary story by writer Edmond Hamilton and penciller Curt Swan, Bruce Wayne's father was killed while working on a serum to cure Superboy of his weakness to Kryptonite. Bruce became Batman to prove Superman's guilt. Frustrated in his efforts to bring Superman to justice, Bruce decided to settle for revenge instead and teamed up with Lex Luthor. When he discovered Luthor had killed his father with a Superboy robot, Batman sacrificed his own life to save Superman, who brought Luthor in for his crime.

THE BAT TRAP

***Detective Comics* #346** ▪ Writer John Broome and artist Sheldon Moldoff told how famous escape artist Carnado and Eivol Ekdal, the mastermind inventor who built apparent deathtraps for Carnado's act, conspired to capture Batman. Unable to defeat a new trap they had invented, they hoped the hero could show them how. Batman managed to blow the trap apart and escape, and then he and Robin tracked the two trappers down. Avoiding an ambush, the heroes captured the crooks and threw them into jail—from which they didn't escape.

INVISIBLE VILLAINS

***Justice League of America* #41** ▪ In this story by writer Gardner Fox and penciller Mike Sekowsky, the Key hypnotized Snapper Carr into drugging the Justice League so that they dissolved the group. The drug made the Key's Keymen henchmen invisible to the Super Heroes, enabling them to commit crimes with impunity. However Super Hero sidekicks, such as Hawkgirl, were immune. Hawkgirl cured Hawkman, they restored the JLA members to normal, and the Key and his gang were soon behind bars. After this debut, the Key became a Batman villain.

ALSO THIS YEAR

March—*World's Finest Comics* #148: Batman and Superman were sent to an alternate world in which their counterparts were a criminal team. The heroes teamed with good versions of Lex Luthor and Clayface to stop their doubles cold.

August—*Metamorpho* #1: After a successful debut in *The Brave and the Bold* #57 (January 1965), Metamorpho got his own title.

August—*Batman* #173: Batman and Robin foiled an attempt by new villain Mr. Incognito to reveal their identities with an X-ray camera. They then stopped a crooked politician who was using a mind-control ray.

August—*Detective Comics* #342: Robin broke up the Robin Gang, a group of young crooks who wore his costume.

December—*Batman* #177: A tiny and giant Batman (the Atom and Elongated Man) helped Batman catch a jewel thief. In the second story, Batman and Robin foiled art thieves who attacked a hopeful press agent who wanted to help with their fake art gallery's PR.

TWO-WAY DEATH TRAP
Batman #166 (September 1964) ● The "New Look" Batman of the mid 1960s was characterized by the iconic pencilling style of artist Carmine Infantino and stories that were grittier and more realistic. In this tale, a crook named Mitch had overheard Batman telling Robin about a nightmare he had had in which he was trapped in a room filling with water while a machine gun fired over his head. Mitch and his partner Beany decided to make Batman's nightmare come true. Fortunately the Dark Knight proved too clever for them.

THE TEEN TEAM

TEEN TITANS #1

Following a strong debut for the Teen Titans in *The Brave and the Bold* #54 in July 1964, DC Comics tapped writer Bob Haney and artist Nick Cardy for the first issue of the team's own book.

By this time, Wonder Girl had joined Robin, Aqualad, and Kid Flash to round out the team. The US government asked the four young heroes to become official members of the Peace Corps so they could help out at a location in the mountains of South America, called Xochatan. A gigantic metal conquistador was wreaking havoc with the Peace Corps' plan to build a dam there. Once the Titans completed their Peace Corps training, they parachuted into Xochatan and battled with the creature.

After they defeated the giant robot, the Teen Titans helped work on the dam to proceed. But when water began to fill the valley, covering an ancient pyramid, a series of superpowered animals with the faces of a man attacked them. The heroes defeated them one by one. As the waters continued to cover the pyramid, the animals' master emerged to threaten the Titans. The "Beast-God of Xochatan" turned out to be a wealthy man who had been run out of the area during a revolt. He had been hiding in the pyramid ever since, and had tried to stop the building of the dam to keep from being flushed out.

JOINING THE CORPS
The U.S. government had taken an interest in the new teenage team and called them to Washington D.C. to give them an official role—despite the fact that Aqualad came from Atlantis and Wonder Girl hailed from Paradise Island.

1966

"Don't despair—I'll leave a clue for you to track me down—if you dare!"

The Cluemaster, *Detective Comics* #351

This was the year Batman and Robin really broke out into the mainstream. The *Batman* TV show starring Adam West as Batman and Burt Ward as Robin debuted in January, showing new half-hour episodes twice a week. The comics might have taken on a more serious tone over the years, but the show played the source material as a campy comedy. DC Comics premiered "Batman with Robin the Boy Wonder" as a newspaper comic strip in May, and the team behind the TV show released a *Batman* film during the show's summer hiatus. Meanwhile the Batman comic books resisted the TV show's camp atmosphere as best they could.

WHAT IF?
Detective Comics #347 ■ Writer Gardner Fox actually appeared in the pages of this unusual tale, which was illustrated by Carmine Infantino. The first part showed how Batman and Robin defeated the Bouncer, but then Fox stepped in and asked, "What if?" The story shifted to show Batman being killed. Robin caught the killer, and in a surprise twist both the Batman and Alfred from Earth-Two showed up to serve as replacements for their deceased counterparts on Earth-One. They had already raised Robin to adulthood in their own universe.

THE MYSTERY OF NIGHTMAN
World's Finest Comics #155 ■ Writer Edmond Hamilton and artist Curt Swan told the story of Batman and Superman's 1000th case together. During the celebration, Batman confessed that a new hero named Nightman had been outdoing him lately. Superman encouraged him to figure out Nightman's secret identity. Batman eventually discovered that Superman had hypnotized him to turn him into Nightman without his knowledge. As a tribute to his friend's skills as a detective, Superman had arranged for Batman to chase himself!

TEEN TROUBLES
Despite the fact that Robin was the only member of the team without superpowers, he regularly proved his worth as a leader and detective, taking on a role like that of Batman in the Justice League.

MARCH

OPPOSITE DAYS
World's Finest Comics #156 ▪ E. Nelson Bridwell helped Edmond Hamilton with the writing, and Curt Swan contributed the artwork for this tale, which introduced the Bizarro Batman. This character and Bizarro Superman came to Earth with Bizarro when Superman and Batman were away on a mission. Unable to keep their Bizarro twins from ruining Metropolis and Gotham City, the heroes flew to the Bizarro planet and started to fix things up. That brought their Bizarro twins zooming home to keep the heroes from doing any more damage to their square planet.

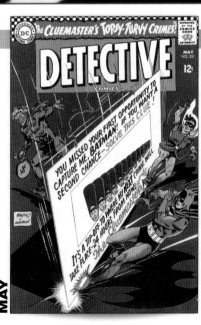

MAY

BEST KEPT SECRETS
Detective Comics #351 ▪ The villainous Cluemaster debuted in this story by Gardner Fox and Carmine Infantino. The Cluemaster gave Batman and Robin clues to his plans—but only so he could trick them into giving him clues to their identities. Fortunately, Dick Grayson's Aunt Harriet (who was now living at Wayne Manor with him and Bruce Wayne) had stumbled upon the entrance to the Batcave, and the heroes' efforts to evade her snooping unwittingly helped them keep the Cluemaster from discovering their secrets, too.

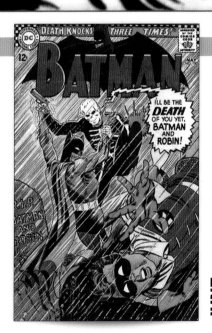

JUNE

DEATH FOR DEATH-MAN
Batman #180 ▪ Batman and Robin faced off against Death-Man—a criminal in a skeleton suit —in this tale by writer Robert Kanigher and artist Sheldon Moldoff. After being captured, Death-Man died in the courtroom the moment he was sentenced to death. He returned to life and to crime, only to die a second time when the heroes captured him again. Batman figured out that Death-Man was faking his demises, reducing his heartbeat and breathing to mimic death. Ironically, Death-Man died for real after being struck by lightning over his own grave.

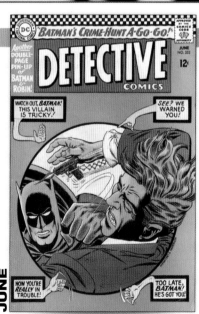

JUNE

BATMAN TELLS THE FUTURE
Detective Comics #352 ▪ In "Batman's Crime-Hunt a Go-Go!," writer John Broome and penciller Sheldon Moldoff told of the time Batman seemed to develop ESP, giving him premonitions of crimes. Two hunches in a row paid off; however, a third turned out to be a false alarm luring Batman and Robin away from a bank robbery. Determined to figure out what was going on, Batman hunted down Mr. Esper, a mind reader who had used super-sonic whispers to suggest the hunches to him. Esper later became the villain known as Captain Calamity.

DEADLY WOMEN
BATMAN #181

Femme fatale and super-villain Poison Ivy made her debut in this issue. The botantist-turned-eco-terrorist had the ability to control plants and seduce men.

In this debut tale, by writer Robert Kanigher and artist Sheldon Moldoff, Poison Ivy appeared at a pop art show featuring portraits of criminal women Dragon Fly, Silken Spider, and Tiger Moth, respectively labeled world public enemy number one, two, and three. She proudly announced in front of Bruce Wayne that *she* was the real public enemy number one, escaping before anyone, including Batman, could catch her. Later, Poison Ivy invited her female criminal rivals and suitors (both Bruce and Batman) to her home. She knocked out her rivals as Batman and Robin punched out their gangs of henchmen. Ivy kissed Batman with drugged lipstick, but with Robin's help he shrugged off its effects and arrested Poison Ivy.

The back-up tale written by Gardner Fox featured the Mystery Analysts of Gotham City. As writer and Analysts member Kaye Daye was about to receive a Sherlock Award for best detective novel, she confessed that someone else had written the book. Batman discovered that the confessor was actually Daye's cousin, who was seeking to inherit their grandfather's wealth.

TRICKY LIPSTICK
Poison Ivy's lipstick was supposedly drugged with a derivative of chloroform, making it easier for her to seduce Batman, but her hold on him seemed to last far longer than the drug.

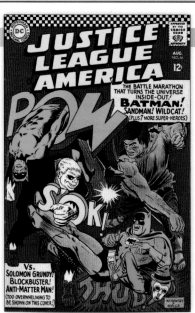

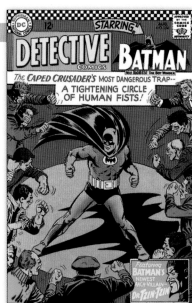

ANTI-HEROES
World's Finest #159 ▪ Anti-Superman and Anti-Batman featured in this tale by writer Edmond Hamilton and artist Curt Swan. Superman and Batman brought Perry White and Commissioner Gordon to the Fortress of Solitude and the Batcave. Soon after, the Anti-Superman and Anti-Batman attacked their namesake heroes. The pair turned out to be Gordon and White, who had been turned evil by a gas released from a bottle during their visit. This issue also marked the debut of Chief O'Hara, a major supporting cast member from the 1966 *Batman* TV show.

POISONED BY IVY
Batman #183 ▪ The impact of the *Batman* TV show was highlighted on this issue's cover. Writer Robert Kanigher and artist Sheldon Moldoff told a story in which Batman continued to be distracted by Poison Ivy. From prison, she sent him a pocket mirror that seemed to hypnotize him, feigned death, begged him to visit her, and when he did, threatened to blow up the jail if he didn't break her out. She then captured him. Batman went on hunger strike rather than join her and her gang. Batman broke free of Ivy's charms and, with Robin, recaptured her.

MIXED-UP WORLDS
Justice League of America #46 ▪ Writer Gardner Fox and penciller Mike Sekowsky brought readers a new meeting of the Justice League and the Justice Society when people were shuffled between the two universes. This not only mixed up the teams but brought Solomon Grundy to Earth-One and sent Blockbuster to Earth-Two. The Spectre discovered the Anti-Matter Man was causing the two worlds to crash together and struggled to stop it. In the following issue, the Earth-One Atom returned the Anti-Matter Man to his own universe.

DOCTOR OF DEATH
Detective Comics #354 ▪ A legendary international criminal known as Dr. Tzin-Tzin came to Gotham City in this story by writer John Broome with pencils by Sheldon Moldoff. While there, Dr. Tzin-Tzin killed an underling who had disappointed him—by frightening him to death. He warned Batman and Robin to keep away from him, but they tracked him down and fought their way through his thugs. Dr. Tzin-Tzin tried to murder Batman with his paralyzing gaze, but Batman managed to toss a Batarang at an intensifying light in the room, shattering the spell.

NOVEMBER

CAT FIGHT

SUPERMAN'S GIRLFRIEND LOIS LANE #70

Batman was caught up in a tale that saw Lois Lane dressed up as Catwoman and Superman transformed into a feline under Catwoman's control.

STEALING A KISS

The first thing Catwoman did when she realized that Superman thought she was Lois Lane in her costume was ask him to give her a super-kiss "to help restore my memory."

In this wacky story, written by Leo Dorfman and drawn by Kurt Schaffenberger, Catwoman kidnapped Lois Lane as she was investigating the Penguin's escape from prison. Catwoman dressed Lois in a costume identical to hers and hypnotized Lois into believing she was Catwoman. Knowing the Penguin would soon arrive at her hideout, Catwoman left Lois to fight her rival villain.

Unaware that they were at Catwoman's hideout, Superman, Batman, and Robin captured the Penguin. While Batman and Robin returned the Penguin to jail, Superman discovered Lois in her Catwoman suit. The hypnotized Lois sent Catwoman's pet lion, tiger, and panther to attack him. Superman gathered up the cats and took them to Metropolis Zoo. By the time he returned, Catwoman had thrown Lois in a cage. Pretending to be his hypnotized girlfriend, Catwoman used a magic wand to change Superman into a cat and locked him in a Kryptonite cage. In the next issue, Lois helped Batman and Robin capture Catwoman and restore Superman to his normal form.

SEPTEMBER

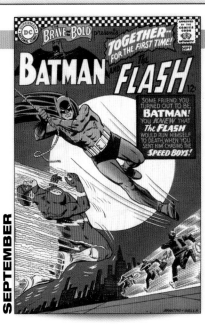

FAST FRIENDS

The Brave and the Bold #67 ● *The Brave and the Bold* was a team-up book, which Batman had starred in before. As of this story by writer Bob Haney and artist Carmine Infantino, he became the mainstay of the title (disrupted only by issues #72 and #73 in 1967). Unable to stop a fast gang of thieves called the Speed Boys, Batman called for help from the Flash, who had secretly been told that his running was killing him. The Flash appeared to die during a chase, but the radioactive isotope used to power the thieves' special shoes revived him.

OCTOBER

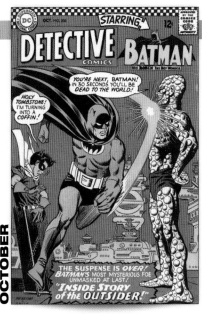

ALFRED RETURNS

Detective Comics #356 ● The Outsider returned with the Grasshopper Twins to attack Batman and Robin in this story by scribe Gardner Fox with art by Sheldon Moldoff. Suspecting the Outsider might be Alfred, the heroes checked on his corpse. They discovered that a scientist had found Alfred in a coma and successfully revived him. The process had transformed Alfred into an evil creature, while morphing the scientist into Alfred's catatonic duplicate. Batman and Robin stopped the Outsider from killing them, and Alfred reverted to his old self.

DECEMBER

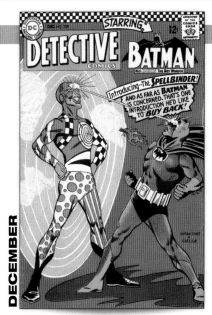

A DEADLY SPELL

Detective Comics #358 ● Delbert Billings, alias Spellbinder, made his debut in this story written by John Broome and illustrated by Sheldon Moldoff. Spellbinder used spinning optics—both on his costume and on separate pinwheels—to hypnotize Batman into frightening dreams while he and his gang committed robberies. A doctor warned Batman that if he died during such a dream, his heart might stop, but Batman refused to give up the chase. Batman eventually managed to overcome Spellbinder's spell and send him and his henchmen to jail.

ALSO THIS YEAR

★ **January 12th**—With Adam West and Burt Ward cast as the Dynamic Duo, the *Batman* TV show premiered on ABC.

April—*Detective Comics #350*: Batman took down the son of an old enemy—the Monarch of Menace—and used him to lure the father to justice.

★ **May 29th**—One month after the cancellation of the "Superman" comic strip, a "Batman and Robin the Boy Wonder" newspaper strip emerged to fill the gap.

June—*Superman's Pal Jimmy Olsen #93*: Jimmy Olsen traveled to Earth X and gained superpowers, becoming Steel-Man.

★ **July 30th**—A *Batman* feature film debuted in movie theaters, starring many key members of the TV show cast.

November—*Batman #186*: The Joker and his new sidekick—little clown Gaggy—stole original items of all kinds, until Batman and Robin put a stop to it.

December—*Justice League of America #50*: Robin joined the Justice League for this battle with the Lord of Time.

THE NEW BATGIRL

DETECTIVE COMICS #359

The original Batgirl hadn't been seen since Schwartz had revamped Batman for the "New Look." Rather than revive her, Carmine Infantino came up with a young woman whose costume mirrored Batman's look.

In this story, written by Gardner Fox and illustrated by Infantino, Barbara Gordon—Commissioner Gordon's daughter and a librarian—originally created her costume for a policeman's ball, but on the way there, she stumbled across Killer Moth and his gang attacking Bruce Wayne. She stopped to save him but made a mess of her costume, so she never made it to the dance.

Later, Barbara brought a rare book to Wayne Manor, where she spotted Killer Moth shooting Bruce Wayne—not knowing it was a dummy. Barbara changed into her costume once again and charged at the Moth-Mob, almost spoiling Batman and Robin's plan to follow the killers to their headquarters. Batman and Robin left her behind so they could pursue the fleeing villains, but Batgirl followed on her custom Batcycle. When Batman and Robin were caught in Killer Moth's trap, Batgirl saved them, earning their respect.

A GIRL OF MANY TALENTS
Despite having a safe job as a librarian, Barbara Gordon was also a first kyu practitioner of judo (also known as a brown belt) and more than capable of taking care of herself.

1967

"That Batgirl sure is tops in my book! Too bad you couldn't be a little more like her, Babs!" Commissioner James Gordon, *Detective Comics #359*

To broaden Batman's appeal to the new readers who had discovered the Caped Crusader through the hit *Batman* TV show, DC Comics redesigned the Batmobile to resemble the one seen on the small screen. They also introduced an all-new Batgirl— drawn by Carmine Infantino, the artist behind 1964's "New Look." She proved popular enough with fans to appear in the TV show's third season later that year. At the same time, DC Comics kept Batman and his expanded family busy, reintroducing old foes such as Scarecrow and revamping Catwoman.

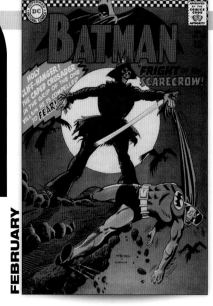

SCARECROW RETURNS
Batman #189 ● Writer Gardner Fox and artist Sheldon Moldoff reached way back to *Detective Comics* #73 (March 1943) to resurrect Scarecrow. Dick Grayson spotted Scarecrow disembarking from a submarine and entering Gotham Park to dig up some long-buried loot. Batman and Robin accosted him but he sprayed them with a fear-inducing compound and escaped. They finally captured Scarecrow trying to rob a philanthropist and frightened him with the sound of police sirens, causing Scarecrow to panic—and get caught.

FUTURE SHOCK
World's Finest Comics #166 ● Writer Jim Shooter joined artist Curt Swan for this futuristic tale, which pitted the Batman and Superman of 2967 against Muto and the Joker of that era. The two villains teamed up to take down Superman, exploiting his weakness to the world's radioactive seawater. Superman retreated to his Fortress of Solitude in the Sun, where the 20th Batman found him. They united to take on the crooks, chasing them through outer space and finally catching Muto—and watching the 20th Joker die.

MAN WONDER

JUSTICE LEAGUE OF AMERICA #55

The Justice League met the Justice Society again in this tale that featured the Robin of Earth-Two, who had now grown up to be a crime fighter on his own.

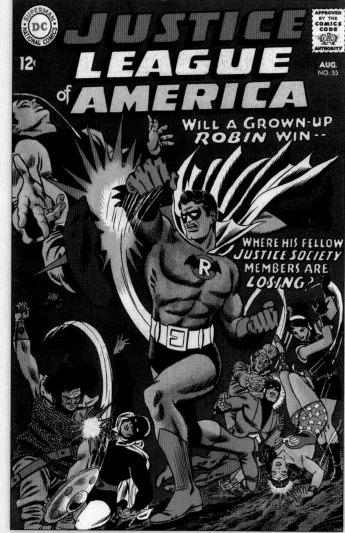

THE NEW MAN

The Robin of Earth-Two was admitted to the Justice Society of America after Batman had semi-retired. Batman was still a part of the Justice Society, but during this particular adventure, he was on a case and couldn't attend the meeting.

Writer Gardner Fox and artist Mike Sekowsky told how the Robin of Earth-Two was admitted to the JSA and helped them solve the mystery of four black spheres that gave their hosts, Gem Girl, How Chu, Money Master, and the Smashing Sportsman, superpowers and turned them evil. The JSA split up to tackle the four new villains, but each team was thrashed. Not even the genie Thunderbolt could stand up to them. Desperate, Johnny Thunder had Thunderbolt bring some of the JLA over to Earth-Two to help out—only to discover that they were having similar problems with these sentient black spheres on their Earth.

In the following issue, the heroes recovered some of the black spheres that had not found hosts and tested them by allowing them to be absorbed by some of their friends. The heroes eventually realized that the best attack involved Johnny Thunder and his awful jokes, which proved remarkably effective at banishing the black spheres.

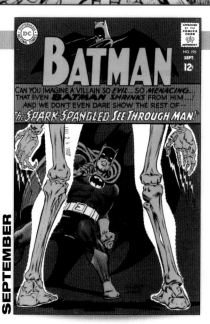

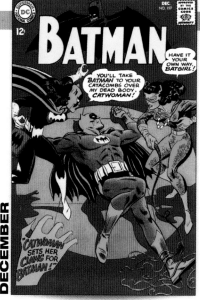

A SHOCK TRANSFORMATION

Batman #195 ▪ Bag O' Bones—a criminal whose flesh was made transparent when he robbed a scientist during an experiment—made his debut in this story by writer Gardner Fox and artist Sheldon Moldoff. The effect also charged him with electricity, with which he shocked the heroes, though it cost him a day of his life for every second he used it. Called the Spark-Spangled See-Through Man on the cover, the character later returned as the Cyclotronic Man and the One-Man Meltdown, changing names as his powers evolved.

GIRL TROUBLE

World's Finest #169 ▪ Writer Cary Bates and penciller Curt Swan told how Supergirl and Batgirl, in their first team-up, were grabbed by a gigantic, gaseous hand. They broke free but then became jealous of Superman and Batman's fame and decided to undermine them. By the time the men figured out what was happening, Superman had lost his powers and Batman's face had changed into someone else's. The girls turned out to be Black Flame (a super-villain from Kandor) and Catwoman in disguise—who then *really* turned out to be Mr. Mxyzptlk and Bat-Mite.

CATWOMAN'S CLAWS

Batman #197 ▪ After Batgirl helped Batman in November's *Detective Comics* #369, Catwoman set out to humiliate her and win Batman's affections. Writer Gardner Fox and artist Carmine Infantino put Catwoman in a "New Look" green costume, in which she pretended to reform to fight crimes rather than commit them. After the heroes discovered she'd staged the crimes she stopped, she caught them in a sonic trap and demanded Batman marry her. He refused, and Batgirl helped him and Robin out of Catwoman's trap to stop her new crime spree.

ALSO THIS YEAR

April—*Detective Comics* #362: The Batmobile appeared with a new design based on the 1966 *Batman* TV show.

May—*Batman* #191: A radioactive villain blackmailed Batman into retiring and auctioning off all his things. Batman did so, but only as a trick to get his foe to reveal himself.

June—*Blue Beetle* #1: Future Batman character the Question debuted.

June—*World's Finest Comics* #167: An alternate history detailed how Lex Luthor became Superman and an orphaned Clark Kent became Batman.

August—*World's Finest Comics* #168: An alien named Xan, bent on vengeance for his father's imprisonment, came to Earth and repowered the Composite Superman.

November—*Detective Comics* #369: Batgirl realized that Batman had contracted swamp fever. Concerned that the fever would hit when Batman was fighting crime, she persuaded Robin to team up with her so they could protect Batman. The duo stopped crooks before Batman could reach them, and he was eventually cured. Meanwhile, Catwoman grew jealous of Batgirl.

FROM ZERO TO FREEZE
DETECTIVE COMICS #373

Batman's old foe Mr. Zero returned with a new name, given to him on the *Batman* TV show: Mr. Freeze. The Caped Crusader had to get hold of the villain's cryothermal gun in order to save the life of Aunt Harriet.

In this story by writer Gardner Fox and artist Chic Stone, Aunt Harriet was undergoing cryogenic surgery when the tool for it failed. Only by capturing Mr. Freeze and taking his cold-gun could Batman and Robin save her life. They found the villain, and Robin fled with Mr. Freeze's spare cold-gun while Batman fought on alone. Mr. Freeze captured him, froze him solid, and then threw him off a roof. Batman managed to burst free from his icy prison and save himself. He had reversed the switch on a thermal unit in his belt, so when Mr. Freeze turned it off in the hopes of freezing his captive, he had really turned it on.

Batman then tracked Mr. Freeze to his hideout and brought him and his gang down while Robin got the spare cold-gun to the hospital, where the doctors were able to save Aunt Harriet's life. In the back-up story, written by Gardner Fox and drawn by Gil Kane, the Elongated Man helped put the Riddler in jail while Batman and Robin were out of town.

PLAN B
Having fought Batman and Robin before as Mr. Zero, Mr. Freeze knew better than to rely on a single weapon that could be taken from him. When Robin snatched the cryothermal gun he was using, Mr. Freeze simply whipped out a replacement and kept fighting.

1968

"Mr. Freeze! That sounds like a campy name dreamed up for a villain in a television program!" Robin, *Detective Comics* #373

The *Batman* TV show ended in March of this year, but Batman's popularity was still riding high. September saw the launch of *The Batman/Superman Hour*, the first animated show in which Batman had ever appeared. In the comics, artist Neal Adams started a long association with Batman, applying his modern style to the tales. Gone was the influence of the TV show's camp humor, Batman stories became darker and more serious. Rather than involving alien invasions or colorful robberies, they dealt with murders, and they featured tough heroes such as the Spectre, the Creeper, and Deadman.

THE ENEMIES WITHIN
World's Finest #173 ■ In this twisted tale by writer Jim Shooter and artist Curt Swan, Batman and Superman stopped Dr. Arron from running horrible experiments on people in the name of science. The doctor later broke out of jail and slipped the heroes a drink that transformed them into their greatest enemies with Batman becoming Two-Face, and Superman turning into Kralik the Conqueror, both physically and mentally. But when Arron was accidentally drugged, too, he changed into a good version of the Composite Superman and saved the day.

BIG FEARS
Batman #200 ■ In this milestone issue, written by Mike Friedrich and drawn by Chic Stone, Scarecrow devised a means of radiating fear into his foes and terrified Batman and Robin. He later arranged for them to catch the Joker, the Penguin, and Killer Moth, each of whom bore clues about Scarecrow's plans. When Batman and Robin finally confronted Scarecrow, he scared them so much they passed out. Thinking about their origin stories gave them the strength they needed to be brave, though, and they frightened Scarecrow into giving up.

NOVEMBER

DEAD BAT WALKING
BATMAN #206

The front cover of this issue showed a man in a Batman costume walking to his execution. Was Bruce Wayne paying the ultimate price for some sort of crime?

Writer Frank Robbins and penciller Irv Novick spun this tale in which a villain known as the Planner became furious at Batman and Robin foiling the crimes he had conceived for others.

When the Gotham Grand Hotel was robbed, Batman and Robin used solid detective work to figure out who did it: Custer's Last Stand, a band of hippie musicians posing as Native Americans who had associations with the Planner. Later, at a gala dinner honoring Batman and Robin, E.G. Never burst in and accused the heroes of hiring him to analyze crimes at his lab and passing off his work as their own. He challenged them to a duel of wits he had rigged in his favor.

Never was actually the Planner, and he set up the heroes for an ambush. They foiled that, but he then arranged for them to arrest a man for a crime actually committed by the Cat-Crook, Never's pawn. Never set up another ambush, planning to shoot the heroes in supposed self-defense, but in the darkness, he shot the Cat-Crook by mistake. The heroes captured Never and arrested him for murder. When the villain was finally executed for his crime, his last wish was to go to the electric chair wearing a Batman costume.

BATMAN'S EVIL TWIN?
The story's last panel showed the same moment as the front cover where 'Batman' was being led to the electric chair—but from the opposite angle. E.G. Never's beard gave away the truth.

APRIL

ENTER THE CREEPER
Showcase #73 ▪ This story introduced the Creeper, alias TV reporter Jack Ryder. He was stabbed trying to rescue Dr. Yatz from a Soviet plot. Yatz gave him a serum that gave him super-strength and stamina, and implanted a device that allowed him to become weightless and invisible. While exposing the secret Soviet cell, the Creeper ran afoul of the police and the criminal underworld. Steve Ditko wrote and drew this story; Don Segall assisted with dialog. In June, Creeper would gain his own series, *Beware the Creeper*, and later become an ally of Batman.

SEPTEMBER

THE DEAD DETECTIVE
The Brave and the Bold #79 ▪ New hero Deadman came to Gotham City to get Batman to help him track down his killer in this story by writer Bob Haney and artist Neal Adams. In Adams' first Batman issue, Deadman possessed Batman and recorded details of his mysterious murder for Batman to play back later. During the investigation, they stumbled across Max Chill, the brother of the man who murdered Batman's parents. Chill was killed, and they didn't find Deadman's murderer, but they stopped a wealthy crime lord living in his private Xanadu.

NOVEMBER

CREEPERS OF THE NIGHT
The Brave and the Bold #80 ▪ Bob Haney and Neal Adams spun the tale of the first meeting between Batman and the Creeper, who had discovered the villain called the Hellgrammite in Gotham City. At first, Batman wanted to arrest the Creeper, but agreed to team up with him against Hellgrammite instead, to stop the monster from turning Gotham City's top crooks into half-insect creatures like himself. By the time they defeated Hellgrammite, Batman had realized the Creeper was a good man, and he decided to allow him to escape from the police.

ALSO THIS YEAR

February—*Batman* #199: Rembrandt Dickens was the cartoonist of Gotham's *Batman* comic book. He turned to crime and poisoned Batman—who used the crook's magazine to track him down for the antidote.

March—*Teen Titans* #14: A mysterious former foe returned as the Gargoyle and sent Aqualad, Kid Flash, and Wonder Girl to Limbo, until Robin set them free.

May—*World's Finest Comics* #175: In Neal Adams's first Batman story; the Batman Revenge Squad teamed with the Superman Revenge Squad to try to destroy the heroes.

May—*Detective Comics* #375: The Batmobile featured a black bat-head painted on the hood.

June—*The Brave and the Bold* #78: Batman joined forces with Batgirl and Wonder Woman in pursuit of serpentine super-villain Copperhead, making his debut.

★ **September 14th—**Batman received his first animated series in *The Batman/Superman Hour*.

December—*Strange Adventures* #215: The first appearance of the Sensei.

BATMAN'S WOMEN
BATMAN #208

In this 80-page giant issue by writer E. Nelson Bridwell and artist Gil Kane, Mrs. Chilton opened her scrapbook to reveal the origins of each of the most important women in Batman's life.

The main story served as a framing device for a number of retold and even reprinted stories. The first featured actor Julie Madison, to whom Bruce Wayne had been engaged. Catwoman appeared in the next segment. Bruce broke up with Julie and started dating nurse Linda Page after that. Later, he began seeing photographer Vicki Vale. After that, Bruce struck up a relationship with Kathy Kane—who, unaware of his secret identity, worked with Batman as Batwoman.

Mystery writer Kaye Daye worked with Batman as a member of the Mystery Analysts of Gotham City. After Alfred seemed to have died, Dick Grayson's Aunt Harriet Cooper moved into Wayne Manor. Officer Patricia Powell worked on a number of cases with Batman, too.

Batman dated playgirl Marcia Monroe for a while, but she left him and later became the villainous Queen Bee to save her father. Poison Ivy tried to seduce Batman later, but failed. The next woman to enter his life was a hero: Batgirl. At the issue's end, Mrs. Chilton revealed that she'd helped raise Bruce as a boy—and that her son Max had recently died fighting Batman and her other son, Joe Chill, had killed Batman's parents.

MRS. CHILTON'S SECRET SORROW
She claimed she was "the most important woman in Batman's life"—for Mrs. Chilton had helped raise the orphaned Bruce. After revealing her scrapbook of Batman's life, she lamented that her sons, Joe and Max (they later changed their name to Chill) had gone to the bad. "Why couldn't you have turned out like Bruce?"

1969

> "Our job is to protect the rights of everyone, not those we just happen to like." Batman to Robin, *Detective Comics #387*

The year marked a huge change for the Batman Family. Both Robin and Batgirl received their own runs of solo stories as back-ups in *Detective Comics*, partly because the Boy Wonder had moved out of Wayne Manor to attend college. Not willing to be an empty-nester in the Batcave, Batman embraced Gotham City instead, leaving the mansion for a penthouse atop the Wayne Foundation building. As part of his move into the heart of the city, Batman embraced social justice, leading an initiative to help the victims of crimes.

BEST FRIEND'S GIRL
Superman's Girlfriend Lois Lane #89 ●
In this imaginary story by writer Leo Dorfman and artist Curt Swan, Bruce Wayne started dating Lois Lane after she broke up with Superman. Bruce had long had a crush on Lois but hadn't said anything out of respect for his friend. When Lois and Bruce were married, Bruce finally revealed to Lois that he was Batman. They later had a son who became Batman Jr. The Gimmick Master tried to force Lois to reveal Batman's identity, but she, Batman, and Superman stopped him cold.

GIRL TROUBLES
Detective Comics #384 ● Writer Gardner Fox and artists Bob Brown and Joe Giella told this issue's lead story in which Batman saved a long-lost heiress from murderous thugs, only to discover that she was an imposter named Colleen Kiernan. Colleen was also attempting to blackmail a local gang boss, who planned to kill her and replace her with a lookalike. Batman sent both crooks to jail. Writer Mike Friedrich and artist Gil Kane created Batgirl's first back-up tale, in which she searched for a man she had taken a fancy to. Her new Batcycle also debuted.

THE WOMEN IN BATMAN'S LIFE

1) Julie Madison 2) Selina Kyle (Catwoman) 3) Linda Page
4) Vicki Vale 5) Kathy Kane (Batwoman) 6) Kaye Daye
7) Aunt Harriet 8) Patricia Powell 9) Marcia Monroe
10) Pamela Isley (Poison Ivy) 11) Barbara Gordon (Batgirl)

MARCH

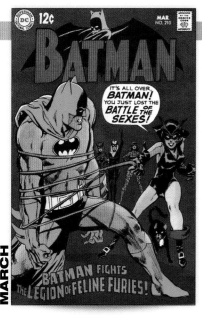

NINE LIVES

Batman #210 ▪ Catwoman showed off her new blue and red costume in this story by writer Frank Robbins and artist Irv Novick. When she got out of jail, Batman and Robin staked out her place, but she seemed to have gone legit. Soon, however, she had lined up eight other women as her proxies, each wearing the same costume. All nine villains attacked Wayne Manor together, hoping to steal a priceless pearl from the Nizam of Nepal. The Caped Crusader foiled Catwoman's plot by planting the pearl in a sticky ball of yarn.

APRIL

STAND-IN FOR MURDER

Detective Comics #386 ▪ Bruce Wayne seemed to have disappeared in a test plane in this story by writer Frank Robbins and artist Bob Brown. In fact it was an actor named Mr. Morse, who sometimes stood in for Bruce; one of Bruce's enemies had murdered him. In the back-up tale, Robin, who had only had a few solo tales until now, started a run of stories in the back of *Detective Comics*, this one written by Mike Friedrich and drawn by Ross Andru. In it, Robin stopped some camp bullies with the help of a lonely kid.

MAY

30 YEARS OF BATMAN

Detective Comics #387 ▪ The main story, written by Mike Friedrich and drawn by Bob Brown, celebrated Batman's 30th anniversary by updating the first Batman story. In it, a young anti-war activist was accused of murdering his father, an atomic chemist who was on the verge of a tremendous breakthrough. Despite the suspicions of Commissioner Gordon and Robin, one of the chemist's lab partners turned out to be the killer. This issue also featured a reprint of that original story, illustrated by Bob Kane.

ROBIN ALONE

World's Finest Comics #184 ▪ In this imaginary tale by writer Cary Bates and artist Curt Swan, the Automator disintegrated Batman while Superman was away and Robin was injured. Robin swore vengeance but, unable to find the killer, took on a new identity and went to college. Years later, the villain Golden Gloves blinded Superman. Superman and Robin followed him to the Automator's hideout. They captured him and discovered that Batman hadn't been killed but teleported away and brainwashed into becoming Golden Gloves.

A NEW ERA

BATMAN #217

In the last *Batman* issue of the 1960s, Dick Grayson graduated from high school and went off to Hudson University. Left on his own once more, Batman decided that it was time for a fresh start.

Writer Frank Robbins and artist Irv Novick kicked off the story with Batman deciding to close down Wayne Manor and move into the skyscraper home of the Wayne Foundation. Bruce directed the Wayne Foundation to set up an assistance program for victims of crime, Victims Inc., and he visited the first beneficiary: a doctor whose husband (also a doctor) had been killed while helping a gunshot victim in their clinic.

Bruce offered the wife of the victim an interest-free, pay-whenever loan to keep the clinic open. Then, as Batman, he investigated her husband's murder. The theory was that the gunshot victim had killed the doctor to keep him from reporting the incident to the police. Batman lured the supposed killer out by leaking word that the second doctor had also seen his face.

A man arrived and shot Batman in the arm before fleeing. Analysis of the bullet showed that it had come from the same gun that had shot the patient and the doctor treating him. Batman realized that the patient hadn't killed the doctor after all. Instead, a third man—who had shot the patient in the first place—had followed the patient to the clinic to finish him off. He had then murdered the doctor and disposed of the patient's body to make it appear that the patient had killed the doctor.

WAR HEROES

***The Brave and the Bold* #84** ■ In this story by writer Bob Haney and artist Neal Adams, Batman flashed back to an adventure during World War II. Winston Churchill sent Bruce on a secret mission, during which he worked with Sergeant Rock and Easy Company. Bruce discovered the Nazis had stored nerve gas in wine bottles at a French estate, and over Rock's objections, he blew up the bridge to the chateau early. Decades later, Rock and Bruce stopped the Nazi commander of the French estate from escaping with stolen gold.

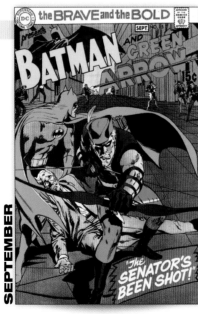

SENATOR WAYNE

***The Brave and the Bold* #85** ■ Scribe Bob Haney and artist Neal Adams teamed up Batman and Green Arrow, who debuted his new costume here. When a senator was shot, the governor asked Bruce Wayne to finish out his term while the senator recovered. While Bruce was thus occupied, Oliver Queen as Green Arrow, took down the Greek crimelord behind the assassination attempt by tricking him into being arrested in an American embassy. Bruce cast the decisive vote for an anti-crime bill before returning to civilian life.

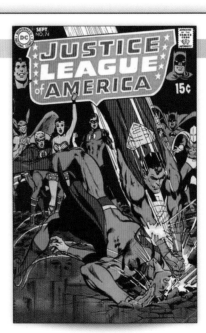

FROM EARTH TO EARTH

***Justice League of America* #74** ■ This was the second half of a two-parter by writer Dennis O'Neil and artist Dick Dillin. In the previous issue, Aquarius erased Earth-Two, but Dr. Fate protected the Justice Society and sent the Red Tornado to Earth-One to alert the Justice League. The Superman of both Earths met—and fought—for the first time. Larry Lance, husband of Black Canary, died to stop Aquarius and save her life. Unable to bear life on Earth-Two without him, Black Canary left for Earth-One instead. She was welcomed by Superman and the JLA.

DEATH AND LOVE

***Detective Comics* #392** ■ Mob hitman Angles Moore seemed to kill Batman in this tale by writer Frank Robbins and artist Bob Brown. In fact, Batman did not die but took Moore's place to infiltrate his boss's gang, and with Robin's help, he pretended his ghost haunted them. In the back-up story by writer Frank Robbins and artist Gil Kane, Batgirl met Jason Bard, who would one day become her fiancé. The two had their first date after Barbara made a bet with another librarian on what book Jason would borrow when they spotted him entering Gotham City Library.

NOVEMBER

DECEMBER

FAMILY MATTERS

Batman #216 ▪ Writer Frank Robbins and artist Irv Novick revealed Alfred's last name as Pennyworth. (The original version—now the butler from Earth-Two—was named Beagle.) In this tale, Batman defended a young woman who turned out to be Alfred's niece. She came to rob Wayne Manor of the original manuscript for Romeo and Juliet to save Alfred's brother Wilfred, who was being held hostage. The girl thought she'd shot her uncle by accident, but the gun was a prop that fired blanks. Batman, Robin, and Alfred saved both her and her father.

VICTIMS AND RIGHTS

Detective Comics #394 ▪ Dakota Jones, a client of the Wayne Foundation's Victim's Inc. program, blamed Bruce Wayne for being shot in the eye during the Gotham Classic Cup while racing against a car Bruce had sponsored. In this story by Frank Robbins with pencils by Bob Brown, it turned out that gangsters had rigged the Wayne car to shoot Jones via a pistol operated by remote control. In the back-up story by Robbins and artist Gil Kane, college freshman Robin wrote home about his investigation of a phony protest group he'd uncovered on campus.

SNAPPER SNAPS

Justice League of America #77 ▪ In this story by writer Dennis O'Neil and artist Dick Dillin, the villain John Dough convinced Snapper Carr to betray his friends in the Justice League. Dough then captured Batman and posed as the Caped Crusader to trick the JLA into getting involved in a riot. He then testified against the JLA, claiming the group planned to overthrow the government. Batman escaped and stopped him and then revealed that Dough was actually the Joker. Snapper confessed he agreed with Dough's diatribes, and he left the JLA.

ALSO THIS YEAR

January—*The Brave and the Bold* **#81:** While Batman dealt with Bork, an invulnerable thug, the Flash scoured the world to discover the source of the crook's power and neutralize it.

March—*Justice League of America* **#70:** The JLA set out to learn the truth about the Creeper, but aliens who had been told the heroes were tyrants, interfered.

May—*The Brave and the Bold* **#83:** Batman took on a troubled new ward, Lance Bruner. When Lance discovered Batman's secret identity, he betrayed him. The Teen Titans intervened, and inspired by Batman's care for Robin, Lance sacrificed himself to save Batman.

June—*Detective Comics* **#388:** The Joker stole an antigravity machine and tried to convince Batman and Robin he had sent them to the moon. Batman and Robin sported new spacesuits.

August—*Detective Comics* **#390:** The villain Masquerader debuted and Robin defeated gangsters trying to engineer a teacher's strike at Gotham High.

1970s

Batman once again became a creature of the night in the 1970s. Back to his noir roots, the Dark Knight Detective surged in popularity once more, helped along the way by some of the industry's finest creators.

The tongue-in-cheek comedy of the 1966-8 *Batman* TV show had greatly altered the public's perception of the character. However, In the late 1960s, Batman's look became a bit darker and more realistic thanks to artists such as Neal Adams, whose version of the character on *The Brave and the Bold* title led to the artist soon making the transition to *Detective Comics* and *Batman*. In 1969, editor Julius Schwartz had sent Robin to college, and almost instantly, Gotham City's skies became darker. Batman was once again a solo hero, and writers Frank Robbins and Dennis O'Neil were given the opportunity to return the Caped Crusader to his roots as a creature of the night and a true Dark Knight Detective.

This gradual darkening of Batman attracted even more talent to Gotham City in the 1970s, from Dick Giordano, who teamed with Neal Adams as an inker and often provided pencils for many other landmark Batman issues, to the writer/artist team of Steve Englehart and Marshall Rogers. Their short partnership resulted in some of the most character-defining stories of Batman's career.

It was a decade of new foes, and one that marked the return of some forgotten ones. New major villains like Rā's al Ghūl, his daughter Talia, and the flying creature Man-Bat crossed the Caped Crusader's path. And old threats like Dr. Hugo Strange and Deadshot were updated and upgraded to premier members of Batman's Rogues Gallery. The 1970s was a time of beautifully realized artwork and gripping noir tales. The Bronze Age of Comics left its mark on Batman perhaps more than any other character.

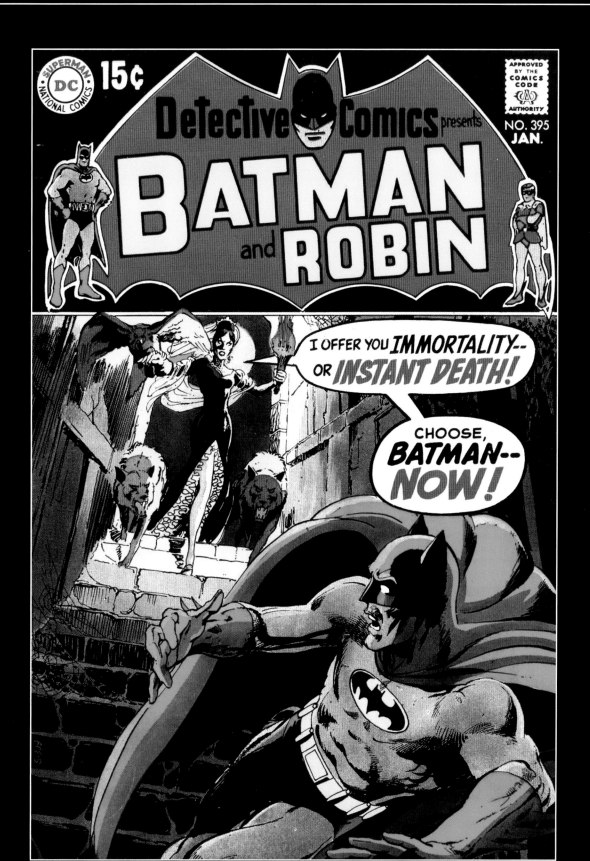

THE SECRET OF THE WAITING GRAVES
DETECTIVE COMICS #395

The new dark tone of Batman's adventures was set in this moody single issue tale that represented a vast departure from the comedic Batman of the 1960s.

Batman had originated as a mysterious creature of the night, and when editor Julius Schwartz paired writer Dennis O'Neil and artist Neal Adams on this landmark issue, that was the direction in which they took the character.
While other artists and writers had already paved the way for the "darkening" of Batman, this issue cemented the look, delivering a shadowy tale that would become a trademark of the decade. The entire 16-page story was set at night, in a macabre environment that would have made Edgar Allan Poe proud. In the story, Dolores and Juan Muerto threw a party at their family's traditional burial ground. There Batman was called into action to save the life of one of the guests from a group of armed assassins. The Dark Knight Detective soon discovered that this party guest was a government agent after the Muertos for possession of Sybil flowers, plants believed to induce hallucinations and offer immortality to their users. Batman was then drugged by the flowers and attacked by trained falcons under the Muertos command. Escaping the falcons and the flowers, Batman hunted the Muertos who fled from him. As they did so, they began to age rapidly, as extreme excitement negated the flowers' effects. The tale ended as Juan and Dolores, reduced to aged bones draped in clothes, fell into their own empty graves.

MEET THE MUERTOS
Dolores and Juan Muerto seemingly had it all. They were a beautiful, mysterious couple whose eccentric party was the talk of Gotham City. But like all Batman villains, they were harboring a dark secret.

1970

"I've never been to a party in a graveyard before!"

Bruce Wayne, *Detective Comics* #395

The decade began with one of the most important pairings in Batman's history: writer Dennis O'Neil and artist Neal Adams. Agreeing almost immediately on the mood and feel of the version of Batman they wanted to explore, this real life Dynamic Duo gave the readership the Batman that many fans were craving. Batman once again became a dark adventurer. The character was back in a more realistic world, even if that landscape often involved him investigating crime in the woods or swamps outside Gotham City proper.

RUNNING ON EMPTY

Kept alive only by the power of their illegal Sybil flowers, the Muertos began to rapidly decompose when they ran from Batman. Their death resembled something out of Gothic literature, a fitting subject matter for a Batman tale.

JUNE

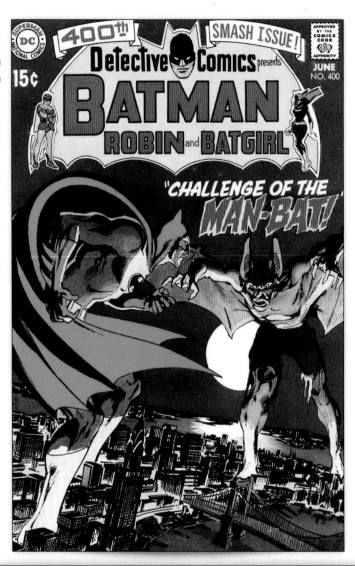

CHALLENGE OF THE MAN-BAT

DETECTIVE COMICS #400

This landmark issue saw the creation of Batman's sometime foe/sometime ally Man-Bat, a misunderstood monster destined for a long life in Gotham City.

Often known for his collaborations with writer Dennis O'Neil, penciller Neal Adams delivered quite a few blockbusters when paired with other writers. A prime example would be this issue where Adams pencilled from a story by writer Frank Robbins, an important Batman contributor in the 1970s.

Following the introduction of the Mayor's public works coordinator Arthur Reeves in issue #399 (May 1970), this comic also featured a Batgirl back-up tale written by O'Neil and drawn by Gil Kane, and the first appearance of a new Batmobile model. But it was the lead feature that would prove most memorable.

This issue's main story focused on bat expert Kirk Langstrom taking the form of a bat-creature when he ingested a serum intended to give him advanced bat-like sonar. In their first encounter, Man-Bat seemed to be on the side of the angels, helping Batman defeat the thieving Blackout Gang. He disappeared into the night at the tale's end, intriguing readers and leaving them eagerly waiting for this bizarre creature's return.

> "I've done it! I now possess a bat's natural sonar!"
>
> Kirk Langstrom, *Detective Comics #400*

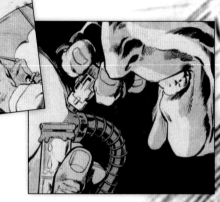

FROM MAN TO BAT
Langstrom had been working on a night-creature habitat for the Gotham Museum of Natural History while secretly experimenting on bats. Interestingly, Man-Bat's wings were not fully formed in this story, despite appearing on the issue's cover and in this story's final panel.

FEBRUARY

SILENT NIGHT OF THE BATMAN

Batman #219 ■ After a story by writer Frank Robbins and artist Irv Novick, readers were treated to a bit of yuletide cheer in a back-up feature by writer Mike Friedrich and penciller Neal Adams. In this often reprinted Christmas classic, Batman was given a break from patrolling Gotham City on Christmas Eve when Commissioner Gordon invited him to police headquarters. As Batman waited expectantly for an emergency call, he sang carols with some of the officers. Amazingly, would-be criminals all around Gotham City ceased their crimes for the night.

MARCH

WILDCAT RETURNS TO THE RING

The Brave and the Bold #88 ■ Normally considered a hero of the Golden Age or of Earth-Two, Wildcat began his long journey to becoming a supporting character of the Caped Crusader with this issue by writer Bob Haney and penciller Irv Novick. In the modern era, Wildcat would become a member of Batman's Network, but in this issue, he and Batman were fairly unfamiliar with each other, despite the story's plot of Bruce Wayne recruiting Wildcat's secret identity, Ted Grant, to coach a youth boxing team.

JUNE

PLENTY OF TWISTS

Batman #222 ■ One pop sensation encountered another when Batman and Robin met the band the Twists. Written by Frank Robbins and drawn by Irv Novick, this story featured the Dynamic Duo investigating the death of one of the Twists' members, Saul Cartwright. Soon the Dynamic Duo deduced that it was the rest of the band that had died in a plane crash, and Saul was the only survivor. This issue also featured a Batman back-up tale by writer Mike Friedrich with Novick once again handling the pencil duties.

OCTOBER

GHOST OF THE KILLER SKIES

Detective Comics #404 ■ While financing a movie about the exploits of the World War I pilot dubbed Enemy Ace, Bruce Wayne could only look on helplessly as one of the film's stunt pilots was killed. Bruce soon caught up with the man responsible for sabotaging the production, Heinrich Franz. As Batman, he had no choice but to take on Franz in a dogfight in this classic Dennis O'Neil-scripted tale illustrated by Neal Adams. This issue also featured a Batgirl back-up story by writer Frank Robbins and drawn by Gil Kane.

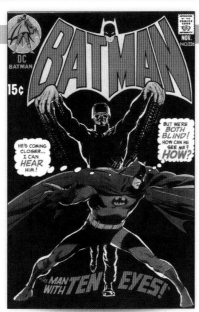

THE BAT-SQUAD

The Brave and the Bold #92 ■ Bruce Wayne seemed to take quite an interest in the movies, because in this atmospheric issue by writer Bob Haney and artist Nick Cardy, he was once again on the set of a film he was financing, this time on the streets of London. When the film's lead was kidnapped, the Caped Crusader teamed up with script girl and karate black belt Margo Cantrell, former Scotland Yard inspector Major Dabney, and former pickpocket and current singer Mick Murdock to form the Bat-Squad and discover this modern-day Scarlet Strangler.

TRICK OF THE EYES

Batman #226 ■ One of Batman's strangest enemies premiered in this issue thanks to the imaginations of writer Frank Robbins and penciller Irv Novick. A Vietnam vet turned security guard, Philip Reardon was blinded in an explosion when thieves blew a safe in the fur store he worked at. Luckily for Reardon, an unorthodox doctor named Dr. Engstrom was able to attach Reardon's optic nerves to his fingertips, allowing him to see out of his fingers, and jumpstarting his criminal career as the Ten-Eyed Man.

THE MAJOR LEAGUE

Detective Comics #405 ■ Batman had his first brush with the mysterious League of Assassins in this issue written by Dennis O'Neil and illustrated by Bob Brown. Assigned by Commissioner Gordon to protect the life of a shipping magnate, Batman crossed paths with Tejja, a member of the shadowy League of Assassins group. Although Batman managed to defeat this new foe, he was left wondering who was running the organization that controlled Tejja. Also included in this issue was a back-up tale starring Batgirl by scripter Frank Robbins and penciller Gil Kane.

ALSO THIS YEAR

February—*Superman's Girl Friend Lois Lane* **#99:** Proving Lois Lane innocent of murder was tougher than expected for Batman in this issue.

March—*Batman* **#220:** A minor love interest for Bruce Wayne debuted in the form of Marla Manning, a reporter whose series of articles had interested the Wayne Foundation's Victims, Inc. Program in *Batman* #217.

March—*Detective Comics* **#397:** Batman tried out a new undersea sled during an investigation.

August—*Detective Comics* **#402:** Man-Bat returned to discover he had bat wings and readers met his fiancée Francine Lee for the first time.

September—*Super DC Giant* **#S-16:** Batman and Metamorpho guest-starred in this "The Best of the Brave and the Bold" issue of a title normally reserved for horror, romance, or western fare.

December—*Batman* **#227:** Artist Neal Adams delivered a great tribute cover to the classic *Detective Comics* #31 (September 1939) by artist Bob Kane.

60L

THE DAUGHTER OF THE DEMON

DETECTIVE COMICS #411

Writer Dennis O'Neil's League of Assassins epic now introduced Talia al Ghūl, a major love interest in Batman's life.

In this issue's lead story drawn by Bob Brown, that also featured a Batgirl back-up tale by writer Frank Robbins and penciler Don Heck, Batman first encountered Doctor Darrk, a leader in the League of Assassins, who first appeared in *Detective Comics* #406 (December 1970). After learning Darrk would be on the Soom Express—a train that traveled through a tiny Asian nation—Batman confronted the notorious doctor when the villain exited the train with a beautiful and mysterious companion. However, Dr. Darrk's virtual army of assassins quickly surrounded Batman.

Taken into captivity and unmasked, Batman met the doctor's companion, Talia, who as it turned out was also a prisoner. Soon, the two were taken to an auditorium where a live bull was let loose on the pair. While Batman rescued Talia and escaped, a final confrontation with Darrk led to Talia shooting the assassin in order to save Batman's life. Simply depicted as a damsel in distress in this issue, the so-called Daughter of the Demon was about to prove herself as much, much more.

MEETING FACE TO FACE

Held in a cell with Batman, beneath an abandoned Buddhist monastery, Talia revealed that her father and Darrk had had a falling out, and she had been kidnapped while studying at the University of Cairo. It was then that she mentioned to Batman that her father's name was Rā's al Ghūl.

"You look familiar— someone I have seen in a photograph, perhaps?"

Talia to the unmasked Batman,
Detective Comics #411

1971

"Ahh... dear Detective! I should have realized I could not escape your scrutiny!"

Rā's al Ghūl to Batman, *Batman* #23

1971 saw the serial nature of Batman's adventures explored further, as writers carried subplots through various issues, often with other stories interrupting them for issues at a time. For instance, Man-Bat's three-part introduction began the previous year in *Detective Comics* #400 (June 1970) and continued into #402 (August 1970), before concluding in #407 (January 1971). Meanwhile, writer Dennis O'Neil spread his League of Assassins epic throughout several titles starting in *Detective Comics* #405 (November 1970) and #406 (December 1970), continuing to #411 (May 1971), and then into *Batman* #232 (June 1971). Both tales introduced major players to Batman's world.

JANUARY

MARRIAGE: IMPOSSIBLE

Detective Comics #407 ● Writer Frank Robbins and artist Neal Adams continued their memorable Man-Bat saga in the lead story of this issue. Also containing a Batgirl back-up feature by Robbins and artist Gil Kane, this issue saw Man-Bat escape Batman when the Dark Knight Detective was attempting to help cure Kirk Langstrom from his bizarre mutation. Langstrom then attempted to marry his fiancée Francine Lee, who had been similarly mutated. In the end, Batman was able to cure both Kirk and Francine with his antidote.

FEBRUARY

WORLD WITHOUT BATMAN

World's Finest Comics #200 ● This issue of *World's Finest Comics* marked the first time Batman was absent from an issue's cover. No longer a co-star of the title that now firmly belonged to Superman, Batman had left the comic with issue #197 (November 1970), allowing Superman to team up with the Flash in the following two issues, and Robin in this issue by writer Mike Friedrich and artist Dick Dillin. While Batman would guest star in the series several times in the coming months, he wouldn't regain a co-starring role until #215 (December 1972–January 1973).

JUNE

THE DEMON'S HEAD

BATMAN #232

This issue would introduce one of Batman's most notorious foes, Rā's al Ghūl, the Demon's Head.

Writer Dennis O'Neil had slowly been telling his League of Assassins epic throughout issues of *Detective Comics* , and was finally ready to introduce the most important behind the scenes player, the powerful terrorist known as Rā's al Ghūl. With a name translating to "the Demon's Head," Rā's piqued Batman's suspicion at their first meeting, but it wasn't until the end of this issue, that would later inspire a two-part episode of *Batman: The Animated Series*, that readers realized just how powerful this new villain was. In this Neal Adams-drawn epic, Robin was kidnapped. After Batman received a ransom letter, Rā's al Ghūl broke into the Batcave with the help of his brawny servant Ubu and called on the Dark Knight to help him find his daughter Talia, who had also been kidnapped. Clues led them to the Calcutta-based cult of killers called the Brotherhood of the Demon and to the Himalayan mountain of Nanda Devi. It was there that a weary Batman decided he'd had enough games. He entered a mountain retreat, rescued Robin, and confronted Rā's. Batman had realized that Rā's was the one responsible for Robin's capture. In a twist ending, the mastermind divulged the reason for this elaborate test: Talia was in love with the Dark Knight and Rā's al Ghūl needed to test his skills in order to determine if Batman was a worthy to be his daughter's mate and the heir to his clandestine organization.

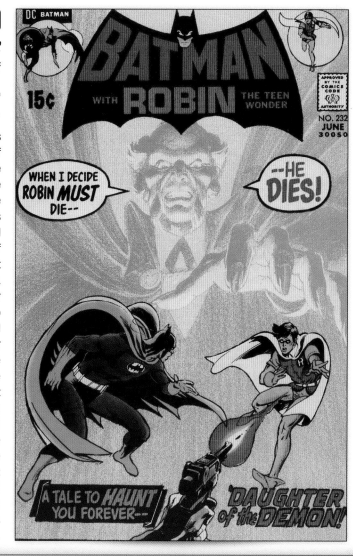

THE DEMON'S TEST

Batman's detective skills kicked in on Rā's al Ghūl's wild goose chase: despite Ubu wearing a mask in Rā's' stronghold, Batman instantly recognized the behemoth he was fighting.

APRIL

SIDESHOW STRANGENESS

Detective Comics **#410** ■ In this issue by writer Dennis O'Neil and artist Neal Adams, Batman was on the trail of murderer Kano Wiggins when he chanced upon a group of former carnival entertainers, including strongman Goliath, the skeletal Charley Bones, the obese Maud, and Flippy, a boy born with flippers for hands and feet. This issue also included a Batgirl back-up by writer Frank Robbins and illustrator Don Heck in which she was tormented by fashion choices—a story that inspired a Killer Croc episode of *Batman: The Animated Series*.

AUGUST

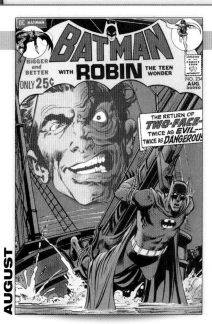

TWO-FACE'S TREASURE

Batman **#234** ■ Two-Face was reintroduced for the Bronze Age in this collaboration by writer Dennis O'Neil and artist Neal Adams. As part of the *Batman* title's new 25-cent format, this was an extra-long 48-page issue that also contained a Robin story by writer Mike Friedrich and penciller Irv Novick as well as a reprint tale by writer Gardner Fox and artist Carmine Infantino from *Detective Comics* #335 (January 1965). But the main star of this volume was Two-Face, seeking a fortune in gold hidden aboard an old ship in this dark and shadowy tale.

DECEMBER

NIGHT OF THE REAPER

Batman **#237** ■ Continuing its 48-page format, this issue of Batman dealt another classic tale by writer Dennis O'Neil and artist Neal Adams, this one based on an idea by artist Berni Wrightson with assistance from writer Harlan Ellison. Also featuring a reprint story from *Detective Comics* #37 (March 1940) by artists Bob Kane and Jerry Robinson and writer Bill Finger, this issue's beautifully rendered lead feature introduced the Reaper, a Holocaust survivor named Doctor Gruener who had been driven to personal vengeance as the macabre Reaper.

ALSO THIS YEAR

December 1970–January 1971— *The Brave and the Bold* #93: Batman entered the House of Mystery in this classic team-up tale.

February—*Justice League of America* #87: Batman temporarily became "King of the World" in this memorable issue.

April—*The Brave and the Bold* #95: Batman met the world's richest woman, Ruby Ryder, during a team-up with Plastic Man.

September—*DC 100-Page Super Spectacular* #6: A classic JLA/JSA team-up was featured in this issue that also included a never before printed Wildcat tale from the 1940s.

October—*Detective Comics* #416: Kirk Langstrom and Francine Lee were officially married despite Kirk's Man-Bat relapse, and Barbara Gordon met an imposter Batgirl in her back-up tale.

November—*Justice League of America* #94: League of Assassins member Merlyn made his deadly debut.

113

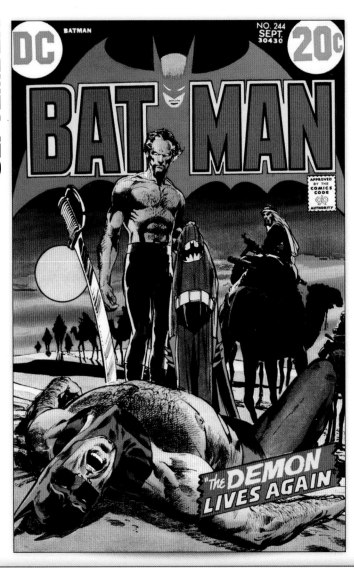

THE DEMON LIVES AGAIN!

BATMAN #244

One of the most iconic fights of Batman's career unfolded in this issue when Batman and Rā's al Ghūl finally engaged in combat.

In the previous issue of *Batman*, written by Dennis O'Neil and drawn by Neal Adams, the Dark Knight traveled to the Swiss Alps to track down the nefarious Rā's al Ghūl, and discovered the villain's lifeless body resting on a slab. Talia escorted Batman out of the chamber, secretly lowering Rā's al Ghūl into a Lazarus Pit, an alchemical solution capable of restoring life, while imparting temporary enhanced strength and insanity to anyone who would bathe in its waters.

At the start of this issue, also by O'Neil and Adams, Rā's al Ghūl faced Batman, making short work of the hero thanks to the chemicals running through his system. He and Talia escaped, and Batman was forced to once again track the Demon's Head to another of his strongholds, this one in a distant desert. Ready to enact his plans of restoring the planet by destroying most of mankind, Rā's first challenged Batman to a duel. Featuring some of the most famous artwork of Neal Adams' career, the Demon's Head battled the Dark Knight in a shirtless swordfight. Batman eventually defeated Rā's, pausing only to kiss Talia one last time.

This issue also featured a Robin story by writer Elliot Maggin and artist Irv Novick. Though less notable than the lead feature, Robin's tale did see the young hero gain a proper Robin Cycle, even if it was blue in this issue, and not the red shade it would take on in later appearances.

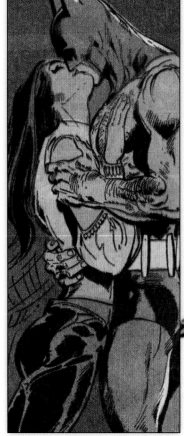

FORBIDDEN FRUIT
There was more than a simple attraction between Batman and Talia. Despite knowing full well who her father was, the Caped Crusader could not help being drawn to this intriguing woman. For her part, Talia found it impossible to choose Batman over her father.

1972

"Your lips are warm, as always! And as always, they chill me... to the marrow!"

Batman to Talia al Ghūl, *Batman #243*

The excitement surrounding writer Dennis O'Neil and Neal Adams' collaborations was still going strong as the two decided to bring an end to their epic Rā's al Ghūl storyline this year. Adams' realistic depiction of the villain who could literally cheat death, as well as his portrayal of Rā's' beautiful daughter Talia, caught the attention of a readership eager to see Batman become a globetrotter combating worldwide menaces. It was a side of the character not truly explored before —just as Batman had never before faced a challenge that tested his mental and physical abilities quite like the villain known as Rā's al Ghūl.

BRUCE WAYNE: EXECUTIONER
***Superboy* #182** ▪ When Superboy learned of the deaths of Thomas and Martha Wayne in this issue by writer Leo Dorfman and artist Bob Brown, he paid a visit to check on their son, Bruce. The Boy of Steel had a keen interest in Bruce Wayne due to his experimental time-scope that allowed him to glimpse Bruce as his ally Batman in the future. After fitting Wayne with a costume, Superboy was surprised to see the inexperienced Wayne adopt the identity of the Executioner as he hunted down a man he mistook for Zodiac Killer, nearly killing his victim in the process.

THE STENCH OF SULPHUR
***Batman* #241** ▪ Writer Dennis O'Neil and penciller Irv Novick introduced the threat of the spy known as Colonel Sulphur. A cutthroat killer with a fake hand that hosted a trick blade, Sulphur kidnapped Mary MacGuffin in this issue, with the intent of trading the woman's safety for top-secret government papers, until Batman stopped him. This issue also featured a Robin story by writer Mike Friedrich and artist Rich Buckler, and a Batman reprint from *Batman* #5 (March 1941) by artist Bob Kane and writer Bill Finger.

JUNE

MEETING MATCHES MALONE

Batman #242 ● Batman met criminal Matches Malone in this issue that saw Matches fire a bullet that ricocheted back into his own chest. His death allowed Batman to later impersonate the criminal and mingle in the underworld, something he would do on many future occasions. This issue with its lead story by writer Dennis O'Neil and artist Irv Novick featured Bruce Wayne faking his own death, as well as a Robin story by scripter Mike Friedrich and artist Rich Buckler, and a reprint tale from *Batman* #7 (November 1941) by artist Bob Kane and writer Bill Finger.

JUNE

RELOCATING BATGIRL

Detective Comics #424 ● While writer Frank Robbins and artist Bob Brown provided an entertaining lead Batman story, the most notable event in this issue came in the form of Robbins' back-up Batgirl tale that he created with the help of artist Don Heck. Barbara Gordon was running for Congresswoman, and recently, as Batgirl had endorsed herself in order to try to win the election. The votes were tallied, and by the end of the issue, Barbara was off to Washington, D.C., to start her new life in Congress.

OCTOBER

GOTHAM CITY'S TOUGHEST COP

Detective Comics #428 ● Destined to be revived decades later as a supporting character in the pages of Robin's ongoing series in the 1990s, Detective Steve "Shotgun" Smith was introduced in this issue by writer Frank Robbins and artist Bob Brown. Batman strongly disapproved of Shotgun's vigilante methods, particularly his willingness to resort to lethal force at any given opportunity. However, the two crime fighters ended up working together when Smith posed as a corrupt cop in order to take down a den of drug dealers.

ALSO THIS YEAR

February—*Batman* #239:** Batman starred in a memorable holiday tale that involved him being assaulted with a Christmas tree.

March—*Batman* #240:** The villainous scientist Dr. Moon debuted.

★ **April—**The "Batman" strip took a bizarre turn when the Caped Crusader took his operations worldwide and hired a new Super Hero named Galexo.

July—*Detective Comics* #425:** With his love interest now in Washington, D.C., Jason Bard took Batgirl's place as the star of this issue's back-up tale.

August—*Justice League of America* #100:** Batman's team hit this milestone issue just in time for another team-up with the Justice Society of America.

SEPTEMBER

THE JOKER'S FIVE-WAY REVENGE!

BATMAN #251

The Joker returned to his murderous self in this chilling issue.

By the 1970s, the Comics Code Authority had become much more lenient than when it first started regulating comic-book content in the 1950s. Writers were once again pushing the envelope when it came to the types of stories they could tell, and how much death and destruction they could get away with. It was the perfect environment for writer Dennis O'Neil and artist Neal Adams to bring back the Joker with their definitive Bronze Age take on the character.

In his very first appearance in *Batman* #1 (May 1940), the Joker was established as an extremely creepy killer, but in the 1950s and 1960s, the character lost his edge, becoming a fairly harmless criminal prankster. Returning the Clown Prince of Crime to his roots, O'Neil and Adams began this tale with Batman being shown a dead body by Commissioner Gordon, a disturbing grin distorting the corpse's facial features. Batman, investigating the death, learned that the Joker had been brutally murdering his former henchmen.

The Clown Prince of Crime managed to kill four of his five former associates by the time the Dark Knight Detective caught up with him at Gotham City's closed aquarium. Batman volunteered to be thrown into a shark tank in order to spare the life of the Joker's fifth intended victim. After killing the shark, Batman chased the Joker on the beach, with Adams including an iconic splash page of Batman in action. Batman took down the villain with a little help from an oil slick in an issue that hid an environmental lesson amidst its dramatic action.

THE JOKER'S JOKE TANK
True to his nature, the Joker double-crossed Batman after the Dark Knight volunteered to be dropped into a shark tank instead of the Joker's intended victim, a former associate named Hooley. When Batman was in the water, the Joker pushed Hooley into the tank as well.

1973

"You're not laughing!? Don't you see the joke?"

Batman to the Joker, *Batman* #251

Having rendered his version of Two-Face and new villains Rā's al Ghūl and Man-Bat, it was time for artist Neal Adams to deliver his iconic version of the Joker to an eager fan base. Paired again with writer Dennis O'Neil, Adams' take on the Joker did not disappoint; the duo gave audiences a villain as true to his roots as their Batman was. Many other writers and artists delivered Batman's shadowy adventures this year, frequently reflecting the character's pulp roots. While a lighter Batman popped up in titles like *World's Finest Comics* and in the new TV cartoon *Super Friends*, Batman remained a creature of the night in most issues.

JANUARY

BATMAN JR., SUPERMAN JR.
World's Finest Comics #215 ▪ Back in *World's Finest Comics* #154 (December 1965), Batman and Superman were given "Super-Sons" in an imaginary tale. And while this issue was relatively unrelated to that previous version, it offered up the same concept for readers, with the "Super-Sons" as teenagers, not children. This time around the "Super-Sons" would become a returning feature, and their mysterious origins would not be revealed until issue #263 (July 1980). This particular tale of Bruce Wayne, Jr. and Clark Kent, Jr. was by writer Bob Haney and artist Dick Dillin.

APRIL

SPOOKY ORIGINS
Detective Comics #434 ▪ Scripter Frank Robbins and penciller Irv Novick introduced a new villain, the green-robed Spook, in this comic, which formed part of a two-issue tale. A master escape artist and showman, the Spook broke criminals out of jail for a fee he called his "Escape Insurance." When Batman located the villain's secret tunnels and trapdoors, the Spook met his match and was taken to prison. There his true identity was revealed. He was Val Kaliban, a murderer supposedly executed on the electric chair ten years prior.

THE JOKER SLIPS UP
Batman was so exhausted after escaping the shark tank that he couldn't catch up to the Joker on the beach. Luckily, the Joker slipped on an oil slick—making the Dark Knight Detective grateful for pollution for the first time in his life!

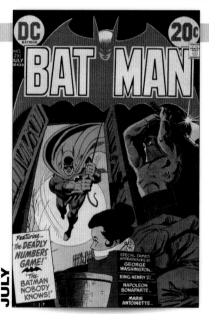

THE BATMAN NOBODY KNOWS!
Batman #250 ■ In a classic back-up tale, writer Frank Robbins and artist Dick Giordano took Bruce Wayne camping with three underprivileged kids. Each child told Bruce Wayne their version of what they thought Batman was like. Their stories ranged from a monstrous Batman to a man wearing rocket-powered wings. But when Wayne decided to put on his costume and surprise the boys, he was laughed at by the children who thought Mr. Wayne was too big for that sort of "kid-stuff."

MANHUNTERS
Detective Comics #437 ■ New DC editor Archie Goodwin scripted the lead feature with artist Jim Aparo. The story focused on Bruce Wayne's character, with Bruce maintaining an aloof and sometimes cowardly playboy persona in order to distance himself from his Batman alter ego. Goodwin also scripted the back-up tale, with artist Walter Simonson. This featured the first chapter of his groundbreaking Manhunter saga, which would revitalize the Golden Age character of the same name, by giving his story a new spin that would involve Batman.

GOTHAM CITY GETS SWAMPED
Swamp Thing #7 ■ A relative newcomer to the DC Universe, the plant creature known as Swamp Thing made his way to Gotham City in this story by writer Len Wein and artist Berni Wrightson. In this first meeting between two mysterious figures of the night, Batman pursued Swamp Thing after being told by Commissioner Gordon that a monster was loose in his city. When he first encountered him, Batman was knocked out cold by Swamp Thing's enhanced strength, allowing the swamp creature to finish his business in the busy metropolis.

ALSO THIS YEAR

February—*Secret Origins* #1: Batman's origin from *Detective Comics* #33 (November 1939) was reprinted along with the origins of many other Super Heroes.

April—*World's Finest Comics* #217: Metamorpho temporarily became the new Composite Superman when he battled the World's Finest team.

June—*Batman* #249: In his back-up feature, Robin gained a Robin Cycle that was green and red.

September 8th: *Super Friends*, a new cartoon featuring Batman and Robin as part of a group of Super Heroes, debuted.

September—*DC 100-Page Super Spectacular* #20: Batman's past battles with Two-Face were explored in this reprint issue that also featured Black Canary.

October—*Superman* #268: Batgirl resumed her costumed career during Clark Kent's visit to Washington D.C.

November—*Batman* #253: Batman crossed paths with pulp hero the Shadow.

BATMAN'S BROTHER
WORLD'S FINEST COMICS #223

It was revealed that Bruce Wayne had an older brother in this mostly forgotten piece of Batman lore that inspired the recent "Court of Owls" storyline.

Written by Bob Haney and drawn by Dick Dillin, what started as a Batman, Deadman, and Superman team-up went on to reveal the existence of Thomas Wayne, Jr. Born three years before Bruce, Thomas was still a baby when he was struck by a car. When they learned that Thomas had incurred irreversible brain damage, the Waynes had him committed to Willowwood Sanitarium. They were tragically killed before they could tell Bruce of his brother's existence.

In this tale, a grown-up Thomas Wayne, Jr. broke out of Willowwood and began a career as the Boomerang Killer. The story ended with Deadman taking possession of Thomas, ready for a second chance at life using Thomas' body. The story would be resolved in *World's Finest Comics* #227 (January–February 1975), when Thomas sacrificed himself to save Batman's life.

This issue's reprints included two Batman/Superman tales by writer Edmond Hamilton and artists Dick Sprang and Curt Swan, and an excerpt from *The Adventures of Superman* radio show.

Decades later, echoing teases in writer Grant Morrison's *Batman: The Return of Bruce Wayne* #5 (November 2010) and *Batman* #702 (October 2010), writer Scott Snyder looked to the lead feature of this issue to inspire his "Court of Owls" epic that would begin in *Batman* #1 (November 2011).

BROTHERLY LOVE
Thomas Wayne, Jr.'s life was dogged by tragedy. After his baby carriage was struck by a car, he was institutionalized by parents who were then murdered. Thomas never knew his brother, although he seemed to recognize him when he died saving Batman's life.

> ### "It's the most stunning... shocking thing that ever happened in my whole life..."
> Batman, *World's Finest Comics* #223

1974

"What if our wolf-like prowler is not wearing a mask?"
Batman to Commissioner Gordon, *Batman* #255

At the beginning of 1974, many of DC Comics' titles were increased to 100-Page "Super Spectaculars," offering many more stories than before for a 50-cent price tag. That format would last for about a year, but in that time period, readers were treated to a variety of material that the shorter comics of the past wouldn't have had room for. While fans were entertained by some classic Batman stories including "Moon of the Wolf" and "Night of the Stalker," the longer format gave the new version of Manhunter room to stretch his legs. It also allowed for the inclusion of many reprint stories that readers might have missed the first time around.

THE SPECTACULAR DETECTIVE
Detective Comics #438 ■ As *Detective Comics'* first "Super Spectacular" 100-page fifty-cent issue, this comic carried reprints of several non-Batman related characters. However, Batman's lead feature was a new tale by writer Archie Goodwin and artist Jim Aparo pitting Batman against Ubu. This volume also contained a reprint Dynamic Duo tale by artist Bob Kane and writer Bill Finger and one other new feature, the latest chapter in the Manhunter saga, written by Goodwin and drawn by Walter Simonson. *Batman* adopted this 100-page format with issue #254 (January–February 1974), too.

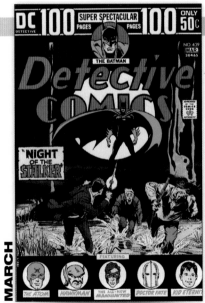

NIGHT OF THE STALKER
Detective Comics #439 ■ Writer Steve Englehart earned his first Batman credit when he created the dialog for this issue's lead feature that was plotted and drawn by Sal Amendola (with co-plot assistance by Vin Amendola). When Batman witnessed a woman shot in cold blood during a robbery, he stalked the thieves to the woods in a dramatic tale full of gripping suspense. This issue also contained a Gardner Fox-scripted Batman reprint drawn by Sheldon Moldoff, Super Hero reprints, and a new Manhunter adventure by writer Archie Goodwin and artist Walter Simonson.

APRIL

MOON OF THE WOLF
BATMAN #255

The inspiration for an episode of *Batman: The Animated Series*, this classic comic introduced Batman to the Werewolf.

Former Olympic athlete Anthony Lupus became plagued with headaches. Unable to alleviate the pain, he looked to Professor Milo, a criminal genius from Batman's past. Milo gave him a serum that cured his headaches, but also transformed him into a werewolf each full moon, with no choice but to do Milo's bidding if he wanted to return to his normal life. Milo wanted nothing less than the death of Batman. Written by Len Wein and drawn by Neal Adams, this grim lead story saw Batman defeat the Werewolf who, presumed dead, headed to Alaska. Dripping with atmosphere, the story brought Professor Milo back into the spotlight as a formidable foe of Batman. This issue also contained "The First Batman," the famous story of Thomas Wayne as Batman from *Detective Comics* #235 (September 1956) by writer Bill Finger and artist Sheldon Moldoff, and other reprinted Batman tales featuring Alfred, Batgirl, Robin, and the "Outsider". As an added bonus, this issue also featured a great two-page visual history of the Batmobile.

BAD MOON RISING
As it turned out, Anthony Lupus had lycanthropy, a disease that should have just given him overly bushy eyebrows or particularly hairy hands. But with Milo's tinkering, it turned Anthony into a full-blown werewolf.

JULY

BREAKING IN BULLOCK
Detective Comics #441 ■ In a story written by Archie Goodwin and illustrated by Howard Chaykin that also introduced the villain known as the Judge, readers met Lieutenant Bullock for the first time. A cop who didn't think much of a "costumed freak" like Batman, he was similar to major supporting character Harvey Bullock who debuted in the 1980s. This issue also featured reprints, Batman reprints drawn by Bob Kane and Jim Mooney and written by Bill Finger, a Batman title page drawn by Sal Amendola, and a Manhunter tale written by Goodwin with art by Walter Simonson.

SEPTEMBER

BATS ON A PLANE
Detective Comics #442 ■ Two masters of sequential storytelling, writer Archie Goodwin and artist Alex Toth, joined forces for an unforgettable Batman lead story entitled "Death Flies the Haunted Sky." A tale of biplanes and dogfights, this issue saw Toth's brilliant high contrast style utilized in all its glory. This issue also included a Black Canary reprint pencilled by Carmine Infantino and a Batman reprint written by Joe Samachson and pencilled by Jerry Robinson, as well as a new Manhunter story written by Goodwin and drawn by Walter Simonson.

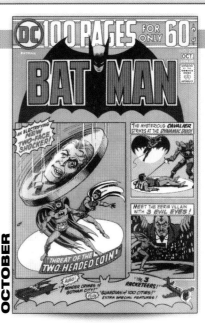

OCTOBER

ENTER ARKHAM ASYLUM
Batman #258 ■ The forbidding Arkham Asylum is almost as much of a character as many of the villainous faces in Batman's Rogues Gallery. This institution made its debut in the lead story of this issue written by Dennis O'Neil and drawn by Irv Novick. Shown from the outside with its name proudly displayed on a plaque during Two-Face's latest escape, Arkham cemented itself into Batman lore. This issue also featured reprints of titles by a host of talent, including artists Bob Kane and Dick Sprang and writers Bill Finger and Gardner Fox.

ALSO THIS YEAR

April—*Limited Collector's Edition* #C-25: This tabloid-sized reprint special focused on Batman stories and included photos from the 1966 *Batman* TV show.

February—*The Brave and the Bold* #111: Batman was forced to team up with the Joker in this intriguing issue.

June—*Famous First Edition* #28: *Detective Comics* #27 (May 1939) was reprinted in tabloid size, and *Batman* #1 (April 1940) would soon receive the same treatment in issue #F-5 (January 1975).

September—*Superman* #279: Batgirl guest-starred in this issue that saw Superman dress up as Batman for the Gotham Charity Folk Festival.

October—*Secret Origins* #7: This origin reprint series came to a close with an issue that featured Robin's origin from *Detective Comics* #38 (April 1940).

October—*Detective Comics* #443: Batman finally met the Manhunter as the character's back-up tale stole the lead feature in this issue.

DRAGGING OUT THE JOKE

THE JOKER #1

While it would only last nine issues, the Joker's ongoing series marked the first time a Batman villain received top billing on his own merit.

The cover featured Catwoman, Two-Face, Riddler, and the Penguin, but there was no question about who the true star of this new series was—the Clown Prince of Crime. Alongside artist Irv Novick, writer Dennis O'Neil gave the readers a bad guy to cheer for when the Joker competed against Two-Face in this premiere issue in order to see who was truly the better criminal. While the Joker escaped the kind of death trap normally reserved for Batman, in the end both criminals were captured and taken back to Arkham Asylum.

As the title continued, the focus was on the Joker's heists and outrageous gags rather than him committing grisly murders (that wouldn't be appropriate for a comic book's protagonist). Artist Ernie Chan, (drawing under the name Ernie Chua), came on board in issue #3 (September 1975) to see another laughing maniac, the Creeper, take on the Clown Prince of Crime. That issue also debuted the newest version of the Jokermobile, while issue #2 spotlighted the Joker's current hideout, the Ha-Hacienda. Later issues would feature Green Arrow, the Royal Flush Gang, Lex Luthor, the Scarecrow, and Catwoman, as the Joker matched wits with any takers that would dare cross his path.

GADGETS AND GIZMOS

While it remained a mystery where the Joker found the time to manufacture all his customized gadgets, they certainly came in handy. In his first issue alone, he escaped incarceration thanks to a giant balloon and a prop gun he switched for his guard's real one.

1975

"Save 'em, Joker! As Queen Victoria remarked—we are not amused!"

Batman, *Batman* #260

The mid-1970s saw Batman and his cast branch out like never before. Even with his adventures confined to mostly *Batman*, *Detective Comics*, and *The Brave and the Bold*, and his participation in *Justice League of America*, Batman was already a major presence on newsstands. Nevertheless, this year saw DC Comics add new titles *The Joker*, *Batman Family*, and *Man-Bat* to their stable. While *Batman Family* would easily be the most successful effort, this willingness to further spotlight the Dark Knight Detective's world would continue into the modern age, in which Batman's cast of characters were accorded many titles.

DETECTIVE GETS EPIC

Detective Comics #444 • While there had been multi-part stories in Batman's past, if these covered more than two issues the stories would often be interspersed with regular, self-contained issues. But with this issue of *Detective Comics*, writer Len Wein and artist Jim Aparo began a five-issue uninterrupted storyline that was quite an event in 1975. In this interesting tale, Batman was framed for murder by his old enemy Rā's al Ghūl. This issue also featured a Robin reprint drawn by Jim Mooney, and other non-Batman related reprint stories.

THE SILVER STANDARD

Detective Comics #446 • In the third chapter of Len Wein and Jim Aparo's five-issue Batman epic, readers met the new villain Sterling Silversmith as part of a larger story featuring Talia, her father Rā's al Ghūl, and the Creeper. In an issue that saw *Detective Comics* lower its price to 25 cents, Sterling still had plenty of room to make an entrance, showing off his suit made of woven silver and steel alloy that could repel bullets. Despite his impressive wardrobe, the silver-obsessed crime boss was no match for Batman.

OCTOBER

DAMNED IF YOU DO

While the Batman titles usually stayed away from the supernatural aspects of the DC Universe, this issue featured a guest appearance by a demon character who might just have been Satan himself. The demon challenged Batgirl and Robin by forcing them to fight Benedict Arnold's ghost.

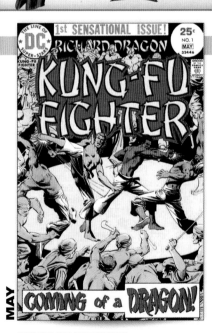

FAMILY MATTERS

BATMAN FAMILY #1

This title was a huge success, making Batman's supporting cast the stars of the show.

When it first hit the newsstands, *Batman Family* was a 50-cent comic featuring a new lead story and several reprints. While it would later contain all-new material, the series would always remain extra-long, even when Batman's other titles reduced in size.

What made *Batman Family* successful was the strength of Batman's supporting cast. This debut issue partnered fan favorites Robin and Batgirl in the dramatic origin of the Batgirl-Robin team, and saw the partners kiss for the first time at the story's end. It would lead to decades' of flirtation between the two Super Heroes.

This issue also featured an interesting sampling of reprint comics, including an Alfred story drawn by Jerry Robinson, and a Batman and Robin tale by writer Gardner Fox and artist Sheldon Moldoff. The comic ended with Man-Bat's first story by writer Frank Robbins and artist Neal Adams from *Detective Comics* #400 (June 1970).

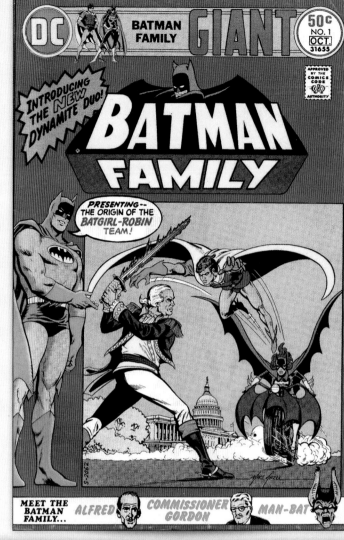

KUNG-FU TEACHER

Richard Dragon: Kung-Fu Fighter #1 ▪
Based on *Dragon's Fists,* a novel by Jim Berry and Dennis O'Neil , this tale drawn by Leopoldo Duranona debuted martial arts expert Richard Dragon. While the new series seemed unrelated to Batman, Richard Dragon and Ben Turner (the future "Bronze Tiger"), would both become supporting characters: Dragon would train Batman allies and be revealed to have taught Batman himself, and Bronze Tiger would murder the original Batwoman after being brainwashed in *Detective Comics* #485 (August 1979).

MAY

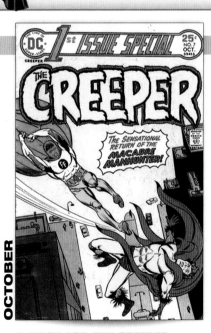

A FIRST FOR THE CREEPER

1st Issue Special #7 ▪ The Creeper took another step toward becoming a regular in Batman's world when he battled the Caped Crusader's villain Firefly in this issue by writer Michael Fleisher and artist Steve Ditko. *1st Issue Special* was a title designed to test out characters that DC Comics was thinking of giving their own ongoing series. Metamorpho starred in issue #3 (June 1975), and Creeper was given the spotlight in this issue. But despite his dramatic battle with Firefly, Creeper wouldn't receive his own title for decades.

OCTOBER

A TWO-FACED LEAGUE

Justice League of America #125 ▪ When a group of space aliens began distributing incredible one-time use power blasts to known criminals of Earth, the Justice League of America found it difficult to counter the mysterious threat. But with the help of Two-Face, the JLA was able to locate the aliens' base and scare them away, if only temporarily. In this story written by Gerry Conway and drawn by Dick Dillin, Two-Face was offered a power blast by the aliens, but upon flipping his trademark coin, opted to help the heroes instead.

DECEMBER

ALSO THIS YEAR

January—*Batman* #260: Batman found that he couldn't contain his laughter when the Joker dumped a large container of drugged coffee on him.

June—*The Superman Family* #171: Batgirl guest-starred in this issue featuring Supergirl and "Cleopatra Queen of America."

August—*Detective Comics* #450: Robin dated new love interest Lori Elton in this issue that also contained the inspiration for a memorable episode of *Batman: The Animated Series.*

August—*Limited Collector's Edition* #C-37: This treasury-sized tabloid featured reprint stories of Batman's greatest villains.

December—*The Brave and the Bold* #123: Metamorpho revealed he knew Batman's secret identity in this issue, but he forgot it less than a decade later.

FAREWELL TO COMEDY
Detective Comics #436 (September 1973)
As exemplified by this image from a moody Nick Cardy cover, the Batman of the 1970s had come a long way from his predecessor of the sci-fi-obsessed 1950s or the swinging 1960s. This Batman helped birth the Bronze Age of comics, establishing himself as a true Dark Knight Detective with the help of ample shadows and creatures that went bump in the night. Often venturing out of Gotham City to derelict houses, swamps, or woods, Batman's detective skills were highlighted like never before. The Dark Knight experienced a long period of solo adventures, unimpeded by teen sidekicks to lighten the mood. This decade also placed greater emphasis on Batman's psyche, his inner demons, and the traumatic events of his childhood.

THERE IS NO HOPE IN CRIME ALLEY

DETECTIVE COMICS #457

Leslie Thompkins was introduced into the Batman mythos in this powerful retelling of Batman's origin story.

Dick Giordano proved that his pencil art was as good as any of the other legends that helped shape the Bronze Age of comics when he teamed with writer Dennis O'Neil to tell a classic Batman story that saw the Dark Knight Detective think back to the night his parents were murdered.

As the story began, an unusually curt Batman dismissed Alfred's suggestion that the hero pursue jewel smugglers who had made the news. The Dark Knight Detective insisted that he had other plans for the evening, and headed to an area of town formerly called Park Row and now referred to as Crime Alley. There he stopped a few minor crimes before meeting with Leslie Thompkins, saving her from a mugging in the process. As he fought off her attackers, Batman remembered the night his parents were murdered and the young social worker who took pity on him and did what she could to help the shattered little boy. That woman was Leslie Thompkins, and every night on the anniversary of his parents' death, Batman came to visit her.

Leslie was depicted as elderly and frail in this, her first appearance, but would be recreated in 1987 as the active head of a medical clinic based in Crime Alley, who would preach non-violence to Batman. Batman's annual visits to Crime Alley would also be adjusted in later years, as the hero would begin to place two red roses on the site of his parents' murder.

NON-VIOLENCE
Leslie Thompkins always preached ending conflicts without the use of violence. When she was later established as knowing Batman's double identity, she'd often voice her disapproval for Batman's methods, even if she thought highly of his results.

1976

"I've been expecting you, Batman—you always come to visit on this day!"

Leslie Thompkins, *Detective Comics #457*

While it wouldn't match the previous year in terms of new Batman-related titles being launched, 1976 would see many new series created that would have significance for the characters in Batman's world. Titles like *The Super Friends* and *The Secret Society of Super Villains* starred Batman or Batman villains in a group setting. Other new books, including *Ragman* and *Kobra*, didn't have anything to do with Batman initially, but would years later when their title characters were incorporated into various Batman series. A year for new titles, 1976 also birthed plenty of new villains to face the Caped Crusader.

SHIVA'S WRATH
Richard Dragon: Kung-Fu Fighter #5 ■
With the martial arts craze going strong in Hollywood, DC Comics indulged in the genre with *Richard Dragon: Kung-Fu Fighter*. But with writer Dennis O'Neil at the helm of the series, it was no surprise that several characters went on to become associated with Batman. Most notable was Lady Shiva, also known as Sandra Woosan, an expert martial artist who debuted in this issue drawn by Ric Estrada. She would become one of the greatest fighters in the DC Universe, and a sometime ally/sometime enemy of the Dark Knight.

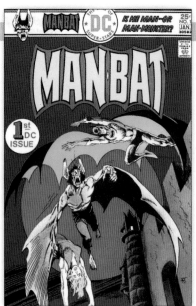

MAN-BAT MISFIRE
Man-Bat #1 ■ Man-Bat took off into the world in his own self-titled ongoing series, which only lasted for two issues. In the first issue, by writer Gerry Conway and artist Steve Ditko, Man-Bat faced the new villain Baron Tyme. The second, and final, volume of the series (February 1975), written by Martin Pasko and drawn by Pablo Marcos, saw Man-Bat take on the Ten-Eyed Man. Unlike his earlier appearances, the Ten-Eyed Man was now clad in a proper costume, cementing his status as a true super-villain.

TWO FOR THE PRICE OF ONE

DETECTIVE COMICS #463

The Black Spider and the Calculator made dramatic debuts in two separate stories in this issue.

The first of several villains to wear the mantle of the Black Spider made his way to Gotham City in this story's lead tale by writer Gerry Conway and artist Ernie Chan. Black Spider's introduction began as drug dealer Slinky Hamilton fled from Batman at Gotham Square Garden, only to die in an explosion when he turned the key on his rigged car. As Batman investigated, he discovered that the person responsible was a vigilante calling himself the Black Spider. Despite the Black Spider viewing his own actions as heroic, his lethal methods put this new purple and orange clad character firmly among the ranks of Batman's Rogues Gallery.

The second villain to debut in this issue was the Calculator, a costumed villain who troubled the Atom in that hero's back-up feature written by Bob Rozakis and drawn by Mike Grell. While the Calculator first fought the Atom and then a variety of other DC Super Heroes, in the 2000s, he would become an evil counterpart to the information guru Oracle. Using his genius behind the scenes rather than directly battling heroes, the Calculator would later offer inside information to the world's super-villains at a price. This would make him not only an enemy of Batman but also an arch-foe of the team of Super Heroes called the Birds of Prey, and their leader, Barbara Gordon.

PURPLE ROGUES

While they didn't have much in common, the Calculator (above) and the Black Spider (below) both shared an affinity for the color purple. Oddly enough, it was the more outlandishly dressed of the pair, the Calculator, who would rise through the ranks of the underworld in later years.

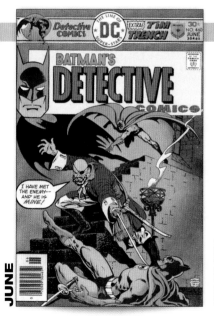

THE STING OF DEFEAT

Detective Comics #460 ▪ The swashbuckling villain Captain Stingaree—a considerable challenge for Batman now and again—debuted in this volume by writers Bob Rozakis and future Batman movie producer Michael Uslan. Drawn by Ernie Chan, this story saw Stingaree launch a campaign against Batman, believing the Dark Knight Detective to be just one of triplets fighting the same cause. Continued into the next two issues, the bizarre story saw Batman hire Stingaree's three brothers to masquerade as Batman in a complicated plot to catch the criminal.

DADDY'S LITTLE GIRL?

Batman Family #6 ▪ This issue featured two all-new lead stories in addition to Alfred and Mad Hatter reprint tales. The first starred Batgirl by writer Elliot S! Maggin and drawn by Jose Delbo, and the second starred Robin in a tale written by Bob Rozakis and drawn by Irv Novick. But it would be Robin's story that was destined to go down in Batman history with its introduction of the Joker's Daughter. Later to be renamed Harlequin, the Joker's Daughter looked exactly like the Clown Prince of Crime, but her true heritage would remain a mystery for several issues.

THE TATTERED TATTERDEMALION

Ragman #1 ▪ Writer Bob Kanigher and co-creator Joe Kubert introduced Ragman, a shadowy figure wearing a suit of tattered rags, in his own first issue, with art from the Redondo Studio. This title only lasted five issues, but further appearances and miniseries in other comics would soon establish the hero firmly in Gotham City. He'd even later join Batman's group of allies called the Network. This original tale showed Ragman's origins as pawnshop owner Rory Regan, who donned his costume for the first time after an electric wire gave him enhanced abilities.

ALSO THIS YEAR

February—*Batman Family* #3: In this issue's lead Batgirl/Robin feature, the two heroes deduced each other's secret identities.

February—*Detective Comics* #456: A new topless version of the Batmobile debuted featuring a large oval bat-symbol on its hood.

February—*Kobra* #1: Kobra, a huge threat to the DC Universe and a future major enemy of Batman and the Outsiders, was unleashed.

April—*Detective Comics* #458: Man-Bat scored his own back-up feature, as promised in the final issue of his own short-lived title.

May—*The Secret Society of Super Villains* #1: Copperhead and Manhunter starred in this new villain-centric series.

June—*Limited Collector's Edition* #C-44: Batman reprints filled this treasury edition that included a blueprint of his new Wayne Foundation Building headquarters.

August—*Batman* #278: Batman faced the Wringer, a new villain with a penchant for wringing the necks of others.

November—*Super Friends* #1: Batman and Robin starred in this new cartoon tie-in title.

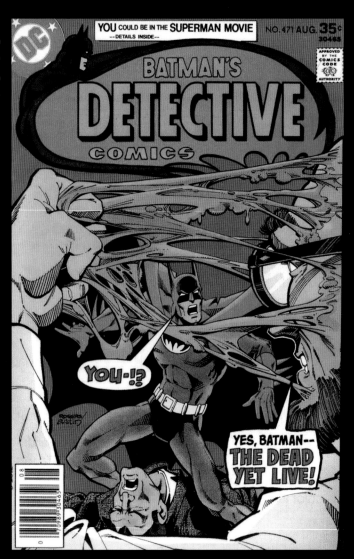

STRANGE BEDFELLOWS

DETECTIVE COMICS #471

The popular Batman writer/artist team of Steve Englehart and Marshall Rogers delivered an unforgettable version of the Caped Crusader.

Paired for the first time on this issue, Englehart and Rogers had both worked with Batman before. Artist Rogers had worked on *Detective Comics* issues as well as on a Man-Bat feature in *Batman Family*; writer Englehart had just delivered a two-part Dr. Phosphorus tale in the two previous *Detective Comics* issues, introducing Batman to his new love interest Silver St. Cloud in issue #470 (June 1977). When the two worked together, readers were treated to a masterful version of Batman, rife with subplots.

After feeling an instant attraction for Silver St. Cloud when they first met at a party on his yacht (a night that also allowed Batman to try out some new scuba equipment), in this issue Bruce Wayne cancelled their planned date to check in to Graytowers in order to recover from a wound received from Dr. Phosphorus. Instead of recuperating, however, Batman faced his old enemy Dr. Hugo Strange.

Through brilliant storytelling, this influential saga continued with Strange trying to auction off the secret of Batman's identity to the criminal underworld before being captured and tortured by Rupert Thorne. Robin then entered the fray, just in time to help Batman in a case against the Penguin in the classic issue #473 (November 1977). With several great stories under their belts, time would prove that Englehart and Rogers were just warming up.

OF MONSTERS AND MEN
Batman discovered that Graytowers was actually run by his old Golden Age foe Hugo Strange, armed with several of his Monster Men. By the end of this issue, Strange had discovered Batman's secret identity, and would parade around in Batman's costume in the very next issue.

1977

"I never have nightmares! I give nightmares!"

Batman, Detective Comics #471

The Bronze Age was starting to gain a golden tint as DC Comics began to explore its roster of Golden Age heroes again, introducing them to a modern audience. A year that saw the Justice Society of America's origin finally told and established Earth-Two's Robin at the forefront of a new title, 1977 would also see the debut of the Huntress, the popular crime-fighting daughter of Batman and Catwoman. Meanwhile, *Batman Family* and *Teen Titans* helped welcome the original Batwoman and Batgirl into Earth-One continuity. The result was a wealth of Batman-related characters on both Earths, offering Batman readers more choice than ever before.

FAMILY REVELATION
Batman Family #9 ▪ The mystery of the teenager posing as the Joker's Daughter came to a head in this Robin/Batgirl adventure by writer Bob Rozakis and artist Irv Novick. After dressing up as Scarecrow's daughter (the Scarecrone), the Riddler's daughter, and the Penguin's daughter, the teen was revealed as Duela Dent, Two-Face's daughter. Duela revealed that her hijinks were meant to show off her skills as a Teen Titans hopeful. This issue also featured an Alfred reprint drawn by Jerry Robinson and a Blockbuster reprint by writer Gardner Fox and artist Carmine Infantino.

LIGHTNING STRIKES
Black Lightning #1 ▪ Writer Tony Isabella and penciller Trevor Von Eeden debuted Black Lightning, who would go on to become an iconic Super Hero of the 1970s and a close personal ally of Batman due to his future status as a founder of the "Outsiders." This landmark issue saw school teacher Jefferson Pierce don a belt that gave him lightning powers as well as a mask/wig to protect his identity as he fought new gang boss Tobias Whale. Clad in his new costume Black Lightning would soon test his abilities when he battled assassin Merlyn in the next issue.

BATWOMAN REEMERGES

Batman Family #10 ● The original Batwoman, Kathy Kane, made her first appearance in the Bronze Age of comics, proving she wasn't merely one of the forgotten elements of the original Batman saga destined to be relocated to Earth-Two. In this story by writer Bob Rozakis and artist Bob Brown, Batwoman reemerged briefly from retirement to team up with Batgirl Barbara Gordon against the Cavalier and Killer Moth. This issue also included two classic Batman and Robin reprints featuring the work of Bob Kane, Bill Finger, France Herron, and Sheldon Moldoff.

...BY DEATH'S EERIE LIGHT!

Detective Comics #469 ● Advertised on the splash page as "the Batman you've been waiting for," this issue certainly didn't disappoint as writer Steve Englehart joined the title, with pencils by Walter Simonson. With a back-up tale by the same creators telling their new villains' backstory, Englehart and Simonson introduced readers to Dr. Phosphorus, who earned a spot in Batman's Rogues Gallery when he poisoned Gotham City's reservoir. This issue also saw the first appearance of corrupt city council chairman and gang boss, Rupert Thorne.

EXTENDED FAMILY

Batman Family #11 ● With this issue, *Batman Family* stopped printing back-up reprints. However, instead of reducing its page count, it continued as a 50-cent title but included even more new stories. This issue not only featured a great Robin/Batgirl tale where the two were "almost" married by writer Bob Rozakis and penciller Curt Swan, but also included two other stories: a Man-Bat feature by Rozakis and artist Marshall Rogers that introduced new villain Snafu, and a Commissioner Gordon/Alfred team-up scripted by Rozakis and drawn by artist Carl Potts.

EARTH-SHATTERING SPECIAL

DC Special #28 ● This anthology issue included three stories that featured Super Heroes battling "Earth Shattering Disasters." In addition to Aquaman and Legion of Super-Heroes sections, there was a main feature by writer Bob Rozakis and penciller John Calnan starring Batman as Gotham City suffered earthquakes. The Dark Knight Detective deduced that these quakes couldn't be from a natural source due to Gotham City being built on bedrock (a fact later forgotten during 1998's "Cataclysm" event), leading him to discover the new villain responsible, the Quakemaster.

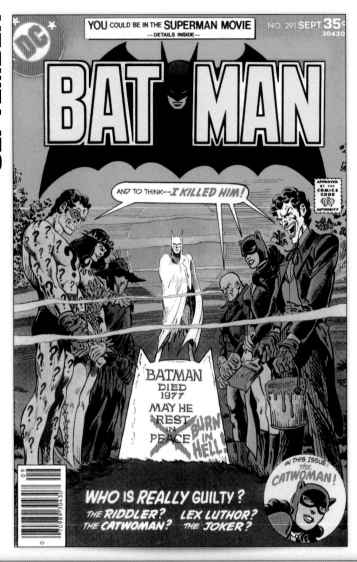

WHO KILLED BATMAN?

BATMAN #291

In a multi-part story, Batman had been killed, and a group of super-villains tried to find out who had done the deed.

Known for his work on many Batman adventures in the 1950s, writer David V. Reed delivered one of his most enjoyable Batman stories in this four-part saga illustrated by John Calnan. When the underworld got word of Batman's death, his greatest villains assembled to undercover the truth about who had had the honor of ending his life. At Colonel Jake "The Claw" Van Cleeve's estate, a mock trial was conducted, led by prosecutor Two-Face. The jury consisted of the Mad Hatter, the Spook, Poison Ivy, Scarecrow, Signalman, and Mr. Freeze, and the judge was none other than Rā's al Ghūl.

In this first chapter, Catwoman admitted to killing her longtime opponent by letting him drown. Two-Face easily picked holes in her story, as he did in the next issue when the Riddler claimed that *he* had murdered Batman. In issue #293 (November 1977), Lex Luthor tried to prove he'd offed the Dark Knight Detective, but was contradicted by guest witness Superman himself. Even the Joker's confession couldn't hold water in this story's final chapter (in issue #294, December 1977), when Batman showed up very much alive after revealing he'd been Two-Face in disguise the entire time. Batman had found the dead body of Jerry Randall, an admirer of his that the Joker had murdered when he mistook him for the real Batman. The entire trial had been an elaborate sting operation for Batman to discover Randall's true murderer.

CATWOMAN'S CLAIM TO INFAMY
According to Catwoman, the villainess murdered the Caped Crusader when she kicked his hand away from a cage the two were floating on after a car wreck landed them in a rushing river. However, Two-Face disproved her case by showing how that particular cage would sink when placed in water.

BATGIRL'S BROTHER

Batman Family #12 ● Barbara Gordon's long lost brother Tony was reintroduced in this issue by writer Bob Rozakis and penciller Jose Delbo. With government help, Tony had been hiding from Communist spies. Tony had first appeared in *World's Finest Comics* #53 (August 1951), and he was destined to fade again into obscurity, just like this issue's new villain, Captain Aero. The issue also featured a Man-Bat tale written by Rozakis and illustrated by Marshall Rogers, and a Robin story scripted by Rozakis and drawn by Irv Novick.

SPECIAL FEATURE

Tony Gordon

When "Batman: Year One" was published in 1987, retelling the origin of Batman and Commissioner Gordon, James Gordon's son would be named James Gordon, Jr. That meant that Batgirl's brother Tony Gordon would be lost to comic book limbo, just as he had been after his first appearance in *World's Finest Comics* #53 (August 1951). Tony died in *Detective Comics* #482 (March 1979).

5-STAR SUPER-HERO SPECTACULAR

DC Special Series #1 ● In this anthology issue that kicked off an ongoing series, Batman starred alongside stories showcasing the Flash, Green Lantern, Aquaman, and the Atom. Batman's tale was inspired by a planned guest-appearance in *Kobra* #8. However, that series folded with issue #7 (April 1977), inspiring writer Martin Pasko and artist Mike Nasser to rework the plot into this seventeen-page showdown between Batman and Kobra that featured a new Batplane and tied up some loose ends from the *Kobra* series.

A NEW BAG OF TRICKS

Black Lightning #4 ● The Batman villain formerly known as Bag O' Bones made his return, now calling himself the Cyclotronic Man. Working for Tobias Whale, the Cyclotronic Man had had his powers improved by the scientists that worked for the 100, Whale's corrupt organization. The Cyclotronic Man kidnapped Jimmy Olsen, drawing out Black Lightning and even, by the issue's end, Superman. The action, by writer Tony Isabella and artist Trevor Von Eeden, continued through the next issue; by issue #6, Black Lightning was fighting the new threat of Syonide.

THE DARK KNIGHT'S DAUGHTER
ALL-STAR COMICS #69

The Huntress, the daughter of Earth-Two's Batman and Catwoman, made her debut in true spectacular Batman fashion.

Batman and Catwoman seemed like the perfect comic book couple, except for their tendency to end up on opposite sides of the law. But in the alternate reality of Earth-Two, the couple was free to marry, so it made sense that Batman would try to create the family he had lost as a young child. Thanks to writer Paul Levitz and penciller Joe Staton, Batman found more than just a daughter in Helena Wayne, the child that he and Selina raised. He would also find a replacement for his lifelong secret career. Now the Commissioner of Gotham City, Bruce Wayne greeted the returning Justice Society members in this issue by charging them with reckless endangerment. In reality, he was being manipulated by Psycho-Pirate, the emotion-altering villain, but with the help of Dr. Fate, Wayne soon came to his senses. He had been grieving, since Catwoman had died a year earlier, so was easy meat for the Pirate. Meanwhile, a mysterious figure watched from the shadows. In the final panel, she stepped into the light and fans caught their first glimpse of Wayne's adult daughter in a purple costume and mask.

Released the same month was *DC Super-Stars* #17, this story, by Levitz and Staton, filled readers in on the history of Bruce Wayne's daughter. The story took them from Bruce's wedding to Selina Kyle, to Helena's birth, to Selina's eventual death. By the issue's end, as Batman retired his cape and cowl in grief, Helena had channeled her sorrow into becoming his crossbow-wielding replacement: the Huntress.

WEAPON OF CHOICE
The Huntress' signature weapon was her crossbow, which was able to collapse and slide into the holster on her leg, Helena made good use of the bow, even into the modern era.

BATGIRL'S BACK
Teen Titans #50 ▪ After Batwoman had officially returned in the pages of *Batman Family* #10 (March 1977), the time was ripe for her sidekick, Betty Kane, the original Batgirl, to return from comic book limbo. In an adventure written by Bob Rozakis and drawn by Don Heck, Batgirl came out of retirement to join forces with Lilith, Hawk and Dove, Beast Boy, Gnarrk, and Golden Eagle to form the Super Hero team Teen Titans West. This issue also saw the return of super-villain Captain Calamity (who debuted in *Detective Comics* #352 (June 1966) and his gang.

DEADSHOT HITS HIS TARGET
Detective Comics #474 ▪ Deadshot adopted his trademark look in this issue by writer Steve Englehart and artist Marshall Rogers. After Silver St. Cloud escorted Bruce Wayne around the latest convention she'd organized, an exhibit full of giant props that served as a tip of the hat to Batman's adventures in the 1950s, Batman was attacked by Deadshot. The villain wore a new costume that included his famous, silenced, wrist-mounted guns. During Batman and Deadshot's fight, Miss St. Cloud got a good look at Batman and realized he was Bruce Wayne.

SPECIAL FEATURE

DEADSHOT
When Floyd Lawton, alias Deadshot, first appeared, he boasted a top hat and tails, and pretended to be a hero. But after a total overhaul by artist Marshall Rogers, Deadshot developed the iconic look that would last for decades. No longer pretending to be something he was not, the assassin-for-hire had guns and a gunsight built into his new suit.

ALSO THIS YEAR

February—*The Brave and the Bold* #132: Batman and Richard Dragon met for the first time and Batman mistook the martial artist for a mugger.

★ **February 12th**—Batman's newest solo cartoon, *The New Adventures of Batman*, debuted thanks to Filmation.

April—*World's Finest Comics* #244: With this issue, *World's Finest Comics* changed format to an all-new "Dollar Comics" anthology that included a new Black Canary back-up tale.

July—*Batman* #289: Batman faced the threat of the Skull Dugger, a murderous foe incapable of feeling joy on his own.

August—*Limited Collector's Edition* #C-51: This issue reprinted Rā's al Ghūl's debut and his first major bout with Batman.

September—*DC Special Series* #1: A secret since the 1940s, the Justice Society's backstory was finally told. Superman coined the name for this group of Super Heroes. The flashback story sent Batman on a mission to fight Nazi forces in which he clashed with Adolf Hitler himself.

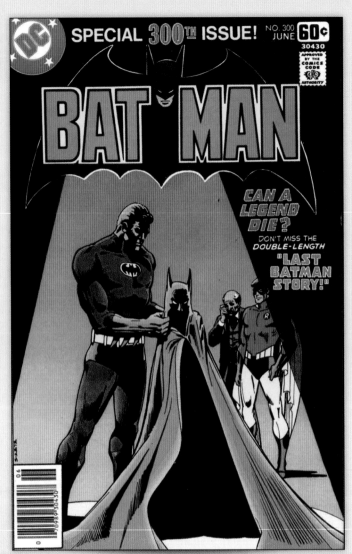

SPECIAL 300TH ISSUE! NO. 300 JUNE 60¢

BAT MAN

CAN A LEGEND DIE?

DON'T MISS THE DOUBLE-LENGTH "LAST BATMAN STORY!"

THE LAST BATMAN STORY?

BATMAN #300

In honor of the 300th issue of *Batman* comics, a possible future for the Dark Knight Detective was revealed.

Crafted by writer David V. Reed and penciller Walter Simonson, this special 34-page issue imagined a possible future where Gotham City had become the hub of Megalopolis-East, a vast urban environment stretching from Boston through New York and from Metropolis to Washington, D.C. In this future, an adult Robin, having adopted the same costume as that of Dick Grayson of Earth-Two, worked occasionally as a crime fighter for the Meg/East interstate police. Meanwhile, Batman remained essentially the same, still fighting his never-ending battle for justice. Armed with a futuristic Batcopter and space-traversing Batwing, Batman maintained his headquarters from below the Wayne Foundation Building, still wearing a costume identical to his standard 1978 attire.

In this adventure, Batman and Robin reunited to destroy the crime syndicate known as Spectrum. Guest-starring an aged Alfred and Commissioner Gordon, this story saw Bruce Wayne, now with silver hair at his temples, contemplate retiring from crime fighting altogether with the hopes of getting married and possibly running for governor.

THE END?
While it seemed like Bruce Wayne was on the verge of retirement at this issue's end, readers were left watching Batman ponder his past, wondering if the Super Hero would ever truly hang up his cape.

"What one man can do, I've done!"

Bruce Wayne, *Batman* #300

1978

"You're always a party-poop—just when I'm beginning to have fun!"

The Joker to Batman, *Detective Comics* #476

Almost as suddenly as they appeared, writer Steve Englehart and artist Marshall Rogers wrapped up their brilliant partnership this year in *Detective Comics*. A short run that would nevertheless go down in Batman history, their collaboration wouldn't be the only thing that ended this year. *Teen Titans* ended its initial run, as did the popular *Batman Family*. While *Batman Family*'s format would be shifted into the pages of *Detective Comics*, the Titans would have to wait two years to return. Fortunately for Robin and his friends, their revival in the 1980s landmark title *The New Teen Titans* would prove their most popular so far.

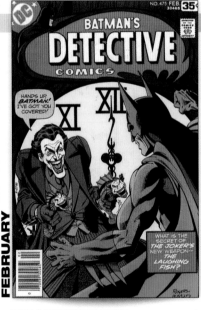

THE LAUGHING FISH
Detective Comics #475 • Writer Steve Englehart and artist Marshall Rogers crafted one of the most iconic Joker stories ever told when the Clown Prince of Crime released a chemical into the waters off Gotham City so that every fish had his signature grin. In the Joker's disturbed mind, he believed he could trademark the fish, making a fortune in royalties. Meanwhile, Batman was involved in a complex relationship with Silver St. Cloud. However, he was soon forced into action against his old foe, putting romance on the back burner.

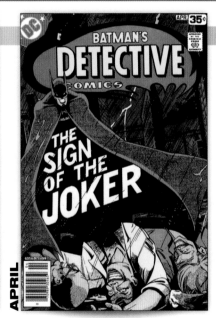

THE COST OF SILVER
Detective Comics #476 • As Batman's battle with the Joker continued from the previous issue, Steve Englehart and Marshall Rogers proved the extent of Bruce Wayne's daily sacrifice when the hero lost his newfound love, Silver St. Cloud. In the previous issue Silver had left Gotham City, unable to deal with Batman's dual identity. She returned to confront him after the hero defeated the Joker. Silver told Batman she loved him, but that she couldn't spend her life worrying about him every night. Then she left him once more, telling him never to call her.

AUGUST

MELTING HEARTS
DETECTIVE COMICS #478

The Clayface family grew to include the newest heir to that villainous legacy with Clayface III, a very different take on a familiar name.

Although the previous issue of *Detective Comics* was mostly a reprint, it included a framing device written by Len Wein and illustrated by Marshall Rogers. Wein had stepped in to fill the very big shoes of departing writer Steve Englehart and managed to deliver an impressive first showing: In that issue's final panel, readers glimpsed the boots of the newest addition to Batman's Rogues Gallery. That murderous criminal would be revealed in this issue as Clayface III, Preston Payne. The Golden-Age Clayface had simply been a masked killer. The Silver-Age Clayface was a shape-shifting thief. However Wein and Rogers' Clayface that debuted for the Bronze Age was very different interpretation. Preston Payne, born with deformed features, used his scientific knowledge to attempt to rectify what nature had gotten wrong. Using a sample of blood from the second Clayface, Matt Hagen, Payne experimented on himself only to wind up an almost formless blob riddled with pain. Forced to wear an exoskeleton to aid movement, he could only alleviate his pain by transferring it to others with a touch. Unfortunately for all involved, that touch killed his victims and reduced them to protoplasmic goo. In this two-part tale, Batman battled Clayface III and ended his reign of terror, discovering that the demented Payne had fallen in love with a wax figure, the only "woman" he could ever truly touch.

THE PAIN OF PAYNE
Very different from the first two Clayfaces, Preston Payne's story had a tragic story. After becoming Clayface, he was forced to rely on an exoskeleton to help his mobility. The suit also increased his strength, making him more of a challenge for Batman.

NO. 478 AUG 30465 35¢

BATMAN'S DETECTIVE COMICS

CLAYFACE IS BACK!

AND THIS GIRL WAS HIS FIRST VICTIM!

YOU, BATMAN, WILL BE HIS NEXT!!

MAY

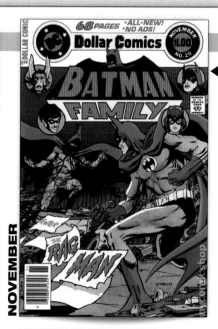

MORE BANG FOR THE BUCK
Batman Family #17 ● With this issue, *Batman Family* included more new material than ever before. First up in this 80-page giant was a Batman and Robin yarn by writer Gerry Conway and artist Jim Aparo. After that, new villain Madame Zodiac debuted to challenge Batgirl, Batwoman, and Huntress in a tale by writer Bob Rozakis and artist Don Heck. Finally, Man-Bat starred in a story also written by Rozakis that was illustrated by Michael Golden. This wonderfully illustrated tale saw the birth of Kirk Langstrom's daughter, Rebecca.

NOVEMBER

THE END OF THE FAMILY
Batman Family #20 ● The *Batman Family* title had reached its end. In the finale, readers saw Ragman's origin retold as he faced the Caped Crusader in the lead feature by writer David V. Reed and artist Michael Golden. Writer Bob Rozakis supplied a Robin and Batgirl story, as well as a Man-Bat tale, illustrated by Don Heck and Michael Golden respectively. And finally, Huntress starred in a back-up tale, thanks to writer Paul Levitz and artist Joe Staton, after starting her own feature in issue #18 (June 1977).

SPECIAL FEATURE

Ragman

Rory Regan's heroic identity as Ragman became more closely related to Batman as of this issue. When Ragman returned for an eight-issue miniseries in 1991, Batman would also guest-star in that title, before Ragman was eventually adopted into Batman's Network of allies.

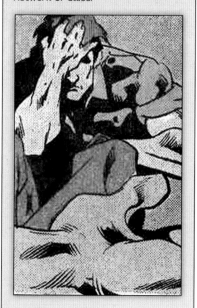

ALSO THIS YEAR

February—*Teen Titans* #53: Robin's team ended its initial run with this flashback story.

★ **April 3rd—*The World's Greatest Heroes*:** A new syndicated daily comic strip debuted in newspapers.

June—*DC Special Series* #15: Batman starred in this special issue that contained three new stories.

July—*Limited Collector's Edition* #C-59: Batman once more starred in a treasury edition, this time featuring his "strangest cases."

August—*Batman Family* #19: A new villain called Raven menaced Robin.

September—*Green Lantern* #108: Hal Jordan battled Replikon, a villain who assumed a bit of Batman's appearance and abilities.

September—*Dynamic Classics* #1: "The Secret of the Waiting Graves" was reprinted in this stand-alone issue alongside a Manhunter reprint.

November—*Batman* #305: Batman met the skull-faced new villain Thanatos.

THE DEATH OF THE BATMAN
ADVENTURE COMICS #462
The original Batman's story ended in this momentous issue when Bruce Wayne of Earth-Two was murdered.

The Justice Society's revival in the pages of *All-Star Comics* had been a rather short one. Despite introducing fan-favorite characters Power Girl and the Huntress, the title ended with issue #74 (September 1978). Luckily for the Society, they soon found a home (albeit a temporary one) in the pages of *Adventure Comics'* new one-dollar anthology format, beginning in issue #461 (January 1979). In this first two-part story, writer Paul Levitz and artist Joe Staton forever altered the world of Earth-Two by killing off the original Batman.

Forced out of retirement when a criminal named Bill Jensen defeated the rest of the Justice Society and demanded to be delivered to Commissioner Bruce Wayne, Batman seemed to somehow understand that this mission would be his last. Summoning unheard-of willpower, Batman fought his way through Jensen's barrage of energy. As Batman did so, enough of his mask was burned off his face for the villain to realize that the man he now faced was his true intended target. In a fiery explosion of rage, Jensen's powers erupted, killing both himself and Batman in the process.

BURYING A BATMAN
Bruce Wayne's funeral was an impressive gathering worthy of an impressive hero. In the next issue, his surviving family, Robin and Huntress, would realize the true villain behind Bill Jensen's bizarre powers, the mystical villain named Fredric Vaux.

1979
"Only legends live forever... not the men who make them."

Helena Wayne, *Adventure Comics #462*

As the decade drew to a close, longtime Batman editor Julius Schwartz finally passed the torch on to Paul Levitz, marking the end of an era. Coincidentally, in the pages of some of Batman's titles, there were also several endings. Batwoman was murdered in *Detective Comics*, while Earth-Two Batman made the ultimate sacrifice in *Adventure Comics*. But with new faces like crazed gang boss Maxie Zeus and business guru Lucius Fox popping up in Gotham City, plus wardrobe changes for some of Batman's classic foes, it seemed a new chapter in Dark Knight's career was just beginning.

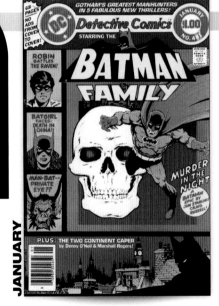

THE DETECTIVE FAMILY
Detective Comics #481 • With this issue, the title adopted the popular multi-story format of *Batman Family*, spotlighting many of Batman's supporting cast. In this issue readers were treated to a Batman tale by writer Dennis O'Neil and artist Marshall Rogers, a Batgirl yarn by writer Bob Rozakis and artist Don Heck, a Man-Bat story by Rozakis and artist Don Newton, and another Batman adventure by writer/layout artist Jim Starlin and finisher P. Craig Russell. This issue also featured a Robin story by Rozakis and Newton that showcased fan-designed costumes for the hero.

THE FINANCIAL FOX
Batman #307 • An indispensible part of Batman's world in both comic books and in subsequent movies, businessman Lucius Fox debuted in this issue by new regular writer Len Wein and artist John Calnan. Established as Bruce Wayne's second-in-command at Wayne Enterprises in a casual conversation between the two in one of this issue's opening scenes, Fox was suddenly a part of Batman's life. Fox was unaware of Batman's double identity, but would grow to respect Wayne. Lucius' daughter Tiffany debuted in the following issue.

MAY

THE CURSE OF CRIME ALLEY
DETECTIVE COMICS #483

Forty years after Batman's first appearance in *Detective Comics*, this anniversary issue introduced new villain Maxie Zeus.

The one-dollar format in *Detective Comics* was still going strong, so when DC Comics decided to celebrate Batman's 40-year anniversary, there was still plenty of room for other features in this issue. In fact, besides Batman's lead story, this issue contained a Batgirl adventure by writer Bob Rozakis and artist Bob Oksner, a Robin story also written by Rozakis yet illustrated by Kurt Schaffenberger, and a second Batman tale dealing with Gotham City's bizarre kangaroo race by writer Dennis O'Neil and penciller Dick Dillin. In addition, this volume featured two non-Batman-related stories, one starring the Human Target, and the other starring the Demon. But of course, the main focus of this issue was its lead tale by writer Dennis O'Neil and artist Don Newton. A sequel to O'Neil's acclaimed "There's No Hope in Crime Alley" from *Detective Comics* #457 (March 1976), this issue saw Batman once again visit Leslie Thompkins on his annual trip to Crime Alley to remember his parents' death. When he encountered some hoods in the employ of debuting mobster Maxie Zeus, Batman stumbled on a plot to kill every resident of a local run-down building in an attempted hit on one of Zeus' enemies. Batman stopped Zeus' horrific crime before it happened, and the villain earned a prominent place on Batman's list of enemies.

A WARNING FOR MAXIE ZEUS
The gang boss believed he was an avatar of Zeus, ruler of the Greek gods. His method of flushing an enemy from an apartment block befitted a cruel deity—he planned to fill the place with poisonous gas. A threatening message from Batman told him that his plan had failed.

COOL CHARACTER
Batman #308 ▪ Mr. Freeze showed off a new look for the Bronze Age of comics in a story by writer Len Wein and artist John Calnan. A bit more appropriate to a life of super-villainy than his bulky Silver Age look, Freeze wore a costume similar to the original he wore as Mr. Zero in *Batman* #121 (February 1959), except it had a blue and white motif. In an era before the invention of Freeze's wife Nora, this issue saw Mr. Freeze trying to unlock the secret to immortality for a beautiful woman named Hildy.

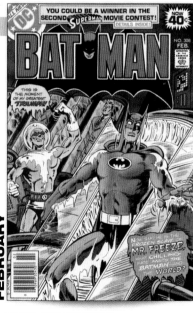

MEDICINE MAN
World's Finest Comics #255 ▪ Writer Bob Haney and artist José Luis García López joined forces to introduce a new character who had worn a costume similar to Bruce Wayne's years before Bruce had been inspired to begin his lifetime of crime fighting. This individual was a Native American medicine man wearing a ceremonial costume meant to stave off a bat-like deity called Gitchka. This issue also included a back-up Creeper tale by writer/artist Steve Ditko as well as stories starring Green Arrow and the Shazam! family.

THE DEATH OF BATWOMAN
Detective Comics #485 ▪ The original female counterpart to Batman, Batwoman Kathy Kane was seemingly murdered by the brainwashed Bronze Tiger in this issue's lead feature written by Dennis O'Neil and illustrated by Don Newton. As it turned out, Bronze Tiger had committed this heinous crime in the name of the Sensei, current leader of the League of Assassins. This volume also included a Robin story by writer Paul Kupperberg and artist Kurt Schaffenberger, a Batgirl tale by writer Jack C. Harris and artist Don Heck, and a Bob Rozakis-scripted Man-Bat yarn drawn by Don Newton.

ALSO THIS YEAR

April—*Batman* #310: The Gentleman Ghost appeared for the first of many conflicts with the Dark Knight.

May—*The Brave and the Bold* #150: Batman teamed up with a mystery guest, who would soon be revealed as Superman.

May—*Batman* #311: Batman debuted a Batmobile that would inspire a toy vehicle.

June—*Batman* #312: Calendar Man finally received a proper costume featuring calendar pages as a cape.

July—*Batman* #313: Lucius Fox's son Tim debuted in this issue.

August—*World's Finest Comics* #258: Batman was turned into a creature in this issue that also included the second part of Black Lightning's new back-up feature.

November—*Best of DC Blue Ribbon Digest* #2: The Dark Knight swung into the smaller digest format in this reprint collection.

December—*Justice League of America* #173: Black Lightning rejected membership in the JLA.

1980s

Few decades would see as much change for Batman as the 1980s. This decade took Batman from being a sometimes-troubled adventurer and team-up partner, to a grim and driven Dark Knight.

With the advent of comic book shops, comic book miniseries, and mature subject matter, comics were growing up. Sophisticated storytelling not intended for the spinner rack at the local grocery store was finding an older reading audience and also mainstream acclaim. For Batman, in particular, this meant an increasing emphasis on limited series aimed at mature readers, including the groundbreaking *Batman: The Dark Knight Returns*.

With the release of *Batman: The Dark Knight Returns*, the character of Batman would never be the same again. Writer/artist Frank Miller delivered what is considered by many to be the quintessential ending of the Batman saga. He then quickly followed this landmark up with the equally definitive origin story of the Dark Knight in the pages of "Batman: Year One." Miller's gritty, hard-boiled vision of Batman became the norm rather than the exception.

In his regular titles, Batman would begin the decade with his adventures in *Batman* and *Detective Comics* often crossing into one another and featuring interlocking subplots. By the end of the decade, each book had a specific feel, as different writer/artist teams were assigned to them. Batman would even gain a few new titles this decade, such as the team book *Batman and the Outsiders*, and the solo ongoing effort by various writers and artists, *Batman: Legends of the Dark Knight*.

It was a decade of much change, as Robin became Nightwing, and a new Robin stepped up to fill the gap, only to later die a grisly death. Batgirl would retire and be paralyzed, and new villains like Killer Croc, Black Mask and the Ventriloquist darkened Gotham City with their presence. There would even be a third Robin by the decade's end, one tailor-made it seemed for the birth of the 1990s.

Batman was once again as dark as he had been portrayed in the 1930s—if not darker. By 1989 and the release of director Tim Burton's acclaimed film *Batman*, the comedic Caped Crusader from the 1960s TV show had clearly been reimagined.

THE LEGEND RETOLD
THE UNTOLD LEGEND OF THE BATMAN #1

In DC Comics' second-ever miniseries, Batman's past was examined in more detail than ever before.

Written by Len Wein, the first issue of this three-part tale was pencilled by John Byrne and issues two and three were drawn by Jim Aparo. The result was a series that served as a modern retelling of many classic Batman tales while adding its own updates.

The story started with an intriguing premise. Batman received a death threat along with a package that contained the remnants of the original Batman costume that his father Thomas Wayne had worn many years before. More dire threats followed, forcing Batman to relive his parents' death and his beginnings as Batman as he continued his investigation.

The second issue focused on the origins of Robin, Alfred, the Joker, and Two-Face, while issue three discussed the past of Commissioner Gordon and Batgirl. This issue also featured the debut of Jack Edison, the master stuntman who helped Batman to update his famous Batmobile from time to time.

In the end, the sender of the original package was revealed to be Robin, who had hoped to banish the demons haunting Batman's tormented mind. The ploy seemed to work: By reliving his traumatic past, the Dark Knight had once again renewed his crime-fighting mission.

1980

"Help? Not at all, Bruce. This is one thing I can handle by myself!"

Robin, *The New Teen Titans* #1

It was Robin's year. The Boy Wonder had grown up to become a Teen Wonder and, thanks to his new title, *The New Teen Titans*, was quickly on his way to becoming his own man. With his various back-up features remaining popular, the presence of Robin was one of the main reasons readers were attracted to The New Teen Titans in the first place. The title's sophisticated storylines and artwork would keep fans coming back for more each month. Robin also stopped by the pages of *The Untold Legend of the Batman*, Batman's first-ever miniseries, playing a major role in that story's outcome.

A CHILLING FINISH
After catching up with Joe Chill in one of this issue's many flashbacks, Batman revealed his double identity to the murderer. The villain then rushed to meet with his fellow criminals, begging them to help him against this man whose parents he'd murdered. Instead, the criminals carried out "their own perverse kind of justice" and gunned Joe Chill down.

THE MAN BEHIND THE MURDER

The Untold Legend of the Batman combined all the various stories of Batman's established origin over the years, including the fact that Batman confronted mob boss Lew Moxon—the man who ordered the death of Bruce's parents—while wearing a Batman costume originally worn by Thomas Wayne.

RAVEN
The daughter of the demon Trigon, Raven was responsible for uniting this incarnation of the Teen Titans. Oddly enough, Robin had met two other characters named Raven, in *Detective Comics* #287 (January 1961) and in *Batman Family* #19 (August 1978).

APRIL

JULY

AUGUST

SEPTEMBER

SUPER-STAR HOLIDAY SPECIAL
DC Special Series #21 • One of the most important creators ever to work on Batman, writer/artist Frank Miller drew his first Batman story in this issue. While it featured five self-contained tales, the story "Wanted: Santa Claus—Dead or Alive," written by Denny O'Neil and pencilled by Miller was the standout. In this story, the Dark Knight encountered retired heist artist Boomer Katz who, in order to go straight, had taken a job as a department store Santa. Batman saved Boomer's life, with the help of an oddly shining star in the sky.

SUNSET FOR THE SUPER-SONS
World's Finest Comics #263 • When they first debuted in *World's Finest* #215 (December–January 1972–1973), the Super-Sons of Batman and Superman became a popular feature. But as Batman and Superman stories became more realistic, these unexplained teen protégés fell out of favor. In this tale, writer Denny O'Neil and penciller Rich Buckler revealed that the adventures of the Sons were computer-generated stories created by Superman's technology. After escaping into the "real world" of Earth-One, the Sons opted to disintegrate themselves.

SWASHBUCKLER SHOWCASE
Detective Comics #493 • As the popular five-story format of *Detective Comics* continued, many unexpected heroes began to pop up in Batman's supporting cast. In this issue's lead feature, Batman tracked the Riddler to Austin, Texas, and encountered the Swashbuckler, a local hero and nephew of the original hero known as the Vigilante, Greg Sanders. In this team-up tale by writer Cary Burkett and artist Don Newton, the two defeated the Riddler, with Batman learning the Swashbuckler's true identity (Michael Carter) along the way.

HUNTRESS STALKS SOLO
Wonder Woman #271 • The Earth-Two daughter of Bruce Wayne and Selina Kyle gained her own regular back-up feature in the pages of *Wonder Woman* in this issue written and pencilled by the Huntress's creators, Paul Levitz and Joe Staton. Huntress's tale, "Into Darkness Once More," had her working at the law firm of Cranston, Grayson, & Wayne. In her secret identity of Helena Wayne, Huntress was surprised by a visit from artist Winston Pitt. Her investigations led her to confront an attempted robbery by Solomon Grundy.

CLASH OF THE TITANS

THE NEW TEEN TITANS #1

One of the Super Hero teams that defined the 1980s with groundbreaking characterization and epic storylines was DC Comics' Teen Titans in the landmark series, *The New Teen Titans*.

Writer Marv Wolfman and artist George Pérez cemented their status as comic book superstars with this series. They took former Titans Robin, Kid Flash, and Wonder Girl, teamed them with former Teen Titans West and Doom Patrol member Changeling, and added new characters Starfire, Raven, and Cyborg. Combining the youthful excitement of teen adventurers with action, humor, and human drama, Wolfman offered an exciting new incarnation of the Teen Titans that was heightened by Pérez's brilliantly detailed artwork.

The series began with the enigmatic mystic Raven recruiting the new Titans team to combat the alien threat of the Gordanians and free their captive, the alien princess Starfire. With a successful first mission under their belts, the team stuck together, and found a home in Titans Tower in New York City. The title rapidly gained in popularity, topping the comics' sales charts in less than six months. This was helped in part by a guest appearance by the Justice League in issue #4, in which Robin rebelled against his overbearing mentor, Batman. *The New Teen Titans* would continue to be one of DC Comic's best sellers for many years to come.

CRIME DOCTOR IN THE HOUSE

Detective Comics #494 ▪ Not glimpsed since the Golden Age of comics, Bradford Thorne, alias the Crime Doctor, made his return in the lead story of this issue by guest writer Michael Fleisher and artist Don Newton, performing heists with the use of anesthesia gas. Also in this issue was a "Tales of Gotham City" story by writer Jack C. Harris and artist Dan Spiegle, a Batgirl tale by writer Cary Burkett and artist José Delbo, a Robin story by Harris and artist Charlie Nicholas, and a Black Lightning yarn written by J. M. DeMatteis and drawn by Gerald Forton.

TITANS TOGETHER

DC Comics Presents #26 ▪ While the cover of this issue focused on the Green Lantern/Superman team-up, it was the free, 16-page preview comic within entitled "Where Nightmares Begin" that stole the show. In that story, by writer Marv Wolfman and penciller George Pérez, the newest incarnation of Robin's famous Super Hero team debuted in the form of the New Teen Titans. The entire tale was told through a vision Robin had of his future, and it served as a successful ad for the first issue of *The New Teen Titans* which would debut the following month.

DEATHSTROKE'S DEBUT

The New Teen Titans #2 ▪ The second issue of *The New Teen Titans* by writer Marv Wolfman and artist George Pérez would be monumental to Dick Grayson for two reasons. Firstly, it introduced one of his greatest foes—assassin-for-hire Deathstroke the Terminator. Deathstroke, aka Slade Wilson, became a lifelong enemy of the Titans when his son and fellow contract killer, Ravager, died battling the youthful heroes. Secondly, when the beautiful alien princess Starfire kissed Robin for the first time, it began a long romance that nearly resulted in marriage years later.

ALSO THIS YEAR

February—*The Brave and the Bold* #159: Batman was forced to team up with his enemy Rä's al Ghül.

March—*DC Comics Presents* #19: Barbara Gordon found herself fighting as Batgirl alongside Superman against a mysterious villain named Doctor Horus.

June—*The Brave and the Bold* #163: Although his title had been canceled in 1978, popular character Black Lightning netted a team-up with Batman in what would serve as a precursor of sorts for 1983's *Batman and the Outsiders*.

September—*Batman* #327: Batman found himself at the mercy of Professor Milo when he checked into Arkham Asylum.

November—*Detective Comics* #496: Batman fought the original incarnation of Clayface, the non-powered actor Basil Karlo. Meanwhile, Batgirl took on the newest rogue in her personal gallery, Dr. Voodoo.

December—*Detective Comics* #497: The Squid, a Gotham City crime boss, debuted in this issue. He succeeded in wounding Batman, but failed to kill him.

THE QUINTESSENTIAL QUINCENTENNIAL
DETECTIVE COMICS #500

To celebrate the 500th issue of his flagship comic, Batman was treated to a super-sized anniversary special with a collaborative cover that spotlighted the issue's guest stars.

REVISIONS
An alternate origin for Batman answered the question of "What if Bruce Wayne's parents had not been killed?" but made clear that all roads eventually led to Wayne becoming the Batman. There is no escaping destiny!

The lead story by writer Alan Brennert and artist Dick Giordano explored Batman's origins by transporting him to an alternate Earth. In this world, Bruce Wayne's parents had not yet been killed. Arriving there with the help of the Phantom Stranger, Batman and Robin successfully prevented the deaths of Thomas and Martha Wayne. However, in the story's epilogue, that world's young Bruce Wayne began a strict training regimen, preparing himself to become the same sort of grim figure of the night that saved his family. It seemed that no matter the circumstances, there was no destroying the legend of Batman.

The issue featured six other tales. Two concentrated on non-Batman related heroes, Hawkman and the Elongated Man. Another featured many of *Detective Comics'* other sleuths, including Slam Bradley, the Human Target, and Mysto the Magician. A fourth was a two-page Batman tale, followed by a prose Batman adventure. Finally, there was a full-length Batman/Deadman team-up. *Detective Comics* #500 proved a memorable milestone for the title that gave DC Comics its name.

1981

"Maybe we ought to get mugged more often."

Thomas Wayne, *Detective Comics* #500

Writer Gerry Conway and artist Don Newton had become the regular team on *Detective Comics* at the tail end of 1980. By the middle of this year, Conway had also taken over the writing in *Batman*. With the same writer handling both main Batman books, easy crossovers between the two titles soon became possible. This method of storytelling swiftly led to interlocking tales that required readers to purchase both *Batman* and *Detective Comics* each month. In the meantime, however, Conway focused on introducing new faces to Batman's world, including Alfred Pennyworth's daughter Julia and a handful of interesting minor villains.

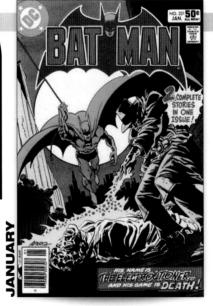

ENTER THE ELECTROCUTIONER
Batman #331 ■ Batman met a self-proclaimed judge, jury, and executioner in the form of the Electrocutioner, an electrically-powered new villain who preyed on criminals who had escaped death row on one legal technicality or another. Plotted by *Batman*'s new regular writer (as of issue #228) Marv Wolfman, with dialog by Michael Fleisher and art by Irv Novick, this story saw Batman face this new costumed threat, who believed himself on the side of the angels. In a back-up tale, Batman disguised himself as a member of Gotham City Police Department.

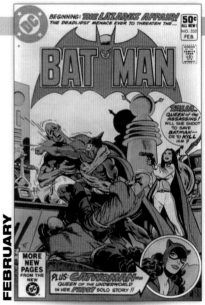

THE LAZARUS AFFAIR
Batman #332 ■ A rare, four-part story began this issue written by Marv Wolfman with art by Irv Novick. When Talia al Ghūl returned to Batman's life, he was too busy dealing with corrupt businessman Gregorian Falstaff to notice that his longtime love interest might have her own agenda. He soon found himself on a globe-spanning adventure alongside Talia, Catwoman, and Robin, discovering that Falstaff was under orders from Rā's al Ghūl. Having defeated Rā's, Batman discovered that for decades, Talia had been using the Lazarus Pit to maintain her youth and beauty.

THE PENGUIN'S PAST

BEST OF DC BLUE RIBBON DIGEST #10

After 40 memorable years as Batman's bird-obsessed number two foe, the Penguin had his bizarre beginnings finally revealed to a curious readership in this completely new origin tale.

In the 1980s, the digest format was usually reserved for reprint tales of momentous stories in comic book continuity. But while the rest of this particular issue did in fact feature reprints, telling the origins of villains Captain Boomerang, the Shark, Parasite, Ocean Master, Shadow Thief, and the Red Dart, the lead story was a brand new tale, detailing the past of the notorious Penguin. Written by Michael Fleisher with pencils by Romeo Tanghal, this story painted a portrait of Oswald Chesterfield Cobblepot, a boy with an overbearing mother who forced him to carry an umbrella everywhere he went. He was teased and nicknamed the Penguin for his wide girth and strange walk. And when his prized bird shop was taken away from him by creditors, Oswald decided to take revenge upon the world as the infamous criminal, the Penguin.

A PRIVATE PENGUIN

Catwoman and the Joker's origins had been outlined in the 1950s, and the Riddler and Two-Face's backstories had been revealed in their debuts. However, it took much longer for Oswald Cobblepot to get his tale out in the open.

ALFRED'S SECRET

Detective Comics #501 ▪ Alfred Pennyworth's past would be explored when writer Gerry Conway and artist Don Newton revealed that Bruce Wayne's longtime butler had a daughter. As it turned out, Alfred had met famous French heroine Mlle. Marie during her time fighting for the French resistance in Nazi-occupied France. Familiar to regular DC Comics readers from her features in *Star Spangled War Stories*, Marie had an affair with Alfred that resulted in the birth of Julia. In her first appearance in this issue, Julia mistook Alfred for her mother's killer.

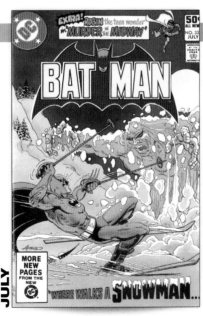

WHERE WALKS A SNOWMAN…

Batman #337 ▪ Regular writer Gerry Conway was assisted by writer Roy Thomas and the pencils of José Luis Garcia Lopez in this issue that introduced Batman to the new threat of the Snowman. When attending a party as Bruce Wayne, Batman noticed that guest Klaus Kristin's shoes were covered in slush. This made Wayne suspect that the Olympic skier might know about a villain called the Snowman. Batman's hunch proved correct, and he discovered that Kristin was both a Yeti and an albino, stealing money to fund his traveling lifestyle.

DIGGING UP THE MOLE

Batman #340 ▪ Writers Gerry Conway and Roy Thomas collaborated with artist Gene Colan for the dramatic return of the Mole, an old Batman villain given a serious upgrade. When he first appeared in *World's Finest* #80 (January/February 1956), the Mole was a tunneling bank robber. But in this issue, he had been transformed into a grotesque creature. It was soon revealed that the Mole had been mutated by chemical waste when he had tunneled out of jail. Reduced to little more than a wild beast wanting revenge, the Mole was finally defeated by Batman.

ALSO THIS YEAR

January—*Best of DC Blue Ribbon Digest* #9: The five-part saga from *Detective Comics* #444–448 was collected in convenient digest form.

March—*DC Comics Presents* #31: Robin crossed Superman's path while investigating a case of hypnosis at the Sterling Circus. Proving a popular partner for Superman, Robin returned to the title with issue #58.

June—*The Brave and the Bold* #175: Superman's girlfriend Lois Lane took a turn teaming up with the Dark Knight Detective.

July—*DC Comics Presents* #35: Man-Bat teamed up with Superman to battle the threat of the Atomic Skull.

September—*Detective Comics* #506: Following a murder, Batman confronted villainess Manikin, only to watch her shed her skin and clothing to reveal nothing more than the body of a mannequin.

CAPITAL HILL

DETECTIVE COMICS #511

This issue paved the way for a thrilling and busy storyline that saw the people of Gotham City vote for a new mayor, the arrival of a new Batman villain, and a shocking announcement by Bruce Wayne.

Hamilton Hill had defeated Councilman Arthur Reeves in the mayoral election when the latter's attempts to reveal Batman's identity, related in previous issues of *Batman* and *Detective Comics*, turned out to be fraudulent.

Hill first appeared in *Detective Comics* #503 (June 1981), and would go on to become a prominent figure as mayor in 1992's popular *Batman: The Animated Series* TV show. But while he would soon cause police commissioner James Gordon to step down from his longtime position, in this issue by writer Gerry Conway and artist Don Newton, Hill's rise to power was overshadowed by the first appearance of new villain Mirage.

Able to project illusions from his wrist jewel, Mirage proved an interesting challenge for the Caped Crusader—one Batman overcame with the help of a special earpiece and sheer force of will. However, the biggest surprise of the issue came when Bruce Wayne stepped down as head of the Wayne Foundation and Wayne Enterprises to concentrate on life as Batman, leaving his business in the more-than-capable hands of Lucius Fox.

SOUND OFF
Batman theorized that Mirage's illusions were created by a combination of audio and visual stimulation. With Robin and Alfred's help, Batman created an earpiece to minimize Mirage's abilities.

1982

"I'm a big girl, Bruce. I can handle disappointments... can you?"

Vicki Vale, *Batman* #344

The Golden Age was back in Batman's world as writer Gerry Conway mined the stories of the 1930s, '40s and '50s to breathe new life into many forgotten members of the Dark Knight's Rogues Gallery. Pitting Batman against the likes of Dr. Death, the Monk, and Hugo Strange, reinvigorated the title—especially when Vicki Vale returned to Bruce Wayne's life. She became a love interest for the hero once again, and future competition for Catwoman and Julia Pennyworth, Alfred's daughter. All the while, the Batman titles were growing more and more interconnected, creating a very streamlined final product fueled by interesting subplots.

TOSSING A NEW DAGGER
Batman #343 ● Unrelated to the original Dagger from *Detective Comics* #174 (August 1951), a new villain emerged boasting the same name in this issue by writer Gerry Conway and artist Gene Colan. Batman first encountered this purple and orange clad villain when Dagger crashed a semitruck with a single knife-throw, and then did the same to the Batmobile. However, Batman ended Dagger's would-be protection racket before he could get it off the ground, discovering that the villain was the owner of the failing blade manufacturer, Rennington Steel.

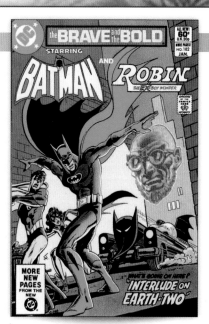

THE DYNAMIC DUO?
The Brave and the Bold #182 ● The Batman of Earth-One found himself in a familiar, yet very different Gotham City when he was suddenly transported to Earth-Two during a lightning storm. In a world where Bruce Wayne had died in the not-too-distant past, Batman teamed up with an adult Robin to defeat a horribly disfigured Hugo Strange. Writer Alan Brennert and artist Jim Aparo pulled out all the stops to please fans of the Golden Age in this memorable tale, even granting cameos to the Batmobile of the 1940s and Catwoman's Pantherjet.

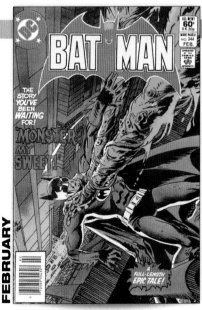

FEBRUARY

MARCH

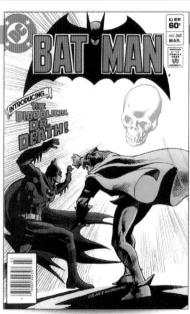

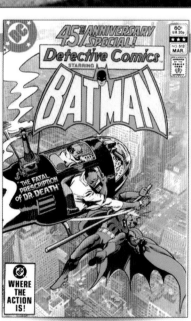

HAPPY AND UNHAPPY RETURNS

Batman #344 ▪ Poison Ivy was back in this issue written by Gerry Conway and pencilled by Gene Colan, but she wasn't the most important woman from Batman's past to resurface. That honor would go to photographer Vicki Vale, who hadn't been glimpsed in Gotham City since *Batman Family* #11 (May–June 1977) Vicki's return to the *Batman* comic helped keep Bruce's romantic life interesting, while Poison Ivy helped keep Batman's world lively. Ivy attempted to wipe out the Wayne Foundation, using a human/plant hybrid monster, but failed.

UNCLE BATMAN

The Brave and the Bold #184 ▪ Helena Wayne, the Huntress (the daughter of Batman's Earth-Two counterpart), arrived on Earth-One to spend Christmas with her "Uncle Bruce" in this tale by writer Mike W. Barr and artist Jim Aparo. However, their holiday was nearly ruined when the Dark Knight found evidence that seemed to point to his late father having bankrolled a notorious Gotham City criminal for his own profit. With the Huntress's help, Batman discovered the real Grinch in this tale was Thomas Wayne's old accountant, Amos Randolph.

DEATH RETURNS

Batman #345 ▪ Following the invention of Earth-Two, Batman's reality began to change. His adventures from the 1930s through the very early 1960s were now said to have occurred on Earth-Two, leaving more modern tales as the basis for the current Batman's adventures on Earth-One. While a bit confusing for some, this concept allowed writer Gerry Conway and artist Gene Colan to reintroduce Golden Age villain Dr. Death aka Dr. Karl Hellfern, seemingly for the first time. Batman and Robin were left in a cliffhanger engineered by this evil chemical expert.

BATMAN TURNS 45

Detective Comics #512 ▪ Writer Gerry Conway and penciller Gene Colan picked up where they left off in this month's *Batman* issue—with Batman and Robin dangling from a bridge, facing death. As this special anniversary issue continued—celebrating *Detective Comics*' 45 years of continued publication —death would prove quite literal in the form of Dr. Death, who had sprinkled a super-allergen dust over Gotham City in an attempt to blackmail it for the antidote. The Dynamic Duo escaped, leaving Batman free to procure the antidote from Dr. Death.

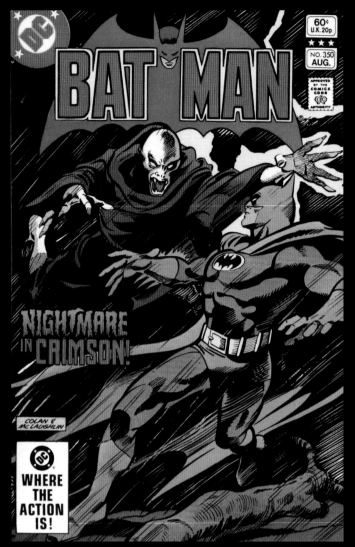

THE CURSE OF THE VAMPIRI

BATMAN #350

In the story "Nightmare in Crimson," Batman faced the vampiric threat of the Monk, a reimagined Golden Age foe who had originally appeared 43 years previously in *Detective* #32 (October 1939).

In this issue by writers Gerry Conway and Paul Levitz and penciller Gene Colan, Batman had become suspicious of his partner's new relationship with the mysterious Dala (which had occurred in February's *Detective Comics* #511). He discovered that she was a vampire lackey of the Monk and had Robin under her hypnotic spell. The Dark Knight's investigation would lead to a bite from the Monk himself, and the start of Batman's transformation into a "vampiri."

As the story continued in August's *Detective Comics* #517, the Monk was revealed to be a cursed plantation owner from the Civil War era named Louis Dubois. It wasn't until September's *Batman* #351 that the Caped Crusader was able to locate the Monk and create a cure for his vampirism with the monster's own blood.

Batman #350 also contained a new Catwoman back-up story, "Those Lips, Those Eyes," by writer Bruce Jones and artist Tony DeZuniga.

FIRST BITE
While there was no indication that they had met before this particular tale, the Golden Age villain, the Monk, had been one of Batman's first foes when he debuted in 1939. This reimagined version quickly got his teeth into the hero.

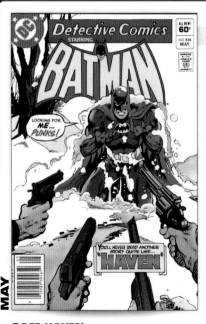

SAFE HAVEN

***Detective Comics* #514** ▪ Following a high-speed chase with Maxie Zeus in woods north of Gotham City, Batman was forced off the icy road into a snow-filled gorge. In this classic tale by writer Len Wein and illustrator Don Newton, Batman was rescued by a burly man named Haven who lived in a modest cabin. Maxie Zeus broke into Haven's home and his men gunned down the peaceful man. Batman defeated Zeus and his thugs, and laid Haven to rest. Also in this issue, Batgirl met new member of her own Rogues Gallery, Lady Viper.

BACK TO THE BATCAVE

***Batman* #348** ▪ Batman and Robin had been through a lot of changes lately. Dick Grayson had dropped out of college, and Bruce Wayne had given up his duties as head of Wayne Enterprises. It was back to the old status quo for Batman and Robin, and there was no better place to do that than Wayne Manor. In this issue written by Gerry Conway and pencilled by Gene Colan, the Dynamic Duo returned to their original Batcave, only to find a visitor waiting for them in the form of Man-Bat. Also in this issue, Catwoman starred in another back-up tale.

SHOT ON TARGET

***Detective Comics* #518** ▪ When crime boss Rupert Thorne learned about Vicki Vale's theory that Bruce Wayne and Batman were the same man, he hired Deadshot to assassinate Wayne in this tale by Gerry Conway and Paul Levitz, drawn by Don Newton. Luckily, Alfred had hired Christopher Chance, the Human Target, to impersonate Bruce following Batman's transformation into a vampiri. "Bruce Wayne" and Batman appeared in the same place at the same time (thereby debunking Vicki Vale's theory) and Batman was able to defeat Deadshot.

A BLIMP ON THE RADAR

***Batman* #352** ▪ Writer Gerry Conway, scripter Paul Kupperberg, and artist Don Newton introduced a new villain to the killer skies in the form of Colonel Blimp. While he piloted a zeppelin armed with a magnet powerful enough to pluck a submarine out of the ocean, the villain's name wasn't exactly one that struck fear into the heart of the readership. The Colonel did, however, give Batman the runaround, and Batman wasn't able to defeat Blimp until part two of the story in *Detective Comics* #519. That issue also saw a brief new costume for Robin—a snowsuit.

BETRAYAL
As if feeling the bite of a vampiri wasn't enough, Batman was soon dealt a blow to the head from a mysterious figure off panel. As Batman discovered his assailant was Robin in *Batman* #350's dramatic finale, he gave a wolf-like scream.

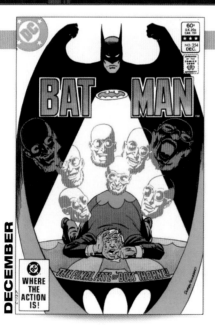

BLACKWING BEGINS
Wonder Woman #297 ● The inspiration for the Batman Incorporated hero Batwing, who would debut in *Batman Inc.* #5 (May 2011), made his first costumed appearance in the Huntress back-up tale of this issue. Based in Huntress's reality of Earth-Two, Blackwing was one of Helena Wayne's co-workers named Charles Bullock, who first appeared in *Wonder Woman* #281 (July 1981). In this story by Joey Cavalieri with art by Joe Staton, Charles, inspired by Batman, wore similar blue threads and set out to fight injustice, but required a timely rescue by Huntress.

THE STRANGE FALL OF THORNE
Batman #354 ● In this thriller by writer Gerry Conway and penciller Don Newton, crime boss Rupert Thorne discovered that he had been "haunted" by the ghost of his enemy, Hugo Strange, via a sophisticated hologram system. Thorne blamed the manipulation on Commissioner Peter Pauling (whom he had put in office), and shot him, receiving a non-fatal bullet wound of his own. Thorne was apprehended by the Dark Knight and survived to see the inside of a jail cell, but Pauling did not. Through it all, Hugo Strange, very much alive, looked on, enjoying his revenge.

BREAKING ANNUAL TRADITION
Batman Annual #8 ● Ever since their inception, Batman's annuals had been reserved for reprints of his more eye-catching stories. But for this annual, DC Comics decided to switch to all-new material. The result was the longest single Batman story ever published to date, a 42-page blockbuster written by Mike W. Barr and illustrated by Trevor Von Eeden. When a mysterious figure calling himself the Messiah of the Crimson Son threatened to destroy Gotham City, Batman began to investigate. He discovered that this new villain was really his old enemy, Rä's al Ghūl.

ALSO THIS YEAR

January—*DC Comics Presents* #41: When villain the Prankster double-crossed fellow-villain the Joker during a treasure hunt, the Clown Prince of Crime was forced to team up with Superman.

April—*Detective Comics* #513: Batman tried on a makeshift Two-Face mask to mess with Harvey Dent's already fractured mind in this issue by writer Gerry Conway and artist Don Newton.

October—*Justice League of America* #207: The Justice League of America joined forces with the All-Star Squadron with part one of the five-part "Crisis on Earth-Prime!" starring the Huntress, among other characters.

NOVEMBER

DECEMBER

143

CROCODILE KILLER
DETECTIVE COMICS #523

Lurking in the shadows was a new, major threat to Gotham City and Batman: a cunning villain with a green, scaly skin who would call himself Killer Croc.

The main story, "Inferno," in this issue by writer Gerry Conway and penciller Gene Colan, revolved around a fight between Batman and Solomon Grundy, that brought Grundy firmly into the ranks of Batman's Rogues Gallery. However, perhaps the most intriguing attraction was a new character, here called only Croc, who spent a short cameo on page six skulking in the shadows. Croc would remain mostly out of sight in this month's *Batman* issue as well, but his true face would finally be shown in *Detective Comics* #524 (March). In that issue, it would become apparent that Croc's skin was covered in green, alligator-like scales, he possessed a devious, criminal mind, and harbored a lust for power. Croc was destined to become a power player in Gotham City, a role he cemented when he murdered the crime boss known as the Squid with a sniper rifle. Soon he would be known as one of the fiercest and most animalistic villains Batman ever faced, adopting the name Killer Croc.

CLOAKED CROC
While he kept to the shadows, Killer Croc was busy making plans to take over Gotham City. In his first appearance, he spoke with a man he had recruited, who had upset him by working with the unpredictable Solomon Grundy.

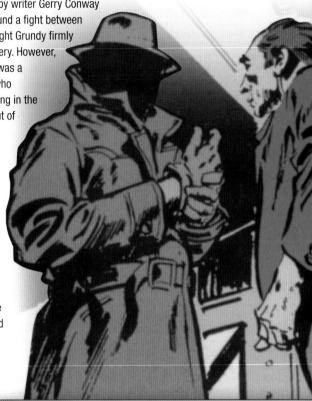

1983

"A buncha outsiders like us? It might work... but we could use a name!"

Metamorpho, *Batman and the Outsiders* #2

1983 ushered in plenty of important new characters to the Batman mythos. From the threat posed by Killer Croc, the Night-Slayer, and Nocturna, to the heroic figures of Geo-Force, Halo, and Katana as members of Batman's new Super Hero team, the Outsiders, the year had plenty of surprises in store for readers. But none of these debuts was as important as the introduction of young circus phenomenon Jason Todd in the pages of *Batman* #357 (March 1983). Jason would soon prove to be Dick Grayson's successor as Robin, and Batman's newest partner against crime.

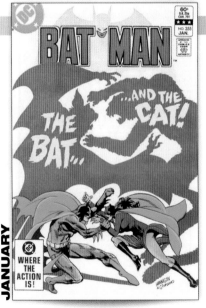

CATTY REACTION
Batman #355 • This issue by writer Gerry Conway and Don Newton shed more light on Batman and Catwoman's longstanding flirtation. When Bruce was driving Vicki home after a date, his car was run off the road by Catwoman's newest Kitty Car. Narrowly saving his life and Vicki's, Batman tracked down Selina. In the ensuing fight, Catwoman spared Batman's life, calling him "Bruce" during the scuffle—thus revealing that she knew the hero's double identity. Also in this issue, Mayor Hamilton Hill restored James Gordon as police commissioner.

COURTING CATWOMAN
The Brave and the Bold #197 • The romance between the Earth-Two Batman and Catwoman was examined in this tale by writer Alan Brennert and penciller Joe Staton. Bruce Wayne was attending a wedding when Scarecrow arrived and gave Bruce a dose of fear gas. This caused him to believe that Batwoman, Robin, Alfred, and Superman had faded away. With no allies, Batman sprang Catwoman out of jail. They tracked down the Scarecrow and on the way learned each other's pasts. They even removed their masks and revealed their mutual feelings.

A BOY NAMED JASON
BATMAN #357

When first introduced, Jason Todd seemed little more than an extra in the Dark Knight's world. But longtime readers might have guessed that history was about to repeat itself…

DÉJÀ VU… AGAIN
Dick Grayson was taking a trip down memory lane when he went to the circus with his old clown friend, Waldo. He was struck by familiar smells like sawdust and cotton candy, but couldn't help but feel a chill run down his spine when he saw the Flying Todds.

This issue, written by Gerry Conway and pencilled by Don Newton, mostly concentrated on the rise to power of Gotham City's newest crime boss, the Squid. However it is best remembered for the brief debut of Jason Todd, destined to be one of *Batman*'s most important characters.

Dick Grayson had grown up. Now leading his own team of Teen Titans, it was becoming clear that serving as Robin was making less and less sense for the adult hero. DC Comics realized that it was time to introduce a replacement. To do so, they returned to the same well that had made Dick such a success in the first place: the circus.

So when Dick visited his friend Waldo the clown at the circus, readers were introduced to an act called the Flying Todds. A family of acrobats, the Todds had a young son, a red-headed phenomenon named Jason. Reminiscent of Dick's circus act, the Flying Graysons, the Todds also belonged to a circus that was being pressured by the local mob, led by up-and-comer Killer Croc. Readers were left wondering if a new, younger partner was in the cards for Batman, and if a similar grisly fate awaited the Todds as had befallen the Graysons.

THE TRAGEDY OF THE TODDS
Detective Comics #526 ■ Killer Croc had been climbing the ranks of Gotham City's underworld, intent on becoming the city's new king of crime. While Batman hunted the Croc, Dick Grayson enlisted the help of the Flying Todds, a circus act whose livelihood was threatened by the villain's protection scheme. This issue by writer Gerry Conway and artist Don Newton served as the finale to Conway's long tenure on *Batman* and *Detective Comics*. To celebrate Batman's 500th appearance in *Detective Comics*, nearly every major member of Batman's Rogues Gallery guest-starred as Killer Croc plotted to kill Batman. While Batman, Robin, Batgirl, Talia, and Catwoman foiled the murder attempt, the Todds ended up as food for Killer Croc's pet crocodiles. In the midst of this tragedy, young Jason Todd took refuge at Wayne Manor. Knowing he was in trouble anyway, he donned a Robin costume and stowed away in the Batmobile, emerging to help Batman defeat Killer Croc.

DAWN OF A DUO
Bravely coping with the death of his parents, Jason seemed to take to the idea of living in Wayne Manor at the story's end. Batman would soon, once again, have a young partner.

THE SAVAGE SKULL STRIKES
Batman #360 ■ *Batman* and *Detective Comics* had evolved into a continuing saga, with subplots and even main storylines carrying over through both titles. So when Gerry Conway parted ways with the Caped Crusader, a new regular writer was needed to handle both titles. That honor fell to Doug Moench who would begin his first of two long tenures with this issue drawn by regular artist Don Newton. Moench's first issue was a stand-alone tale that introduced readers to a new Batman villain, the cop-killing slasher calling himself the Savage Skull.

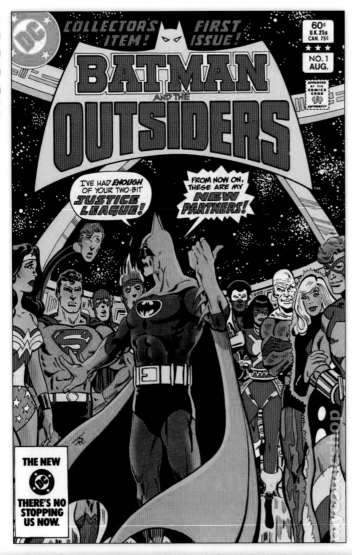

INSIDE THE OUTSIDERS
BATMAN AND THE OUTSIDERS #1

The cover alone was enough to make the title a hit. In dramatic fashion, Batman was quitting the fabled Justice League of America to join a new ragtag group of Super Heroes calling themselves the Outsiders.

Writer Mike W. Barr and artist Jim Aparo were about to launch Batman into a new phase of his career. When Bruce Wayne's loyal C.E.O., Lucius Fox, went missing during a business trip to the country of Markovia, Batman appealed to the Justice League for help. But due to the politics surrounding Markovia's ongoing violent revolution, the JLA decided not to interfere. Infuriated by the team's decision, Batman resigned from the League, and employed hero Black Lightning to help him track down Fox.

Batman soon found himself teaming with a female samurai called Katana, longtime hero Metamorpho, the Earth-powered prince of Markovia dubbed Geo-Force, and a mysterious teenage girl possessing powerful color auras, whom Batman named Halo. Together, they battled the corrupt forces of the revolution's leader, Baron Bedlam, ultimately saving Lucius and Markovia.

By issue #3, Batman had set up his new Super Hero team in the abandoned Batcave below the Wayne Foundation Building in the heart of Gotham City. They proved their worth as they defeated new super-villain Agent Orange and, in the following issue, One-Man Meltdown (formerly the Cyclotronic Man and, before that, Bag O'Bones). However, it was issue #5 that really cemented the team's place as a major DC institution when the title crossed over with *The New Teen Titans* issue #37 (December 1983) in a two-part tale that saw Batman and Robin finally coming to terms with one another as equals.

QUITTING THE LEAGUE
Batman believed that his allies in the Justice League had become his friends. Yet when they refused to bend the rules to help out one of Bruce Wayne's most loyal employees, Batman decided that he had no place in the institution that the JLA had become.

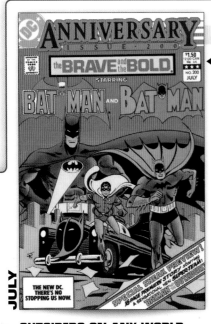

OUTSIDERS ON ANY WORLD
***The Brave and the Bold* #200** ● Batman's time in *The Brave and the Bold* came to a close with this final issue, but his team-up adventures were just beginning. This oversized issue by writer Mike W. Barr and artist Dave Gibbons also featured a sneak peek of Batman's new ongoing title by Barr and artist Jim Aparo, *Batman and the Outsiders*. In the issue's main story, a new Earth-Two super-villain called Brimstone awoke from a coma to discover that the Caped Crusader of his world had died, so he transferred his mind into his Earth-One counterpart to battle Batman.

SPECIAL FEATURE

THE OUTSIDERS IN ACTION

The Brave and the Bold #200 served as the first appearance of the Outsiders, despite the fact that the team was already fully formed during this initial story. Katana, Geo-Force, and Halo all appeared for the first time in this tale that showcased Katana's martial arts skills as well as the powers of her heroic teammates.

FILLING THE VOID
***World's Finest Comics* #293** ● After dealing with the threat of Anthrax in the previous issue, Batman and Superman met two more new challengers—Null and Void—in this tale written by David Anthony Kraft and pencilled by Adrian Gonzales. Null and Void were seasoned criminals whose powers activated when they touched each other's palms: Null could negate light and sound, while Void could teleport items through his form. The duo planned one last heist, but Superman and Batman caught Void red-handed, while Null escaped.

NOCTURNAL NIGHTMARES
***Detective Comics* #529** ● A new Gotham City femme fatale debuted in this issue, alongside her tormented admirer. Writer Doug Moench and artist Gene Colan introduced readers to the Thief of the Night (later called the Night-Slayer), a shadowy burglar who would play a major role in Batman's life. Readers also caught their first glimpse of Nocturna, an astronomer on Wayne's payroll named Natasha Knight, whose skin was bleached white following a laser accident. Nocturna would become an integral part of Moench's first tenure on the *Batman* titles.

BARON BEDLAM
The corrupt leader of the revolution in Markovia, Baron Bedlam was defeated by Batman and the Outsiders. Geo-Force threw Bedlam to the angry populace and let them decide the rebel's fate.

ROBIN TAKES FLIGHT
Batman #366 ▪ Jason Todd first wore Dick Grayson's classic costume in this issue by writer Doug Moench and penciller Don Newton. In Guatemala, Batman found himself staring down the barrel of the Joker's machine gun. Luckily, Robin swooped in to save the day, and delivered a swift kick to the Joker, setting up the villain for defeat. Despite having dyed his hair black to match Grayson's and donning a Robin costume he'd found in Dick's closet, Jason was scolded by the Dark Knight for having the audacity to wear the uniform of a true hero.

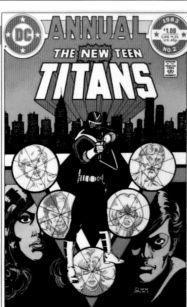

THE SMILE OF CHESHIRE
The New Teen Titans Annual #2 ▪ While she wouldn't go on to become a major member of Batman's Rogues Gallery, the newest villain to debut in the pages of *The New Teen Titans* would become a repeated thorn in the sides of Barbara Gordon's future team, the Birds of Prey. The murderer in question was named Cheshire. In this tale by writer Marv Wolfman, co-plotter and layout artist George Perez, and finisher Pablo Marcos, Cheshire showed off her penchant for poisons and toxins, and held her own against powerhouses Starfire and Kid Flash.

SPECIAL FEATURE

CHESHIRE
A deadly murderer, Cheshire would have a romance with Green Arrow's sidekick Speedy before becoming a founding member of the Ravens, a group of female criminals that often clashed with Black Canary and Oracle.

ALSO THIS YEAR

April—*Captain Carrot and his Amazing Zoo Crew!* #14: Batmouse debuted as a member of Earth-C Minus's JLA: the Just'a Lotta Animals.

August—*Batman* #362: The Riddler's origin story was reexamined for a more modern audience.

October—*Justice League of America* #119: Black Canary's origin was revised, revealing that she was the daughter of the crime-fighting heroine of the same name.

BATMOUSE

DECEMBER

147

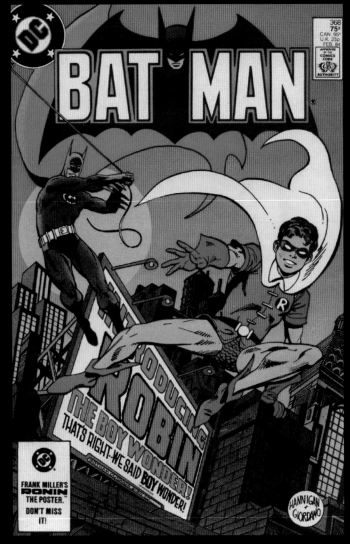

THE SECOND SIDEKICK
BATMAN #368

From this issue's first page, it was clear that Jason Todd had passed his baptism of fire and earned his place fighting by Batman's side. All he needed was a crime-fighting name.

The coveted title of Robin still belonged to Dick Grayson, but with a cover that trumpeted the return of "Robin the Boy Wonder," this issue by writer Doug Moench and artist Don Newton promised to be a historic moment in the Dark Knight Detective's career.

When it came to claiming the title of Robin for his own, luck turned out to be on Jason Todd's side. While Crazy Quilt was plotting the death of his archenemy Robin in a deserted warehouse somewhere in Gotham City, Dick Grayson paid a visit to the Batcave to hand over his mantle and costume. Dick wanted to become his own man, and he could think of no better successor than Jason Todd. Delighted, Jason changed out of the makeshift uniform he had put together in *Detective* #526 (May 1983) and officially became Batman's young partner as Robin, the Boy Wonder.

Jason Todd served faithfully as the new Robin until his untimely death years later at the hands of the cruel and sadistic Joker in *Batman* #428 (December 1988). Todd returned almost two decades later in the "Hush" storyline.

RITE OF PASSAGE
Dick Grayson presented Jason Todd with the original Robin costume that he had worn during his time as Batman's sidekick. Over the years the costume would undergo several redesigns.

1984

"I've come to pass on the mantle of Robin. Take it, Jason. You've earned it."

Dick Grayson, *Batman* #368

Team books became a major factor in Batman's life, with his own strike force, the Outsiders, proving a hit with readers. Robin's team title, *The New Teen Titans*, received a major boost in the form of the "The Judas Contract" event, and the book branched out into two separate titles. The direct market of the comic book store was becoming increasingly important. It enabled DC Comics to experiment with page count and utilize better-quality paper—something they couldn't do with subscriptions or newsstand editions. New printing paper enabled artwork to "pop" more than ever, literally signaling a brighter future for the DC Universe.

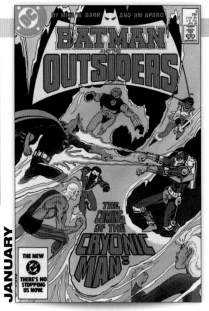

THE CRYONIC MAN COMETH
Batman and the Outsiders #6 ▪ The Outsiders found themselves up against the Cryonic Man, who debuted in this issue by writer Mike W. Barr and artist Jim Aparo. Able to project gases that could freeze victims instantly, the Cryonic Man proved a challenge for the fledgling team. He wasn't stopped until the following issue, when he tried to kidnap Katana and transfer her organs to his dying love. Meanwhile, in their civilian identities, Katana and Black Lightning began new jobs as the manager of a Japanese bookstore and an English teacher.

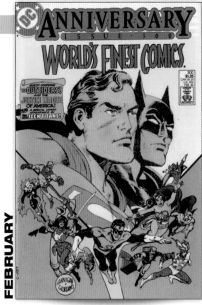

THREE HUNDRED OF THE FINEST
World's Finest Comics #300 ▪ In an oversized $1.25 issue, writers David Anthony Kraft and Mike W. Barr served up a tribute to the Superman/Batman team, with the help of artists Ross Andru, Mark Texiera, and Sal Amendola. Guest-starring the Justice League, Sgt. Rock, and the Outsiders, this issue also featured a cameo by the New Teen Titans supplied by writer Marv Wolfman and artist George Pérez. When earthquakes struck Earth's major cities, Superman and Batman discovered the cause—a cosmic being named Zeta and his connection to the Cosmic Tree.

ROBIN NO MORE

The New Teen Titans #39 ▪ On the cusp of the earth-shattering "The Judas Contract," which would begin in *Tales of the Teen Titans* #42 (May 1984), writer Marv Wolfman and artist George Pérez were shaking up the world of the Teen Titans. First Kid Flash decided to retire from the Super Hero life. Then, no longer happy in the role he had begun playing aged just eight, Robin announced that he was also retiring. He declared that he was simply Dick Grayson for now. He would not return as Titans' field leader until he had decided his place in the world.

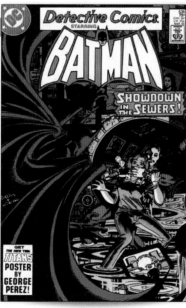

THE DOCTOR IS IN

Detective Comics #536 ▪ In this issue, writer Doug Moench and artist Don Newton introduced the threat of Dr. Fang, a former boxer with a set of teeth that would put Dracula to shame. He wouldn't encounter Batman and Robin until *Batman* #370 (April 1984), but Dr. Fang would prove just as intimidating as his name implied. Fang's spooky caped appearance alone was enough to give fledgling Robin Jason Todd a nasty fright, making the mysterious villain's escape from his first encounter with the Dynamic Duo all too easy.

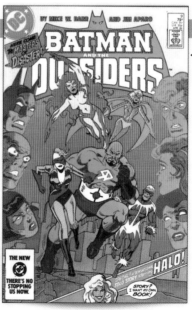

THE MASTERS OF DISASTER

Batman and the Outsiders #9 ▪ Their leader, the water-powered New-Wave, had debuted in the previous issue; now the Masters of Disaster sealed their reputation as the Outsiders' greatest foes in this two-part tale by Mike W. Barr and Jim Aparo. This formidable team of villains, which would return several times, was made up of New-Wave, hot-temperatured Heatstroke, cold-generating Coldsnap, earth-moving Shakedown, and air-manipulating Windfall. This issue also marked the first appearance of Geo-Force's future wife, Denise Howard.

ENTER DENISE

When Brion Markov went to register for graduate school and became lost, a kind young woman named Denise Howard helped him, and the two struck up an instant friendship. That friendship soon blossomed into romance, and it was not too long before the pair married.

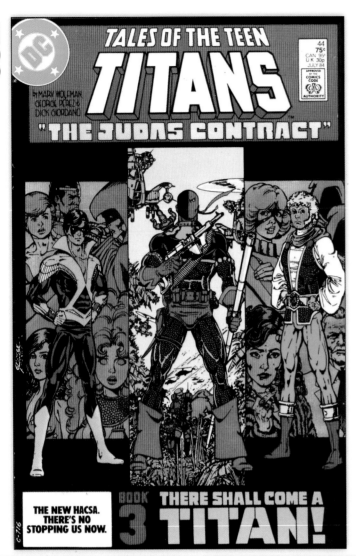

THE NEW HACSA.
THERE'S NO
STOPPING US NOW.

BOOK 3

THERE SHALL COME A
TITAN!

NAMING NIGHTWING

TALES OF THE TEEN TITANS #44

In an epic to end all Teen Titans epics, Dick Grayson adopted a new name and costume, an identity that would finally establish him as his own man in the DC Universe.

The story that gave Dick Grayson a new crime-fighting persona was the four-part "The Judas Contract," by writer Marv Wolfman and artist George Pérez, beginning in *Tales of the Teen Titans* #42 (May 1984). The tale revolved around Titans member Terra's betrayal of the team.

A double agent working for Deathstroke the Terminator, Terra's treachery became apparent when the Titans began to disappear one by one while in their supposedly secret civilian identities. Terra revealed her true colors when she attacked Raven and gave Deathstroke the information he needed to defeat Starfire, Wonder Girl, Changeling, and Cyborg. She thus fulfilled the contract that Deathstroke's son, the Ravager, was never able to complete.

Knowing that the Titans needed him, Dick donned a new costume, inspired by Batman, and another of his childhood heroes, Superman. He even adopted a crime-fighting name from Superman's Kryptonian heritage, calling himself Nightwing. Dick teamed up with another son of Deathstroke's, a hero called Jericho, and the two took the fight to Deathstroke's door in Book 4 of the story, in the pages of July's *Tales of the Teen Titans Annual* #3. Clad in a snowsuit version of his new uniform, Nightwing rescued his teammates with the help of Jericho in a fight that Terra would be unable to walk away from.

MATURITY
Dick's Nightwing costume was the polar opposite of his old, brightly colored Robin outfit. In shades of blue with yellow highlights, the dramatic and bold costume signified Grayson's new maturity as a Super Hero in his own right.

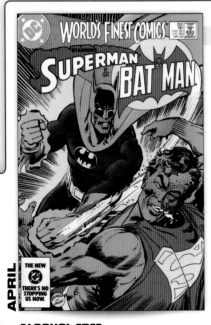

ALCOHOL FREE
World's Finest Comics #302 ● While Superman and Batman slugged it out in this issue's main story, written by Cary Bates and pencilled by Neal Adams, it was the back-up tale by writer David Anthony Kraft and artist David Mazzucchelli that stole the show. A rare early example of Mazzucchelli's Batman before his ground-breaking "Batman: Year One" story in February 1987, this tale featured Superman and Batman doing something quite out of the ordinary for the duo: having a drink at a local bar (even if that drink was just a tall glass of milk).

THE MAN BEHIND THE BAT
Batman and the Outsiders #13 ● At the end of this title's previous story, Batman was poisoned by a blow dart. In this one-year-anniversary issue written by Mike W. Barr and pencilled by Dan Day, the team had to keep the near-delirious hero on his feet to work the poison through his system. The Outsiders achieved this by tricking Batman into reliving his tragic origin. When the scenario was interrupted by new villain Mayme, Batman sprang into action, cheating death. Batman then unmasked himself, proving his loyalty to the Outsiders.

SPECIAL FEATURE

REVELATION
After the Outsiders risked their lives to save him from a deadly toxin, Batman rewarded the team by revealing his true identity to them. In a surprising gesture of camaraderie, Batman pulled back his cowl and acknowledged that he was the handsome millionaire Bruce Wayne.

THE NEW, NEW TEEN TITANS
The New Teen Titans #1 ● The advent of the direct market and comic book stores freed DC Comics to experiment with limited series and with vibrant white Baxter paper. The company relaunched *The New Teen Titans* in this deluxe format. Still in traditional newsprint, *Tales of the Teen Titans* began reprinting the Baxter title, allowing fans to follow Titans' adventures no matter where they shopped. It was clear that the Titans' popularity would continue apace, enhanced by the bright colors only possible in this upgraded format.

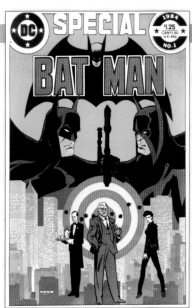

FEAR HIS WRATH
Batman Special #1 ▪ Writer Mike W. Barr and artist Michael Golden teamed up on this issue, which introduced the Wrath, essentially Batman's equal and opposite. The Wrath's criminal parents had been shot dead 25 years ago by a young beat cop named James W. Gordon. Clad in a costume similar to Batman's, the Wrath hunted Gordon, only to have his attempts on the commissioner's life foiled by the Dark Knight. Having kidnapped Leslie Thompkins, hoping to trade her life for Gordon's, the Wrath plummeted to his death during a fight with Batman.

SPECIAL FEATURE

BLIND RAGE
After the Wrath seemingly succeeded in killing Commissioner Gordon, he was enraged to discover that Batman helped stage Gordon's phony death with the use of a bulletproof vest. Channeling the full force of his fury, the Wrath fought the Dark Knight before falling off a large building.

PATRIOTS ACT
Batman and the Outsiders Annual #1
The Outsiders were having a busy year. While facing Maxie Zeus and his New Olympians in the pages of *Batman and the Outsiders*, they were fighting the Force of July zealots, including Major Victory, Lady Liberty, Mayflower, Silent Majority, and Sparkler in this special by writer Mike W. Barr and pencillers Jerome Moore, Alex Saviuk, Jan Duursema, and Rick Hoberg. The same issue debuted a costume change for Geo-Force who swapped his brown and tan uniform for the green and gold colors of the Markovian flag.

ALSO THIS YEAR

April—*Infinity Inc.* #1: This issue not only told the backstory of the next generation of Earth-Two heroes, it also saw Huntress and Power Girl leaving the JSA in a huff.

July—*Super Powers* #1: Toy company Kenner Products released a popular line of DC Super Hero and super-villain action figures called the Super Powers Collection, featuring many characters from Batman's world. Each figure was accompanied by a mini comic book. This issue provided a related five-issue regular-size miniseries.

November—*Wonder Woman* #321: Huntress starred in her final back-up tale titled "The Final Blackout."

December—*Man-Bat vs. Batman Special* #1: Three of Man-Bat's earliest battles with Batman from *Detective Comics* #400, #402, and #407 were reprinted on better paper in this special.

December—*World's Finest Comics* #310: Batman and Superman met a new hero in the form of Sonik.

BATMAN'S WORLD IN CRISIS

CRISIS ON INFINITE EARTHS #1

Virtually every significant DC Comics character was involved in *Crisis on Infinite Earths*. A number of them would cease to exist altogether as DC Comics replaced the concept of the Multiverse with a single, simpler continuity.

1985 was the 50th anniversary of DC Comics, and Executive Editor Dick Giordano was keen to honor that occasion with a major celebration. Besides the massive *Who's Who* project that would attempt to catalog every major character in the company's history, writer Marv Wolfman was employed to help streamline the complex various realities of the DC Universe into one succinct timeline.

Under Wolfman's eye, the project grew in scale and scope, tying into most of DC Comics' line and making it the largest crossover ever for the company. With a cast that included nearly every major DC Comics character and featuring beautiful, detailed artwork by George Pérez, the 12-issue series served as a fitting tribute to DC Comics, as heroes of many worlds attempted to battle the cosmic threat of the Anti-Monitor.

DEMISE OF THE FLASH
When Barry Allen appeared before Batman to warn him about the dying multiverse, he was shot by the Joker. With his last breath, the Flash implored Batman to save his loved ones before it was too late. With that, Allen disintegrated in front of a shocked Batman.

1985

"He said the Earth was dying. That's what the Flash said. What's going on here?"

Batman, *Crisis on Infinite Earths #2*

DC Comics was celebrating 50 years of publishing comics, and they weren't about to let that milestone pass without commemorating it in a large-scale fashion. Leading the celebratory projects was *Crisis on Infinite Earths*, a 12-issue maxiseries that, seemingly accidentally, created the blueprint for future company-wide crossover events. Batman and his supporting cast soon found themselves guest-starring in a variety of titles as nearly every Super Hero in DC Comics' long history teamed up to fight for the common good. It was an exciting time to be a DC Comics fan, and the continuity ramifications of *Crisis on Infinite Earths* would be felt for years to come.

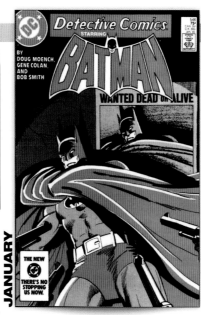

ONYX'S ORIGIN

Detective Comics #546 • The lead story by writer Doug Moench and artist Gene Colan featured Gotham City's Mayor Hamilton Hill and the Night-Slayer. However, it was the Green Arrow back-up tale—a regular feature in *Detective Comics* since issue #521 (December 1982)—that made this issue memorable. Written by Joey Cavalieri and pencilled by Jerome Moore, the story introduced readers to Onyx, a female vigilante who became a major player in Green Arrow's world, and a member of Batman's supporting cast in the 2000s.

THE GHOST OF THE BATMAN

America vs. the Justice Society #1
On Earth-Two, Batman seemed to be haunting the Justice Society from beyond the grave, with help from writer Roy Thomas, co-plotter Dann Thomas, and penciller Rafael Kayanan. Batman's diary had accused the JSA of aiding Hitler during World War II. When Clark Kent's paper, *The Daily Star*, printed the story, Superman surrendered to the authorities, despite knowing that the diary was full of untruths. As the four-issue series continued, Robin and Huntress helped to exonerate the JSA.

AUGUST

DONNING THE BLACK MASK
BATMAN #386

In this issue, Gotham City crimelord Black Mask, leader of the False Face Society gang and one of the most fearsome villains in Batman's world, made his murderous bow.

INITIATION
To join Black Mask's twisted False Face Society, his lackeys had to take masks designated to them out of the now empty ebony coffin that used to contain Roman's mother. Black Mask believed these disguises held "spirit power."

Writer Doug Moench and artist Tom Mandrake would make an important contribution to the Batman mythos with the villain Black Mask. This issue not only debuted the twisted gangster, but detailed his origin as well. Born into a wealthy Gotham City family, Roman Sionis's twisted nature gradually manifested itself. As an adult, he angered his parents by dating a model named Circe. To get his revenge, he burned the family house down, killing his parents and gaining control of their company, Janus Cosmetics. Sionis soon drove the company to the verge of collapse, but was saved by a bailout from the Wayne Foundation. Obsessed with masks, and driven past the edge of sanity, Roman carved an ebony shard from his mother's casket into a mask and started a criminal empire that targeted the man he blamed for his misfortune: Bruce Wayne.

FEBRUARY

THE OTHER DARK KNIGHT
Batman #380 ▪ Anton Knight was obsessed with his adopted sister, Natalia (Natasha) Knight, alias Nocturna. His obsession changed him from the Thief of the Night into the Night-Slayer. Nocturna shot Anton, choosing Batman over him, but the Night-Slayer clung to life. In this issue by writer Doug Moench and new series penciller Rick Hoberg, Anton took revenge. He defeated Batman and convinced an amnesiac Dark Knight that *he* was the true Night-Slayer (until the next issue). Dr. Fang caught a stray bullet during the fight and was killed.

MARCH

DARKWOLF RISES
Detective Comics #548 ▪ While he wasn't destined to become one of Batman's greatest adversaries, new villain Darkwolf gave it his best shot. In a story written by Doug Moench and illustrated by *Detective Comics*' new penciller, Pat Broderick, the terrorist Darkwolf took a room full of people hostage at the Egyptian Embassy. A clash with Batman forced him to flee the scene. This issue also continued the interesting love triangle involving Batman, Vicki Vale, and Alfred's daughter, Julia Remarque, recently hired at *Picture News*.

DOUBLE IDENTITY
Superman #405 ▪ Clark Kent donned a Batman cowl along with his Superman costume in this story by writer Craig Boldman and penciller Alex Saviuk. When Kent was visiting the father of his childhood friend Lana Lang at a museum, Lana accidentally played the Syrinx of Arcadia, pipes that only Superman's ears could hear. As a result, Clark sprouted horns where the "ears" on Batman's cowl were located. Superman borrowed the Dark Knight's look for a bit until he could find a cure for this magical affliction.

APRIL

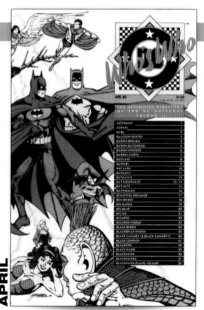

WHO'S BATMAN?
Who's Who: The Definitive Directory of the DC Universe #2 ▪ Begun in March, Who's Who was a 26-issue maxiseries with all-new artwork and detailed histories. An A-Z encyclopedia of DC Comics characters, *Who's Who*'s had a large staff that varied from issue to issue. Under the helm of writer/editor Len Wein, issue #2 from Automan to the Blackhawks, included entries on Earth-One and Earth-Two Batman, Bat-Mite, and Batwoman. *Who's Who* spun off into two updates, in 1987 and in 1988, and was published in a loose-leaf format in 1990.

153

TRAPPED IN A FANTASY WORLD
SUPERMAN ANNUAL #11

Both Batman and new Robin Jason Todd guest-starred in this memorable Superman annual written by legendary talent Alan Moore and illustrated by his frequent collaborator, Dave Gibbons.

The story "For The Man Who Has Everything" began when Batman, Robin, and Wonder Woman traveled to the Fortress of Solitude in the arctic to celebrate Superman's birthday. As Jason got his first glimpse inside the Fortress, and even a kiss hello from Wonder Woman, he was shocked to find the party already crashed by the villain Mongul who had trapped Superman in a blissful fantasy world inside his own mind, using an alien plant known as the Black Mercy. Working together, the heroes freed Superman and managed to ensnare Mongul in his own cruel trap.

Moore had Batman and Robin stop by in another of his monumental Superman tales the following year in the second half of the two-part "Whatever Happened to the Man of Tomorrow" in *Action Comics* #583 (September 1986).

BAD DREAMS IN THE FORTRESS OF SOLITUDE
Batman found Superman under the dream-like spell of a mysterious organism stuck to his chest. After being freed from its grip, Superman found out alien invader Mongul was responsible and made quick work of him.

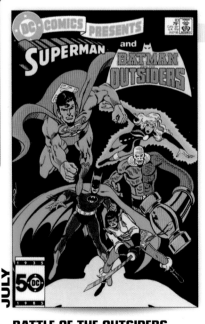

JULY

BATTLE OF THE OUTSIDERS
DC Comics Presents #83 ● Writer Mike W. Barr found the perfect counterpart to battle his team of Outsiders in the form of the 1960s Batman villain the Outsider in this team-up with Superman drawn by Irv Novick. When delivering refreshments to the Batcave, Alfred tripped and injured his head, allowing the powerful Outsider to gain control over him once again. Fortunately, Batman, Metamorpho, Halo, and Katana discovered and defeated the true mastermind behind the villain's return—the evil genius Ira Quimby, also known as I.Q.

AUGUST

EVE OF DESTRUCTION
Batman and the Outsiders #24 ● Life continued to be a rollercoaster for the Outsiders. More of Halo's origin was revealed, Metamorpho's roots were explored, and Geo-Force picked a fight with Superman in *Batman and the Outsiders* #19 (March 1985). But those adventures paled in comparison to the threat of Kobra, one of the team's greatest foes. In this issue by writer Mike W. Barr and new regular artist, Alan Davis, Kobra's right-hand woman, Lady Eve, was introduced. Eve and Kobra would prove quite a problem for the Outsiders.

SEPTEMBER

NOT YET A LOOKER
Batman and the Outsiders #25 ● Her husband Greg thought her beautiful, but Emily Briggs strongly disagreed. Debuting in this issue by writer Mike W. Barr and artist Alan Davis, Emily complained to a complete stranger about missing out on a promotion because of her looks. In issue #31 (March 1986), she would be transformed into stunning psionic superheroine Looker. Soon to join the Outsiders, Looker would add an interesting dynamic to the mix as she discarded her old life for the shallow rewards of being judged solely on her image.

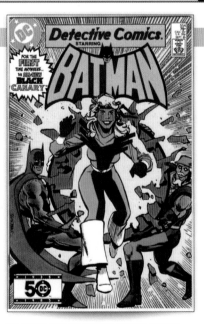

BLACK CANARY'S NEW LOOK
Detective Comics #554 ● This issue featured a moody lead story, written by Doug Moench and illustrated by Klaus Janson, concerning a bomb threat in Gotham Harbor. However Janson's cover—an homage to *Flash Comics* #92 (February 1948) which launched Black Canary's first solo series—emphasized the book's back-up story, written by Joey Cavalieri and drawn by Jerome Moore. It introduced a new costume for Black Canary with a definite 1980s feel. A Green Arrow supporting character, Black Canary's prominence on the cover hinted at her future status in Gotham City.

A SPOTLIGHT ON THE FUTURE

DC Spotlight #1 ● Distributed at comic conventions, this rare prose issue made comic book history. Writer/editor Robert Greenberger commissioned a series of articles to tease upcoming events in the world of DC Comics. The last few pages previewed Frank Miller's artwork from the groundbreaking series, *Batman: The Dark Knight Returns*. Accompanying an interview with Miller were early designs of what a 50-year-old Batman would look like. *DC Spotlight* also provided the first glimpse of Alan Moore's *Watchmen*.

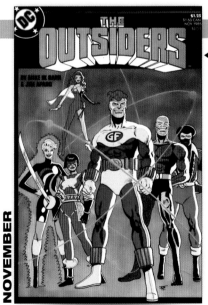

NOVEMBER

OUTSIDE GOTHAM CITY

The Outsiders #1 ● Like the popular New Teen Titans and Legion of Super-Heroes teams, the Outsiders, were upgraded to the bright world of Baxter paper with this new ongoing series. Written by Mike W. Barr and drawn by Jim Aparo, this issue debuted Looker in full costume, showed the team's new HQ off the coast of Santa Monica, California, and featured the threat of the android Nuclear Family. The earlier title, *Batman and the Outsiders,* would also soon change its name to *Adventures of the Outsiders* with issue #33 (May 1986).

WHAT A LOOKER!

Emily Briggs was a sheepish bank teller who underwent a metahuman transformation and became the hero Looker. She joined the Outsiders after helping to rescue them when they were captured by the Masters of Disaster, but she was always distant from her other teammates. Despite this, she won Batman's trust.

ALSO THIS YEAR

April—*Wonder Woman* #324: Future Outsider Gardner Grayle earned an upgrade to Super Hero status as he donned the uniform of the new Atomic Knight.

July—*Batman Annual* #9: Four sides of the Caped Crusader were examined in this all-new annual: as a boy, as a vigilante, as a detective, and as a man.

July—*The Best of DC Blue Ribbon Digest* #62: Batman's best tales from 1984 were reprinted in digest form, including the Batman Special # 1, *Detective Comics* #'s 537 and 539, and Batman # 372.

December—*Shadow of the Batman* #1: The highlights of writer Steve Englehart and Marshall Rogers's work on Batman were reprinted on vibrant Baxter paper in this five-issue series.

December—*Batman and the Outsiders Annual* #2: Metamorpho had been wooing his longtime love, Sapphire Stagg, ever since his first appearance way back in *The Brave and the Bold* #57. In this issue, the two finally tied the knot.

YEAR ONE

Batman #407 (May 1987) ▪ Artist David Mazzucchelli and writer Frank Miller re-established Batman after the reality-warping events of 1985's *Crisis on Infinite Earths*. The Dark Knight's universe was a clean slate and, for the first time, a modern origin was put in place in "Batman: Year One" that added extra grit and realism to Gotham City. The Dark Knight's early years now revealed a fallible hero, an approach that would influence generations of Batman writers and artists.

THE DARK KNIGHT GETS DARKER

BATMAN: THE DARK KNIGHT RETURNS #1

One of the most important comic books in Batman's history, *Batman: The Dark Knight Returns* was a four-part, deluxe-format epic that that helped change the entire landscape of comic books.

Acclaimed for his work on the miniseries *Ronin*, writer/artist Frank Miller delivered this masterpiece with the help of atmospheric inker Klaus Janson and brilliant colorist Lynn Varley. Innovative for its storytelling techniques, sophistication, and willingness to push the limits of noir and the Super Hero genre, *The Dark Knight Returns* made an immediate impact.

The book told the story of a 50-something Bruce Wayne, who had retired as Batman and sunk into a life of extreme sports and alcohol. But with Gotham City becoming the worse for Batman's absence, Wayne found himself donning cape and cowl again and tangling with his old enemy Harvey Dent. After taking down the sadistic leader of the city's Mutant gang, Batman then fought the Joker, who had returned to challenge his greatest enemy. The series also included an epic battle with Superman, who was ordered by the President of the United States to end the "dangerous" movement Batman's presence had sparked in Gotham City.

A story rife with political and social commentary, *Batman: The Dark Knight Returns* paved the way for more adult storytelling in comics. Batman would take a darker tone in the decades to come. The voice of Alfred also changed. Thanks to Miller, he now possessed a dry wit rarely glimpsed during his first 40-plus years in comics.

TAKING A TANK TO A GUN FIGHT
When confronting the Mutant Leader, Batman drove a new tank-like version of the Batmobile, bombarding the Mutant gang members with gunfire. In keeping with Batman's modus operandi, the bullets he fired were rubber. It was in this scene that the young Carrie Kelley first teamed with her hero. She would soon be given Batman's blessing to continue her career as Robin.

1986

"You don't... get it, boy... This isn't a mudhole... it's an operating table. And I'm the surgeon." Batman takes down the Mutant Leader, *Batman: The Dark Knight Returns* #2

This was the year that changed everything. Three of the comic world's most enduring titles would be released in 1986: the real-world approach to Super Heroes titled *Watchmen*, the gripping holocaust tale *Maus*, and writer/artist Frank Miller's seminal *Batman: The Dark Knight Returns*. More than any other character, Batman would never be the same, as future writers drew upon the dark possibilities of the topics that Miller opened up. Comic books were now reaching and challenging adult audiences. Controversial subjects became fair game and sophisticated storytelling techniques allowed for powerful books unlike any that had come before.

THE JOKER'S FINAL JOKE

When *Batman: The Dark Knight Returns* began, the Joker had "retired." He remained at Arkham Asylum, having lost his trademark smile during Batman's absence. But when his "darling" returned on the scene, so did the Joker. The Joker and Batman battled at an amusement park, and the Joker deliberately broke his own neck so that the Dark Knight would be accused of murder.

A FEMALE ROBIN

When Miller began sketching the bulky Batman he had in mind for Dark Knight Returns, he quickly realized that the hero needed a Robin to contrast with and really show off Batman's powerful frame. Enter Carrie Kelley, the first female Robin, and a small spunky foil to Bruce's gritty and grim demeanor.

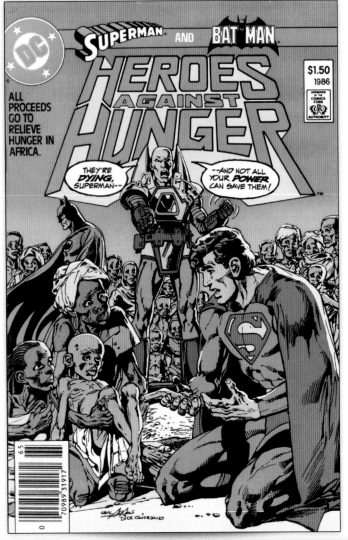

THE GOOD FIGHT

SUPERMAN AND BATMAN: HEROES AGAINST HUNGER #1

This special issue teamed Superman, Batman, and Lex Luthor against an opponent that even their combined forces could not easily defeat—hunger in Ethiopia.

FACE TO FACE WITH FAMINE
Even the normally hard-hearted Lex Luthor was moved to tears by the terrible plight of the Ethiopian famine victims.

Organized and plotted by writer/artist Jim Starlin and artist Bernie Wrightson (the latter providing character designs as well), this one-shot, titled "A Song of Pain and Sorrow!," included contributions by more than 40 other writers and artists, not to mention a slew of talented inkers, letterers, and colorists. All those involved donated their time and efforts for the cause of famine relief in Africa, which had been highlighted the previous summer by the massive Live Aid rock concerts in Philadelphia and London.

With all proceeds going to charity, this special featured a great cover pencilled by Neal Adams and an impressive back cover by Bill Sienkiewicz. In addition, legendary comic book talents such as Jack Kirby, Joe Kubert, and Carmine Infantino offered a few pages in what shaped up to be a worthy, all-star event.

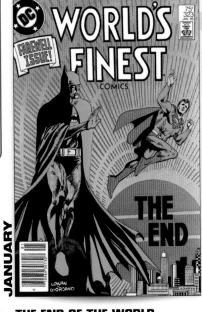

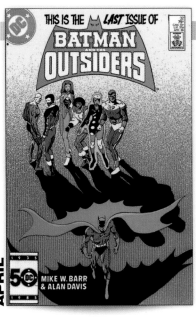

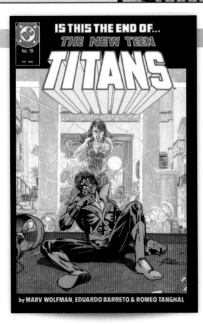

THE END OF THE WORLD

World's Finest Comics #323 ▪ It seemed that Batman stories were heading somewhere other than Metropolis for the time being, so fans had to say goodbye to this long-running DC Comics staple. While the letters column promised that *World's Finest* would return soon, it would be almost two decades before Batman and Superman's partnership would receive another ongoing series, in the 2003 title *Superman/Batman*. Writer Joey Cavalieri and penciller José Delbo saw the heroes off in style as they faced the new menace of the mystical villain Nightwolf.

THE END OF EARTH-TWO

Crisis on Infinite Earths #12 ▪ This year-long maxiseries came to a halt in this issue by writer Marv Wolfman and co-plotter and penciller, George Pérez. As the Anti-Monitor threatened Earth-One, millions of shadow demons flooded the planet, causing death and destruction in their wake. Among the casualties were the original Dove and Earth-Two's Robin and Huntress. The Anti-Monitor was defeated and the multiverse was no more. All that was left was one Earth, one Batman.

LEAVING THE OUTSIDERS

Batman and the Outsiders #32 ▪ Batman had little time for Super Hero team-ups in his gritty war against crime. Believing he had taught the Outsiders everything they needed to know to become an independent force, he left the team in this issue, putting them through one final test by disbanding the team completely. The Outsiders proved their resolve by refusing to break up in this story by writer Mike W. Barr and artist Alan Davis. In the very next issue, the book's title changed to *Adventures of the Outsiders*, as the heroes renewed their claim in the DC Universe.

THE NEWEST TEEN TITANS

The New Teen Titans #19 ▪ Jason Todd followed his predecessor as Robin by briefly joining the New Teen Titans in this issue by writer Marv Wolfman and penciller Eduardo Barreto. With Starfire away on her home planet, Nightwing searching for Raven, Cyborg injured, and Changeling disillusioned, Wonder Girl had to recruit a short-lived new group of heroes when the government called. The roster included Jason Todd's Robin, Hawk, Speedy, Aqualad, and Wally West, the Flash. The story showed Jason stepping out from Batman's shadow.

DEALER OF DESOLATION
An alien calling himself the Master, who gained power from "lifelessness and from voids," had been shooting down famine relief planes. Superman, Batman, and Lex Luthor's combined forces eventually gave him the boot— back through his own dimensional portal.

MAY

CAPTURED ON FILM
Batman #395 ▪ In this start of a three-part story, writer Doug Moench and artist Tom Mandrake introduced the villain Film Freak. A failed actor who had faked his death to gain popularity that never came, Burt Weston reenacted scenes from hit movies when committing crimes. Thwarted by Batman and Catwoman or by Robin and film-buff Harvey Bullock, the Film Freak attempted to murder Alfred's daughter Julia. The Dynamic Duo overcame the villain by the next issue, undeterred by the Film Freak dressing up like a giant ape.

RETURN TO THE BIG LEAGUES
Justice League of America #250 ▪ This issue, by writer Gerry Conway and artist Luke McDonnell, returned the Dark Knight to the Justice League as the team's leader for the next year. Normally hesitant about joining any organization, Batman answered a JLA emergency alongside former members Green Lantern (Hal Jordan), Green Arrow, Superman, and Black Canary. After this team saved the current JLA from an extraterrestrial threat called Junior, Batman realized that the new JLA, comprised of mostly rookie heroes, needed his expertise.

JULY

PUTTING A HEX ON BATMAN
Hex #11 ▪ In the title *Hex*, writer Michael Fleisher and artist Mark Texeira had sent Wild West gunslinger Jonah Hex into a post-apocalyptic future. In New York City, Hex was tricked into hunting the "Batman" of this future, named Cohen, whose parents had been murdered. Inspired by Batman, Cohen had developed his own Batsuit and an operations base inside the Statue of Liberty. After fighting Hex, Cohen then found himself partnering with the gunslinger to battle three giant robots. They were victorious in the next issue, but Cohen disappeared, presumably killed in action.

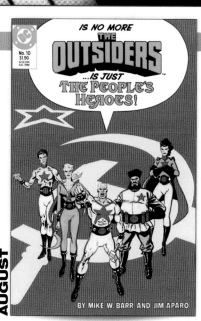

AUGUST

THE PEOPLE'S HEROES
The Outsiders #10 ▪ The Cold War came to California when the Outsiders found themselves battling the super Soviets known as the People's Heroes in this three-part tale by writer Mike W. Barr and artist Jim Aparo. The team of villains included the super-strong Hammer, blade expert Sickle, the explosive Molotov, the expert athlete Bolshoi, and the psionic-powered Pravda. This issue also featured one of the back-up tales the title was quickly becoming known for, an inspiring Geo-Force character study by Barr and artist Jerry Ordway.

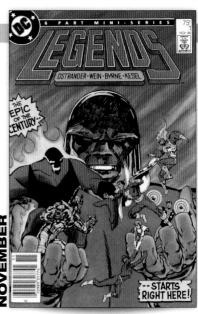

THE USUAL SUSPECTS

Detective Comics #566 ■ Writer Doug Moench ended his tenure on *Detective Comics* with this issue, which featured art by Gene Colan, who would also soon end his time in Batman's world. Here, the pair presented the most famous faces in Batman's Rogues Gallery as Batman and Robin perused their crime files, reading dossiers on dozens of their worst enemies as they tried to discover who had sent them an ominous note that read, "Know your foes." The mystery would not be solved until the final issue of Moench's first run, *Batman* #400.

THE ORIGINAL'S ORIGIN

Secret Origins #6 ■ The Batman of Earth-Two's origin was retold in this issue, which also featured Halo of the Outsiders. When the title first started, a Golden Age character featured in one issue and the next starred a modern character. But from now, Golden Age and Modern Age stories were combined in each issue. To kick things off, Earth-Two Batman's history was chronicled by writer Roy Thomas and artist Marshall Rogers, while Halo's story, in which she sported a new white costume, was told by writer Mike W. Barr and artist Dick Giordano.

SWAMP THING VS. GOTHAM CITY

Swamp Thing #52 ■ When police arrested Abby Cable for her relationship with Swamp Thing, her husband, Gotham City paid the price. In this two-part tale by writer Alan Moore and artist Rick Veitch (and artist John Totleben in issue #53), Swamp Thing turned Gotham City into a chaotic, natural wonderland. Confronting Swamp Thing in a tank-like Batmobile, the Dark Knight realized that the monster's cause was just, and convinced police to free Abby. However, in a cruel twist engineered by Lex Luthor, the authorities seemingly destroyed the plant elemental.

THEY ARE LEGENDS

Legends #1 ■ Following *Crisis on Infinite Earths*, DC Comics decided to make epic crossovers an annual event. Scribes John Ostrander and Len Wein teamed with penciller John Byrne for this six-issue series, which pitted dozens of Super Heroes against the forces of Darkseid. The series saw the debut of the new Suicide Squad, a government-led team of super-villains and the death of Batman's old enemy Blockbuster. But the biggest development happened in the series' final issue (April 1987) when Batman joined the new JLA alongside other major DC heroes.

OCTOBER

BREAKOUT DILEMMA
BATMAN #400

Nearly every member of Batman's Rogues Gallery was broken out of jail by Rā's al Ghūl the anniversary of the night Batman began his crime-fighting campaign.

With this oversized issue, *Batman* reached its 400th issue—a landmark that was also the swan song of writer Doug Moench. In the story "Resurrection Night," Rā's al Ghūl engineered a massive breakout of Batman's archfoes from Arkham Asylum, including the Joker and the Penguin. He then offered to kill the villains off if Batman would agree to join his campaign of international eco-terrorism with a view to becoming his successor as leader. Batman resolutely refused, but was faced with a deadly situation: The escaped villains had captured Alfred, Commissioner Gordon, Harvey Bullock, Julia Pennyworth, and Vicki Vale. Luckily, the Dark Knight, with help from Robin, Talia, and Catwoman, managed to round up the villains before Rā's' plan could escalate any further.

This massive issue contained a script by Moench with pencils by Steve Lightle, George Pérez, Paris Cullins, Bill Sienkiewicz, Arthur Adams, Tom Sutton, Steve Leialoha, Joe Kubert, Ken Steacy, Rick Leonardi, Brian Bolland, Mike Grell, Michael Kaluta, Bernie Wrightson, and Steve Rude, as well as an introduction by the master of horror himself, Stephen King.

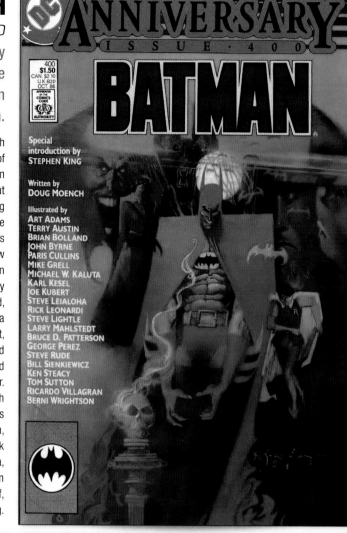

Special introduction by STEPHEN KING

Written by DOUG MOENCH

Illustrated by
ART ADAMS
TERRY AUSTIN
BRIAN BOLLAND
JOHN BYRNE
PARIS CULLINS
MIKE GRELL
MICHAEL W. KALUTA
KARL KESEL
JOE KUBERT
STEVE LEIALOHA
RICK LEONARDI
STEVE LIGHTLE
LARRY MAHLSTEDT
BRUCE D. PATTERSON
GEORGE PEREZ
STEVE RUDE
BILL SIENKIEWICZ
KEN STEACY
TOM SUTTON
RICARDO VILLAGRAN
BERNI WRIGHTSON

BATMAN PIN-UP
Not every artist that contributed to this issue participated in the story. Some, like Steve Rude, were commissioned for a pin-up drawing in a gallery section, giving readers an extra "bonus feature."

MEETINGS AND MAGPIES
The Man of Steel #3 ■ In the wake of *Crisis on Infinite Earths*, writer/artist John Byrne was reinventing Superman for a new generation. This story redefined the Superman/Batman team. Batman visited Metropolis and, for the first time, tangled with the Man of Steel. Viewed as a vigilante by Superman, Batman managed to manipulate the hero into helping him defeat the murderous thief Magpie. The tale established the pair as uneasy allies rather than friends, laying the foundations for decades of team-ups between the world's finest partners.

SPECIAL FEATURE

TENSE MEETING
Superman's first post-Crisis meeting with Batman was a far cry from their relationship of old. The two were immediately distrustful of each other. While they formed an uneasy truce, each kept an eye on the other until they could establish a more solid relationship. They would eventually become close friends and allies, facing many adversaries together.

DECEMBER

A NEW DYNAMIC DUO
Detective Comics #569 ■ Writer Mike W. Barr and artist Alan Davis became the new regular team on *Detective Comics* with this issue. The pair started their run by establishing Batman and Robin's relationship and then throwing Catwoman into the mix. Aided by Davis' stylish work and under the guidance of new Batman group editor Dennis O'Neil, Batman and Robin took on the Joker, but arrived too late to save Catwoman from his evil scheming. The Joker and the nefarious Dr. Moon had altered her mind, returning Selina to her thieving roots.

ALSO THIS YEAR

April—*Outsiders* #6: A villain called the Duke of Oil debuted, rampaging through the Outsiders' new oil rig hideout.

July—*Last Days of the Justice Society of America* #1: The Justice Society of Earth-Two went on one last adventure in this special featuring guest appearances by the Batman of both Earth-One and Earth-Two.

August—*Batman Annual* #10: Evil genius Hugo Strange was the starring villain in this entertaining annual.

December—*'Mazing Man* #12: Frank Miller lent his talents and his *Dark Knight Returns* version of Batman and Robin to the final cover of *'Mazing Man*.

December—*Batman* #402: Batman battled an imposter wearing his costume.

BATMAN: YEAR ONE
BATMAN #404

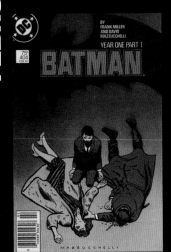

Writer Frank Miller had told the definitive end to Batman's story in the previous year's epic *Batman: The Dark Knight Returns.* He would contribute an equally powerful origin story for the Dark Knight with "Batman: Year One."

During the creation of *Batman: The Dark Knight Returns*, Dennis O'Neil had rejoined DC comics as Batman's group editor. Formerly a writer who had helped to redefine the Caped Crusader in the 1970s, O'Neil decided to shake up Batman's life from his editorial chair. He hired Frank Miller and artist David Mazzucchelli, who created a stunning work of contemporary storytelling—a four-issue flashback tale chronicling Bruce Wayne's return to Gotham City as an adult and, inspired by a bat flying through his study window, his evolution into Batman.

The future commissioner of Gotham City James Gordon, given more depth and personality than ever before, played an equally important role in this series. His wife Barbara was introduced to readers in issue 405 (March 1987), and his son James Gordon Jr. was born by issue 407 (May 1987). Also of note was the first actual appearance of Detective Sarah Essen, a policewoman that Miller had established as Gordon's wife in the future world of *The Dark Knight Returns.* After her debut in issue 405, she and Gordon began an affair that further humanized the cop. With breathtaking shadowy, realistic art, a fascinating story of one man's pursuit of an insane mission, and an examination of a corrupt city and its equally corrupt police force (given life with the debut of Gordon's partner, Detective Flass), "Batman: Year One" stands as one of the Caped Crusader's greatest stories, only rivaled by Miller's own *Dark Knight Returns.*

1987

"Your feast is nearly over. From this moment on—none of you are safe."

Batman to the guests assembled at the mayor's mansion—*Batman* #405.

Frank Miller proved that he was not finished with Batman when he rewrote the character's history in "Year One," assisted by editor Dennis O'Neil, who had returned to the character he'd helped shape over a decade before. This four-issue series ran through the regular Batman title, and paved the way for dozens, if not hundreds of stories set in the early years of the Dark Knight's career. But "Year One" was not 1987's only groundbreaking title. New team concepts like the Suicide Squad and an incomparable new take on the Justice League sprang up, creating an intriguing variety of styles and sub-genres for Batman fans.

COMING HOME
Bruce Wayne returned home to his father's mansion after years away from Gotham City. Wayne was a man on mission, determined to see his plan come to fruition. The only problem was, Bruce wasn't sure how best to go about fighting crime in his hometown.

BRUCE'S FIRST FORAY
Bruce Wayne took a walk through one of Gotham City's worst neighborhoods. Looking for trouble, Wayne found it in the form of prostitute Selina Kyle, who would later be inspired by his example to become Catwoman.

BECOMING THE BAT

Bruce Wayne was brooding on the murder of his parents when a startling event triggered a long-buried childhood fear: A bat smashed through the window of his study. Bruce resolved to "become the bat"—and strike terror into the minds of Gotham City's criminals as Batman.

CORRUPTION IN THE G.C.P.D.

Detective Flass was as corrupt as a Gotham City cop could get, and when James Gordon arrived in Gotham City, he instantly disagreed with his partner's methods. Their clashes would be some of the most memorable moments in "Batman: Year One," and show just how tough a cop Jim Gordon really was.

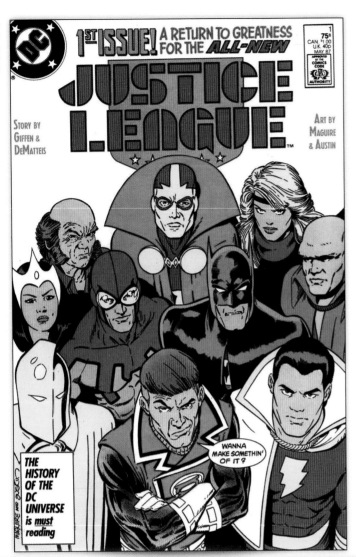

A LEAGUE OF THEIR OWN

JUSTICE LEAGUE #1

Batman was back leading the Justice League, but this wasn't the JLA of old. The "A" had been dropped entirely, and the series would be dubbed *Justice League International* by issue #7 (November 1987).

The title was the least of the book's innovations. In this new Justice League incarnation by writers Keith Giffen and J.M. DeMatteis and penciller Kevin Maguire, a new tone was apparent. Giffen and DeMatteis introduced humor into the world of DC Comics' top-tier team, making their adventures refreshing and fun. Combined with Maguire's knack for hilarious facial expressions and moment-to-moment panel storytelling, the League's adventures came to resemble an absurdist comedy or a Super Hero sitcom. However, just when the reader least expected it, Giffen and DeMatteis would introduce a powerful scene of raw emotion or tension.

Starring lesser-known faces of the DCU, with a few heavy hitters like Batman and Captain Marvel added to the mix, the series was jam-packed with memorable moments. For Batman fans, the high point came in issue #5 (September 1987), when tensions boiled over between Batman and the hot-headed Green Lantern, Guy Gardner. Agreeing to settle their differences in a fight, Batman ended their argument with a single punch—an event Gardner's teammates never let him live down. By issue #7 (November 1987), the book's title had changed to *Justice League International*.

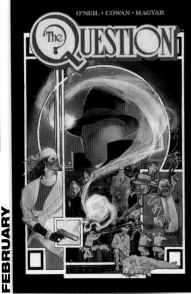

WHO IS THE QUESTION?

The Question #1 ● While helming Batman's adventures as his main editor, writer Dennis O'Neil penned the adventures of vigilante detective the Question alongside penciller Denys Cowan. The series established the faceless vigilante, also known by his real name Charles Victor Szasz and by his public persona of Vic Sage, in Batman's world. In his debut, the Question was badly beaten by Lady Shiva. Sage received a visit from Batman in issue #2, before training with martial-arts supremo Richard Dragon and finding a new direction in life.

THE FIRST DETECTIVE

Detective Comics #572 ● *Detective Comics* was 50 years young, and writer Mike W. Barr was on hand to wish it a happy birthday. Its first issue in March 1937 didn't feature the Batman, but did include the first appearance of Slam Bradley. So Barr chose Bradley to co-star in this issue, which was illustrated by Alan Davis, Terry Beatty, Carmine Infantino, and E.R. Cruz. Barr also included the Elongated Man and introduced Batman to Sherlock Holmes by the end of the issue. This tale also featured a pin-up by Batman legend Dick Sprang.

BACK IN THE RANKS

The Outsiders #17 ● While Batman would debut as a founding member of the newest incarnation of the Justice League in two months time, he returned to his own team, the Outsiders, with this issue by writer Mike W. Barr and artist Jim Aparo. Batman found himself working alongside his old allies when they rescued him from a cult that worshipped the powerful villain Eclipso. In the second half of the story, which appeared in the following issue, Batman and the Outsiders defeated Eclipso, encouraging the Dark Knight to rejoin their ranks.

SUICIDE MISSION

Suicide Squad #1 ● Much like *Justice League*, *Suicide Squad* was another new DC Comics title spinning out of the *Legends* miniseries. And also like *Justice League*, this series proved to be full of twists and turns. Written by John Ostrander with art by Luke McDonnell, the premiere issue of *Suicide Squad* saw several super-villains embark on missions for the U.S. government's Task Force X to win "get out of jail free" cards. With both Deadshot and Bronze Tiger more or less permanent members, the Suicide Squad would later include other Batman-related characters.

BATMAN VS. GUY GARDNER
Batman wasn't prepared to take lip from anyone, even when those snarky remarks came from a bearer of the world's most powerful weapon. To Batman, Green Lantern Guy Gardner was just an annoyance he could easily beat, despite Gardner's near limitless abilities.

BATCAVE WEST
The Outsiders #19 ▪ In this issue by writer Mike W. Barr and artist Jim Aparo, the Outsiders helped Batman, now back on the team, move into his new West Coast hideout, Batcave West, located inside a mountain. Meanwhile, the team inducted former Master of Disaster Windfall, only to discover that she was a clone. Only after a battle with the Masters of Disaster next month, did the real Windfall join. This issue also featured a fun back-up tale by Barr and artist Dan Spiegle in which Halo dreamed that she was an adult and Katana was her kid partner.

JUNE

THE NEW JASON TODD
Batman #408 ▪ Up to this point, Jason Todd's origin had been a virtual carbon copy of Dick Grayson's. However, with the clean slate offered by *Crisis on Infinite Earths*, writer Max Allan Collins decided to make the characters more different. In this issue drawn by Chris Warner, the Dark Knight fired Dick Grayson for his own good after Robin was nearly killed by the Joker. Soon afterward, Batman met the boy who would become the second Robin when he caught street urchin Jason Todd trying to steal the tires off the Batmobile.

A NEW ROBIN
Before Jason became Robin, Batman enrolled him in the Crime Alley school called Ma Gunn's School for Boys. By the next issue (illustrated by Ross Andru), Jason discovered that Ma Gunn was training her students in the ways of crime, and helped Batman shut down her activities. After learning Two-Face had killed Jason's father, Batman decided to take the boy in as his partner, and the career of the second Robin began.

JULY

LADY CLAY STRIKES
The Outsiders #21 ▪ Mining Batman's past led to writer Mike W. Barr reinventing several Batman foes in a new super-villain team, Strike Force Kobra. Alongside artist Jim Aparo, Barr introduced a new Zebra-Man, Planet-Master, and a Clayface, in the form of Lady Clay. The team also included new villains Elemental Woman, a take on the classic Elemental Man from *Detective Comics* #294 (August 1961), and a creature made of pure energy known as Spectrumonster. Barr introduced another new foe, Fusion, in September's *The Outsiders* #23.

AN AFFAIR TO REMEMBER
A temporary truce with Rā's al Ghūl allowed Batman and Talia to reveal their feelings for each other. So much so, that this volume included a rare bedroom scene involving the two.

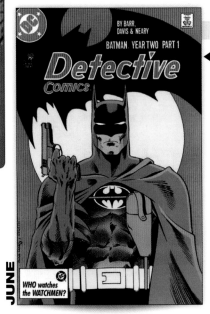

BATMAN: YEAR TWO
Detective Comics #575 • Writer Mike W. Barr and artist Alan Davis concocted a powerful, four-part tale (the last three installments were drawn by Todd McFarlane) of Batman's second year fighting crime. The story told of Bruce's brief love affair with Rachel Caspian, whose father was revealed to be a vigilante called the Reaper. The miniseries also saw Batman meet his parents' killer, Joe Chill. Batman was robbed of his chance of vengeance by the Reaper, who killed Chill before Batman could decide whether to pull the trigger of the very gun that had shot his own parents.

FEAR THE REAPER
No relation to the original Reaper from *Batman* #237 (December 1971), this Reaper was established to have stalked Gotham City's streets many years ago before Batman's time. With guns embedded in his scythes, he proved a difficult challenge for the Caped Crusader.

THE RIGHT TO REMAIN SILENT
Batman #412 • Writer Max Allan Collins' tenure as the regular *Batman* writer came to a close with this issue pencilled by Dave Cockrum. For his final effort, the acclaimed *Dick Tracy* comic strip writer delivered a new villain to Batman's Rogues Gallery in the form of the Mime. Classically trained in her craft, Camilla Cameo was a successful mime artist whose 15 minutes of fame had passed far too quickly for her liking. She became a murderous villain, lashing out at anyone who created the "noise" that she detested so much.

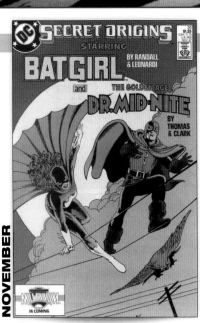

BECOMING BATGIRL
Secret Origins #20 • Issue #13 (April 1987) of *Secret Origins* had shown that Nightwing Dick Grayson's backstory hadn't changed much since *Crisis on Infinite Earths*. However, Batgirl Barbara Gordon's origin was overhauled in this issue. Writer Barbara Randall and penciller Rick Leonardi revealed that Barbara was not Commissioner Gordon's daughter, but his niece. The daughter of Jim's widower brother Roger, Babs went to live with Jim when her alcoholic father died. Idolizing Batman, Barbara trained to become a Super Hero—Batgirl.

SEPTEMBER

SONS AND DAUGHTERS
BATMAN: SON OF THE DEMON

Batman's first-ever official graphic novel was memorable for a passionate romance between the Dark Knight and Rā's al Ghūl's daughter, Talia.

In this 78-page, oversized spectacular, writer Mike W. Barr and artist Jerry Bingham delivered an exciting tale of a globe-trotting Batman forming an uneasy alliance with Rā's al Ghūl. The Demon's Head was usually one of the Dark Knight's most fearsome foes but here they joined forces against a demented terrorist named Qayin, who had invented a weapon that could control the weather. As Batman and Rā's al Ghūl tracked down Qayin—a threat even more dangerous than Rā's al Ghūl himself and the murderer of Talia's mother—Batman and Talia grew closer than ever before. After Qayin was killed in a final battle with Rā's al Ghūl, it was revealed that Talia had given birth to Batman's child without his knowledge and given the baby up for adoption. Writer Grant Morrison later revived the idea of Batman and Talia's child in his "Batman and Son" storyline, beginning in *Batman* #655 (September 2006).

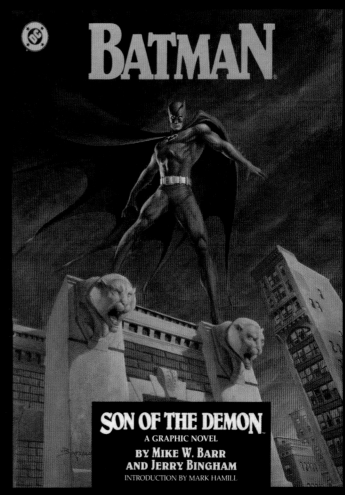

BATMAN

SON OF THE DEMON
A GRAPHIC NOVEL
BY MIKE W. BARR
AND JERRY BINGHAM
INTRODUCTION BY MARK HAMILL

NOVEMBER

ATOMIC ALLY
The Outsiders #25 ▪ With Batman back on the team and new member Windfall adjusting to life as a Super Hero, it seemed that the Outsiders' roster had stabilized. But writer Mike W. Barr and artist Jim Aparo had a surprise for the group in the form of Gardner Grayle, the Atomic Knight, who helped the Outsiders fight the threat of Major Disaster. The battle cost them Station Markovia, their oil-rig HQ, but the Atomic Knight stayed with the Outsiders for the rest of this particular incarnation. He was especially drawn to Windfall, despite the difference in their ages.

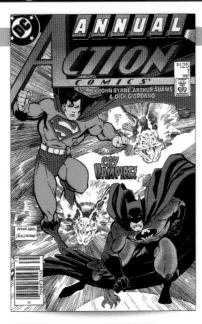

CREATURE OF THE NIGHT
Action Comics Annual #1 ▪ Despite decades of publication, *Action Comics* had not received its own annual until this issue by scribe John Byrne and artist Arthur Adams. In a spooky tale, set in rural Fayerville, Batman went undercover as "Mr. Smith" to investigate a series of grisly murders. Realizing he needed help, Batman called Superman. The two encountered a seemingly innocent young woman named Elly Mae Skaggs, who called herself Skeeter. The vampiric Skeeter overpowered Superman, but Batman ran her through with a wooden stake.

DUMMY LOVE
Batman Annual #11 ▪ Alan Moore crafted yet another timeless tale in this annual. It featured the art of George Freeman and starred Clayface III, Preston Payne. Payne's touch rendered anyone he came in contact with into protoplasmic goo. Obsessed with a store mannequin, Payne went to any lengths to obtain the inanimate object, including murder. When Batman finally caught up with the villain, the Dark Knight arranged for the dummy to live with Payne at Arkham Asylum. However, in time, Clayface grew to despise the "woman" he had so desired.

ALSO THIS YEAR

April—*Superman* #4: Future Gotham City cop and love interest of Batwoman, Captain Maggie Sawyer debuted.

May—*Detective Comics* #574: In a precursor to "Batman: Year Two," Batman's origin was reexamined, focusing in part on the gun that killed Bruce's parents.

September—*Teen Titans Spotlight* #14: Nightwing went solo for an issue in this new Titans title.

September—*Superman* #9: The Joker brought his particular brand of terror to Metropolis to face the Man of Steel.

November—*Detective Comics* #580: Disturbed actor Paul Sloane was reintroduced as a pawn of Two-Face in this first part of a two-part tale.

December—*Batman* #414: A serial killer, Frank "Cutter" Thompson, killed a young social worker and incurred Batman's vengeful wrath.

INVENTING THE VENTRILOQUIST
DETECTIVE COMICS #583

The Ventriloquist and his puppet Scarface debuted in this memorable issue, soon becoming one of the most notorious "pairs" of super-villains in the Dark Knight's modern era.

Artist Norm Breyfogle had drawn a few *Detective Comics* issues in the past year, but it wasn't until this memorable issue that he became the regular artist for the title, joining forces with writers Alan Grant and John Wagner. Besides beginning Grant and Breyfogle's tremendous run, this issue also debuted perhaps their greatest achievement, the new villain Ventriloquist and his wooden puppet, Scarface.

Mentally disturbed, the Ventriloquist played the role of a mild-mannered right-hand man. His violent split personality emerged in the form of the bloodthirsty Scarface, the mobster puppet he kept with him at all times. The two had such distinct personalities that even the Ventriloquist's henchmen spoke directly to Scarface, rather than to the man controlling him. Destined to become one of Batman's most notorious enemies and and also to feature in several Batman cartoon series, the Ventriloquist fit right in with the Dark Knight's twisted pantheon of classic foes.

1988

"All it takes is one bad day to reduce the sanest man alive to lunacy."

The Joker, *Batman: The Killing Joke*

DC Comics was realizing how to utilize the great potential of one-shots and prestige-format graphic novels and miniseries in order to create powerful stories. Unhindered by monthly continuity, these new direct-market formats enabled writers and artists to take their time and tell a complete story the way they needed to tell it. The result was works like this year's *Batman: The Killing Joke*, one of the most powerful and important Joker stories to date. Also of note was *Batman: The Cult*, a four-issue prestige series that altered the entire landscape of Gotham City for the duration of its self-contained tale.

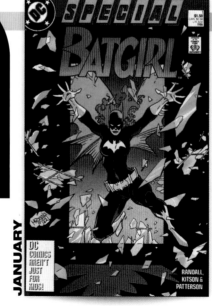

THE LAST BATGIRL STORY
Batgirl Special #1 ■ In a story set before *Batman: The Killing Joke* (July 1988), in which Batgirl Barbara Gordon was crippled, scribe Barbara Randall and penciller Barry Kitson retired Batgirl after one final adventure in her first solo comic. A female killer called Slash was murdering men. Batgirl found herself trapped between Slash and Cormorant, a hired killer. After defeating Slash just as the villainess shot and killed Cormorant, Barbara decided to give up being Batgirl, hoping that another young heroine might replace her.

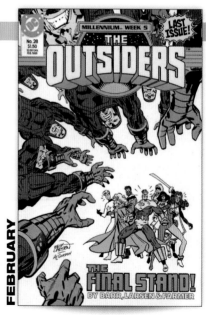

THE END OF THE OUTSIDERS
The Outsiders #28 ■ 1988's epic DC Comics crossover was entitled *Millennium*, and while it mostly revolved around the Green Lantern cast, the Outsiders would feel the effects of the eight-issue miniseries, too. This tie-in issue by writer Mike W. Barr and artist Erik Larsen was the last of their ongoing series. In the previous issue, regular character Dr. Helga Jace had betrayed the team to alien robots the Manhunters. This final chapter saw the Outsiders fighting the Manhunters. Sadly, Looker was depowered and Halo left in a coma.

WHEN ROBINS MEET
Batman #416 ■ Nightwing and Jason Todd, the new Robin, met for the first time in this tale by Jim Starlin and artist Jim Aparo. In a story set a year earlier, Robin was caught off-guard by criminals working in a cocaine lab and had to be rescued by Nightwing. Dick Grayson's history was revised to allow for Jason's new origin when Dick visited the Batcave. Bruce admitted that he had taken Jason on because he missed his partnership with Grayson. This issue saw Nightwing come to terms with being replaced as Robin.

MARCH

TEN NIGHTS OF THE BEAST
Batman #417 ■ Beginning with this issue, Jim Starlin penned the four-part miniseries "Ten Nights of the Beast," drawn by Batman veteran Jim Aparo and with covers by Mike Zeck. A Cold War nightmare full of political intrigue and action, this series introduced the assassin KGBeast, a hulking, cybernetically-enhanced martial-arts expert. The Beast's real name was Anatoli Knyazev, and he was the best agent that the Soviet Union had ever produced. The Beast made his way to Gotham City, killing over a hundred people before the Dark Knight outsmarted the brute.

SPECIAL FEATURE

BURIED BUT FAR FROM DEAD
The KGBeast proved a formidable opponent to Batman and Robin when they tried to stop the cyborg villain from executing ten high-ranking U.S. officials in his mission to disable the Star Wars space program. The Dark Knight buried the assassin alive, but would face him again in the future.

APRIL

TO CATCH A RAT
Detective Comics #585 ■ Writers John Wagner and Alan Grant and artist Norm Breyfogle introduced the Ratcatcher in this two-part story. When former exterminator Otis Flannegan was sent to prison for murder, he sought revenge by kidnapping the judge and others he viewed responsible for his incarceration, and holding them captive in his sewer lair. Able to control rats to do his bidding, the Ratcatcher proved quite a challenge for Batman. Using his strength and survival instincts, Batman overcame the Ratcatcher, making a long-time enemy.

MOORE'S GREAT JOKE
BATMAN: THE KILLING JOKE

After *Batman: The Dark Knight Returns* and "Batman: Year One," fans couldn't wait for the next big Batman story. Expectations were more than met by writer Alan Moore and artist Brian Bolland's *Batman: The Killing Joke.*

Regarded by many fans as the finest Joker story to date, *The Killing Joke* was perhaps the most disturbing Joker story as well, prompting DC to place the warning "Suggested For Mature Readers" on its back cover. Jumping back in time from the present day to the past, this beautifully illustrated tale told Joker's origin, presenting him as a failed comedian talked into donning the guise of criminal the Red Hood to support his family. When an encounter with the Batman sent him falling into a vat of chemicals, the Joker was born.

Meanwhile, in the present, the Joker barged into Commissioner Gordon's home, shooting and crippling his daughter Barbara in a shockingly violent scene. In an attempt to drive Gordon insane, the Joker then stripped the commissioner naked and made him view pictures of his injured and bleeding daughter while held captive on a perverse carnival ghost train.

The Joker's attempt to show that madness is the only logical option when faced with the random pointlessness of human existence failed, however. Despite all of his efforts, Gordon retained his sanity, and Batman brought the villain to justice once more. In the story's powerful final scene, Batman and the Joker shared a melancholy joke, both understanding the tragic inevitability of their continued conflicts.

Full of gorgeous illustrations and almost lyrical in its delivery, *Batman: The Killing Joke* remains the definitive Joker story and yet another high point in the career of Alan Moore.

NO LAUGHING MATTER
Having quit his job at a chemical plant, the man who would become the Joker found that he could not support his wife and unborn child as a stand-up comedian. Crime seemed the only option.

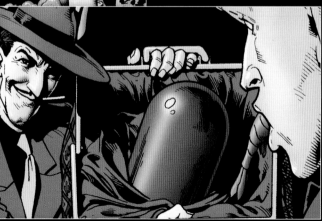

THE RED HOOD
His sanity threatened by the death of his wife in a household accident, the man was easily persuaded to take part in a robbery of the chemical plant where he once worked. The gang tricked him into wearing a red hood, so that a notorious criminal by that name would get the blame.

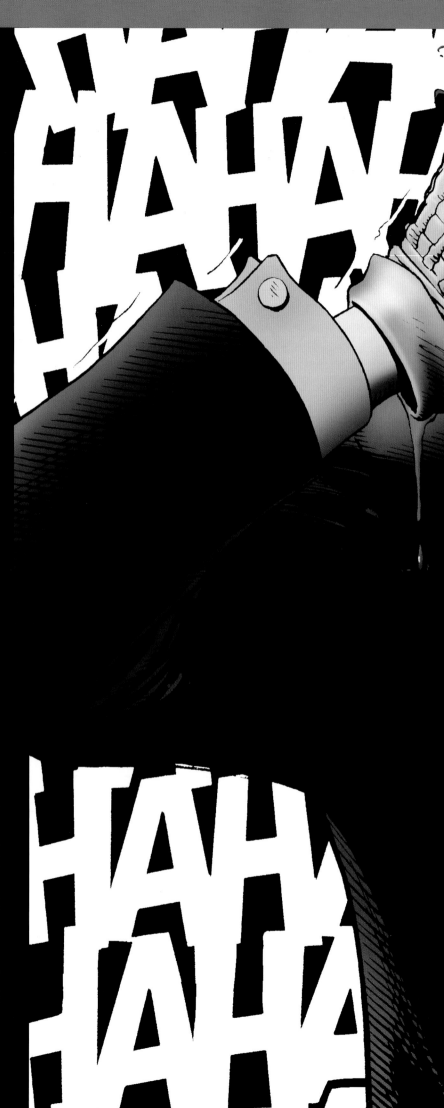

THE JOKER CALLS
Commissioner Gordon and his daughter Barbara never suspected that an early evening knock on the door would bring sudden terror and lasting pain into their lives.

IN COLD BLOOD
In an unprovoked act of violence, the Joker deliberately shot the defenseless Barbara, leaving her crippled for life.

THE EDGE OF MADNESS
The Joker tried everything his fertile mind could come up with to drive Commissioner Gordon insane. Somehow Gordon managed to keep his mind intact.

"You must realize by now that you and I are on the same side in this battle against evil."

Deacon Blackfire, *Batman: The Cult*

HARVEY'S HIDDEN DEPTHS

Checkmate #1 ● Gotham City cop Harvey Bullock showed there was more to him than met the eye when this new title debuted. Written by Paul Kupperberg with pencils by Steve Erwin, this ongoing series dealt with a superspy organization known as Checkmate whose agents were based on chess pieces. Bullock spent the majority of this issue recruiting the character Black Thorn into Checkmate's ranks. Despite his previous bumbling appearances in *Batman* titles, it seemed that Harvey had now become a major player in global peacekeeping.

CORROSIVE CONTRIBUTION

Detective Comics #587 ● Writers John Wagner and Alan Grant teamed with artist Norm Breyfogle to create a new Batman villain—the Corrosive Man—in this three-part tale. Serving life in Gotham City jail, murderer Derek Mitchel escaped, only to be trapped in a waste explosion at Dispo-Chem (Gotham) Inc. Granted an acid touch and now impervious to gunfire, Mitchel became the Corrosive Man. He wreaked havoc in the following issue, hunting for Mr. Kadaver, an old double-crossing associate. The final chapter saw a sleek, but short-lived, version of the Batmobile.

THE ANNUAL TREATMENT

Detective Comics Annual #1 ● Dennis O'Neil stepped out of his editorial role once again to chronicle a Batman adventure for *Detective Comics'* first annual. Illustrated by artist Klaus Janson, Batman and Talia al Ghūl hunted for the Penguin, who had stolen a poison from Rā's al Ghūl. In addition, Batman first met Lady Shiva, when she tried to recruit him to aid martial-arts master O-Sensei. In this three-part story, Batman, Green Arrow, and the Question teamed up to help Shiva fulfill a promise the O-Sensei had made years ago: to be buried alongside his wife.

CATWOMAN IN ACTION

Action Comics Weekly #611 ● Now a weekly anthology title, *Action Comics* began a Black Canary feature in issue #609 (July 1988) when she burned her 1980s uniform in favor of her classic fishnets look. By this issue, Catwoman nabbed a four-part feature with the help of writer Mindy Newell and penciller Barry Kitson. Sporting her purple costume with the dress replaced by pants, Catwoman was joined by Nightwing in issue #613 (August 1988) who netted his own six-part feature by writer Marv Wolfman and penciller Chuck Patton.

AUGUST

CULT CLASSIC

BATMAN: THE CULT #1

The Dark Knight clashed with Deacon Blackfire's vast army of Gotham City's homeless and disaffected, and fell under the villain's evil, mystic spell.

The teaming of powerful storyteller Jim Starlin with horror artist Bernie Wrightson proved a resounding success when the two paired for this four-part prestige format tale. Batman was drugged and taken underground beneath Gotham City by a mysterious cult worshipping their modern day messiah, Deacon Blackfire. It fell to Robin to free the Dark Knight from the cult's hold on his mentor's mind. Blackfire was a charismatic butcher who kept himself looking young by bathing in his victims' blood. The cult leader soon had a firm grasp on the city, using its homeless and destitute to isolate the metropolis by cutting off its entry and exit points and conquering its people in his name.

Luckily for Gotham City, Batman and Robin escaped Blackfire's lair and brought the fight to the city streets in a giant new monster truck model of the Batmobile. The Dynamic Duo successfully stopped the underworlders and then unleashed them on the villainous Deacon Blackfire himself.

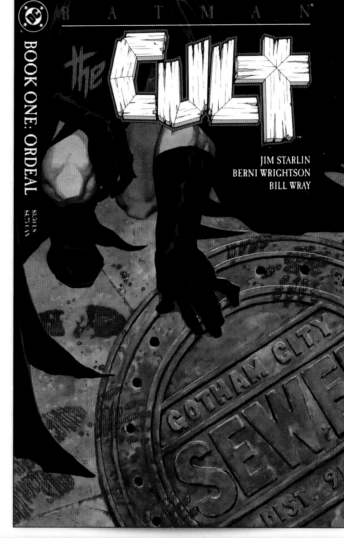

TOTEMIC POWER
Deacon Blackfire showed a drugged and brainwashed Batman the massive totem that represented the nexus of his perverse power. Batman could not help but be awed. His conversion to Blackfire's cult seemed complete.

NOVEMBER

THE UNDIPLOMATIC JASON
Batman #424 • Ever since his reinvention, Jason Todd had had anger issues. In this issue by writer Jim Starlin and artist M.D. Bright, they boiled over when he discovered model Gloria Stanson severely beaten by a thug named Felipe Garzonas. When Gloria hanged herself after being threatened by Felipe, Robin challenged Garzonas on his balcony. Seconds later, Felipe fell to his death. Batman confronted his young partner, and Robin maintained that Garzonas had slipped after he spooked him, leaving an air of doubt with both Batman and readers.

THE HYPNOTIC KILLER
Detective Comics #592 • Writing partners Alan Grant and John Wagner, alongside artist Norm Breyfogle, crammed one last great new Batman villain into the year when they crafted Cornelius Stirk. A cannibalistic serial killer whose diseased mind led him to feed on his prey's fear, Stirk possessed the ability to change his appearance and project mental images through a form of advanced hypnosis. In this two-part tale, Batman tracked down the murderer with the help of another newly-designed Breyfogle Batmobile, which had debuted in the previous issue.

DEADSHOT TAKES AIM
Deadshot #1 • The Batman foe and star of the current *Suicide Squad* series, Deadshot featured in his own four-issue miniseries written by John Ostrander and Kim Yale, and illustrated by Luke McDonnell. Retelling Floyd Lawton's fall from scion of a wealthy family to assassin, the story examined why Deadshot pulled his shots around Batman and why he seemed to have a death wish. Readers were introduced to Deadshot's ex-wife, Susan Lawton, as Deadshot went on a quest to save his kidnapped son, Eddie, who was killed before he could rescue him.

ALSO THIS YEAR

January—*The Saga of Rā's al Ghūl #1:* Rā's al Ghūl's early stories were reprinted on deluxe Baxter paper in this four-issue series.

February—*Suicide Squad #10:* Batman stopped by the Suicide Squad to give them a piece of his mind.

May—*Action Comics #600:* Superman faced off with Man-Bat in this 80-page giant anniversary special.

August—*Justice League International #16:* Batman disguised himself as—Bruce Wayne!

September—*Batman #423:* The many interpretations of Batman's public persona were examined in this interesting tale.

October—*Best of the Brave and the Bold #1:* Neal Adams' art was celebrated in this six-issue Baxter collection of his classic *Brave and the Bold* stories.

November—*Black Orchid #1:* Acclaimed writer Neil Gaiman lent his considerable talents to this prestige format three-issue series beautifully illustrated by Dave McKean that guest-starred Poison Ivy.

THE DEATH OF JASON TODD

BATMAN #428

With this four-issue tale, readers were given an unprecedented opportunity to decide the outcome of a crucial episode in Batman's life: Should Robin Jason Todd live or die?

The pre-*Crisis on Infinite Earths'* version of Jason Todd as Robin hadn't matched Dick Grayson for popularity, and Jason's post-*Crisis* reintroduction as a young thief who partnered with Batman had also received a mixed reception. So DC Comics decided to let the readership decide whether or not Batman truly needed a Robin.

The four-part "A Death in the Family" hit stands with *Batman* #426 (December 1988), thanks to writer Jim Starlin and artist Jim Aparo. As the gripping story unfolded, Jason Todd discovered that his true mother was still alive. She was a doctor named Sheila Haywood working in an Ethiopian refugee camp. However, the Joker had been blackmailing Sheila and forced her to hand Jason over to his tender mercies. After beating Jason with a crowbar, the Joker tied Sheila up in a building set to explode, with her son Jason's near-lifeless body close by.

It was at that point (issue #427) that the fans became involved. In the back of the issue, two 1-900 numbers were listed: one for readers to call if they wanted Jason to live, and one for them to call if they wanted him to die. The voting was close, but in issue #428 Jason Todd was killed while still trying to save his mother's life. Arriving just too late to save Jason, Batman was devastated and guilt-ridden.

UTTER DEVASTATION
When Batman came across the body of his sidekick, he was appalled to realize that Jason Todd had fallen victim to one more example of the Joker's unbridled cruelty. One look told Batman that he had lost Jason for good.

1989

> "No, Alfred. I'll handle this by myself. No help from now on... that's the way I want it."
> Bruce Wayne to Alfred Pennyworth, *Batman #428*

Not since 1966 and the hit *Batman* TV series had "Bat-Mania" so gripped the country. Tim Burton's film *Batman*, starring Michael Keaton as Batman and Jack Nicholson as the Joker, was released, causing a publicity frenzy. Times Square boasted a Batman logo billboard for the movie, the Prince soundtrack topped the album chart, and black Batman logo T-shirts became a fashion hit. The comics were also working up their own major events, including the death of one Robin and the birth of another. And in the landmark *Batman: Arkham Asylum* graphic novel by Grant Morrison, artist Dave McKean used a painterly style that was well ahead of its time.

ORACLE'S ODYSSEY
Suicide Squad #23 ▪ Barbara Gordon wasn't the type to retire. Despite receiving a crippling injury at the hands of the Joker in *Batman: The Killing Joke*, the tenacious heroine was back, using her skills as computer expert Oracle to benefit the Super Hero community. In this issue by writers John Ostrander and Kim Yale and artist Luke McDonnell, Oracle made contact with the Suicide Squad in a simple voice broadcast via computer. Barbara became an important asset to the team and later worked directly from the Squad's headquarters at Belle Reve Prison.

MEET JOE POTATO
Detective Comics #594 ▪ Gotham City had seen its fair share of private eyes, but none quite like the gumshoe concocted of writers Alan Grant and John Wagner and artist Norm Breyfogle. Plump and garbed in a trench coat the same shade as his namesake, Joe Potato made his debut by firing his gun at a speeding Porsche on a city street. After the Dark Knight realized that Joe Potato was on the right side of the law, the two ended up combining forces to stop a mad bomber named Ed Hallen targeting drug users and dealers.

SPECIAL PLEADING
Batman planned to take revenge on the Joker, who had become the new Iranian Ambassador to the U.N. Superman was asked to persuade Batman not to cause an international incident. Batman did not respond kindly.

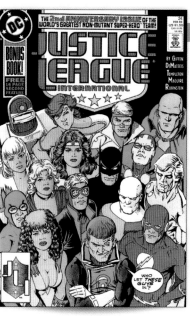

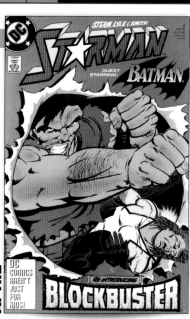

CATWOMAN LASHES OUT
Catwoman #1 ▪ In her first series of her own, Catwoman's past was re-examined, picking up where "Batman: Year One" left off. Written by Mindy Newell with pencils by J.J. Birch, this four-issue mature readers' series looked at Selina's life as a victim and a prostitute, until she discovered her own inner strength and evolved into Catwoman. This miniseries saw Wildcat train Catwoman and debuted Maggie Kyle, Selina's sister, a nun calling herself Sister Magdalene. By the second issue, Selina was wearing the gray costume first seen in "Batman: Year One."

EUROPEAN JUSTICE
Justice League International #24 ▪ Thanks to its blend of humor and drama, the Justice League was a hit again. DC Comics branched out the title in the form of *Justice League Europe*, but before it could premiere in April, the League had to recruit enough members, as in this issue by the writing team of Keith Giffen and J.M. DeMatteis, and artists Ty Templeton and Kevin Maguire. The JLI threw a meet-and-greet for heroes that Batman attended. The team for Justice League Europe was picked by the businessman behind the League, Maxwell Lord.

BATMAN'S NEW BLOCKBUSTER
Starman #9 ▪ The original Blockbuster had died in the pages of *Legends* #3 (January 1987), but that didn't deter his brother, Roland Desmond, from taking on the role and fighting Will Payton aka Starman, with the help of scribe Roger Stern and penciller Tom Lyle. Despite Starman's many powers, he was initially defeated by this mysterious new Blockbuster. Batman helped the rookie Starman overcome the villain. It was revealed that Roland's powers were derived from a combination of steroids and the gene bomb let off during the *Invasion* miniseries (October 1988).

BACK IN THE HUNT
Huntress #1 ▪ A popular character, the Earth-Two daughter of Batman and Catwoman had no place in the post-*Crisis* DC Universe. But when writer Joey Cavalieri and artist Joe Staton reintroduced Huntress in the pages of her first ongoing series, it only took a few tweaks to transform Helena Wayne into a permanent fixture in Batman's world. Now named Helena Bertinelli, Huntress was reimagined as a mob boss' daughter who witnessed the murder of her family. The killer was a costumed villain called Omerta, hired by a rival mafia family.

BLIND JUSTICE
DETECTIVE COMICS #600

This landmark issue, part of Batman's 50th anniversary adventure, provided new insights into the Dark Knight's origin and his training to become Gotham City's guardian.

A screenwriters' strike in Hollywood allowed writer Sam Hamm (one of the screenwriters of the summer's blockbuster *Batman* movie) to turn his hand to the world of comic books in this three-issue storyline, which began with *Detective Comics* #598.

Delving into Batman's past and training, Hamm and artist Denys Cowan simultaneously examined the Dark Knight's present, revealing the depth of Bruce's tortured obsession with fighting crime. The storyline introduced a new love interest for Batman in the form of Jeannie Bowen. It also marked the debut of the assassin Henri Ducard (in issue #599, April 1989) who had helped train Bruce Wayne during his early years. In an interesting piece of comic-to-movie symmetry, Ducard would play a major role in the 2005 film *Batman Begins*.

The story pitted Batman against the corrupt, mind-possessing scientist Dr. Kenneth Harbinger who, using implanted bio-chips, could remotely operate murdering villains called Bonecrushers. The three oversized issues also celebrated Batman's legacy, featuring galleries by some of the biggest names in comics and film, including Bob Kane, Terry Gilliam, Adam West, Stan Lee, Julius Schwartz, Penn and Teller, Will Eisner, Neal Adams, Dick Sprang, Mike Mignola, David Mazzucchelli, and Kyle Baker, among many other industry luminaries.

HENRI DUCARD
A minor presence in the Batman comics, Ducard would go on to appear in a handful of Robin comics and little else before Liam Neeson portrayed him in the film *Batman Begins*.

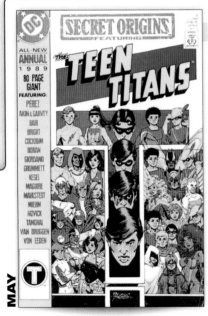

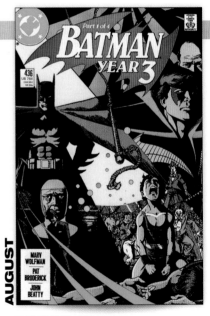

FLAMEBIRD FLAMES ON
Secret Origins Annual #3 ▪ As a Super Hero, Bette Kane took the name of Flamebird, the partner of Nightwing in Kryptonian lore. The original Batgirl pre-Crisis, her origins were revised in this issue by writer George Pérez to make her a tennis pro inspired by Robin to become a crime fighter. This oversized issue also retold the history of the Teen Titans and was drawn by a variety of artists, including pencillers Tom Grummett, Grant Miehm, Irv Novick, Michael Bair, Trevor Von Eeden, and Dick Giordano, with Pérez himself providing *Who's Who* profiles at the back.

THE MANY DEATHS OF BATMAN
Batman #433 ▪ Writer John Byrne teamed with artist Jim Aparo for this three-issue arc. In this first issue, told with only two words of dialogue, Batman's body was found and he was pronounced dead. Commissioner Gordon took off Batman's cowl—revealing a blond man who was not Bruce Wayne. Then another body, dressed as Batman, turned up… One of Batman's trainers, explosives expert Fredrick Stone, was killing off Bruce Wayne's instructors. He feared that some villain would discover his past connnection to Batman and murder him.

MAKING MAHAKALA
Detective Comics #601 ▪ Alan Grant became the solo writer on *Detective Comics* with this issue that ushered in yet another new character co-created with artist Norm Breyfogle. In this three-part tale, Batman was involved in a high-speed chase that ended with the driver of the other car disintegrating before his eyes. Soon, the Dark Knight would be forced to enter the realm of magic and sorcery, joining forces with Etrigan the Demon to defeat the demon Mahakala. This issue also debuted Breyfogle's new Batmobile design.

BATMAN: YEAR 3
Batman #436 ▪ After the success of "Batman: Year One" and "Batman: Year Two," editor Dennis O'Neil and writer Marv Wolfman made the series a trilogy with this four-issue tale illustrated by Pat Broderick and with powerful covers by George Pérez. Dick Grayson's origin was examined, as was that of gangster Anthony Zucco, the murderer of Dick's parents, who was gunned down just as he was being paroled from prison. Also of note was a new, boxy version of the Batmobile, and a brief appearance of a young boy named Tim Drake—the next great Robin.

A MIND NOT HIS OWN
Jeannie Bowen had been separated from her brother Roy Kane when she was two years old after their parents were killed in a car crash. With Bruce Wayne's help, she later found her brother. She discovered that he had become a guinea pig in Dr. Harbinger's Bonecrusher experiments.

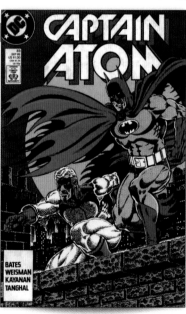

ORIGINS OF THE SUPER-VILLAINS
Secret Origins Special #1 • Three of Batman's most notorious foes starred in this first ever special for the ongoing *Secret Origins* series. The Riddler, Two-Face, and the Penguin featured in this extra-long issue, which included a framing story written by rising star Neil Gaiman with pencils by Mike Hoffman. Writer Alan Grant and artist Sam Keith tackled the Penguin's origin tale, while scribe Mark Verheiden and penciller Pat Broderick retold Two-Face's story. Gaiman wrote the Riddler's tale, with the help of artist Bernie Mireault, focusing on the villain's temporary fall.

THE MUD PACK
Detective Comics #604 • Writer Alan Grant and artist Norm Breyfogle's four-part "The Mud Pack" story featured every incarnation of the shape-shifting villains. The original Clayface, Basil Karlo, brought together Preston Payne (Clayface III), Sandra Fuller (Clayface IV or Lady Clay), and a sample of the deceased Matt Hagen (Clayface II) who had died during *Crisis on Infinite Earths*. After uniting the team, Karlo used DNA from each member to give himself powers as the Ultimate Clayface. The series also guest-starred a mysteriously repowered Looker.

BATMAN VS. THE MANHUNTER
Manhunter #17 • The newest heir to the Manhunter name, Mark Shaw, had already tussled with the Batman villain Catman in issue #13 of his title (May 1989). But in this issue by scripter Kim Yale from a plot by Yale and John Ostrander, penciller Grant Miehm brought Manhunter onto Batman's turf. When both the Manhunter and Batman were on the trail of the newest incarnation of villain Sportsmaster, the two butted heads over their respective motives for crime-fighting. In the end, Shaw left Gotham City, with no plans of returning soon.

THE GOTHAM CITY GAUNTLET
Captain Atom #33 • Batman seemed to be popping up in almost every DC comic book, especially those starring lesser-known heroes. One of those books was *Captain Atom*, where Batman guest-starred in order to help train a recently depowered Cap fight crime without any enhanced abilities. Written by Cary Bates and Greg Weisman with pencils by Rafael Kayanan, this issue saw Captain Atom and Batman uncover a murder plot hatched by the Scarecrow. Cap proved that he had the mental stamina to be a Super Hero, with or without powers.

A SERIOUS HOUSE ON A SERIOUS EARTH
BATMAN: ARKHAM ASYLUM

Few comic book writers have ever gotten inside the heads of Batman's Rogues Gallery to the extent that Grant Morrison did in this hardcover graphic novel illustrated by innovative artist Dave McKean.

Setting their tale inside the asylum's walls and forcing the reader to explore this shadowy old establishment alongside Batman, Morrison and McKean created an unsettling tale of horror and tragedy that is genuinely disturbing and haunting.

When the insane inmates rioted inside Arkham, the Joker requested Batman's presence. With several hostages at the Clown Prince of Crime's mercy, the Dark Knight had no choice but to accept the invitation. As shown through McKean's daring and purposefully chaotic artwork, once inside, Batman was forced into a game of hide and seek with the Joker, touring the asylum in the process. As Batman ran a gauntlet of his foes, it became clear to readers that Morrison had developed his own interpretations of the personalities and manias of the inmates. Maxie Zeus' god complex was explored, Mad Hatter's perverse obsessions were discussed, and Killer Croc's brute animalistic nature was examined. In addition, flashbacks revealed the slow descent into madness of Amadeus Arkham, the institution's founder. Batman himself, as soon as he entered the Asylum, was revealed as a brutal, unsympathetic character as haunted by demons as the villains.

Today, *Batman: Arkham Asylum* remains one of the greatest Batman stories ever told, and also serves as a highly important work that influenced not only the comic book medium, but also the world of video games. Many of its themes and ideas reappear in the smash-hit 2009 video game, *Batman: Arkham Asylum* and its sequels.

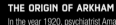

THE ORIGIN OF ARKHAM
In the year 1920, psychiatrist Amadeus Arkham inherited the family mansion following the seeming suicide of his insane mother. Fascinated by one of his patients, homicidal maniac "Mad Dog" Hawkins, Arkham resolved to turn the house into an asylum for the mentally ill, and told his wife Constance and daughter Harriet of his plans.

SPELLBOUND
In time, the malignant spirit haunting Arkham drove Amadeus insane and led his wife to commit suicide. In his cell, Arkham scratched a "holding spell," to keep the evil spirit from escaping the building.

THE DARK KNIGHT'S GUIDE
When Batman entered Arkham Asylum's portals the first person he saw was the leering Joker, whom Batman assumed had taken control. The Joker introduced Batman to the remaining staff and some of the insane inmates.

FINISHING ARKHAM'S WORK
The deadliest threat in Arkham was not the Joker. Staff member Dr. Cavendish, holding Nurse Adams hostage, asserted that Batman was the incarnation of the evil haunting the asylum. Cavendish had fomented the riot to draw Batman inside, where be belonged.

TOSS OF A COIN
Should Batman be allowed to live? The Dark Knight let Two-Face decide. If his silver dollar fell unmarked side up Batman would go free. Two-Face flipped the coin—and Batman was released from Arkham. No one knew that Two-Face had cheated his own coin— and in the process won his own personal victory.

A LEGEND IS BORN
BATMAN: LEGENDS OF THE DARK KNIGHT #1

With the modernization of Batman in "Batman: Year One" and a smash-hit Batman film, the time was ripe for DC Comics to deliver a new Batman title.

Not since the 1940s had Batman seen an ongoing solo title created in his honor. But this Batman title would be strikingly different to those that came before. *Legends of the Dark Knight* would be the first ongoing Batman title created specifically for the direct market of comic book stores. The idea of this title was to allow rotating teams of writers and artists to offer their own interpretations of events in Batman's life, with each team only staying on for one story arc before the next one arrived. While not originally intended to fall within the boundaries of conventional Batman continuity, the first storyline, "Shaman," tied directly in with "Batman: Year One," setting a standard that many subsequent stories followed. The result was an exploration of the early years of Batman's life by some of the finest writers and artists that comics had to offer.

In "Shaman," a five-issue story by writer Dennis O'Neil and penciller Ed Hannigan, readers were treated to one of Bruce Wayne's final travels before his return to Gotham City and his creation of the Batman. While tracking a killer named Tom Woodley in Alaska, Wayne nearly froze to death before being rescued by a Shaman in a bat mask. As the story continued, Bruce returned to his family home, only to encounter Woodley again, as well as a crazed cult committing human sacrifices. Batman triumphed over both threats, realizing his right to wear the symbol of the bat in the process.

VARIANT COVERS
The first issue of this title came with an extra wrap-around cover to clearly show its Batman logo. For fun, DC Comics provided four different colors for that cover, unwittingly creating one of the first examples of a variant cover.

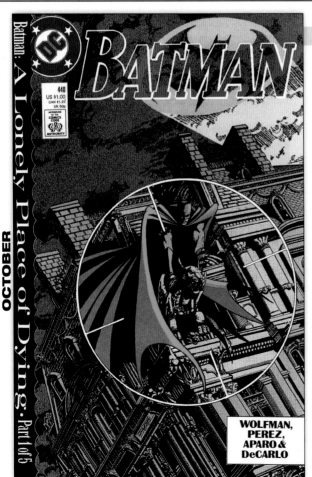

WOLFMAN, PEREZ, APARO & DeCARLO

A LONELY PLACE OF DYING
Batman #440 ● The stage was set for a new Robin, and writers Marv Wolfman and George Pérez had just the candidate in mind: Timothy Drake. At the beginning of this five-part series, which crossed into the pages of *The New Titans* and was drawn by Jim Aparo, Pérez, and Tom Grummett, the brilliant young Tim Drake deduced Batman's alter ego and tried to reunite him with his old partner, Dick Grayson. However, when the threat of Two-Face loomed large, Tim was forced to don a Robin costume himself in *Batman #442*.

THE THIRD ROBIN
Tim Drake had been forever scarred when he saw Dick Grayson's parents plummet to their deaths at the circus. But when he figured out that Grayson was really Robin, he began a journey that would eventually lead to him adopting the Boy Wonder persona himself. He'd still have to face plenty of training before Batman allowed him to officially become his newest Robin.

ANNOUNCING ANARKY
Detective Comics #608 ● Drug-dealing musician Johnny Vomit had been electrocuted and an anarchy symbol sprayed over his unconscious body. A new vigilante was in Gotham City. Wearing a yellow mask and a red-robed costume, "voice for the people" Anarky doled out his own brand of justice based on his political beliefs. The Dark Knight soon apprehended him and discovered that he was a teenager named Lonnie Machin. However, unknown to Batman, Anarky had the last laugh, spray-painting his symbol on the back of Batman's cape.

CULT OF CHUBALA
Between his bouts with Woodley, Batman stumbled upon a cult committing human sacrifices. In order to defeat the cult's leader, the Dark Knight appeared like some sort of supernatural being thanks to his own brand of smoke and mirrors.

HERALDING HAROLD
The Question #33 ■ When his mother rejected him due to his short stature and inability to speak, Harold Allnut left Gotham City and headed to the Question's home of Hub City in this issue by writer Dennis O'Neil and penciller Denys Cowan. With his genius-level mechanic skills Harold would soon become a major supporting character in Batman's world as the Dark Knight's personal inventor and tinkerer. But for this issue, Harold was content simply to prove his worth by rescuing Hub's mayor and her innocent child from a killer named Cathy Fregosi.

BATMAN VS. THE RIPPER
Batman: Gotham by Gaslight ■ This story presented a Batman that no one had seen before and ushered in an entire series of Elseworlds tales that placed heroes in times and places that would have been inconceivable in the normal DC Universe. Writer Brian Augustyn and artist Mike Mignola transported Bruce Wayne from present-day Gotham City to the year 1889. Batman, plagued by the death of his parents in a stagecoach holdup, was just starting his crime-fighting career. He would soon face his first super-villain—Jack the Ripper.

SPECIAL FEATURE

MEETING JACK
When Jack the Ripper traveled to Gotham City to continue his murder spree, he soon met the city's new protector. By the story's end, Batman discovered that the Ripper was his own uncle, Jacob Packer. This hit prestige format special later spawned a sequel in Batman: Master of the Future (December 1991).

ALSO THIS YEAR

January—Secret Origins #36: Neil Gaiman gave readers a rare glimpse into the inner workings of Poison Ivy's mind.

March—The Question #26: The Riddler's real name was revealed to be Edward Nashton.

May—Justice League America #26: Batman and the Huntress crossed paths for the first time.

★ **June 23rd:** Director Tim Burton portrayed Batman once more as a dark creature of the night in his blockbuster film *Batman*, starring Michael Keaton in the title role and Jack Nicholson as the Joker.

★ **November 6th—**A new incarnation of the *Batman* comic strip returned to newspapers.

1989—Batman Annual #13: Alfred's origins were examined in this issue that also featured a lead Two-Face story, plus a variety of Who's Who entries.

1989—Detective Comics Annual #2: Batman recalled that as a teenager he trained with cop Harvey Harris and the pair investigated a series of gruesome murders.

183

1990s

The 1990s was an unprecedented decade of expansion for Batman. Since his creation in 1939, Batman had largely been confined to his own two monthly titles, various team-up or team books, and starred in a 1960s TV series. However, after 1989's hit Batman film, Batman became the subject of a blockbuster movie franchise in the 1990s.

The Dark Knight would see two new ongoing titles thrive at the beginning of the decade—*Batman: Legends of the Dark Knight* and *Batman: Shadow of the Bat*. His sidekicks would also earn their own titles. Robin, Nightwing, and former Batgirl Barbara Gordon starred in new monthly comics as more and more miniseries and one-shots were published, taking advantage of a sales boom that saw comic book stores opening across the country.

The 1990s was also the decade of the crossover. Not only did DC Comics run epic storylines through many of its own titles, but the 90s saw a level of cooperation never seen before with other publishing companies. And in his own titles, the Dark Knight saw a major change in his world in the 19-part "Knightfall" event that would shake up Gotham City like never before.

Ushering him through all these events were several key writers and artists. Writer Chuck Dixon arrived at DC Comics with the first ever Robin miniseries, and soon found himself a longtime fixture in Gotham City. Writer Doug Moench returned for a second, and equally memorable run on *Batman*, made all the more dramatic by the highly imaginative and moody covers, and later interiors, by artist Kelley Jones. And writer Alan Grant and artist Norm Breyfogle shared their talents in *Batman*, *Detective Comics*, and *Batman: Shadow of the Bat*, continuing to deliver their brand of villains fitting for a more violent and edgy era.

Above all else, the Batman titles managed to stand on a foundation of solid storytelling in the 1990s, creating comics that contained as much substance as style.

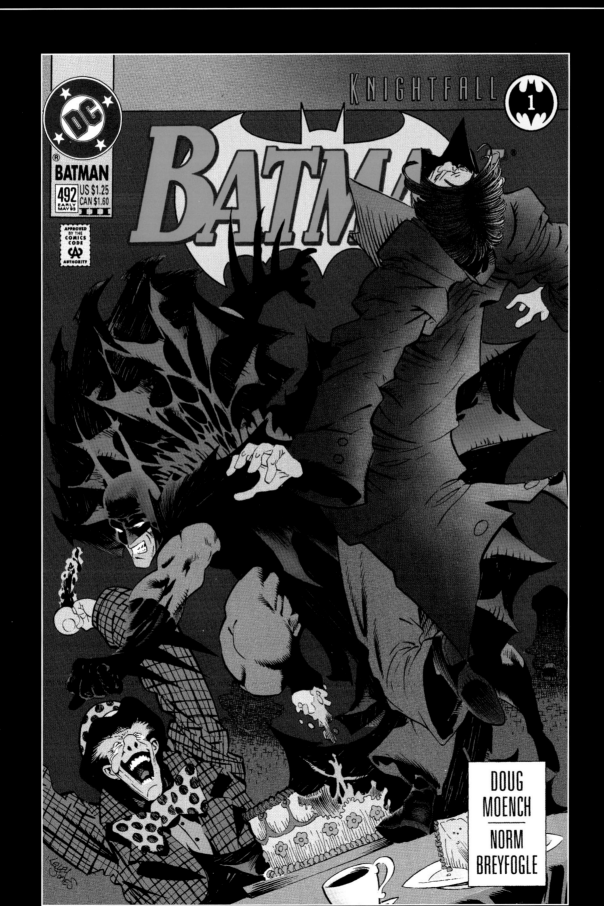

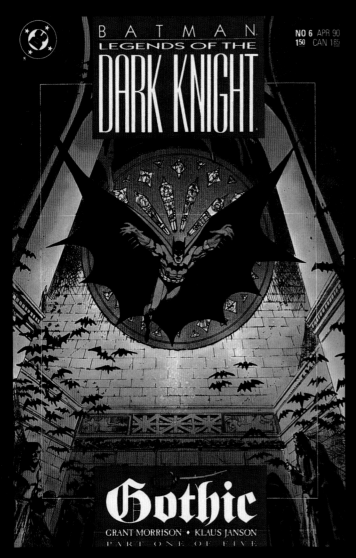

WHISPERS AND LEGENDS
BATMAN: LEGENDS OF THE DARK KNIGHT #6

The Dark Knight faced a seemingly supernatural threat that he had first encountered during his school days: Mr. Whisper, the man without a shadow.

Following Dennis O'Neil's classic "Shaman" arc in the first issues of *Legends of the Dark Knight*, Grant Morrison stepped up to the plate to pen the title's next five-issue storyline, illustrated by Klaus Janson. During young Bruce's hated time in private school, the enigmatic Mr. Winchester had been his headmaster. The cruel Winchester was feared by Bruce's peers, who claimed that he possessed no shadow.

Many years later, when Bruce had become Batman, he was plagued by recurrent nightmares of his private school, in which his father returned from the dead, but with his mouth stitched shut.

At the same time someone was murdering Gotham City's gang bosses. Strange as it seemed, the culprit had to be Winchester. Batman journeyed to Austria to investigate Winchester's past. He discovered that he was a very long-lived monk named Manfred who had made a pact with the devil. Now calling himself Mr. Whisper, the villain attempted to release a plague on present-day Gotham City, only to be defeated by Batman on his return. The series was reprinted as trade paperback *Batman Gothic* in 2007.

NIGHTMARE MESSENGER
Recurring bad dreams about his father haunted Bruce Wayne reminding him of his miserable time in private school. In one nightmare, his father, Thomas Wayne, appeared with his mouth sewn up, prompting Bruce to wake up screaming. Bruce became convinced that this nightmarish image of his father held a message for him.

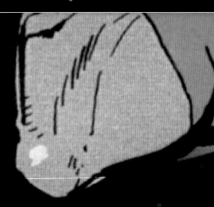

1990

"You may join me—and my *daughter*—or you will perish."

Rā's al Ghūl to Batman, *Bride of the Demon #1*

With Batman still very much in the spotlight after his hit Warner Bros. film *Batman*, his comics continued to mature, focusing on storylines that were as intriguing as any political thriller or horror tale. In addition, excitingly different art styles took the character out of his illustrative "comfort zone." The hardcover *Batman: Digital Justice* by writer/artist Pepe Moreno, which experimented with computer-rendered imagery, proved that there was plenty of new territory for Batman to explore. The most notable character development of the year was Tim Drake's progress toward making the mantle of Robin unquestionably his own.

MARCH

FROM KGB TO NKVD
Batman #445 ■ In this issue, Batman tangled with a foe named Slasher who was armed with a buzz-saw gauntlet. However, a far greater challenge awaited the Dark Knight in this three-issue arc by writer Marv Wolfman and artist Jim Aparo: the NKVDemon. This protégé of the KGBeast was out for revenge for his mentor's defeat at Batman's hands. The NKVDemon (real name Gregor Dosynski), proved nearly as skilled as his predecessor when Batman confronted the killer on his home turf of Moscow. This issue also reintroduced Vicki Vale into Batman's life.

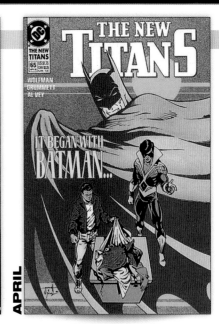

APRIL

ROBIN IN TRAINING
The New Titans #65 ■ Nightwing's team of Titans had dropped the "Teen" part of their name with issue #50 (December 1988) to signify that the sidekicks had grown up and created their own legacy. In this issue by the title's longtime writer Marv Wolfman and regular artist Tom Grummett, Nightwing further proved that point by training a member of the next generation of Super Heroes—Tim Drake. This stand-alone tale shed light on the methods of the adult Dick Grayson, revealing his keen observational skills and methods of combating the drug trade.

"Be thankful that you will soon die *cleanly*. You will be spared the *pestilence*... millions sneezing and spitting *blood*..."

Mr. Whisper, *Batman: Legends of the Dark Knight* #10

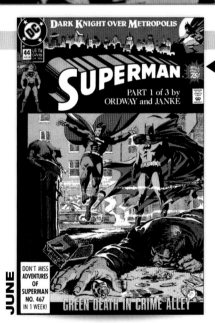

JUNE

DARK KNIGHT IN METROPOLIS

Superman #44 ▪ Batman appeared in Metropolis and in each of Superman's three ongoing titles in this three-part adventure. Thanks to writer/artists Jerry Ordway and Dan Jurgens, and the writer/artist team of Roger Stern and Bob McLeod, the story provided a rare glimpse of the post-Crisis World's Finest duo in action. After Superman and Batman had defeated Dr. Moon and Intergang, Superman handed Batman a Kryptonite ring. Superman knew that if he ever lost control of his powers he could trust Batman to use the ring to keep him in line.

SPECIAL FEATURE

WORKING TOGETHER

Batman made a rare appearance in Metropolis as he and Superman worked together to solve a crime wave caused by Mr. Moon and Intergang. This tale was one of Batman and Superman's first team-ups after their initial meeting.

THE PENGUIN AFFAIR

Batman #448 ▪ In the 1990s, crossovers between *Batman* and *Detective Comics* were rare, as each title had its own creative team. However, part two of this three-part tale took place in *Detective Comics* #615 (June 1990). Co-plotted by *Batman* writer Marv Wolfman and *Detective Comics* writer Alan Grant, and drawn by Jim Aparo, Norm Breyfogle, and Mark Bright, this battle of wits between Batman and the Penguin introduced the villain's right-hand woman Lark and brought genius mechanic Harold Allnut into Batman's world.

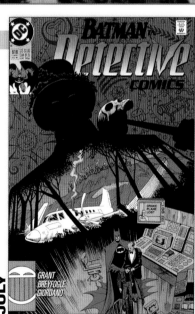

JULY

ONSLAUGHT OF THE OBEAH MAN

Detective Comics #618 ▪ Tim Drake had been training to be Robin for a while, but wasn't quite ready yet. With this issue written by Alan Grant, with layouts by Norm Breyfogle and finishes by Dick Giordano, readers met the Obeah Man, the head of a voodoo cult, who kidnapped Tim's parents. In a suspenseful, four-issue arc, Tim tried to keep hope alive as Batman hunted the villain. Finally, in issue #621 (September 1990), Tim's mother Janet died and his father Jack was paralyzed, fulfilling the tragic fate that seemed a tradition in Robin origin stories.

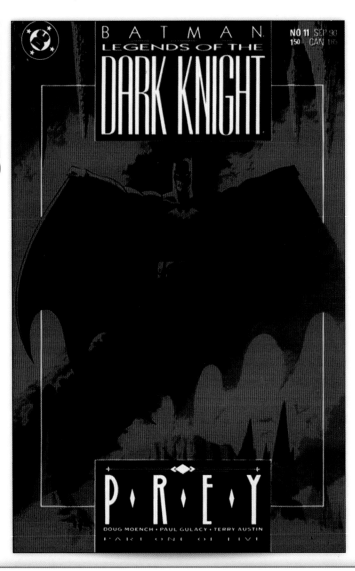

PREY

BATMAN: LEGENDS OF THE DARK KNIGHT #11

Evil mastermind Hugo Strange was back in Gotham City. This time he was a psycho psychiatrist both obsessed with Batman and determined to destroy him.

No stranger to Batman's world, Doug Moench scripted the next five-issue installment in this flashback series with the help of artist Paul Gulacy. A brilliant reintroduction of Hugo Strange set in the days after "Batman: Year One," "Prey" focused on Strange's obsession with the Batman and his manipulation of police Sergeant Maxwell Cort into a killer called the Night-Scourge. Moench and Gulacy also threw Catwoman into the mix, cladding the thief in a purple version of her gray "Year One" costume. This series also reintroduced the Batmobile, revealing the first time Batman ever took the famous car (redesigned for this series) out for a drive in issue #15 (February 1991), as well as the Bat-Signal, first used by James Gordon in issue #12 (November 1990).

OBSESSED WITH BATMAN

When twisted psychiatrist Hugo Strange donned his own version of the Batman costume, he was filled with a perverted sense of purpose and glee. Each time he wore the costume he believed that he gained a fresh insight into the way Batman's mind worked. His interest in the Dark Knight quickly became an obsession.

DARK KNIGHT, DARK CITY

***Batman* #452** ● Writer Peter Milligan penned this memorable three-issue storyline, illustrated by Kieron Dwyer and with cover art by Mike Mignola, in which the Riddler proved that he was still a serious threat to Batman. In this entertaining tale of cruelty and the occult, a demon named Barbathos had possessed the Riddler, turning him from an eccentric criminal into a ruthless murderer. After capturing Batman, the Riddler tried to sacrifice the hero in order to control Barbathos, but was stopped by the demon, who claimed to be the dark city of Gotham City itself.

WORLDS APART

***World's Finest* #1** ● Writer Dave Gibbons and artist Steve Rude lent their storytelling skills to this three-issue prestige format miniseries. Contrasting Superman's world of Metropolis, full of light and hope, with Batman's existence in a Gotham City, full of shadows and crime, this series took a look at the past of the two heroes, and shed light on their similarities as orphans. Centering around the Midway Orphanage, this entertaining tale pitted the two heroes against the Joker and Lex Luthor, and introduced a Steve Rude-designed Batmobile.

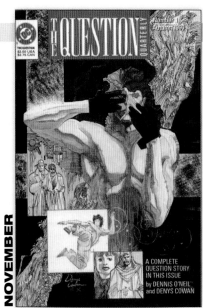

THE QUESTION RETURNS

***The Question Quarterly* #1** ● The Question's first title had been a monthly. The character returned in this new series, which delivered the same intriguing storylines, beginning with this issue by the team of writer Dennis O'Neil and artist Denys Cowan. The quarterly format would only survive for five issues; however, the Question would bounce back in the special *The Question Returns* (February 1997), as a member of a team called *The L.A.W.* (September 1999), and again in a self-titled six-issue miniseries in January 2004.

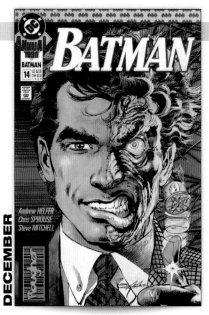

TWO SIDES TO TWO-FACE

***Batman Annual* #14** ● In perhaps the greatest Two-Face origin story to date, writer Andrew Helfer and artist Chris Sprouse made Harvey Dent more three-dimensional than ever before. Carrying on the look and feel of "Batman: Year One," this extra-long tale was set in the days when James Gordon was still a police captain, and Harvey Dent was Gotham City's star district attorney. Introducing Harvey's abusive father, along with Harvey's suppressed split personality, this tale influenced 1992's *Batman: The Animated Series* among other reinterpretations of Harvey's tragic fate.

DECEMBER

A ROBIN FOR THE 1990S
BATMAN #457

Tim Drake was about to prove his worth at last, and a grateful Batman would officially reward him with the mantle of Robin.

In a story that had begun with issue #455 (October 1990), Batman had battled the Scarecrow's latest scheme, only to become a captive of the so-called "Master of Fear" at the start of this Alan Grant/Norm Breyfogle issue. While using the Dark Knight as a guinea pig to test his latest fear gases, Scarecrow was unprepared for an attack from a young boy clad in a red ski mask. That boy was Tim Drake, who was aware that he hadn't earned the mantle of Robin, but knew he needed to act. Fighting through his fear to defeat the villain, Tim saved Batman's life, and by page 20, Batman finally addressed him as "Robin."

But Tim Drake wasn't just a carbon copy of the previous Robins, and Batman, as well as DC Comics editorial, decided to gift the boy with a new take on the familiar uniform. Robin's new costume featured a cape that was yellow on the inside and black on the outside, a streamlined Utility Belt, long green pants, and black ninja tabi boots. The costume also included a redesigned "R" logo that Robin could use as a shuriken when the need arose. The result was a new Robin for a new era.

A MODERN ROBIN
Tim Drake's new Robin costume was a sleeker, more intimidating version of the costume worn by Dick Grayson and Jason Todd. Designed to give Drake the most efficient means of fighting crime, the costume also symbolized his status as a brand-new Robin for a brand-new age.

GRANT · BREYFOGLE · MITCHELL

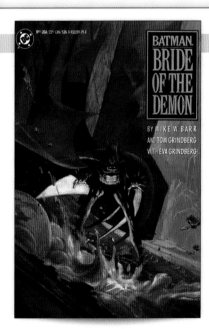

THE DEMON WITHIN
Batman: Bride of the Demon ■ With art by Tom Grindberg, writer Mike W. Barr returned to chronicle a new Rā's al Ghūl story in this sequel to his popular 1987 graphic novel *Batman: Son of the Demon*. In his quest for an heir, Rā's sought out aging actress Evelyn Grayce and rejuvenated her in a Lazarus Pit. Rā's also planned to poison the planet with excess ozone, to heal the hole in the ozone layer. Rā's al Ghūl's plans ended explosively, thanks to Batman. In the final page, Evelyn revealed that she was pregnant with the Demon Head's child.

BATMAN GOES DIGITAL
Batman: Digital Justice ■ Today, computer graphics are an commonplace occurrence. Comics are colored, lettered, even "pencilled" and "inked," via computer. In 1990, lettering was still done on art boards, and coloring through hand-painted color guides. So when Pepe Moreno wrote and illustrated this hardcover graphic novel that was entirely computer generated, it stood out on comic shelves. Chronicling a digital Batman's fight with a computer virus version of Joker, *Digital Justice* was a technological milestone for DC Comics and Batman.

A NEW DIMENSION
Batman 3-D ■ Batman hadn't had a new story in 3-D since the 1950s; editor Archie Goodwin thought it was high time that changed. With writer/artist John Byrne and 3-D effects expert Ray Zone, Goodwin created this oversized comic, which came with bat-shaped red and blue 3-D glasses. The issue's main story featured Two-Face, the Penguin, and the Riddler; it also reprinted "The Robot Robbers," drawn by Curt Swan, from *Batman Adventures in Amazing 3-D* (December 1953). A gallery section featured 3-D pin-ups by many of Batman's finest artists.

ALSO THIS YEAR

January—*Batman* #443: The start of a two-part tale, this issue introduced a new Crimesmith: Dr. Jeffrey Fraser, a brilliant scientist and media personality with a double life as a criminal mastermind.

March—*Sandman* #14: The serial killer Fun Land debuted, a character who would later join Batman's Rogues Gallery.

August—*The Huntress* #17: The vigilante Huntress clashed with Batman in this three-issue story.

August—*Secret Origins* #50: Batman and Robin's first meeting was retold as a prose story as part of the final issue of *Secret Origins*.

October—*Detective Comics* #622: This three-issue story featured a comic book within a comic book. Bruce Wayne was none too pleased by a Batman backstory invented by a comic book writer in Gotham City, in which Batman made a pact with the devil to purge the world of evil.

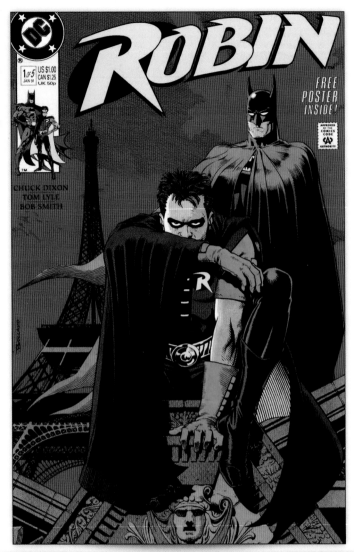

ROBIN LEAVES THE NEST

ROBIN #1

In April of 1940, the character of Robin debuted in *Detective Comics* #38. Nearly 51 years later, the hero finally received his own title, even if the character wearing the costume had changed.

Writer Chuck Dixon and artist Tom Lyle's incarnation of Robin was a major moment in the history of the world's most famous sidekick, and would lead to Dixon's long and successful association with the Batman books.

In this five-issue series, Tim Drake journeyed to Paris to help perfect his skills as Robin and, more importantly, cement his own identity as a Super Hero. What he found was an adventure that debuted two new villains: gang member Lynx (in issue #1), and the blind martial-arts master King Snake (in issue #2). This series also featured the assassins Henri Ducard and Lady Shiva, the latter training Robin and enabling him to discover a special liking for the weapon known as the bō a long, wooden, martial-arts staff.

By the series' end, Robin had indeed become his own man. He had successfully taken down King Snake as well as the vengeful Lynx. He had also firmly rejected Lady Shiva's invitation to become her agent of death.

LYNX OF THE GHOST DRAGONS

Lynx was the codename for the woman known as Ling, whom Robin met and fell for while in Paris. When King Snake gouged out one of her eyes, Lynx blamed Robin for the deed and swore revenge. Lynx would eventually become leader of the Chinese gang known as the Ghost Dragons when they moved to Gotham City.

1991

"You make me sound like a knight errant sent out on some glorious quest..."

Tim Drake, *Robin* #1

Batman's reach and influence in the world of comic books was expanding. Just as Catwoman had two years before, Robin branched out into his first miniseries. By 1993, both characters would have their own ongoing titles. Meanwhile, Batman continued to inspire prestige-format specials. The character crossed over with properties from other comic book companies but, in his own titles, also found his supporting cast beginning to grow as Gotham City seemed to be ever expanding in scope and scale. Batman was well on his way to becoming DC Comics' most popular character.

NEW FAMILIAR FACES

Batman #458 ▪ The Caped Crusader gained a new partner in this issue written by Alan Grant and drawn by Norm Breyfogle. Hailing from the pages of *The Question* and the recent "The Penguin Affair" *Batman/Detective Comics* crossover, hunchback technician Harold Allnut was found living in an abandoned building and serving as the neighborhood "Mr. Fixxit." Seeing the young mute's talent, the Dark Knight relocated Harold to the Batcave where he became Batman's resident inventor. This issue also saw the return of Sarah Essen, who resumed her courtship with Commissioner Gordon.

SOUL DESTROYER

Detective Comics #625 ▪ Marv Wolfman and penciller Jim Aparo introduced serial killer Abattoir in this issue. Believing he could absorb his victims' souls, Arnold Etkar, alias Abattoir, escaped Arkham Asylum, and struck at a fundraiser for prospective Mayor Henry Etchison. Party guest Bruce Wayne quickly changed into Batman. While he didn't defeat Abattoir in their first battle, the Dark Knight Detective soon discovered Etchison and Etkar were cousins. Etchison had arranged Etkar's asylum escape so that Abattoir could kill his wife. With their crimes revealed, the cousins were soon apprehended.

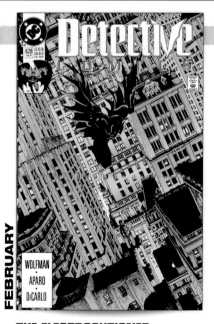

FEBRUARY

THE ELECTROCUTIONER

Detective Comics #626 ■ Writer Marv Wolfman and artist Jim Aparo continued their run on *Batman* by introducing the second villain to bear the name of the Electrocutioner. The original had died in the pages of *Vigilante*. Clad in a red costume and with his skull-like face partially exposed, this new villain employed a so-called "'lectronic lash" and worked for the mob, hunting down criminals that were suspected of stealing from other gangs. Deducing that Jim Gordon was the Electrocutioner's next target, Batman donned a white, padded costume to defeat this foe.

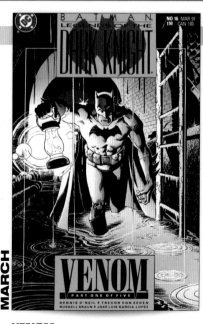

MARCH

VENOM

Batman: Legends of the Dark Knight #16 The strength-enhancing drug that would later help villain Bane defeat Batman debuted in this five-issue arc written by Dennis O'Neil and drawn by Trevor Von Eeden and Russell Braun. This story saw Batman fail to save a young girl due to the limits of his physical strength. The girl's father, Randolph Porter, gave Batman the designer drug Venom to improve his crime-fighting performance. However, the Dark Knight became addicted to the drug and was forced to lock himself in the Batcave to detox. He then put a stop to the career of Venom's corrupt creator.

BATMAN'S FIRST CASE

Detective Comics #627 ■ In a tribute to Batman's 600th appearance in *Detective Comics*, Batman's first adventure by artist Bob Kane and writer Bill Finger (May 1939), "The Case of the Chemical Syndicate," was reprinted, as was its reinterpretation from *Detective Comics* #387 (May 1969) by writer Mike Friedrich and artist Bob Brown. To bring this classic tale up to date, editor Dennis O'Neil employed the current creative teams on *Detective Comics* and *Batman*—respectively writer Marv Wolfman and artist Jim Aparo, and writer Alan Grant and penciller Norm Breyfogle.

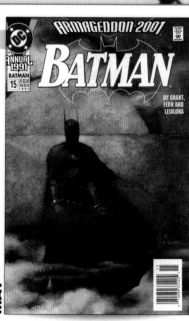

MAY

THE LAST BATMAN STORY

Batman Annual #15 ■ As part of DC Comics' crossover, *Armageddon 2001*, this story was set in the future of the year 2001, where a tyrant named Monarch ruled with an iron fist. After discovering Monarch used to be a Super Hero, a time traveler named Waverider headed to 1991 to deduce the villain's identity by meeting Super Heroes of the present day, and traveling into their possible futures. Waverider traveled into Batman's future in this issue by writer Alan Grant and penciller Jim Fern, where he discovered that the Dark Knight had been framed for several murders.

CIRCLE OF VIOLENCE

BATMAN: FULL CIRCLE

As the title suggested, Batman was forced to revisit the most traumatic incident of his childhood, coming face to face with the son of the murderer of his parents, a criminal by the name of Joseph Chill.

MIKE W. BARR   ALAN DAVIS   MARK FARMER

In writer Mike W. Barr's memorable "Batman: Year Two" storyline, Batman had fought a villain named the Reaper, a murderous vigilante who shot the killer of Bruce Wayne's parents, Joe Chill. In this aptly-named prestige-format sequel, Barr introduced Joseph Chill, the son of Joe Chill and the newest heir to the Reaper mantle. Set in the early days of Batman's career when Dick Grayson was just learning the ropes as Robin, this series featured the sleek art of Alan Davis, the original artist from "Year Two." While Batman eventually bested the new Reaper, he stopped just short of killing him in front of Joseph's child, Joey. The circle of violence that had began with Batman's father and the Reaper's father was finally at an end.

A FALSE TALE
Joseph Chill's son Joey tracked down his father in Gotham City as he wanted to live with him. At first Joey was unaware of his father's criminal identity as the Reaper. To explain his twisted mission, the Reaper told Joey a false story about Batman so that the little boy believed that Batman was evil.

RETURN OF THE BAT-HOUND
Batman #462 ▪ This three-part tale saw the return of a 1950s character, Ace the Bat-Hound, although the "Bat-Hound" part of his name was dropped. The scripting of Alan Grant and the pencils of Norm Breyfogle gave a modern twist to the character. Ace crossed Batman's path when, journeying to California in the Batmobile, the Dark Knight nearly ran over the dog. After Ace's elderly owner passed away, following a skirmish with a kidnapper named Two-Hearts, the hound came to reside in the Batcave.

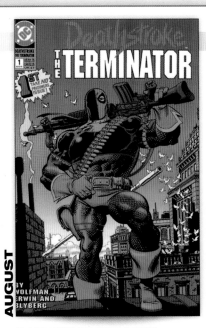

A STROKE OF BAD LUCK
Deathstroke: The Terminator #1 ▪ The longtime foe of Robin and the Teen Titans and a future member of Batman's Rogues Gallery, Deathstroke earned his own series, thanks to writer Marv Wolfman and penciller Steve Erwin. Slade Wilson was a mercenary for hire but, as Deathstroke he had his own code of honor. In this debut issue, Slade's history was recounted, featuring a cameo by the original Robin, Dick Grayson. It also included the first appearance of a new Ravager, Bill Walsh, Slade's former rival.

ROBIN RETURNS
Robin II #1 ▪ Tim Drake's first miniseries had been a hit and, after he starred in the three-part story "Shadow Box" that began in Batman #467 (August 1991), DC Comics wasted no time delivering a sequel. Reuniting writer Chuck Dixon and artist Tom Lyle, the series featured variant covers, a rarity for DC at the time as well as hologram stickers, a first for a Batman title. Readers witnessed this new Robin's first ever fight with the Joker, an adventure made all the more tense by Joker's violent history with the last Robin, Jason Todd.

DUEL
Batman: Legends of the Dark Knight Annual #1 ▪ Writer Dennis O'Neil took Batman back to a monastery where he had trained as a young man. Then Batman embarked on a quest through a demon-filled cavern, a vampire-occupied castle, a city invaded by aliens, a past filled with gangsters, and a haunted battlefield—adventures revealed to have been hallucinations. The main story was handled by artist Jim Aparo, each hallucination was drawn by different artists, including Keith Giffen, Joe Quesada, Tom Lyle, and Dan Spiegle.

DECEMBER

THE IDIOT ROOT

Batman #472 • In this four-part crossover with *Detective Comics* (continuing into #639), writer Peter Milligan and artists Norm Breyfogle and Jim Aparo introduced a pair of new villains: the Queen of Hearts and the Idiot. The Queen of Hearts was a serial killer, obsessed with cutting out her victims' hearts. The Idiot was a disembodied product of four people's subconscious who consumed minds by bringing others into his Idiot Zone via a drug, the Idiot Root. Batman managed to triumph over both weird foes in this reality-bending tale.

ENTER ELSEWORLDS

Batman: Holy Terror • "In Elseworlds, heroes are taken from their usual settings and put into strange times and places—some that have existed, or might have existed, and others that can't, couldn't or shouldn't exist. The result is stories that make characters who are as familiar as yesterday seem as fresh as tomorrow." With that introduction, *Batman: Holy Terror* became the first Elseworlds special. This tale by writer Alan Brennert and artist Norm Breyfogle featured a Gotham City ruled by the church and Batman as a vigilante man of the cloth.

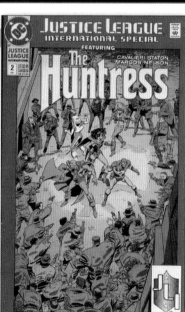

THE END OF THE HUNTRESS?

Justice League International Special #2
The Huntress was given one final hurrah with this issue. Helena's usual team of scripter Joey Cavalieri and artist Joe Staton featured the Huntress seeking the help of the JLI when a cop-killer, calling himself the Hunter, appeared in New York City. Realizing that the violent vigilante was a former ally, the Huntress fought the Hunter, only to later watch him die in a police shootout. The last page showed Helena discarding her costume in an incinerator, hoping to lead a normal life.

ALSO THIS YEAR

March—*Batman* #460:** Catwoman gained a new young civilian sidekick—a girl named Arizona.

April—*Superman Annual* #2:** This *Armageddon 2001* tie-in depicted a future where Batman and Superman were forced to square off in the climax.

August—*Detective Comics* #633:** The strange new villain called the Synaptic Kid first appeared.

November—*Black Canary* #1:** The future Bird of Prey was rewarded with her first-ever four-issue miniseries, leading to an ongoing series in January 1993.

December—*The New Teen Titans Annual* #7:** With the identity of super-villain Monarch still a mystery, Waverider visited a possible future where Dick Grayson, unaware that he would turn into Deathwing, was leading a new group of Titans.

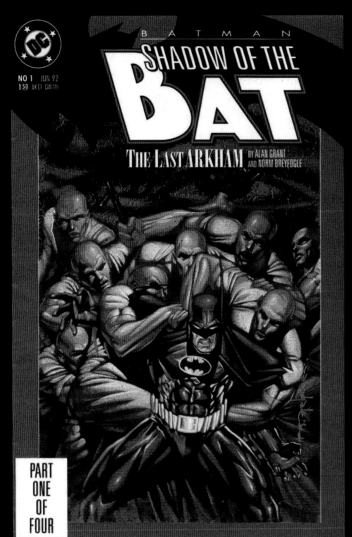

BATMAN
SHADOW OF THE
BAT
NO 1 JUN 92
150 UK £1 CAN 195
THE LAST ARKHAM BY ALAN GRANT AND NORM BREYFOGLE

PART ONE OF FOUR

THE LAST ARKHAM

BATMAN: SHADOW OF THE BAT #1

When the movie *Batman Returns* hit cinema screens in 1992, DC Comics launched a new Batman solo series—*Batman: Shadow of the Bat*—thereby giving the hero four monthly titles all of his own.

Editor Dennis O'Neil and his staff recognized the importance of giving *Shadow of the Bat* its own identity to help set it apart on the stands. A border was added to the covers, and artist Brian Stelfreeze was hired to paint his stylized version of the Caped Crusader. The result was a bold statement and Stelfreeze would remain its cover artist until issue #49 (April 1996). Issue #1 was a special deluxe edition, packaged in a polybag that included a bookmark, blueprints of Arkham Asylum, mini-posters of the covers of issues #1 and #2, and a 3-D fold-out model of the asylum, occupied by a host of Batman's enemies.

Shadow of the Bat was writer Alan Grant's newest forum to tell Batman stories on a monthly basis, along with his partner, artist Norm Breyfogle. The pair introduced the new head of Arkham, Jeremiah Arkham, as well as the new villain Mr. Zsasz. This first four-part arc saw Batman imprisoned in the redesigned Arkham Asylum in order to deduce how Zsasz was escaping and going on his murder sprees. The man-mountain known as Amygdala debuted in issue #3 and, in its second storyline, the villain Black Spider met his apparent end in issue #5, letting readers know that in this fast-paced new title, anything was possible.

THE MURDEROUS MR. ZSASZ
When he first appeared, the serial killer known as Mr. Zsasz had already racked up over 47 known kills. For every person he murdered, Zsasz slashed a tally mark on his own body, soon becoming covered in the disturbing scars.

1992

"If I'm an angel, why do I need a bulletproof vest?"

Azrael, Batman: Sword of Azrael #1.

Batman Returns, the sequel to 1989's *Batman* film by director Tim Burton, premiered and Batman fever swept the country once more. The hit film encouraged DC Comics to increase the number of Batman titles. The new monthly title *Batman: Shadow of the Bat* was launched, and Batman miniseries and one-shots became a frequent sight at comic stores, a tradition that continues to this day. In the fall, the soon-to-be-hit cartoon *Batman: The Animated Series* debuted, giving Batman another comic book title, *The Batman Adventures*, as well as a continued heroic presence on toy aisles.

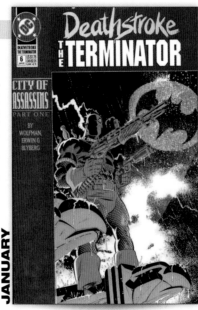

JANUARY

DEATH COMES TO GOTHAM CITY
Deathstroke: The Terminator #6 ● Slade Wilson, alias Deathstroke, came to Gotham City in this four-part tale by writer Marv Wolfman and artist Steve Erwin. Deathstroke kidnapped hitman Jeremy Barker from police custody in order to ferret out a traitor inside the police force and clashed with Batman for the first time. Much to the readership's shock, Deathstroke actually defeated the Dark Knight in hand-to-hand combat in a violent confrontation in issue # 7 (February 1992), although Slade could only barely walk away from it afterward himself.

FEBRUARY

DESTROYER
Batman #474 ● Academy Award-winning production designer Anton Furst was put in the spotlight in the first-ever crossover between *Batman*, *Detective Comics* (#641) and *Batman: Legends of the Dark Knight* (#27). After seeing Furst's designs for the movie version of Gotham City in the 1989 film *Batman*, editor Dennis O'Neil hired the artist to concoct a Gotham City for the comics. Furst's creations graced the covers of these three issues by writers Alan Grant and O'Neil himself, alongside artists Norm Breyfogle, Chris Sprouse, and Jim Aparo.

MEETING MONTOYA
Batman #475 ■ Not too many police officers were especially well known in Gotham City. However, in this issue, written by Alan Grant and drawn by Norm Breyfogle, a rising star in the police department was revealed—James Gordon's new assistant, Renee Montoya. Soon to be a fixture on the G.C.P.D., the resourceful Renee would go on to become a regular supporting character in the upcoming *Batman: The Animated Series*. She would later become a Super Hero in her own right as the next Question in the 2006 maxiseries, *52*.

MARCH

SPECIAL FEATURE

RENEE MONTOYA
Renee Montoya began her career as Commissioner Gordon's assistant, but soon found herself the longtime partner of one of Gotham City's most interesting cops, Harvey Bullock. Bullock and Montoya were shown working together in *Batman: The Animated Series*, and soon developed a deep camaraderie in the comics.

DARK NIGHTS
Batman: Gotham Nights #1 ■ In this four-issue series, writer John Ostrander and penciller Mary Mitchell focused on the ordinary citizens of Gotham City. From a hopelessly romantic clerk at a donut counter to an elderly man who was once a patient of Dr. Thomas Wayne, average Gothamites were the focus, as Batman crossed their paths (sometimes at the wheel of a slightly redesigned Batmobile). Still relevant to this day, *Gotham Nights* earned a sequel, four-issue miniseries by the same creative team in March 1995.

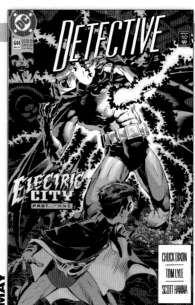

ELECTRIC CITY
Detective Comics #644 ■ After writing Robin's first two miniseries, Chuck Dixon became the new writer on *Detective Comics*, starting with this issue with the help of the pencils of Tom Lyle and the inks of Scott Hanna. In this three-part tale, Dixon introduced the electric-powered Buzz Galvin, who survived being sentenced to the electric chair to take revenge on his enemies. But even more of a milestone than the introduction of this sadistic murderer was the first appearance of the third, and longest-lasting Electrocutioner, Lester Buchinsky.

MAY

SPOILER ALERT
DETECTIVE COMICS #647

Writer Chuck Dixon fleshed out the character of Tim Drake using the brilliant groundwork already laid, and also provided him with a great supporting cast, with Spoiler making her debut.

This three-part story not only added a future love interest to Robin's world, but served to delineate the humble beginnings for a character who would one day become a hero in her own right.

The character in question was Stephanie Brown, alias crime fighter Spoiler. The daughter of the villain Cluemaster, Spoiler set out to foil her deadbeat dad's criminal career by sending the police and the Dynamic Duo hints about his latest schemes.

With the energetic pencils of Tom Lyle debuting her in style, the new vigilante Spoiler would later become a recurring character in Robin's future ongoing series, be promoted to Robin herself, and then take over the job of Batgirl. An equal-parts bright and tragic future awaited Ms. Brown, as it did for the other character to debut in this issue, Gotham City's latest mayor, Armand Krol.

CHUCK DIXON
TOM LYLE
SCOTT HANNA

THE CLUEMASTER
Like many of Batman's foes, the Cluemaster was thwarted by the Dark Knight and sent to Blackgate Prison. Upon his release, he abandoned his usual *modus operandi* of leaving clues and planned a major heist with a gang in exchange for a percentage of their profits. His plan took a murderous turn, and he encountered Batman and Robin once more.

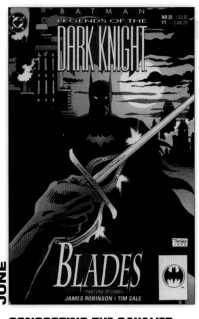

CONCOCTING THE CAVALIER
Batman: Legends of the Dark Knight #32
James Robinson penned this memorable three-issue story arc starring a reinvention of one of Batman's most underrated foes, the Cavalier. With the storytelling help of artist Tim Sale, Robinson created a new Cavalier that was a better fit for the tone of the flashback continuity of *Legends of the Dark Knight*. Named Hudson Pyle, this Cavalier was a stuntman turned vigilante who wanted to compete with Batman to be Gotham City's number one hero. However, he was secretly as corrupt as his original namesake.

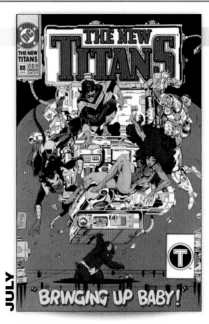

NIGHTWING'S NEW LOOK
The New Titans #88 • Dick Grayson was given a new Nightwing costume in this issue by writers Marv Wolfman and Len Wein and artist Tom Grummett. After his original costume was shredded during a fight with Deathstroke in issue #86 (May 1992), Nightwing decided an upgrade was in order. Designed by Mirage, posing as Starfire, the new costume replaced his low V-neck, high-collar look with something more up to date. It came complete with yellow material between his arms that allowed Nightwing to glide on wind currents.

HEALERS AND HARPIES
Batman #481 • Over a half-decade after his tenure as the regular writer on both *Batman* and *Detective Comics*, Doug Moench returned to script Batman alongside another longtime Batman contributor, artist Jim Aparo. While the pair's first effort began like an average Maxie Zeus story, in a quiet, two-page scene, Moench introduced a new love interest for Bruce Wayne, physical therapist Dr. Shondra Kinsolving. The two-part tale also saw the debut of a new villain obsessed with Maxie Zeus, the weapons expert known as the Harpy.

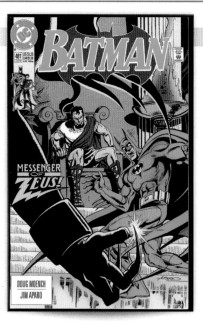

A BULLET FOR BULLOCK
Detective Comics #651 • Harvey Bullock took center stage in this self-contained issue by writer Chuck Dixon and *Detective Comics'* new regular penciller, Graham Nolan. Only Nolan's second issue, this entertaining tale would later be adapted into an episode of the TV show *Batman: The Animated Series*. When death threats escalated into an attempt on Bullock's life, the longtime Gotham City cop teamed up with Batman and discovered that the culprit was none other than Bullock's landlord, who wanted Harvey out of his rent-controlled apartment.

WATCHING DAD
Spoiler had no truck with her father Cluemaster's criminal ways, and used a surveillance device to overhear his plans.

NOVEMBER

DOUG
MOENCH
JIM
APARO

BATMAN GETS ANIMATED
The Batman Adventures #1 ■ DC Comics decided to match the tone and all-ages appeal of the *Batman: The Animated Series* TV show with this new series. It was set firmly in the universe of the animated continuity pioneered by producer/character designer Bruce Timm and his colleagues. The series focused on innovative, self-contained stories by writer Kelley Puckett and penciller Ty Templeton. Artist Mike Parobeck began pencilling the title with issue #7 (April 1993). A popular series, after issue #36, the title was restarted as *Batman & Robin Adventures*.

VOWS
Batman: Legends of the Dark Knight Annual #2 ■ In this rare present-day issue of *Legends of the Dark Knight*, writer Dennis O'Neil and artist Michael Netzer decided to marry off Commissioner Gordon to his longtime love, Sarah Essen. But things turned sour quickly when Flass, Gordon's old partner from "Batman: Year One," reappeared in his life, kidnapping Gordon's son, James Gordon Jr. The tale revealed that Gordon's first wife Barbara was very much alive, despite the commissioner's previous statements on the matter.

LEGEND OF THE DARK MITE
Batman: Legends of the Dark Knight #38 Bat-Mite was back, courtesy of writer Alan Grant and artist Kevin O'Neill, in this self-contained story. Implied to be a drug-induced hallucination of a criminal named Overdog, Bat-Mite's existence in the modern DCU was left to the reader to determine. Showcasing one of the most unusual Batmobile designs to date, the issue also earned a sequel of sorts in 1995 with the prestige-format one-shot by the same creative team entitled *Batman: Mitefall*, a parody of 1993's "Knightfall" crossover event.

HEAVY METAL
Batman #486 ■ Black Mask had escaped Batman in the previous issue and, while neglecting his body's need for sleep in a mad search for the gang boss, the Dark Knight encountered Metalhead, a criminal trying to work his way into Black Mask's crew. Batman defeated this new spikey-topped foe, but was clearly quite the worse for wear in this issue by writer Doug Moench and artist Jim Aparo. That made it doubly difficult for the Caped Crusader to defeat his next new enemy, who debuted in the following issue, an assassin known as Headhunter.

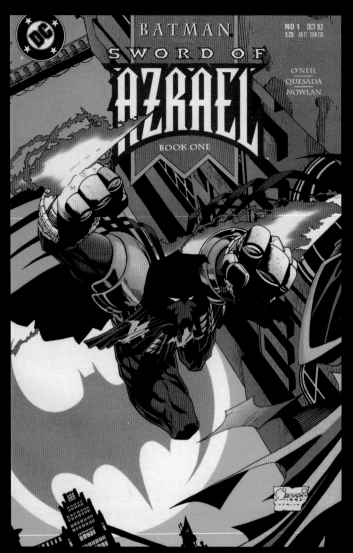

A PORTRAIT OF AZRAEL AS A YOUNG MAN

BATMAN: SWORD OF AZRAEL #1

Readers weren't aware of it at the time, but writer Dennis O'Neil and artist Joe Quesada were about to introduce one of the biggest characters in Batman history: Azrael the Avenging Angel.

In this four-issue mini series, fans met Jean-Paul Valley for the first time, an average young man whose life would go from the mundane to the fantastic when he discovered the body of his father, limp and dying at his back door, wearing the costume of the so-called avenging angel, Azrael.

Jean-Paul grew up believing he was an ordinary person but, in truth, he had been brainwashed from birth by "the System," a training method developed by the mysterious and ancient Order of St. Dumas. Jean-Paul's father had been the Order's assassin, killing its enemies as the need arose. And Jean-Paul had been groomed to be his father's successor.

Embarking on a journey that would take him to a remote village in Switzerland to be trained by the ogre-like Nomoz, Jean-Paul soon adopted the mantle and flaming dagger gauntlets of Azrael. However, with Batman's help, the young man eventually overcame his programming, deciding that his future was his own.

Beautiful to look at and featuring the debut of Azrael's arch foe, Carleton LeHah, this action-packed series set the stage for Jean-Paul Valley to begin appearing regularly as a supporting character in Batman's monthly titles. The hero would begin training with the Dark Knight, preparing for a new career that would soon surprise thousands of readers.

DESTINY CALLING
Jean-Paul Valley went from nobody to masked avenging angel Azrael when he discovered his father's dead body in the costume. While Azrael's methods were questionable, Batman saw something in the young man.

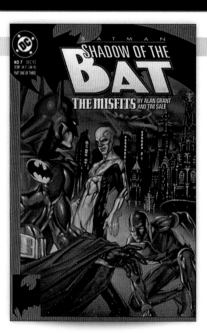

DISCOVERING THE DEMON

Batman: Birth of the Demon • The third and final installment of the Rā's al Ghūl hardcover trilogy arrived in this origin volume by writer Dennis O'Neil and artist Norm Breyfogle. Centuries ago, when a king's son was dying, his physician discovered the Lazarus Pit. The prince used the pit's healing properties, but went mad and killed the physician's wife. Framed for the murder and caged in the fierce desert sun with his wife's rotting corpse, the physician sought revenge against the prince, and took the name of Rā's al Ghūl, "The Demon's Head."

GENERAL MISCONDUCT

Detective Comics #654 • Writer Chuck Dixon and artist Mike Netzer collaborated on this tale that debuted the General, a future Robin foe. The General was a young, psychotic boy called Ulysses Hadrian Armstrong, who attended military school and became an expert military strategist. Bored, he left the school and headed for Gotham City, where he set about recruiting a gang. He masterminded a raid on the national guard armory and acquired vast amounts of weaponry—sending a message to rival gangs and resulting in Batman being shot and injured.

THE MISFITS

Batman: Shadow of the Bat #7 • Writer Alan Grant introduced a new team mostly comprised of failed former Batman villains in this three-part tale drawn by Tim Sale. Dubbed the Misfits, this team included the lucky new villain Chancer and classic foes Calendar Man, Killer Moth (wearing a newly designed costume), and Catman, in his new look that debuted in *Detective Comics* #612 (March 1990). A serious threat when united, the team was eventually defeated with the help of a new invisible vigilante named Nimrod the Hunter.

BEAUTIES AND THE BEAST

Robin III: Cry of the Huntress #1 • Following the holograms offered in Robin's second miniseries, this six-issue tale featured special "motion" covers in addition to the regular newsstand editions. A precursor to Robin's upcoming ongoing title, this series by writer Chuck Dixon and artist Tom Lyle fleshed out Robin's supporting cast, including his future girlfriend, Ariana Dzerchenko, who debuted this issue. In the story, a bond formed between Robin and the Huntress, and the villain KGBeast returned, clad in a new costume.

SEEING RED

BATMAN & DRACULA: RED RAIN

One of Batman's most beloved Elseworlds tales pitted the Dark Knight against another creature of the night: Dracula.

This compelling graphic novel by writer Doug Moench and penciller Kelley Jones saw Batman turned into a vampire himself, much to loyal Alfred's astonishment. *Red Rain* proved that artist Kelley Jones had a bright future in Gotham City thanks to his shadowy pencils. This special spawned two blood-sucking sequels in the form of *Batman: Bloodstorm* and *Batman: Crimson Mist*, and even inspired two different action figures.

BITE OF THE VAMPIRE
Batman's climactic fight with Dracula led to him being bitten by the vampire. Batman later discovered that he was a vampire himself—and declared he would live forever.

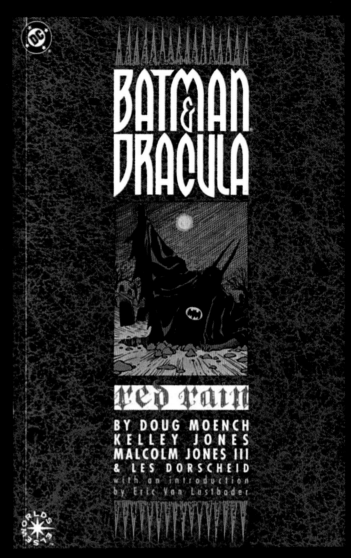

BATMAN & DRACULA

red rain

BY DOUG MOENCH
KELLEY JONES
MALCOLM JONES III
& LES DORSCHEID
with an introduction
by Eric Van Lustbader

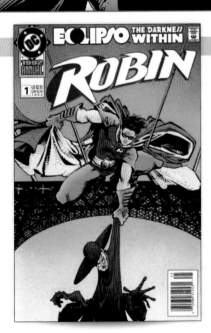

TOTAL ECLIPSE

Robin Annual #1 ■ Even before his ongoing series began, Robin scored his first annual, thanks to writers Alan Grant and John Wagner and artists Tom Lyle and Scott Hanna. As part of DC's crossover event *Eclipso: The Darkness Within*, Anarky found one of the magical villain Eclipso's black diamonds, further corrupting the young vigilante. Meanwhile, Batman and the Joker were both eclipsed in *Batman Annual #16*, a giant eclipsed monster raged in *Detective Annual #5*, and Black Canary was eclipsed in *Green Arrow Annual #5*.

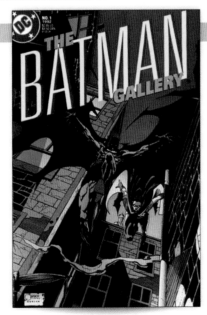

A GALLERY OF STARS

The Batman Gallery ■ In this special one-shot, a host of famous images from Batman's history were reprinted. This "gallery" issue led to many other similar one-shots, featuring new artwork by the best in the business. This particular special featured a cover by Joe Quesada, and reprinted artwork from the likes of Bob Kane, David Mazzucchelli, Neal Adams, Frank Miller, Carmine Infantino, Dick Sprang, Brian Bolland, Todd McFarlane, Dick Giordano, Jerry Robinson, Marshall Rogers, and Sheldon Moldoff, among many other luminaries.

NIGHT TERRORS

Batman: Night Cries ■ Writer Archie Goodwin's skill at crafting complex, emotional tales was apparent in this hardcover graphic novel. Painted by artist Scott Hampton, the book's beautiful appearance only made its ugly subject matter more powerful. Dealing with a serial killer who murdered abusive parents, this story entered disturbing territory, taking the Dark Knight out of his comfort zone. In parallel with the main plot, the tale also dealt with the break-up of Commissioner Gordon's first marriage, and his own anger issues.

ALSO THIS YEAR

March—*Batman: Legends of the Dark Knight #28*: This three-part story featured the villain Two-Face and his "freak show" army.

★ June 19th—*Batman Returns*: Tim Burton's second smash-hit Batman film starred Michael Keaton once again as the Dark Knight, Danny DeVito as the Penguin, and Michelle Pfeiffer as Catwoman.

August—*Superman: The Man of Steel #14*: Current Robin Tim Drake partnered with Jimmy Olsen in this vampire-hunting tale.

★ September 5th—*Batman: The Animated Series*: Producer Bruce Timm and a host of talented artists and writers created this legendary cartoon series starring the voices of Kevin Conroy as Batman and Mark Hamill as the Joker.

October—*Deathstroke: The Terminator #15*: This issue marked the debut of Slade's daughter Rose Wilson, destined to become the vigilante Ravager.

November—*Batman: The Blue, the Gray, and the Bat*: Batman tried his luck in the Wild West in this Elseworlds tale.

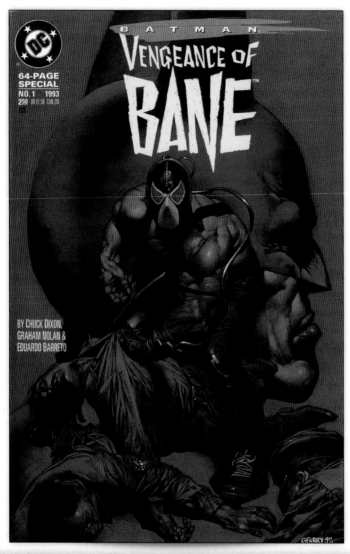

BANE BEGINS

BATMAN: VENGEANCE OF BANE #1

Fans came face-to-face with one of the most important Batman villains of the 1990s—Bane. His harrowing origin story was detailed in this special 64-page one-shot by writer Chuck Dixon and artist Graham Nolan.

Bane was born in a prison called Peña Duro on the island of Santa Prisca. The law stated that the innocent child must serve out his father's life sentence, surrounded by some of the country's most dangerous criminals. When Bane's mother died, the young boy came under the protection of two inmates: Zombie, who had cared for Bane's mother during her death, and Trogg, who protected the child from the other savage inmates. One day, the boy stabbed a would-be attacker to death, earning him a place in the prison's isolation chamber, it's so-called "hole."

Alone in a chamber that flooded every night, with only rats, crabs, and fish to eat, Bane grew into a man, dreaming of slaying his fears, which he pictured in the form of a bat-creature. When he was finally released from the hole, he met another ally, Bird, who told him about Gotham City and its champion, Batman. Bane set his sights on defeating Gotham City's guardian, and trained his body and mind to perfection. When the prison doctors experimented on him with the designer steroid Venom, Bane knew he was ready. With Trogg, Zombie, and Bird's help, he escaped prison, killing the warden. Bane traveled to Gotham City, where he met Batman, and sized up his opponent for the battle to come.

A DOSE OF VENOM
While in prison, Bane had become respected and feared by the other inmates. He was the obvious choice when the warden needed a strong subject to continue his experiments with the addictive steroid Venom. Bane survived when other test subjects had died.

1993

"I will meet this Batman some day. I will destroy him."

Bane, *Batman: Vengeance of Bane #1*

Just as the editors of the Superman titles were shaking up the Man of Steel's world by killing off the famous Super Hero, the staff on the Batman books were coincidentally plotting a similar large-scale story for Batman. They planned to injure the Dark Knight and replace him with a new Caped Crusader. In a shocking crossover event, fans met a Batman who wore sophisticated armor, clawed gauntlets that fired mini Batarangs and Bat-lines, and a cape that he'd soon replace with sharp, wing-like extensions. By the year's end, the Dark Knight would be darker than ever. Fans wondered if the original Batman would ever return.

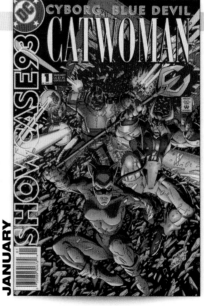

BATMAN'S NEW SHOWCASE
Showcase '93 #1 ● DC Comics brought back the classic *Showcase* title for this 12-issue anthology series. Each comic included three stories, with an ever-shifting roster of characters, writers, and artists and with a Batman character always in the lead role. This first issue starred Catwoman in what was the start of a four-part story by writer Doug Moench and artist Ed Hannigan. Other Batman-related characters featured in the series included Robin, Huntress, Deathstroke, Katana, Two-Face, Deadshot, the Creeper, and Geo-Force.

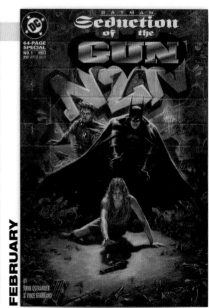

DEALING WITH GUNS
Batman: Seduction of the Gun Special #1
Writer John Ostrander and artist Vince Giarrano tackled the tough subject of gun ownership in this 64-page special. When a criminal informant named Freddie Lasker gave up information on a gang deal, he called his daughter Louisa and instructed her to keep his gun on her at all times. Despite the help of Todd Richards, Tim Drake's undercover identity in this issue, Louisa was killed by the story's end. The issue's strong anti-gun message reflected the personal standpoint of Batman himself.

AUGUST

CATWOMAN STEALS THE SPOTLIGHT
CATWOMAN #1

With the success of *Batman Returns* raising Catwoman's profile, the time was right for the feline fatale to steal an ongoing series all her own.

Selina Kyle, alias Catwoman, had been a major player in Gotham City and in Batman's Rogues Gallery ever since her debut in *Batman* #1 (April 1940). While she'd starred in her own back-up tales, multi-part adventures in anthology titles, and in her own four-issue miniseries, everyone's favorite cat burglar had yet to gain her own ongoing series. That all changed when writer Jo Duffy and artist Jim Balent debuted Catwoman's new monthly title in style with an embossed cover and a new costume that she'd premiered in the pages of *Batman* #498 (August 1993), written by Doug Moench and drawn by Jim Aparo. In that issue, Catwoman and her new "flunky" Leopold, had been recruited by Bane. The "Knightfall" villain required her to fence her ill-gotten goods exclusively through his organization, and to periodically work for him as a thief. It was this added tie-in to the "Knightfall" saga that would make the Catwoman title relevant from the beginning, and add the extra layer of excitement needed to successfully launch her as a major player in Gotham City.

WHEN SHE'S BAD, SHE'S VERY, VERY BAD...
CATWOMAN
#1
AUGUST 1993
195
by JO DUFFY, JIM BALENT & DICK GIORDANO

THIS KITTY'S GOT CLAWS
Catwoman was more than a match for Gotham City's police force thanks to her superior fighting skills. Martial arts training and amazing gymnastic agility gave her the edge in almost any situation.

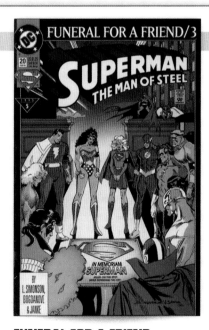

FUNERAL FOR A FRIEND
Superman: The Man of Steel #20
In the biggest comic book event of 1993, Superman was killed fighting Doomsday in *Superman* #75 (January 1993). As a longtime ally of the Man of Steel, Batman wanted to attend the funeral, but couldn't do so in public. Instead, in this story by Louise Simonson and penciller Jon Bogdanove, Batman kept watch from the rooftops, stopping a terrorist from disrupting proceedings. Batman guest-starred in *Superman* #76 (February 1993), mourning the death of Superman with other heroes.

APRIL

THE BEGINNING OF THE END
Batman #489
Now a part of Batman's inner circle, Azrael had been undergoing training from Robin since the previous issue, wearing a new, ninja-like costume. But in this issue by writer Doug Moench and artist Jim Aparo, Azrael was temporarily forced to fill Batman's shoes when an emotionally and physically exhausted Bruce Wayne was unable to go into action. After meeting with his new doctor, Shondra Kinsolving, Wayne collapsed, leading Azrael to don Batman's uniform to confront a rampaging Killer Croc.

BREAKOUT!
Batman #491
After testing Batman with a Venom-enhanced Riddler in the previous issue, Bane was finally ready to make his move on Gotham City in this issue by writer Doug Moench and artist Jim Aparo. Striking with the utmost precision, Bane led an assault on Arkham Asylum, freeing many of the institution's most dangerous inmates. Meanwhile, Azrael was continuing his own personal transformation, having his hair trimmed short and switching from glasses to contact lenses. A war was coming, and the players were all in place.

JULY

BATMAN ANNUAL 17
BLOODLINES
OUTBREAK
BY MOENCH & BARRETO

GOTHAM CITY GOES BALLISTIC
Batman Annual #17
DC's summer crossover, "Bloodlines," saw alien parasites coming to Earth, feeding on its inhabitants and unlocking powers in survivors. In Gotham City, a new vigilante with armored skin called Ballistic was born when police officer Kelvin Mao was bitten by one of the aliens. Ballistic proved himself in a team-up with the new Batman (driving a new model Batmobile), as did another so-called New Blood, Joe Public in *Batman: Shadow of the Bat Annual* #1 (May 1993) by writer Alan Grant and artist Trevor Von Eeden.

KNIGHTFALL

BATMAN #492

For the first time in his career, Batman was going to meet his match. Pushed to the brink of exhaustion, the Dark Knight would taste defeat battling Bane.

Every man has his breaking point, and the Dark Knight reached his in this 19-part crossover—the first of many epic, multi-part stories starring Batman. Beginning with this issue by writer Doug Moench and artist Norm Breyfogle, "Knightfall" featured an already fatigued Batman attempting to deal with an unprecedented crisis. A mysterious new villain named Bane had secretly loosed all of Batman's most dangerous foes on Gotham City. In this initial chapter, Batman and Robin took down the Mad Hatter during a bizarre tea party. Meanwhile, the Film Freak was murdered by Bane when the villain tried to track down Bane in Gotham City.

To help highlight the importance of this series, nearly every issue's cover was drawn by artist Kelley Jones, whose exaggerated proportions and moody atmosphere immediately caught fans' attention. In addition, each issue featured a slowly eclipsing, circular bat-symbol on its cover, symbolizing Batman's waning strength. This symbol eventually turned from yellow to red by the crossover's end.

"Knightfall" continued into *Detective Comics* #569 and its following seven issues, featured in *Showcase '93* for two issues, and continued in the pages of *Batman* as well until it reached its conclusion in *Batman* #500 (October 1993). Chronicled by writers Moench and Chuck Dixon and artists Breyfogle, Jim Aparo, Jim Balent, Graham Nolan, Klaus Janson, and Mike Manley, this series saw the Dark Knight battle Mad Hatter's gang, Amygdala, the Ventriloquist, Mr. Zsasz, Killer Croc, the Joker, Cornelius Stirk, Scarecrow, Cavalier, Firefly, Poison Ivy, Riddler, Two-Face, and Bane's three henchmen before the main event in *Batman* #497 (July 1993). That issue saw a thoroughly exhausted Caped Crusader return to Wayne Manor to find Bane there waiting for him. The criminal had forced Batman to run his gauntlet and, after deducing his civilian identity, was ready to claim his position as the king of Gotham City. To readers' astonishment, Bane did just that—breaking Batman's back during a brutal encounter. With Bruce Wayne suddenly out of action, a new hero, Jean-Paul Valley, was left with the daunting task of becoming Gotham City's new Batman.

NO ESCAPE FOR BRUCE
Wayne Manor had always been a place where Bruce Wayne could retreat if his life as Batman grew too intense. While he rarely took a break, in *Batman* #497, the Dark Knight finally realized that, having recently battled villain after villain, he badly needed to get some rest. However, Bane was waiting for him, determined to catch Batman off guard and at his weakest.

TIME FOR TEA
When the Mad Hatter noticed a falcon following him, he had the bird caught and tagged with a homing device. After inviting Batman to a "tea party," Hatter forced a group of criminals to wear his mind-controlling hats and attack Batman. Meanwhile, Hatter told Film Freak to follow the falcon. Film Freak tracked it to Bane's henchman Bird, and was promptly killed. Bane was determined to keep his master plan to defeat Batman secret.

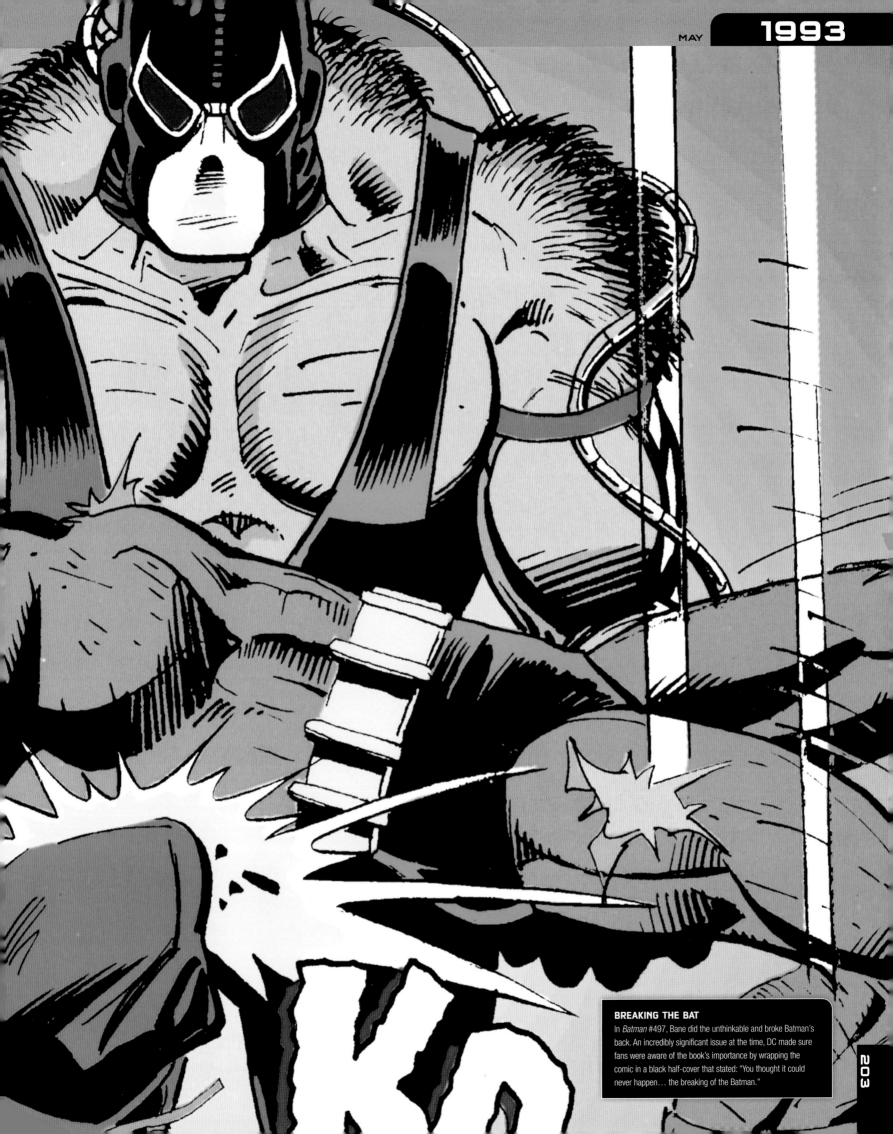

BREAKING THE BAT

In *Batman* #497, Bane did the unthinkable and broke Batman's back. An incredibly significant issue at the time, DC made sure fans were aware of the book's importance by wrapping the comic in a black half-cover that stated: "You thought it could never happen… the breaking of the Batman."

KNIGHTFALL'S END

BATMAN #500

The Dark Knight had fallen. In this epic conclusion to the "Knightfall" crossover, former Azrael Jean-Paul Valley donned a new Batman costume to take down Bane.

Bane had freed Batman's greatest enemies from Arkham Asylum and brought the hero to the point of exhaustion before breaking his back in July's *Batman* #497. Robin and Batman's trainee, Jean-Paul Valley, procured a spinal trauma drug called Decadron for Wayne, but it was clear that Gotham City needed a Batman.

When Bruce Wayne regained consciousness in *Batman* #498 (August 1993), he asked Jean-Paul to step up to the plate. While Dr. Shondra Kinsolving helped Bruce recover, Jean-Paul donned the Batman mantle and headed out on patrol. As Bruce Wayne searched for the suddenly missing Dr. Kinsolving, Jean-Paul succeeded in finding Bane in Gotham City. Bane defeated the new Batman, causing Jean-Paul to head back to the cave and don a new, full-body armor in this milestone issue by writer Doug Moench and pencillers Jim Aparo and Mike Manley.

Featuring an edition with a foil-embossed cover and a regular edition, *Batman* #500 included two postcards that showcased the classic Batman and the new version. In this extra-long issue, the new Batman again confronted Bane and, aided by his new costume, brutally defeated him. There was a new Batman in Gotham City, one about to start his own "Knightquest."

A DARKER DARK KNIGHT

When Bruce Wayne tasked Jean-Paul Valley with taking over as Batman, the former Azrael donned a metallic, sinister version of the Dark Knight's costume. Owing to brainwashing he had received from the Order of St. Dumas, Valley's Batman was as violent and ruthless as some of the criminals he sought to apprehend.

GREETING GEIST
***Detective Comics Annual* #6** • In a crossover with the event "Bloodlines," a hero with invisibility powers debuted thanks to writer Chuck Dixon and artist Jim Balent. A bite from an alien parasite turned Chem-Max employee Dwayne Geyer into the Super Hero Geist, the Twilight Man. Meanwhile, in the pages of *Batman: Legends of the Dark Knight Annual* #3 (November 1993), writer Dennis O'Neil and artists Mike Manley, Luke McDonnell, Gray Morrow, and Ricardo Villagran introduced two more New Bloods: Cardinal Sin and the Samaritan.

BIRTHDAY BAT-GALLERY
***Batman: Legends of the Dark Knight* #50** For this extra-long, special anniversary issue, writer Dennis O'Neil and artist Bret Blevins revealed the first meeting of the Batman and the Joker. Despite mistaking his opponent for a normal clown in their first encounter, Batman later defeated the villain, realizing the monster he had helped create. This issue also included a gallery section including work from Jim Lee, Howard Chaykin, Phil Winslade, P. Craig Russell, Tim Bradstreet, Kevin Nowlan, and many other talents.

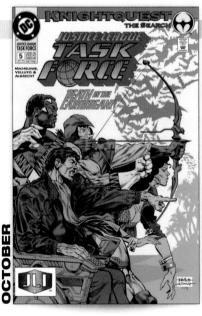

THE SEARCH BEGINS
***Justice League Task Force* #5** • In this newest Justice League title that featured a rotating team of heroes (Nightwing took part in *Justice League Task Force* #1 (June 1993)), "Knightquest: The Search" began as a wheelchair-bound Bruce Wayne headed to Santa Prisca and employed the help of Super Heroes Bronze Tiger, Gypsy, and Green Arrow to help find the missing Dr. Shondra Kinsolving. She had been kidnapped by her stepbrother, the debuting villain Benedict Asp in this two-part story by writer Dennis O'Neil and artist Sal Velluto.

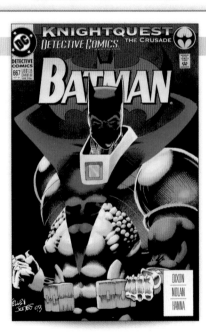

KNIGHTQUEST
***Detective Comics* #667** • Writer Chuck Dixon and artist Graham Nolan ushered in the start of "Knightquest," the latest epic crossover in the Batman books, with this issue. This crossover was divided into two parts: "The Crusade," featuring Jean-Paul Valley's adventures as the new Batman, and "The Search," featuring Bruce Wayne's own adventures. This issue began "The Crusade" and featured new, western-themed villains, the Trigger Twins, and a Harold Allnut-designed Batmobile that ran on Gotham City's underground train tracks.

ROBIN LEAVES THE NEST
ROBIN #1

Following the success of Batman's titles in recent years, and with longtime Batman supporting character Catwoman nabbing her own book, Robin earned his very own title.

In order to gain as much attention as possible for this series' initial issue, *Robin* #1 featured an embossed cover and tied into the events of the hit "Knightfall" series. Robin soon found the new Batman literally at his throat. Jean-Paul Valley seemingly had no place for a Robin in his borderline-obsessive crusade against crime, and would go so far as to physically attack the Boy Wonder. With Bruce Wayne unavailable to guide him, Robin decided to fight crime on his own terms, going solo with the help of his new transforming car nicknamed the Redbird. Besides declaring Robin's independence as a hero in his own right, this first issue by writer Chuck Dixon and artist Tom Grummett also saw an upcoming challenge for Tim Drake in the form of Cluemaster and his lackeys, who included a new, not-so-bright villain known as Czonk. The series also brought back "Shotgun" Smith, a sheriff's deputy operating in the Gotham City suburbs who had first debuted in *Detective Comics* #428 (October 1972).

TIME TO SPLIT UP?
Although he regretted his actions later, the mentally unstable Batman attacked Robin in the Batcave, causing a rift between the two crime fighters. It was certainly time for Tim Drake to step out of this new Batman's dark shadow.

INSIDE THE OUTSIDERS
Outsiders #1 ▪ Writer Mike W. Barr brought the Outsiders team back, sans Batman, in this issue. The group's new roster included Geo-Force, Katana, a resuscitated Halo, and a re-powered Looker, all clad in new costumes, plus new heroes Technocrat, Wylde and Faust, the son of DC Comics villain Felix Faust. Beautifully drawn by Paul Pelletier, the debut issue came in two versions, an Alpha and Omega variant. Each featured a great cover by Travis Charest and told a different half of the story of how the Outsiders reformed to face their vampiric new foe, Roderick.

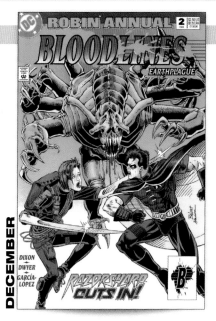

ROBIN MEETS RAZORSHARP
Robin Annual #2 ▪ In another crossover with the "Bloodlines" event, writer Chuck Dixon and artist Kieron Dwyer introduced Robin to the Psyba-Rats, a team of young New Blood hackers led by Razorsharp, a teenage girl capable of turning her arms and legs into blades. The team included two other members, Hackrat and Channelman. The "Bloodlines" event would conclude in *Bloodbath*, a two-issue series debuting in December. The Psyba-Rats would return several times in Gotham City, and even earned their own three-issue miniseries in April 1995.

THE SHORT HALLOWEEN
Batman: Legends of the Dark Knight Halloween Special #1 ▪ The team of writer Jeph Loeb and artist Tim Sale first left their mark on the Caped Crusader with this prestige-format special. Set in a Halloween of Batman's past, and introducing corrupt love interest Jillian Maxwell, this series showed a wonderfully paced and illustrated Batman vs. Scarecrow battle that would excite readers enough to earn two sequel specials in the next two years, followed by the pair's seminal maxiseries *Batman: The Long Halloween*.

ALSO THIS YEAR

April—*Batman: Shadow of the Bat* #11: While already contending with the return of Kadaver, Batman found himself chasing a burglar named the Human Flea.

August—*New Titans* #100: After years of dating, Nightwing and Starfire were about to marry when their wedding was interrupted by a corrupted form of Raven.

September—*Superman: Speeding Bullets:* This Elseworlds novel posed the question: What if the Waynes had discovered Clark's rocket ship?

October—*Batman: Shadow of the Bat* #19: A bloodthirsty, trigger-happy murderer, the Tally Man, seemed a perfectly appropriate foe to face the new, more violent Batman.

★ **December 25th—*Batman: Mask of the Phantasm:*** Batman's first animated movie hit theaters. Kevin Conroy voiced Batman, Mark Hamill voiced the Joker, and Dana Delany voiced Batman's love interest, Andrea Beaumont.

November—*Batman: Shadow of the Bat* #21: The Hood helped Bruce Wayne get closer to tracking down Benedict Asp and his captive, Shondra Kinsolving.

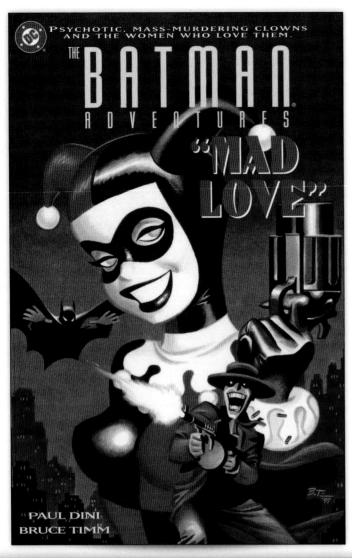

PSYCHOTIC, MASS-MURDERING CLOWNS
AND THE WOMEN WHO LOVE THEM.

THE BATMAN ADVENTURES "MAD LOVE"

PAUL DINI
BRUCE TIMM

LOVE SICK

THE BATMAN ADVENTURES: MAD LOVE

One of the most popular Batman characters to debut in recent years, Harley Quinn, with her quirky personality and bizarre infatuation with the Clown Prince of Crime, earned her own origin tale.

Two of the top names from TV's *Batman: The Animated Series,* writer Paul Dini and artist/co-plotter Bruce Timm, decided to flesh out the character of Harley Quinn in this 64-page stand-alone special set firmly in the animated universe. The Joker's quirky and feisty female sidekick/love interest debuted in the acclaimed Batman cartoon episode "Joker's Favor" (September 1992), and soon became a fan sensation. Later adapted into an episode of *The New Batman Adventures,* this tale revealed that Harley had been a psychologist named Harleen Quinzel studying the Joker at Arkham Asylum. She soon grew obsessed with the criminal, and the two began a relationship after she adopted her own costumed persona. A tragic tale of abuse, love, and dedication, this powerful story offered insight into not just the character of Harley Quinn, but into the unhinged mind of the Joker.

HIGH-FLYING HARLEY
While Harley Quinn won a gymnastic scholarship to Gotham State University, her real goal was to earn a degree in psychology. This she did by any means necessary, short of actually studying and applying herself. Instead, she used her feminine wiles to charm and manipulate her professors into getting ahead.

1994

"Face it, Harl. You're... hopelessly in love with a murderous, psychopathic clown."

Harley Quinn, *The Batman Adventures: "Mad Love"*

The Batman titles had discovered the power of the crossover. Azrael's time as the Dark Knight was nearing its end, and the same fans that had welcomed a change in Batman's status quo were eagerly anticipating the return of the original. Following the success of "Knightfall" and "Knightquest," Jean-Paul Valley's brief reign as Batman ended in another epic crossover: "KnightsEnd." As soon as Bruce Wayne regained his mantle, he was thrown into a company-wide event called "Zero Hour." He then embarked upon another multi-part crossover in the form of "Prodigal." For Batman, 1994 was a year of tumultuous stories with big casts.

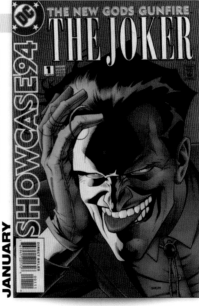

ANOTHER SHOWCASE
Showcase '94 **#1** ● This popular anthology title returned, once again focusing on Batman characters in each lead story. Following a dark, two-issue Joker tale by writer James Robinson and artist Christian Alamy, was a memorable two-issue spotlight on the former inmates of Arkham by writer Alan Grant and artist Tim Sale that introduced new villain Dr. Faustus. By issue #5 (May 1994), another villain, Deathangel, debuted in a Huntress/Robin tale written by Chuck Dixon and drawn by Phil Jimenez. Other future stars would include the Penguin and the Ventriloquist.

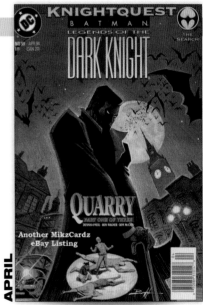

QUARRY
Batman: Legends of the Dark Knight **#59**
"Knightquest: The Search" concluded in this three-issue series written by Dennis O'Neil and illustrated by Ron Wagner (#59) and Eduardo Barreto (issues #60 and #61). While Benedict Asp tried to weaponize the healing abilities of his hostage and stepsister Dr. Shondra Kinsolving, Bruce Wayne pushed his broken body to the limit to rescue her. Wayne found Shondra just as she killed Asp. She healed Bruce, but the trauma she'd been through reduced her mind to that of a young girl.

SCRIBBLE SCRITCH

VIOLENT MOOD SWINGS
The Joker and Harley Quinn's relationship may have been dysfunctional, but they could not do without each other. The Joker's psychotic mood swings endangered Harley's life, but she remained devoted to her beloved "puddin'."

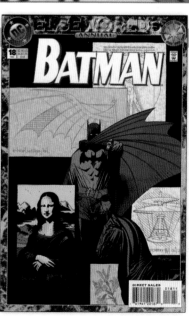

ONE-MAN ARMY
Detective Comics #674 ● Batman Jean-Paul Valley had already become a more violent crime fighter than Bruce Wayne. In this two-issue storyline by writer Chuck Dixon and artist Graham Nolan, the Super Hero upgraded his arsenal to match that of the assassins Gunhawk and Gunbunny. By issue #675 (June 1994), available in a deluxe embossed variant and a newsstand edition, the new Batman added a rapid-fire function to his gauntlet-launching Batarangs, and donned new armor with wing-like extensions in place of a cape.

CREATURES OF CLAY
Batman: Shadow of the Bat #27 ● In issue #25 (March 1994), a fight with the Corrosive Man caused Batman to refine his helmet and cape. In this two-part story by writer Alan Grant and artist Bret Blevins, those adjustments came in handy when he faced Lady Clayface and Clayface III, Preston Payne. The two Clayfaces had begun a romance, poisoned by Payne's need to murder in order to cease his own pain. Their infant child, Cassius Payne, was introduced to the readership, before Azrael defeated them in this second half of the tale.

BATMAN VS. THE OUTSIDERS
Outsiders #7 ● New Batman Jean-Paul Valley, visited the new Outsiders in this two-part story by writer Mike W. Barr and penciller Paul Pelletier. Featuring the second appearance of the villain Sanction—who debuted in issue #2 (December 1993)—the story saw the team clash with Batman just as Halo was seemingly killed. Halo would return from the dead in a new body in the following issue. Joining the team in issue #9 (July 1994) was Superman character the Eradicator, who debuted in *Action Comics Annual* #2 (May 1989).

BATMAN'S RENAISSANCE
Batman Annual #18 ● Artist Bob Kane had long cited the work of Leonardo Da Vinci as one of his inspirations for creating Batman. When DC Comics decided to dedicate their 1994 annuals to Elseworlds tales, writer Doug Moench and artist Frederico Cueva chose to find parallels between the Dark Knight's origin and that of a boy from Da Vinci's time who became his own version of Batman. Meanwhile, in another Elseworlds story in *Detective Comics Annual* #7, scripter Chuck Dixon and artist Enrique Alcatena examined Batman's life if he had been a pirate.

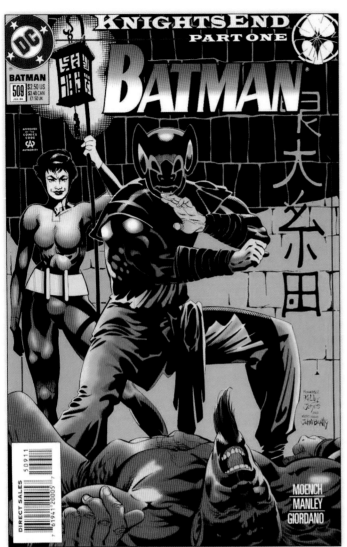

KNIGHTSEND

BATMAN #509

When the new Batman allowed Abattoir to fall to his death, fans realized that Jean-Paul Valley had crossed a line. They were ready to welcome Bruce Wayne back in the role.

With so many gun-toting, extremely violent characters in favor at other comic book companies, DC Comics editor Dennis O'Neil wondered what would happen if Batman was replaced by a hero who possessed many of those qualities. So O'Neil and his team created the concept of "Knightfall". However fans didn't take to the idea of an "extreme" Batman for long—hence "KnightsEnd," a final, ten-part crossover (accompanied by two "Aftermath" issues). The series featured numbered chapters and a slowly shattering Azrael Batman symbol on each cover. This symbol gradually fell away to reveal the classic, iconic bat-symbol. "Knightsend" crossed over into all the Batman titles: *Batman*, *Detective Comics*, *Batman: Shadow of the Bat*, *Robin*, *Catwoman*, and *Batman: Legends of the Dark Knight*.

Healed, but out of practice, Bruce Wayne began to train with Lady Shiva, wearing a bat mask Tengu costume. While Shiva trained Wayne by setting her enemies on him, Jean-Paul Valley slowly descended into madness brought on by the brainwashing "system" in his mind. Wayne finally reclaimed his Batman costume and defeated Azrael in a climactic battle in the Batcave, ending this saga by writers Doug Moench, Alan Grant, Chuck Dixon, Jo Duffy, and Dennis O'Neil and artists Mike Manley, Bret Blevins, Graham Nolan, Ron Wagner, Tom Grummett, Jim Balent, Ray Kryssing, and Barry Kitson.

TENGU BATMAN
Part of Bruce Wayne's recovery program involved rebuilding his fighting skills. He did so under the relentless tutelage of Lady Shiva, until he was once more ready to take up the mantle of Batman.

THE DARKER SIDE OF HUNTRESS
Huntress #1 ● Helena Bertinelli, the Huntress, returned to star in her own title in this four-issue series written by Chuck Dixon and drawn in a moody, shadowy style by artist Michael Netzer. In this series, which established why the Huntress's crime-fighting methods were too extreme even for the Dark Knight himself, Huntress met a new ally in the form of police Detective Sergeant Dan Holtz. As she dealt with her past childhood trauma, Huntress fought the new armored villain called Redzone, the brother of her old foe, Omerta the Silencer.

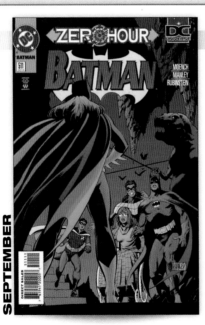

BATGIRL RETURNS?
Batman #511 ● DC Comics' major crossover of 1994 was published in the form of the five-issue crisis in time miniseries called "Zero Hour." In this important series, the DC Universe's conflicting time issues were streamlined, but not before anomalies in the timestream popped up briefly here and there. This tie-in issue by writer Doug Moench and artist Mike Manley saw Batman bring one of his older Batmobile models back into commission, just as a younger version of Barbara Gordon appeared in Gotham City wearing her Batgirl garb.

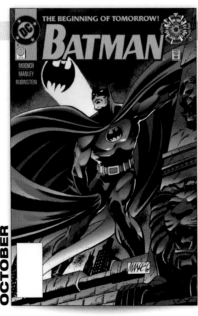

STARTING AT ZERO
Batman #0 ● As part of the "Zero Hour" event, every DC Universe title was granted a #0 issue that told a character's now-streamlined origin and sometimes teased events to come. These issues served as a useful starting point for new readers as well as a way for older fans to discover new titles. In this issue by writer Doug Moench and Mike Manley, Bruce's life was recalled, including his first meeting with Alfred, his parents' death, and his career as Batman, including his injury at Bane's hands and his recovery.

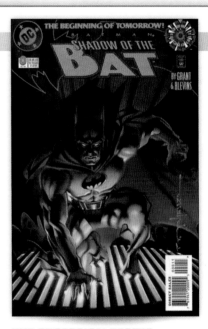

THE OBSESSION BEGINS
Batman: Shadow of the Bat #0
Picking up where Batman #0 left off, this issue written by Alan Grant and drawn by Bret Blevins concentrated on Bruce Wayne's training to become Batman, and his civilian mask as a playboy. It discussed how Alfred and Dr. Leslie Thompkins were concerned for the boy when he seemed obsessed with subjects varying from lip reading to gymnastics. Meanwhile, Batman was also shown in action on the present-day streets of Gotham City, hunting down the mob hitmen known as the Stone Brothers.

ALL TOMORROW'S PARTIES

In this tale from Batman's past, Bruce Wayne is shown developing his playboy billionaire persona, and the resulting ups-and-downs of this experiment. In later years he would play the part to perfection, but it was a long, hard road to success.

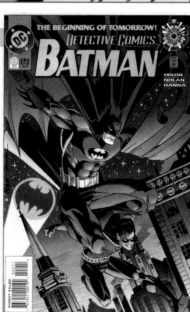

THE DETECTIVE'S NEW START

Detective Comics #0 • Writer Chuck Dixon and artist Graham Nolan created this memorable "Zero Hour" tie-in issue that continued to examine Batman's origin from a fresh perspective. In "Choice of Weapons," Batman reminisced about his early years, recalling his original designs for the Dark Knight's costume, his appropriating a design for the Batmobile from WayneTech, his exploration of the Batcave, and his development of the first Batarangs and Utility Belt. Batman also found time to rescue two kidnapped children.

ANOTHER NEW BATMAN

Robin #0 • After showcasing a team-up between the teenage Dick Grayson and the teenage Tim Drake in issue #10 (September 1994) thanks to the time anomalies of "Zero Hour," writer Chuck Dixon and artist Tom Grummett decided to examine further the Grayson/Drake brotherly relationship. This issue saw Nightwing discuss his past with Robin and his near-death experience at the hands of the villain Two-Face. But at the issue's end, it was Batman who revealed the biggest surprise when he asked Dick Grayson to take over as the Dark Knight.

BEFORE YEAR ONE

Catwoman #0 • Batman's feline fatale was granted her own zero issue in this effort by writer Doug Moench and artist Jim Balent. Expanding upon Catwoman's modern origin from "Batman: Year One," Moench and Balent revealed that Selina Kyle's father had drunk himself to death. This led to her placement at the Seagate orphanage, where she first began to develop a fondness for prowling rooftops at night. By the issue's end, Selina had not only escaped the institution, but had ensured that her records were entirely erased from its files.

PRODIGAL

BATMAN #512

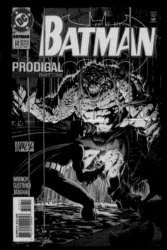

The Batman titles ended the year in the same grand fashion that they had begun it with this 12-part crossover that saw Dick Grayson assume the mantle of the Batman.

Bruce Wayne had some unfinished business to take care of without his Batman costume. Bruce realized that he could no longer look to an outsider like Azrael to deputize for him in Gotham City. He asked the one man he trusted more than anyone else—his former ward, Dick Grayson.

Reluctantly taking his mentor's place, Nightwing adopted the identity of Batman and began a series of adventures that pitted him against several of Batman's most dangerous enemies. "Prodigal" crossed from the pages of *Batman*, to other titles including *Batman: Shadow of the Bat*, *Detective Comics*, and *Robin* and was written and illustrated by a variety of talent: scribes Doug Moench, Alan Grant and Chuck Dixon, and artists Mike Gustovich, Bret Blevins, Lee Weeks, Phil Jimenez, Graham Nolan, Ron Wagner, M.D. Bright, and John Cleary. Also included in this series in the pages of *Robin* #12 (December 1994), was the first appearance of Dana Winters, Tim Drake's future step-mom.

With Robin by his side, Dick Grayson's first act as Batman was to take down Killer Croc. Although full of self-doubt and still haunted by the memory of a boyhood failure against Two-Face, Dick continued to fight through Gotham City's underworld, defeating the Ventriloquist and the Ratcatcher before being forced to confront Two-Face once more. While Grayson overcame his fears as well as Two-Face, he soon came to feel that he was Batman—but Batman wasn't him!

After facing down the Tally Man, Dick returned to the Batcave to find Bruce Wayne waiting for him. The two had a long overdue heart-to-heart and Dick Grayson returned to his role as Nightwing, while Bruce Wayne took back his familiar cape and cowl.

THE SUBSTITUTE

Bruce Wayne had been forced to reclaim his Batman mantle in order to put an end to Jean-Paul Valley's descent into madness as the Dark Knight. However, Bruce was not ready to take on the role of Batman quite yet. He needed time, and he could conceive of no better substitute for him in the interim than his original partner, Dick Grayson.

CROCODILE HUNTER

Dick Grayson's first mission as Batman saw him partnered with Robin to hunt down Killer Croc. Using a "borrowed" WayneTech speedboat, the two caught up to the primal villain, defeating him with a bit of ingenuity and teamwork.

ALSO THIS YEAR

March—*Catwoman* #8: Catwoman faced the new threat of Zephyr.

September—*Detective Comics* #678: Bruce Wayne found new evidence that Joe Chill might not have been his parents' killer.

September—*Superman: The Man of Steel* #37: Superman faced many different versions of Batman.

October—*Batman: Legends of the Dark Knight* #0: Pages from upcoming stories were teased and presented as different interpretations of Batman.

November—*Batman: Legends of the Dark Knight* #65: The Joker reformed his ways for a time after believing he had killed the Batman. He assumed the identity of Joseph Kerr and started over with a new neighborly love interest, Rebecca Brown.

December—*Batman: Castle of the Bat:* This prestige-format Elseworlds special served as a Frankenstein/Batman mash-up.

December—*Batman: In Darkest Night:* This Elseworlds story examined what Batman's life would be like if he had become a Green Lantern.

TROIKA

BATMAN #515

Batman's costume saw a redesign, taking it from the "underwear on the outside" look, to a sturdier and more streamlined Batsuit.

Cover artist Kelley Jones took over the interior art as the new regular artist on *Batman*, in a tale that featured the Dark Knight trying out a new Batsuit—a gray Kevlar bodysuit with spikes on the wrists and calves, and a dark navy cape. While facing up to the return of the Dark Rider, a villain who had debuted in *Batman* #393 (March 1986), as well as the KGBeast, Batman continued to adjust his costume, settling on a look that was in a darker shade of gray and navy than his previous uniform and without the "underwear on the outside."

"Troika" was a four-part series that pitted Batman against the combined forces of several former Soviet enemies: the aforementioned Dark Rider and KGBeast, as well as Romana Vrezhenski, who first appeared in *Robin* #12 (December 1994), and Colonel Vega (who debuted in *Batman: Shadow of the Bat* #21, November 1993). Batman eventually took the Troika team down, thereby preventing a nuclear catastrophe.

This short crossover was written by Doug Moench, Alan Grant, and Chuck Dixon, and illustrated by Kelley Jones, Barry Kitson, Graham Nolan, and Tom Grummett. To make it stand out on the racks, each issue came in both a newsstand edition and in a special embossed edition.

A NEW LOOK FOR BATMAN
Resuming his role as Batman, after handing the cape and cowl to Dick Grayson in the "Prodigal" adventure, "Troika" saw Batman experimenting with radical new costume designs.

1995

> "The world is full of... lost and desperate people who have no one to ask for help. From now on, they'll have me."
>
> Nightwing, *Nightwing* #4.

Finally, Batman was back. Bruce Wayne, the one true Dark Knight, returned to the role in the "Troika" crossover, and this time he planned on staying put for quite a while. With steady creative teams in place on both *Batman* and *Detective Comics*, and both Nightwing and Azrael earning solo attention, fans were treated to a stable Gotham City once more, just in time for the June release of the third Batman film of the era, *Batman Forever*. Batman merchandise was once again flooding toy stores, and the Caped Crusader's comic book presence continued to grow.

HOLIDAYS ON ICE
The Batman Adventures: Holiday Special #1 ▪ Later the blueprint for an episode of *The New Batman Adventures*, the title's sole holiday special collected vignettes by writer Paul Dini teamed with artists Dan Riba, Bruce Timm, Ronnie Del Carmen, Glen Murakami, Kevin Altieri and Butch Lukic, with Bruce Timm and Ronnie Del Carmen co-plotting their chapters. The stories were Christmas and New Year's tales starring Clayface, Harley Quinn and Poison Ivy, the Joker, Commissioner Gordon and, of course, Mr. Freeze.

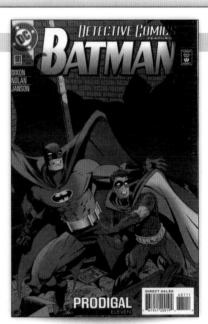

ENTER STEELJACKET
Detective Comics #681 ▪ A new high-flying foe was introduced to Batman's Rogues Gallery in this issue written by Chuck Dixon with art by Graham Nolan. As the "Prodigal" crossover neared its finale, Robin came into conflict with an armored assassin named Steeljacket. Capable of flight and possessing sharp metal claws similar to those formerly sported by Azrael during his stint as Batman, Steeljacket proved a tough enemy. Gotham City also gained an ally in the person of Det. Mackenzie "Hardback" Bock, Lieutenant Sarah Essen's new assistant.

FEBRUARY

AZRAEL'S SECOND CHANCE
AZRAEL #1

After giving up the mantle of Batman, Jean-Paul Valley was homeless and suffering from hallucinations. The Dark Knight stepped in and gave the former Batman a new direction: to become Azrael once more.

Having introduced Azrael in *Batman: Sword of Azrael* #1 (October 1992), writer Dennis O'Neil returned to pilot the character's life as the confused, homeless Jean-Paul Valley wandered the streets of Gotham City. With the able help of penciller Barry Kitson, O'Neil introduced Jean-Paul to fellow homeless man and former psychiatrist Brian Bryan. Jean-Paul came to Bryan's rescue when he was being attacked by street thugs, and Bryan took Jean-Paul back to the homeless shelter where he was staying. Following a fire at the shelter, the Dark Knight visited Jean-Paul hoping to help get his meandering life back on track. Batman revealed to Jean-Paul the location of the headquarters of the Sacred Order of St. Dumas—the secret cult that had had such a traumatic impact on Valley's psyche. He then handed Valley his original Azrael costume, setting the former hero on a new quest of self-discovery. Jean-Paul recruited his new friend Bryan and the two headed to Europe. There they discovered a corrupt Order of St. Dumas under the leadership of Brother Rollo and encountered the beautiful, enigmatic Sister Lilhy, who joined them on their adventures.

PURGING THE SYSTEM
The System had done a number on Jean-Paul Valley, and he was having trouble telling reality from fantasy. He needed a dramatic change in his life. The mysterious Bryan Brian would prove to be a major force for that change.

MAY

MONKEY BUSINESS
Detective Comics #685 • Writer Chuck Dixon and artist Steve Lieber concocted a new enemy to challenge the Dark Knight in the form of Silver Monkey in this two-part tale of martial-arts intrigue. A recurring character in the comics, the Silver Monkey would go on to star in several episodes of 2013's animated series *Beware the Batman*. Dixon would shortly introduce another new villain in the pages of *Detective Comics,* with the help of artist Graham Nolan. Issue #687 (July 1995) marked the debut of modern-day pirate Cap'n Fear.

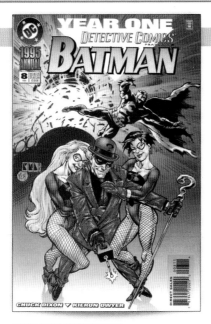

RIDDLER REVEALED
Detective Comics Annual #8 • The Riddler's origin was retold and expanded upon in this issue by writer Chuck Dixon and artist Kieron Dwyer. It also introduced Riddler's two henchwomen, Query and Echo. This new version of Riddler's backstory revealed that the criminal's obsession with riddles had started at a very young age. As an adult, Edward Nigma decided to quit his job as a delivery man to become a thief, only to find that his new career lacked satisfaction unless he left a challenging riddle for the police to solve as a clue.

MEMOIRS OF A MAN-BAT
Batman: Legends of the Dark Knight Annual #5 • Man-Bat's origin was re-evaluated and given a modern spin in this issue, which served as part of DC Comics' "Year One" themed annuals. In previous origin tales, Batman's first meeting with Man-Bat happened later in his career, after Robin had left for college. In this retelling, written by Chuck Dixon and illustrated by Enrique Alcatena, Man-Bat's metamorphosis from Kirk Langstrom to a giant bat-creature occurred earlier in the timeline, before Batman adopted the yellow oval on his chest.

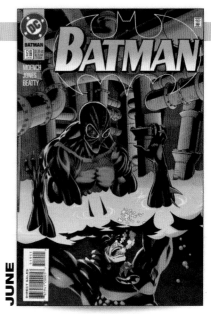

PLAYING POLITICS
Batman #519 • While the main focus of the issue, penned by Doug Moench and drawn by Kelley Jones, was to showcase the Dark Knight's defeat of the second Black Spider, the most significant continuity developments lay in the details of the story. In the subplot, longtime police commissioner James Gordon was demoted and replaced by his wife, Sarah Essen. Readers also received their first glimpse of Marion Grange, Gotham City's latest mayoral candidate. This issue marked the first use of a thicker, slicker paper in the pages of *Batman*.

JUNE

A QUARTERLY CHRONICLE
THE BATMAN CHRONICLES #1

The Dark Knight added yet another ongoing title to his impressive lineup of comics with this quarterly book.

An anthology title with three stories in each volume, the premier issue of *The Batman Chronicles* began with a Huntress tale by writer Chuck Dixon and artist Lee Weeks. This saw Commissioner Gordon run into trouble as he was taking the subway home from work one night, when a group of criminals calling themselves the Tranz-It Authority attempted to hijack the train. Fortunately, Huntress showed up and she and Gordon joined forces to take down the criminals. While not exactly approving of Huntress, Gordon couldn't help but be reminded of his daughter Barbara Gordon when the Huntress was shot in the stomach during their adventure. Unlike Barbara, however, Huntress was saved by her Kevlar body armor, preventing another senseless tragedy.

This issue also featured an Anarky story written by Alan Grant and pencilled by Stewart Johnson, and a short feature following the life of a criminal's mask by writer Doug Moench and penciller Brian Apthorp.

GORDON UNDER FIRE
Commissioner Gordon always managed to remain cool and collected when faced with thugs and criminals of all kinds. His public connection to Batman often placed him in danger, but Gordon refused to take their relationship for granted.

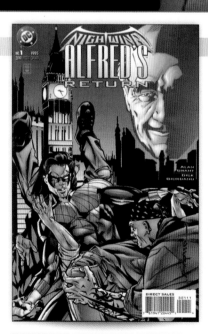

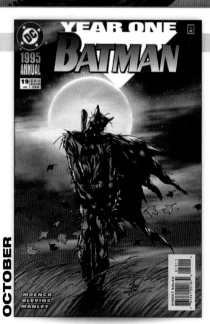

THE HOUND OF HELL
***Catwoman Annual* #2** ▪ Selina Kyle's life as a prostitute was explained in this "Year One"-themed issue writen by Jordan B. Gorfinkel, with breakdowns by Jim Balent and finishes by James A. Hodgkins. A botched jewel heist led to Selina being kidnapped and forced into prostitution. While she soon returned to her thieving ways after the heat had died down, Selina also began to train in a dojo, meeting her enemy, the future villain Hellhound in the process. This issue also served to introduce the corrupt former commissioner of police, Peter Grogan.

MOUSE TRAP
***Robin* #18** ▪ Before new regular penciller Mike Wieringo took over the art chores on *Robin* in the next issue, artist Mike Parobeck stopped by to draw this issue from a Chuck Dixon script. It featured the debut of a criminal computer hacker known as the Mouse. Pamela Sweigeld got her start in crime by donning an old *Nutcracker* mouse costume she possessed and attempting to take revenge on her employer. In issue #21 by Dixon and Wieringo, Robin would face another new threat in the form of martial artist Dragoncat.

BRINGING HOME THE BUTLER
***Nightwing: Alfred's Return* #1** ▪ Two of Batman's most important supporting characters got their first special in the form of this stand-alone issue by writer Alan Grant and artist Dick Giordano. While Nightwing had had a mini-series teased for years in letter columns and the like, for now he'd have to settle for this story in which he ventured to London, England, to talk Alfred into returning home to Gotham City and resuming his role as Batman's butler. And, after an adventure featuring Alfred's old love interest, Joanna Clark, that's exactly what Nightwing did.

ORIGINS OF FEAR
***Batman Annual* #19** ▪ The Scarecrow was given a modern origin in this "Year One" annual written by Doug Moench and drawn by Bret Blevins. Psychologist Jonathan Crane was fired from his job as a college professor specializing in the study of fear for shooting a live gun off in class. He retaliated by murdering the dean along with his four regents, literally scaring them to death. Donning the guise of Scarecrow and armed with fear-inducing gas and a style of fighting that seemed like a macabre dance, Scarecrow was truly a creature of nightmare.

ANARKY IN GOTHAM CITY
Former child prodigy Lonnie Machin created the costumed identity of Anarky to spread his message of political and philosophical anti-statism. He and Batman soon found each other on opposing sides.

NOVEMBER

UNLEASHING CHAOS

Underworld Unleashed #1 ▪ Writer Mark Waid and artist Howard Porter spearheaded DC Comics' latest crossover event in this three-issue miniseries that saw many of Batman's enemies given a power upgrade by the demon Neron. Blockbuster, Copperhead, and Killer Moth (now called Charaxes) were among those whose abilities and appearances were drastically altered in this debut issue. Two other titles tied into this epic event: *Underworld Unleashed: Batman: Devil's Asylum* and *Underworld Unleashed: Patterns of Fear.*

NOVEMBER

CASTING HER SPELL

Detective Comics #691 ▪ In another issue tying in with the *Underworld Unleashed* storyline, a new version of the Batman villain Spellbinder, appeared for the first time, thanks to writer Chuck Dixon and artist Staz Johnson. Initially a lackey for the original Spellbinder, Delbert Billings, Fay Moffit killed Delbert. In exchange for her soul, Fay was given the power to distort visual perceptions by the demon Neron. The new Spellbinder immediately proved herself far superior to her predecessor and quite a challenge for the Dynamic Duo in this two-part story.

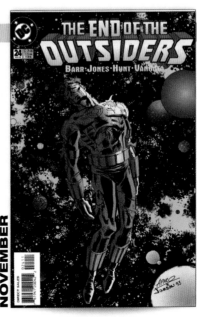

NOVEMBER

ENDINGS AND BEGINNINGS

Outsiders #24 ▪ The Outsiders' series reached its conclusion with this issue by the team's longtime writer Mike W. Barr and penciller Casey Jones. As the team returned from space from a battle with Eclipso, Barr and Jones saw them off in style, ending the tale with the wedding of Geo-Force to his lover Denise Howard. Guests at the happy occasion were the Atomic Knight, Windfall, and Metamorpho (who all three had recently received costume updates), as well as Black Lightning, Katana, Faust, Halo, Technocrat, Looker, and Bruce Wayne himself.

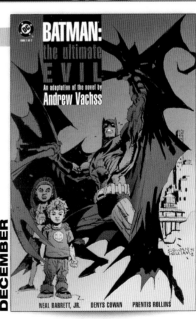

DECEMBER

A DISTURBING EVIL

Batman: The Ultimate Evil #1 ▪ Adapted from the novel of the same name by writer Andrew Vachss came this two-issue prestige-format series scripted by Neal Barrett, Jr. and drawn by Denys Cowan. When Bruce Wayne crossed paths with the beautiful Debra Kane, an albino woman working for Gotham City's child-protection services, Batman was smitten, even escorting her around Gotham City in a new model Batmobile. Batman soon found himself uncovering a web of pedophile tourism, a crime that deeply disturbed the Dark Knight.

BY DENNIS O'NEIL, GREG LAND & MIKE SELLERS

NIGHTWING NO MORE?

NIGHTWING #1

At long last, Nightwing was given a miniseries of his very own by the capable team of writer Dennis O'Neil and artist Greg Land.

As well as a new series, Dick Grayson was also given a new costume designed by Harold Allnut in the second issue of this four-issue story, changing his blue and gold duds to a new black and blue costume complete with arm gauntlets that served as a Utility Belt of sorts. The future indeed looked bright for the longtime crime fighter.

But when this series first began, Nightwing looked to be on his way to becoming a thing of the past. In fact, in the first issue, he took off his costume and retired from crime fighting altogether. When he later discovered a note relating to the death of his parents, Dick donned new Nightwing gear in an adventure that led him to the principality of Kravia. With the help of a tragic figure and near love interest named Miggy Webster, Nightwing realized how important a role he played in the lives of so many people, and renewed his career as a hero.

FAILED ROMANCE
Miggy Webster was a sweet young woman who was in love with Dick Grayson, and the two dated briefly. However, upon learning of Grayson's role as Nightwing, she realized that they could never be more than friends.

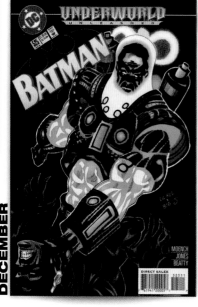

MOENCH
JONES
BEATTY

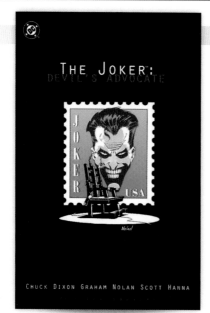

CHUCK DIXON GRAHAM NOLAN SCOTT HANNA

GRANT
APTHORP
WOCH

DIXON ▼ ARMSTRONG ▼ CAMPANELLA

COLD CASE
Batman #525 ▪ Mr. Freeze saw a dramatic upgrade in this *Underworld Unleashed* tie-in by scripter Doug Moench and penciller Kelley Jones. Wearing a new suit that featured wrist-mounted freezing guns, Mr. Freeze looked more intimidating than ever. When Mr. Freeze resurfaced in Gotham City, murdering elderly people in a cryogenics scam, Batman once again bested his foe, despite Freeze's new weaponry, by shattering his helmet with an antique shield and causing him to overheat.

THE JOKE'S ON JOKER
The Joker: Devil's Advocate ▪ Batman's ethics were tested when he was forced to save the life of the Joker in this deluxe hardcover graphic novel written by Chuck Dixon and pencilled by Graham Nolan. In this tale, postage stamps featuring famous comedians were poisoned, killing anyone who licked them; victims' faces were frozen in a rictus grin. The Joker was caught and convicted, but then Batman discovered that he was innocent of this particular murder spree. The Dark Knight had to save the Joker from the electric chair.

FIRST DOSE OF POISON
Batman: Shadow of the Bat Annual #3 ▪ In another "Year One" themed annual, Poison Ivy nabbed the spotlight thanks to scripter Alan Grant and penciller Brian Apthorp. Infatuated with Batman, Ivy watched him from afar even as she committed her plant-based murders. Set in the early days of Batman's career, this issue featured a Poison Ivy more powerful than that in her debut in *Batman* #181 (June 1966). However, it paid tribute to that comic by including cameos by rock-musicians-turned-criminals Silken Spider, Dragon Fly, and Tiger Moth.

RETELLING ROBIN
Robin Annual #4 ▪ Rather than delve into the recently told origin of the current Robin, Tim Drake, in this "Year One" annual, writer Chuck Dixon and artist Jason Armstrong took the opportunity to retell Dick Grayson's story instead. Focusing mostly on Batman's investigation into the death of Dick's parents, circus acrobats the Flying Graysons, this issue showed Dick's life in Gotham City's youth center before he was adopted by Bruce Wayne and let in on Gotham City's greatest secret—the true identity of Batman.

INTO THE BLACK AND BLUE
Nightwing's sleek new black and blue costume featured arm gauntlets with compartments that stored, among other things, tracers, smoke pellets, gas capsules, sedative darts, and a stun gun.

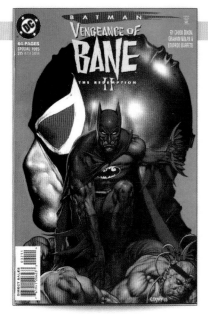

BANE'S BACK
Batman: Vengeance of Bane II: The Redemption ■ Writer Chuck Dixon and artist Graham Nolan revived the blockbuster villain in this sequel to the one-shot that introduced Bane. In this 64-page special, Bane went from being an overweight inmate at Blackgate prison fighting addiction to the steroid Venom, to becoming a drug-free athlete in his prime. It seemed that incarceration had had a healthy effect on Bane as he escaped prison helped by new allies: the electric-powered Galvan and the Ratcatcher.

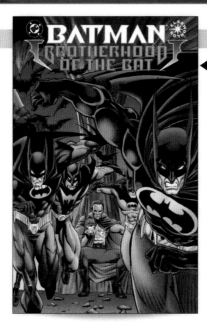

BAND OF BROTHERS
Batman: Brotherhood of the Bat ■ Unused costume designs for Batman were put to good use in this prestige-format Elseworlds one-shot written by Doug Moench, with art by Jim Aparo, Jim Balent, Bret Blevins, Norm Breyfogle, Vince Giarrano, Tom Grummett, Mike Manley, and Graham Nolan. Set 50 years into the future, Rā's al Ghūl had unleashed a plague and formed an army of "Batman impersonators." With Bruce Wayne dead, it was up to Tallant, the son of Wayne and Talia al Ghūl and the true heir to Batman's cowl, to stop Rā's' scheme.

SPECIAL FEATURE

LIKE FATHER…
Talia revealed to her son Tallant that his father was the original Batman. Realizing his heroic legacy, Tallant decided to take up his father's mantle and become a new Dark Knight.

ALSO THIS YEAR

March—*Detective Comics* #683: The Penguin evolved from a comical, bird-themed villain into a mob boss in this issue that introduced his brilliant henchman Actuary as well as his club, the Iceberg Lounge.

April—*Wonder Woman* #96: The Joker paid the Amazing Amazon a visit in this two-part tale.

April—*Catwoman* #20: Always fashionable, Catwoman tried out a temporary green and black jungle costume in this issue.

May—*Catwoman Annual* #2: Major villain Hellhound debuted in this flashback issue, as did Commissioner Grogan.

★ **June 16th:** *Batman Forever* was released, directed by Joel Schumacher and starring Val Kilmer as Batman, Jim Carrey as the Riddler, Tommy Lee Jones as Two-Face, and Chris O'Donnell as Robin.

June—*Batman: Riddler* and *Batman: Two-Face*: Both villains had a special issue, due to their appearance in *Batman Forever*.

October—*Batman: Manbat* #1: A tale of Batman and Man-Bat's family set outside regular continuity via the Elseworlds imprint.

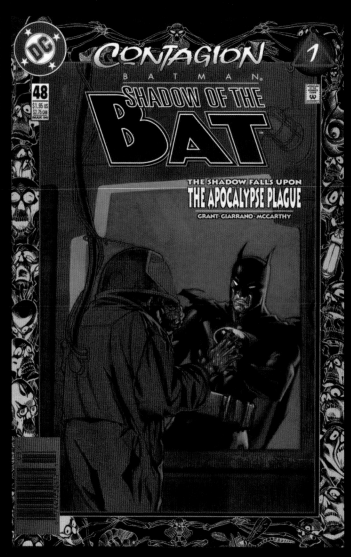

CONTAGION
BATMAN: SHADOW OF THE BAT #48

Robin looked set to succumb to a plague-like virus called "the Clench" in this 12-chapter epic crossover tale that spanned *Detective Comics, Robin, Azrael, Catwoman, Batman,* and *The Batman Chronicles* as well as this title.

Each issue of this event included a macabre border on its cover, and a number (except for *The Batman Chronicles* #4 (February 1996)) to help readers follow the story throughout the various titles. "Contagion" was created by a large list of talent, including writers Alan Grant, Chuck Dixon, Dennis O'Neil, Doug Moench, Garth Ennis, and Christopher Priest. Artists included Vince Giarrano, Tommy Lee Edwards, Mike Wieringo, Barry Kitson, Jim Balent, Kelley Jones, Graham Nolan, John McCrea, Matt Haley, and Frank Fosco.

The story revolved around a deadly plague that came to Gotham City after escaping a lab at the Order of St. Dumas. Referred to as the Apocalypse Filovirus and nicknamed "the Clench," the strain was brought to Gotham City by an infected man named Daniel Maris. As he succumbed to the fast-killing virus, with his eyes and nose bleeding and open sores forming all over his body, Maris revealed that he knew of one plague survivor in a small town in Greenland. Soon, Robin, Catwoman (clad in a new white camouflage costume that she debuted in *Robin* #27 in March 1996) and Azrael were searching for the survivor, coming into conflict with a new bounty hunter called Tracker in the process.

After securing a blood sample from the survivor, Robin began showing signs of the Clench. With the help of Nightwing and the Huntress, Batman worked tirelessly to limit the chaos of a quickly-dying city, but failed in using the blood sample to create an antidote. Luckily, Azrael discovered the antidote in a tome from the Order of St. Dumas, and rushed to Gotham City, saving the lives of countless citizens, including Robin himself.

SNOW FIGHT
Catwoman and Robin clashed in Canada when both were searching for the sole survivor of the plague that had ravaged Gotham City. They then decided to join forces.

1996

"This place is hopelessly lost to corruption and injustice and violence. I'm going to like it here" Nightwing, *Nightwing* #3

After a brief respite, the Batman titles returned to the landscape of epic crossovers. Beginning with "Contagion," and then continuing on with "Legacy," the Dark Knight's comics embarked on large-scale adventures before giving the readers a break from big events with a series of "1 of 1" stand-alone tales. These self-contained stories returned to the "old-fashioned" idea of a single self-contained story in each issue. This year also placed a strong emphasis on artwork, from the eye-popping paintings of Alex Ross's *Kingdom Come* miniseries, to the brilliant line work contained in the miniseries *Batman: Black and White.*

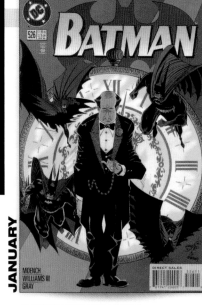

A RIDE FOR THE '90S
Batman #526 ▪ First teased in the Elseworlds special of behind-the-scenes designs, *Batman: Knightgallery* (September 1995), the latest Batmobile model debuted in this issue by writer Doug Moench and artist J.H. Williams III. A design that would later be made into a Hallmark ornament, the new Batmobile included special thrusters, an ejection seat, and scratch and shatter-proof high-impact polymer, all of which were utilized in this issue that showcased the Batmobile's new function as well as Batman's rededication to his life fighting crime.

LOCKDOWN
Robin #24 ▪ Dealing with Charaxes, a newly-transformed insectoid beast that was originally villain Killer Moth, Robin had his hands full. But in this Chuck Dixon-written issue pencilled by Aaron Lopresti, a new character stepped in to rescue Robin and apprehend the monstrous villain. Familiar to fans of *Batman: The Animated Series*, the mystery man in question was Lock-Up, a character adapted from the hit cartoon. Specializing in security systems, Lock-Up captured and held villains in his own prison, thinking himself above the traditional rule of the law.

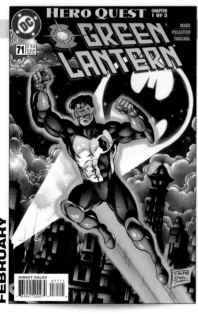

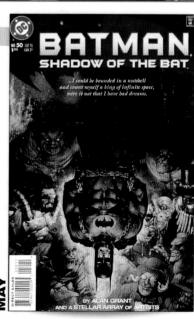

FEBRUARY

APRIL

MAY

HERO QUEST

Green Lantern #71 ▪ Kyle Rayner had recently taken over the role of Earth's Green Lantern from Hal Jordan, who had gone on a mad rampage, attacking some of the members of the Green Lantern Corps. In order to better learn how to be a Super Hero, Kyle embarked on a "Hero Quest" that first took him to Gotham City. In this story by writer Ron Marz and penciller Paul Pelletier, Kyle officially met Batman for the first time as he helped stop the Checquered Gang. Sadly for Kyle, however, Batman had no interest in tutoring him in the ways of being a Super Hero.

THE KILLER SKIES

Man-Bat #1 ▪ Kirk Langstrom's monstrous alter ego received a three-issue starring role thanks to writer Chuck Dixon and penciller Flint Henry. Having devolved into little more than a flying animal, Man-Bat was the prime suspect when the police began to discover bodies that could only have been killed by something savage and capable of flight. Much to the relief of Man-Bat fans, by issue #2, the true killer was revealed to be the villain Steeljacket. And what's more, by issue #3, readers were treated to the first appearance of Kirk's half-bat son, Aaron.

TAKING A HIT

Hitman #1 ▪ A new type of "hero" received his own ongoing series in *Hitman*, an-offbeat and darkly comedic title dealing with the adventures of New Blood and hired hitman Tommy Monaghan. Written by Garth Ennis and illustrated by John McCrea, the first three issues of this series dealt with Hitman taking out a contract on the Joker, which led him into direct conflict with the Dark Knight. The fight was short, yet not sweet for the Caped Crusader. He punched Tommy in the gut, and Hitman responded by promptly vomiting on Batman's boots.

GRANT'S GALLERY

Batman: Shadow of the Bat #50 ▪ Writer Alan Grant showed off many of his co-creations in this 50th issue special pencilled by Bret Blevins, Norm Breyfogle, Vince Giarrano, Barry Kitson, and Dave Taylor. When Batman found himself trapped in a nightmare thanks to the new villain Narcosis, he was forced to fight the Ventriloquist, Amygdala, the Tally Man, the Corrosive Man, Mahakala, and many more products of Grant's imagination. Batman finally combated these villains by conjuring other heroes to help him, including Anarky, the Hood, and Pagan.

KINGDOM COME

Mark WAID Alex ROSS

BATMAN'S FUTURE KINGDOM

KINGDOM COME #1

Two superstar comic book creators, artist Alex Ross and writer Mark Waid, came together to craft one of the most enduring visions of DC Comics' future ever created with the series *Kingdom Come*.

Artist Alex Ross had wowed the comic book world with his highly realistic painterly style. So when he came to DC Comics to debut an even bigger story, fans couldn't have been more excited. Teaming with Ross on this prestige-format four-issue project was another comic book talent known for his encyclopedic knowledge of the DC Universe, writer Mark Waid.

While this Elseworlds tale starred Superman, Wonder Woman, and many other DC Super Heroes, Batman played a major role in the storyline. After his identity was made public, Bruce Wayne patrolled Gotham City from the Batcave beneath a destroyed Wayne Manor, sending out drones to keep his city under control. Later in the series, he joined forces with Lex Luthor in a clandestine double cross to destroy Luthor's organization from within. A year later, Batman met with Superman and Wonder Woman, who shared the news that Diana was pregnant with Clark's child and they wanted Bruce to be a godparent!

This monumental series also introduced readers to Batman's son, Ibn al Xu'ffasch as well as Dick Grayson's daughter, Nightstar.

BAT SENTRIES
Too old to patrol the streets of Gotham City by himself every night, Bruce Wayne employed remote operated Bat Sentries to help keep Gotham City safe.

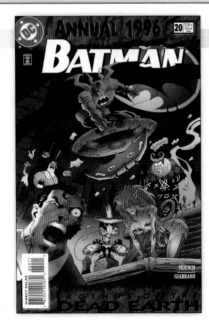

THE ORIGIN OF ORACLE

The Batman Chronicles #5 ▪ Soon after Mr. Zsasz's origins were explored by writer Alan Grant and artist Jennifer Graves in *The Batman Chronicles* #3 (January 1996), writers John Ostrander and Kim Yale delved into another important character. They looked in detail at how Barbara Gordon evolved into Oracle with the help of Richard Dragon in a tale drawn by Brian Stelfreeze. This issue also contained a James Gordon story written by Howard Chaykin and co-plotted and pencilled by Tommy Lee Edwards, and a chapter from Alfred's early life.

LEGENDS OF THE DEAD EARTH

Batman Annual #20 ▪ DC Comics decided on giving this year's annuals the theme of "Legends of the Dead Earth," where stories of our planet were told and retold by future generations on different worlds. This resulted in tall tales that starred familiar, yet radically different, Super Heroes. *Batman Annual* #20, by writer Doug Moench and artist Vince Giarrano, told the story of a flying Batman and his partner, Darkbird. Meanwhile, in *Detective Comics Annual* #9, writer Chuck Dixon and artist Flint Henry told tales of villains like Bane-a-Gator, Three-Face, and the Jokester.

BLACK, WHITE & READ ALL OVER

Batman: Black and White #1 ▪ In what would prove to be one of the most impressive displays of comic book artistry ever to grace Batman's world, the four-issue miniseries *Batman: Black and White* debuted thanks to editors Mark Chiarello and Scott Peterson. Each issue of this remarkable series contained five short, self-contained stories foregoing the use of color in order to really draw attention to the ink work involved. In addition, every issue featured a cover by A-list artists, as well as inspired inside front and back cover pin-ups.

NEW VIEWS

Several writers and artists tackled Batman and his world in this groundbreaking series, including Ted McKeever, Joe Kubert, and José Muñoz. Each artist added a new facet to Batman's complex and engaging story, and the series soon became a fan favorite.

JUNE

TWO BIRDS WITH ONE COMIC

BLACK CANARY/ORACLE: BIRDS OF PREY #1

One of the most enduring female teams in the DC Universe was created when computer expert Oracle teamed with fellow longtime Super Hero and martial artist Black Canary, forming the Birds of Prey.

While this one-shot was a single self-contained extra-long story that paired Barbara Gordon with Black Canary, the Birds of Prey idea soon earned a four-issue miniseries in September of the same year with *Birds of Prey: Manhunt*, followed by four quarterly specials, and eventually, an ongoing series. This particular issue, by writer Chuck Dixon and artist Gary Frank, told the tale of Oracle contacting Black Canary in order to help take down the Green Brotherhood, eco-terrorists led by multibillionaire Nick Devine. In honor of the occasion, Canary ditched her blonde wig and fishnets in favor of dyeing her hair blonde and adopting a new costume given to her by Oracle. With Oracle supplying the information and Black Canary supplying the physical legwork, including a fight with the villain and fellow martial artist Lynx, the team proved a perfect partnership, as readers heartily agreed.

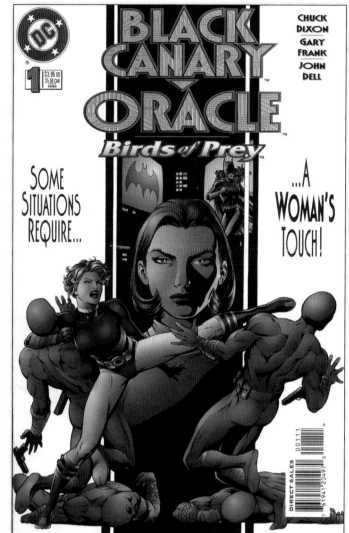

LEGACY

Detective Comics #700 ● While it began in two prelude issues in *Batman* and *Batman: Shadow of the Bat*, the 10-part "Legacy" crossover officially began in this anniversary issue. As well as a parchment-wrapped deluxe format, it was also available in a newsstand edition. Written by Chuck Dixon and drawn by Graham Nolan, this issue saw Batman discover who was behind the Clench plague: Rā's al Ghūl. "Legacy" continued through the bat-books, climaxing in a Batman/Bane rematch that saw the Dark Knight triumph over Rā's al Ghūl's new lackey.

AUGUST

TALIA'S SUITOR

Rā's al Ghūl had tried to get the Batman to take over his empire and marry his daughter Talia on several occasions. But when Batman refused, Rā's tested a new possible candidate, the villain Bane.

AUGUST

G.C.P.D. BLUE

Batman: G.C.P.D. #1 ● The good men and women of the Gotham City Police Department, along with the not-so-good, found a moment in the spotlight in this four-issue limited series written by Chuck Dixon and drawn by longtime Batman artist Jim Aparo. An interesting glimpse inside police work akin to a primetime TV drama, this series dealt with issues that only arise when living in a city full of super-villains, like the Polka-Dot Man filing a police brutality complaint against Harvey Bullock. Batman and Robin made a cameo appearance.

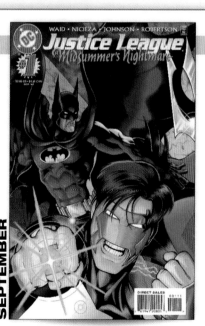

SEPTEMBER

THE RETURN OF THE LEAGUE

Justice League: Midsummer's Nightmare #1 ● In what would serve as a lead-in to 1997's smash hit, *JLA*, the big seven members of the Justice League—Batman, Superman, Green Lantern, the Flash, Wonder Woman, Martian Manhunter, and Aquaman—were reunited for a new generation. Written by Mark Waid and Fabian Nicieza and illustrated by Jeff Johnson and Darick Robertson, this series saw Batman and Superman wake from a dream to recruit the rest of the League when combatting the threat of Dr. Destiny and the new villain Know Man.

CARMINE FALCONE
Carmine "The Roman" Falcone was Gotham City's most notorious mob boss and clashed with Batman on more than one occasion.

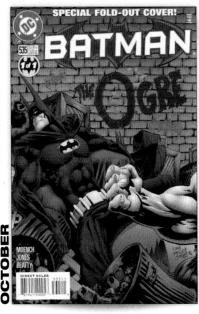

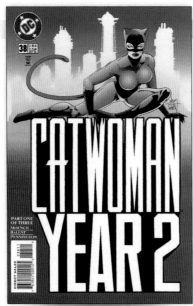

SPECIAL FEATURE

TORQUE

The Blüdhaven Police Department was riddled with corruption, and one of the worst offenders was Inspector Dudley Soames. By *Nightwing* #27 (January 1999) Soames would become a super-villain in his own right. After having his head literally twisted around on his shoulders by Blockbuster, he would adopt the name Torque.

1 OF 1

Batman #535 ▪ With some readers exhausted from the grand-scale multi-part crossovers that many books had been employing since 1993's "Knightfall," increasingly Batman titles began to proudly bear a "1 of 1" emblem on their covers, indicating that the story inside was a self-contained tale that didn't continue elsewhere. In this one-off story available in a newsstand edition or in a deluxe edition with a foldout cover, writer Doug Moench and artist Kelley Jones introduced a pair of new villains into Batman's world with the Ogre and the Ape.

CATWOMAN: YEAR 2

Catwoman #38 ▪ Selina Kyle welcomed Doug Moench as the new regular writer on her title with this three-issue flashback series-within-a-series, detailing events from her second year in costume. Illustrated by Catwoman mainstay Jim Balent, this series saw Catwoman progress from her gray costume to a purple uniform that better fitted her self-proclaimed status of "dark royalty." This series also saw Selina tangle with Two-Face, the Joker, and the Penguin when they decided to pool their efforts and kill Catwoman once and for all.

NIGHTWING'S NEW TOWN

Nightwing #1 ▪ After 56 years, Dick Grayson was awarded his own ongoing series, written by Chuck Dixon with pencils by Scott McDaniel. Gotham City was becoming a little crowded when it came to Super Heroes, so Dick was dispatched further south to the harbor town of Blüdhaven. Investigating a case for Batman, Nightwing soon realized that Blüdhaven was even more corrupt than Gotham City, prompting him to move there for good. This debut installment also included the first appearance of Blüdhaven's nefarious Chief of Police, Delmore Redhorn.

DECEMBER

TAKING A HOLIDAY
BATMAN: THE LONG HALLOWEEN #1

In this epic 13-part tale, the Dark Knight Detective entered the world of the mob as he sought to track down Holiday, a mysterious villain who systematically murdered a victim on each major holiday.

Writer Jeph Loeb and artist Tim Sale had drawn much acclaim for their annual *Batman: Legends of the Dark Knight* Halloween specials, so much so that editor Archie Goodwin expanded the duo's exposure by giving them a 13-issue series set firmly in Batman's early days, and telling a year-long murder mystery.

Not only did this beautifully drawn series feature a host of Batman villains, it also picked up where "Batman: Year One" left off. It introduced new members of mob boss Carmine "the Roman" Falcone's crime family, including his daughter, Sophia, as well as the main villain, known as Holiday, whose identity wouldn't be revealed until issue #12 (December 1997). The story served to retell Two-Face's origin, revealing the corruption of Harvey Dent that was firmly a part of his character before he became a super-villain. The series also showed the villain Calendar Man in a serious light, and brought Solomon Grundy firmly back into Batman's world. *Batman: The Long Halloween* soon became a best-selling series.

BATMAN THE LONG HALLOWEEN · JEPH LOEB & TIM SALE · A Dark Knight Halloween Special · CRIME in Thirteen Parts

GOTHAM CITY'S TOP COP
Batman: Gordon's Law #1 ● Jim Gordon had recently regained his position as police commissioner of Gotham City, and now, thanks to writer Chuck Dixon and artist Klaus Janson, he received his first miniseries. In this four-issue story, readers saw Gordon take action on his own while trying to deduce the culprit of a federal reserve heist. In June of 1998, Gordon earned another four-issue miniseries entitled *Batman: Gordon of Gotham*. This second volume focused on Gordon's life in Chicago before he arrived in Gotham City.

MAN OF CLAY
Batman: Legends of the Dark Knight #89 ● The second and perhaps most memorable Clayface received a modern retelling of his origin thanks to writer Alan Grant and artist Enrique Alcatena. Thief Matthew Hagen was posing as an "adventurer," when he was caught double-crossing his employer. While hiding out in an underwater cave, Hagen fell into a pool of bizarre mud that transformed him into the malleable Clayface. In order to stop him, Batman changed his own appearance, adopting the identity of criminal "Matches" Malone in this two-part tale.

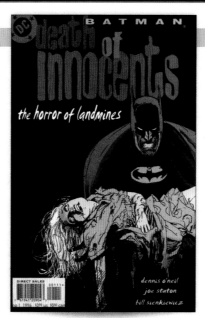

THE HORROR OF LANDMINES
Batman: Death of Innocents ● Writer Dennis O'Neil and artist Joe Staton joined forces to increase awareness of the issue of landmines in this one-shot special. Aided by inker Bill Sienkiewicz's powerful style, this issue began with an introduction about the dangers of landmines by Senator Patrick Leahy from Vermont. And after the comic book's tragic tale, in which Batman witnessed the death of a young girl, Colonel David H. Hackworth, Jody Williams, and Jerry White offered nonfiction information regarding the horrors of these deadly weapons.

ALSO THIS YEAR

January—Catwoman #28: Computer hacker Giz and masked thief Slyfox debuted.

February—Black Lightning #13: Batman guest-starred to bid farewell to Black Lightning as his series came to a close.

March—Action Comics #719: Batman and Superman teamed up when the Joker nearly killed Lois Lane in this one-off tale.

May—Batman #530: Deadman guest-starred in this comic available with standard or glow-in-the-dark covers.

September—Catwoman #37: Selina Kyle faced a literal Catwoman when she met Panara for the first time.

October—Total Justice #1: Tying in to a new toy line came this miniseries where Batman teamed with other DC heroes.

November—Batman & Robin Adventures Annual #1: Paul Dini returned to comics to pen a sequel to the film *Batman: Mask of the Phantasm*.

December—Azrael Plus #1: Azrael and the Question took on a terrorist group.

225

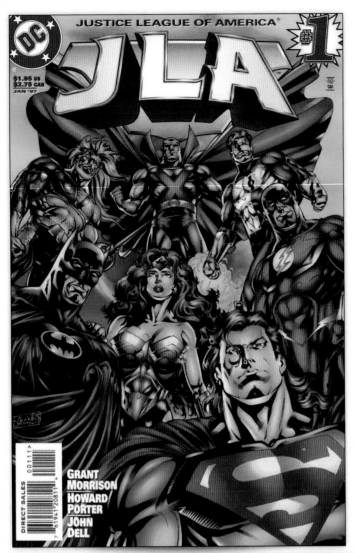

NOT YOUR FATHER'S JUSTICE LEAGUE

JLA #1

The original big seven heroes of the Justice League were back, but with a modern twist in this ongoing series. It was Batman who came to the fore when the JLA had to deal with a villainous Martian super team.

By the late 1990s, the Justice League of America had fallen out of the spotlight due to the lack of superstar team members like Batman or Superman. Home to the likes of Metamorpho, Nuklon, and Ice Maiden, the JLA was no longer the center of goings-on for the DC Universe. It was time to change that.

Enter fan-favorite scribe Grant Morrison and new dynamic penciller, Howard Porter. The pair set out to establish just how important the Justice League was by first telling a four-part arc that pit the Super Heroes against the Hyperclan, a so-called Super Team that was actually made up of white Martians, bloodthirsty aliens from a different tribe on Mars than the one that had birthed Manhunter. Outwardly, the Hyperclan looked to be heroes. In reality, the villains had decimated the headquarters of the former League, and reduced Metamorpho to an inert form.

Knowing that Batman might look out of place on a team with powerhouses like Superman, Wonder Woman, Green Lantern, Aquaman, the Flash, and Manhunter, Morrison showcased Batman's detective skills and fearlessness in this first arc. The Dark Knight Detective was seen defeating the Hyperclan when the rest of his team had been captured during a conflict that destroyed Batman's latest Batplane model. With great stories and renewed popularity, the JLA was truly back.

THE WATCHTOWER
The Justice League's new base on the moon was a state-of-the-art fortress known as the Watchtower. It offered unparalleled protection and technology, as well as stunning views of the Earth, the home the heroes had sworn to protect.

1997

"Ready when you are."

Batman, JLA #3

In order to keep things fresh in Batman's world, editor Dennis O'Neil declared that there would be no inter-title crossovers in any of the Batman titles for at least one year. So while Batman guest-starred in many other comics, in his own family of books his adventures were contained to each individual title. The result was an entire line of great starting points for new readers, some of whom were beginning to discover comics after this year's final installment of the 1990s' Batman movies, *Batman & Robin*. Movie excitement once again caused a surge in Batman's popularity, and the Batman comics benefited from the exposure.

THRILLS FROM THE 60S
Thrillkiller: Batgirl & Robin #1 • Writer Howard Chaykin and painter Dan Brereton teamed up to deliver this three-issue Elseworlds miniseries set in 1961 that starred a different kind of Dynamic Duo. Batgirl and Robin were pop icons in this tale, while Bruce Wayne was a police detective, and the Joker was a woman named Blanca Steeplechase. A popular series, *Thrillkiller* earned a sequel in the form of the prestige-format special *Thrillkiller '62* (April 1998) that paired Batgirl with new partner, Batman, as Bruce Wayne became a different kind of detective.

LADY OF THE NIGHT
Nightwing #4 • It was time for Nightwing to start building his own Rogues Gallery, and the team of writer Chuck Dixon and artist Scott McDaniel were certainly up to the task. In this issue, they introduced Lady Vic, a contract killer who considered herself a bit of a "workaholic." Meanwhile in his private life, Dick Grayson took a day job at a cop bar called Hogan's Alley to learn information that might help Nightwing on his missions. But he continued to be stymied in his attempt to find out what his mysterious landlady, named Bridget Clancy, actually looked like.

SURROUNDED
Batman found himself surrounded by members of the Hyperclan during his mission, but the resourceful Dark Knight managed to make short work of the threat.

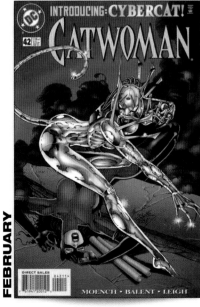

THE OTHER CATS

Catwoman #42 ■ Catwoman met two would-be successors to her crown in the form of She-Cat and Cyber-C.A.T. In this tale written by Doug Moench and illustrated by Jim Balent, audiences first met She-Cat when she robbed the Gotham Museum of Natural History. Immediately after, they met Cyber-C.A.T., a cybernetic engineer who developed armor capable of shooting lasers and equipped with thermal vision, radar, and razor-sharp claws. Cyber-C.A.T. quickly made life difficult for Selina Kyle, marking her as her enemy due to Catwoman's thieving history.

PLAYING DETECTIVE

Robin #38 ■ Roy Raymond Jr. shared the name of his father and fellow famous TV detective, but when he first appeared in this issue written by Chuck Dixon and illustrated by Staz Johnson, he possessed none of his father's bravery or integrity. Relying on paid information to make his busts that were later recreated in hokey dramatizations, Roy Raymond Jr. failed to impress Robin when they first crossed paths. However, Roy would later become a Super Hero in his own right when he donned the mantle of Owlman in *Outsiders* #15 (April 2009).

THE GHOST AND THE GIRL

Batman #540 ■ While not a crossover, coincidence dictated that Batman and Spectre appeared in each other's titles this month. In the pages of *Spectre* #51 (March 1997) by writer John Ostrander and artist Tom Mandrake, the Spectre traveled into the mind of the Joker, while in *Batman* #540 and #541 (April 1997), writer Doug Moench and artist Kelley Jones pit the ghostly Spectre against Batman, believing the Dark Knight a murderer. Issue #540 also introduced a new love interest for Bruce Wayne, radio talk show host Vesper Fairchild.

BAT VERSUS CAT

Batman/Wildcat #1 ■ Writers Chuck Dixon and Beau Smith teamed up with penciller Sergio Cariello for the fight of the century told over three issues. Spearheaded by Lock-Up and corrupt former boxer Ernie Chubb, an underworld fighting show called The Secret Ring was kidnapping criminals and forcing them to fight to the death. But when a fake Wildcat was killed on one of the videotaped "episodes," both Ted Grant and Bruce Wayne took interest, breaking up the fighting ring, but not before they were forced to fight each other. Villain Monsoon also debuted.

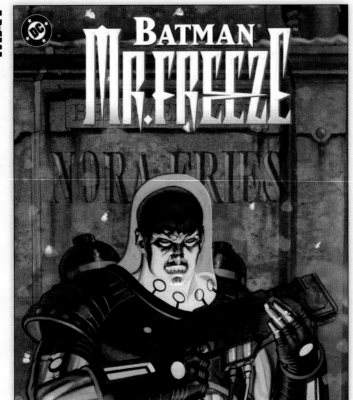

HEART OF ICE

BATMAN: MR. FREEZE

Mr. Freeze gained a tragic origin in this special that humanized this iconic member of Batman's Rogues Gallery.

Despite being in comics for over three decades, Mr. Freeze had only been given a true origin story in the landmark *Batman: The Animated Series* TV show thanks to writer Paul Dini. In this issue, one of the prestige-format specials meant to attract readers excited about June's upcoming *Batman & Robin* film, Dini retold his tragic love story in comic book form with the help of artist Mark Buckingham. Also released at this time were *Batman: Poison Ivy*, *Batman: Bane*, and *Batman: Batgirl*, three other prestige-format specials celebrating characters from the same big-budget movie.

Brilliant molecular biologist Victor Fries was working for tech company Gothcorp in the field of cryogenics when his beloved wife Nora contracted a rare, terminal form of cancer. Gothcorp ordered Fries to shut down his costly research, but he continued in secret, freezing his wife Nora's body to save her until a cure for her condition could be found. When Fries' boss, Ferris Boyle, stormed into Fries' lab and ordered it shut down Fries seized a security guard's gun. It went off when Boyle attacked him, causing coolant to escape and turn Fries into Mr. Freeze. To survive, Fries was thereafter forced to wear a suit that maintained his body at freezing temperatures.

Armed with his deadly Freeze Gun, Mr. Freeze later attacked Boyle and Batman intervened, leading to a struggle in which the frozen body of Mr. Freeze's beloved Nora shattered in pieces. Henceforth, Mr. Freeze turned all his attention to making the Dark Knight's life as miserable as his own.

Paul Dini
Mark Buckingham
Wayne Faucher

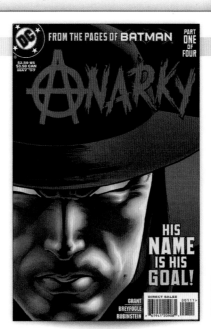

NIGHTWING OR NITE-WING

Nightwing #8 ▪ After discovering the mob boss of Blüdhaven was actually the now hyper-intelligent Blockbuster (due to an upgrade by Neron during the *Underworld Unleashed* event) in the previous issue, Nightwing's Rogues Gallery continued to grow. In this issue, writer Chuck Dixon and artist Scott McDaniel introduced the mentally unhinged Tad Ryerstad. Shown beating up a homeless man for dirtying "his" block, Tad would adopt the Nite-Wing identity in issue #21 (June 1998), becoming a dangerous and violent version of Dick Grayson's famous alter ego.

LOSING FACE

Batman #542 ▪ The team of writer Doug Moench and artist Kelley Jones introduced Joseph Zedno, the newest villain to cross paths with Batman, in his persona as Faceless. Zedno was fired from the Post Office following too many complaints about undelivered mail. This caused his already unstable mind to slip further away from reality. Zedno began calling himself Faceless, intent on using violence to ensure that the people in his life never thought he was a nobody ever again. He also dressed up as each of his intended victims.

THE RISE OF ANARKY

Anarky #1 ▪ Anarky received his first shot at elevating his comic book status in this four-issue miniseries by writer Alan Grant and artist Norm Breyfogle. Using a variety of techniques, Anarky succeeded in fusing the two halves of his brain together in this series that guest-starred Etrigan, Darkseid, and Batman. The tale proved popular enough to earn the vigilante his own short-lived ongoing series by the same creative team that debuted in May 1999, giving the character a new costume to combat the threats he faced.

MAGIC SHOW

Batman: Legends of the Dark Knight #95
Writing partners Dan Abnett and Andy Lanning teamed up with artist Anthony Williams for this three-issue tale. Touring Europe after college and before becoming Batman, Bruce Wayne came upon the myth of the Magician, an ancient "bogey man" challenging Romania's corrupt regime. Unable to stop the Magician's murder spree then, Batman had a second chance when the "killer" came to Gotham City. Batman soon discovered that there was more than one of these costumed mystery men.

FREEZE FRAME
Batman dodged as Mr. Freeze fired his Freeze gun. The blast hit the cryogenic chamber containing the biologist's dying wife, killing her. Instead of taking the blame, Mr. Freeze blamed Batman and swore revenge.

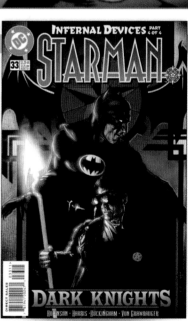

A BAD SIGNAL

Hitman #15 ● In the six-part "Ace of Killers" storyline, Hitman teamed up with Catwoman by summoning her in a very unusual way. With the help of writer Garth Ennis and artist John McCrea, Hitman found himself up against a demon named Mawzir. With no idea how to beat such a powerful foe, Hitman knew he needed an ally, so he chose someone who apparently knew the demon personally. By using a dead cat and a spotlight, Hitman concocted a "cat-signal" and convinced Catwoman Selina Kyle to join his bizarre crusade.

ATTEMPTED MARRIAGE

Nightwing Annual #1 ● The theme running through 1997's DC annuals was "Pulp Heroes," with each volume garnished with a cover that looked more like a pulp novel than a comic book. Each issue also featured a tagline of sorts running down the side of the cover, including "Suspense Detective" and this issue's "Young Romance." Writer Devin Grayson and artist Greg Land supplied Nightwing's chapter, which saw the former Boy Wonder undergo a fake marriage to a woman named Emily Washburn in order to discover who had murdered her last three husbands.

A REAL GEARHEAD

Detective Comics #712 ● Writer Chuck Dixon and artist Graham Nolan created a new foe for Batman to battle when an escaping criminal named Nathan Finch fell through the ice of a frozen lake and had to have his arms and legs amputated. A technical genius, Finch became a cyborg calling himself Gearhead. Gearhead later appeared on the 2005 cartoon *The Batman*. He was even later made into an action figure in the tie-in toy line, but due to legal reasons, the name on his packaging had to be changed to Metal Head.

THE TRUTH ABOUT GRUNDY

Starman #33 ● Jack Knight had taken over the role of Starman in writer James Robinson's critically acclaimed *Starman* title. In this issue, drawn by Tony Harris and Mark Buckingham, Batman traveled to Opal City along with the Floronic Man to help shed some light on the mystery of Solomon Grundy. Traveling into the mystical realm of the Green, the two heroes discovered that there were many sides to Solomon Grundy, each taking its turn to become his dominant personality every time the monster died and was reincarnated.

OFF ON A TANGENT

TANGENT COMICS: THE JOKER

A new take on the Joker was created when the Tangent Universe emerged out of a series of one-shot specials.

During the Silver Age of Comics, existing DC Comics' character names like the Flash and Green Lantern were applied to brand new heroes, ignoring past continuity. These new characters became popular and soon the Golden Age versions were brought back to meet them, giving rise to the alternate realities of Earth-One and Earth-Two.

Writer/artist Dan Jurgens utilized that idea for a series of one-shots that birthed the Tangent Universe. Included in this new line was writer Karl Kesel and artist Matt Haley's new take on the Joker as a female anarchist. Also of note to Batman fans was Nightwing, a team of covert agents in a title written by John Ostrander and drawn by Jan Duursema, and the Secret Six, the Tangent Universe's version of the JLA, which included a version of the Joker in its roster.

Tangent released another batch of specials in September 1998 that included new Joker and Nightwing specials, alongside the Tangent version of Batman by writer/artist Dan Jurgens and finishing artist Klaus Janson. The Tangent Universe saw a revival in May 2008 with a 12-issue maxiseries called *Tangent: Superman's Reign*.

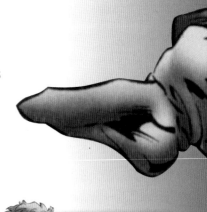

FAST-MOVING TARGET
Officer John A. Keel found the Joker an intriguing quarry. The free-spirited vigilante even offered Keel a bottle of soda in a generous gesture.

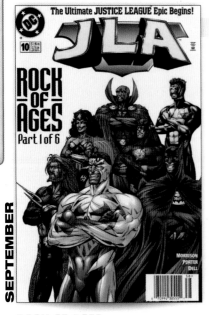

ROCK OF AGES

JLA #10 ■ One of the more unique Batman villains debuted in the first chapter of this six-part epic by writer Grant Morrison and artist Howard Porter. Not quite a living entity, this "new enemy" was an energy construct created to look exactly like the Batman. The only differences were that this entity was made out of purple "hard light" and wore a skull over of the famous bat-symbol on his chest. To make matters worse, this Hard-Light Batman was being controlled remotely by the Joker, one of the members of the newly re-established Injustice Gang.

SECRETS OF SUCCESS

***Batman: Secret Files and Origins* #1**
A modern spin on the classic *Who's Who* series from 1985, this comic was one of a series of specials published by DC Comics that told the histories of their characters in comic form and through text dossiers. Batman's origin was recounted by writer Devin Grayson and Staz Johnson, the Batcave was toured by writer/artist Graham Nolan, and writer Chuck Dixon and artist Jim Aparo detailed how Bruce Wayne gets all his toys into the Batcave. It also featured text pieces and pin-ups by other top talent.

ARMING THE CAT

***Catwoman* #50** ■ Selina Kyle had never been one for a stable wardrobe. Even before she nabbed her own ongoing series, her costumed had changed time and time again. So it was no surprise that she showed off a new underwater costume in issue #48 or that in this anniversary issue, she debuted a new armored costume. Thanks to writer Doug Moench and penciller Jim Balent, Catwoman donned this temporary armor in order to better combat Cyber-C.A.T. after the suit was designed for her by her ally, Clutterbuck.

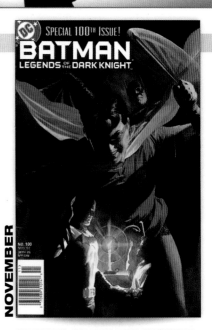

LEGENDS OF THE BOY WONDER

***Batman: Legends of the Dark Knight* #100**
While *Legends of the Dark Knight* had previously been a title focusing on Batman's solo adventures from the past, for this extra-long anniversary issue, writer Dennis O'Neil and artist Dave Taylor brought Robin into the mix, for a retelling of Dick Grayson's classic origin. This issue also featured a Jason Todd story written by James Robinson and drawn by Lee Weeks, and a pin-up gallery featuring star artists, such as Frank Miller and Joe Quesada, all wrapped up in a great Alex Ross painted cover.

"How do I look gentlemen? I'm a woman of many hats you know!"

The Joker, *Tangent Comics: The Joker* #1

THE MANY FACES OF THE JOKER
A revamped version of the Joker's Daughter, Harlequin, the Joker was portrayed by three different women. They included Lori Lemaris, a Superman supporting character, and the bookish Mary Marvel, familiar to Shazam! fans.

THE PENGUIN'S TRUE FACE
Batman #548 ▪ The Penguin returned to his thieving roots in this two-part tale by writer Doug Moench and artist Kelley Jones. Not content with being an everyday crime boss, the Penguin took a hands-on approach, leaving a Penguin egg in place of the diamond that he stole during his first robbery. The story also featured the return of the Penguin's Aviary lair. Part two, in *Batman* #549 (December), featured a close-up of Penguin's face on the cover as part of the "Faces of the DC Universe"-themed covers that spanned the entire Super Hero line.

CREEPING BACK
The Creeper #1 ▪ Gotham City's most bizarre Super Hero was back in his own title thanks to writer Len Kaminski and artist Shawn Martinbrough. This post-*Infinite Crisis* version of the Creeper was no longer an exaggerated persona that Jack Ryder used to scare criminals, but a dark, troubled personality. The Creeper was now also armed with a laugh that caused pain to anyone within earshot. This version of the character was short-lived; another Creeper was revealed in June 2003 in *Beware the Creeper*, published in DC Comics' Vertigo imprint.

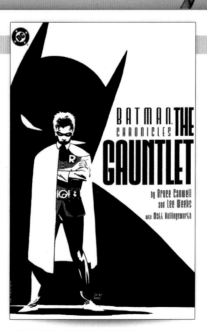

ROBIN'S FINAL EXAM
Batman Chronicles: The Gauntlet ▪ Written by Bruce Canwell with art by Lee Weeks, this prestige-format one-shot showed Dick Grayson, hoping to take up the mantle of Robin, engaged in a fast-paced, dangerous game of hide-and-seek with Batman. As his final initiation into the role, Grayson had to undergo a field test to prove to Batman that he was ready to share the dangers of fighting crime. Given a six-hour head start, Robin had to to stay hidden from Batman until the following sunrise in order to graduate to the role of Robin.

BATMAN
SHADOW OF THE BAT

73

$1.95 US
$2.75 CAN
APR 98

CATACLYSM

ONE
GRANT,
BUCKINGHAM
& FAUCHER

DIRECT SALES

Orbik

073 11>

CATACLYSM
BATMAN: SHADOW OF THE BAT #73

When a 7.6 earthquake struck the unprepared East Coast city of Gotham City, the once grand metropolis was reduced to a rubble-filled disaster area in this 18-part epic crossover series.

Like "Contagion" before it, this massive crossover event would affect all of Gotham City. Following the earthquake, only a handful of properties were still standing. While Bruce Wayne had earthquake-proofed his company's constructions, Wayne Manor itself wasn't immune to the devastation, and the once proud building was horribly damaged. The death toll in Gotham City was high, and soon a madman calling himself the Quakemaster began to claim the carnage as his own creation.

Writer Alan Grant and penciller Mark Buckingham kicked off the epic storyline in the pages of *Shadow of the Bat* (after a prelude issue in *Detective Comics* #719 (March 1998) written by Chuck Dixon). The story soon crossed into the ongoing titles *Nightwing*, *Batman*, *Azrael*, *Catwoman*, *Robin*, and *The Batman Chronicles*. This 18-part series included three one-shot specials, *Batman: Blackgate: Isle of Men*, *Batman: Huntress/Spoiler: Blunt Trauma*, and *Batman: Arkham Asylum: Tales of Madness*.

By the end of the series, it was soon discovered that the "Quakemaster" was merely a fake persona orchestrated by the Ventriloquist. But the damage from the quake itself wasn't something Gotham City could as easily overcome, and following "Cataclysm," was a looser set of related titles, sold under the banner "Aftershock."

TECTONIC MYSTERY
After a massive earthquake hits Gotham City, scientists and geologists struggle to discover the source of the quake, an event unusual for both Gotham City and the east coast of the United States.

1998

"I guess you could say I was a child of the love generation."

Prometheus, *Prometheus* #1.

In terms of Batman's life story, 1998 served almost as a prequel to a main event. While it contained its fair share of new characters, the year's big crossover event, "Cataclysm," set the stage for "Aftershock" and "Road to No Man's Land" by delivering a powerful earthquake to the unprepared Gotham City, and altering the landscape of Batman's home dramatically. By early 1999, Gotham City would be shut off from the rest of the world, and Batman's comics would interconnect in the largest crossover ever attempted in the Batman stable. 1998 was the necessary set-up, and would serve as the appetizer for the changes in store for 1999.

JANUARY

GIVING CHASE
Batman #550 ▪ A new fixture in the DC Universe debuted in this anniversary special in the person of Cameron Chase, an agent for the Department of Extranormal Operations. When Dr. Peter Malley accidentally merged with a tissue sample from Clayface Cassius Payne, Clay-Thing was born. With Batman's help, Chase contained the threat before spinning off into her own self-titled series. This issue, by writer Doug Moench and pencillers Kelley Jones and J.H. Williams III, came in a deluxe version with trading cards and a standard newsstand edition.

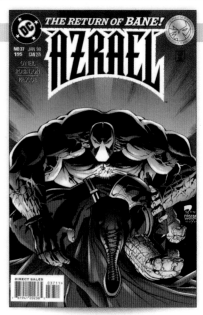

THE RETURN OF BANE
Azrael #37 ▪ Bane got the chance to challenge Azrael to a rematch in this second chapter of a four-part arc by writer Dennis O'Neil and artist Roger Robinson. And unfortunately for Azrael, the rematch didn't go so well, as Bane thoroughly trounced him in this issue with the help of a Venom-induced Bird. But not satisfied with this victory, Bane then injected Azrael with Venom. However, Azrael overcame the need for the drug, and found the inner strength to defeat Bane in their third bout in *Azrael* #39 (March 1998).

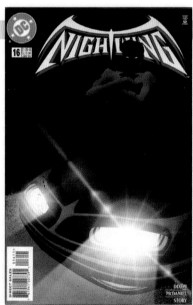

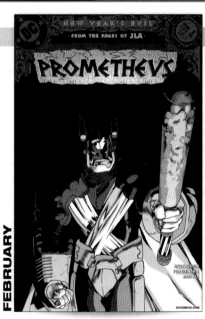

FEBRUARY

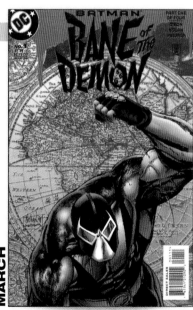

MARCH

THE NIGHTWING-MOBILE

***Nightwing* #16** ▪ While he usually relied on a motorcycle or swinging from rooftops to get around Blüdhaven, Nightwing—and writer Chuck Dixon and artist Scott McDaniel—decided that there were some situation that required a proper automobile. So in this issue, Dick Grayson built a car with a souped-up engine that had a multiple chassis to blend in easily on the street. While the "Nightwing-mobile" wasn't that impressive to look at, it certainly got the job done. In issue #18 (March 1998), Grayson invested in a boat with a bit more flash and style.

NEW YEAR'S EVIL

***Prometheus* #1** ▪ As part of the "New Year's Evil" series of one-shots featuring super-villains, fans met the newest Batman foe, thanks to writer Grant Morrison and artist Arnie Jorgensen. Prometheus was the son of a Bonnie and Clyde-like couple, whose hair turned white when his parents were killed during a shootout with police. After training himself in a variety of disciplines and creating a helmet that allowed information on his opponents to be downloaded directly into his central nervous system, Prometheus set his sights on taking down the JLA.

A NEW KIND OF DEMON

***Batman: Bane of the Demon* #1** ▪ Rā's al Ghūl had been searching for an heir to his empire for some time, and in this four-issue series by writer Chuck Dixon and artist Graham Nolan, the Demon's Head realized that Bane just might be the man he was looking for. While searching the globe for his birth father, Bane encountered Rā's al Ghūl's daughter Talia, and was brought home to meet her father. In this prequel to the "Legacy" crossover, Bane fought his way into Rā's al Ghūl's good graces and even had a brief romance with Talia.

PROMETHEUS UNBOUND

***JLA* #16** ▪ Disguised as the Super Hero Retro, new villain Prometheus snuck into the JLA's Watchtower headquarters just as Huntress joined the team based on Batman's recommendation. In this two-part story written by Grant Morrison and illustrated by Howard Porter and Arnie Jorgensen (in issue #17), Prometheus took out the League's members one by one. When Batman was defeated, all hope looked lost even when the Dark Knight contacted the JLA's secret member, Oracle. Eventually, it was Catwoman's sudden appearance that forced the villain to retreat.

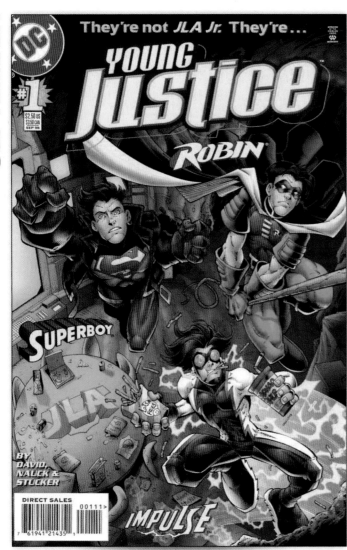

They're not *JLA Jr.* They're...

YOUNG JUSTICE #1

ROBIN
SUPERBOY
IMPULSE

BY DAVID, NAUCK & STUCKER

DIRECT SALES

JLA JR.
YOUNG JUSTICE #1

TRICK OR TREAT?
The heroes of Young Justice faced old and mischievous foe Mr. Mxyzptlk shortly after they formed their team. The young heroes would come across all sorts of adversaries, all while based out of their secret headquarters in Happy Harbor.

With *Young Justice*, new generation Super Heroes Superboy, Robin, and Impulse, the Flash's new semi-sidekick, gained their own team-up series.

The Young Justice team first appeared in a one-shot entitled *Young Justice: The Secret* #1 (June 1998) that was part of DC's "Girlfrenzy!" series of specials. Written by Todd Dezago and illustrated by Todd Nauck, this special brought the trio of teen heroes together, and also introduced Young Justice's future teammate, the ethereal Secret.

The Young Justice team then starred in a two-issue prestige series called *JLA: World Without Grown-ups* written by Dezago and illustrated by Mike McKone and Humberto Ramos. In this series the group fully established their Super Hero team and discovered the site of their future hideout, the Justice League's former headquarters located in a cave in Happy Harbor. After this, the team was finally given its own ongoing title, *Young Justice*, written by Peter David and illustrated by Todd Nauck.

This first issue saw the team investigate a disturbance at a nearby archaological dig, only to come into contact with female villain the Mighty Endowed. Combining humor, super heroics, and drama, this series proved to be a DC Comics staple.

NIGHT OF THE HUNTRESS
Nightwing/Huntress #1 ■ Writer Devin Grayson brought her enthusiasm for the character Nightwing to this four-part series that was drawn by Greg Land and Bill Sienkiewicz. When Huntress was on the tail of criminal Frankie Black for the murder of an undercover policewoman, Nightwing crossed Helena's path, since he had firsthand knowledge of Black's innocence. Their resulting investigation developed into a romantic fling. However this fizzled out when it became clear that Huntress was using Nightwing to become part of Batman's inner circle.

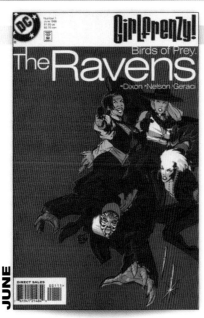

QUOTH THE RAVENS
Birds of Prey: The Ravens #1 ■ As part of a series of female-centric specials called "Girlfrenzy!," readers met the Birds of Prey's super-villain equivalent called the Ravens. Written by Chuck Dixon and drawn by Nelson DeCastro, this one-shot served as the Birds of Prey's final special. The title paired the Ravens team leader Cheshire with Pistolera (formerly named Gunbunny), and new villains Vicious and Termina. Also in the "Girlfrenzy" line was *Batman: Batgirl*, a flashback tale featuring the menace of serial killer Mr. Zsasz.

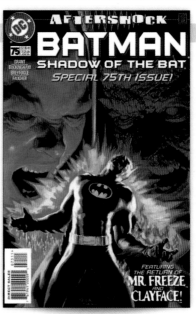

FIRE AND ICE
Batman: Shadow of the Bat #75 ■ In this extra-long anniversary issue, writer Alan Grant and artist Mark Buckingham brought back Ultimate Clayface Basil Karlo, last seen falling deep inside the earth in *Detective Comics* #607 (October 1989). In this "Aftershock" issue, Clayface was freed from his earthly prison thanks to Gotham City's earthquake, and quickly displayed his new heat-generating powers. Meanwhile, Mr. Freeze was busy stockpiling diamonds needed to power his suit, until Batman pitted the two villains against each other.

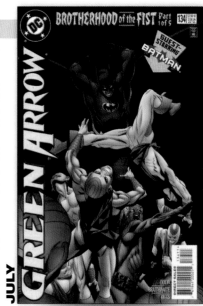

BROTHERHOOD OF THE FIST
Green Arrow #134 ■ Writer Chuck Dixon staged his own five-part mini-crossover event through the four titles he was writing at the time—*Green Arrow*, *Detective Comics*, *Robin*, and *Nightwing*—that explored the martial artists of the DCU. Drawn by Doug Braithwaite, Alex Maleev, Scott McDaniel, and William Rosado, this series pit the Monkey Cult against Batman and other Super Heroes in order to redeem the honor of Silver Monkey for his past failures. This first chapter also debuted the snow camouflage option of Batman's photo-reactive suit.

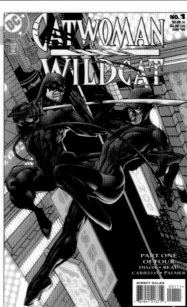

BRUTALE TRUTH

***Nightwing* #22** ● Dick Grayson met a vicious new enemy in this issue by writer Chuck Dixon and artist Scott McDaniel. Aptly named Brutale, this hired killer set his sights on Nightwing after being hired by Blüdhaven's crime boss, Blockbuster, to kill the injured Nite-Wing, whom they'd mistaken for Dick Grayson himself. Nightwing managed to take down Brutale and the villain Stallion, and saw to it that Nite-Wing made it safely to Leslie Thompkins' clinic in Gotham City. Unfortunately, to do so, Dick had to ditch new love Bridget Clancy on their first date.

THE NAIL IN THE COFFIN

***Justice League: The Nail* #1** ● Artist Alan Davis tried his hand at writing and pencilling in this three-issue prestige-format Elseworlds tale. A nail gave the Kents a flat tire, so they never discovered Kal-El when his rocket ship crash-landed on Earth. Without Superman to sway public opinion in their favor, Super Heroes were viewed as threats, especially after Batman killed the Joker when the villain murdered Robin and Batgirl. This story also saw Black Canary form her own team of Outsiders and Catwoman adopt the identity of Batwoman.

ROBBING THE CAT'S CRADLE

***Catwoman/Wildcat* #1** ● Writers Chuck Dixon and Beau Smith once again teamed with artist Sergio Cariello to partner Wildcat with another character from Batman's world, Catwoman. In this four-issue story, Wildcat and Catwoman met up in Las Vegas, although Ted Grant failed to recognize Selina since she'd changed so much from the young girl he originally trained. But in their costumed alter egos, the pair soon found themselves facing new villains Clawhammer and Redblade, as a romance began to bloom between the two cat-themed adventurers.

REMEMBERING THE 80S

***Batman: 80-Page Giant* #1** ● A long-lost classic DC Comics format was revived with the return of *80-Page Giants*, including this first volume of Batman stories. Among the tales featured were a Bruce Wayne story by writer Ron Marz and artist Rodolfo Damaggio and a Penguin tale by writer/artist Rick Burchett. Writer Chuck Dixon and artist Flint Henry told a Harvey Bullock yarn, while writer Doug Moench and penciller Tommy Castillo focused on Huntress. Commissioner Gordon, the Ventriloquist and other members of Batman's cast also featured.

BATMAN BEYOND THE BEYOND

BATMAN #1,000,000

As part of November's DC One Million crossover, nearly every DC Universe title was granted a 1,000,000th issue.

When the JLA journeyed to the future of the 853rd century at the invitation of that time's Justice Legion A, Batman declined to go. Nevertheless, he found himself waking up in the far future and meeting a robot named Robin, the Toy Wonder, thanks to writer Doug Moench and artist Yvel Guichet.

Discovering that his essence had been sent to the year 85,271, Batman explored Pluto, the planet-sized equivalent of Arkham Asylum, with the help of this future's Batmobile, a vehicle called the Omnibat. The story continued into the pages of *Catwoman #1,000,000* by writer Devin Grayson and penciller Jim Balent, in which Batman was aided by the future Catwoman. Batman then escaped this prison planet with the help of the robotic Robin, who sacrificed himself to the 853rd-century version of the Joker, the Laugher, in *Robin #1,000,000* by writer Chuck Dixon and artist Staz Johnson.

THE ONCE AND FUTURE BAT
Unsurprisingly, Batman's finely-tuned survival skills managed to kick in quickly, despite being sent to the far future against his will. Although he was an android, Robin, the Toy Wonder, felt a profound sense of loyalty to the hero.

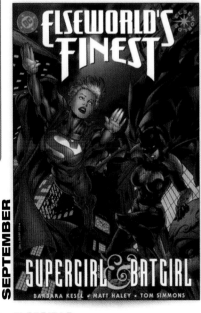

ELSEGIRLS
Elseworld's Finest: Supergirl & Batgirl
In this prestige-format Elseworlds tale, a new take on the World's Finest team was delivered to readers, courtesy of writer Barbara Kesel and plotter/artists Matt Haley and Tom Simmons. In this setting, Batgirl Barbara Gordon was exercising a draconian level of control over Gotham City, even keeping the powerhouses of the Justice Society in check. However, when a muscle-bound version of the Joker kidnapped Lex Luthor, Batgirl was forced to team up with this world's Supergirl to take on the villain.

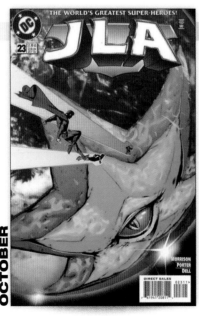

JUSTICE LEGION A
JLA #23 ■ The Batman of the year 85,271 made his debut on the final page of this issue by writer Grant Morrison and artist Howard Porter. While the bulk of this issue focused on the Justice League fighting the alien Starro, the cliffhanger featured the first appearance of Justice Legion A, a team of future Super Heroes. The sudden appearance of these characters from the 853rd century led directly into *DC One Million* #1 (November 1998), the start of a four-issue event, written by Grant Morrison and drawn by Val Semeiks.

THE FUTURE IS NOW
Batman: Shadow of the Bat #1,000,000
After the Batman of the 853rd century explored the Gotham City of the present day in this issue written by Alan Grant and pencilled by Mark Buckingham, he met up with Nightwing in this month's *Nightwing #1,000,000*, written by Chuck Dixon and illustrated by Scott McDaniel, before ending his adventures in our era in *Detective Comics #1,000,000* by Dixon and penciller Greg Land. These three issues revealed that the personality of this new Batman was similar to that of the Dark Knight of the present.

BETTERING BATGIRL
Legends of the DC Universe #10 ■ Writer Kelley Puckett and artists Terry Dodson and Kevin Nowlan regaled readers with this two-part story that revealed how the original Batgirl was trained by the Batman. When he discovered her hair tie at a crime scene, Batman confronted Barbara Gordon about her double identity. Instead of letting Batman shut down her nightly activities, Babs convinced him to train her for a time. This story also saw Barbara start her college education at Gotham State University, even as her father became suspicious of her double life.

DESTINY DUO
Batman found himself teaming up with a robotic Robin in one of the strangest takes on the Dynamic Duo in *Batman #1,000,000*.

DECEMBER

ROAD TO NO MAN'S LAND
Azrael #47/Batman: Shadow of the Bat #80 ▪ In a first for the Batman titles, two comic books became one in an extra-long flipbook issue. Written by Dennis O'Neil and Alan Grant and drawn by Roger Robinson and Mark Buckingham, this interesting comic began the epic Batman crossover event "Road to No Man's Land." This double feature also served to introduce new villains Nicholas Scratch, a former astronomer turned murderous rock star, and Wax Man and Pinhead, two rather deformed Arkham inmates.

WAYNE GOES TO WASHINGTON
Batman #560 ▪ After the Clench virus and the recent earthquake, Batman realized his city needed his help more than ever. So in this three-part story by writer Chuck Dixon and artist Jim Aparo, Bruce Wayne headed to Washington D.C. to plead for federal aid. There, Wayne was opposed by Nick Scratch who had public opinion on his side. Soon, Gotham City was declared a disaster area, and citizens were given 48 hours' notice to evacuate. The city was shut off from the rest of the world, now overrun by the freed madmen of Arkham Asylum.

VILLAINS FROM SCRATCH
Detective Comics #727 ▪ After Firefly was horribly burned in an arson attempt before being brought down by Nightwing and Robin, activist and murderer Nick Scratch employed the help of some new faces in his campaign to destroy Gotham City. Writer Chuck Dixon and artist William Rosado introduced the deadly Dynamiteer as well as the jackhammer-armed threat of Tumult. And while they were unable to save Gotham City from the rising tide of popular apathy, Nightwing and Robin managed to take down Scratch's men one by one.

ALSO THIS YEAR

February—*Catwoman #54*: New regular scribe Devin Grayson came aboard *Catwoman*, starting with this issue.

June—*Batman: Scottish Connection*: The beautiful work of artist Frank Quitely was showcased in this prestige-format special that took Batman to Scotland.

June—*Batman #555*: Batman utilized an appropriately-themed Humvee of sorts before switching to a new version of his monster truck Batmobile in *Detective Comics #725* (September 1998).

July—*Legends of the DC Universe #6*: Robin (Dick Grayson) teamed up with Superman for the first time in this new flashback ongoing series.

September—*Batman Annual #22*: Batman was haunted by the ghost of Abattoir, the villain whom Azrael had allowed to die.

December—*JLA/The Titans #1*: Nightwing's allies were pitted against Batman's in this three-issue series.

237

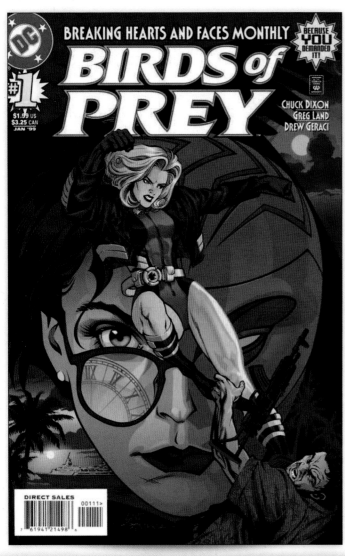

WING AND PREYER

BIRDS OF PREY #1

The *Birds of Prey* pairing of longtime Super Hero Black Canary and computer expert and former Batgirl, Oracle, was set to be a true success for DC Comics.

It had taken quite a while before the Birds of Prey team finally achieved their own ongoing monthly. Once the series began, with this issue by writer Chuck Dixon and artist Greg Land, *Birds of Prey* became a hit. In fact, by the series' end 10 years later, the only all-female DC Comics title that had as many issues to its credit was *Wonder Woman*.

Relying on high-octane adventure stories often set in different exotic locales around the globe, *Birds of Prey* continued the team-up adventures of Black Canary and Oracle, despite Canary having no idea who the voice on her computer screen belonged to. Besides beginning the Birds' monthly exploits, this issue also reintroduced a familiar face into Barbara Gordon's life, her ex-fiancé, private eye Jason Bard.

SAME BIRD, NEW TRICKS

No longer possessing superpowers of any sort, Black Canary was forced to rely on her years of experience, her martial arts training, and plenty of hi-tech gadgets to help her succeed in her missions.

1999

"Gotham's my town. I intend to fight for it."

Harvey Bullock, *Batman: No Man's Land #1*

By 1999, crossovers had become commonplace in Batman's world. Epic storylines often continued from one title to another, changing the landscape of Gotham City and the lives of its inhabitants. But the Batman offices soon developed a story so big it couldn't be contained, even in a 19-part crossover! Editor Dennis O'Neil and his staff unveiled a year-long Batman epic that would cross through the main core titles and tie in with supporting books such as *Robin*, *Catwoman*, and *Nightwing*. Dubbed a "megaseries" by O'Neil, "No Man's Land" defined Batman's world for a year, placing the Dark Knight in a challenging new setting.

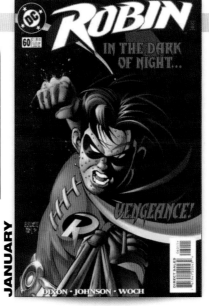

MEETING MR. DRAPER

Robin #60 • Tim Drake utilized the fake persona he invented in *Robin* #22 (October 1995) to great effect in this issue by writer Chuck Dixon and artist Staz Johnson. Stephanie Brown, the adventurer known as the Spoiler, had become pregnant before she started dating Tim. Deciding to have the baby but give it up for adoption due to her young age, Stephanie needed her Super Hero boyfriend around in her civilian life. So Tim appeared as Alvin Draper, and was able to be there for Stephanie when she gave her child up in issue #65 (June 1999).

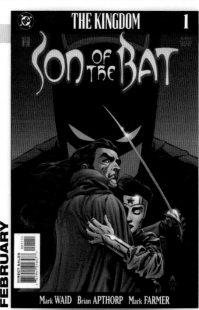

THE KINGDOM OF WAID

The Kingdom: Son of the Bat #1 • Writer Mark Waid returned to the world of *Kingdom Come*, and partnered several different artists to create two bookend volumes simply titled *The Kingdom*, and a series of specials. One of these was this volume drawn by Brian Apthorp, starring Batman's son, Ibn al Xu'ffasch. This special told a bit of Ibn's origin as well as when he killed his grandfather, Rā's al Ghūl. Also of note was *The Kingdom: Nightstar* #1, written by Waid and drawn by Matt Haley, which starred the daughter of Nightwing and Starfire.

VIRTUAL FRIENDS
Originally, Oracle and Black Canary only communicated from a distance via computers or through miniaturized communication systems. Years later, they would meet face to face and their friendship would continue to grow.

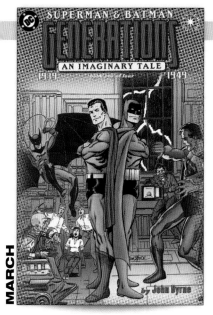

MARCH

GENERATION GAP
Superman & Batman: Generations: An Imaginary Tale #1 ▪ Writer/artist John Byrne returned to the Man of Steel and paired him with the Caped Crusader in this four-issue prestige-format Elseworlds series. Instead of having the comic take place in "comic book time," in which the characters rarely age, Byrne set his story in real time, starting in 1939 and continuing into the present as the heroes aged, and saw new faces accept the Batman role. This series earned a sequel four-issue series in August 2001, and a 12-issue series in March 2003.

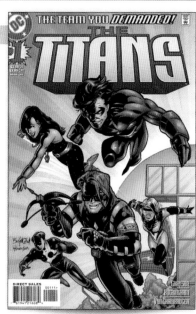

FROM TEENS TO TITANS
The Titans #1 ▪ The original Teen Titans had grown up, so writer Devin Grayson and artist Mark Buckingham decided to showcase the heroes in a new title featuring the adult lives of the classic former sidekicks. With Nightwing on board as team leader, and funded by the undersea treasures discovered by Tempest (formerly Aqualad), teammates Donna Troy (formerly Wonder Girl), Arsenal (formerly Speedy), and the Flash (formerly Kid Flash) reunited, along with new teammate Jesse Quick and members from other Titans eras: Argent, Damage, Cyborg, and Starfire.

THE FUTURE OF ANIMATION
Batman Beyond #1 ▪ Terry McGinnis, the Batman of the future of the DC Animated Universe appeared for the first time in comic book form in this six-issue series by writer Hilary J. Bader and artist Rick Burchett. While the first two issues simply adapted the two-part series premier of the *Batman Beyond* cartoon, the rest of the series told new, self-contained tales, with issues three through six drawn by Joe Staton. By November, the series proved popular enough to graduate to an ongoing series written by Bader with art by Craig Rousseau.

APRIL

THE FINEST YEARS
World's Finest #1 ▪ The Batman/Superman relationship was examined throughout the characters' modern history in this 10-chapter series written by Karl Kesel and illustrated by Dave Taylor, Peter Doherty, Graham Nolan, and Tom Morgan. Issues one and 10 were delivered as prestige-format bookends, and the remaining middle issues were done in a standard "floppy" format. Each issue examined a different fictional year in the careers of the Dark Knight and the Man of Steel, from one of their earliest team-ups to an adventure that took place a year earlier.

NO MAN'S LAND

BATMAN: NO MAN'S LAND #1

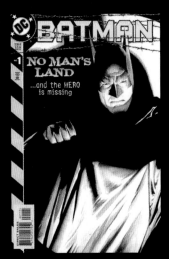

Gotham City had been rocked by the Clench virus and a cataclysmic earthquake. But these were minor problems compared to the chaos unleashed when the city was turned into No Man's Land. Batman was needed. But where was he?

The stories in the loose crossover dubbed "Road to No Man's Land" paved the way for Gotham City being isolated from the rest of the country. This special began the year-long megaseries "No Man's Land" in earnest. Available in a standard cover as well as in a motion-lenticular deluxe cover, both featuring the artwork of Alex Ross, this special by writer Bob Gale and penciller Alex Maleev set up the status quo in the city. With military surrounding its perimeter, Gotham City had indeed become a No Man's Land. Only the stubborn, the loyal, or the crazy remained within its near lawless environs.

As a result, gangs ruled the city. Ninety-three days had gone by and there was no sign of Batman. Various groups claimed different sections of town as their own. One of those groups was the G.C.P.D., the police officers who had stayed behind to protect their city. Other sections were run by Two-Face, the Penguin, Poison Ivy and other infamous faces from Batman's Rogues Gallery. Each claimed their territory by tagging it with their particular spray-painted sign. Finally, on the last page of this special, a mysterious caped figure spray-painted the symbol of the bat for all Gotham City to see.

In "No Man's Land," multi-part stories would continue from one title into the next, creating a weekly experience for the reader. The core story took place in the pages of *Batman: Shadow of the Bat*, *Batman*, *Detective Comics*, and *Batman: Legends of the Dark Knight* as readers watched each group battle for new ground. Each arc was written and illustrated by a different creative team, most of them new to telling stories in the world of Batman.

The story from the *Batman: No Man's Land* special continued into *Batman: Shadow of the Bat* #83 (March 1999) by Gale and Maleev, shocking readers with the introduction of a new Batgirl dressed in black before Batman himself returned (having swapped his sleek Utility Belt for his old-fashioned pouch belt) in the next part of that creative team's

story in *Batman* #563 (March 1999). *Batman: Legends of the Dark Knight* #120 (August 1999) by writer Greg Rucka and artist Mike Deodato revealed that the new Batgirl was actually Huntress in disguise, and *Batman: Shadow of the Bat* #88 (August 1999), by Rucka and artists Dan Jurgens and Bill Sienkiewicz, introduced readers to the idea of Poison Ivy's skin taking on a new green hue.

"No Man's Land" was truly unexplored territory for the Dark Knight and, as the hero plotted to take back his city, readers were treated to Batman stories that were full of thrilling surprises for the cast and the city they still called home.

THE BLUE BOYS
The Gotham City Police Department had its hands full in No Man's Land, and its leader, James Gordon, had been pushed to the limit of his endurance. Batman, the man he once trusted, was absent when the city needed him most. Gordon felt betrayed by his longtime ally, going so far as to smash the Bat-Signal.

THE VILLAINS RUN WILD

When Arkham Asylum opened its doors and lets its inmates run free in the closed off No Man's Land of Gotham City, several super-villains battled for territory. As they attempted to stake their claims over parts of the city, they wondered where the Joker was. When would the Clown Prince of Crime make his move?

THE NEW FACE OF BATGIRL

BATMAN #567

The mysterious Cassandra Cain debuted in this issue as the newest incarnation of Batgirl. Unable to talk, read, or write, the heroine would only communicate through body language, and would eventually be welcomed into Batman's inner circle.

Written by Kelley Puckett and illustrated by Damion Scott, this two-issue "No Man's Land" story introduced the silent heroine who wore Huntress's makeshift Batgirl uniform. Cassandra was raised by assassin David Cain, who also first appeared in this issue. He had not taught her to talk or to read, but instead she was instructed on how to decipher other people's body language and to predict their next move.

Realizing her father, who had been one of Bruce Wayne's instructors, did not have good intentions, Cassandra soon rejected his ways. She soon found an ally in Oracle, who started to teach her to read. And it was that friendship that led to Oracle giving the young heroine her blessing in regards to taking over the Batgirl mantle in *Batman: Legends of the Dark Knight* #120 in a story by writer Greg Rucka and artist Mike Deodato. That issue also saw Batgirl join Batman's inner circle that included Azrael, Robin, Nightwing and Oracle in a renewed effort to take back Gotham City.

KILLER CAIN
Batman trained with many unsavory types while acquiring the necessary skills to become the Dark Knight. That meant knowing his enemies, and David Cain certainly became one of them, especially when Batman learned of the horrors Cain put his daughter through.

> ## "I recognize this. It's the mark of Cain."
>
> Barbara Gordon, *Batman #567*

THE MAN IN BLACK

Superman: The Odyssey ■ Co-writers Graham Nolan and Chuck Dixon took a vacation from Gotham City to chronicle an early adventure of Clark Kent before he became Superman. While this prestige-format one-shot, that was pencilled by Nolan, mostly focused on Clark's travels to the country of Bhutran, it also showed a brief meeting between Kent and Bruce Wayne when Wayne was training before his time as the Batman. To Kent, Wayne was just a mysterious American in black, but they'd meet again in a sequel to this issue in *Superman* #710 (June 2011).

I DOUBLE DARE YOU

Nightwing #32 ■ A duo of acrobatic criminals made their debut in Blüdhaven in this issue written by Chuck Dixon and illustrated by Scott McDaniel. Dubbed Double Dare, Margot and Aliki Marceau were part of the Cirque Sensationnel, a popular circus in town for only a week. When not dealing with this pair of high-altitude thieves in this three-issue story, Nightwing was busy, in his real identity of Dick Grayson, training to become a member of the Blüdhaven's police force, in order to seek out corruption inside the organization.

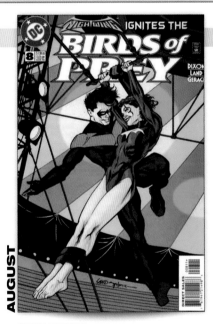

LOVE BIRDS

Birds of Prey #8 ■ Barbara Gordon and Dick Grayson seemed an inevitable couple, but the two never quite got together romantically, at least not until the seeds were planted in this memorable issue by writer Chuck Dixon and penciller Greg Land. Both needing some downtime, Grayson took Gordon to the circus, where the two spent time on the trapeze. And while Barbara continued to keep Grayson at arm's length until the two finally kissed in *Nightwing* #38 (December 1999), this issue showed readers just how deeply Nightwing cared for his longtime crush.

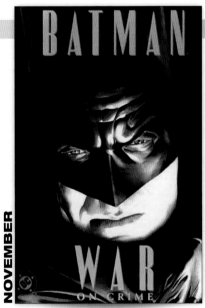

THE GREAT WAR

Batman: War on Crime ■ In this graphic novel, comic book superstars writer Paul Dini and artist/co-plotter Alex Ross tackled Batman's never-ending crime-fighting mission. This was their second treasury-sized, prestige-format graphic novel in their new series spotlighting DC Comics' major Super Heroes. What had started with their painted opus *Superman: Peace on Earth* (January 1999) took a darker turn with this this self-contained story of the Dark Knight's perpetual fight against violent crime in the mean streets of Gotham City.

HER PUDDIN'

Like any couple, Harley and the Joker had their ups and downs. Good times were spent robbing, pillaging, and attempting to murder Batman. Bad days usually involved crazed attempts on Harley's life by the Clown Prince of Crime.

HERE COMES HARLEY

BATMAN: HARLEY QUINN #1

Since her debut in the *Batman: The Animated Series* TV show, Joker's love interest/sidekick Harley Quinn had become a fan favorite. She would soon become a hit in comics, too.

Despite her popular appearances in several animated universe DC Comics titles, Harley Quinn still had to debut in the DC Universe proper. That changed with this prestige-format special, by writer Paul Dini alongside artist Yvel Guichet.

In this issue, Dini delved into Harley's past, making several alterations from her animated origin. Now merely an intern at Arkham Asylum who fell madly in love with the Joker, Harleen Quinzel was locked away after she freed her "Puddin'." But when Gotham City was reduced to a "No Man's Land," she found her way to freedom and decided to adopt a costume and join forces with the Joker, calling herself Harley Quinn. After a few weeks of toying with Harley, the Clown Prince of Crime did what came naturally. He locked Harley in a rocket in an attempt to murder her. Barely surviving her crash landing, Harley met up with Poison Ivy, who gave her new friend a formula that made her immune to toxins. As a side effect, the elixir increased Harley's flexibility, strength and agility. Thus empowered, Harley Quinn was truly unleashed on Gotham City to continue her obsession with the Joker.

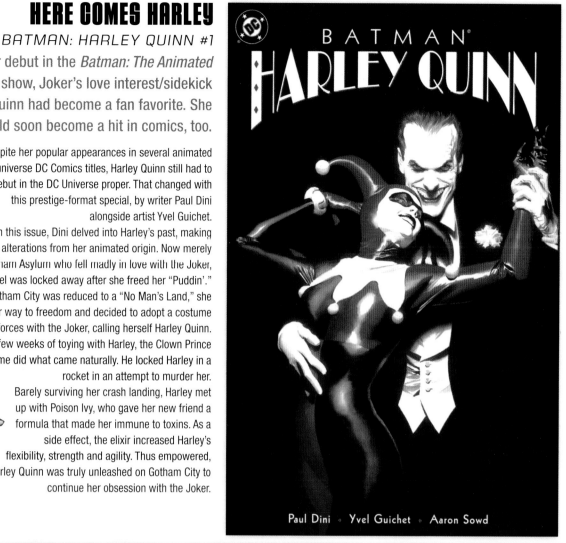

BATMAN® HARLEY QUINN

Paul Dini • Yvel Guichet • Aaron Sowd

TROPHIES AND TRAGEDIES

The Batman Chronicles #19 ● Writer Steve Englehart teamed with artist Javier Pulido to introduce Viveca Beausoleil into Bruce Wayne's past in a lead story of tragic romance. Also included was a Huntress tale by writer Joseph Harris and artist Eric Battle, and a modern update of the Penny Plunderer by writer/artist Graham Nolan that explained the presence of the giant penny in the Batcave. This was the second Batcave feature that Nolan had authored, having previously recounted the origin tale of the Batcave's Tyrannosaurus Rex.

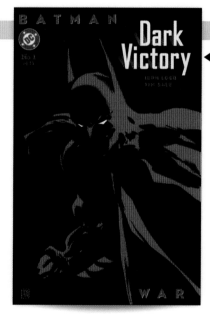

HALLOWEEN GETS LONGER

Batman: Dark Victory #1 ● The fan-favorite team of writer Jeph Loeb and artist Tim Sale joined forces again to tell the latest chapter in their saga of the early years of Batman's career in this 13-issue sequel to *Batman: The Long Halloween* (complete with a bonus #0 issue offered to customers of *Wizard Magazine*). In this moody tale, Gotham City was haunted by a serial murderer. Called the Hangman, this new killer targeted Gotham City cops, first killing Chief Clancy O'Hara, a character that was a nod to the classic *Batman* TV show of the 1960s.

SPECIAL FEATURE

HANGMAN KILLER

Who was the killer that left unfinished games of Hangman at each murder scene? There were several suspects. In this story, which also told a modern origin of the original Robin, the Hangman was revealed to be mobster Sofia Falcone Gigante.

ALSO THIS YEAR

★ **January 10th:** Batman's next phase in animated life came in the form of *Batman Beyond*, a new series set in the future with Terry McGinnis as a youthful Batman.

March—*Azrael #50*: Jean Paul Valley's title began to bear the subtitle "Agent of the Bat." He also acquired a new costume.

May—*Catwoman #68*: Selina Kyle changed her costume to an all-purple look.

July—*Fanboy #5*: In this issue, the various eras of Batman's history each received a bit of good-natured ribbing.

July—*Young Justice: No Man's Land Special #1*: Robin and company met new villain and plant creation of Poison Ivy, Ferak.

October—*Nightwing: Secret Files and Origins #1*: This issue marked the debut of the assassin Shrike, a major Nightwing foe.

December—*Batman: No Man's Land: Ground Zero #1* It was revealed that Batman had various Batcaves in Gotham City.

1999—*Doctor Mid-Nite #1*: A new Doctor Mid-Nite and The Terrible Trio starred in this three-issue prestige-format series.

2000s

As Batman entered the new millennium, the character began to undergo a great deal of change. Batman's comic books also received a shake-up, with new titles and unforgettable, landmark storylines such as "Hush" and "Batman and Son."

As the Dark Knight's longtime editor Dennis O'Neil retired, "No Man's Land," the largest crossover epic in the character's history, came to its dramatic close. The 2000s saw first Bob Shreck and then Mike Marts edit the Batman titles and also the return of some of Batman's greatest creators. Among that number were Frank Miller, Matt Wagner, and writer Jeph Loeb, who had quickly become a fan favorite due to his collaborations with Tim Sale in the late 90s. This time, Loeb partnered with legendary artist Jim Lee, and the result was "Hush," a blockbuster comic title if ever one deserved the name. The series also introduced readers to the new villain Hush, who would quickly rise up the ranks of great Batman enemies.

New ongoing titles made their debut, including *Batman: Gotham Knights*, *Batgirl*, and a highly acclaimed new volume of *Catwoman*. The 2000s would see the birth of new incarnations of the *Teen Titans*, *Outsiders*, *Justice League of America*, and Batman's first ongoing police drama, *Gotham Central*. Harley Quinn also received her own title, having been introduced into the DC Universe at the end of the 1990s.

Writer Grant Morrison began his greatest Batman epic to date, "Batman and Son," a story that began in 2006 in the pages of *Batman*, and wound through several titles before coming to its conclusion in 2013 in the final issue of *Batman Incorporated*. The series would introduce Damian Wayne, the newest Robin, Bruce Wayne's own son. The tale offered readers an intriguing new look at the character of Batman, taking the Caped Crusader of the 2000s into a bold new direction, while simultaneously celebrating every single decade that had come before.

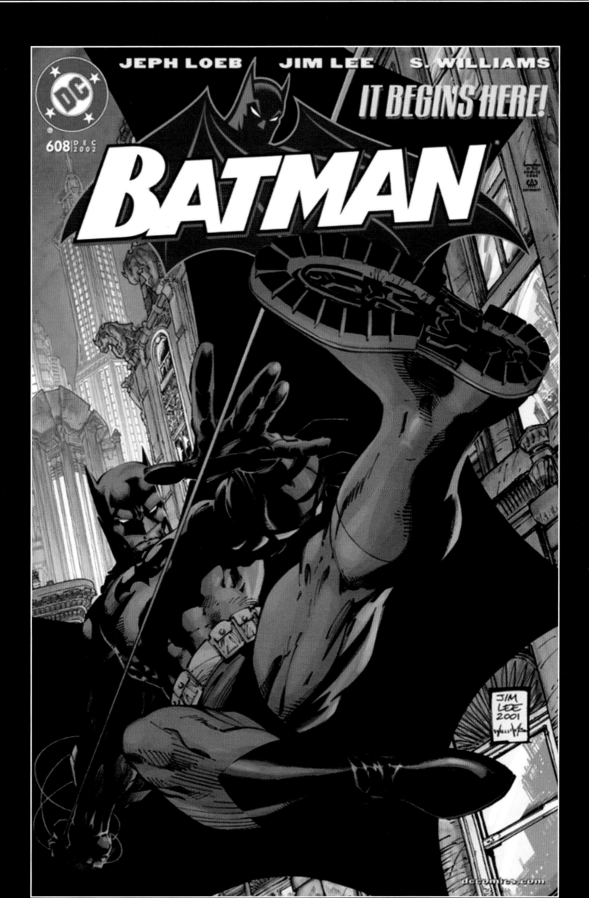

BATMAN'S NEW COLORS
DETECTIVE COMICS #742

This issue redefined the look and content of *Detective Comics,* distinguishing the title from other Batman books.

A stand-out writer in the "No Man's Land" event, Greg Rucka was handed the reins of *Detective Comics,* alongside artist Shawn Martinbrough. They delivered realistic stories focused on the Gotham City Police Department and Batman's role as a detective. To visually distinguish the title from other Batman books, Martinbrough employed a minimal color palette, using shades of only one or two colors per issue. This gave the book a feeling of realism balanced with noir, and matched the tone of Rucka's writing, which introduced readers to many new G.C.P.D. faces, including, in this issue, Crispus Allen. Batman employed a new model Batmobile in this issue, as well as a streamlined set of gadgets.

While this first issue offered a Brian Stelfreeze cover, *Detective Comics* would soon host Dave Johnson artwork on its exterior, the artist who would develop the look of Batman's new costume in the wake of "No Man's Land." Essentially, Johnson took Batman back to his "Year One" style, keeping the pouch belt from "No Man's Land," but adding "underwear" and a black bat-symbol on his chest, sans yellow oval.

By *Detective Comics* #743 (April 2000), the covers of each Batman book received a new, stylish title logo crafted by designer Chip Kidd. The sophisticated look indicated the new direction of Batman's titles. This was emphasized by Rucka and Martinbrough's introduction of several long-lasting characters in that issue, villainess Whisper A'Daire and her assistant Kyle Abbot, and Gotham City Mayor Daniel Dickerson.

IN LOVING MEMORY
After her death at the hands of the cruel Joker, Commissioner Gordon honored his wife's memory with a plaque at the G.C.P.D., but it was cold comfort to the gaping hole her passing had left in his heart.

2000

"I have razorangs and bloodseekers. Smart guys run."

Owlman, *JLA: Earth 2*

As the "No Man's Land" crossover came to a close at the beginning of the year, it became clear that the Batman books needed redefinition. Each of Batman's four titles was overhauled and given its own distinct identity. *Batman: Legends of the Dark Knight* returned to its roots as a flashback title serving up longer stories; *Batman* focused on Super Heroics; *Detective Comics* dealt with the G.C.P.D. and the Dark Knight's role as a detective; and *Batman: Shadow of the Bat* was replaced by a new title, *Batman: Gotham Knights,* which focused on Batman's personal life and his human side. The result was a title for every type of Batman fan.

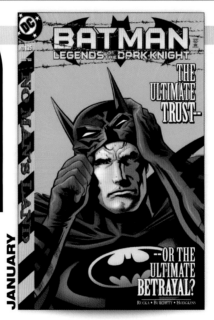

THE MAN BEHIND THE MASK
Batman: Legends of the Dark Knight #125
Batman's first true ally in Gotham City had been Jim Gordon, but after the Dark Knight's absence during the first three months of "No Man's Land," Gordon had lost faith in him. In this issue by writer Greg Rucka and artist Rick Burchett, Gordon aired his grievances. Their conversation culminated with an ultimate display of trust when Batman unmasked in front of his friend. Gordon refused to look at Batman's face, but he appreciated the gesture just the same, and he and Batman resumed their partnership.

LEX LUTHOR TO THE RESCUE?
Batman #573 ● Batman and his allies were gaining quite a bit of ground in the "No Man's Land" of Gotham City. But just as things were looking up, writer Greg Rucka and penciller Sergio Cariello brought the ultimate villain to town: Lex Luthor. The corrupt industrialist skirted the law, putting dozens of construction crews to work inside Gotham City. Meanwhile with the tide of popular opinion on Gotham City's side, Lucius Fox campaigned to reopen the city in the second chapter of this two-issue story in *Detective Comics* #740 (January 2000).

'TEC TALK
Commissioner Gordon investigated the death of a police officer who had "TEC 742" written on his palm. While the phrase was a license plate number in the story, it was also a nod to the issue itself, *Detective Comics* #742.

JOKER'S ENDGAME
Detective Comics #741 ▪ "No Man's Land" came to its dramatic climax in the three-part "Endgame" story by writers Greg Rucka and Devin Grayson and pencillers Damion Scott and Dale Eaglesham. As the military delivered supplies and things slowly began to return to normal in Gotham City, the Joker surfaced. Nearly killing the Huntress in a violent battle, the Joker then shot and killed Sarah Essen Gordon before giving himself up to police in a powerful finale that saw the newly reinstated Commissioner Gordon reduced to tears.

SPECIAL FEATURE

GORDON DOWN
Batman comforted a distraught Jim Gordon after his wife was shot and killed by the Joker, as the events of the past year finally took their toll on everyone. Despite the Joker's arrest, the trail of death and destruction he had left in his wake would take a long time to set right.

LIBERTY AND JUSTICE
JSA: The Liberty File #1 ▪ A new Elseworlds franchise originated with this two-issue, prestige-format series by writer Dan Jolley and co-writer and artist Tony Harris. The series reimagined the JSA as members the Bat (Batman), the Clock (Hourman), and the Owl (Dr. Mid-Nite) as they faced the threat of a white-skinned man with green hair named Jack the Grin during World War II. The story spawned a two-part sequel in February 2003 called *JSA: The Unholy 3*, and a six-part series starting in February 2013 entitled *JSA Liberty Files: The Whistling Skull*.

SPECIAL FEATURE

WAR STORY
This Elseworlds story *JSA: The Liberty File* was set during the years of World War II. Although it deposited Batman in a different time and place, familiar elements—including the Batmobile—still made an appearance, albeit in period style.

BATMAN GOTHAM KNIGHTS NO. 1 MAR '00

IN THIS ISSUE:
BATMAN
BLACK & WHITE
WARREN
ELLIS
JIM
LEE

GRAYSON
EAGLESHAM
FLOYD

JOHNSON

BLACK KNIGHTS, WHITE KNIGHTS

BATMAN: GOTHAM KNIGHTS #1

Batman: Gotham Knights cast new light on the Dark Knight's world and his personality, as well as upon those of his supporting cast.

In what served as the fourth core Batman title and a replacement for the recently canceled *Batman: Shadow of the Bat*, *Batman: Gotham Knights* #1 was written by Devin Grayson and illustrated by Dale Eaglesham. This particular issue established the new look for the rebuilt Wayne Manor.

Another innovation of this new title was the eight-page black and white back-up tales in each issue that showcased constantly shifting creative teams. This premier issue showcased the writing of Warren Ellis and the artistry of Jim Lee in the story "To Become the Bat," and many other stars would follow in the issues to come, continuing the tradition established in the highly acclaimed *Batman: Black and White* miniseries (June 1996).

In fact, in September of 2002, a hardcover volume of these back-up tales was published as *Batman: Black and White: Volume Two*, that included 40 new pages of material unique to that publication. A *Volume Three* was also produced in the series in May 2007 that collected the rest of these memorable short stories that continued through issue #49 of *Batman: Gotham Knights* (March 2004).

THINGS TO COME
One of Jim Lee's earliest Batman tales was this Warren Ellis-penned story full of the dramatic poses, panels, and panoramas that would become his trademark in 2002's "Hush" storyline.

BATMAN OF ACTION

Batman #575 ■ In the wake of "No Man's Land," most of Batman's titles were given new creative teams. On *Batman*, writer Larry Hama came aboard alongside *Nightwing* alumni, artist Scott McDaniel. The two helped establish the Super Hero side of Batman's personality, relying on dynamic action and more traditional bouts with super-villains, such as Batman's fight with this issue's new character, patriotic fanatic Banner. In the following issue, readers were treated to a glimpse of Batman's newly redesigned, multi-level Batcave.

SPECIAL FEATURE

BANNER
Gotham City had barely recovered from "No Man's Land" when the fanatic Banner reared his head. Batman had to defeat this misguided patriot before he went too far.

BATMAN GETS REAL

Realworlds: Batman ■ Similar in concept to Elseworlds, "Realworlds" took place in a different universe than the proper DCU: our own. In this prestige-format special, writers Christopher Golden and Tom Sniegoski and artist Marshall Rogers told of a man named Charlie who believed he was Batman, emboldened by the premier of the 1989 *Batman* film. Meanwhile, a different version of a Batman from our world premiered in *Realworlds: Justice League of America* by writer J.M. DeMatteis and artist G.L. Barr in this tale about childhood friends reuniting.

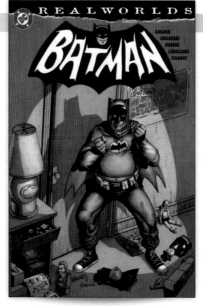

ROBIN'S PRIVATE LIFE

Robin #75 ■ Writer Chuck Dixon and artist Pete Woods moved Tim Drake to private school Brentwood Academy in issue #74 (March 2000) with Alfred along to cover for Tim during his excursions as Robin. By issue #75, Tim started to learn skateboarding stunts with the help of a girl named Star. He then employed a skateboard during his subsequent adventures. Everything was new for Tim Drake, including his villains. Upcoming debuts included the flying bounty hunter Jaeger in issue #76 (May 2000) and the magical Arrakhat in issue #78 (July 2000).

BATGIRL'S BREAKTHROUGH
BATGIRL #1

While there had been several women behind the mask of Batgirl over the years, Cassandra Cain would be the first to receive her own ongoing series.

Writers Scott Peterson and Kelley Puckett navigated this newly christened Batgirl out of the realm of "No Man's Land" and into her new heroic career path with the help of lively penciller Damion Scott. Working closely with Oracle Barbara Gordon, Batgirl attempted to adjust to her new life, but had a difficult time dealing with the fact that she'd never learned to speak. Her cruel father, David Cain, one of the world's premier assassins, had only taught her to communicate via body language. While this helped to make her a tremendous hand-to-hand fighter, able to predict her opponent's every move in a split second, it made establishing any degree of normality in her life that much more difficult. By issue #4, however, Batgirl saved the life of a man with psychic powers who used his abilities to instantly teach her English. While she still struggled to form words, Batgirl suddenly found that she could understand the world in a new, more fulfilling way.

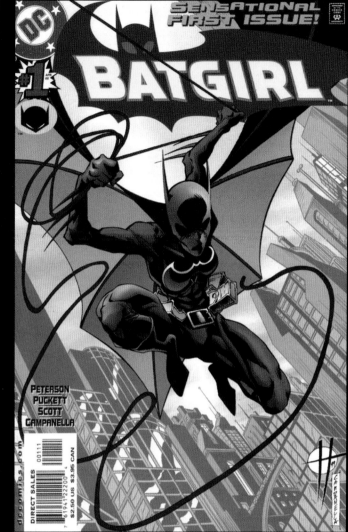

THE NEW BATGIRL
Cassandra Cain went from fighting on the streets to fighting crime in Gotham City as the newest incarnation of Batgirl. The original Batgirl, Barbara Gordon, trained Cain to use her skills wisely and to their best effect. It was not long before Cain would don the Batgirl costume—with her own special modifications.

APRIL

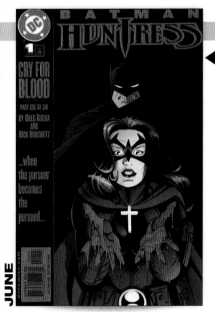

BLOOD ON HER HANDS
Batman/Huntress: Cry For Blood #1
In this six-issue series by writer Greg Rucka and artist Rick Burchett, Huntress's life and origin were revised, shedding new light onto her tragic past. Readers discovered that only Helena Bertinelli's brother and parents were murdered rather than her entire extended family. The Question then took her to Richard Dragon for training. Huntress returned to Gotham City with renewed purpose, only to seemingly give up her role as a vigilante after seeing that her parents' murderer was permanently dealt with.

JUNE

SPECIAL FEATURE
MARK OF THE BEAST
Helena Bertinelli witnessed the murders of her parents and older brother when she was eight years old, yet her life was spared. Trying to find out why, she hardened herself to life as an orphan and trained to become the vigilante Huntress.

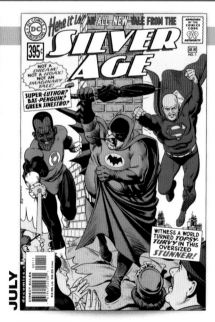

SEARCHING FOR LOIS
Action Comics #766 • After bringing the Joker and Harley Quinn to Metropolis in the previous issue, writer Joe Kelly delivered a powerful Batman team-up story. In this character study, drawn by Cary Nord, Superman enlisted the Dark Knight's help to find his wife, the kidnapped Lois Lane. As they hunted for Lois, the benefits and reasoning behind each Super Hero's methods became apparent. While they approached their careers quite differently, both Batman and Superman's strategies proved effective as they found Lois alive and well at the story's end.

JULY

WINNING SILVER
Silver Age #1 • Writer Mark Waid and penciller Terry Dodson delivered this special, which kicked off a string of one-shots revitalizing famous titles from DC Comics' Silver Age. Issue #1 saw Batman and Penguin mystically swapping bodies as well as the debut of interplanetary conqueror and super-villain Agamemno. In future one-shots, Batman fans would be treated to a *Silver Age: The Brave and the Bold* special, and a new 7 Soldiers of Victory team featuring Batgirl, Shining (Atomic) Knight, and Metamorpho in the *Silver Age: Showcase* special.

TOWER OF BABEL

JLA #43 ● After writer Grant Morrison had left *JLA*, Mark Waid took over the writing chores for the title with this memorable four-issue story that pitted Rā's al Ghūl against the Justice League. Always a tough adversary, in this Howard Porter pencilled arc the infamous Demon's Head was armed with information on how to defeat the Justice League that he'd appropriated from Batman's own files. By this series' final issue—guest pencilled by Steve Scott—the team defeated Rā's al Ghūl's forces, only to vote Batman out of its ranks for breaching their trust.

ORCHESTRATING ORCA

Batman #579 ● The team of writer Larry Hama and artist Scott McDaniel introduced a new Batman villain into the fold with Orca, a whale-themed villain thief seeking revenge against those that she viewed as Gotham City's corrupt elite. In this three-part story, Batman donned a new underwater costume (in issue #580 (August 2000), in order to seek out the villain who turned out to be Dr. Grace Balin, an employee of the Gotham Aquarium. She had been changed into the monstrous form of Orca by drinking a gene-altering chemical formula.

SIEGE: A FINAL TRIBUTE

Batman: Legends of the Dark Knight #132 Writer Archie Goodwin had had an impact on comic books owing to his innovative storytelling and editorial expertise. However, after being commissioned by editor Andy Helfer for the five-issue arc "Siege," Archie was unable to complete the assignment for health reasons. Writer James Robinson was hired to finish this interesting examination of the new mercenary Brass, and the Wayne legacy. Aided by the art of Marshall Rogers, this story was a fine tribute to Goodwin's brilliant body of work.

LIKE FATHER, LIKE DAUGHTER

Batman: Gotham Knights #6 ● When writing "Batman: Year One," Frank Miller had neglected to include Barbara Gordon, the famous Batgirl, as Commissioner James Gordon's daughter. This caused Barbara to be retroactively established as the commissioner's niece. However, in this issue by writer Devin Grayson and artist Paul Ryan, Barbara discovered that Jim Gordon had once had a romance with her mother, suggesting that it was more than likely that Barbara Gordon was in fact the commissioner's own flesh and blood.

OCTOBER

MISCHIEVOUS MXYZPTLK

In true frustrating fashion, Mr. Mxyzptlk did not make restoring things to their proper reality easy when the Joker wreaked havoc with his new powers. However, he did pop in from time to time and help Superman figure things out, which ultimately allowed the Man of Steel to save the day.

FROM JOKER TO KING
EMPEROR JOKER #1

The Joker popped up as the main villain of a crossover in the Superman titles when he tricked the Man of Steel's mischievous, 5th-dimensional enemy Mr. Mxyzptlk into giving him near-omnipotent powers.

In this special by writer Jeph Loeb and artist Ed McGuinness, which began in *Superman* #160, the Man of Steel found himself trapped in a bizarre parody of the reality he knew, populated by new additions to his Rogues Gallery. As the story continued into the pages of *The Adventures of Superman, Superman: The Man of Steel*, and *Action Comics*, writers J.M. DeMatteis, Mark Schultz, and Joe Kelly and artists Mike Miller, Doug Mahnke, and Kano revealed more and more of this insane world before finally letting the audience know that the mastermind behind all the insanity was none other than the Clown Prince of Crime himself. Following the original four chapters and the special *Emperor Joker* #1 "The Reign of Emperor Joker (Part I of V): It's a Joker World, Baby, We Just Live In It!," written by Kelly and Loeb and pencilled by Duncan Rouleau, Todd Nauck, Carlo Barberi and Scott McDaniel, the chaos once again returned to Superman's four monthly books. In the end, Superman overcame the Joker and made the villain lose his newfound powers by exploiting the Joker's main weakness: his obsession with the Batman.

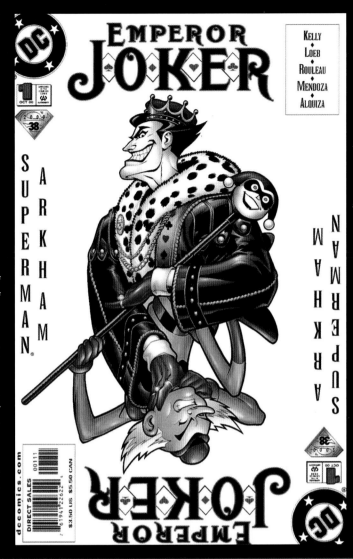

A DANGEROUS EGO

Batman: Ego ● In this powerful, prestige-format tale by writer/artist Darwyn Cooke, criminal Buster Snibbs had ratted out his boss, the infamous Joker, to the Batman. After hearing the Joker was planning to pay his family a visit when next he escaped custody, Buster killed his family before shooting himself, unable to bear the idea of the Joker getting his hands on those close to him. After witnessing Buster's death, Batman returned to the Batcave and, stricken by guilt, embarked on his own personal "psychotic slide into the heart of darkness."

THE HUNT FOR ORACLE

Birds of Prey #21 ● In this final chapter of a four-part crossover with Nightwing by writer Chuck Dixon and artist Butch Guice, teammates Oracle and Black Canary finally met face to face for the first time. In an attempt to locate and kill Oracle, Blockbuster hired a small army of familiar faces, including new villain and motorcycling expert Thrilldevil who debuted in *Nightwing* #46 (August 2000). In the climax, Black Canary saved Oracle's life and Barbara revealed her secret identity to her partner, showing how much she respected and trusted Canary.

THE BAT MANHUNTER

Martian Manhunter #22 ● In this interesting, self-contained flashback story written by John Ostrander and drawn by Tom Mandrake, the Super Hero known as the Martian Manhunter used his shape-shifting powers to become his own more literal version of a "Batman," in order to draw out the Caped Crusader and meet him for the first time. When circumstances led to the Manhunter's true Martian form being revealed to the Dark Knight, Batman agreed to keep the alien's secret, despite not trusting this strange visitor.

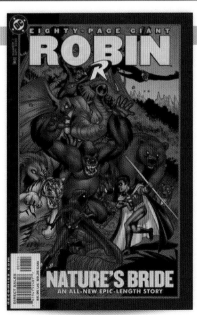

THE BRIDE FROM HELL

Robin Eighty-Page Giant #1 ● In his first ever *Eighty-Page Giant*, Tim Drake attended the wedding of his dad Jack to physiotherapist Dana Winters. In this story written by Chuck Dixon and drawn by Diego Barreto, Dana was possessed by the spirit of Ravenna, a foe from the Justice Society's early days. By teaming up with guest stars Black Canary, Spoiler, and Wildcat, Robin saved his father's wedding. In December, Nightwing had his own *Eighty-Page Giant*, meeting new villain Hella, courtesy of Dixon and artists Manuel Gutierrez and Mike Collins.

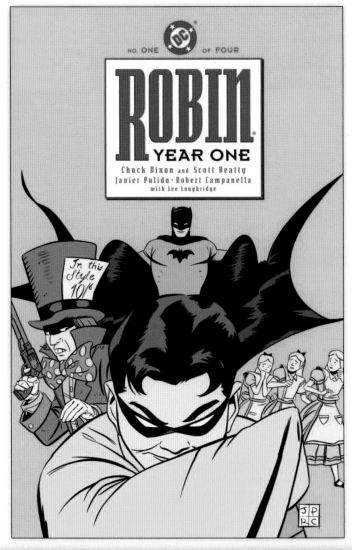

LEARNING TO FLY

ROBIN: YEAR ONE #1

This poignant story told of Dick Grayson's formative years as Robin in a four-issue prestige-format miniseries.

Other "Year One" titles had focused on a character's origin. However, instead of retelling Dick's origin story, this tale by writers Chuck Dixon, Scott Beatty and artists Javier Pulido and Marcos Martin, focused on his early days as Robin, showing him putting Batman's lessons to use in the field. Dick soon discovered that fighting crime at Batman's side was not the fun escapade that he imagined, but a life and death affair.

The story showcased a disturbing kidnapping case by the Mad Hatter and battles with the super-villains Two-Face, Killer Moth, Blockbuster, and Mr. Freeze, in which Dick acquitted himself with great courage. When Dick was beaten up by Two-Face, Batman decided that the mantle of Robin was too dangerous. Dick ran away and became involved with a junior league of assassins led by a martial artist named Shrike who had been hired by gangsters to assassinate Two-Face. Eventually, Dick rejoined Batman (who allowed him to become Robin again) and foiled Shrike's plot. Shrike's pupil, Boone, would go on to adopt that same moniker years later as an enemy of Nightwing's.

The book also examined the young sidekick's private life as he began attending public school at Bristol Middle School and attempted to develop his own life away from the cave, even dating a girl named Jenny Noblesse.

TIME FOR ROMANCE
Despite a secret life as Robin, homework, and lessons from Alfred, Dick Grayson found time for romance with new girl in town Jenny. After saving her from the Mad Hatter, Dick went rollerblading in the park with her.

BATMAN MEETS ZEISS

Batman #582 ● Ed Brubaker became a regular Batman scribe with this issue, partnering with artist Scott McDaniel. The story featured a new villain named Zeiss. Equipped with a pair of high-tech goggles wired to his brain and capable of storing Batman's tactics and movements for future exploitation, martial artist Zeiss was determined to prove himself the superior fighter. Batman would face the villain in the following issue, Zeiss would escape, leaving Batman to wonder who had hired this dangerous new threat.

COPS AND ROBBERS

Nightwing #48 ● Nightwing met a new ally and enemy in this two-part tale by writer Chuck Dixon and penciler Greg Land. The new ally was Dick Grayson's new field training officer, Sgt. Amy Rohrbach of the Blüdhaven Police Department, who would become more than just a superior officer—a good friend. The new enemy was Sylph, an expert at manipulating a micro-thin interwoven synthetic polymer that was as strong as it was flexible. The material proved a dangerous weapon when she wrapped Nightwing in it and dumped him on the highway.

BRUCE GETS A BABYSITTER

Detective Comics #751 ● Just a month after the 64-page anniversary issue of *Detective Comics* #850 hit the stands, writer Greg Rucka and artist Shawn Martinbrough debuted a major new character and love interest into the life of Batman: Sasha Bordeaux. WayneCorp's second in command, Lucius Fox told Bruce Wayne that he needed a bodyguard and he introduced martial artist Sasha. Backed into a corner by Fox and his own board of directors, Bruce's double life as Batman was made that much harder now that he had a live-in employee to avoid.

HAVOC BY HARLEY

Harley Quinn #1 ● Joker's girlfriend received her own series thanks to writer Karl Kesel and artist Terry Dodson. In this debut issue, guest-starring the Joker and Poison Ivy, Harley's insanity took center stage. Readers were treated to an opening sequence drawn in the style of *Batman: The Animated Series*, the TV show that introduced Harley into Batman's world. With plenty of faces from Batman's Rogues Gallery popping up through the series, Harley stepped out from the Joker's shadow and became her own woman, albeit an extremely unbalanced one.

THE FAR SIDE OF THE MIRROR

JLA: Earth 2 ● Writer Grant Morrison revisited the Pre-Crisis idea of an evil version of the DC Universe where the Super Heroes were villains and vice versa. This new dimension was introduced to the JLA when they were contacted by that Earth's Alexander Luthor. The issue showcased a world dominated by the JLA's corrupt equivalent, the Crime Syndicate of Amerika. One of its members was Batman's polar opposite, Owlman, a villain having an affair with that world's Wonder Woman, named Superwoman. *JLA: Earth 2* was a dark, modern twist on a classic idea, beautifully rendered by artist Frank Quitely.

WHAT CAN THE MATTER BE?
Luthor's discovery of a universe composed of matter rather than antimatter caused consternation among the members of the Crime Syndicate of Amerika (clockwise from top)—Ultraman, Owlman, Johnny Quick, Power Ring, and Superwoman.

2001

"Children, pull on your tights—and give them hell."

Batman, *The Dark Knight Strikes Again* #2

As longtime Batman editor Dennis O'Neil handed over the keys of Gotham City to Bob Schreck, the Batman titles continued to go in interesting directions. Writer Greg Rucka gave supporting player Sasha Bordeaux a bigger role in Batman's life as she uncovered his secret and began to fight by his side. The Joker was handed his own DC Universe crossover, as dozens of super-villains found themselves bearing the Clown Prince of Crime's signature grin and mania. And soon, writer/artist Frank Miller made his return to Batman, authoring one of the most highly anticipated sequels in comic book history.

JANUARY

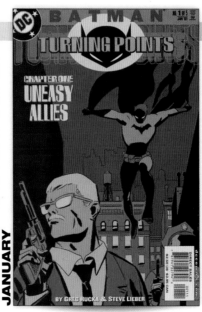

UNLIKELY PARTNERS
Batman: Turning Points #1 ■ Batman and Jim Gordon's friendship was examined in this five-issue weekly series by writers Greg Rucka, Ed Brubaker, and Chuck Dixon, and artists Steve Lieber, Joe Giella, Dick Giordano, Brent Anderson, and Paul Pope. With each issue set in a different era of Batman's career, from Robin's debut, to Jason Todd's death, to the present introduction of Gotham City's new Chief of Police, Michael Akins (in #5), readers gained a better understanding of the tumultuous relationship between Gotham City's top cop and Batman.

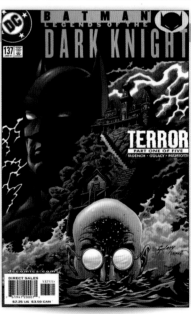

TERROR
Batman: Legends of the Dark Knight #137
Writer Doug Moench and artist Paul Gulacy concocted this five-part sequel to their famous "Prey" collaboration that began in *Batman: Legends of the Dark Knight* #11 (September 1990). Here, Batman faced not only the return of Hugo Strange and Catwoman, but also the threat of Scarecrow. When Strange returned to Gotham City, murdering people in Batman's costume and manipulating Scarecrow to do his bidding, Batman (with the help of his new Batboat) had to foil the mastermind.

OFFICER DOWN

BATMAN #587

Commissioner James Gordon had been shot by an unknown assailant. The Gotham City Police Department was determined to track down his would-be murderer.

The story "Officer Down" by writer Greg Rucka and artist Rick Burchett, beginning in this issue, was just seven parts, despite crossing through the pages of *Robin, Birds of Prey, Catwoman, Nightwing, Detective Comics,* and *Batman: Gotham Knights.* Also written by Ed Brubaker, Chuck Dixon, Bronwyn Carlton, Devin Grayson, and Nunzio DeFilippis and drawn by the Pander Brothers, N. Steven Harris, Mike Lilly, and Mike Collins, "Officer Down" centered around the hunt for Commissioner James Gordon's assailant. As Jim Gordon fought for life in the hospital, Oracle led the manhunt for his attacker. Eventually, the trail led to a corrupt cop named Jordan Reynolds, who later mysteriously disappeared, with all signs pointing to Harvey Bullock having something to do with his death. By the story's end, despite a speedy recovery, the commissioner decided to retire from the police force. Michael Akins took his place as Gotham City's new police commissioner.

CATWOMAN: MURDERER?

When Commissioner James Gordon saw Catwoman prowling the street, he attempted to arrest her, but he was suddenly gunned down before Selina's eyes. Selina herself was an initial suspect for the shooting.

BATMAN 587

GREG RUCKA • RICK BURCHETT • RODNEY RAMOS | Part I

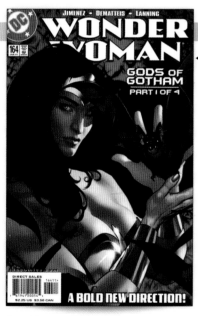

GODS OF GOTHAM CITY

Wonder Woman #164 ■ The inmates at Arkham received a divine upgrade in this four-issue tale by writer/artist Phil Jimenez and co-scripter J.M. DeMatteis. When Deimos, god of terror, merged his form with the Joker, his sister Eris, goddess of discord, took possession of Poison Ivy's form, and his brother Phobos, god of fear, took up residence in Scarecrow's body. This godly trio, the children of Wonder Woman's longtime foe, the god of war Ares, terrorized Gotham City, forcing Batman and Wonder Woman to pool their resources to stop them.

SPECIAL FEATURE

Batman, God of Fear

During the battle with Deimos, Phobos took control of Batman, altering his form drastically. But with Wonder Woman's coaching, Batman's superior willpower managed to chase the god out, enabling the god Ares to ban Phobos and his siblings from the mortal plane.

WORKING GIRL

Action Comics #773 ■ In Metropolis, Lex Luthor had decided to run for President of the United States of America, and despite Superman's opposition, had won the election. Busy with a whole new set of responsibilities, Luthor needed to take a break from his duties as the CEO of LexCorp. In exchange for three hundred years of her father's research, passcodes for his accounts, and information on his contacts, Talia al Ghūl became CEO of Luthor's company, and would soon adopt the name of Talia Head for her public persona.

THIS ISSUE: BATMAN DIES!

Nightwing #52 ■ A clear theme ran through the Batman titles this month, with each issue advertising Batman's death on its cover. While some of these "deaths" were just a single panel, this issue's death of the Dark Knight took place at Catwoman's hands during a dream she had in the book's intro. But even more notable, was the ensuing team-up between Selina Kyle and Nightwing that took place in this story by writer Chuck Dixon and artist Greg Land. The partnership culminated in a kiss between the two characters.

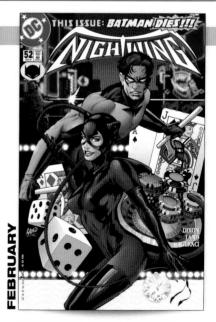

NEVER PLAY WITH MATCHES
BATMAN #588

For some time, Bruce Wayne had occasionally adopted the criminal persona of "Matches" Malone to infiltrate Gotham City's criminal community. But who was the original "Matches?"

Readers—and Batman's own allies for that matter—believed that "Matches" Malone was merely a creation of Bruce Wayne's imagination. In this three-part story by writer Brian K. Vaughan and artist Scott McDaniel, Batman revealed the truth.

The real "Matches" Malone was actually a small-time criminal, specializing in fraud and arson, who came from Hoboken, New Jersey. He had acquired the nickname "Matches" because he always carried a stick match ready to fire up. Batman had adopted his identity believing that the criminal had died years ago, shot by a ricocheting bullet. Impersonating Matches by adopting the criminal's trademark mustache, plaid suit, tinted glasses, and New Jersey accent, enabled Bruce to gain valuable information about Gotham City's's gangs. In this story, Bruce, disguised as Matches, successfully infiltrated the Ventriloquist and Scarface's mob in order to foil a heist of illegal, armor-piercing ammunition. When Batman showed up and collared most of the gang, the Ventriloqust assumed that Matches had tipped off the Dark Knight.

The dramatic last page revealed that the unfortunate Matches Malone was in fact alive and had returned to Gotham City. Scarface and the Ventriloquist gunned him down, believing that he had double-crossed them.

EMPTY THREAT
In order to convincingly infiltrate Gotham City's underworld, Batman masqueraded as the criminal "Matches" Malone, who found himself "threatened" by Batman (really Nightwing in disguise).

AZRAEL'S MAKEOVER
Azrael #75 ● Jean-Paul Valley once again felt the need for a wardrobe change, this time with the help of writer Dennis O'Neil and artist Sergio Cariello. In this extra-sized climax of the three-part "Losses" tale, Jean Paul designed a new costume for himself and confronted a different Azrael, who had taken enigmatic femme fatale Sister Lilhy hostage. After defeating his enemy, Jean-Paul decided to take up residence in a temple built by the Order of St. Dumas. He would soon renew his life as Azrael with the help of new assistant Harold Allnut.

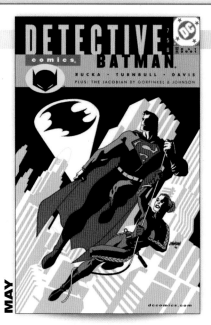

SECRETS AND SUPERMEN
Detective Comics #756 ● In Superman #168 (May 2001) by writer Jeph Loeb and artist Ed McGuinness, Bruce Wayne revealed that he was secretly bankrolling Clark Kent's newspaper, the *Daily Planet*. Lois visited Gotham City to team up with Batman in an attempt to steal the famous Kryptonite ring from the new U.S. president, Lex Luthor. In this issue by writer Greg Rucka and artist Koi Turnbull, not only did the two pull off the heist with the help of Superman, but Wayne's bodyguard, Sasha Bordeaux, discovered her employer's double identity.

SNOW BIRD
Robin #89 ● Tim Drake tried out a new look in this issue by writers Chuck Dixon and Scott Beatty and penciller Pete Woods. Needing a break from Gotham City after Batman revealed Tim's secret identity to his former girlfriend, Spoiler Stephanie Brown, in issue #87 (April 2001), Tim took a road trip with a friend that soon progressed into a battle against the fanatical Kobra cult. When heading to the country of Bhutran in the Himalayas to further confront Kobra in this issue, Robin donned a special costume to combat the cold—a hooded snowsuit.

BATMAN GETS BIZARRE
Bizarro Comics #1 ● A legion of underground comics talent united to create spins on classic DC characters in this hardcover special. Featuring a cover by Simpsons creator Matt Groening, this volume included a Batman tale by writer Chip Kidd and artist Tony Millionaire, a Batman and Robin versus the Eraser yarn by writer Eddie Campbell and artist Hunt Emerson, and a Batcave story by writer Paul Pope and artist Jay Stephens, among many other shorts. Bizarro Comics would spawn a sequel in February 2005 with *Bizarro World*.

INNOCENCE LOST

***Batman* #591** ■ Bruce Wayne's life got just a bit more complicated thanks to writer Ed Brubaker and artist Scott McDaniel when several faces from Wayne's past resurfaced. Gangster Lew Moxon and his daughter Mallory had made quite an impression on Bruce when he and Mallory had shared a mutual bout of puppy love many years ago. When, as an adult, Mallory returned to Gotham, Bruce realized that his feelings for this beautiful woman conflicted with Lew Moxon's business, especially as Moxon had the super-villain Zeiss on his payroll.

THE FAMILY YOU CHOOSE

***Batman: Gotham Knights* #17** ■ In this issue, writer Devin Grayson and artist Roger Robinson concluded Batman's two-part battle with new villain Matatoa who, after killing a Maori shamen was cursed as a vampiric "Devourer of Souls." The villain had to keep killing to survive, but believed that the cycle could be broken if he could consume the soul of an undefeated warrior—such as Batman. Matatoa claimed that he would then take over as Gotham City's immortal defender. For a moment, Batman was almost persuaded—until Nightwing intervened.

SPECIAL FEATURE

Dick Grayson Adopted

At the conclusion of the main story, came a low-key, but nonetheless major change in the Batman/Nightwing relationship: Batman officially adopted Dick Grayson, a symbolic gesture that showed Grayson how much Bruce really cared for him. The penultimate page revealed the adoption certificate, witnessed by Alfred Pennyworth and Dr. Leslie Thompkins.

THE DEMON LAUGHS

***Batman: Legends of the Dark Knight* #145**
In the conclusion to this four-issue arc, writer Chuck Dixon and artist Jim Aparo showed the Joker in a new light. After the Clown Prince of Crime was shot eight times by Talia al Ghūl, Batman was forced to dip the Joker in the mystical Lazarus Pit in order to save his life and discover Rā's al Ghūl's location. While the Pit's revivifying effects created temporary insanity in a normal person, in the Joker's case they provided a brief moment of clarity, in which he regretted all the heinous crimes he had committed.

257

THE DARK KNIGHT RETURNS

THE DARK KNIGHT STRIKES AGAIN #1

Frank Miller returned to the future of the Caped Crusader that he had originally mapped in the *Batman: The Dark Knight Returns* limited series.

With this three-issue prestige format story, writer/artist Miller once again set the scene for a large-scale Batman adventure. This time he utilized more of the DC Universe's most famous characters and set the story in a Gotham City of the future.

Former Robin Carrie Kelley had adopted the roller-skating persona of Catgirl and was leading Batman's army of "Batboys" against an oppressive government run by Lex Luthor. Meanwhile, the Dark Knight started a campaign to free his old allies the Atom, Plastic Man, and the Flash from captivity.

The story, which also starred Wonder Woman and Superman, once again took Batman into extreme territory. A killer had been terrorizing Gotham City clad in various costumes including those of Legion of Super-Heroes member Cosmic Boy and Superman foe, Mr. Mxyzptlk. In this limited series' third and final issue, the villain met up with an aged Dark Knight for a showdown in the Batcave. In a surprising twist, the murderer was revealed to be former Robin, Dick Grayson. Grayson had gone insane and, despite having gained superpowers, was dispatched fairly easily by his former mentor who even decapitated the Grayson at one point during the story's bizarre climax.

HERE COME THE BATBOYS!
Batman: The Dark Knight Returns had ended with Batman taking charge of an army of former gang members. In *The Dark Knight Strikes Again*, this army called itself the Batboys.

TARGET PRACTICE

Nightwing: The Target • Dick Grayson nabbed a rare, prestige-format one-shot in which he adopted a new costume as the crime-fighting Target thanks to writer Chuck Dixon and artist Scott McDaniel. When Dick was framed for beating and killing a young teen by a few corrupt members of the Blüdhaven Police Department, Batman insisted that Grayson should clear his name without using his Nightwing identity and attracting attention to the Dark Knight's world. So Grayson became the Target, a new temporary identity that he promptly retired after proving his innocence.

THE ORPHEUS ORIGIN

Batman: Orpheus Rising **#1** • While Gotham City already had its fair share of Super Heroes, the metropolis welcomed a newcomer in this five-issue miniseries when writer Alex Simmons and artist Dwayne Turner introduced Orpheus. However, the welcome wasn't exactly a warm one. Batman considered the fledgling crime fighter an amateur and wanted him out of Gotham City, and the police wanted Orpheus for questioning. Despite this, Orpheus managed to set up shop, both as a vigilante and in his civilian identity of Gavin King.

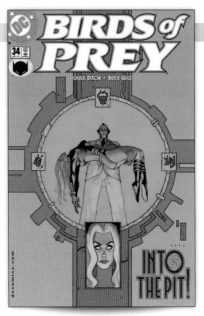

REMEMBERING HOW TO CRY

Birds of Prey **#34** • Black Canary wasn't the best at choosing relationships with the opposite sex, but when she unwittingly started dating Rā's al Ghūl in issue #31 (July 2001) in the first part of this story by writer Chuck Dixon and guest penciller Mike McDonnell, she reached her dating low. After discovering her mistake, Black Canary tried to escape, and was injured in the resulting battle. In this issue by Dixon and artist Butch Guice, Black Canary was healed in a Lazarus Pit. She recovered and also regained her famous Canary Cry power.

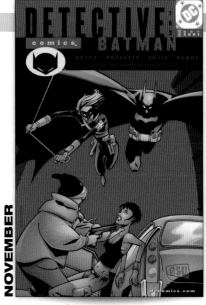

BATMAN'S NEW SIDEKICK?

Detective Comics **#762** • Knowing the double identity of her boss, Bruce Wayne, bodyguard Sasha Bordeaux needed a way to do her job and protect him in both of his personas. To that end, writer Greg Rucka and artist Rick Burchett had Batman give Sasha her own costume to protect her identity as she ventured out with the Caped Crusader on his patrols. This issue also saw Harvey Bullock quit the G.C.P.D., owning up to his actions in "Officer Down," and the final Slam Bradley back-up story written by Ed Brubaker and drawn by Darwyn Cooke.

DECEMBER

HE WHO LAUGHS LAST
JOKER: LAST LAUGH #1

The Clown Prince of Crime took center stage in the DC Universe when he became the subject of this company-wide crossover event.

Revolving around this six-issue miniseries written by Chuck Dixon and Scott Beatty and illustrated by Pete Woods, Marcos Martin, Walter McDaniel, Andy Kuhn, Ron Randall, and Rich Burchett, this event tied into a variety of Super Hero titles, and also included the *Joker: Last Laugh Secret Files* and *Origins* special. After inciting a riot at his current prison, the Slabside Penitentiary, the Joker gassed his fellow prisoners, in essence creating an entire super-villain army of pale-faced Jokers. The Jokers escaped, forcing nearly the entire DCU into action against them. The story reached its disturbing climax when Nightwing, under the impression that Robin had been killed during the chaos, took the Joker on and savagely beat the criminal mastermind. While he was soon resuscitated, Joker had been technically "killed" by Grayson for a few brief moments, causing Nightwing to live with the shame of letting the Joker get the better of him.

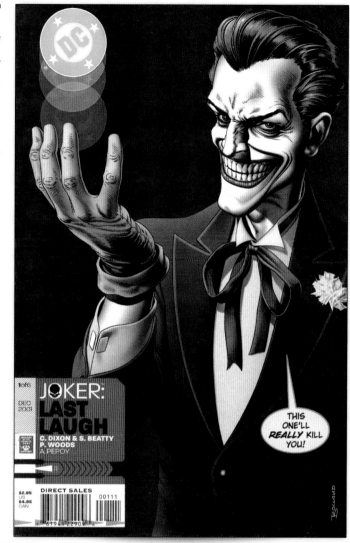

JOKING AROUND
Powerful criminals, many of whom already possessed enhanced metahuman abilities, became as unpredictable and unstable as the Joker in this epic crossover.

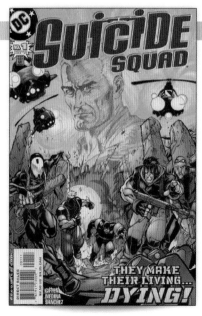

DEATH SQUAD
***Suicide Squad* #1** ▪ This series marked the return of the government-sponsored super-villain team Suicide Squad. Graced by the dialogue of scripter Keith Giffen and artwork by Paco Medina, this first issue featured the supposed death of Cluemaster. While the series only lasted 12 issues, despite the quality storytelling, the Squad would be resurrected again in November 2007 for an eight-issue miniseries by writer John Ostrander and penciller Javier Pina. This showcased the death of former Outsider Windfall in issue #7 (May 2008).

HERE COMES SANTA KLAUS
***Batman* #596** ▪ Writer Ed Brubaker and penciller Scott McDaniel gave the holidays a sinister twist in this issue, titled "City on Fire," when they introduced the new Batman villain Santa Klaus as part of a *Joker: Last Laugh* tie-in. First appearing briefly in this month's *Joker: Last Laugh* #5, the murderous Santa Klaus interrupted Batman's battle with the villain Zeiss when Klaus opened fire on a Gotham City street. While Santa Klaus didn't prove much of a threat, he unwittingly helped to buy Zeiss the time to escape the Dark Knight's grasp.

AN OFFICER OF INTUITION
***Detective Comics* #763** ▪ The main story by writer Greg Rucka and artist Shawn Martinbrough in this issue featured a Sasha Bordeaux/Huntress team-up that tied in to the "Joker: Last Laugh" crossover event. However, the real star of this book was new character Josie Mac, debuting in a back-up feature by writer Judd Winick and artist Cliff Chiang. An officer for the Gotham City Police Department, Josephine MacDonald had the uncanny ability to locate missing items, as if the inanimate objects could speak to her.

ALSO THIS YEAR

March—*Batman: Gotham Noir:* This Elseworlds one-shot set in 1949 cast Jim Gordon as an alcoholic private eye caught up in city corruption and framed for murder.

April—*Green Arrow* #1: The original Green Arrow was resurrected in this ten-issue story that guest-starred Batman.

April—*The Batman in Nine Lives:* This interesting Elseworlds take on Batman was a hardcover special that opened sideways to create a widescreen effect.

★ November 17th: Cartoon Network debuted the next chapter in producer Bruce Timm and company's animated DC Universe with the new cartoon *Justice League*.

December—*Nightwing* #62: Nightwing villains Leather and Meathead debuted in this *Joker: Last Laugh* tie-in issue.

December—*Gotham Knights* #22: The cockroach-comprised entity of Kafka premiered in this *Joker: Last Laugh* tie-in.

A NEW LOOK FOR CATWOMAN

CATWOMAN #1

Selina Kyle was at a crossroads, and it would take writer Ed Brubaker and artist Darwyn Cooke to turn her life around. The result was a radically different Catwoman.

Catwoman's first ongoing series was nearing its 100th issue and DC Comics decided to give the character a fresh start with this debut issue. In order to build reader interest in Selina's new direction, Brubaker and Cooke had first partnered on a series of back-up tales in *Detective Comics*, starting with issue #759 (August 2001). These stories reintroduced readers to tough private detective Slam Bradley, one of the title's original stars. Bradley would go on to become an integral supporting character in *Catwoman*. By first featuring him in *Detective Comics*, DC Comics gave fans a glimpse of the sophisticated storytelling that would grace Brubaker's critically acclaimed run on the title.

Catwoman #1 began with Selina Kyle, inspired by Batman's example, reevaluating her life and returning to Gotham City's troubled East End. Pondering her past, she wondered at what point she stopped defending the powerless in her neighborhood and began only to care about herself and her life as a thief. Outfitted with a new costume, Catwoman resolved to return to her roots and protect the innocent of her neighborhood. She soon got the chance to do just that when, reunited with her old friend Holly Robinson, she battled a terrifying, shape-changing murderer who was preying on the East End's community of prostitutes.

2002

"Like the view? It's about the only thing you're going to catch tonight."

Catwoman, Batman #608

Crossover events such as 1999's "No Man's Land" had proved an excellent method of attracting readers to Batman's group of titles, and DC Comics believed the time was ripe to unleash another. The year would see the huge "Batman: Murderer?" crossover, followed quickly by the "Batman: Fugitive" resolution to the story. The superstar team of writer Jeph Loeb and artist Jim Lee then commenced the epic "Hush" storyline in the pages of *Batman*. An enduring hit, "Hush" renewed an old idea at DC: Pair some of the biggest names in comic books together and the readers will quickly follow.

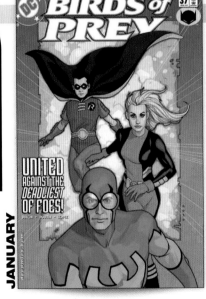

A VILLAIN TO RELISH
Birds of Prey #37 ■ Characters from *Batman: The Animated Series* and *The New Batman Adventures* often surfaced in the mainstream DC comic book universe. Harley Quinn and Lock-Up were just two examples. However, few would have predicted writer Chuck Dixon and penciller Marcos Martin bringing the animated villain Condiment King into the pages of *Birds of Prey*. With a gun firing spicy mustard, the Condiment King proved only a minor distraction for Black Canary and guest-stars Blue Beetle and Robin.

ANIMATED JUSTICE
Justice League Adventures #1 ■ After the success of *Batman: The Animated Series* and *Superman: The Animated Series*, producer Bruce Timm and company decided that the next step would be a cartoon *Justice League*. Tying into that show was *Justice League Adventures*, a title that featured stories set within the continuity of the new cartoon. The first issue was written by Ty Templeton and pencilled by Min S. Ku. The title lasted for 34 issues before being relaunched in November 2004 as *Justice League Unlimited*.

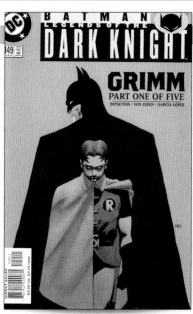

GRIMM LEGENDS

***Batman: Legends of the Dark Knight* #149**
Batman met the threat of new villain Mother Grimm
in this five-issue flashback tale written by J. M.
DeMatteis and pencilled by Trevor Von Eeden. Issue
#100 had introduced Robin to the series, setting the
stage for this storyline, narrated by the Boy Wonder.
Here, the Dynamic Duo fought and defeated Mother
Grimm, a twisted thief who fooled children into
believing she was a caring old woman. Also debuting
was Grimm's disturbed twin sister, Cyanide, a
manipulator of deadly toxins.

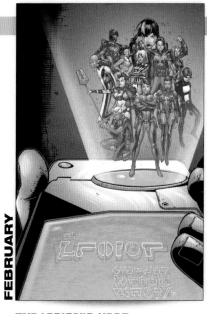

FEBRUARY

THE LEGION'S HEAD

***Legion* #3** ▪ After their acclaimed run on the
12-issue maxiseries *Legion Lost*, writers Dan
Abnett and Andy Lanning and penciller Olivier
Coipel relaunched the adventures of the 31st-century
heroes known as the Legion of Super-Heroes in this
new ongoing series. Fans of the future heroes were
in for a surprise in issue #3 when it was revealed
that the president of the United Planets, Leland
McCauley, had a sinister secret. He was not the
noble man he pretended to be, but Batman's
old enemy, Rā's al Ghūl.

MARCH

THE SOUND OF DEATH

***Green Arrow* #12** ▪ Batman's presence had
been felt from the start in writer Kevin Smith's
relaunched *Green Arrow* series in April of 2001.
In this issue, written by Smith with art by Phil Hester,
the Riddler appeared as well as Onomatopoeia, a
new sound-effects spouting villain. The villain proved
popular, later joining Batman's Rogues Gallery in the
Batman: Cacophony miniseries. As Green Arrow
continued his new adventures, the trend of
Batman-related guest stars continued, including
the return of Catman in issue #16.

ONOMATOPOEIA

A darkly disturbing serial killer,
Onomatopoeia lived a normal life in
suburbia by day, and stalked and killed
Super Heroes by night. First setting
his sights on Green Arrow's son, the
villain later decided he wanted
Batman's cowl among his trophies.

GREG RUCKA • RICK BURCHETT • KLAUS JANSON

BRUCE WAYNE: MURDERER?

BATMAN: THE 10 CENT ADVENTURE #1

This prologue chapter issue brilliantly set the scene for the upcoming epic crossover "Bruce Wayne: Murderer?"—and it went on sale for only ten cents!

The majority of this issue by writer Greg Rucka and artist Rick Burchett retold Batman's origin and brought new readers up to speed with Bruce Wayne's fledgling partnership with his bodyguard Sasha Bordeaux. The main event didn't occur until its final two pages, when Bruce discovered the dead body of his former girlfriend, Vesper Fairchild, on the floor of Wayne Manor. To make matters worse, the police were also on scene, with every intention of arresting Bruce Wayne for murder. The "Bruce Wayne: Murderer?" crossover officially began in Detective # 766, released the same week as the *10 Cent Adventure*. Also written by Greg Rucka, but with pencils by Scott McDaniel, the issue kicked off with Sasha Bordeaux and Bruce Wayne both being interrogated by police. Unfortunately, since the duo had been out on crime-fighting patrol at the time of the murder, neither had a usable alibi.

As the story continued, crossing over into the pages of *Batgirl*, *Nightwing*, *Batman: Gotham Knights*, *Birds of Prey*, *Robin*, and *Batman*, Batman's allies rushed to offer whatever help they could. While Batgirl discovered Batman's secret identity and some of his closest allies began to doubt his innocence, Bruce Wayne was sent to prison to await trial. Instead of trusting those close to him, in the twelfth and final issue of the crossover, Bruce Wayne did the unthinkable and escaped from prison.

VESPER FAIRCHILD
Vesper Fairchild became an unwitting pawn in a much larger game when she was murdered. Her desperate 9-1-1 call seemed to implicate Bruce Wayne, her former boyfriend.

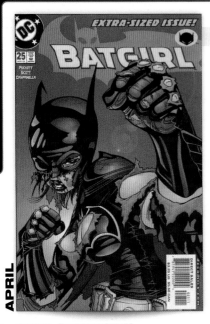

SHIVA SHOWDOWN
Batgirl #25 ▪ Cassandra Cain had been through many trials as Batgirl, but none would compare to her showdown with arguably the world's most dangerous martial artist, Lady Shiva. In this extra-sized issue by writer Kelley Puckett and artist Damion Scott, Shiva easily bested and killed Cassandra. However, discovering that Cassandra had wanted to die to atone for killing a man when she was only eight years old, Lady Shiva brought Batgirl back to life with a blow to the chest. When the two battled once again, Cassandra Cain emerged the victor.

DIXON'S DEPARTURE
Robin #100 ▪ Writer Chuck Dixon had long been chronicling the adventures of Tim Drake, and was more than a little responsible for Tim's success as a popular successor to the Robin legacy. When Dixon left the title with its one hundredth issue, many fans were sad to see him go. Dixon's final issue featured the art of penciller Pete Woods and also introduced a new writer, Jon Lewis, to Robin's world. The story concerned Tim Drake leaving Brentwood Academy to move back in with his father due to Jack Drake's money issues.

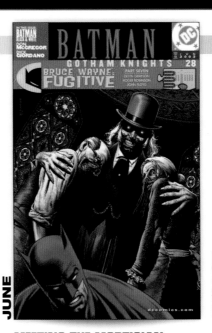

MEETING THE MORTICIAN
Batman: Gotham Knights #28 ▪ As the events of "Bruce Wayne: Fugitive" continued through the Batman titles, a new villain emerged in *Gotham Knights*, thanks to writer Devin Grayson and artist Roger Robinson. When bodies began disappearing from the G.C.P.D.'s morgue, Batman encountered an army of the undead led by a mysterious undertaker named the Mortician. Able to make the dead his mindless minions, the Mortician was obsessed with his parents' death. That was one obsession Batman could easily identify with.

A CATWOMAN CAPER
Catwoman: Selina's Big Score ▪ Darwyn Cooke was both writer and artist of this hardcover graphic novel. *Selina's Big Score* introduced a colorful bunch of characters including intel deliverer Swifty, hard-talking driver Chantel, and master thief Stark. A fast-paced heist set immediately before Selina's second ongoing series, this tale explained how Selina had enough money to embark on a new life as a crime fighter. Beautifully colored by artist Matt Hollingsworth, this special also featured a spectacular gallery section by top DC Comics artists.

APRIL

BRUCE WAYNE: FUGITIVE
BATMAN #600

Batman celebrated his title's 600th anniversary in shocking fashion—by ending the existence of Bruce Wayne.

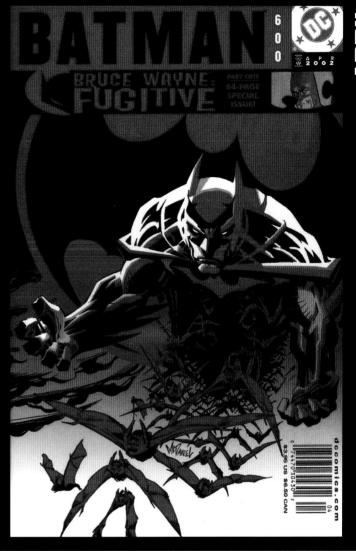

Now a fugitive from justice following the events of "Bruce Wayne: Murderer?," Batman returned to the Batcave to start a new life, rejecting his Bruce Wayne identity. However, his allies didn't quite see eye to eye with him on that front. In this 64-page special by writer Ed Brubaker and artist Scott McDaniel, which served as the first chapter in the "Bruce Wayne: Fugitive" crossover, Batman and Nightwing fought a vicious battle in the Batcave when Dick refused to allow his mentor to make such an extreme life choice.

Like "Bruce Wayne: Murderer?", "Fugitive" ran through nearly all the Batman-related titles, lasting for 18 issues. As the epic story continued, *Batman* #601 debuted new villain Nicodemus, and Nightwing and Oracle searched for clues to Bruce's innocence in the pages of *Nightwing* and *Birds of Prey*.

After Batman came to his senses and realized that he needed Bruce Wayne in his life, the murderer of Vesper Fairchild was revealed as assassin David Cain, Batgirl's father. Cain had been hired to frame Bruce Wayne by Lex Luthor, who hated Wayne for ruining his bid to take over Gotham City in the final chapters of "No Man's Land." By *Batman* #605 (September 2002) Batman had bested Cain, and Bruce Wayne was soon cleared of all charges.

DISSENTION IN THE RANKS
Bruce Wayne's decision to abandon his Batman identity did not sit well with his friends, especially Dick Grayson. When Nightwing confronted Batman about the situation, it quickly turned ugly and a vicious fight broke out. The two eventually mended fences and resumed their deep bond.

SEPTEMBER

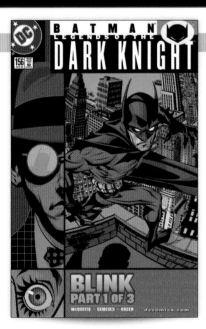

BLINK
***Batman: Legends of the Dark Knight* #156**
Batman met one of his strangest allies in the form of a blind con man named Lee Hyland in this three-part story set in Batman's past and written by Dwayne McDuffie and pencilled by Val Semeiks. The Dark Knight was on the trail of a murderer, and Hyland become involved in the investigation. Despite being blind, Hyland was able to see through the eyes of those he came into physical contact with. After touching the serial killer Batman was tracking, he helped to bring the villain to justice.

NOVEMBER

TARANTULA, TOO
***Nightwing* #71** ▪ Writer Devin Grayson came aboard *Nightwing* as the regular scripter with this issue drawn by penciller Rick Leonardi. Grayson was quick to introduce the hero to a new future love in the form of Catalina Flores. While she remained out of costume in her first appearance, Catalina would soon don the costume of Tarantula, taking her inspiration from the Golden Age hero and original Tarantula, Jonathan Law. Throughout her career, this new female Tarantula would walk a fine line between heroism and villainy.

BROTHER OF THE BAT?
***Batman: Gotham Knights* #33** ▪ Bane returned to Wayne Manor with the help of *Gotham Knight*'s new regular writer, Scott Beatty, and penciller Mike Collins. This time around, Bane came in peace. Clutching a photo of his mother side by side with Thomas Wayne, Bane believed that he and Bruce Wayne might be brothers. While it was later revealed, in issue #47 (January 2004), that Bane's true father was the villain King Snake, Beatty had nevertheless started his run with a bang, and would continue to introduce plenty of surprises to Batman's world.

DECEMBER

ALL IN THE FAMILY
***Batman: Family* #1** ▪ After teasing the characters Tracker in *Detective Comics* #773 (October 2002), and Bugg in *Detective Comics* #774, writer John Francis Moore and artists Rick Hoberg and Stefano Gaudiano launched this eight-issue miniseries. Tracker and Bugg were part of the Network, a gang that included Athena, Mr. Fun, Doctor Excess, Freeway, Technician, and Suicide King. The series also introduced Tim Drake's future girlfriend, Tam Fox, a daughter of longtime Batman supporting character Lucius Fox.

HUSH

BATMAN # 608

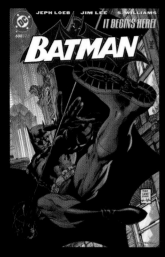

A blockbuster story crammed with unforgettable life-altering events for the Dark Knight and the characters in his world.

Ever since his landmark work on both *Batman: The Long Halloween* and *Batman: Dark Victory*, Jeph Loeb had been a favorite with Dark Knight fans. Expectations were running high when the writer teamed up with superstar penciller Jim Lee for an epic, 12-issue Batman storyline entitled "Hush." The story featured stunning new realizations of many of Batman's best known characters. It also introduced readers to a host of newly designed gadgets for Batman, including a new Batmobile in issue #615, a new Batplane, Batboat and parachute Batsuit in issue #616, and a new Batcycle in issue # 617.

The first issue of "Hush" began with Batman battling a newly upgraded Killer Croc, and ended with Batman falling off a rooftop during a flirtatious chase with Catwoman. More surprises were in store in the following issue as Huntress debuted a new costume and a matching armored motorcycle, and the newest menace in Batman's life premiered in the form of the mysterious, bandage-wrapped Hush.

In keeping with Loeb's typical storytelling style, Batman soon began to run a gauntlet of his most famous foes, owing to Hush's scheming. After battling Poison Ivy, the Joker, Harley Quinn, Rā's al Ghūl, Scarecrow, Clayface, and a mind-controlled Superman, Batman finally faced Hush himself, deducing that the villain was his embittered childhood friend, Thomas Elliot.

With the help of a newly healed Harvey Dent, now without his Two-Face facial scars, Hush was defeated, but at the price of the life of Batman's ally, Harold Allnut. In the concluding chapter, *Batman* #619 (November 2003), Batman discovered that the true mastermind behind Hush's crimes was none other than the Riddler. The longtime villain had finally solved Gotham City's greatest riddle: "Who is that under Batman's mask?"

CROC 2.0

Killer Croc was never one of Batman's most handsome foes, but thanks to the Riddler's machinations, the villain was mutated even further by a virus, gaining an even more brutish appearance and personality.

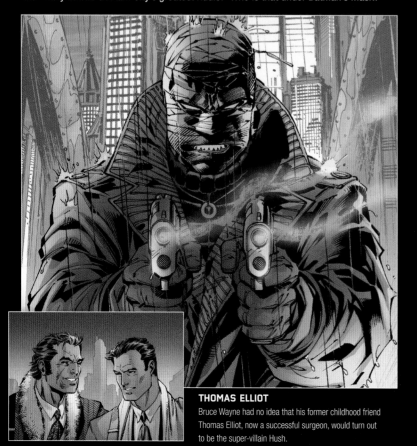

THOMAS ELLIOT
Bruce Wayne had no idea that his former childhood friend Thomas Elliot, now a successful surgeon, would turn out to be the super-villain Hush.

ALSO THIS YEAR

April—*The Batman in Nine Lives*: This Elseworlds graphic novel was set in a 1940s Gotham City ridden with organized crime.

October—*JLA* #69: Nightwing joined the JLA in a time-spanning epic that would see Batman die for a brief time.

October—*Gotham Girls* #1: This tie-in miniseries starred the five Gotham Girls of the third season of the animated series: Catwoman, Harley Quinn, Poison Ivy, Batgirl, and Renee Montoya.

★ **October 9th**—The *Birds of Prey* live-action TV show debuted on The WB TV network starring Huntress and Oracle.

November—*Birds of Prey* #47: Oracle regained feeling in her legs and Black Canary gained a new costume.

ED BRUBAKER • GREG RUCKA • MICHAEL LARK

dccomics.com

ON PATROL

GOTHAM CENTRAL #1

This new ongoing series was a finely detailed, hard-hitting police drama, telling realistic, behind-the-scenes stories of the lives of the members of the Gotham City Police Department.

In what would become a highly acclaimed fan-favorite series, writers Ed Brubaker and Greg Rucka teamed with artist Michael Lark to deliver *Gotham Central*, a rare look at the difficulties of doing police work in a city populated by super-villains, madmen, underworld gangs, and a crime-fighting Batman.

In this debut issue, readers were introduced to Detective Marcus Driver as he lost his partner Charlie in an attack by Mr. Freeze. As the story progressed, Detective Romy Chandler was introduced, as well as a host of other new cops. In addition, Metropolis' Maggie Sawyer was promoted to Captain.

By issue #3, a new Firebug was terrorizing the city. The fast-growing readership quickly realized that in this creative team's capable hands, even minor villains would pose a real and present danger to the brave men and women of the G.C.P.D.

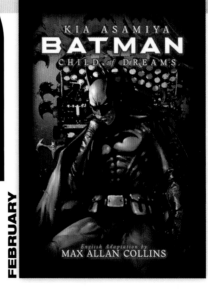

FROZEN OUT
Acting on a misleading tip-off, Detectives Marcus Driver and Charlie Fields were confronted by Mr. Freeze. Charlie was frozen stiff and Marcus injured by the villain's Freeze Gun. But why had Freeze let Marcus live?

2003

"Never is a long time. I know."

Rā's al Ghūl, *Batman: Death and the Maidens #1*.

After the success of the "Hush" story arc, DC launched the latest blockbuster title for the Dark Knight in the form of *Superman/Batman*, a modern take on the original *World's Finest* series. The Gotham City Police Department were handed their own highly acclaimed comic title, and *Outsiders* and *Teen Titans* both launched new, successful runs. Even *Birds of Prey* was reinvented for a new era, showing DC's dedication to keeping its team books fresh and interesting with bold new directions and equally bold creators.

KIA'S DREAM
Batman: Child of Dreams ▪ Acclaimed Manga artist and writer, Kia Asamiya lent his talents to the landscape of Gotham City in this graphic novel that spanned over 300 pages. Translated into English by a voice familiar with chronicling Bruce Wayne's adventures, writer Max Allan Collins, this epic story followed a Japanese reporter named Yuko Yagi who traveled to Gotham City in an attempt to nab an interview with the Dark Knight. This hardcover introduced a new model of the Batmobile as well as a new villain, in the form of a Batman imposter.

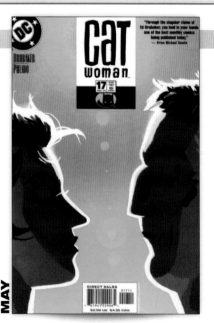

TRUE ROMANCE
Catwoman #17 ▪ The new Catwoman title was quickly becoming renowned for its storytelling and daring use of innovative panel structure. This issue by writer Ed Brubaker and artist Javier Pulido was certainly no exception. The use of titles for the various chapters added to the drama, heightening the creative team's powerful characterizations. The plot's most significant event was the beginning of a passionate romance between Catwoman and Slam Bradley, jump-started by a kiss on the last page of the previous installment.

BEFORE ORACLE

BATGIRL: YEAR ONE #1
The quality of writers Chuck Dixon
and Scott Beatty's *Robin: Year One*
miniseries seemed near-impossible to
top, but the duo arguably did just that
in this beautiful, nine-issue series
illustrated by Marcos Martin.

The story began with a young Barbara Gordon who
desperately wanted to follow in her adopted father's
footsteps and become a police officer. Unfortunately for
her, James Gordon forbade Barbara from doing just that,
forcing the intelligent young library researcher to pursue
other avenues. After training in the martial arts, Barbara
made her own female Batman costume and took on
Killer Moth, just as she had in her original debut in
Detective Comics #359 (January 1967). But in this
updated version, Batgirl soon found herself being
brought back to the Batcave, in order for Batman to test
her skills. While she didn't exactly pass his exam, Robin
became sympathetic to her case and supplied her with
some fancy tools, and later even with her own cycle.
After a literal trial by fire battling Killer Moth and his new
partner Firefly, Batgirl finally proved her worth and was
accepted into Batman's ranks, even teaming with Black
Canary in the process. This series also served to
introduce one of Barbara's old love interests, a young
police officer named Jason Bard.

MOTH ATTACK
Similar to Batgirl's first appearance in
Detective Comics #359 (January 1967),
the fledgling heroine was forced to fight
Killer Moth while dressed in her Batgirl
costume for a fancy-dress ball.

FEBRUARY

THE DEATH OF AZRAEL
***Azrael* #100** ● In issue #97 (February 2003),
writer Dennis O'Neil and artist Sergio Cariello pitted
Azrael against the devilish Nicholas Scratch once
again, but this time cladding the villain in a white
version of Azrael's original costume. Feeling that
his identity was being usurped by Scratch, Azrael
confronted him in this issue wearing his old costume,
only to be riddled with bullets fired by the assassin
Carleton LeHah. Jean-Paul Valley was seemingly no
more, leaving only Batman to put an end to Scratch's
latest nefarious scheme.

JUNE

COMRADE BATMAN?
***Superman: Red Son* #1** ● What if Superman's
rocketship had landed in the Soviet Union rather than
in Smallville, Kansas? That was the question writer
Mark Millar and artists Dave Johnson and Killian
Plunkett posed in this three-issue prestige-format
Elseworlds series. In this reality, Batman's parents
were murdered by the head of the N.K.V.D., a man
named Pyotr Roslov whom Batman was later forced
to team up with to attempt to bring Superman down.
This striking take on the World's Finest duo later
inspired a Batman action figure from DC Direct.

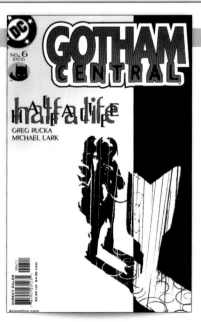

HALF A LIFE
***Gotham Central* #6** ● Gotham City cop Renee
Montoya saw her life put under the microscope by
writer Greg Rucka and artist Michael Lark in this
acclaimed five-part story. When Renee's personal life
was put on display by an anonymous photo sent to
her workplace, her life veered in a direction she had
not expected. Two-Face set her up for a murder he
had committed. Renee was forced to deal with the
super-villain's advances until Batman stepped in
during a fight between Renee and Two-Face that
would have led to one of them being killed.

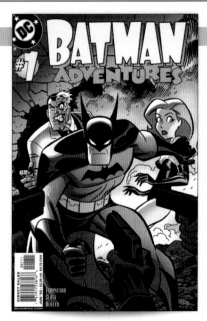

THE ADVENTURES CONTINUE
***Batman Adventures* #1** ● While *Batman: The
Animated Series* and *The New Batman Adventures*
had long since stopped producing new episodes for
television, the DC Animated Universe retained
its popularity. To further celebrate the world that
producer and designer Bruce Timm helped create,
writer Ty Templeton and penciller Rick Burchett
supplied the first issue of this new ongoing series.
This second volume of *Batman Adventures* debuted
many familiar Batman villains for their first outing in
the famous animated style.

THE RESIDENTS OF HELL

ARKHAM ASYLUM: LIVING HELL #1

Writer Dan Slott would prove his skill for creating new villains in this six-issue collaboration with artist Ryan Sook that took a look inside the walls of the fabled Arkham Asylum.

Following new character Warren White, a billionaire criminal who chose to stay at Arkham rather than spend time in an actual prison, this first issue debuted more than its fair share of new villains, including the cult leader Death Rattle, the violent Junkyard Dog and Lunkhead, the murderous graffiti artist Doodlebug, and Jane Doe, a killer who murders others so she can impersonate them. This introductory issue also introduced Aaron Cash, an Arkham guard with one arm (thanks to Killer Croc) who would become a regular supporting character in Batman's world.

As the series progressed, and White began to realize how dire his situation truly was, readers met new villain Humpty Dumpty in issue #2 (August 2003)—a villain obsessed with taking things and people apart just to put them back together again.

The story concluded in a riot that summoned the supernatural and White lost his hair, nose, and ears before the violence was curbed by Batman in a new model Batmobile. Driven half-insane by his terrible ordeal, and filing his teeth to points, White became Arkham's new crime lord, the Great White Shark.

WARREN WHITE
Arrogant and blissfully unaware of the terrifying nature of Arkham and its residents, White was in for the shock of his life. Called "new fish" by the other inmates, White would soon evolve from a cowering prisoner to a cold and calculating "shark."

PREDATOR AND PREY

Birds of Prey #56 ▪ Writer Gail Simone would begin what would become her breakthrough work on a series for DC Comics with the help of artist Ed Benes, taking the Birds of Prey in a new direction. When Black Canary was kidnapped by two new villains named Savant and Creote, not only would Canary escape with the help of new Birds member Huntress, but she'd even manage to help convert both criminals later on down the road into heroic supporting characters thanks to the always helpful meddling and planning of Oracle.

SUPER HERO TRIO

Batman/Superman/Wonder Woman: Trinity #1 ▪ Legendary storyteller Matt Wagner headed to DC Comics to write and illustrate this three-issue prestige-format series that retold the original meeting between Batman and Superman and heroine Wonder Woman. This series told the story of Rä's al Ghül teaming with Superman clone Bizarro. The series introduced Wagner's interesting new Batmobile and submarine designs, and included the first kiss between Batman and Wonder Woman in issue #3 (November 2003).

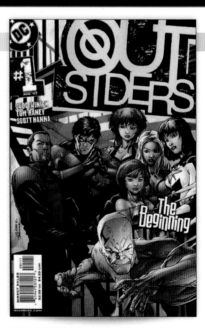

NIGHTWING AND THE OUTSIDERS

Outsiders #1 ▪ Writer Judd Winick and artist Tom Raney's Outsiders were quite different from their predecessors. Spinning out of the *Titans/Young Justice: Graduation Day* miniseries (July 2003), this series saw Nightwing join a team that included many DCU veterans as well as the debut of Black Lightning's daughter Thunder, her later lover, the powerhouse Grace Choi, and a piece of Metamorpho who developed his own personality and later called himself Shift.

REVIVING THE REVIVAL

Teen Titans #1 ▪ When writer Marv Wolfman and artist George Perez revived *The New Teen Titans* in 1980, it became one of the best-selling titles for years. In this issue, writer Geoff Johns and artist Mike McKone successfully reunited the young heroes. After the *Titans/Young Justice: Graduation Day* miniseries that chronicled the end of the two teams, a clean slate meant that a new incarnation of the Teen Titans could emerge. With members from Young Justice alongside classic Titans, the team once again boasted genuine star power.

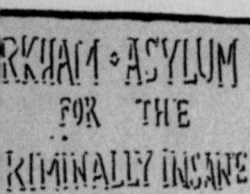

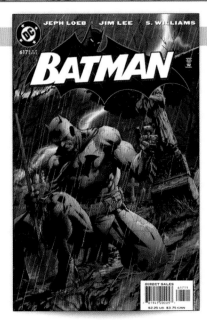

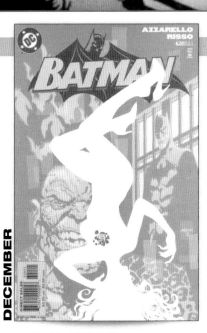

OCTOBER

DECEMBER

JASON TODD, ALIVE?

Batman #617 ▪ As part of their dramatic "Hush" epic, writer Jeph Loeb and artist Jim Lee ended this issue with Hush unmasking himself, revealed now as Jason Todd. But by the next issue, "Jason" would be exposed as Clayface in disguise. Later, readers would find out that even that ruse was more than it appeared. That particular Clayface was actually a new version, a man named Johnny Williams, whose connection to Hush was revealed in *Batman: Gotham Knights* #68 (October 2005) in a story by writer A.J. Lieberman and penciller Al Barrionuevo.

DEATH BECOMES HER

Batman: Death and the Maidens #1 ▪ In what was intended to be the final Rā's al Ghūl story, writer Greg Rucka and artist Klaus Janson created this series that delved into the family tree of the Demon's Head while also examining what was behind Batman's pursuit of an impossible justice. Having introduced Rā's al Ghūl's daughter Nyssa Raatko in a feature in *Detective Comics* #783 (August 2003), Rucka and Janson went on to explain her vendetta with her father, culminating in Rā's' death and Nyssa's takeover of his empire—with his blessing.

BROKEN CITY

Batman #620 ▪ Editor Bob Schreck gave two more big name creators a shot at the Batman when he hired writer Brian Azzarello and artist Eduardo Risso for a six-issue noir thriller. Investigating another case, Batman happened upon the murder of a child's parents that mirrored the death of his own. As he continued his manhunt, meeting a new pair of villains—Fatman and Little Boy—in *Batman* #623 (March 2004) and #621 (January 2004) respectively, Batman would discover the identity of the murderer from his least likely assistant—the Joker.

SOFT TARGETS

Gotham Central #12 ▪ Writers Ed Brubaker and Greg Rucka took a turn at handling Batman's greatest foe when they collaborated on this four-issue arc with artist Michael Lark. Telling the tale of a sniper loose in Gotham City, the creative team started off with a bang when the assassin shot and killed Mayor Dickerson. When another high-profile target was killed, the detectives soon realized the Joker was behind the deaths. This realistic thriller saw the debut of corrupt cop Jim Corrigan as well as the first appearance of Mayor David Hull in issue #13 (January 2004).

RETURN OF THE WORLD'S FINEST
SUPERMAN/BATMAN #1

Batman and Superman were back in action as DC Comics' most iconic duo, this time utilizing a title that was a bit more direct in a modern update to the classic *World's Finest Comics* series that ran for decades.

With artist Ed McGuinness on tap to pencil the series, writer Jeph Loeb used his experience handling both Batman and Superman to deliver a fan-favorite series that attempted to give each Super Hero equal time in the spotlight.

A high-octane title that was meant to be one of the most important comics in DC Comics' lineup at the time, Loeb and company wasted no time in shaking up the lives of both Superman and Batman. In this first six-issue arc, a giant asteroid made of Kryptonite was seen heading on a collision course with Earth. President Lex Luthor publicly blamed Superman for this incoming disaster and declared the Man of Steel a public enemy. After loosing a host of super-villains and Super Heroes upon Superman and Batman, Luthor's madness soon became apparent as he continually injected himself with a Kryptonite-laced version of the drug Venom.

Realizing that they needed to end Luthor's reign of terror for good, Superman and Batman invaded the White House with help from their respective crime-fighting "families." Lex Luthor showed his true colors to the world in a crazed attempt to end Superman's life. However, the World's Finest team triumphed. Luthor was thrown out of office while Talia Head, CEO of LexCorp, purposely bankrupted his company. Superman and Batman also managed to destroy the Kryptonite asteroid with the help of the brave Captain Atom, who piloted a massive spaceship that shared the likeness of the classic villain known as the Composite Superman.

Superman/Batman proved to be a long-lasting title for DC Comics. This inaugural story would later be adapted into a direct-to-DVD animated movie in 2009 entitled *Superman/Batman: Public Enemies*, and action figures would also be created.

VILLAINS UNITED
As President of the United States, Lex Luthor was able to influence popular opinion like never before. In an attempt to defeat Superman, Luthor publicly placed a $1 billion bounty on the Super Hero's head, causing dozens of super-villains to crawl out of the woodwork.

"THE SAME, SPLIT DOWN THE MIDDLE"
The *Superman/Batman* title shone light on its two main protagonists by having them tell a simultaneous narrative. The device contrasted the two characters, underlining the differences that defined these Super Heroes.

ALSO THIS YEAR

January—Harley Quinn #26: The new creative team of writer A.J. Lieberman and penciller Mike Huddleston signed on to fuel Harley's monthly antics.

February—Detective Comics #777: Paul Sloan was reintroduced into Batman's life, now calling himself Charlatan in this issue that also featured part two of the back-up "Spore" story.

June—Power Company #15: This action-packed issue featured a memorable fight between the newest Manhunter, Kirk DePaul, and Batman.

★ **July 19th**—Robin appeared on Cartoon Network's new *Teen Titans* cartoon, starring alongside Beast Boy, Starfire, Cyborg, and Raven.

September—Batgirl #42: Dr. Death returned to Gotham City sporting a new look.

November—Batman: Detective No. 27: Michael Uslan told his own Elseworlds tale in this hardcover featuring a world where Bruce Wayne was the world's greatest detective, without his Batman identity.

2004

"Frankly, I don't care what they call me, as long as I'm free to protect my city."

Batman, *DC: The New Frontier* #1.

It was Spoiler's year in the spotlight, and unfortunately for Stephanie Brown, things weren't going to end well. The longtime supporting character finally hit the big leagues when she adopted the mantle of Robin in Tim Drake's absence. She was the first female Robin in mainstream continuity, but Stephanie's tenure in the Robin suit was treated with little fanfare. However, when Tim reclaimed his title and Stephanie returned to her identity of the Spoiler, she'd find herself accidentally triggering this year's definitive Batman event in the 25-issue saga "War Games."

JANUARY

THE BREAK-UP

Nightwing #87 ▪ While their relationship harked back to their days as Robin and Batgirl, Nightwing and Oracle finally broke off their relationship, in this issue by writer Devin Grayson and artist Patrick Zircher. After fighting the new Tarantula in a crowded restaurant, Dick and Barbara took their date to the Gotham City Amusement Mile where they had a much needed heart-to-heart. Tired of Grayson's over-protective attitude, Barbara called off their relationship, devastating Nightwing in a way no super-villain ever could.

WONDER BATWOMAN

JLA #90 ▪ Batman was battling a new villain in Gotham City called the Steel Fang and called Wonder Woman for help. However, his true reason for asking Diana to his city was to discuss the mutual attraction the two had been feeling since their kiss in *JLA* #74 (December 2002). In this heartfelt tale by writer Joe Kelly and penciller ChrisCross, Wonder Woman saw a glimpse of a possible future life with Batman by using the Martian Manhunter's device called the Transconsciousness Articulator. However, despite the machine's influence, they decided to remain friends.

FRONTIER LIVING

DC: THE NEW FRONTIER #1
The Silver Age of the DC Universe received a glorious reinterpretation in this fresh new take on classic heroes, tropes, and storylines.

When the original Justice Society publicly retired after ignoring an order to take off their masks before Congress, Batman became a wanted vigilante, even staging a fight with Superman to keep his freedom. New heroes began to appear in this new world, culminating in a battle against a living island. Writer/artist Darwyn Cooke, with colorist Dave Stewart, created a rich and vibrant story where heroes fought for truth and justice amongst the suspicion and paranoia of the McCarthy era, and new twists on old relationships made readers sit on the edge of their seats.

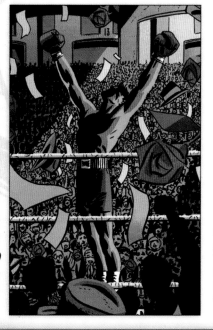

UP FOR THE FIGHT
Another star of The New Frontier, Ted Grant, alias Wildcat, proved himself the people's champion in a brilliant sequence by Darwyn Cooke in issue #2.

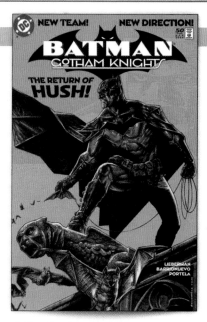

NO STOPPING THE TITANS
Teen Titans Go! #1 ▪ As part of DC Comics' new Johnny DC line, an all-ages selection of comic book titles suitable for kid readers, writer J. Torres and artist Todd Nauck debuted this new ongoing title, which tied into the *Teen Titans* animated series on Cartoon Network. Capturing the energy of the popular cartoon as well as its action-packed style, this title even included exaggerated cartoony (large head, small body) looks for the characters that ran along the bottom of pages. There were also jokes and fun riddles that were not part of the actual story.

ROBIN ROGUES
Robin #121 ▪ Bill Willingham joined *Robin* as its regular writer, and quickly began to make the Super Hero's life as busy as possible. In this issue, Willingham and artist Rick Mays debuted the supernatural foe who would soon call himself Johnny Warlock. They also included new character Darla Aquista, who would become a magical powerhouse herself by issue #137 (June 2005) and later adopt the name Laura Fell. After rewarding Robin with his own cycle in issue #122, Willingham then introduced the armored assassin, Scarab, two issues later.

PERFECT STRANGERS
Batman: Room Full of Strangers ▪ Writer/artist Scott Morse created this inventive whodunit starring the now-retired Jim Gordon and a young boy named Graham who believed that his father was the Batman. While vacationing at the Inn at Hidden Cove, ex-Commissioner Gordon was thrust back into detective work when a fellow hotel guest was killed. What followed was a tragic tale of a mother dying of cancer, a violent criminal, and a boy imitating his hero, even to the extent of putting his own life in danger.

THE RETURN OF HUSH
Batman: Gotham Knights #50 ▪ Writer A.J. Lieberman took over the writing chores on Gotham Knights with this issue that started the sequel to the popular "Hush" series drawn by new regular artist Al Barrionuevo. This elaborate six-part story saw Hush team with Prometheus in issue #52 (June 2004), who would be revealed as an impersonator in *Faces of Evil: Prometheus #1* (March 2009). This arc also revealed a bit more insight into the Joker's origin from *Batman: The Killing Joke* (July 1988), even revealing Joker's first name, Jack.

WILLINGHAM · SCOTT

ROBIN

126

THE GIRL WONDER!

DIRECT SALES

$2.25 US $3.50 CAN

THE NEW ROBIN

ROBIN #126

Former Spoiler Stephanie Brown was promoted to Robin's position when Tim Drake could no longer continue. Her tenure as the Girl Wonder would be the shortest of any Robin on record.

In the previous month's *Robin* #125 by writer Bill Willingham and artist Francisco Rodriguez de la Fuente, Tim stepped down as Batman's partner when his father Frank Drake discovered his double life.

And that's where Stephanie Brown, alias crime-fighting vigilante Spoiler, came in. In this issue by Willingham and artist Damion Scott, Stephanie took over from Tim, with Batman promising to fire her the first time she disobeyed one of his commands. As it turned out, readers wouldn't have to wait long for that to happen. In issue #128 (September 2004), Stephanie leaped into action to help save Batman during a battle with the assassin Scarab, who was hunting down and eliminating boys who fitted Robin's profile. Despite his new, high-tech armor, Batman wasn't faring very well. However, when Stephanie's Robin rushed in to help him, things went from bad to worse. Scarab took her captive, forcing Batman to let Scarab escape in order to spare Stephanie's life. Batman had forbidden Robin to leave her post in the Batplane, and since she had contradicted a direct order, he fired her.

To add insult to injury, Batman also demanded that Stephanie give up crime fighting altogether, even in her former identity of Spoiler.

TAKING DIFFERENT PATHS
Tim had promised his father that he would retire his Robin persona and live an ordinary life. His grilfriend Stephanie still wished to continue fighting crime as Spoiler. When she thought Tim had eyes for another girl at Memorial High, jealousy fueled her desire to take Tim's place at Batman's side as Robin.

LICENSE TO DRIVE!

JOYRIDE

***Teen Titans* #9** ▪ A new model of the Batmobile debuted in this issue, thanks to writer Geoff Johns and artist Mike McKone. When the Teen Titans needed to investigate a strange epidemic among fortune-tellers in the Bay Area of San Francisco, Robin suggested they travel in style in a Batmobile that he had shipped to the city. This particular model featured a smokescreen device, oil slicks, and anti-White Martian rays. However, it couldn't protect against Kid Flash, who managed to flip the car when he drove it, getting Robin in trouble with Batman.

THE NEW GIRL IN TOWN!

FISHING FOR HEROES

***Superman/Batman* #8** ▪ After a Superboy/Robin team-up in the previous issue by writer Jeph Loeb and artist Pat Lee, Loeb began the second major story arc on this title in this issue, drawn by superstar Michael Turner. Equipped with a new model Batboat and a new underwater uniform, Batman chanced upon a Kryptonian ship in the waters off Gotham City that contained Superman's cousin, the newest version of Supergirl. While Batman viewed her with suspicion at first, he would soon see Supergirl as an ally by the end of this six-issue epic.

BATMAN HARLEY and IVY

THE DESTRUCTIVE DUO

***Batman: Harley and Ivy* #1** ▪ Writer Paul Dini and artist Bruce Timm crafted this tale set in the DC Animated Universe and starring the odd couple of Harley Quinn and Poison Ivy. In this three-issue series, the girls had a brush with Batman, staged a breakout at Arkham Asylum and, in issue #2, fought new villains Slash and Burn. In issue #3, the two femme fatales even attacked Bruce Timm and Paul Dini. The creative team featured as the directors of a Harley and Ivy movie in Hollywood. The real Harley and Ivy decided to take over the production.

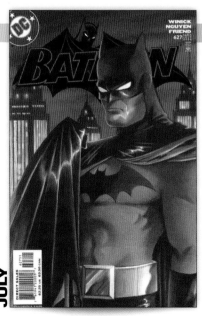

WINICK NGUYEN FRIEND 627

BATMAN

SCARE TACTICS

***Batman* #627** ▪ Coming on board as the regular Batman team with the previous issue, writer Judd Winick and artist Dustin Nguyen began the four-issue tale "As the Crow Flies," which saw Scarecrow's monstrous transformation into Scarebeast. To combat this new threat, Batman would adopt an armored suit in issue #630 (September 2004), only to discover that the real mastermind behind Scarecrow's rampages was Crane's assistant, Dr. Linda Friitawa. The albino villainess debuted in this issue, and adopted the name Fright in the story's finale.

> "Let's get one thing straight. You're on probation... No second chances."
>
> Batman, *Robin* #126

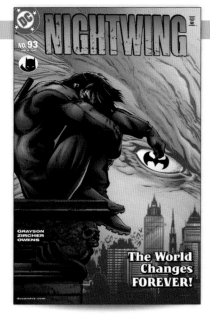

NIGHTWING'S NIGHTMARE

Nightwing #93 ▪ Writer Devin Grayson and artist Patrick Zircher would cause plenty of controversy when Nightwing was attacked by the villainess Tarantula in this issue. After a violent confrontation with his arch-foe Blockbuster, in a moment of weakness, Nightwing stood by and let Tarantula murder the crime boss in cold blood. Traumatized by the event, Nightwing was in a state of emotional shock. Seeing this, Tarantula took advantage of Nightwing in a disturbing sequence that would continue to affect the Super Hero for some time.

RETURN OF THE DRAGON

Richard Dragon #1 ▪ Richard Dragon found himself starring in a new ongoing series by writer Chuck Dixon and Scott McDaniel, albeit with a few changes. Revising Dragon's history somewhat, this new series saw a younger version of the martial arts master, now trained by Ben Turner, the Bronze Tiger. Revealed to be one of Batman's trainers in issue #3 (September 2004), this youthful version of Richard Dragon still contained all the skill of the previous interpretation, quickly earning Nightwing's respect in the title's second issue.

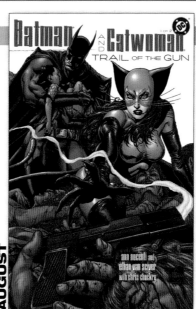

GUN CONTROL

Batman and Catwoman: Trail of the Gun #1 ▪ Catwoman earned a new variation of her gray costume in this two-issue, prestige-format series written by Ann Nocenti and illustrated by Ethan Van Sciver that dealt with a gun that never missed its target. Dubbed a "smart gun," this one-of-a-kind, heat-seeking firearm was loose on the streets of Gotham City, just as Catwoman was framed for murder. Including a debate on gun control, this series saw Batman finally regain the prized gun. Selina Kyle was soon cleared of the charges against her.

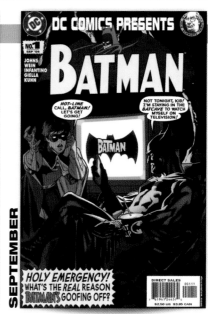

REMEMBERING JULIUS

DC Comics Presents: Batman #1 ▪ When editor Julius Schwartz passed away, DC Comics released a series of specials as a tribute to the man who had been one of the most influential pilots of the DC Universe. Owing to Schwartz's role in guiding the era of the "New Look" Batman in the 1960s, writer Geoff Johns and artist Carmine Infantino told a modern Batman tale that included a 1966-flavored TV show version of the Dynamic Duo. Batman and Robin investigated when the actor playing Batman on TV was accused of killing the actor playing Robin.

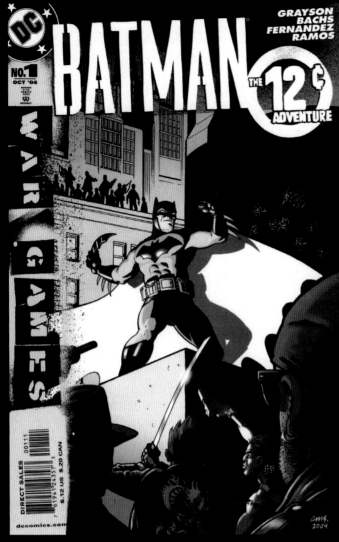

WAR GAMES

BATMAN: THE 12 CENT ADVENTURE #1

A perfect entry point for new readers as the start of the 25-issue crossover "War Games," *Batman: The 12 Cent Adventure* would waste no time in triggering the biggest gang war in the history of Gotham City.

Written by Devin Grayson with pencils by Ramon Bachs, this issue showed a misguided Spoiler attempting to prove herself in the eyes of the mentor that rejected her, Batman. Spying on a meeting that involved every major gang in Gotham City, Spoiler watched in horror as a gun battle broke out that resulted in several dead mob bosses and their enforcers, including costumed villains Hellhound and Silver Monkey. This meeting would later be revealed to have been orchestrated by Spoiler, who was following a gang infiltration procedure she'd discovered on Batman's computer. However, this strategy was supposed to involve Batman's alter ego, "Matches" Malone.

As this series continued through the pages of *Detective Comics*, *Batman: Legends of the Dark Knight*, *Nightwing*, *Batman: Gotham Knights*, *Robin*, *Batgirl*, *Catwoman*, and *Batman* over the course of the next three months, each title's creative teams dealt with the fallout of Spoiler's actions.

New hero Orpheus, and his right-hand woman and former Green Arrow supporting character, Onyx, tried to fight the gangs from inside, but were no match for the the new Gotham City crime boss rising to power in the chaos, Black Mask.

FLASH BACK
Batman's battle with Spoiler reminded him of another headstrong youth—Robin. In dealing with Spoiler, the girl he refused to mentor, he was reminded of the start of his relationship with Robin, which had far better results.

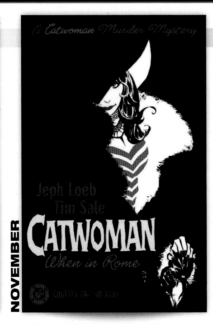

ON THE HUNT

Manhunter #1 ● Writer Marc Andreyko and penciller Jesus Saiz debuted the newest heir to the Manhunter title in this new ongoing series. While she'd later become a fixture in Gotham City, Los Angeles-based federal prosecutor Kate Spencer showed ties to the Caped Crusader right from the get-go. When she was unable to convince a jury about the guilt of the Batman villain Copperhead, Spencer donned armor from an evidence locker, including Azrael Batman's old gauntlets, to pursue life as a lethal crime fighter called the Manhunter.

DO AS THE ROMANS DO

Catwoman: When in Rome #1 ● Continuing their storyline from *Batman: The Long Halloween* and *Batman: Dark Victory*, writer Jeph Loeb and artist Tim Sale reunited on this six-issue series that detailed Selina Kyle's adventures in Italy. This series saw Selina and the Riddler head to Rome, quickly meeting Christopher Castillo, a hitman called "The Blond." When Southern Italy's so-called boss of bosses, Don Verinni, was killed via Joker Venom, Catwoman found herself in a mystery that involved stolen Gotham City weapons and the Wonder Woman villain, the Cheetah.

TITANS OF TOMORROW

Teen Titans/The Legion Special #1 ● In a tale that began in *Teen Titans* #16 (November 2004) by writer Geoff Johns and artist Mike McKone, the Titans were taken into the future to team with the Legion of Super-Heroes. In this issue, written by Mark Waid and Johns and pencilled by Ivan Reis, Joe Prado, and Barry Kitson, the Titans battled the Fatal Five. They ended up in another possible future where Tim Drake was now a lethal version of Batman, as readers would see when the story continued in the pages of *Teen Titans* #17 (December 2004).

STRIKE WHILE THE IRON'S HOT

The Batman Strikes! #1 ● The Johnny DC imprint for younger readers gained another long-lasting title in the form of this series, which tied in to *The Batman* cartoon that aired on The WB network. While this first issue was written by Bill Matheny and starred the Penguin, after a while, the title would switch formats to accommodate rotating writers. However, the artist on this first issue, Christopher Jones, would continue to illustrate the bulk of the series, only interrupted by a handful of guest artists in the title's 50-issue run.

CARNAGE
Gotham City's new crime lord, Black Mask, cut a swath of chaos and death throughout the major metropolis, unintentionally aided by the foolish actions of Spoiler. The latter's mistakes would have lasting repercussions for many years.

HAWKS OF PREY
Birds of Prey #74 ■ Writer Gail Simone and artist Ed Benes added another new member to the Birds of Prey in this extra-sized issue. In it, Oracle gained a new mobile headquarters in the form of the plane called the Aerie One. And to pilot the craft was the Birds' newest member, the legendary Lady Blackhawk. In the issue's back-up tale, Eduardo Barreto pencilled a Simone script that starred that very heroine. Not stopping there, Simone would debut a new villain in the very next issue drawn by Joe Prado and Ed Benes, the magical Black Alice.

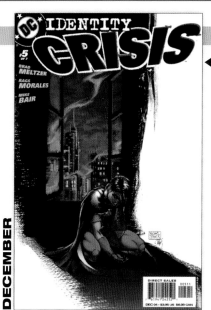

THE ROBIN CURSE
Identity Crisis #5 ■ Unlike the former Robins, Tim Drake was not an orphan, and his father Jack was still a big part of his life. But in this seven-issue miniseries by writer Brad Meltzer and artist Rags Morales, Jack Drake was murdered by the super-villain Captain Boomerang as part of a larger mystery thriller. This powerful issue dealt with a helpless Batman trying to get Robin to his father's side before it was too late. Tim realized that he was not immune to the pain that went with the territory of being a hero in Batman's war against crime.

SPECIAL FEATURE

DEARLY DEPARTED
Tim Drake learned a hard lesson when he was unable to save his father from being killed by the villain Captain Boomerang—not even Batman's superior skills and experience could soften the blow. Yet another of Batman's wards was now an orphan, and it would take years for the wounds to heal.

ALSO THIS YEAR

★ **July 23rd:** *Catwoman* stole some time on the big screen in her first self-titled feature, albeit in the form of new character Patience Phillips, in this movie starring Halle Berry.

★ **July 31st:** The animated TV show *Justice League* evolved into the acclaimed *Justice League Unlimited*, featuring a larger cast and connecting story threads.

September—*Justice League Elite* #1: Batgirl went undercover for Batman as Kasumi in this new 12-issue Justice League tie-in title.

★ **September 11th:** Batman saw a facelift in the form of a new animated series titled simply *The Batman* that featured a more youthful Bruce Wayne and a creatively redesigned Rogues Gallery.

December—*Solo* #1: This new ongoing series spotlighted a different artist each issue, often featuring collaborations with various writers. The first issue starred Batman and Catwoman.

CITY OF CRIME

DETECTIVE COMICS #800
This landmark issue ushered in a new exploration of Batman's world after the "War Games" series. It also signaled the beginning of a new saga, "City of Crime," with a special prelude story titled "In the Dark."

The main story of this comic was written by Andersen Gabrych and pencilled by Pete Woods, showed the status quo of Gotham City after the "War Games" crossover. However, starting with the next issue, back-up write David Lapham would become the new pilot of *Detective Comics*.

In his 12-part series, set in the days before "War Games," Lapham teamed with artist Ramon Bachs and took a look at the city's darkest corners. When spoiled 14-year-old heiress Haddie McNeil died of a drug overdose, Batman felt responsible, despite barely knowing the child. So, when a similar young girl named Cassie Welles was kidnapped, Batman became obsessed with her case. Disguised as a construction worker named Donnie Malloy, Batman uncovered a mysterious group of entities called the Body. While he defeated this bizarre group with the help of a new model Batmobile, Batplane, and Batcopter, Batman eventually realized that Cassie Welles had been murdered by her own mother. He had overlooked a prime suspect out of a misguided sense of guilt.

A MEETING OF MINDS
After the tumultuous events of "War Games," circumstances had led to Batman being wanted by the police. Despite the Dark Knight's outlaw status, James Gordon remained loyal to his old friend.

2005

"Nuts? You want to see nuts, kid? I'll show you nuts!"

Batman, All Star Batman and Robin the Boy Wonder #2.

While it began as a year of follow-up stories that showcased Batman's world after the traumatic events of "War Games," 2005 would soon transition into a year of anticipation, as big events and storylines began to be teased in many of Batman's titles. *Infinite Crisis*, DC Comics' most ambitious crossover storyline since the likes of *Crisis on Infinite Earths* or *Zero Hour*, would soon change the status of the DCU as a whole. But before that could happen, several series served as prequels that would only build excitement in the readers. *Villains United* and *The O.M.A.C. Project* were two such miniseries, each promising something big on the horizon.

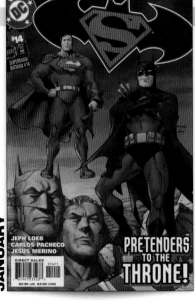

ABSOLUTE POWER
***Superman/Batman* #14** ● Writer Jeph Loeb continued his epic storylines with this five-issue arc pairing with artists Carlos Pacheco and Ivan Reis. In this tale, the 31st-century Legion of Super-Villains'—Cosmic King, Lightning Lord, and Saturn Queen adopted the young Bruce Wayne and baby Kal-El. In this new reality, Superman and Batman grew up to become cruel dictators, until real history was eventually restored and the Legion of Super-Villains' world-conquering masterplan was exposed and foiled.

KNIGHT OF JUSTICE
***JLA Classified* #1** ● Writer Grant Morrison and artist Ed McGuinness jumpstarted this new Justice League ongoing series that would use various creative teams. In this three-part story, Morrison once more utilized the super team the Ultramarine Corps, which included England's version of Batman, the Knight, in a new costume. Formerly known as the Squire when he first appeared in *Batman* #62 (January 1951), Cyril Sheldrake was revealed to be the current Knight in *JLA* #26 (February 1999), alongside his own Squire, Beryl Hutchinson.

THE FIRST JOKE

BATMAN: THE MAN WHO LAUGHS
This first meeting between the Dark Knight and the Joker was a modern retelling of a classic encounter that first appeared in *Batman* #1 (April 1940).

The Joker's definitive origin story was considered by many to be *Batman: The Killing Joke* (July 1988). When writer Ed Brubaker and artist Doug Mahnke set their sights on telling the first Batman/Joker meeting, they had little interest in rehashing the origin of the Clown Prince of Crime. Instead, they began this prestige-format one-shot tale with the Joker having already adopted his new super-villain identity. After dozens of bodies were discovered in an abandoned factory with rictus expressions on their faces, the Joker made himself known to the public by killing a reporter on camera, and threatening to kill a wealthy man, Henry Claridge, by midnight. While he succeeded in carrying out the murder, the Joker's real ploy was to let loose the criminally insane inmates of the Williams Medical Center while the police attempted to protect Claridge. The Joker continued his reign of terror and assassinations. At one point, even Batman was a target, saved just in time by his butler, Alfred. Batman eventually confronted the Joker at the Gotham Reservoir. The Joker was about to release poison into Gotham City's water supply, but Batman prevented this by blowing up the viaduct that led to the city. Batman then defeated the Joker and had him imprisoned in newly-reopened Arkham Asylum.

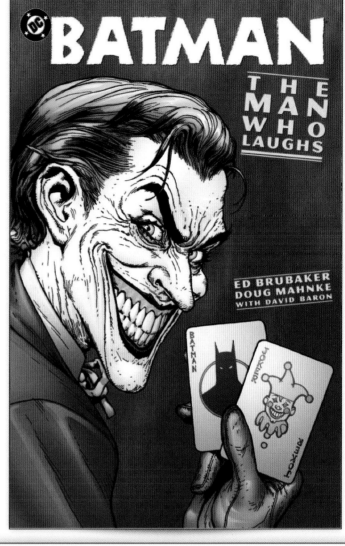

THE JOKER'S CALLING CARD

After announcing on television that Arkham Asylum was to reopen, the reporter collapsed. Her hair turned green; her skin turned white; her red lips stretched into a hideous grin. A new, deadly villain was at large in Gotham City.

A NEW RED HOOD

When Jason Todd returned, as if from the dead, he was shocked to discover that Batman had not avenged his "death" by killing the Joker. This caused a rift between the Dark Knight and his former sidekick, leading Jason into criminality as the Red Hood.

UNDER THE HOOD

Batman #635 ■ Is Jason Todd back from the dead? That was a question readers began asking during Clayface's impersonation of Jason in *Batman* #617 (September 2003), and again in *Batman* #630 (September 2004) when Alfred seemed to discover Jason's mask after Batman battled what he thought was a hallucination of Todd in the previous issue. In this four-part arc by writer Judd Winick and penciller Doug Mahnke, Jason Todd was indeed alive, adopting the criminal persona of the Red Hood and attempting to take over Gotham City's drug trade.

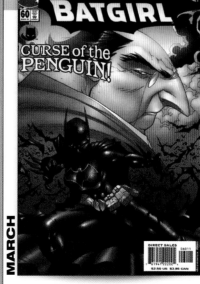

THE BATGIRL CAVE

Batgirl #60 ■ Scripter Andersen Gabrych and artist Alé Garza established a new life for Batgirl as a resident of Blüdhaven. For the first time living life on her own terms, Cassandra Cain moved to the city's Fort Joseph district. With the help of Bruce Wayne's near-limitless funds, she was given an old carriage house that, from the outside, looked run-down and empty. But once inside, the newly-renovated building included a pole that Batgirl could slide down to enter her own "Batcave," a repurposed subway station, complete with a computer and motorcycle.

ROOFTOP RUMBLE

Cassandra Cain had little time for relaxation in her new home town. She was given a tough Blüdhaven welcome in full-on training sessions with martial arts expert and trained assassin Onyx.

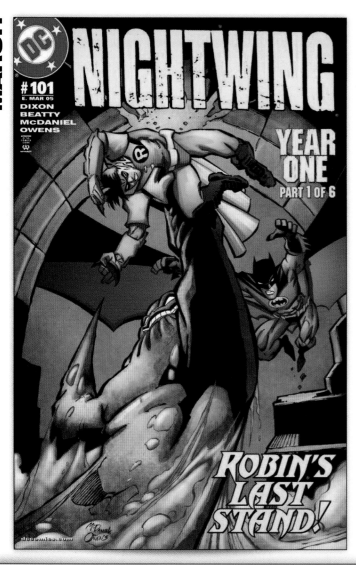

NIGHTWING: YEAR ONE

NIGHTWING #101

Readers got to witness Robin's transition from young Teen Wonder to a hero in his own right in this six-issue series within a series that followed up Nightwing's 100th issue anniversary.

As they had done with their previous *Robin: Year One* and *Batgirl: Year One* miniseries, writers Chuck Dixon and Scott Beatty, together with artist Scott McDaniel, began their story when Dick Grayson was nearing adulthood and developing his own life with college and the Teen Titans.

After a battle with Clayface in which Grayson tried out a new snowsuit costume, Batman and Robin argued over Robin being absent from Gotham City too many times when the Dark Knight had needed him. Fired from his position as Robin, Grayson met with Superman, who shared with him the legend of the Kryptonian hero, Nightwing.

After spending some time at the circus with the hero Deadman (who also influenced Grayson's style), Grayson adopted the name of Nightwing, and soon teamed with Batgirl. Finally, after teaming up with the new Robin, Jason Todd, Nightwing found peace with his new life. Alfred made him a new Nightwing costume featuring a yellow trim so that Dick would forever remember his time as Robin the Boy Wonder.

CLAYFACE TRIUMPHANT?
Batman and Robin had their hands full when Clayface fought them to a near standstill, but Dick Grayson did not disappoint his mentor and helped defeat the morphing villain thanks to some slick moves and a few cool new gadgets.

RALLYING AGAINST ROBIN
Robin #135 ■ Now partnered with artist Damion Scott, writer Bill Willingham continued to churn out a variety of new villains for Robin to face during his monthly adventures. In *Robin* #133 (February 2005), Robin and guest star Batgirl faced the not-so-dire threat of the villain Gas Bag. In this month's issue, Robin was pitted against a new villain, the highly skilled Rising Sun Archer, as well as the horse-bound Dark Rider, a character seemingly unrelated to the espionage-based villain who debuted in *Batman* #393 (March 1986).

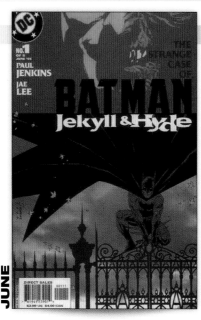

HYDING THE TRUTH
Batman: Jekyll & Hyde #1 ■ Two-Face's twisted mind was explored by writer Paul Jenkins and artists Jae Lee and Sean Phillips in this six-issue series. When a mother and her children were murdered, Batman suspected there was more to the crime than a psychotic father. Batman discovered that Two-Face had caused a rash of murders using a gene manipulation formula that brought out the subject's dark side. While Batman stopped Two-Face's scheme, he discovered that Harvey Dent had had a brother Murray who died a tragic death.

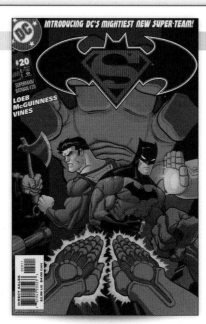

THE END OF THE BEGINNING
Superman/Batman #20 ■ Writer Jeph Loeb began his final major arc on this title with his original partner in crime, artist Ed McGuinness. In what was revealed to be an elaborate reality-warping battle between the Joker and Mr. Mxyzptlk, readers were introduced to Batzarro, a bizarre counterpoint to Batman. Full of new characters from weird worlds, issue #22 (October 2005) saw Tim Drake as a future version of Batman Beyond, as well as the Kryptonite Batman. In the following year, issue #25 (May 2006) saw the birth of the Composite Superman-Batman.

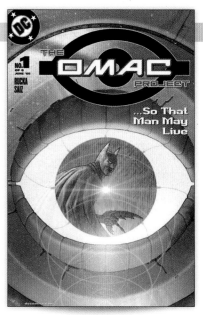

BIG BROTHER
The O.M.A.C. Project #1 ■ Batman's paranoia and advanced technology were used against him in this six-issue miniseries by Greg Rucka with art by Jesus Saiz. Former Justice League organizer Max Lord manipulated Batman's Brother Eye satellite technology to create a cyborg-soldier army designed to combat meta-humans. Batman had created Brother Eye to watch over the Super Hero community after Zatanna and the JLA messed with his memories as revealed in *Identity Crisis* #6 (January 2005), but he never thought it would be used against innocents.

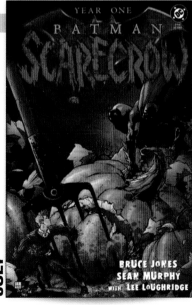
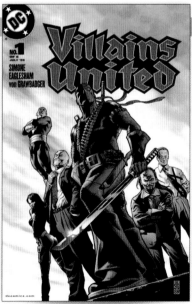

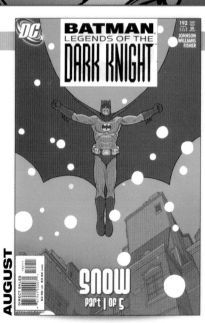

JULY

AUGUST

BEFORE THEY WERE FILM STARS

Year One: Scarecrow #1 ● Giving readers a crash course in the two villainous stars of the new Warner Bros. film *Batman Begins*, DC Comics launched this two-issue, prestige-format series that told a revised version of Scarecrow's origin by writer Bruce Jones and future superstar artist Sean Murphy. Meanwhile, in a similar two-issue series *Year One: Rā's al Ghūl* (June 2005), writer Devin Grayson and artist Paul Gulacy told a tale of Batman versus the threat of Rā's al Ghūl from beyond the grave, involving reanimated corpses and new vehicles for Batman.

VILLAINS VS. VILLAINS

Villains United #1 ● Writer Gail Simone and artist Dale Eaglesham would revitalize an old DC Universe name with a brand new concept in this six-issue series. When the Calculator, Deathstroke, Talia al Ghūl and several other super-villains attempted to unite the costume-clad underworld under their rule, only a few declined. Of those, Catman, Deadshot, and Birds of Prey foe Cheshire created a new team of antiheroes—the Secret Six. They went on to face threats like a new Hellhound and female Crazy Quilt, who debuted next issue.

SILVER ST. CLOUD RETURNS

Batman: Dark Detective #1 ● The team of writer Steve Englehart and artist Marshall Rogers reunited in this six-issue sequel to their classic work of the late 1970s. When attending a fundraiser for United States Senator Evan Gregory, Bruce Wayne ran into Gregory's fiancée, Silver St. Cloud. Wayne had to dispel the memories of their past romance, as he was quickly forced into an adventure that pitted him against the Joker and Two-Face. This tale highlighted the tragic sacrifices that the Dark Knight's troubled life required.

DEEP FREEZE

Batman: Legends of the Dark Knight #192 ● Mr. Freeze's origin and costume were tweaked in this five-issue arc written by J.H. Williams and Dan Curtis Johnson and illustrated by the brilliant Seth Fisher. When his wife started showing signs of a degenerative disease of the central nervous system, Victor Fries attempted to freeze her body using technology he developed at his work at Neodigm. His attempt to save his wife seemingly killed her, permanently transforming Fries' body chemistry as well. And so Mr. Fries became Mr. Freeze.

FRANK MILLER + JIM LEE

SCOTT WILLIAMS + ALEX SINCLAIR

BATMAN & ROBIN THE BOY WONDER

ISSUE NO. 1

SPRINGING SURPRISES

ALL STAR BATMAN AND ROBIN THE BOY WONDER #1

When writer Frank Miller returned to Batman, it was always a big deal. Miller had earned his place as an icon in Gotham City lore.

Together with penciller Jim Lee, Miller delivered a series that took place in a reality that began with Miller and David Mazzucchelli's "Batman: Year One" and was set to end with Miller and Klaus Janson's *Batman: The Dark Knight Returns* and Miller's *The Dark Knight Strikes Again*. The 10-issue series focused on the first pairings of *Batman* and Dick Grayson. This first issue portrayed the shooting of Dick's acrobat parents at the conclusion of their circus act, and the now-orphaned Dick's recruitment into Batman's war against crime.

This series featured a flying Batmobile that could transform into a submarine, Batman hitting Robin in the face on multiple occasions, and a risqué liaison between Black Canary and the Dark Knight. In addition, there was a scene where a painted yellow Batman and Robin taunted Green Lantern while sipping lemonade in a completely yellow room intended to negate Lantern's powers.

THE DARING YOUNG MAN
Columnist and socialite Vicki Vale was overjoyed to get a date with Gotham's most eligible bachelor, Bruce Wayne. To her surprise, the date was a trip to the circus—to witness the death-defying act of Dick Grayson of the Flying Graysons. She couldn't help but wonder why Bruce was so interested in the boy. Then a murderer struck...

WILLINGHAM McDANIEL OWENS

ROBIN

139

VILLAINS AND VETERANS
Robin #139 ▪ The second villain to call himself Junkyard Dog debuted in this issue by writer Bill Willingham and artist Scott McDaniel. As one of the parade of hitmen contracted by the Penguin to kill Robin, this new Junkyard Dog had an appearance like his namesake, and controlled a pack of feral, man-eating canines. This issue also included the second appearance of the Veteran, a vigilante who, according to legend, served in every major war of the United States' long history, and would become something of an ally to the Boy Wonder.

GOTHAM CENTRAL

NO. 33 SEPT 05

RUCKA
BRUBAKER
KANO
GAUDIANO

DEAD ROBIN
Gotham Central #33 ▪ In this four-part arc written by Ed Brubaker and Greg Rucka and pencilled by Kano, the action started right away when police discovered the body of a young boy who looked exactly like Robin. Fortunately for Batman, the victim wasn't Tim Drake. Unfortunately for the G.C.P.D., when another body dressed in a Robin uniform showed up in the following issue, it seemed the city had a new serial killer on its hands. Later, in a twisted attempt to be a small part of Batman's world, the killer turned himself in.

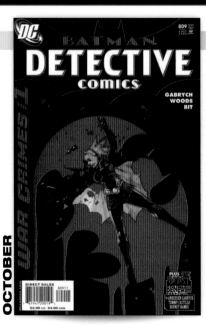

809

BATMAN

DETECTIVE COMICS

GABRYCH
WOODS
BIT

WAR CRIMES
Detective Comics #809 ▪ Writers Andersen Gabrych and Bill Willingham penned this four-issue epilogue to the "War Games" crossover that dealt with the repercussions of Spoiler's death. Pencilled by Pete Woods and Giuseppe Camuncoli, this series saw the return of Cluemaster, now hideously scarred after his stint with the Suicide Squad. Following a tip-off, Batman discovered not only Black Mask wearing his cape and cowl, but also that Dr. Leslie Thompkins had allowed Stephanie Brown to die, forcing Batman to banish Thompkins.

BATMAN
JOURNEY INTO KNIGHT

HELFER
HUAT

DARK KNIGHT DAWNING!

KNIGHT'S SKYE
Batman: Journey into Knight #1 ▪ While much had been written about Bruce Wayne's transformation into Batman, his role in returning to Wayne Industries and reclaiming his birthright after training to become the Dark Knight had been mostly glossed over. Writer Andrew Helfer and artist Tan Eng Huat remedied that with this 12-issue flashback series. It showed a young and inexperienced Batman learning to deal with new love interest, Skye, and a deadly virus being spread around Gotham City by a knowing carrier.

A NEW BRAND OF JUSTICE

Justice #1 ● Set in its own Elseworlds-like alternate reality, this 12-issue series became the next big project for show-stopping painter Alex Ross. Together with scripter Jim Krueger and artist Doug Braithwaite, Ross delivered this epic tale of a united cast of villains attempting to appear as heroes in the public eye, while systematically attacking the Justice League. This exciting series featured a new Batmobile design and a new Batman armor that served as a tribute to the George Barris-designed Batmobile from the 1960s Batman TV show.

DECEMBER

NIGHTWING, THE TERMINATOR?

Nightwing #113 ● Still reeling from his traumatic failure to stop Tarantula from killing Blockbuster in *Nightwing* #93 (July 2004), Nightwing adopted a new name and costume for himself. In this issue by writer Devin Grayson and artist Phil Hester, Nightwing temporarily donned a red and black uniform and began calling himself Renegade. Dick Grayson's life changed even more dramatically when he took on a young partner in the form of Deathstroke's daughter, Rose, also known as Ravager, in an attempt to steer her away from her villainous life.

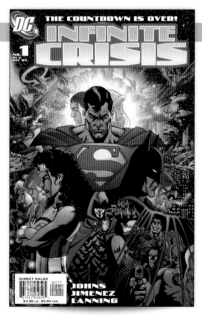

RETURN OF THE CRISIS

Infinite Crisis #1 ● The DC Universe had become a decidedly violent place. This seven-issue series saw Batman, an aging Superman, and Wonder Woman join the rest of the DCU heroes in the thick of a cosmic event that reshaped reality. Thanks to writer Geoff Johns and the illustrators Phil Jimenez, Jerry Ordway, George Pérez, Ivan Reis, and Joe Bennett, *Infinite Crisis* also gave birth to a new Spectre in the form of former G.C.P.D. detective Crispus Allen. He had died in *Gotham Central* #38 and would become the Spectre in *Inifinite Crisis* #4.

ALSO THIS YEAR

January—*Batman: Legends of the Dark Knight* #185: The Riddler received a temporary makeover in this five-issue arc.

★ **April 8th:** Ace the Bat-Hound made his debut in the new cartoon *Krypto: The Superdog*.

★ **June 15th:** The Batman film franchise was restarted with *Batman Begins*, an origin tale of the Dark Knight directed by Christopher Nolan and starring Christian Bale.

July—*Detective Comics* #806: In this two-part Alfred origin back-up tale, the famous butler's surname was revealed to be Beagle, like his former Earth-Two counterpart.

December—*Batgirl* #69: Mr. Freeze's wife Nora Fries was transformed into the alchemical Lazara following immersion in a Lazarus Pit.

December—*Birds of Prey* #87: Having set up their new base in Metropolis in the previous issue, the Birds met Black Spider III, Derrick Coe.

SHOOTING FOR THE STARS
All Star Batman and Robin the Boy Wonder
#6 (September 2006) ■ Beginning his major work
with Batman at the start of the decade with "Hush," artist
Jim Lee continued on with the Dark Knight in *All Star
Batman and Robin the Boy Wonder*, with writer Frank
Miller. The two applied a gritty look to Batman, and the
character was often depicted with an unshaven face, as
in this image. Lee would redesign the character's look in
the next decade with his art for *Justice League*. Lee was
just one of the many comic book stars that flocked to
Batman in the 2000s, giving the Caped Crusader
additional prestige and mainstream attention.

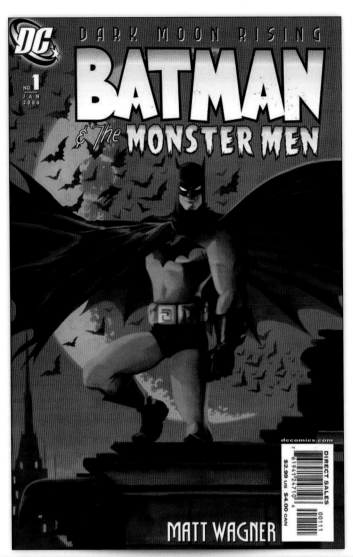

DARK MOON RISING
BATMAN & THE MONSTER MEN

NO. 1
JAN 2006

DIRECT SALES

$2.99 US $4.00 CAN

dccomics.com

MATT WAGNER

MONSTERS OF ALL SIZES

BATMAN AND THE MONSTER MEN #1

Batman encountered his notorious old foe, the mad psychologist and scientist Dr. Hugo Strange and his Monster Men in this new six-part story that paid homage to *Batman* #1 (April 1940).

Returning to Batman's "Year One" era, writer/artist Matt Wagner utilized the Monster Men from that original issue, as well as their creator, Dr. Hugo Strange. The scientist, together with his assistant Sanjay, had been experimenting with genetic manipulation on patients at Arkham Asylum. The results were devastating as Dr. Hugo Strange and Sanjay produced a race of cannibalistic Monster Men who needed regular feeding. Batman had to go and investigate.

The story delved into the Dark Knight's past, including his relationship with his Golden Age socialite girlfriend, Julie Madison. With a brilliant sense for the look and feel of Gotham City, *Batman and the Monster Men* would be a welcome update to the Dark Knight's lore.

STRANGE TIMES
Dr. Hugo Strange seized his opportunity to bring Gotham City to its knees and control the city with a plan that was both simple and efficient. The one thing he did not count on was the tenacity of the city's protector—Batman.

2006

"There goes my vacation."

Batman, *Batman* #655

Beginning at the tail end of 2005, the epic crossover *Infinite Crisis* caused a great deal of fallout in the DC Universe and in Batman's world. A blockbuster series that saw a new earth born out of the continuity of the past, *Infinite Crisis* caused every DCU title to jump "One Year Later" into the aftermath of the event, revealing new costumes, status quos, and a fresh and intriguing DC Universe that was totally accessible to new readers. Meanwhile, the maxiseries *52* debuted, set to fill in lapses in time in that mysterious missing year in in Gotham City's and Batman's story.

GETTING A TAPEWORM

Robin #144 • Robin's world had never been more chaotic. As Tim Drake faced an onslaught of villains in this issue, he encountered the new threat of the segmented villain Tapeworm. Written by Bill Willingham and illustrated by Scott McDaniel, this issue tied in to the events of *The O.M.A.C. Project*, in which a multitude of android O.M.A.C.s were causing massive destruction in Blüdhaven. This issue also saw the Warlock's Daughter join the supernatural team called Shadowpact, which included Ragman in its ranks.

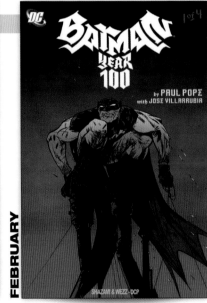

100 YEARS OF SOLITUDE

Batman: Year 100 #1 • Writer/artist Paul Pope contributed his abilities to the Caped Crusader on this four-part prestige-format Elseworlds tale. It presented a Gotham City that, in the year 2039, was virtually a police state. Batman had been labeled an outlaw vigilante by the federal government and was wanted for murder. This Batman wore fake fangs during his missions to exploit his own urban legend to his advantage. He also employed a team of partners, ranging from a rebellious police coroner and her daughter to Robin, a mechanical expert.

EARLY ADVENTURE
When Hugo Strange's Monster Men menaced Gotham City, Batman used his still-developing skills to meet this latest threat head-on. It would help make him the hero he remains to this day.

APRIL

THE MOTHER OF ALL ENDINGS

Batgirl #73 ▪ As Batgirl's first series drew to a close, the troubled heroine would finally confirm her suspicions regarding the identity of her long lost mother. Readers already knew that Batgirl was raised by her father, assassin David Cain. Now writer Andersen Gabrych and artist Pop Mhan revealed that her mother was martial arts master Lady Shiva. After discovering how corrupt her family tree was, Batgirl battled Shiva, defeating and impaling her on a hook above a Lazarus Pit. Cassandra Cain then walked away, seemingly giving up on her life as Batgirl.

THE DEATH OF BLACK MASK

Catwoman #52 ▪ In recent years, Gotham City gang boss Black Mask had become a thorn in Catwoman's side. In this issue by writer Will Pfeifer and artist Pete Woods, the skull-faced villain finally pushed Catwoman too far. When Black Mask carved a bloody message in Slam Bradley's chest, Catwoman went hunting him. She was nearly gunned down, but finally cornered the villain. Holding a gun to his head, Catwoman threatened to kill him. She then followed through on the threat, shocking readers by actually pulling the trigger.

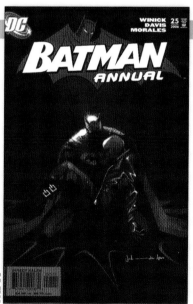

MAY

FROM ROBIN TO RED HOOD

Batman Annual #25 ▪ The secrets behind Jason Todd's return from the dead were finally revealed in the first *Batman Annual* in six years. In this story written by Judd Winick and drawn by Shane Davis, the villain Superboy-Prime unwittingly resurrected Jason by causing a time ripple. Jason recovered fully following a dip in a Lazarus Pit. This issue also included an unpublished page from "A Death in the Family" by writer Jim Starlin and penciller Jim Aparo that had been set to print in case readers voted for Jason's survival during that eventful 1989 storyline.

JUNE

COURTING KATE

52 #7 ▪ As DC Comics prepared to jump its titles one year in advance in the wake of the *Infinite Crisis* event, writers Geoff Johns, Grant Morrison, Mark Waid, and Greg Rucka, and breakdown artist Keith Giffen, working alongside many other artists, delivered a weekly series to fill in the missing year. Focusing on minor characters like the Question, this series also premiered several heroes, including a new Batwoman. She debuted as Renee Montoya's ex-girlfriend, the wealthy Kate Kane in this issue drawn by Ken Lashley.

DC

BATMAN

Detective Comics.

817
MAY
2006

YEAR 1 LATER

dccomics.com

DIRECT SALES
$2.50 US $3.50 CAN

ROBINSON • KIRK • CLARKE

THE SHARK BITES

DETECTIVE COMICS #817

To build up excitement for the new reality of the post-*Infinite Crisis* DC Universe, most of DC Comics' Super Hero titles jumped ahead in time. Labeled "One Year Later," they often revealed major changes to the characters.

Writer James Robinson was tasked with writing the introduction to the Gotham City of "One Year Later." Eight-issue crossover "Face the Face" alternated between *Detective Comics* and *Batman* and featured artists Leonard Kirk, Andy Clarke, Wayne Faucher, and Don Kramer. This issue marked the return of Commissioner Gordon and Harvey Bullock to the police force, as well as the arrival of newcomer Jamie Harper.

Absent during much of those 52 weeks in question, the Dark Knight had placed the city under the watch of Harvey Dent. Harvey's Two-Face personality had seemingly disappeared after plastic surgery by Tommy Elliot in the "Hush" storyline of 2002 and 2003, leaving only the just partner Batman used to rely on during his early years. Meanwhile, a new killer had emerged, murdering super-villains. KGBeast, Magpie, the Ventriloquist, and Orca died before Batman and his new ally, private detective Jason Bard, discovered the criminal behind the assassinations: the Great White Shark and his hitman, the new Tally Man (who debuted in *Detective Comics* #819, July 2006).

"Face the Face" introduced a new Batmobile and Batplane and saw Harvey Dent reclaim his Two-Face personality. Killer Moth was back in human form and in a new costume, and Bruce Wayne officially adopted Tim Drake as his son.

THE GREAT WHITE SHARK
Crooked financier Warren White had sought to escape jail by pleading insanity. Ironically, he had been driven truly insane in Arkham Asylum. Skin disfigured by frostbite, teeth filed to points (hence his moniker) White was now Gotham City's top crime boss.

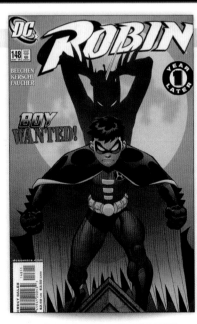

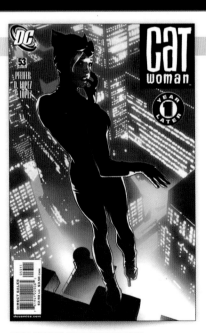

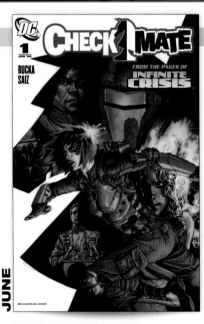

THREE'S A CROWD

Nightwing #118 ■ The mentally unbalanced Jason Todd temporarily gave up his Red Hood identity to assume the uniform of Nightwing in this "One Year Later" tie-in title written by Bruce Jones and drawn by Joe Dodd. Dick Grayson put a stop to Jason's deadly impersonation, but not before another person tried out the Nightwing costume—Dick's new girlfriend, Cheyenne Freemont, who debuted this issue. Born a metahuman, Cheyenne would wear the suit in issue #121 (August 2006), before quickly retiring from the Super Hero game.

FLYING IN A NEW DIRECTION

Robin #148 ■ Tim Drake's world changed drastically in this issue, which jumped ahead in time as part of the "One Year Later" event. The story featured Robin clad in a new red and black costume that seemed to take its color scheme from *The New Batman Adventures* cartoon. Robin's look would later be credited to honoring the colors of his friend, Superboy, who had died during *Infinite Crisis*. Written by Adam Beechen and drawn by Karl Kerschl, this comic wasted no time shaking things up, killing off the villains Lynx and Nyssa Raatko.

THE NEW CATWOMAN

Catwoman #53 ■ Selina Kyle's life had changed dramatically in this "One Year Later" tie-in title written by Will Pfeifer and pencilled by David Lopez. Giving birth to a baby girl that she named Helena, Selina passed on her Catwoman mantle to her longtime friend Holly Robinson. As readers puzzled over the mystery of who could be the father of Selina Kyle's child, Holly began her career as the new Catwoman. She first clashed with Wonder Woman villain Angle Man and then, in the following issue, with the latest incarnation of the villain Film Freak.

LONG LIVE THE QUEEN

Checkmate #1 ■ In *Detective Comics* #774 (November 2002), Bruce Wayne's former bodyguard Sasha Bordeaux was recruited into the government organization Checkmate after being wrongly convicted of involvement in the murder of Vesper Fairchild. Fans caught a glimpse of Sasha's new life as a superspy in 2005's *The O.M.A.C. Project* miniseries, but in this new ongoing title written by Greg Rucka and illustrated by Jesus Saiz, Sasha would really get her chance to shine as the Black Queen of Checkmate's chess-like structure.

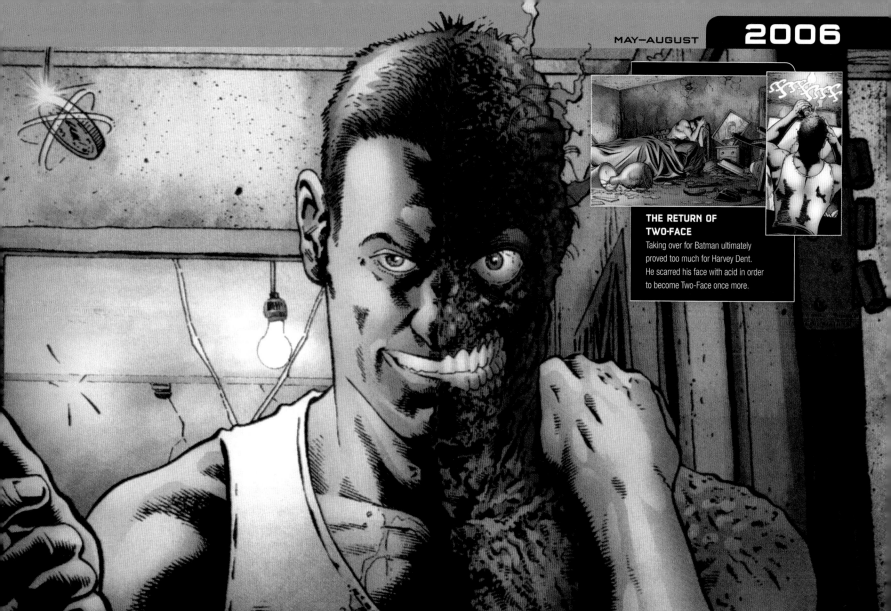

THE RETURN OF TWO-FACE
Taking over for Batman ultimately proved too much for Harvey Dent. He scarred his face with acid in order to become Two-Face once more.

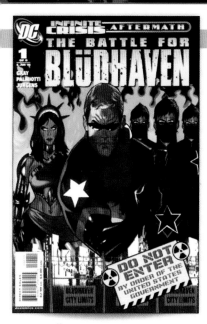

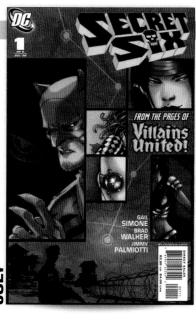

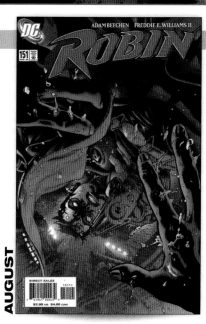

BAD BLÜD
Infinite Crisis Aftermath: The Battle for Blüdhaven #1 ▪ In the pages of *Infinite Crisis* #4 (March 2006), the giant chemical monster known as Chemo was dropped on an unsuspecting Blüdhaven, killing millions of people and effectively rendering the city an uninhabitable wasteland. In this six-issue series, writers Justin Gray and Jimmy Palmiotti and artists Dan Jurgens and Gordon Purcell examined the ruins of Nightwing's former hometown. This series starred the Teen Titans as well as many Outsiders-related characters.

SIX SHOOTERS
Secret Six #1 ▪ Spinning out of the events of the Villains United miniseries and the *Infinite Crisis* miniseries came this six-issue series by writer Gail Simone and artist Brad Walker. Featuring Catman (wearing a new, white, snow-camouflage costume in this issue) and Deadshot, this series also included new team member Jervis Tetch. Seemingly developing mind-controlling abilities, Tetch was left for dead by his cutthroat teammates at this series' end. This story also introduced Cheshire's baby, the father of whom was none other than Catman himself.

A DODGY SOCIAL LIFE
Robin #151 ▪ Writer Adam Beechen and series regular artist Freddie E. Williams II introduced a new annoyance into Robin's life: wannabe Super Hero Dodge. Possessing teleportation powers, Dodge continued to pop in and out of Robin's life, although clearly not welcome there. On the flipside, the previous issue debuted a much more welcome presence in Robin's life, love interest Zoanne Wilkins. Tim finally dated her in issue #159 (April 2007), only to see the party crashed by another new annoyance, a super-villain named Jitter.

STRUCK BY WONDER
Teen Titans #37 ▪ In the wake of Superboy's tragic death during the *Infinite Crisis* miniseries, the Boy of Steel's former girlfriend Wonder Girl and his best friend Robin were both having quite a hard time adjusting to their loss. In this issue by writer Geoff Johns and penciller Tony S. Daniel, Robin and Wonder Girl's grief led to the beginnings of a romance between the two teens, one that would not end until issue #55 (March 2008). Johns and artist Carlos Ferreira introduced Talon, the partner to Earth-Three's Owlman, in the following issue.

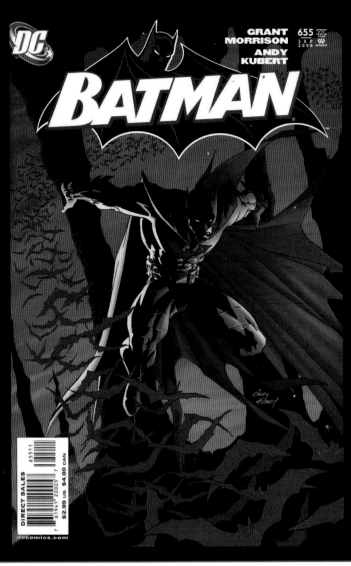

GRANT
MORRISON
655

ANDY
KUBERT

BATMAN AND SON
BATMAN #655

The character of Damian Wayne was introduced in this issue. He would have a far-reaching impact on the Dark Knight's world.

With this issue, drawn by Andy Kubert, writer Grant Morrison would begin a seven-year stint chronicling the adventures of the Caped Crusader. Originally planning it as a simple story arc, Morrison soon realized he had a much larger story to tell.

Damian Wayne was Batman and Talia al Ghūl's son—perhaps the same child mentioned in Mike W. Barr and Jerry Bingham's *Batman: Son of the Demon* hardcover (1987). Damian was raised via test tube, in order to be the perfect heir for Rā's al Ghūl's corrupt empire.

After Batman battled Talia's Man-Bat army, the villainess left Damian in the Dark Knight's care. Soon the headstrong, assassin-trained Damian defeated Robin and took his place. He also snuck out and killed the super-villain the Spook. After foiling Talia's latest terrorist scheme, Batman saw Damian return to his mother's side, leaving the Dark Knight with more questions than answers.

Showcasing a new version of the Batcave (complete with poles like the classic 1960s TV show), and Batmobile, a rocket, and a parachute costume for Batman, this four-issue arc also introduced Bruce Wayne love interest Jezebel Jet.

NOW WE SHALL SAY HELLO
In this issue, readers were only vouchsafed a glimpse of Damian Wayne as he stood in the shadows of Talia's army of Ninja Man-Bats.

ORIGINS AND ENDINGS
52 Series #21 ● In this issue of *52*, written by the braintrust of Grant Morrison, Greg Rucka, Mark Waid and Geoff Johns and drawn by Keith Giffen and Joe Bennett, readers met the third Blockbuster. While this issue heralded a new beginning, there were plenty of endings in issue #25 (October 2006), drawn by Joe Bennett, Dale Eaglesham, Phil Jimenez, and Patrick Olliffe, when crime boss Bruno Mannheim killed several Batman villains: Mirage, Kiteman, and the Sewer King (a character who oddly enough made his comic book debut in that same issue).

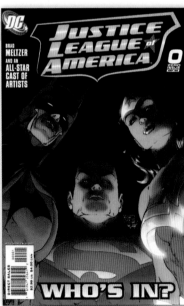

HISTORY IN THE MAKING
Justice League of America #0 ● The newest incarnation of the Justice League would begin the following month thanks to the writing of Brad Meltzer and the pencilling of Ed Benes. The team would include not only Batman, but also former Outsiders Black Lightning and Geo-Force. Before embarking on this new era, however, Meltzer delivered this stand-alone, flashback tale that reestablished the League's original founders as Superman, Wonder Woman, and Batman, and reexamined their past, present and future.

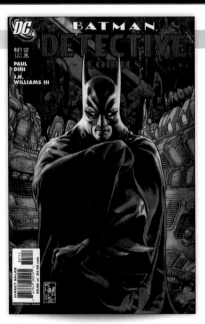

NEW VILLAINS
Detective Comics #821 ● Writer Paul Dini came aboard *Detective Comics* as its new ongoing writer with this issue. Overflowing with new characters and ideas, Dini teamed with artist J. H. Williams III to invent the thieving villain Façade. In the very next issue, Dini and artist Don Kramer would introduce Roxy Rocket to the DC Universe, a high-flying villainess who committed her crimes aboard a small, flying rocket. Roxy Rocket first appeared on *The New Batman Adventures* cartoon, and her roots in animation mirrored those of Dini himself.

DARK VENGEANCE!
Birds of Prey #96 ● While writer Gail Simone and artist Paulo Sequeira may have led audiences to believe that a new Batgirl had arrived in the pages of *Birds of Prey* in this issue's final sequence, the character they were truly introducing was a far cry from the classic version. Originally imitating Batgirl, the heroine in question, real name Charlotte "Charlie" Gage-Radcliffe, later adopted the name Misfit. A lighthearted teleporter with a battle cry of "Dark vengeance," Misfit would soon force her way into Oracle's inner circle.

JUST JOKING AROUND
The story began with the Joker fighting a mysterious Batman imposter with the aid of a new Joker-themed helicopter. The Joker then took a bullet to the head just as the real Batman arrived to take down his imitator.

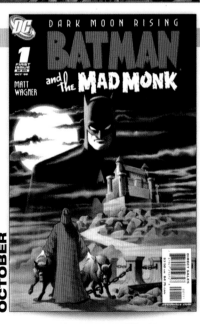

OCTOBER

THE MOON OF THE MONK

Batman and the Mad Monk #1 ▪ The second in his "Dark Moon Rising" series, writer/artist Matt Wagner dug up another Golden Age gem in the person of the Mad Monk in this six-issue follow up to *Batman and the Monster Men*. Elaborating on the vampiric Monk and his female partner, Dala, this series dealt with his cult of would-be vampire followers. Batman ended the Monk's campaign with the help of a terror-inspiring Batmobile, but a romance between Julie Madison and Bruce Wayne couldn't survive the story's traumatic events.

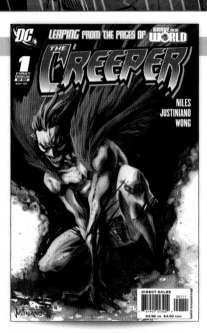

THE CREEPER GETS THE JOKE

The Creeper #1 ▪ Writer Steve Niles re-envisioned the Creeper in this six-issue series. Pencilled by Justiniano and Steve Scott, this new version of Jack Ryder's alter ego debuted in the special *Brave New World* #1 (August 2006). Talk show host Ryder became the Creeper when he was injected by Dr. Vincent Yatz with an experimental serum that had been partially made with the Joker's Joker Venom. This series also introduced the new Gotham City villain Axeman in issue #2 (November 2006).

DECEMBER

NIGHTWING'S NEW YORK

Nightwing #125 ▪ Now that he had moved back to New York City in *Nightwing* #118 (May 2006), Dick Grayson was once again in the city he called home during his long tenure with the New Teen Titans. So it seemed only natural that former Titans writer Marv Wolfman became Grayson's new scribe as of this comic, alongside artists Dan Jurgens and Norm Rapmund. Wolfman introduced new villain Raptor in this issue, as well as the killers known as the Bride and Groom in issues #128 (March 2007) and #129 (April), respectively.

ALSO THIS YEAR

January—*Robin* #144: Tim Drake faced the new threat of segmented villain Tapeworm in this *The O.M.A.C. Project* tie-in.

February—*Robin* #145: This issue introduced the twelve angry men of villain team the Jury.

April—*Batman: Legends of the Dark Knight* #200: This longstanding Batman staple celebrated its bicentennial issue.

April—*Green Lantern* #9: Batman guest-starred in this issue that saw the Dark Knight try on a Green Lantern ring.

May—*Birds of Prey* #92: Black Canary's soon to be adopted daughter, Sin, debuted.

June—*Man-Bat* #1: this five-issue series starred Man-Bat, Batman, Hush, and the Flash villain Murmur.

November—*Krypto: The Superdog* #1: Ace, the Bat-Hound starred in the first issue of this six-issue animated tie-in Johnny DC title for younger readers.

December—*Detective Comics* #824: Narcoleptic villain Mr. ZZZ and the diminutive Little Italy debuted.

FINDING THE BATMAN

52 SERIES #47

While it continued to tell the stories of some of the more minor characters of the DC Universe, the weekly *52* maxiseries also took the Dark Knight on a spiritual journey.

As early as *52* #30 (November 2006), Batman became a major focus of this epic series. In that issue, by writers Geoff Johns, Grant Morrison, Greg Rucka and Mark Waid, breakdown artist Keith Giffen, and penciller Joe Bennett, readers glimpsed a brief history of the Caped Crusader, including him wearing a costume extremely similar to his suit used in *Detective Comics* #27 (May 1939), a touch that had previously been erased from continuity. After that, readers followed Bruce Wayne as he attempted to find himself and his resolve. Meeting with the mysterious Ten-Eyed Surgeons of the Empty Quarter, Bruce had his inner demons "sliced" away, cutting out all his paranoid, fearful urges he'd been allowing to corrupt his life in recent years.

By this issue, pencilled by Giuseppe Camuncoli, Batman had travelled to the mysterious city of Nanda Parbat, accompanied by Robin. There he participated in an ordeal called *Thörgal*, sealing himself inside a dark cave for seven days. When Bruce finally stepped out into daylight once again, having survived this trial, he was Batman once again —a new and improved version, ready to start over in Gotham City.

BATMAN RISES AGAIN
Bruce Wayne wasn't exactly a kinder Batman when he left Nanda Parbat, but he wasn't the often arrogant Dark Knight he had been. His paranoia had been stripped away and the the darkness cleansed from his soul.

2007

"Face down in blood and vomit... Must be a better way to strike terror into the hearts of criminals."
Batman, *Batman* #665

Batman was in need of a personality adjustment, and writer Grant Morrison was just the man for the job. Over the years, Batman had slowly gone from being a no-nonsense tactician to a cold, sometimes cruel, crime fighter. Morrison set out to reclaim the less grim adventurer spirit of 1970s comics, using the theory that Batman is always trying to improve himself. After giving Bruce Wayne the hero's journey he deserved in the pages of 2006's *52* maxiseries, Morrison developed Batman's people skills in the *Batman* title, giving the Caped Crusader a new outlook on life, but without diminishing his established character.

JANUARY

A NEW QUESTION

52 Series #38 • After forming a bond with her new mentor, the Question, Renee Montoya was distraught to lose him in this issue by writers Geoff Johns, Grant Morrison, Greg Rucka, and Mark Waid, breakdown artist Keith Giffen, and penciller Joe Bennett. The Question died before he could see the mystical land of Nanda Parbat. Penciller Giuseppe Camuncoli had Montoya arrive there and train with Richard Dragon in issue #41 (February 2007) before she adopted the mantle of the new Question in issue #48 (April 2007), pencilled by Darick Robertson.

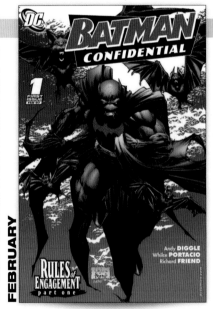

FEBRUARY

A TECHNICAL UPGRADE

Batman Confidential #1 • As *Batman: Legends of the Dark Knight* was ending publication in the following month with issue #214, *Batman Confidential* stepped up to replace the flashback title. This ongoing series started with a six-issue arc by writer Andy Diggle and artist Whilce Portacio. Their storyline reintroduced Lucius Fox, changing his backstory to better match the one used in the 2005 film *Batman Begins* by making him an expert at Wayne Aerospace. It also introduced a new Batmobile, the first Batplane, and a new Batcycle.

APRIL

THE SMILE WIDENS
BATMAN #663

Writer Grant Morrison continued his Batman saga in this special self-contained issue that was written entirely in prose.

Accompanied by disturbing digital imagery supplied by artist John Van Fleet, this issue was written in ten chapters, depicting the Joker's latest murder spree of his former clown lackeys. This story not only featured Harley Quinn in a primary role, but it also guest-starred some of the Joker's other past henchmen, including two familiar faces from the landmark graphic novel, *Batman: The Killing Joke* (July 1988). Highlighting Morrison's theory that the Joker changed his personality every few years, this story involved Joker showing off his new visage. A long cut at the corner of each side of his mouth made his grotesque smile all the more macabre. Apparently more psychotic than ever, the Joker even tried to kill Harley Quinn in the story's climax. However, Harley defended herself, apologizing to the Joker at the same time in a sad display of love. In the end, Batman dragged the defeated Joker away, knowing full well that he'd face the villain again one day.

DIGITAL JUSTICE
Artist John Van Fleet tried a new take on his customary style with his use of digital imagery in this story. The three-dimensional effect of Fleet's work really helped give the story more impact.

SLAYRIDE
Detective Comics #826 ▪ Writer Paul Dini proved his knack for creating memorable stories with this issue drawn by artist Don Kramer. When Robin wrecked his motorcycle while fleeing from criminals, he took refuge in a stranger's car. Unfortunately, that stranger was the Joker. In this tense thriller, Joker gassed Robin and strapped him in the passenger seat before driving around Gotham City, running down as many innocents as he could. After witnessing all too much horror, Robin finally managed to get free and stop the laughing maniac.

SELINA'S SECRET
Catwoman #62 ▪ Written by Will Pfeifer and drawn by David López, this issue of *Catwoman* was the one that many fans had waited months for. Because in this comic, Selina Kyle finally revealed that the father of her daughter Helena was Sam Bradley Jr., the son of Catwoman's friend and ex-lover, Slam Bradley. Sam had debuted in *Catwoman* #27 (March 2004) by writer Ed Brubaker and artist Paul Gulacy, and would later adopt the vigilante identity of Smart Bomb. He died soon after he and Selina had their romantic fling.

SCARFACE'S MOLL
Detective Comics #827 ▪ Writer Paul Dini and artist Don Kramer introduced a new Ventriloquist in this self-contained issue. Following in the footsteps of the deceased Arnold Wesker, female crime boss Peyton Riley adopted the damaged puppet Scarface and his personality. The Ventriloquist was an appropriate role for the villainess, as Peyton hid her own scarred visage behind her blonde hair. Mentally unbalanced and believing herself Scarface's lover, Peyton was later revealed to be the former fiancée of Tommy Elliot, the super-villain known as Hush.

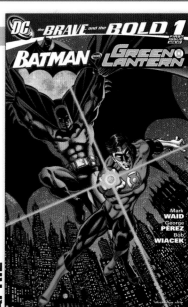

BRAVER AND BOLDER
The Brave and the Bold #1 ▪ Team-ups were once again fashionable thanks to writer Mark Waid and artist George Pérez. Unlike the original *The Brave and the Bold* series, this modern take often utilized multiple-issue story arcs. In another big change from the classic series, Batman did not appear in every issue. However, the Caped Crusader did manage to grab the title spot in four out of the first six issues, teaming with Green Lantern, Blue Beetle, and the Legion of Super-Heroes, and even merging temporarily with Fatal Five member Tharok.

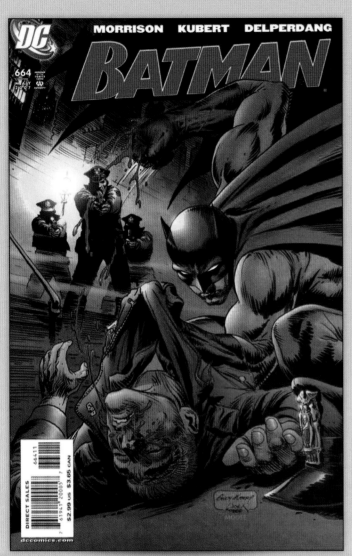

BATMAN OR BANE?

BATMAN #664

Writer Grant Morrison and artist Andy Kubert continued their run on *Batman*, introducing a second imposter wearing a Batman costume.

In this two-part tale, the mystery surrounding recent odd happenings in Gotham City deepened as the Dark Knight met the second of three imposters. A police officer, like the previous Batman impersonator glimpsed in *Batman* #655 (September 2006), this "Batman" had been killing prostitutes while pumped up on the drug Venom and Hugo Strange's monster serum. Looking more like Bane than his namesake, this twisted "Batman" trounced the Dark Knight, leaving him barely able to trudge to his penthouse in the city and regroup. In the next issue, Robin mowed down this imposter with a motorcycle before Batman took on the vicious brute and finally overcame him.

NOT FULLY FOCUSED

Batman was distracted when he first encountered this new threat, explaining his quick defeat at the hands of this imitator. He was thinking back to the first Batman imposter, and more than that, his Black Casebook, a notebook detailing unexplained experiences and past missions.

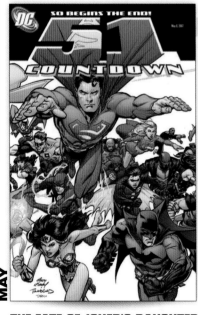

THE FATE OF JOKER'S DAUGHTER

Countdown #51 ▪ In this new weekly series, birthed from the success of DC's previous 52 series, writer Paul Dini headed a team of writers and artists, counting backwards to DC's newest epic crossover miniseries, *Final Crisis*, which would begin the following year. This first issue featured a script by Dini and pencils by Jesús Saiz, and saw the death of Duela Dent, the sometime hero, sometime villain also known as the Joker's Daughter and Harlequin. Soon after, it was revealed that the mysterious Duela was actually a citizen from Earth-Three.

ROBIN AND BATGIRL

Nightwing Annual #2 ▪ Dick Grayson and Barbara Gordon's romance was examined in this flashback tale, written by Marc Andreyko and pencilled by Joe Bennett. In *Nightwing* #117 (April 2006), by writer Devin Grayson and artist Brad Walker, Nightwing proposed to Oracle. In the next issue, a year had passed owing to the "One Year Later" event, and Dick was dating a new young woman, Cheyenne Freemont. This issue revealed why Barbara had rejected Dick's proposal, while portraying the history of their love affair.

THE RETURN OF THE CLUB

Batman #667 ▪ Writer Grant Morrison and artist J.H. Williams revitalized the 1950s concept of the International Club of Heroes when Batman and Robin headed to the island of reclusive millionaire Jonathan Mayhew in this three-issue story. Each hero was depicted in a different art style, and most in updated costumes. This murder mystery introduced criminal organization the Black Glove and its shadowy leader, soon revealed as Dr. Hurt. The story also featured a corrupt Wingman, working for John Mayhew, murder his former friends Legionary and Dark Ranger.

A MAGICAL CHILDHOOD

Detective Comics #833 ▪ As he had done in *Batman: The Animated Series*, writer Paul Dini delved into Batman's boyhood and his past with the magical hero Zatara. With the help of artist Don Kramer in this two-part story, Dini revealed that Zatara's daughter, Zatanna, had been a childhood friend of Bruce Wayne's, helping him to deal with his parents' murder. Bruce would later be trained in part by Zatara, while Zatanna would go on to become a Justice League member, even flirting with the idea of a romance with the Dark Knight.

JULY

A BRAVE NEW BATMAN

BATMAN #666

The future of a Gotham City protected by Damian Wayne as Batman was glimpsed in this stand-alone issue that teased quite a few new Batman villains.

This self-contained issue written by Grant Morrison and illustrated by Andy Kubert starred Damian Wayne as an adult Batman of the future battling a devil-like figure in a Batman costume (later revealed to be the third Batman imposter from our era). In this possible future, Damian donned a Batman costume in order to mete out his own harsh brand of justice to the villains of Gotham City. Barbara Gordon was Gotham City's commissioner of police, resolved to bring Batman in. While the story mostly focused on a showdown between Damian and the Batman imposter, it also introduced villains Morrison would later introduce into regular continuity: Professor Pyg, Phosphorus Rex, Jackanapes, Max Roboto, and Flamingo.

MORRISON KUBERT DELPERDANG

666 JUL 2007

BATMAN

DIRECT SALES

$2.99 US $3.65 CAN

A FUTURISTIC BATMOBILE

In this story, Batman piloted a Batmobile that resembled a bobsled. Damian had very little in common with his father Bruce Wayne, apart from a similar taste in uniforms.

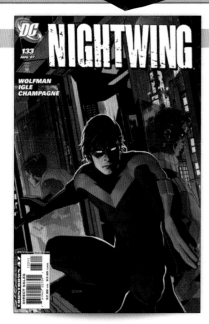

WOLFMAN IGLE CHAMPAGNE

NIGHTWING

133 AUG 07

OCTOBER

BEDARD SCOTT HAZLEWOOD

BIRDS of PREY

109

MARRY GREEN ARROW?! ARE YOU SERIOUS?!!

DIRECT SALES

$2.99 US $3.65 CAN

DECEMBER

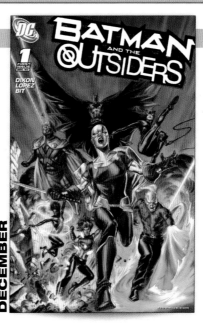

BATMAN AND THE OUTSIDERS

1 FIRST ISSUE

DIXON LOPEZ BIT

STAYING VIGILANT

Nightwing #133 ▪ This tale was a blast from the past in more ways than one for Dick Grayson. He came face to face once more with his first love from his teenage days as Robin—treacherous femme fatale Liu, who made her debut in this issue. Written by Marv Wolfman and illustrated by Jamal Igle, this issue also announced that a new Vigilante was waiting in the shadows. After coming into conflict with Nightwing, the Vigilante would soon move to Gotham City and even earn his own ongoing series in February 2009.

WINGING IT

Birds of Prey #109 ▪ With this issue, writer Tony Bedard stepped up as the new regular *Birds of Prey* writer, accompanied by Nicola Scott as penciller. However, after Bedard's first four issues, writer Sean McKeever came onboard the title for five issues, bringing with him the new Super Hero, Infinity, in issue #114 (March 2008). When Bedard returned, he would quickly help the Birds improve their status quo. By issue #119 (August 2008) the team had relocated to Platinum Flats, California, to start a new, exciting chapter in their lives.

OUTSIDERS TO THE OUTSIDERS

Batman and the Outsiders #1 ▪ While writer Chuck Dixon and artist Julian Lopez's new incarnation of the Outsiders was closer to the original than the previous version, this new Batman strike force was still quite different from Batman's original 1983 team. Comprised of core members Batman, Katana, Thunder, Grace, Batgirl, Metamorpho, Geo-Force, and new character REMAC, this new team often added extra muscle on missions, including the likes of Catwoman, Green Arrow, Nightwing, and Martian Manhunter.

ALSO THIS YEAR

January—*Batman* #659: This four-part arc featured aptly named new villain Grotesk.

January—*Birds of Prey* #100: This extra-sized anniversary issue introduced an old rival of Oracle's, the new Spy Smasher, Katarina Armstrong.

May—*Detective Comics* #829: The terrorist Vox debuted in this two-part tale.

September—*Black Canary* #1: This four-issue series featured the villain Merlyn.

September—*Batman Confidential* #7: A retelling of the Joker's origin made him a criminal before his transformation.

October—*Batman Annual* #26: Rā's al Ghūl's origin was retold and White Ghost, Rā's son Dusan al Ghūl, debuted.

November—*Superman/Batman* #40: Batman shared a brief romantic moment with Bekka, wife of Orion, in part four of the six-issue "Torment" epic.

December—*Gotham Underground* #1: The Batman Family battled criminals looking to muscle in on territory recently vacated by deceased gang boss Black Mask.

THE DEMON'S HEAD RETURNS

THE RESURRECTION OF ROBIN #168

The world believed him dead, but Rā's al Ghūl had found a way to keep his soul alive. If he wanted it to stay that way, he'd have to transfer his spirit into a body of flesh and blood.

In *Batman* #670 (December 2007), the prelude issue to the "Resurrection of Rā's al Ghūl" crossover by writer Grant Morrison and artist Tony Daniel, Rā's had looked to Damian Wayne as his most logical option as a host for his soul. However, Damian had escaped his grandfather's grasp and turned to his father, Batman, for help.

Writer Peter Milligan and artist Freddie E. Williams II continued the tale with this issue, which introduced the villain Detonator, an assassin working for the Sensei, the martial artist controlling a splinter group of the League of Assassins. Batman was soon drawn into an adventure that would see him don corrupting mystical armor known as the Suit of Sorrow. Also written by Fabian Nicieza and Paul Dini, and illustrated by Don Kramer, Ryan Benjamin, David Baldeón, and Carlos Rodriguez, this series would see Rā's return, albeit in the body of his secret offspring, his albino right-hand man, the White Ghost. This series also saw the return of the little known villains Silken Spider, Tiger Moth, and Dragonfly, and debuted a new Batman snowmobile as well as assassin Maduvu in *Nightwing* #138 (January 2008), and killers Shellcase and Razorburn in *Batman* #671 (January 2008).

THE WHITE GHOST
Unable to take Damian's form, Rā's decided to transfer his soul into his son, the mysterious White Ghost. A story very much about the father/son dynamic, this crossover also revealed that the Sensei was Rā's al Ghūl's own father.

2008

"You're wrong! Batman and Robin will never die!"

Batman, *Batman* #676

In 2008, Grant Morrison changed the Batman continuity in a way that had not been done since the days before *Crisis on Infinite Earths*. He stated that every Batman story had actually happened. As Morrison continued as the regular writer of Batman and developed the climactic "Batman: R.I.P." event, he began to refer to obscure incidents from Batman's life, such as some of the weirder sci-fi stories from the 1950s. In addition, previously forgotten characters such as the original Batwoman returned to continuity. This approach created a new landscape for the Caped Crusader that appealed to fans of the older material and current material alike.

THE FINAL COUNTDOWN
Countdown #14 ▪ As the weekly saga neared its conclusion, writers Paul Dini and Tony Bedard and pencillers Peter Woods and Tom Derenick gave Jason Todd a new identity, albeit briefly. He adopted the identity of Red Robin in an Alex Ross-designed costume that had debuted in the *Kingdom Come* miniseries (May 1996). An exploration of the DC multiverse, *Countdown* also gave birth to a series of specials that began this month, as well as a miniseries in February, *Countdown Arena*, that saw versions of Batman from different realities doing battle.

BOOSTER SHOT
Booster Gold #5 ▪ Time-traveling Super Hero Booster Gold did his best to save Barbara Gordon from the fate that she'd suffered in *Batman: The Killing Joke* (1988). With the help of writers Geoff Johns and Jeff Katz and penciller Dan Jurgens, Booster Gold went back in time to stop the Joker from severely injuring Barbara Gordon. Instead, he found himself bested by the Clown Prince of Crime, despite repeatedly returning to that fateful night. Booster soon realized that some events, no matter how tragic, could not be altered in the timestream.

FEBRUARY

AND THEN THERE WERE THREE

BATMAN #672

The third and final Batman impersonator debuted in this three-part story drawn by Tony Daniel that continued writer Grant Morrison's epic Batman narrative.

A former cop, Michael Lane wore an altered version of the Batman suit when he took Commissioner Gordon hostage and successfully defeated Batman. Seeing a vision of Bat-Mite, Batman began to take a trip through his subconscious and his personal history. Through this narrative vehicle, Morrison was able to change the details of the death of Joe Chill, revealing a new version of Batman's early days in which the hero tracked down his parents' murderer while wearing a costume very similar to the one that debuted in the pages of *Detective Comics* #27 (May 1939).

By the third chapter in this story, Batman awoke as Lane's prisoner and discovered that the Batman impersonator was one of three cops brainwashed by Dr. Simon Hurt, a man the Dark Knight had considered an ally when they originally met in *Batman* #156 (June 1963). Batman escaped, but so did Lane, leaving Batman to wonder if there was some sinister force pulling these impersonators' strings.

THE THIRD BATMAN
The final Batman imposter wore the costume of the demonic villain from *Batman* #666 (July 2007). While the character had a decidedly modern look, the bulk of this storyline dealt with elements from the Batman comics of the 1950s mostly forgotten by continuity—until now.

MARCH

GLOBETROTTER

Detective Comics #840 ■ It seemed there was no slowing down writer Paul Dini's imagination, especially when combined with the talents of new series artist Dustin Nguyen. As the two began their partnership in this issue, they debuted a new villain, the map-obsessed Globe. In the following issue, they introduced the handywoman of deathtraps known as the Carpenter, a member of the Wonderland Gang. Not to be outdone, writer Peter Milligan paired with Nguyen on *Detective Comics* #842 (May 2008), to introduce yet another new rogue, Gotham Jack.

APRIL

RETURN OF THE WRATH

Batman Confidential #13 ■ In the third arc of this flashback series, Batman faced the heir to the Wrath, a villain who had debuted in *Batman Special* #1 (April 1984). Written by Tony Bedard and pencilled by Rags Morales, this four-issue story was set in the years when Dick Grayson was still wearing his original Nightwing uniform. The new Wrath in this tale began his crime career where his predecessor left off, setting his sights on Commissioner Gordon. However, he too proved no match for Gotham City's original Caped Crusader.

TERROR TITANS

Teen Titans #56 ■ While the DC Universe had long had its own Clock King, that super-villain had had very little to do with Batman. However, when *Batman: The Animated Series* debuted a new Clock King named Temple Fugate, readers began to confuse the two very different characters. In this issue written by Sean McKeever and illustrated by Eddy Barrows, a Fugate-like version of Clock King made his comic debut, challenging Robin, Ravager, and their allies alongside a new version of the contortionist assassin villain Copperhead.

JUNE

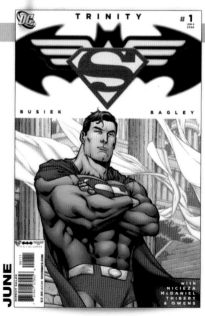

THREE FOR ALL

Trinity #1 ■ Following the weekly series *52* and *Countdown* came DC's newest weekly 52-issue title, Trinity. Written by Kurt Busiek and illustrated by Mark Bagley, this series examined a world in which Superman, Batman, and Wonder Woman were elevated to the status of gods. Trinity also featured back-up tales, with the added help of writer Fabian Nicieza and artist Scott McDaniel, among other artists. Showcasing Earth-Three's Riddler, a character called Enigma who had debuted as the Quizmaster in *JLA Secret Files and Origins* #4 (November 2004).

BATMAN: R.I.P.

BATMAN #676

In what would be the ending of merely the first of three major acts in writer Grant Morrison's Batman opus, the crossover "Batman: R.I.P." began with this issue.

While the titles *Nightwing*, *Robin*, *Batman and the Outsiders*, and *Detective Comics* all boasted the "R.I.P." logo on their masthead, the main story of the "Batman: R.I.P." epic was confined to the pages of *Batman*, and was delivered by Morrison and artist Tony Daniel.

In the previous issue of *Batman*, Bruce Wayne's love interest, Jezebel Jet, discovered the playboy's alter ego as the Dark Knight while Nightwing and Robin faced a minor league villain called the Ray-Gun Raider. Following quickly on its heels, this issue introduced the Club of Villains, the center of the organization known as the Black Glove. Led by Dr. Simon Hurt, the Club included hunchback Le Bossu, mime Pierrot Lunaire, the disturbing Charlie Caligula, the poisonous Scorpiana, the powerful King Kraken, the Australian criminal Swagman, and the deadly El Sombrero, whose costume had been worn by John Mayhew in *Batman* #669 (November 2007). But as the story continued and Batman welcomed Jezebel Jet into his Batcave, a graffiti image on the Batcomputer that read "Zur-En-Arrh" would change everything.

Years ago, Batman began keeping his "black casebooks," journals filled with the extraordinary events for which he had no explanation. Fearing that one day his mind might become unbalanced, he created the trigger phrase "Zur-En-Arrh" that would eliminate every facet of his personality that wasn't entirely Batman. With his "secret self" now unlocked, Batman donned a bizarre purple costume, (a homage to one he had worn in *Batman* #113 back in January 1958), only to discover that Jezebel Jet was actually a member of the Black Glove. With the help of Nightwing, Robin, and the Club of Heroes, Batman triumphed over the villains and chased the fleeing Dr. Hurt, who tried to convince him that he was his father, Dr. Thomas Wayne. The story ended as mysteriously as it had begun. Both Dr. Hurt and Batman were aboard a helicopter that came down in flames in the sea near Gotham City, seemingly killing them both.

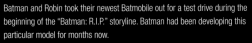

TEST DRIVE
Batman and Robin took their newest Batmobile out for a test drive during the beginning of the "Batman: R.I.P." storyline. Batman had been developing this particular model for months now.

THE BLACK GLOVE
Dr. Hurt's Club of Villains included: (from left to right)
Charlie Caligula, King Kraken, El Sombrero, Pierrot
Lunaire, Dr. Hurt, Scorpiana, and Swagman.

RECRUITMENT JOKE
Playing out murder fantasies
in his mind, the Joker was
persuaded by the Black Glove
to become one of its members.
This led to a disturbing
showdown at Arkham Asylum
between the Clown Prince of
Crime and the Dark Knight. During
their fight, Joker sliced his own
tongue down the center, giving
him a serpentine appearance.

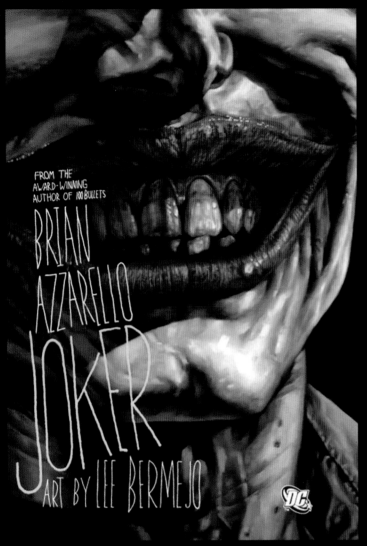

FROM THE AWARD-WINNING AUTHOR OF *100 BULLETS*

BRIAN AZZARELLO

JOKER

ART BY LEE BERMEJO

SETTING THE JOKER FREE
JOKER GRAPHIC NOVEL #1

In this hardcover graphic novel, a crafty Joker took steps to reclaim the criminal underworld after his release from Arkham Asylum.

Writer Brian Azzarello and artist Lee Bermejo took on the Clown Prince of Crime when they crafted this hardcover graphic novel about the Joker's latest release from Arkham Asylum. A sequel of sorts to their *Lex Luthor: Man of Steel* miniseries from 2005, *Joker* employed a similar tone and visual style, yet was told in a more realistic fashion. Shrouded in a noir Gotham City, and told from the perspective of new henchman Johnny Frost, the story centered around the Joker regaining his crime empire, initially by recruiting Killer Croc and Harley Quinn to his cause.

Reimagined by Bermejo, the Joker in this tale was a cunning crime boss, whose chaotic behavior greatly disturbed Frost, eventually driving him to violently lose control. Dark and relentless, *Joker* gave readers a new take on the power structure of Gotham City's underworld and, before the story's final confrontation between the title character and his nemesis Batman, showcased redesigns for many of the Dark Knight's Rogues Gallery.

ART OF THE CLOWN
Bermejo's use of shadows and hard, angular shapes added to the stylish noir feeling of this graphic novel.

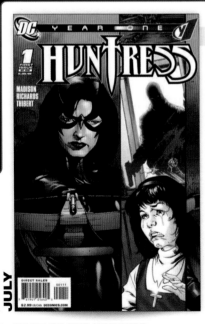

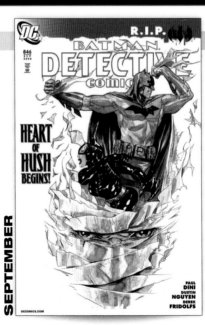

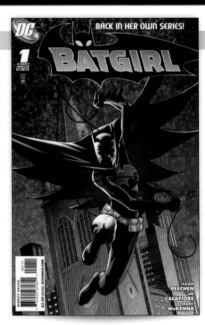

YEAR OF THE UPDATES
Huntress: Year One #1 ▪ To breathe new life into some longstanding characters, DC Comics released a group of six-issue "Year One" miniseries, updating each character's origins. Huntress' origin was examined by writer Ivory Madison and artist Cliff Richards. Also receiving new origins were Black Lightning, in a series written by Jen Van Meter and drawn by Cully Hamner, Metamorpho, courtesy of writer/artist Dan Jurgens and artists Jesse Delperdang and Mike Norton; and the Teen Titans, thanks to writer Amy Wolfram and artist Karl Kerschl.

THE SPOILS OF WAR
Robin/Spoiler Special #1 ▪ Writer Chuck Dixon had returned as Robin's regular writer with *Robin* #170 (March 2008). Teasing the return of Spoiler by introducing new vigilante Violet in that issue with artist Chris Batista, Dixon revealed Stephanie Brown to be alive in *Robin* #172 (May 2008). By #174 (July 2008), Dixon explained that Dr. Leslie Thompkins had faked Spoiler's death to get Stephanie away from the dangers of Gotham City. This issue, drawn by Rafael Albuquerque and Víctor Ibáñez, explained Stephanie's return.

HEART OF HUSH
Detective Comics #846 ▪ Billed as a tie-in with the "Batman: R.I.P." epic, this issue began writer Paul Dini and artist Dustin Nguyen's "Heart of Hush" story, in which Tommy Elliot returned to plague Bruce Wayne, by literally removing Catwoman's heart. Introducing the interesting new rogue Dr. Aesop at the story's beginning, this five-issue arc revealed new insight into Hush's origin as Batman saved Selina's life and discovered that Hush had endured extensive plastic surgery in an attempt to look exactly like Bruce Wayne.

DADDY'S GIRL
Batgirl #1 ▪ While her ongoing series had been canceled, that didn't stop Cassandra Cain from going on one final self-titled outing in Gotham City in the form of this six-issue miniseries written by Adam Beechen and illustrated by Jim Calafiore. Explaining Batgirl's recent manipulation by Deathstroke, this series also introduced another of David Cain's students, the vigilante named Marque. But more importantly, in this series' final issue, Bruce Wayne offered to adopt Cassandra as his own daughter, officially cementing her place in the Batman family.

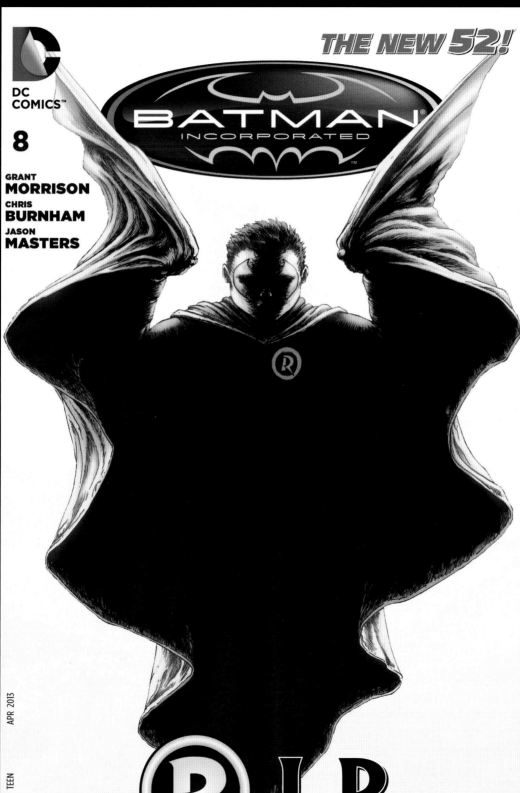

WHAT'S UP, DOC?

BATMAN/DOC SAVAGE #1
This one-shot introduced an alternate universe's version of the Batman, a gun-toting Dark Knight living in a pulp-styled reality.

In the first scene of this stand-alone special writer Brian Azzarello and artist Phil Noto proved that their Batman was a far cry from the Bruce Wayne of the main DC Universe. Because in that very scene, Batman pulled two handguns from his shoulder harnesses and engaged in a gun battle.

This issue was a precursor to the six-issue miniseries called *First Wave* (May 2010) a pulpish examination of many classic characters including Batman, Doc Savage, and the Spirit. This particular tale introduced Bruce Wayne to Doc Savage, the touted adventurer known as the Man of Bronze. Crossing paths with Savage at a party, Bruce threw a punch at him, in order to learn a little more about this man's fighting style. He soon got the chance to find out even more when the two became unlikely allies by the story's end.

The story continued into the pages of the *First Wave* miniseries thanks to the efforts of Azzarello, now paired with artist Rags Morales. A comic spanning from actual jungles to concrete jungles, *First Wave* felt like a modern take on a classic adventure movie serial.

THE BRAVE AND THE BRONZE
When Doc Savage promised to rid Gotham City of its mysterious Batman, Bruce Wayne sized up the adventurer at a party before breaking into his hotel to gain more info on the hero.

2010

"He was my brother, my best friend. I had a job to do and I never let him down."

Dick Grayson about Bruce Wayne, *Batman and Robin #7*

Readers were certainly enjoying exploring the possibilities of a DC Universe without Bruce Wayne, but fans knew it was only a matter of time before the original Batman appeared to claim his mantle. But before the real Dark Knight returned, readers were treated to plenty of fun "false alarms." The "Blackest Night" miniseries event introduced readers to the reanimated corpse of a faux Batman, a concept explored in the pages of *Batman and Robin*. Meanwhile, Bruce Wayne attempted to fight his way through time itself in the pages of *Batman: The Return of Bruce Wayne* as Grant Morrison wrapped up the second act of his epic story.

SPIDER INFESTATION
Red Robin #6 ▪ Red Robin crossed paths with Rā's al Ghūl's League of Assassins in this tale by writer Christopher Yost and artist Marcus To, in which the League was currently at war with enemies known as the Council of Spiders. After meeting new League member Expeditor in the previous issue, Red Robin met Council member Recluse in this tale, as well as members Sac and Goliath. The Council member known as the Wanderer debuted in this issue, while the rest of the Spiders (Wolf, Funnel, Widower, and Tangle) introduced themselves in the next issue.

STAY OF EXECUTION
Catwoman #83 ▪ In a creative Blackest Night tie-in event, several long-canceled ongoing series were "resurrected" for one final issue. Catwoman faced an undead Black Lantern Black Mask in her new final issue, by writer Tony Bedard and artists Fabrizio Fiorentino, Ibraim Roberson, and Marcos Marz. The Question also received a special new final issue—one that saw Renee Montoya battle a Black Lantern version of her former mentor Vic Sage, thanks to writers Dennis O'Neil and Greg Rucka, and penciller Denys Cowan.

BLACK LANTERN BATMAN

BLACKEST NIGHT #5

The apparent corpse of Bruce Wayne's
Batman was brought back to life
as a Black Lantern in this major
DC Universe event.

The bodies of the dead were rising all over the
DC Universe. Deceased Super Heroes and
super-villains alike were rising from their
graves as they were granted the dark powers
that came with wearing a Black Lantern ring.
Ominously, the villain helping to usher in all
this chaos, Green Lantern foe Black Hand,
had dug up Batman's skull in *Blackest Night
#0* (June 2009), a teaser for this upcoming
miniseries event by writer Geoff Johns and
artist Ivan Reis.

This eight-issue epic truly began with *Blackest Night* #1 (September
2009) as the Black Lanterns began to rise. By issue #3 (November 2009),
the reanimated corpses of villains like Copperhead, Deacon Blackfire, the
Ventriloquist, and Magpie had joined the Black Lantern Corps, and caused
trouble for the current Batman, Dick Grayson, in the pages of the three-
issue spin-off *Blackest Night: Batman* miniseries that began the
previous month thanks to writer Peter Tomasi and artist Adrian Syaf.
A reanimated Azrael made his way into issue #4,
leading up to this issue that saw the birth of Black Lantern
Batman. The living would soon triumph over the dead,
but the mystery of Batman's corpse would remain
just that for the time being.

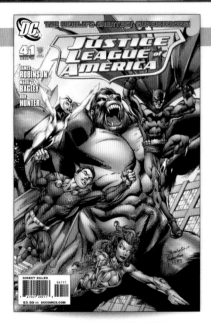

IN THE BATMAN'S LEAGUE

Justice League of America #41 ● Dick
Grayson discovered that more came with the Batman
mantle than simply his responsibilities in Gotham City
in this tale when the hero joined the Justice League
of America. Written by James Robinson and drawn by
Mark Bagley, this issue saw Grayson officially accept
League membership when his former Titans ally,
Donna Troy, recruited him. Along with Legion hero
Mon-El who took the place of Superman, Grayson,
and Donna formed a next generation trinity as the
heart of this newest League incarnation.

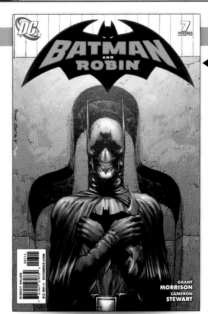

BACK FROM THE DEAD?

Batman and Robin #7 ● In this three-issue
story by writer Grant Morrison and artist Cameron
Stewart, Dick Grayson took what he assumed to be
Batman's corpse to a Lazarus Pit, meeting Batwoman
there in the process. Instead of bringing Batman back
from the grave as he intended, Grayson instead
unwittingly resurrected a Batman clone created in the
workshop of Darkseid's lackeys. After which Dick
managed to resurrect Batwoman as well when she
was mortally injured, and the two teamed up to take
down this perverse version of Batman.

SPECIAL FEATURE

RISING AGAIN

Darkseid's men created an army of
Batman clones to do their master's
bidding. It was the corpse of one of
those clones that Superman found in
Final Crisis #6 (January 2009), and
that Dick Grayson finally brought back
to life via a Lazarus Pit in *Batman and
Robin* #8 (April 2009).

THE MAN BEHIND THE MASK

Batman #697 ● The new Black Mask revealed
his secret identity in this issue by writer/artist Tony
Daniel. After keeping fans in the dark since his
Batman: Battle for the Cowl series of the previous
year, Daniel showed audiences that the mystery man
behind the mask was none other than Jeremiah
Arkham, finally pushed over the ledge of sanity. With
a little help from the Network, Batman defeated Black
Mask only to face a new threat in the following issue
in the form of the villain Blackspell in a tale by Daniel
and artist Guillem March.

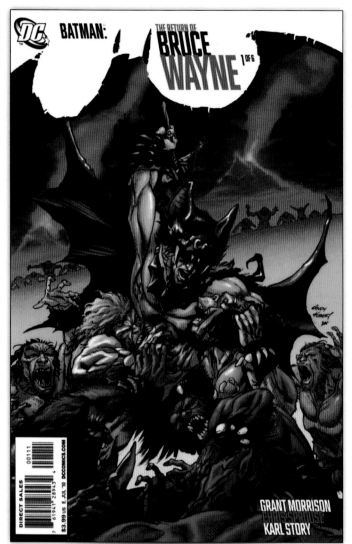

THE "MAN OF BATS"

BATMAN: THE RETURN OF BRUCE WAYNE #1

Not even time itself could stop the pure willpower that is Batman. Displaced in time by Darkseid during the *Final Crisis* miniseries, Batman fought his way through the ages to return to his proper era.

In this six-issue series by writer Grant Morrison and pencillers Chris Sprouse, Frazer Irving, Yanick Paquette, Georges Jeanty, Ryan Sook, Pere Perez, and Lee Garbett, readers were finally updated on what had been happening to Bruce Wayne since Darkseid shot him with his fabled Omega Effect. Believed dead in his own time, Wayne had actually traveled back to a prehistoric era. Called "Man of Bats" by the men of this time, Wayne fought the villain Vandal Savage, while dressed in the fur of a giant bat. After falling over a giant waterfall, however, Wayne woke up in a quite a different time period—a time of Pilgrims and witch hunts in early America.

Infused with the Omega energy, Wayne continued to jump through time, even as Superman, Green Lantern, and Booster Gold hunted for him, their adventures chronicled in the six-issue *Time Masters: The Vanishing Point* miniseries by writer/artist Dan Jurgens from September 2010. After battling pirates and cowboys, Wayne finally awoke in a time just after his parents had been killed, discovering a cult that involved Dr. Hurt, John Mayhew, and human sacrifice.

Jumping forward in time once more, Batman became saturated with Omega energy, and was rescued by Red Robin, Superman, Wonder Woman, and a few other allies. Batman was back, but he wasn't quite ready to leave the shadows yet.

GRANT MORRISON
CHRIS SPROUSE
KARL STORY

SAVAGE TIMES

A longtime enemy of many characters in the DC Universe including the Flash, Vandal Savage was an immortal who would go on to amass quite a great deal of power through the years. But as a simple caveman, he was no match for Batman.

JOINING THE FLOCK

Birds of Prey #1 • Newly resurrected hero Hawk and his longtime partner Dove entered the realm of Batman-supporting players. Starting in this issue, they joined the Birds of Prey in a new ongoing series that tied in to the events of the DC comics crossover maxiseries "Brightest Day." The team also included returning characters Oracle, Black Canary, Huntress, and Lady Blackhawk as writer Gail Simone and artist Ed Benes reestablished the team in Gotham City and introduced them to the villain known as the White Canary.

BEYOND THE CARTOON

Batman Beyond #1 • Terry McGinnis returned to comics in this six-issue series by writer Adam Beechen and artist Ryan Benjamin. Not quite based in the animated world of the cartoon with the same name, this series blended that version with the comic series, introducing characters like Hush into Batman Beyond's world, as well as a new Catwoman. In March 2011, Batman Beyond nabbed another chance at an ongoing series by the same creative team and even guest-starred with Superman Beyond in *Superman/Batman Annual* #4 (August 2010).

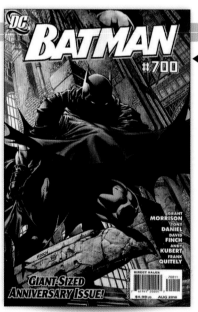

700 AND COUNTING

Batman #700 • In an extra-long anniversary issue written by Grant Morrison, artists Tony Daniel, Frank Quitely, Scott Kolins, Andy Kubert, and David Finch told three tales of Batmen past, present, and future. Bringing back 1950s Batman supporting character Professor Carter Nichols, Morrison also renamed the second Mad Hatter as Hatman in this tale that introduced the future threat of Two-Face-2. This issue included a gallery section featuring a variety of artists, a tour of the modern Batcave, and even a glimpse into several possible futures.

THE THREE BATMEN

Bruce Wayne, Dick Grayson, and Damian Wayne all shared the spotlight as Batman in the tales in this issue. By the comic's end, Damian Wayne was even shown in one of the possible futures as the mentor to Batman Beyond.

BRUCE'S SAFETY BELT
Bruce Wayne was understandably confused when he woke up in a prehistoric era. Luckily he had his wits about him, as well as his Utility Belt. Even during the challenging environment of the Dawn of Man, Batman kept calm and triumphed over adversity.

LOST AND FOUND
Red Hood: The Lost Days #1
The final missing secrets of Jason Todd's resurrection were revealed in this six-issue miniseries by writer Judd Winick and artists Pablo Raimondi, Cliff Richards, and Jeremy Haun. After rising from the grave thanks to Superboy Prime's alterations to the time stream, Jason's body was a wandering, near mindless soul. Talia al Ghūl brought Jason back to his true self via a dip in the Lazarus Pit and later even shared a brief romance with him in a story that saw Jason find renewed purpose as the Red Hood.

A HERO BY PROXY
Batgirl #12 ● Stephanie Brown got her own Oracle of sorts when Barbara Gordon's protégé, the Calculator's daughter Wendy Kuttler, became the new information guru called Proxy thanks to writer Bryan Q. Miller and artists Lee Garbett and Pere Perez. In a nod to the *Super Friends* show, Wendy had first debuted with her brother Marvin in *Teen Titans* #34 (May 2006). This wouldn't be the first time animated characters made their mark on Batgirl's series, as the Gray Ghost/Mad Bomber appeared in #9 (June 2010).

A CONTINUING ODYSSEY
Batman: The Odyssey #1 ● Writer/artist Neal Adams returned to the character of Batman with this series that took place in its own slightly altered continuity. Originally labeled as a 12-issue maxiseries, it was split into one six-issue miniseries, followed by another seven-issue miniseries that began in December 2011. In a world where Batman used a gun in an early adventure and Dick Grayson wore the Neal Adams-designed Robin costume, this series also starred another memorable Adams creation, Man-Bat.

THE MISSING CHAPTER
Batman #701 ● Even as he brought the Dark Knight back to the present in other titles, writer Grant Morrison returned to *Batman* for two issues to fill in audiences on what happened between the final pages of "Batman: R.I.P." and Batman's battle with Darkseid in *Final Crisis*. Drawn by Tony Daniel, the story began as Batman survived the helicopter crash with Dr. Hurt, and, after searching for the villain in a submarine, was asked by Superman to investigate the death of a New God. This led to his capture by Darkseid minions and the events of *Final Crisis*.

NOVEMBER

MAKING HER GETAWAY

Batman #703 ▪ The heir to the title Getaway Genius debuted in this stand-alone issue by writer Fabian Nicieza and artist Cliff Richards. Making her debut with the use of a gravity-defying sailboard, this new thief, who possessed invisible cloaking technology, was actually Olivia Reynolds, the daughter of the original Getaway Genius. Not to be outdone when it came to introducing new characters, writer/artist Tony S. Daniel debuted the vigilante Peacock in the following issue (January 2011) to kickstart his next story arc, "Eye of the Beholder."

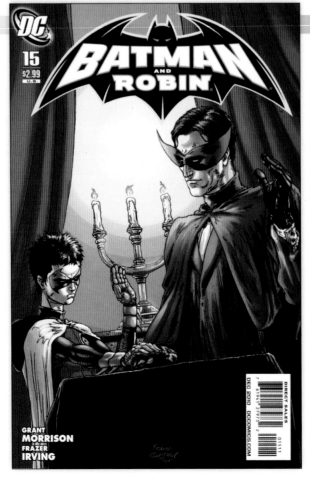

BATMAN RETURNS

Batman and Robin #15 ▪ In issue #10 of this series by writer Grant Morrison and Andy Clarke, Dick Grayson as Batman began to investigate clues around Wayne Manor that seemed to point to Bruce Wayne being alive. Soon, Grayson discovered a hidden chamber in the Manor just as the home went under attack by Dr. Hurt's forces. As the story continued and Frazer Irving took up the art chores with issue #13, Dr. Hurt seemed to get the upper hand. That is, until the true Batman arrived.

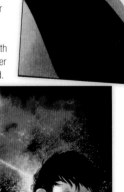

WHO IS DR. HURT?

It was revealed that Dr. Hurt was really Thomas Wayne, a black sheep of the Wayne family who lived in the 1760s and tried to summon a demon named Barbatos. Batman faced off with the villain in *Batman and Robin #16* (January 2011), featuring the art of Cameron Stewart, Christ Burnham and Frazer Irving, but it was the Joker who ended the threat of Dr. Hurt once and for all.

COMING HOME

BRUCE WAYNE: THE ROAD HOME: BATMAN AND ROBIN #1

Batman observed Gotham City from the shadows, discovering everything he had missed while being displaced in time.

"Bruce Wayne: The Road Home" was an event spread over eight one-shots with interlocking covers, each featuring a different Gotham City character or team of characters. Starting in this *Batman and Robin* issue, the story continued into *Red Robin*, *Batgirl*, *Outsiders*, *Catwoman*, *Commissioner Gordon*, *Oracle*, and *Rā's al Ghūl*. An event that reaffirmed the status quo of present-day Gotham City, these issues were written by Fabian Nicieza, Bryan Q. Miller, Mike W. Barr, Derek Fridolfs, Adam Beechen, and Marc Andreyko. They were drawn by Cliff Richards, Ramon Bachs, Pere Pérez, Javier Saltares, Peter Nguyen, Szymon Kudranski, Agustin Padilla, and Scott McDaniel.
In order to better spy on his allies and gain an assessment of their job performance, Bruce Wayne adopted the uniform and name of the Insider with the help of Red Robin. His new suit included technology that could make him appear invisible, teleport and fire heat vision and other forms of energy, as well as employ super-speed. As he revealed himself one by one to his friends and co-workers, Batman assessed his network and even managed to stop Rā's al Ghūl from killing Vicki Vale, although Vicki did learn the Dark Knight's secret identity in the process.

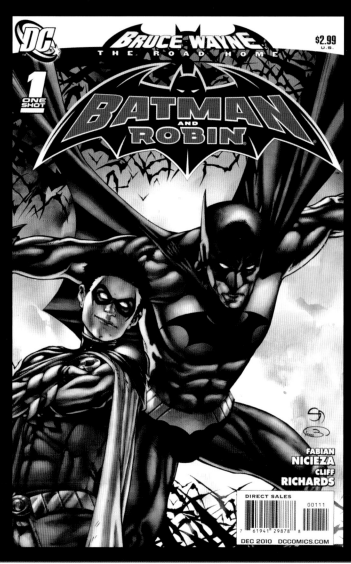

THE INSIDER

Bruce Wayne had always lived a secretive life. Even though he had become less paranoid and controlling in recent years, he still felt the need to observe his many allies without their knowing that Batman had returned to Gotham City. The high-tech Insider suit was his way to doing just that, although it didn't seem to fool those closest to him.

THE BRITISH BATMAN

Knight and Squire #1 ▪ The so-called Batman and Robin of England, the current Knight and the female Squire who'd made her first appearance in *JLA* #26 (February 1999), were given a bit more exposure in their own six-issue miniseries. Written by Paul Cornell and drawn by Jimmy Broxton, the story included many of the Knight's supporting characters like Jarvis Poker and the Milkman. Wanting to keep an authentic English feel to the series, Cornell even included a guide to cultural references in the back of the issue to help key in American readers.

SPECIAL FEATURE

JARVIS POKER

England's own version of the Joker was named Jarvis Poker. However, unlike the true Clown Prince of Crime, Jarvis could never bring himself to commit crimes—a fact he revealed while talking to the Knight at a bar called The Time in a Bottle.

ROBIN OR RED ROBIN?

Teen Titans #88 ▪ Damian Wayne followed in Robin tradition when he briefly joined the Teen Titans at the behest of his mentor in this issue by the series' new creative team, writer J.T. Krul and artist Nicola Scott. Insisting on leading the team that also included the newly-returned Ravager among its ranks, Damian lost interest rather quickly when Red Robin also returned to the Titans' roster in issue #91 (March 2011). It seemed there really wasn't room for two of Batman's sons in the Teen Titans, and Robin soon returned to Gotham City.

ALSO THIS YEAR

March—*Detective Comics* #861: Batwoman's final arc in Detective Comics began, featuring the new villain Cutter.

April—*Justice League: Cry For Justice* #7: In the final issue of this miniseries also featuring Batwoman, Green Arrow killed the villain Prometheus.

July—*Outsiders* #30: After the debut of new Masters of Disaster Mudslide and Dust Devil in *Outsiders* #27 (April 2010), this issue introduced new Outsiders member Freight Train who later joined the Batman Inc. team.

July—*Gotham City Sirens* #12: Catwoman's sister Maggie adopted the super-villain identity of Sister Zero.

September—*Batman: Streets of Gotham* #14: The villain who would become known as Skel debuted just as Two-Face earned his own back-up feature.

★ **November 26th—**The new Cartoon Network animated series *Young Justice* debuted starring Robin.

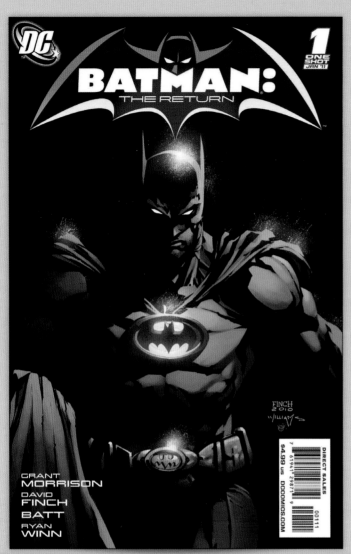

RETURNING TO THE FRAY
BATMAN: THE RETURN #1

Bruce Wayne was officially back as Batman in this issue, which saw the hero prepare for a battle to come, complete with a new costume.

During his travels through time in the previous year's miniseries *Batman: The Return of Bruce Wayne*, Batman had witnessed a glimpse of the future, and thus knew of a coming menace called Leviathan. Batman needed to create a new way to battle the forces of evil. He was thinking outside the box, and outside Gotham City.

After introducing Oracle to a WayneTech innovation called Internet 3.0, Bruce Wayne visited Lucius Fox at that company to discuss with him new weapons that they were creating to help Batman's war on crime. After asking Fox to paint two of the company's new jet-suits to look like Batman and Robin, the Dynamic Duo took to the skies of Yemen to combat a mysterious new villain who looked somewhat like Batman, but wore a glowing red visor over his eyes. A major player in the coming months, this new threat was revealed in the issue's end to be under the command of a group called Leviathan, ruled by a dark figure in a shadowy mask.

The third and final act of writer Grant Morrison's massive Batman tale had begun, and the outcome promised to shake up the Dark Knight's world yet again.

SUITED UP
Batman's new costume included his iconic yellow oval chest emblem, which he could light up to project his symbol if the need arose. The costume also featured bat-themed insignia on his Utility Belt.

2011

"Tonight's the night, father. It's time for a change."

Batman, *Batman and Robin #1*

Bruce Wayne was back, but that didn't mean he was the only Batman. As Bruce traveled the globe organizing his new team, Batman Incorporated, Dick Grayson remained the Batman of Gotham City. At least until the universe changed. In late 2011, DC released 52 new titles, each starting with a #1 issue. Among these, *Detective Comics* and *Batman* were restarted, and Batman's continuity would be adjusted to reflect a new timeline. DC Comics did release a series of "Retroactive" specials dealing in characters from past eras like the Reaper from "Batman: Year Two," yet the emphasis was firmly on starting a fresh continuity that was accessible to new readers.

THE BLACK MIRROR
Detective Comics #871 • Superstar writer Scott Snyder began his tenure on the Batman titles alongside popular artist Jock in this issue. First battling new villain the Dealer (who premiered in the following issue), Grayson would debut new flight armor in issue #873 (March 2011), and then fight a slightly more fearsome update of Tiger Shark in issue #878 (August 2011). Meanwhile, in a back-up tale written by Snyder and drawn by Francesco Francavilla, readers were reintroduced to James Gordon, Jr. who would soon become a chilling villain in his own right.

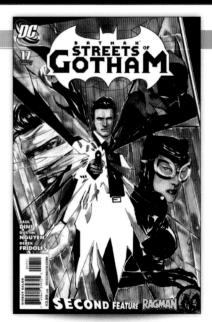

BUGS AND RAGS
Batman: Streets of Gotham #17 • Writer Paul Dini introduced another new enemy to Gotham City thanks to artist Dustin Nguyen. Bedbug first appeared in this issue, armed with a battalion of bedbugs that turned citizens into sleepwalking criminals. Meanwhile, the hero Ragman earned his own back-up feature written by Fabian Nicieza and with art by Szymon Kudranski that pitted him against Firefly, and gave him a bit more attention, as did his one-shot from December of the previous year, *Ragman: Suit of Souls*.

JANUARY

LORD DEATH MAN

This first issue saw the return of the skeletal villain Lord Death Man, as well as the first appearance of new hero Mr. Unknown. By the end of this two-issue arc, Batman would recruit Mr. Unknown into his team's ranks, with a little help from Catwoman.

GOING GLOBAL

BATMAN INCORPORATED #1

With a deadly threat waiting on the horizon, the Dark Knight began to branch out his activities, taking the Batman's methods to a global level.

On the final two pages of writer Grant Morrison's last issue of *Batman and Robin* (#16, January 2011), Bruce Wayne admitted in a press conference that he had been financing Batman's career for years. Wayne and Batman were ready to begin a new chapter in Batman's career, taking his operations to the global arena as they began *Batman Incorporated*. This new series took off where that issue left off, as Morrison moved Batman titles once again. Aided by artist Yanick Paquette on this first story arc, Batman traveled to Japan to recruit a Batman Inc. member in that country. Kathy Kane returned to Batman continuity in issue #3 (March 2011), establishing her relationship with Batman in the following issue, drawn by Chris Burnham. That issue also included the first appearance of villain Dr. Dedalus. Meanwhile, in issue #5 (May 2011), Batman Inc.'s ranks continued to grow as heroes such as Batwoman, the Hood, and El Gaucho appeared, along with the new armored hero of Africa, Batwing. After eight issues, and many new members from Batman's Club of Heroes, the first volume of this series was followed by the prestige-format special Batman Incorporated: *Leviathan Strikes!* (February 2012), that revealed Talia al Ghūl as the mastermind behind the Leviathan crime network.

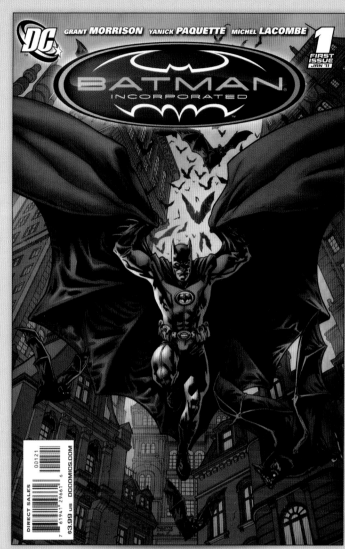

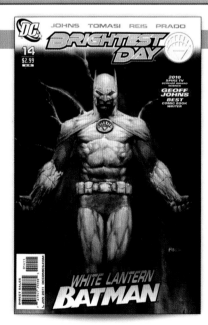

WHITE LANTERN BATMAN

Brightest Day #14 ■ In this 24-issue series (which also had an additional #0 issue) the fallout of the *Blackest Night* miniseries was examined by following many of the characters resurrected at the end of that crossover event. In this issue by writers Geoff Johns and Peter Tomasi and artist Ivan Reis, the newly-revived Deadman began to date heroine Dove. However, the main event for Batman fans was when Batman briefly gained the White Lantern power ring, changing his costume to reflect this extremely temporary new power set.

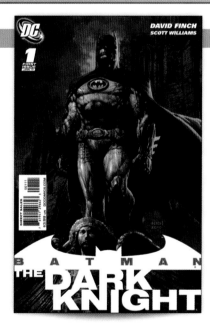

DARK KNIGHT RETURNS...TWICE

Batman: The Dark Knight #1 ■ Writer/artist David Finch saw the birth of his own Batman title in the form of this new ongoing series that allowed the popular artist to explore his own Batman stories. In this first issue, Finch introduced a love interest from Bruce Wayne's childhood, Dawn Golden. While a solid seller for DC, *Batman: The Dark Knight* only lasted five issues before it was restarted with a new #1 issue in November as part of DC's New 52 initiative. That issue would see Finch gain co-writer Paul Jenkins, and debut the villain the White Rabbit.

FEBRUARY

PROMISES, PROMISES

Red Robin #18 ■ In the previous issue, Red Robin had had a heartfelt reunion with Batman, one that saw the Dark Knight uncharacteristically drop his guard to show his "son" how much he cared about him. Red Robin had also commenced a romance with the new Lynx in that issue. In issue #18, Red Robin was in Russia with Tam Fox investigating a wealthy businessman and encountering another female vigilante, Promise. This issue also guest-starred former Teen Titans member Red Star, thanks to writer Fabian Nicieza and artist Marcus To.

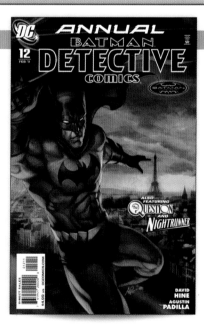

"LE BATMAN"

Detective Comics Annual #12 ■ A new addition to Batman Incorporated emerged in the form of parkour expert Nightrunner. In this story by writer David Hine and artist Agustin Padilla, Dick Grayson and Bruce Wayne encountered this new hero in France. This story continued into *Batman Annual* #28 that featured artwork by Andres Guinaldo and a Veil story by writer Paul Tobin and artist Ramon Bachs. In addition to the main tale, *Detective Comics Annual* #12 included a Question back-up feature and Nightrunner's origin tale.

EVERYTHING CHANGED IN A FLASH

FLASHPOINT #1

In what would become one of DC's most important events, the five-issue *Flashpoint* series changed the entire landscape of the DC Universe for what seemed like forever.

Writer Geoff Johns and penciller Andy Kubert put the Flash at the center of 2011's major crossover event. In this series, Barry Allen woke up in a different reality where Batman was Thomas Wayne, a casino owner who had lost his son, inspiring his life as a crime fighter willing to kill if necessary. Metamorpho seemingly didn't exist, and in his place was the flighty Emily Sung, alias Element Woman. Meanwhile, Aquaman and Wonder Woman engaged in a war that threatened to destroy all of mankind.

As the Flash recruited Batman to try and put the world back the way the speedster knew it should be, readers were treated to several tie-in miniseries, including a three-issue series entitled *Flashpoint: The Outsider* by writer James Robinson and artist Javi Fernandez, as well as the three-issue *Flashpoint: Deadman and the Flying Graysons* miniseries by writer J.T. Krul and artists Mikel Janin and Fabrizio Fiorentino.

In the end, the Flash discovered that he had caused the shift in reality himself by traveling back in time to save his mother from being killed. He soon corrected his mistake, but in doing so, altered reality once more.

As he saved the world, the Flash witnessed the traditional DC Universe merge with the Vertigo and Wildstorm Universes, creating a single new continuity.

A VERY DIFFERENT BATMAN

The Batman of the Flashpoint universe was a cold man, willing to kill his enemies, such as the villainous Reverse-Flash (below). When the Flash later set the universe straight, Batman was back to his usual, non-lethal self, even if he was wearing a new costume designed for this slightly different reality.

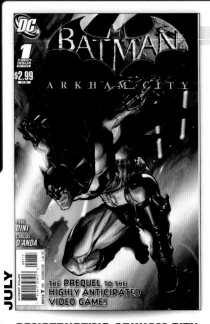

CONSTRUCTING ARKHAM CITY

***Batman: Arkham City* #1** ▪ In 2009, the hit video game *Batman: Arkham Asylum* debuted. 2011 saw the release of its even more popular sequel, *Batman: Arkham City*. Apart from influencing the direction and costumes of a few Batman villains in the comics and inspiring a toy line, these games also inspired this five-issue miniseries, bridging the gap in story between the two games. Written by Paul Dini with art by Carlos D'Anda, this series would prelude June 2012's effort, *Batman: Arkham Unhinged*.

GOTHAM CITY'S FIRST FAMILIES

***Batman: Gates of Gotham* #1** ▪ Writer Scott Snyder would add intrigue to the history of Gotham City in this five-issue series co-written by Kyle Higgins and Ryan Parrott. Drawn by Trevor McCarthy, Dustin Nguyen, and Graham Nolan, this series introduced the villain known as the Architect, who began destroying Gotham City's famous bridges. This series starred Cassandra Cain as Black Bat, saw a new Batboat design, and delved into the past of Gotham City's most influential families: the Waynes, the Elliots, the Cobblepots, and the Kanes.

TRAGEDY OF THE WAYNE FAMILY

***Flashpoint: Batman: Knight of Vengeance* #1** ▪ In this powerful reimagining of the Batman legend, writer Brian Azzarello and artist Eduardo Risso, joined forces for a three-issue examination of *Flashpoint*'s Batman, Thomas Wayne. Wearing a slightly different uniform to that of his son in the regular DC Comics' continuity, Thomas Wayne had lost Bruce in a mugging, inspiring him to become Batman. In a shocking turn of events, as this series progressed the Joker of this world was revealed to be Martha Wayne, driven insane by the death of her son.

SPECIAL FEATURE

MARTHA WAYNE

The Joker's identity as Martha Wayne was kept secret for half of this miniseries. This clever twist made the Joker a part of the Batman story from the beginning, and all the more tragic a figure.

SEPTEMBER

BATMAN GOES RETRO
Batman: Retroactive: The 1970s #1
A celebration of the past, DC Comics released a series of "Retroactive" specials and Batman nabbed three of them. One focused on the 1970s, one on the 1980s, and the last on the 1990s. Each contained a new story as well as a reprint from the era. In this 1970s issue, a new Terrible Trio was introduced that included Lucius Fox's son, Tim, thanks to writer Len Wein and artist Tom Mandrake. This issue also featured a reprint of a tale by Wein and artist John Calnan from *Batman* #307 (January 1979).

NOVEMBER

A NEW BRAND OF JUSTICE
Justice League #1 ▪ The Justice League was formed for the first time in the landscape of the fresh universe of the New 52 thanks to writer Geoff Johns and artist Jim Lee. Set five years in the past, this first, six-issue arc explained how Batman joined forces with Superman, Wonder Woman, Aquaman, Green Lantern, the Flash, and Cyborg in order to battle the forces of Darkseid. Batman also starred in *Justice League International* #1 (November 2011), written by Dan Jurgens and drawn by Aaron Lopresti.

THE JOKER LOSES FACE
Detective Comics #1 ▪ For the first time, Batman starred in a first issue of *Detective Comics* as the title was restarted to reflect the revised continuity of DC Comics' New 52 universe. Written and drawn by Tony S. Daniel, this issue introduced Batman's most recent Batmobile model and a camera-equipped Batarang called the Ro-Bat, both designed for the New 52. After meeting with a now younger, red-haired Commissioner Gordon, Batman chased and defeated the Joker, leaving him at Arkham Asylum as the villain had planned all along.

SPECIAL FEATURE

FACE-OFF
The Joker wanted new villain the Dollmaker to operate on him. After entering the Joker's cell at Arkham Asylum, the Dollmaker removed the skin from the Joker's face in a bizarre ritual of rebirth.

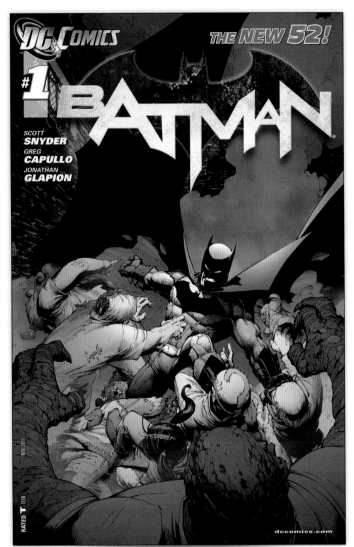

THE COURT OF OWLS
BATMAN #1

In an unprecedented event, Batman's longstanding title was restarted with a new number 1 issue to set the stage for the powerful "Court of Owls" seven-issue storyline.

Writer Scott Snyder was paired with superstar artist Greg Capullo for this new series. Clad in his Jim Lee-designed New 52 suit, Batman stopped an Arkham Asylum breakout before attending a fundraiser as Bruce Wayne. It was here that Bruce met Lincoln March, a current mayoral candidate. By issue #2 (which also saw a new Batcycle model), March was attacked by one of the Talons, a group of resurrected assassins of mysterious origin.

The Dark Knight began looking into the Talons' history and deduced that the killer worked for the Court of Owls, a secret society of Gotham City's elite, previously thought to be an urban legend. Following a trail that revealed Court of Owls strongholds in Wayne-owned buildings, Batman found himself in a massive labyrinth built by the Court underneath the city and was attacked by a Talon.

In issue #5 (March 2012), Snyder and Capullo invited readers to turn the comic in several different directions to follow the story, creating a disorienting effect. While Batman defeated the Talon and freed himself from captivity in the following issues, it was apparent that the threat of the Court of Owls was only just beginning.

FAMILY MAN
Bruce Wayne's family had grown since he began his career six years prior. When attending the fundraiser, not only did Dick Grayson, the current Nightwing attend, but so did Red Robin, Tim Drake, and Robin, Damian Wayne.

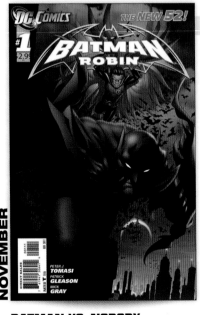

BATMAN VS. NOBODY
Batman and Robin #1 • Readers were witness to an interesting father/son dynamic in the pages of this restarted title. Written by Peter J. Tomasi with art by Patrick Gleason, the story saw new villain Nobody kill new Batman Inc. member Ravil, the Batman of Moscow. As the story continued in the next issue, while buying a Great Dane named Titus for Damian, Bruce discovered that Nobody was Henri Ducard's son, Morgan. This issue debuted a spherical Batgyro, while issue #3 showcased a new Batplane, and issue #5 (March 2012) saw a new glowing red Batmobile.

BATWOMAN'S BREAKTHROUGH
Batwoman #1 • With her ongoing series teased back in January of this year with the release of the special Batwoman #0, Kate Kane's series was held back a bit to fit seamlessly in with the rest of the New 52. Written and drawn by J.H. Williams III and co-written by W. Haden Blackman, this title featured a romance between Kate Kane and G.C.P.D. cop Maggie Sawyer. Meanwhile, Kate began training her cousin and former Flamebird, Bette Kane, as Batwoman took on the mysterious new threat of the ghostly Weeping Woman.

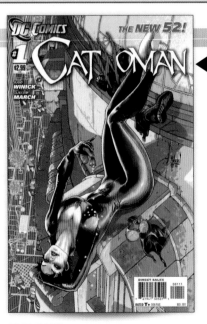

CAT CALL
Catwoman #1 • Writer Judd Winick and artist Guillem March showed quite a revealing side of the feline fatale in this issue that explained the Batman/Catwoman dynamic in no uncertain terms. After escaping a firebombed apartment and battling a Russian gangster, Catwoman retreated to a penthouse hotel room only to be paid a visit by Batman. In the fairly controversial scene that followed, the two became quite intimate, explaining their new physical relationship. In the New 52's reality, Selina did not know Batman's true identity.

SPECIAL FEATURE

CAT AND BAT
In the streamlined reality of the New 52, Catwoman had no idea who Batman was under his cowl. And she didn't really seem to care, either, as long as their romantic relationship could continue.

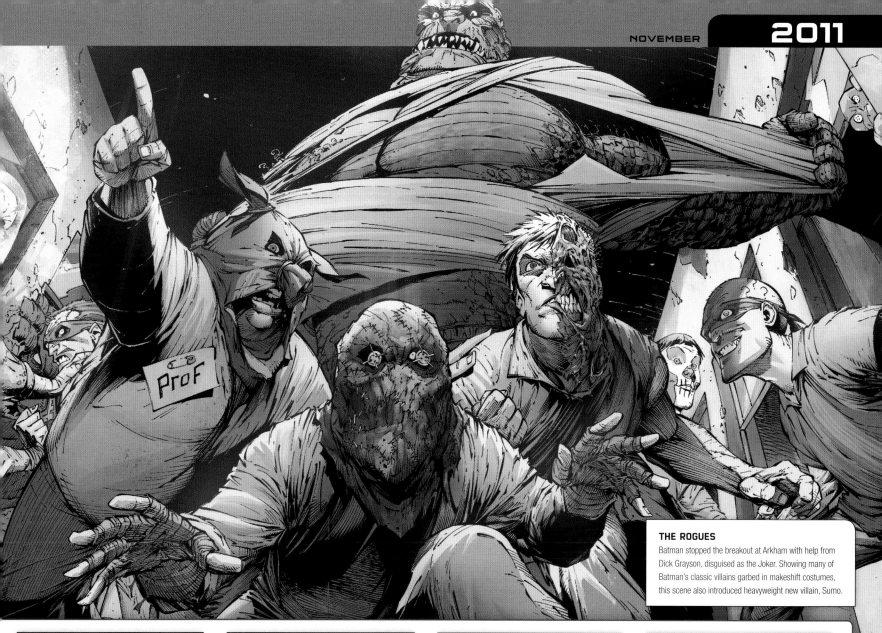

THE ROGUES
Batman stopped the breakout at Arkham with help from Dick Grayson, disguised as the Joker. Showing many of Batman's classic villains garbed in makeshift costumes, this scene also introduced heavyweight new villain, Sumo.

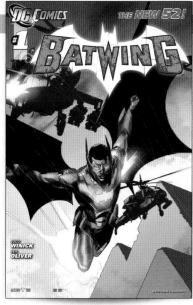

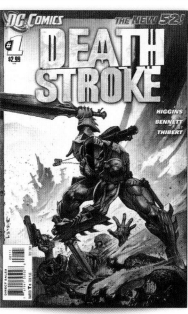

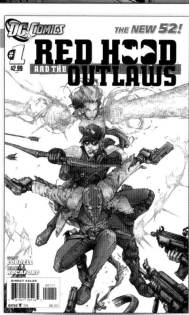

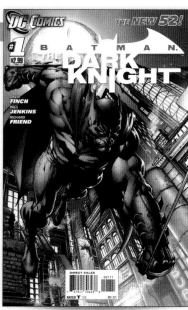

TAKING WING
Batwing #1 • Batman Incorporated member Batwing was given his own ongoing series thanks to writer Judd Winick and artist Ben Oliver. The armored Batman equivalent of Africa, David Zavimbe fought crime by day as a police officer, and by night as Batwing. In this issue that introduced Batwing's first true super-villain in the form of Massacre, readers also met supporting character Kia Okuru, examined Batwing's secret hideout the Haven, and met Matu Ba, David's trusted aid and former worker at a child soldier rescue organization.

A TOUCH OF DEATH
Deathstroke #1 • One of the DC Universe's premier mercenaries was back in his own ongoing series thanks to writer Kyle Higgins and artist Joe Bennett. Equipped with a new armored uniform, Deathstroke found himself out of his element when he was forced to work with a team of young mercenaries called the Alpha Dawgs. However, in true Deathstroke fashion, after Slade and his team had dealt with their target—a German scientist dealing in biological weapons—Slade gunned down the Dawgs, refusing to allow his "competition" to run free.

OUTLAW JUSTICE
Red Hood and the Outlaws #1 • Jason Todd found himself at the helm of a new team of heroes in this ongoing series by writer Scott Lobdell and artist Kenneth Rocafort. Sporting a new look that resembled an earlier costume design, albeit now with a red bat-like symbol on his chest, Jason, as the Red Hood, joined forces with the former Green Arrow partner Arsenal, and an alien princess. These three vigilantes banded together and became fast allies. No matter their differences, they all shared a desire to work outside the constraints of the law.

TWO BECOME ONE
Batman: The Dark Knight #1 • Writer/artist David Finch returned *Batman: The Dark Knight* to the stands with the help of co-writer Paul Jenkins. While the original series had begun at the start of 2011 and only ran five issues, it was decided to relaunch the title in order to have the series restart with the rest of the New 52 books. In this issue, Batman faced a new threat: the mysterious, Alice in Wonderland-themed female villain, the White Rabbit. This issue also saw Two-Face become enhanced by Venom and start calling himself One-Face.

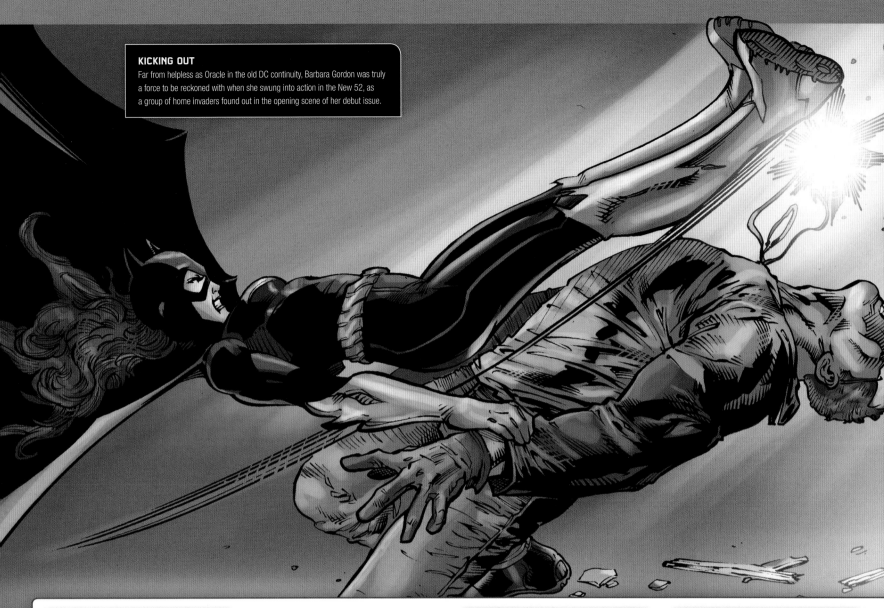

GOTHAM CITY'S HEX

***All-Star Western* #1** • Batman's cast of characters usually stayed away from DC Comics' stable of great western characters. While famous scarred gun-slinger Jonah Hex had met Batman before, their two worlds only rarely collided. That changed in this new title for Jonah Hex's adventures by writers Jimmy Palmiotti and Justin Gray and artist Moritat. In this issue, Jonah Hex's exploits took place in the Gotham City of the 1880s as Dr. Amadeus Arkham, the founder of Arkham Asylum, became one of Hex's supporting characters.

SPECIAL FEATURE

THE FIRST BATCAVE

Hex and Arkham encountered a giant prehistoric bat and an ancient tribe of Native Americans while underneath Gotham City searching for missing children in issue #6 (April 2012). When they emerged above ground, they found themselves at Wayne Manor, the home of Alan and Catherine Wayne.

HARLEY'S NEW LOOK

***Suicide Squad* #1** • The classic concept of super-villains forced to go on government missions was reestablished in this ongoing effort by writer Adam Glass and artist Federico Dallocchio. Harley Quinn played a major role, clad in a drastically different costume. By issue #7 (May 2012), Harley received a new origin when it was revealed that the Joker had shoved her in a vat of chemicals that altered her hair and skin color, as well as her mind. Deadshot, Black Spider, and Birds of Prey supporting character Savant also served as Squad members.

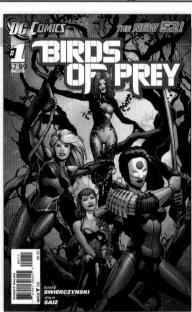

GETTING THE GIRLS TOGETHER

***Birds of Prey* #1** • Featuring all-new costumes for each of its members, the New 52's Birds of Prey debuted in this issue by writer Duane Swierczynski and artist Jesus Saiz. A title that concentrated on action, this series introduced new Birds member Evelyn Crawford, a.k.a. Starling. Originally consisting of leader Black Canary, Starling, Poison Ivy, and Katana, the team eventually included Batgirl. While her past would remain a mystery in this issue, Black Canary's history would be explored further in 2012's new title *Team 7*.

HAUNTED BY THE JOKER

While she was facing her fears as Batgirl, Barbara was plagued by the horrific night that the Joker shot her three years prior, a pivotal point in the character's life originally told in 1988's *Batman: The Killing Joke*.

BATGIRL'S BACK

BATGIRL #1

In the landscape of the New 52, Barbara Gordon returned to a life of adventure as Batgirl once again.

While there had been two ongoing *Batgirl* titles in the past, neither had starred Barbara Gordon, despite her continued status as the most recognizable Batgirl in comic books. Writer Gail Simone and artist Adrian Syaf rectified this oversight with a new ongoing title centering on Barbara Gordon. Now she was back in the thick of the action as Batgirl and clad in a new costume.

In the reality of the New 52, Batgirl had been shot and paralyzed by the Joker, just as in the traditional post-Crisis DC Universe. However, instead of becoming the information guru Oracle, Barbara had recovered from her seemingly life-changing wound to start life as Batgirl again.

This issue saw Barbara move in with new roommate Alysia Yeoh and come into conflict with a villain known as the Mirror. While she defeated Mirror by issue #4, issue #5 (March 2012) introduced another threat in the form of Gretel, and issue #7 (May 2012) debuted the villain Grotesque. Batgirl certainly had her hands busy and, despite lingering feelings of self-doubt and the traumatic effects of the Joker's savagery, soon regained her crime-fighting confidence.

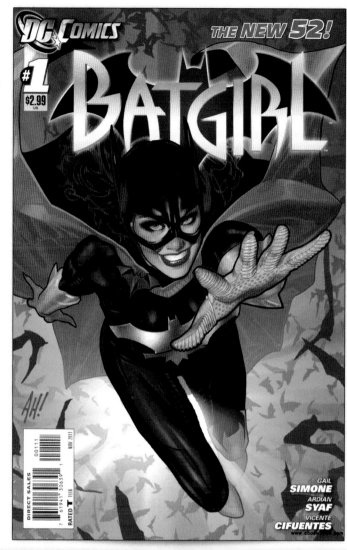

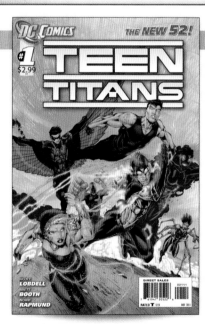

RED ROBIN'S FLIGHT

Teen Titans #1 ■ The biggest New 52 changes surrounded the origin of the various Robins. atman had only been fighting crime for six years in this revamped universe, so the tenures of each Robin had to be shortened dramatically. In this issue by writer Scott Lobdell and artist Brett Booth, Tim Drake was established as Red Robin. Armed with new glider wings and a very different costume, Red Robin helped found the Teen Titans. Titans' villain Deathstroke also received his own ongoing series thanks to writer Kyle Higgins and artist Joe Bennett.

THE RETURN OF NIGHTWING

Nightwing #1 ■ Dick Grayson was back as Nightwing in this series, having left his life as Batman far behind him. But that didn't stop Dick from changing his color scheme a bit, switching to a black and red uniform in this issue written by Kyle Higgins and drawn by Eddy Barrows. This debut issue introduced readers to a face from Grayson's circus past, Raya Vestri. Nightwing also faced a new threat in the assassin Saiko, a killer equipped with deadly claws, unusually out to murder Dick Grayson, rather than his Super Hero alter ego.

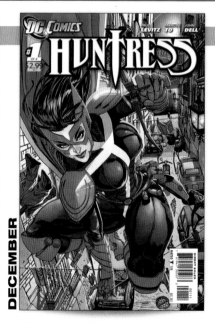

HELENA WHO?

Huntress #1 ■ In this six-issue series, Huntress's co-creator, writer Paul Levitz hinted that Helena Bertinelli might be closer to the original Huntress than anyone suspected. The main focus of this series, drawn by Marcus To, centered on Huntress shutting down a women slavery ring in Italy. But the biggest development for the character was when she met up with the New 52's version of Power Girl in the final issue. Power Girl revealed the two were partners, implying that Helena Bertinelli was truly Earth-Two's Helena Wayne.

ALSO THIS YEAR

January—*Batman and Robin* #17: The villain with a hole in her head named Absence debuted in a three-issue arc.

February—*Red Robin* #18: After a heartfelt reunion with Batman in the previous issue and the start of a romance with Lynx, Red Robin met the vigilante Promise.

March—*Young Justice* #0: A new ongoing series revived the *Young Justice* title tying in to the cartoon of the same name.

April—*Superman/Batman* #81: Superman traveled to a magic-based world and met a very different version of Batman.

April—*Superman* #708: Superman's legacy inspired the future hero SuperBatman in this issue.

July—*Red Robin* #23: A new Black Spider debuted, hot on the heels of issue #20's new villain Romeo Void, and before the villain Cricket debuted in issue #25.

December—*Penguin: Pain and Prejudice* #1: The Penguin earned a starring role in his own five-issue miniseries.

BATMAN FOR A NEW GENERATION
Justice League #2 (December 2011) ■ Batman
and Superman had been almost instant buddies in the
1950s and uneasy allies when they met in the 1980s.
However, in the pages of the New 52's *Justice League*
#2, by writer Geoff Johns and artist Jim Lee, the two
began their association at each other's throats.
Fortunately, the World's Finest bond proved too strong to
alter for long, and the two heroes soon began to work
together as frequent partners both within and apart from
the Justice League.

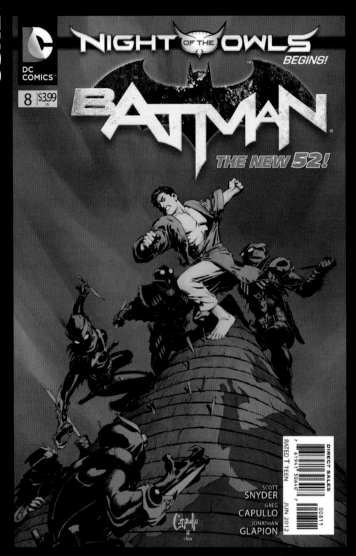

NIGHT OF THE OWLS

BATMAN #8

Batman had escaped the elaborate, insanity-inducing labyrinth employed by the corrupt secret society known as the Court of Owls, but his struggle evolved with this issue into the crossover "Night of the Owls."

In this story by writer Scott Snyder and artist Greg Capullo, Batman was back in Wayne Manor, following his escape from the labyrinth in *Batman* #6 (April 2012). Soon, countless Talons attacked the house and Bruce was once again fighting for survival. Retreating to the Batcave, Bruce confronted a Talon and, with the help of Alfred, trapped the assassin. Meanwhile, the Court's attacks on Gotham City began in full when an army of Talons was set on the city's most respected figures. This crossover also saw Talons challenge the protagonists of *All-Star Western*, *Batman: The Dark Knight*, *Batman and Robin*, *Batwing*, *Batgirl*, *Red Hood & the Outlaws*, *Nightwing*, *Catwoman* and *Birds of Prey*.

The action concluded in *Batman* #10 (August 2012) when Batman discovered the Court of Owls had been betrayed and poisoned by a traitor. He tracked down this villain, discovering that he was the man Batman had known as politician Lincoln March. The man had survived a murder attempt organized by his former allies in the Court and taken his revenge. In a final revelation, the man announced he was Thomas Wayne, Jr., Bruce's younger, forgotten brother. Dressed in flying owl armor, Thomas battled Batman through the Gotham City skies until Batman defeated him.

2012

"You're not my brother. You're a lunatic in a bird suit..."

Batman to "Lincoln March," *Batman* #11

To keep up the energy of the New 52, DC Comics introduced a few new series, including the Court of Owls related title Talon. Meanwhile, nearly every existing comic was granted a zero issue that offered insight into the history of its title character. Batman even returned to the crossover format, when the series "Night of the Owls" and "Death of the Family" passed through the majority of the Batman family titles. While the main story took place within the *Batman* title itself, the other issues added to the scope of the drama, creating even more excitement for the readership.

A LIFE BEYOND

Batman Beyond Unlimited #1 • This new digital-first ongoing series featured a Batman tale by writer Adam Beechen and artist Norm Breyfogle and a Justice League Beyond story by writers Derek Fridolfs and writer/artist Dustin Nguyen. This series ended with issue #18 (September 2013), a comic that introduced Batgirl Beyond thanks to writer Scott Peterson and artist Annie Wu. It was then restarted in October of that year as *Batman Beyond Universe*. That title featured Batman now pairing with former Nightwing, Dick Grayson.

DANGER VIA DANIEL

Detective Comics #6 • *Detective Comics* had featured quite a few debuts since its restart thanks to the imagination of its writer/artist Tony Daniel. In issue #2 (December 2011), Bruce Wayne's new love interest Charlotte Rivers appeared, and issue #5 (March 2012) introduced gang boss Mr. Mosaic and the Penguin's new floating Iceberg Casino. By this issue, Daniel premiered new villains Snakeskin, Mr. Toxic, Hypnotic, and Mr. Combustible, a great new lineup of criminals that seemed to fit right in with the rest of Batman's classic Rogues Gallery.

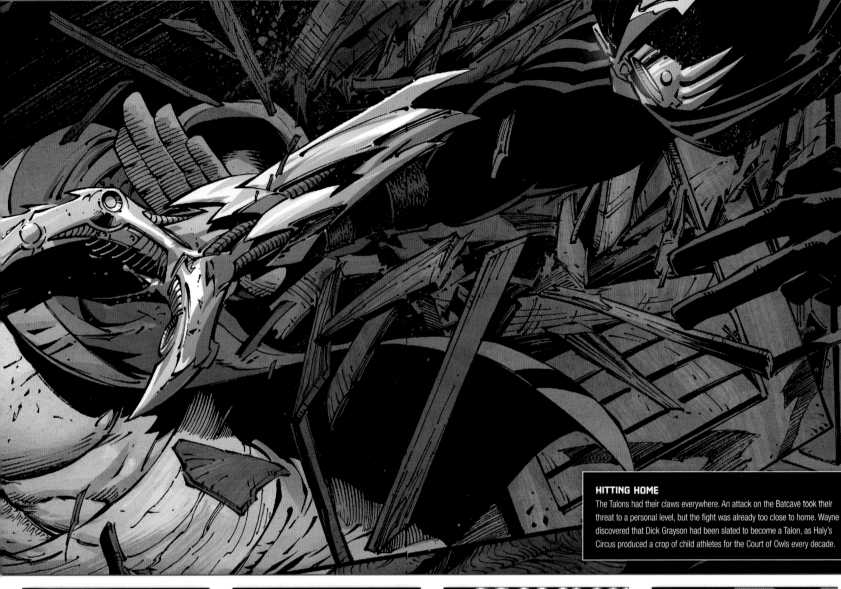

HITTING HOME
The Talons had their claws everywhere. An attack on the Batcave took their threat to a personal level, but the fight was already too close to home. Wayne discovered that Dick Grayson had been slated to become a Talon, as Haly's Circus produced a crop of child athletes for the Court of Owls every decade.

SPARKS FLYING

Catwoman #7 ▪ Catwoman was meeting plenty of new people in the universe of the New 52. In issue #4 (February 2012), she came across her old friend and fellow thief Gwen Altamont and fought the female metahuman named Reach. By this issue, writer Judd Winick and artist Adriana Melo introduced Selina to another likeminded bandit, the electrically charged Spark. The two soon found themselves allies, even as their new enemy, the disturbed Dollmaker, who debuted in *Detective Comics #2*, began her reign of terror in this issue.

A DESIGNER'S TOUCH

Batman: Death By Design ▪ Writer and designer Chip Kidd was given the chance to leave his mark on Batman alongside artist Dave Taylor in this hardcover graphic novel. Known for designing several Batman-related books, as well as for his work on the Batman title logos in the early 2000s, Kidd came up with a Batman tale set in a Golden Age continuity all its own, showcasing a Batman with a slightly different bat-symbol on his chest. Depicted in mostly black and white with touches of color for emphasis here and there, this memorable tale featured the Joker.

HOME AWAY FROM HOME

Worlds' Finest #1 ▪ With a bit of clever wordplay in this series' title apostrophe placement, Huntress and Power Girl were given their own comic now that they had been revealed as the Robin and Supergirl of Earth-Two. With the heroines stranded on Earth-One, this issue by writer Paul Levitz and pencillers George Pérez and Kevin Maguire explained how Helena Wayne had adopted the identity of Helena Bertinelli after the real Bertinelli had died. This issue saw Power Girl adopt her name and costume as new villain Hakkou battled the pair of displaced heroines.

GOATBOYS AND BAT-COWS

Batman Incorporated #1 ▪ After a brief hiatus, this Grant Morrison-written series returned, drawn by Chris Burnham. In an issue that debuted Damian Wayne's new pet, a cow nicknamed Bat-Cow (inspired by the Bat-Cow from *Tiny Titans #17* (August 2009), this story introduced the assassin Goatboy, as well as Batcave West, a headquarters in San Francisco. It also showcased the new Outsiders, a team including Halo, Looker, Freight Train, Katana, Metamorpho, and Red Robin that had debuted in *Batman Incorporated #6* (June 2011).

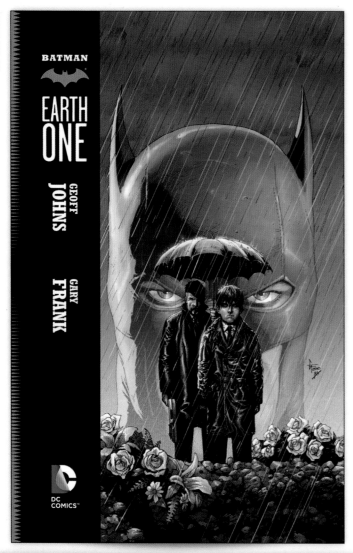

BATMAN
EARTH ONE
GEOFF JOHNS
GARY FRANK
DC COMICS™

ANOTHER EARTH, ANOTHER BATMAN

BATMAN: EARTH ONE

The Batman mythos was reimagined in this alternate take on the hero's origin in this hardcover special. It brought together writer Geoff Johns and artist Gary Frank for their first Batman story.

In October of 2010, the hardcover *Superman: Earth One* debuted, establishing a new continuity for the Man of Steel. This younger version of the hero was meant to attract knew readers by starting the character's origin and adventures over from scratch and reinventing elements of his history along the way. That volume was meant to be just the first in this series of alternate universe hardcovers, and soon writer Johns and artist Frank delivered Batman's first foray into the world of Earth-One.

In this new reality, Thomas Wayne was running for Mayor of Gotham City when he hired his old friend, the tough-as-nails Alfred Pennyworth, to be the head of security for him once elected. But when the Waynes were killed and their son Bruce orphaned, Alfred instead became 'butler' and mentor to the boy who would go on to become the Batman.

Establishing a fledgling Batman, prone to making mistakes, Earth-One gave the Dark Knight a new costume, complete with his famous yellow oval chest emblem. This hardcover special also depicted Oswald Cobblepot as Gotham City's corrupt mayor, and introduced the serial killer on Cobblepot's payroll, Birthday Boy, who had a gruesome method for dispatching his teenage victims.

ALFRED GETS TOUGH
No longer the mild-mannered gentleman's gentleman, in Earth-One, Alfred Pennyworth was a hard man who was trained in the ways of security. This was also the approach taken towards Alfred in the 2013 animated series *Beware the Batman*.

BATMAN'S BEGINNING AND END

Earth 2 #1 ▪ Long associated with Golden Age heroes, writer James Robinson concocted the Earth–Two of the New 52 with artist Nicola Scott. As Earth-Two fell siege to Darkseid's forces, its Batman gave his life to fight the villains. Meanwhile, Batman's daughter, the Robin of this world, Helena Wayne, piloted a new Batplane through a boom tube alongside Supergirl, unwittingly entering the dimension of Earth-One. While Batman was dead, an old foe of his soon reared his undead head when Solomon Grundy attacked Earth-Two in issue #3 (September 2012).

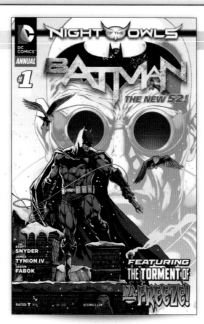

FROZEN OBSESSION

Batman Annual #1 ▪ In this surprising issue, writers Scott Snyder and James Tynion and artist Jason Fabok added a new dimension to the motivation of the tragic Dr. Victor Fries. Wearing a new "bare arms" version of his Freeze suit, Mr. Freeze went on a violent quest for his love Nora. However, in this story, it was revealed that Nora was never Mr. Freeze's wife, but a woman named Nora Fields who'd had her body frozen in the 1960s due to a heart condition. Victor had become obsessed with her, but had never even met "his Nora."

THE POWER OF BLACK MASK

Detective Comics Annual #1 ▪ Black Mask had traditionally been more of a psychological threat for Batman and his allies as a gang leader and psychotic sadist, but in this issue by writer Tony S. Daniel and artists Romano Molenaar and Pere Pérez, his status as a powerhouse was reaffirmed. In *Detective Comics* #9 (July 2012), it was revealed that Roman Sionis' skull-like Black Mask gave him mind control powers. And in this issue that also introduced a new villain called Mad Bull, Black Mask had a mind control showdown with the Mad Hatter.

LIFE LESSONS

Detective Comics #0 ▪ After writer/artist Tony Daniel ended his writing tenure on *Detective Comics* with issue #12 (October 2012), an issue that saw Batman debut a new hang glider costume, writer Gregg Hurwitz joined forces with Daniel's pencils in this flashback issue. Readers saw Bruce Wayne training in the Himalayas and meeting love interest Mio, whose betrayal would temporarily deter Bruce from romantic relationships. Later on, in issue #21 (August 2013), Mio would arrive in Gotham City as the assassin Penumbra.

LEARNING CURVE
In *Batman: Earth One*, Batman was a novice and often made rookie mistakes that left him injured. While he originally wore a black bat on his chest, his emblem would evolve into a yellow oval as his skills improved.

BEFORE ZERO YEAR

Batman #0 ▪ Writer Scott Snyder and artist Greg Capullo teased their upcoming "Zero Year" revamp of Batman's origin with this issue featuring a new take on the classic Red Hood, now the leader of the Red Hood Gang. Meanwhile, Bruce Wayne was newly returned to Gotham City from his training years, now living in a brownstone he had converted into a high-tech headquarters. This issue also featured a back-up tale written by James Tynion IV and illustrated by Andy Clarke that showcased the Robins before they joined Batman, and the first use of the Bat-Signal.

SPECIAL FEATURE

THE RED HOOD GANG

This prelude to "Zero Year" established the Red Hood from Batman's past as a criminal mastermind. This new villain was a far cry from the blackmailed Red Hood that became the Joker in 1988's *Batman: The Killing Joke*.

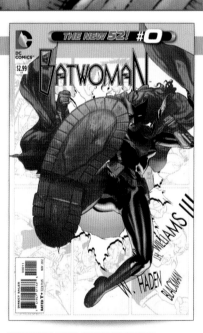

BEHIND THE BATWOMAN

Batwoman #0 ▪ While she'd already received one *Batwoman* #0 special, Kate Kane proved worthy of another in this flashback story written and illustrated by J.H. Williams III and co-written by W. Haden Blackman. Flashing back to her childhood and the bond she formed with her father when her sister Beth seemingly died, Kate's transition from aimless party girl to determined vigilante was explored as she faced rigorous training at the hands of her father after being inspired to fight crime from her own past tragedies and a chance encounter with the Batman.

BATGIRL'S BACKSTORY

Batgirl #0 ▪ Idolizing her father, James Gordon, from an early age, Barbara strived to be just like him, mastering skills like martial arts and ballet early in life. Visiting her father at work in this flashback issue by writer Gail Simone and artist Ed Benes, Barbara tried on a mock Batman costume to stop an escaping prisoner. She soon adopted a gray Batman-like bodysuit and a Nightwing-like mask, becoming Batgirl. In this newly designed costume, Batgirl was soon earning the respect of both Batman and the original Robin, Dick Grayson.

NOVEMBER

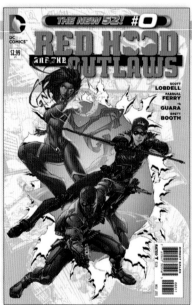

THE SECOND ROBIN

Without knowing it, Jason Todd had been a secret pet project of the Joker for years. The Joker had faked the death of Jason's mother from an overdose, and arranged for his father to be imprisoned. After Jason was adopted by Batman as the next Robin, the villain revealed that Jason's mother was alive, only to kill both Todds during their family reunion.

RAINING CATS AND DOGS

Catwoman #0 • Catwoman received a new origin in this flashback issue by writer Ann Nocenti and artist Adriana Melo. As a young child, Selina Kyle moved in and out of foster homes, and was even forced to steal for the profit of the Oliver's Group Home. She finally landed on her feet in a city office, only to have her boss push her off a rooftop when she tried to research her own file. Just like in the 1992 film *Batman Returns*, Catwoman was born that night when Selina's life was saved by an awning and a group of curious cats.

SHARPENING TALON

Talon #0 • This zero issue began a new ongoing series starring Calvin Rose, a Talon who escaped from the corrupt life of the Court of Owls. A natural escape artist with a tortured past, Rose was sentenced to die by the Court after he rejected their brutal training and refused to murder a mother and her child. In this series by writers James Tynion IV and Scott Snyder and artist Guillem March, Rose took the fight to the weakened Court of Owls with the help of Sebastian Clark, an enemy of the Court who debuted in the following issue.

BOY IN THE HOOD

Red Hood and the Outlaws #0 • Jason Todd's tragic past was told in this flashback tale by writer Scott Lobdell and artists Pasqual Ferry, Ig Guara, and Brett Booth. Born to a mother with drug issues and a criminal father, Jason practically raised himself, and was soon forced to live on the streets. When he tried to steal drugs from Dr. Leslie Thompkins, Jason met the Batman, and soon found himself living in Wayne Manor. After six months of intensive training, Jason became the second Robin, wearing a uniform different from Dick Grayson's New 52 Robin suit.

CHILL IN THE AIR
BATMAN: THE DARK KNIGHT #0

Bruce Wayne's youth was explored in this flashback issue that retold the murder of his parents and his determination to find the gunman, Joe Chill.

Part of DC Comics' zero issue releases that told the origins of each issue's title character or characters, this comic by writer Gregg Hurwitz and pencillers Mico Suayan and Juan Jose Ryp informed readers of the days and years following Bruce's parents' death. Following the shooting of Thomas and Martha Wayne, Bruce Wayne headed into Gotham City by himself one night, obsessed with discovering their killer. He encountered a homeless man who had witnessed the event, but instead of giving the young boy information, the man stole Thomas Wayne's watch from Bruce. Years passed, and Bruce trained his mind and body at the Roxbury Fielding Academy. At age 18, he went back to that same alley and tracked down the homeless man who'd stolen from him. He told Bruce that the name of the man who had shot his parents was Joe Chill. Wayne then took his watch back from the homeless thief. Bruce tracked down Chill, but instead of finding a hired killer or a cog in some larger conspiracy, the man was nothing more than a drunk. Chill had chanced upon the Waynes and killed them merely to buy himself another bottle of booze. Directionless, Bruce left Gotham City to continue his training, wanting to discover what the world had to offer him.

FINDING JOE CHILL
Bruce Wayne had spent most of his young life trying to join the dots on some vast conspiracy involving his parents. He had even investigated the legendary Court of Owls as a possible group responsible for his parents' deaths. But in reality, a random act of violence took Thomas and Martha Wayne's lives, revealing the need for someone like Batman in the world.

THE NEW 52! #0

DC COMICS
$2.99 US

BATMAN THE DARK KNIGHT

GREGG **HURWITZ**
MICO **SUAYAN**
JUAN JOSÉ **RYP**

DIRECT SALES 00011

FINCH 2012

RATED **T** TEEN   NOV 2012

A NEW KIND OF SOLDIER

***Batwing* #0** • The majority of Batwing's origin was revealed in issue #4 (February 2012) by writer Judd Winick and artist ChrisCross, but in this flashback issue, Winick teamed with Marcus To to tell the rest of the tale. A child soldier who committed heinous acts of violence before he could even fully understand them, David Zavimbe soon realized the horrors of his life and changed his ways with the help of Matu Ba. Becoming a vigilante as an adult, David was soon recruited by Batman into Batman Incorporated, and given a flying set of armor.

ROBIN MEETS SUPERGIRL

***Worlds' Finest* #0** • Writer Paul Levitz and artists Kevin Maguire and Wes Craig told a tale from Helena Wayne's past, before she adopted the identity of the Huntress. Set when Helena was still living on Earth-Two, the young heroine debuted her new crime-fighting identity of Robin with a little help from her mother, Catwoman. In this tale, the Catwoman of Earth-Two was killed while wearing a costume similar to the one Huntress would later adopt. Distraught over the loss of her mother, Helena met Earth-Two's Supergirl this issue, forming a lasting bond.

DADDY ISSUES

***Batman and Robin* #0** • Damian Wayne's origin was further examined in this flashback issue by writer Peter J. Tomasi and artist Patrick Gleason. Grown in an incubator womb, Damian Wayne was trained in the arts of death by his mother Talia al Ghūl since birth. The young boy quickly became interested in his father when he discovered Batman's costume in a trunk in his mother's room, and was finally introduced to him on this issue's last page, a panel drawn in a near-identical composition to the final splash page of *Batman* #656 (October 2006).

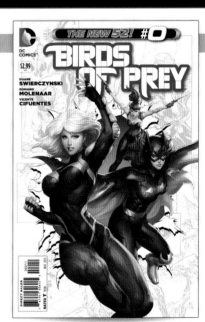

MEETING OF THE BIRDS

***Birds of Prey* #0** • Writer Duane Swierczynski and penciller Romano Molenaar explained how Dinah Lance got the name Black Canary in this flashback tale. Getting a job with the Penguin in order to spy on a meta-terrorist group known as Basilisk, Dinah adopted her codename due to the Penguin's penchant for having his help employ bird-themed monikers. There she met Starling, and the two hit it off, so much so that when push came to shove and Batgirl crashed Penguin's party, Starling opted to join forces with the two heroines and quit her day job.

THE JOKER COMES CALLING
The Joker paid a visit to Wayne Manor, attacking and kidnapping Alfred. This event forced Batman to confess to his team about an encounter with the Joker from years ago when the villain might have had the opportunity to learn Batman's alter ego.

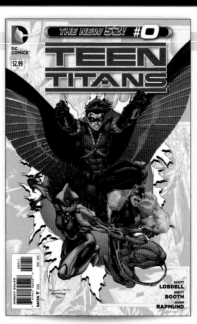

ROBIN RETELLING

Nightwing #0 • Dick Grayson's early life with Haly's Circus was chronicled by writers Tom DeFalco and Kyle Higgins and artist Eddy Barrows. After his circus-performing parents were murdered by Tony Zucco, Dick took to patrolling the city streets in search of the villain, leading to Bruce Wayne taking the boy in to live at Wayne Manor. Grayson soon deduced Wayne's alter ego, and began training with Batman. He adopted the identity of Robin—complete with a newly designed New 52 costume—when Batman's life was in danger from Lady Shiva.

RED ROBIN REDO

Teen Titans #0 • Written by Scott Lobdell and pencilled by Tyler Kirkham, this story revealed the drastically different origin of Red Robin. In this tale, Tim was a determined athlete and student obsessed with discovering Batman's identity and replacing the deceased second Robin, Jason Todd. To that end, Tim hacked into the Penguin's bank account and stole his fortune just to gain Batman's attention. It worked, but also forced Tim's parents to relocate for their own safety, and Tim to change his last name to Drake as he became Batman's newest partner, Red Robin.

BATMAN COMES TO SMALLVILLE

Smallville: Season Eleven #5 • The popular *Smallville* television show had ended, but that didn't stop DC from continuing the adventures of its star, a young Clark Kent. In this digital-first issue, fans of the CW hit met *Smallville*'s version of Batman courtesy of writer Bryan Q. Miller and artist ChrisCross. Partnered with a female Nightwing (Barbara Gordon), Batman wore a grayish blue armored batsuit. Soon drawn to Metropolis when he heard of the whereabouts of Joe Chill, the Dark Knight attacked the Man of Steel at the issue's end.

BLACK AND BLUE

DC Universe Presents #13 • In this title that featured ever-changing lead characters and creators, longtime Batman ally Black Lightning was granted a new start and costume. Written by Marc Andreyko and illustrated by Robson Rocha and Eduardo Pansica, this four-part story saw schoolteacher Jefferson Pierce meet co-star and partner in the form of Blue Devil. Still a fledging Super Hero, Black Lightning originally mistook Blue Devil for a threat before teaming with the young hero to help defeat a villain familiar to Black Lightning fans, Tobias Whale.

DEATH OF THE FAMILY

BATMAN #13

In a similar fashion to the "Night of the Owls" crossover, writer Scott Snyder and artist Greg Capullo told the next major Batman event that had ramifications in the other Batman titles.

Before the Joker could once again terrorize Gotham City, he needed to put his face on. Literally. Having had the skin on his face removed in *Detective Comics* #1 (November 2011), the Joker broke into the G.C.P.D. in the first issue of this "Death of the Family" crossover event in order to steal his face back and reattach it in crude fashion. In order to emphasize this bizarre event in the life of the Clown Prince of Crime, DC decided to print many of the "Death of the Family" tie-in issues with a die-cut second cover that allowed readers to remove Joker's skin mask and reveal one of the Batman cast underneath. This created an interesting look for this crossover that bled into issues of *Batgirl*, *Catwoman*, *Suicide Squad*, *Batman and Robin*, *Detective Comics*, *Nightwing*, *Red Hood and the Outlaws*, and *Teen Titans*.

The main storyline ran through Snyder and Capullo's *Batman*. In this first issue, after donning a mechanic's overalls, the Joker kidnapped Alfred. He would later kidnap the rest of the Batman's inner circle, while claiming to know Batman's secret identity. Batman held fast to the idea that the Joker did not really know his alter ego. And even though Batman successfully ran Joker's gauntlet through Arkham Asylum and freed his team, the Joker's manipulation had created a rift in the formerly tight-knit Batman family.

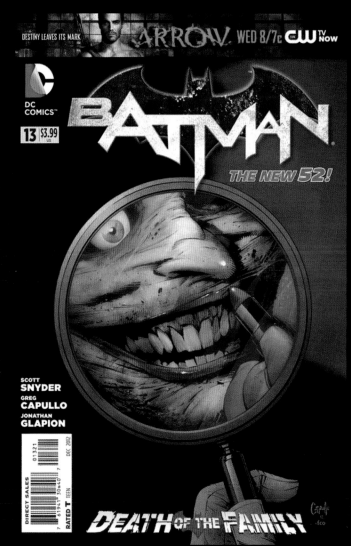

SCOTT **SNYDER**
GREG **CAPULLO**
JONATHAN **GLAPION**

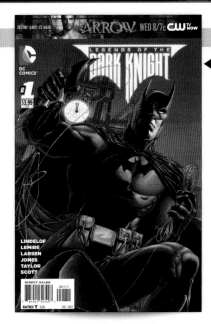

A NEW KIND OF LEGEND

Legends of the Dark Knight #1 ● When the New 52 debuted, each issue was available digitally on the same day as the book's physical release. However, DC Comics had begun to offer original online content as well, and this new, out-of-continuity title was one of several series that collected those digital stories in print form. An anthology title, this first issue featured a story written by Damon Lindelof and drawn by Jeff Lemire as well as tales by writer Jonathan Larsen and artist J.G. Jones, and writer Tom Taylor and penciller Nicola Scott.

SPECIAL FEATURE

Talent Showcase

Reminiscent of 1989's successful *Batman: Legends of the Dark Knight* ongoing series, this new *Legends of the Dark Knight* series featured constantly shifting writers and artists, from new faces to tried and true comic book stars.

THE RISE OF THE EMPEROR

Detective Comics #13 ● The new creative team of writer John Layman and artist Jason Fabok joined *Detective Comics* just in time to introduce the Penguin's new right hand man, Ignatius Ogilvy. While he seemed a loyal servant at first, Ogilvy would soon be revealed to be every bit as cunning as his employer. In fact, by issue #15, Ogilvy usurped the Penguin's criminal throne and replaced him as the new Emperor Penguin. This issue also featured a back-up story written by Layman and drawn by Andy Clarke.

ALSO THIS YEAR

February—*Nightwing* #4: Nightwing faced a new enemy in the putty-like Spinebender in this issue, and cult leader Paragon in issue #10 (August 2012).

April—*Hawk and Dove* #6: New 52's Blockbuster debuted in Hawk and Dove's new series alongside guest-star Batman.

June—*The New 52: Free Comic Book Day Special Edition* #1: A new version of the classic Question debuted with a more mystical origin than his predecessor.

★ July 20th—Director Christopher Nolan completed his Batman film trilogy with *The Dark Knight Rises*, starring Christian Bale as Batman and Tom Hardy as Bane.

August—*Batman and Robin* #10: Villain Terminus debuted, wanting to watch Batman die before his own untimely death.

October—*National Comics: Looker* #1: Looker was reinterpreted as a vampire without her telekinetic powers in this special seemingly set in an alternate continuity.

December—*Birds of Prey* #13: After Poison Ivy betrayed her team in issue #11, the Birds met new vigilante, Condor.

THE DEATH OF DAMIAN WAYNE
BATMAN INCORPORATED #8

Batman's son Damian was brutally murdered by the criminal forces led by the boy's own mother, Talia al Ghūl.

Talia al Ghūl had placed a bounty on her own son's head in this series by writer Grant Morrison and artist Chris Burnham. Her actions had forced Damian Wayne to adopt the identity of Redbird in issue #3 (September 2012). Despite a glimpse into Damian's future in issue #5 (January 2013), the young hero was doomed to die a tragic death in this issue. In fact, Morrison had planned Damian Wayne's death since he first introduced the character, but what had started as a simple arc for Batman grew to become a mammoth opus.

After killing the Super Hero Knight in issue #6 (February 2013), the mysterious Batman-like villain Leviathan battled Robin during a siege of the Wayne Enterprises building. Despite Damian's best efforts, the imposter ran him through with a sword. Damian was buried in the following issue. In the end, the world mourned the death of another Robin, and Batman mourned the loss of his son.

ROBIN'S LAST STAND
Despite Batman banning him from combat, Robin could not sit on the sidelines and watch his father do all the work. He donned his Robin flight suit and stormed the Wayne Enterprises Building, facing the forces of Leviathan head on.

2013

"If we ever needed Batman we need him right now, Bruce."

Bruce Wayne, *Batman Incorporated* #13.

For the first time since 1987's monumental "Batman: Year One," Batman's origin was given a modern take with "Zero Year," cementing the idea that the New 52 version of Batman's past was quite different from the one readers had been following up until the "Flashpoint" event. "Zero Year" proved to be much more than simply a story arc; the series inspired tie-in issues in the pages of *Nightwing, Batgirl, Batwing, Birds of Prey, Catwoman, Detective Comics, Red Hood and the Outlaws,* and even *Action Comics, The Flash, Green Arrow,* and *Green Lantern Corps.* "Zero Year" presented a Batman for a new generation and was a defining series for Batman.

THE SON OF BATMAN
Batman had held a dead Robin in his arms before, but Damian's death was even more of a tragedy. After all, Damian was Bruce Wayne's very own flesh and blood.

FINAL FIGHT
Referring to Damian as
his "brother," "twin," and "rival,"
the imposter Batman engaged in a deadly
swordfight with the young hero. Bested by the
hulking villain, Robin pleaded with his mother to
call him off. In the end, Robin had given all he
had, but it just wasn't enough.

ZERO YEAR

BATMAN #21

In this monumental collaboration between writer Scott Snyder and artist Greg Capullo, Batman's origin was given a revamp for the first time since "Batman: Year One," back in 1987.

Batman had tried out a Batman Beyond prototype suit and an orange and black airtight suit when he fought Clayface in the previous issue. These innovations would pale in comparison with the far-reaching changes, both to his costume and to his life, that the epic "Zero Year" storyline would bring. Set in the Gotham City of six years ago, this origin story showcased an early version of the Batsuit with purple wrist-length gloves—a nod to his look in *Detective Comics* #27 (May 1939).

In this first issue, Bruce Wayne had not yet adopted his Batman identity. He was simply establishing his home in Gotham City. By the next issue, Bruce began to wage war with new criminal the Red Hood. It wasn't until the extra-long issue #24 (December 2013) that he'd don his Batman suit and battle the Red Hood's forces. The result was a climactic fight at the A.C.E. Chemical factory in which the Red Hood plunged into a tank of chemicals. Batman had just witnessed the birth of the Joker.

UNCLE PHILIP
Bruce's uncle, Philip Kane, debuted in this issue, which also featured a back-up tale written by Scott Snyder and James Tynion IV, and drawn by Rafael Albuquerque. Philip would later come into conflict with the Riddler before dying as a member of the Red Hood's gang.

KATANA CUTS IN

Katana #1 • The Japanese Super Hero Katana, wielder of the magical Soultaker Sword and a longtime Batman ally, gained her first-ever ongoing series with this issue. With a new membership in the Justice League of America, this founding Outsiders member had never been more in the spotlight. This issue was written by Ann Nocenti and drawn by Alex Sanchez, and by issue #3, Katana would also meet another face familiar to Outsider fans, the New 52 version of the Creeper, who had debuted as Jack Ryder in *Phantom Stranger* #7 (June 2013).

JUSTICE FOR CATWOMAN

Justice League of America #1 • In the same month that Batman tried out a new underwater costume in the pages of *Justice League* #17, *Justice League of America* debuted, featuring members Catwoman and Katana. Offered with 53 different covers of the characters holding up various flags (including a flag for each of the 50 states), this issue was written by Geoff Johns and illustrated by David Finch. This comic also debuted the mysterious new villain called the Outsider, who would later be revealed to be Earth-Three's nefarious Alfred Pennyworth.

GOTHAM CITY GETS LITTLE

Batman: Li'l Gotham #1 • In 2009's *Batman Annual* #27, readers glimpsed a two-page story by writer Derek Fridolfs and writer/artist Dustin Nguyen. Set in a light-hearted cartoony world featuring a short and stubby Batman in a painterly wash style, this series proved popular enough to earn its own digital-first comic starting this month. Lasting for 12 issues chock-full of dozens of villains and supporting characters, this new series focused on Batman's adventures during the holidays, and even earned its own action figure line from DC Collectibles.

BATWING 2.0

Batwing #19 • In *Batwing* #16 (March 2013), writer Fabian Nicieza and artist Allan Jefferson introduced the Sky-Pirate. This new villain would soon kill Batwing's aid Matu Ba, starting a chain of events that saw the original Batwing step down from his position at Batman Incorporated. In this issue by writers Jimmy Palmiotti and Justin Gray and artist Eduardo Pansica, Lucius Fox gifted Batman with an improved Batwing suit. Little did Lucius realize that the man set to wear it was his own son and Batman's first choice for Batwing, new character Luke Fox.

WORLD'S APART
BATMAN/SUPERMAN #1

The World's Finest partnership was back in this ongoing title, with Batman receiving top billing in an adventure that led them to meeting older versions of themselves from an alternate world.

In the landscape of the New 52, Batman and Superman weren't quite the bosom buddies they'd been in previous continuities. While it had been established in the pages of *Justice League* that the two had begun to work together, how that team-up began remained a mystery. Writer Greg Pak and artists Jae Lee and Ben Oliver decided to fill in that gap, while giving readers a new take on this classic pairing. When they met as Clark Kent and Bruce Wayne in Gotham City years ago, Clark didn't much care for Bruce's holier-than-thou attitude when he showed him photos of three Wayne Enterprises employees who'd recently been murdered in Superman's home town Metropolis. But when things began to go astray with his investigation, Batman got his first glimpse of the Man of Steel in impressive action.

SETTING THE MOOD
Featuring moody artwork that matched the story perfectly, Batman/Superman saw the two heroes soon meet their counterparts from Earth-Two. The World's Finest team of that world was older and wiser than their brash doppelgangers.

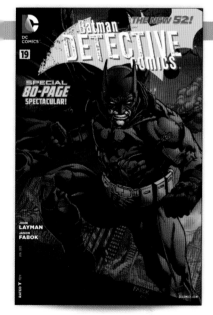

THE 900
***Detective Comics* #19** • *Detective Comics* had reached its 900th issue, but due to the numbering restart in the New 52, the title was only at issue #19. However, DC Comics decided to celebrate the milestone anyway with this 80-Page issue showcasing the birth of the New 52's Man-Bat. Writer John Layman supplied three stories starring Kirk Langstrom. They were illustrated by Jason Fabok, Andy Clarke, and Jason Masters, respectively. This issue also featured a Bane story by writer James Tynion IV and artist Mikel Janin.

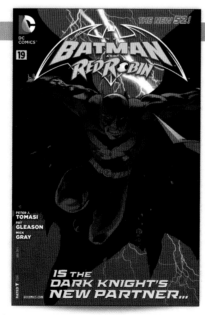

BATMAN AND—?
***Batman and Red Robin* #19** • DC Comics employed foldout covers in most of its Super Hero titles this month to reveal a surprise. In this issue by writer Peter J. Tomasi and artist Patrick Gleason, the surprise was Carrie Kelley—Robin from 1986's *Batman: The Dark Knight Returns*—appearing in modern continuity. Carrie debuted as Damian Wayne's former acting teacher, and would soon become Batman's dog walker. This month also signaled the comic's first of many title changes, as it co-starred a variety of partners due to Robin's death.

EARTH-TWO'S NEW BATMAN
***Earth 2 Annual* #1** • While the Bruce Wayne of Earth-Two had died during that world's struggle with Darkseid in *Earth 2* #1 (July 2012), a new Batman debuted in this annual by writer James Robinson and artists Cafu and Julius Gopez. First emerging from the shadows when the military agent known as the Atom encountered trouble, this mysterious new red and black clad hero faced off with the villain Mister Icicle, killing the villain after defeating him. While he possessed the same level of determination, this new Batman clearly lacked Bruce Wayne's principles.

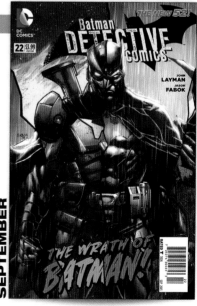

RENEWED WRATH
***Detective Comics* #22** • The classic villain the Wrath was reintroduced to Batman and the New 52 universe with a little help from writer John Layman and artist Jason Fabok. In an issue that also introduced the Wrath's literally short-lived partner in crime, Scorn, the villain began to sully Batman's reputation in Gotham City, having a very similar appearance to the Dark Knight. This issue also featured the continued adventures of Man-Bat in its back-up tale, scripted by Layman and illustrated by Andy Clarke.

THE CRIME SYNDICATE
Just like the heroes of the New 52 reality, the villains of the Crime Syndicate also received costume makeovers. Pictured here in their new uniforms are (from left to right): Power Ring, Deathstorm, Owlman, Ultraman, Superwoman, Johnny Quick, and Atomica.

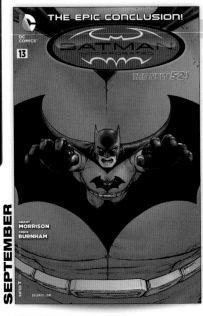

SEPTEMBER

THE DEATH OF TALIA
Batman Incorporated #13 ▪ In the finale to writer Grant Morrison's tenure on the Batman titles, the threat of Leviathan came to an end. After Batman injected himself with a form of Man-Bat Kirk Langstrom's serum to become a real bat in issue #10 (June 2013), he attacked Talia al Ghūl's forces and defeated her Batman imposter, only to discover that he, too, was his "son," a hastily grown monstrosity who looked like Damian. While Talia killed this "son" in issue #12, Kathy Kane emerged from the shadows in this issue and killed Talia.

OCTOBER

THE NEWEST OWLMAN
Justice League #23 ▪ In this finale to the six-part "Trinity War" crossover that passed through the pages of *Justice League of America* and *Justice League Dark*, writer Geoff Johns and artist Ivan Reis unveiled the true masterminds between the recent infighting among the various Justice Leagues. As it turned out, on the same day the League first fought Darkseid five years ago, the Outsider, Earth-Three's Alfred Pennyworth, traveled to Earth-One. And in this issue's final page, the new Crime Syndicate finally followed, including Owlman, Earth-Three's Thomas Wayne Jr.

THE JOKER'S DAUGHTER
Catwoman #23 ▪ When Catwoman was on a mission to find a man named Rat-Tail, she headed to the unknown territories below Gotham City, including a town run by Dr. Phosphorus. After teaming with Phosphorus' daughter Tinderbox in the previous issue, Catwoman tried to broker a peace alliance between two underground civilizations in this issue by writer Ann Nocenti, co-plotter and breakdown artist Scott McDaniel, and artist Rafa Sandoval. In the process, she came across the Joker's Daughter, a new villain who wore the Joker's old skin mask.

NOVEMBER

VENTRILOQUISM AND ILLUSIONS
Batman: The Dark Knight #23.1 ▪ Villains Month hit DC Comics, and with it came special point issues of many of the company's most popular titles. Each special focused on a different villain, and each was crafted with a standard cover or with a highly sought after 3-D motion cover. This particular issue debuted the New 52's version of the Ventriloquist and Scarface, a deranged killer with telekinetic powers thanks to writer Gail Simone and artist Derlis Santacruz. Other Batman villains saw the spotlight, including the Joker's Daughter in issue #23.4.

NOVEMBER

EVIL WINS
FOREVER EVIL #1

In this seven-issue series, Nightwing had to pay the ultimate price when the Crime Syndicate from Earth-Three took over the entire world.

Writer Geoff Johns and artist David Finch revealed the true definition of evil in this series, which took place after the Crime Syndicate had defeated and seemingly killed the entire Justice League. In a world with no electricity, Nightwing had been captured by the villains and his identity revealed. Seeing this, Batman emerged from the shadows to team up with Catwoman, Lex Luthor, and a host of traditional villains in an attempt to win back his world and rescue his former sidekick. Batman briefly used a Sinestro Corps ring that changed his costume into a yellow and black uniform.

Batman's team gained Deathstroke's help when the villain switched allegiances, killing the villain Copperhead in the process. Batman's team then successfully breached the Syndicate's headquarters as Black Manta killed the Outsider. Batman then discovered Nightwing hooked up to a Murder Machine; the only way to free his ally would result in Dick Grayson's death.

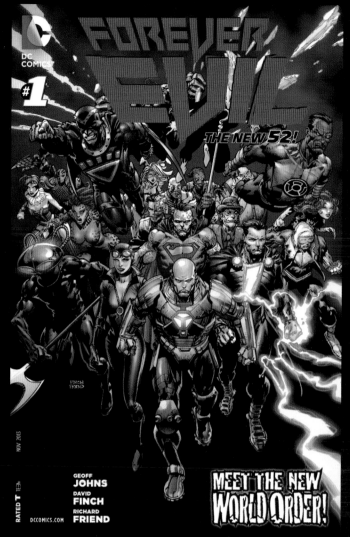

GEOFF **JOHNS**
DAVID **FINCH**
RICHARD **FRIEND**

DECEMBER

BLACK, WHITE, AND BATMAN

Batman: Black and White #1 ■ In this sequel to the popular miniseries of 1996, a new six-issue black and white Batman anthology was released for a new era. Like the previous incarnation, this series was edited by Mark Chiarello and filled with DC Comics' most shining artistic stars. This first issue alone included stories by writer Chip Kidd and artist Michael Cho, writer/artist Neal Adams, writer Maris Wicks and artist Joe Quinones, writer John Arcudi and artist Sean Murphy, and writer Howard Mackie, and illustrator Chris Samnee.

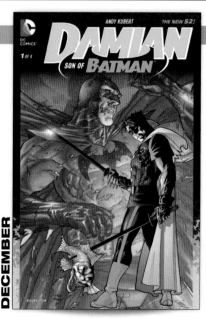

FROM ROBIN TO BATMAN

Damian: Son of Batman #1 ■ Although Damian Wayne had died in the mainstream DC Universe, this series imagined a world in which the young Robin had lived, leading up to when he donned the Batman costume glimpsed in *Batman* #666 (July 2007). Showcasing the death of Dick Grayson as Batman in this first of four issues, writer/artist Andy Kubert showed Damian's fall from hero to murderous vigilante. After a fight with an aged Bruce Wayne that left the original Batman near death's door, Damian changed his ways and his take on Batman's uniform.

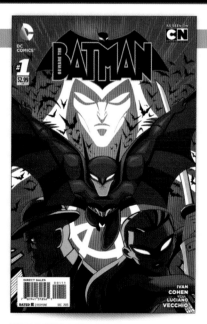

VILLAINS BEWARE

Beware the Batman #1 ■ To tie in with Cartoon Network's new computer-animated cartoon *Beware the Batman* came this new all-ages comic of the same name. Just like its related animated series, this one saw Batman teaming with a much tougher reinterpretation of Alfred Pennyworth as well as fledgling Super Hero, Katana. While this comic would rotate writers and artists, the first issue was written by Ivan Cohen and drawn by Luciano Vecchio. In a series that emphasized lesser-known villains, this debut effort featured the villain Anarky.

ALSO THIS YEAR

January—Detective Comics #14: Poison Ivy and Clayface "married" before Batman debuted a new temporary orange and black costume in the following issue.

March—Batman and Robin Annual #1: Damian tried out his *Batman* #666 costume when Bruce Wayne was away.

March—Batwoman #16: Bette Kane adopted the new identity of Hawkfire.

★ **April 23rd:** The humorous *Teen Titans Go!* cartoon debuted on Cartoon Network.

★ **July 13th:** Batman's first computer-animated series *Beware the Batman* began.

September—Batman '66 #1: Fans of the 1960s *Batman* TV show were rewarded with a new ongoing series set in the world of the tongue-in-cheek show.

September—Superman Unchained #2: Batman wore a new armored Batsuit capable of evading even Superman's sight.

December—Batman and Two-Face #24: Crime family leader, Erin McKillen, was revealed to have poured acid on Harvey Dent's face and killed his wife Gilda.

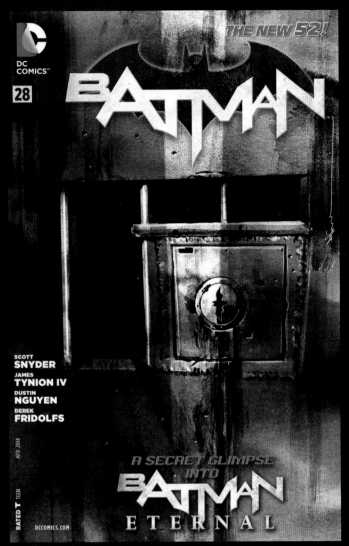

SCOTT
SNYDER
JAMES
TYNION IV
DUSTIN
NGUYEN
DEREK
FRIDOLFS

APR 2014

RATED T TEEN

DCCOMICS.COM

BATMAN ETERNAL
BATMAN #28

Readers were given a glimpse of the upcoming weekly *Batman Eternal* series in this sneak peak issue.

Written by Scott Snyder and James Tynion IV and pencilled by Dustin Nguyen, this stand-alone preview issue interrupted "Zero Year" to give readers a glimpse into the future of Gotham City. A big part of that future was Harper Row, a character who had first appeared in *Batman* #7 (May 2012). Harper had appeared a few times since, and her relationship with Batman had been developed in issue #18 (May 2013) in an issue written by Snyder and Tynion IV, with art by Andy Kubert and Alex Maleev. But it wasn't until this issue that Harper was shown to be one of Batman's partners, adopting the costumed identity of Bluebird.

In this bold new landscape, Gotham City had a strict 8 p.m. curfew, and Bluebird and Batman were forced to break into Gotham City's only nightclub in order to meet with the city's new kingpin of crime, Selina Kyle. There they were permitted to glimpse the person they had come for, touted as the only one who knew how to stop a coming threat. That person was Stephanie Brown, alias the Spoiler, making her New 52 debut in this story, which would lead into Batman's first weekly comic: *Batman Eternal*.

TAKING ON CATWOMAN
Batman and Bluebird stormed Catwoman's stronghold, fighting their way to a meeting with Selina Kyle. Having risen to power after the events of *Forever Evil*, Selina seemed intrigued by the pair of heroes, finally offering to reveal her little secret to them.

2014

"It's pretty obvious, isn't it? We're the good guys."
Bluebird, *Batman* #28

The first half of 2014 promised plenty of new additions to Batman's universe. In addition to the new crime fighter Bluebird, this year would see the debut of a future Batman in the title *Justice League 3000*, and the start of the first ever large-scale weekly Batman series, Batman Eternal. Meanwhile, a lighter side of the Dark Knight and company popped up in new all-ages titles, and Harley Quinn starred in a new self-titled series. The Caped Crusader had stayed the course for 75 years and to celebrate, the New 52 offered up its own version of the 1939's monumental *Detective Comics* #27.

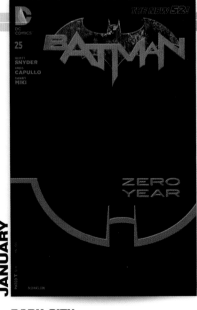

DARK CITY
Batman #25 ▪ The second arc of "Zero Year" was announced in dramatic fashion with this all-black cover with embossed logos. Written by Scott Snyder and illustrated by Greg Capullo with a back-up tale by writers Snyder and James Tynion IV and artist Andy Clarke, this issue saw the Dark Knight test drive a prototype Batmobile as he faced the Riddler who had blacked-out the whole of Gotham City. This issue also introduced a revamped version of the now-grotesque Dr. Death, while the next issue premiered Batman's first New 52-continuity Batboat.

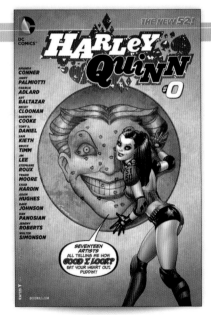

HARLEY'S HUNT
Harley Quinn #0 ▪ Back in her own ongoing series, Harley Quinn's new lease on life was celebrated by writers Amanda Conner and Jimmy Palmiotti in this special #0 issue. This was one of many issues DC Comics offered with an alternative "We Can Be Heroes" blank cover, created to raise money for famine relief in Africa. This teaser issue showed Harley Quinn breaking the fourth wall to talk directly to her writers as a variety of superstar artists, including newcomer Jeremy Roberts, winner of a talent contest, tackled her adventures.

CRACKING THE WHIP
Selina Kyle, new boss of Gotham City's underworld, was determined to show Batman who was in control.

SPOILER ALERT
A popular character who had served Batman in the previous continuity as both Robin and Batgirl, the Spoiler added to the dramatic tension at the end of this issue.

FEBRUARY

BATMAN 3000

Justice League 3000 #1 ● The future reality of the Legion of Super-Heroes was explored by writers Keith Giffen and J.M. DeMatteis and artist Howard Porter. After the Fatal Five ransacked the Earth, the planet was in desperate need of heroes. Enter a new Justice League and their own Batman. Clad in a red and black uniform, this Batman was Bruce Wayne's genetic sample brought back to life in a Cadmus lab by the scientists nicknamed the Wonder Twins. Lacking the motivation of the death of his parents, Batman only had half the memories of the original.

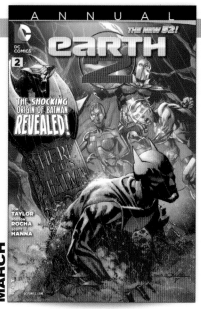

MARCH

FATHER OF THE YEAR

Earth 2 Annual #2 ● The second Batman of Earth-Two debuted in the previous year's annual, yet his origin had remained a secret until this issue by writer Tom Taylor and artist Robson Rocha. In this story, readers learned that the new Batman was Thomas Wayne, Bruce's father. Thomas had survived Joe Chill's bullet and faked his own death to protect his still living son. He then began injecting himself with a strength-enhancing drug called Miraclo in order to gain revenge on his old enemy Frankie Falcone before adopting the Batman mantle when Bruce died.

A NEW CHEMICAL CASE

Detective Comics #27 ● In honor of Batman's 75th birthday, writer Brad Meltzer and artist Bryan Hitch told a modern version of "The Case of the Chemical Syndicate," and writer John Layman began "Gothtopia" with artist Jason Fabok. This crossover would pass through *Batwing*, *Batgirl*, *Catwoman*, and *Birds of Prey*. This celebratory issue also featured the work of writers Gregg Hurwitz, Peter J. Tomasi, Mike W. Barr, Scott Snyder, writer/artist Francesco Francavilla, and artists Neal Adams, Ian Bertram, Guillem March, and Sean Murphy.

ALSO THIS YEAR

January—*Scooby-Doo! Team Up* #1: Scooby-Doo teamed up with Batman and Robin in this first issue of this team-up miniseries that would later include characters like Bat-Mite and the Teen Titans.

February—*Teen Titans Go!* #1: The animated adventures of the Teen Titans received a second chance at an ongoing tie-in series to match their new cartoon.

March—*Batman and Robin Annual* #2: A flashback tale teamed Batman and Dick Grayson (in his New 52 Robin costume) in this issue.

April—*Justice League* #25: Readers learned how Earth-Three's Owlman, Thomas Wayne Jr., had murdered his brother Bruce and their parents with the help of his butler, that world's Alfred Pennyworth.

April—*Batman: Joker's Daughter* #1: This one-shot saw the popular Joker's Daughter once again in a starring role.